The Great 1

OTHER BOOKS BY SAMUEL ELIOT MORISON

Samuel Eliot Morison 1887–1976

The Great Explorers

THE EUROPEAN DISCOVERY
OF AMERICA

SAMUEL ELIOT MORISON

OXFORD UNIVERSITY PRESS

New York   Oxford

Oxford University Press

Oxford   New York   Toronto
Delhi   Bombay   Calcutta   Madras   Karachi
Petaling Jaya   Singapore   Hong Kong   Tokyo
Nairobi   Dar es Salaam   Cape Town
Melbourne   Auckland

and associated companies in
Beirut   Berlin   Ibadan   Nicosia

The Great Explorers: The European Discovery of America, first published in 1978 by Oxford University Press, Inc., is a new edition of material selected from two earlier volumes, *The European Discovery of America: The Northern Voyages, A.D. 500–1600*, Copyright © 1971 by Samuel Eliot Morison, and *The European Discovery of America: The Southern Voyages, 1492–1616*, Copyright © 1974 by Samuel Eliot Morison

First issued in paperback in 1986 by Oxford University Press, Inc.,
200 Madison Avenue, New York, New York 10016

Oxford is a registered trademark of Oxford University Press

Library of Congress Cataloging in Publication Data

Morison, Samuel Eliot, 1887–1976.
The Great Explorers

Originally published in 2 v. in 1971–74.
Includes bibliographical references and index.
1. America—Discovery and exploration.
2. Voyages and travels.   I. Title.
E101.M852   1978   970.01   77-21831
ISBN 0-19-502314-5
ISBN 0-19-504222-0 (pbk.)

6 8 10 9 7

Printed in the United States of America

Preface to *The Northern Voyages*

This volume devoted to European voyages to North America prior to 1600 should replace John Fiske's classic *Discovery of America* (2 vols., 1893) and supplement an irreplaceable work, the first four volumes of Justin Winsor's *Narrative and Critical History of America* (1884–89). Nobody in the present century has followed Winsor in attempting to cover the entire field of New World discovery.

All honest efforts to throw light on historical darkness, such as this era, have my enthusiastic support. But it has fallen to my lot, working on this subject, to have read some of the most tiresome historical literature in existence. Young men seeking academic promotion, old men seeking publicity, neither one nor the other knowing the subject in depth, only a particular voyage or a particular map, write worthless articles; and the so-called learned journals are altogether too hospitable to these effusions. Some of these stem from mere personal conceit; others from racial emotion. Canada and the United States seem to be full of racial groups who wish to capture the "real" discovery for their medieval compatriots. They argue that Columbus and Cabot had so many predecessors as to deserve no more credit than a person who buys a ticket for a cruise at a tourist agency.

The cartographical aspect deserves special notice. Literary evidence of these early Northern Voyages must be supplemented by that of early maps showing bits and pieces of the New World. Most of these are in European libraries or museums. I have attentively examined almost every one, as even the excellent Edward Luther Stevenson full-scale black-and-white photographs do not bring out every detail of a colored original. Several learned and excellent studies of these maps, especially of the projections they used, have been published by R. A. Skelton, G. R. Crone, Heinrich Winter, and others. But nobody has yet penetrated the secret of how the maps were made. Did the cartographer call on individual discoverers and explorers, record what they said, and borrow their own charts? Did he simply depict his own notion of the relation of early North American discoveries to Asia, and dub in the names of bays and promontories told to him by the sailors, or even make them up? Peculiar features of early maps, which may have been nothing but a draftsman's whimsy, have inspired pages of vain conjecture. Dozens of islands, rocks, and shoals that do not, and never did, exist are depicted on charts of the Atlantic, even down to the nineteenth century; and some have been avidly seized upon as evidence of pre-Columbian voyages. Williamson well observed, "All this map interpretation is hopelessly uncertain, and from it one may argue almost anything that comes into one's mind. The historian wants written statements."

Alas, he does not often find them, for the earliest period. He has to apply his background knowledge, his common sense, and (rarest of all qualifications) his personal knowledge of sailing to make sense out of the sources. Accordingly, I have handled cartographical evidence with respect, but somewhat gingerly, ever conscious that I am writing a history of voyages, not of maps.

The reproduction of old maps in a book presents typographical problems. Nobody likes a big pull-out; but if the size is too much reduced, one cannot read the names of places. I have tried whenever possible to obtain a photo directly from the map, and to keep the scale as big as possible by using only the immediately relevant portion. Most of the libraries and museums in Europe and America which possess these treasures have been very generous, helpful, and reasonable in their charges about reproduction.

The pursuit of suitable illustrations of places discovered by the early explorers has been interesting and time-absorbing. Not one government in the New World, to my knowledge, has made a complete photographic coverage of its shores. Hence I have been compelled to cover them by air, and do my best to photograph them from the fast-flying Beechcraft of my friend James F. Nields. The results, as the reader will observe, are very spotty, but the best I can offer.

Finally, there is oral evidence. We have precious little of that for so early a period, a notable exception being the Eskimo tradition about Frobisher; but as oral evidence I would include what professional sailors have taught me about coastal and blue-water sailing, and what fishermen have told me about their art. Just as old Horace wrote that his rustic poems came not only from personal experience but from his farmer Ofellus, *rusticus abnormis sapiens;* so much of what I know comes from a succession of Maine sailors who initiated me into the mysteries of the sea. Among these, I am especially indebted to Enos Verge, *nauta abnormis sapiens,* who sailed with me for years, mostly from Nova Scotia to Cuba. My knowledge of seafaring, acquired from such oral sources and from books over a period of seventy years, enables me to stretch back across the centuries and understand not only the triumphs of the navigators but their day-by-day problems. And, of late, Alan Villiers has been very generous to me from his vast fund of sea experience.

There is something very special about these northern voyages. In contrast to the fair winds that Columbus experienced and which made an outward Atlantic crossing easy from the navigator's point of view, anything might happen to you in the North Atlantic, even in summer; and in the sixteenth century everyone but French fishermen avoided sailing in winter. Westerly gales hurled crested seas against your little bark and forced it to lay-to for days; easterly gales drenched the sailors with chilling rain; fierce northerlies ripped their sails and cracked their masts. Between weather fronts even the whisper of a wind would often die and a white calm descend, so calm that one might think that the winds were worn out; then the fog closed in and the sea became a shimmering mirror reflecting the filtered rays of the sun. In high latitudes in summer one could forget whether it was day or night, while the sails slatted monotonously and the yards and rigging dripped rime. Plenty of men died on these northern voyages, but never of thirst. In a big fishing fleet, two centuries later, days of white calm might pass with jollity and humor from ship to ship, but for little knots of men confined to a small vessel, and no other human being within a thousand miles, the experience might be maddening. In the era of discovery, sailors would break out their sweeps and try to row their heavy vessels out of the calm, just to have something to do. It was a life for strong men and boys, not for women; the Greenlanders did indeed take women on their short voyages to Vinland, but there is no record of French or English taking them to America before Cartier's second voyage; and they were *forçats*, convicts.

People ask me to compare the hazards of the early navigators and those of the modern single-handed breed. The Atlantic was crossed many years ago by a Gloucester fisherman rowing a dory; and since Captain Slocum sailed around the world in his little *Spray*, with not one modern gadget, there have been countless one-man ocean crossings and a number of non-stop circumnavigations with self-inflicted hardships perhaps equal to those of the crews of Cabot and Frobisher. But these modern "loners" know where they are going; they have accurate charts, many instruments, and an auxiliary engine; they are in communication with the world by radio; naval vessels, airplanes, and coast guards shepherd them, drop food and water, and even, on occasion, take them on board for a rest; and, perhaps most important, they have no unruly, timid, and suspicious crew to govern and cajole into doing their duty.

Consider also the hazards of a sixteenth-century navigator exploring an unknown coast in a square-rigged vessel, incapable of quick maneuvering like a modern sailing yacht. With an onshore wind, the discoverers had to sail close to shore if they wanted to learn anything; yet it was always risky, especially on a fog-bound coast like Newfoundland. Submerged just below the surface, rocks capable of ripping the guts out of a ship were difficult to see in northern waters—dark green, opaque waters, not transparent like those of the Caribbean and the Coral Sea. Every harbor you entered added a new risk, even if a boat were sent ahead to sound. Would your anchor hold, or was the bottom hard rock, eel grass, or kelp, along which your hook would skid like a sled, requiring quick and efficient action to prevent your ship's crashing? If the wind is offshore when you sight land, you might be blown seaward again and have to beat back, which could take weeks—we shall see many instances of this. As Alan Villiers wrote, "The plain everyday difficulties of handling these ships . . . are already so forgotten as to seem incredible. Their means of movement was the wind properly directed to their sails. . . . They had to *fight* for their way, fight for their lives at times." * And so many lost their lives: John Cabot, both Corte Reals, Sir Humfry Gilbert, for instance. North America became a graveyard for European ships and sailors.

I wish that everyone who imagines that the "perils and dangers of the sea" have vanished before modern science would read Captain K. Adlard Coles's *Heavy Weather Sailing* (1967), with its hair-raising stories of sailing yachts no smaller than those of the era of discoveries, but laden with gadgets. There you have first-hand accounts of some of the hazards that the early navigators encountered as a matter of course—enormous freak waves, pitch-poling, capsizing; and although hurricanes were rarely encountered on these northern voyages of discovery, very strong gales and immense seas were common. Please remember, too, that these seamen had no storm warnings, no "law of storms" enabling them to evade the eye; and that even sailing in a fleet gave little protection. Under certain conditions a ship that foundered, like Gilbert's, or crashed on a lee shore, could expect no help even from another ship within sight. There is no basis of comparison between the astronauts who first landed on the moon on 20 July 1969, and discoverers like Columbus, Cabot, Verrazzano, and Cartier. Those four were men with an idea, grudgingly and meanly supported by their sovereigns. The three young heroes of the moon landing did not supply the idea; they bravely and intelligently executed a vast enterprise employing some 400,000 men and costing billions of dollars; whilst Columbus's first voyage cost his sovereigns less than a court ball; and Cabot's, which gave half the New World to England, cost Henry VII just fifty pounds. The astronauts' epochal voyage into space, a triumph of the human spirit, was long prepared, rehearsed, and conducted with precision to an accurately plotted heavenly body. Their feat might be slightly comparable to Cabot's if the moon were always dark and they knew not exactly where to find it—and if they had hit the wrong planet.

Abbé Anthiaume, a pioneer historian of French navigation, wrote many years ago of the early explorers by sea, "What superhuman energy a captain needed to triumph over these terrors of the ocean,

---

* Alan Villiers, *Captain James Cook* (1967), pp. 146-47.

to free his mind of ancient prejudices . . . and to carry his crew through these obscurities! . . . He knew very well that he risked his life and that of his shipmates for a hypothesis." The Abbé asks us to remember the common sailor who, "lost in an immensity of ocean that he suspected to be endless," imagined an island behind each cloud on the horizon, and anxiously followed with his eyes the birds which, as evening fell, flew in the same direction, hoping to be able, like them, to sleep ashore again.

Finally, I am highly conscious of writing amid "the tumult of the times disconsolate"—as Longfellow wrote of the 1860's. And to those now whimpering about the state of the world, and especially Americans predicting the collapse of society, I will say, "Have faith! Hang on! Do something yourself to improve things!" What if England and France had given up trying to establish colonies after the failures we are about to relate, and had become ingrown like certain other European countries, or Japan? What if they had written off North America as worthless, for want of precious metals? Where, then, would you be?

Just before the discovery of America, thinking men in western Europe believed that their world, already crumbling, would shortly crash; the stately Nuremberg Chronicle dwelt on "the calamity of our time . . . in which iniquity and evil have increased to the highest pitch," and gave its readers six blank pages to record events from 1493 to the end of the world. Nevertheless, a new era of hope and glory and enlargement of the human spirit, some aspects of which we shall now relate, was about to begin.

In human affairs there is no snug harbor, no rest short of the grave. We are forever setting forth afresh across new and stormy seas, or into outer space.

I must here make a special tribute to those who have been with me all the way: my beloved wife Priscilla, who has not only accompanied me around the world in my quest for material, but has heard, read, and corrected my prose and created perfect conditions for work, whether in Boston, Northeast Harbor, or overseas. Second, my secretary Antha Eunice Card, who not only with exemplary cheerfulness has typed and retyped my drafts, but on occasion pointed out *le mot juste*, and executed many pieces of research. Third, my daughter Catharine Morison

Morison, Nields, and Obregón setting forth to check on Leif Ericsson and John Cabot, 1968. Photo by Señora Obregón.

Cooper who has acted as my London agent and has been assiduous in looking up the scattered facts on early shipping in the British Museum and the National Maritime Museum at Greenwich (two institutions to which I am greatly indebted), and obtaining photographs of persons, places, and ships. Finally, James F. Nields of Ware, Massachusetts, and Mauricio Obregón of Bogotá, Colombia, both eminent in the new world of aviation, who have flown me, in Nields's plane, along the coasts discovered by Cabot, Cartier, and Verrazzano.

"Good Hope"   S. E. Morison
Northeast Harbor, Maine
January 1971

Preface to *The Southern Voyages*

In this volume I return to Columbus, of whom I have been an almost lifelong student, and carry the story of the Southern Voyages down to 1616 when Le Maire and Schouten discovered Cape Horn. The core of this volume, however, relates to the work of three of the greatest navigators of history, Columbus, Magellan, and Drake, and the story of their voyages is told in greater detail than those of the others, partly because of their importance, but also because we know more about them. My readers should not expect accounts of the great conquests such as Mexico, Peru, New Granada, and Brazil—or of the colonial wars such as the Franco-Spanish quarrel over Florida. In a book of this scope I have had to limit the story to voyages—to how the conquerors got here.

Pray keep in mind the vast length of these Southern Voyages compared with the Northern. The crossing of the North Atlantic from Bristol in the west of England to St. John's, Newfoundland, is only 1940 nautical miles, and 700 miles more will take a ship to Quebec. The entire coastal voyage from New York around Florida to Galveston, Texas, is only 1887 miles. Columbus's great circle distance from Gomera, his 1492 jumping-off place in the Canaries, to San Salvador in the Bahamas, was 3116 nautical miles, whilst his shortest transatlantic crossing, from Gomera to Dominica in 1502, measures 2500 miles. But suppose your destination to have been the Strait of Magellan. First, you have a 1529-mile sail from Cadiz to São Vicente in the Cape de Verdes; then a 1616-mile ocean crossing direct to Pernambuco (Recife), just under the bulge of Brazil, and after that you must coast South America for 2062 miles to reach Montevideo, touching at Rio de Janeiro halfway. If you cross the River Plate and continue along Patagonia to the entrance of the Strait of Magellan, you would have to cover another 1254 nautical miles.* So it is no wonder that the Southern Voyages, at least those south of the Caribbean, required months rather than weeks, or that their leading problem was food. You seldom hear of food giving out on a Northern transatlantic voyage in the sixteenth century, but on Southern Voyages scurvy and starvation were commonplace; and very many, perhaps a majority of the men who set out on them, never returned.

What made them do it? I wish I knew. Was it mere adventure and glory, or lust for gold or (as they all declared) a zeal to enlarge the Kingdom of the Cross? Bernal Diaz del Castillo well said, in his *Historia Verdadera* of the conquest of Mexico, "We came here to serve God, and also to get rich." One quality all these mariners had in common with the ancient Greeks was restlessness. Just as Ulysses, returning home to Penelope after infinite pains and wanderings, had to make one last voyage; just as Alexander, after marching to northern India, regretted there were no more worlds to conquer; so these paladins of discovery never had enough. Columbus could have settled for a castle in Spain and a pension after any one of his first three voyages; but he always had to make one more. Sebastian Cabot held an honorable and lucrative position in Spain, but he had to go to sea and prove himself a sailor. Drake sailed around the world, brought home (some say) a million pounds in booty, bought a country estate, and set up as an English squire; but, at the first call, off again to sea went he, and at sea he left his bones. And many other examples of this restlessness my readers will see.

---

* These figures are for the shortest, great circle course between two points, except where I have followed modern steamship courses in Brown's Almanac, or "stepped it off" on a modern chart. The actual course sailed, owing to wind fluctuation and other causes, was always considerably longer. For the 1492 calculations, see John W. McElroy in *American Neptune*, I (1941), pp. 215–16. Columbus estimated that he had sailed 3466 nautical miles.

Few of the sources and other writings on voyages south of the Caribbean are in English. The historians who have mainly concerned themselves with these voyages have been Spaniards, Portuguese, Brazilians, Uruguayans, Argentinians, Chileans, and Paraguayans. And so are practically all those now living. Their works, many in the form of short magazine articles, are almost never reviewed or even noticed in England or North America. Thus, most readers in English-speaking countries have never heard of such important figures as Ladrillero, Loaysa, and Sarmiento de Gamboa. The greatest of all, Columbus, Magellan, and Drake, are indeed well known; but I have contributed something new in retracing their courses at sea.

T. S. Eliot's injunction in his *East Coker*, "Old men ought to be explorers," has appealed to me; and I would add, "Young historians, too!" In the 1930s I followed Columbus across the Atlantic and around the West Indies in barquentine *Capitana* and ketch *Mary Otis*, to write *Admiral of the Ocean Sea* and *Christopher Columbus, Mariner*. In 1963 Mauricio Obregón flew me around the Caribbean, with his wife and David Crofoot as photographers, and my wife as passenger, resulting in *The Caribbean as Columbus Saw It* (1964). In preparation for the volume at hand, Obregón and James F. Nields flew me in the latter's Baron Beechcraft to cover landfalls and routes of Pinzón, Cabral, Vespucci, and Cabot along the coast of Brazil and (following Cabeza de Vaca's second stupendous walk) to Asunción, Paraguay. In May 1973 my daughter Emily Beck and my old friend John Gordon accompanied me to California, where the United States Coast Guard lent us a cutter to check up on Drake's landing. Everywhere the navies of the United States and Great Britain have afforded me assistance, as did the navies of Brazil, the Argentine, and Chile in their waters.

I cannot claim to have followed the discoverers of the River Plate under sail; but I have flown over that great inland waterway where the adaptable Spaniards rowed, towed, and kedged their *bergantinas* for thousands of miles. There is nothing like a personal visit to newly discovered lands to bring home to one the pioneers' dangers and difficulties. My admiration for them increases with time. For years I have been living with the records of heroic navigators and with the ordinary grousing, grumbling, believing but blaspheming mariner. God bless 'em all! The world will never see their like again.

Maps are still a problem. The difficulties inherent in reproducing old maps in a book of this format are still insurmountable; so in this volume I have largely substituted original maps by Vaughn Gray, for which my readers will doubtless be grateful. Fortunately there is now available a quarto edited by W. P. Cumming, R. A. Skelton, and D. B. Quinn, *The Discovery of North America* (New York: American Heritage Press, 1972), an ideal companion to my *Northern Voyages* and, to a lesser degree, to this volume. Here these three cartographical scholars have produced in color some of the most important mappemondes such as the Cantino (1502), the Vespucci (1526), the Ribero (1529), the Royal Library of the Hague (1540), and the Rotz (1542), which include parts of Florida, California, and Central and South America, and have added hundreds of black-and-white maps and illustrations. Yet even they have been unable to make the toponymy of the oldest maps legible, and for that the scholar must still resort to the old folio reproductions, and the modern *Portugaliae Monumenta Cartographica* (1960), and *Mapas Españoles de América Siglos XV–XVII* (Madrid, 1951, Duke of Alba head of the editorial board).

For want of facts from which to generalize, dialectic has played an inordinate part in the history of American discovery. "Occam's Razor," a principle of the schoolman William of Occam that in explaining obscure matters, imaginary things should never be postulated as existing,* is so frequently violated that mythical coasts and islands have become almost as substantial as New York. I am all in favor of Occam's Razor, and would rather leave something unexplained than create imaginary links in a shadowy chain. Now that my English colleague Parkinson has formulated "Parkinson's Law," I venture to add two principles which, if you will, you may call "Morison's Musings":—(1) The invention or publication of some new method of navigation does not prove that it was promptly used at sea, as the school of the late Professor E. G. R. Taylor generally assumes; and (2) No theory is valid that makes nonsense of what follows. To illustrate the second point: If there were any truth in the theory now favored by several English geographers, that men of Bristol discovered Newfoundland in 1480, the prudent and economical Henry VII would never have called it the "New Isle," much less rewarded John Cabot for discovering it. Whilst

---

* As he put it, *Entia non sunt multiplicanda praeter necessitatem.*

crackpot theories about Columbus continue to proliferate, and Portuguese historians still claim that their compatriots were first everywhere, I do not have to deal with so much nonsense here as in my *Northern Voyages*. Nobody has yet claimed that Vikings sailed through the great Strait before Magellan, but my revered master Leo Wiener insisted that Africans were in Mexico ahead of Cortés, and Professor Cyrus W. Gordon of Brandeis University has Phoenicians swarming over Brazil even before that.

A word as to dates. All to 1582 are in the Julian Calendar. The Gregorian Calendar, which we still use, went into effect that year in Spain, Portugal, Italy, France, and certain provinces of the Netherlands; but the Protestant countries stuck to the Julian for a century or more after that. Dates of round-the-world voyages are one day too early from Guam westward (as Elcano and Drake later discovered), because sailors knew no international date line. Another source of misunderstanding is the nautical day used in ships' logs, which began at noon until well into the twentieth century. That is why, for instance, the pilot Albo's dates often differ from Pigafetta's on Magellan's voyage.

Many, many people have helped me. First, as always, my wife, to whose blessed memory this volume is dedicated. Miss Antha E. Card, my devoted and efficient secretary for twenty-three years, performed numerous research tasks besides typing and retyping, checking, and compiling the index. Librarians, notably Miss Wallis of the British Museum and Mr. Trout of the Harvard Map Room, have been most helpful. Airlifts by Messrs. Obregón and Nields were indispensable. My daughter Catharine Cooper performed valuable research at the British Museum and Greenwich, and helped me with the conclusion. Her sister Emily (Mrs. Brooks Beck) accompanied me to California to study Drake. My grandson Lt. (j.g.) Samuel Loring Morison USNR, at present in the Naval Intelligence Division at Washington, looked up such essential factors as tides and phases of the moon. Among my Harvard colleagues, Professors John H. Parry and Francis M. Rogers have been very helpful, Rogers particularly so with his knowledge of navigation, of early Portuguese voyages, and of the Iberian languages. He also read and criticized the entire typescript. Professor Rogers has also been of great assistance about Spanish and Portuguese spellings and accents, which differ in the two languages. For instance, *historia*, Spanish for "history," has no accent; *história*, the Portuguese word, has. After consulting with several Spanish scholars, I decided to place no accent on short words like *Rio*, *Luis*, *Maria*, and *Bahia*, and largely to suppress the circumflex accent in Portuguese. Of foreign historians, Capitão-de-mar-e-guerra Avelina Teixeira da Mota of Lisbon, Capitão-de-mar-e-guerra Max Justo Guedes of the Brazilian Navy, Colonel Rolando Laguarda Trías of the Uruguayan Army, Captain Laurio H. Destéfani of the Argentine Navy, and Dr. Ricardo Donoso of Santiago de Chile have given me freely of their time, advice, and wisdom. Nor have I forgotten old friends like Paul and Susy Hammond who helped me to organize and conduct the Harvard Columbus Expedition.

But, alas, this preface is written under the shadow of a great grief, the loss of my beloved Priscilla, still sharing my life as we approached the end of a long literary voyage. She accompanied me almost everywhere by land, sea, and air; her sparkling account of *Our Magellan Expedition from the Distaff Side* has been privately printed for distribution among our friends. Besides her innate and wonderful qualities of beauty, wit, gaiety, and grace, and her lovely singing and speaking voice, Priscilla was an excellent critic; and almost every page of this volume prior to the chapters on Drake, I read aloud to her before grievous pain made it impossible for her to pay attention. Her favorite criticism, born of her early experience on charitable boards, was, "Sam, that sounds like the secretary reading the minutes of the last meeting!" Any passage thus castigated was summarily removed or rewritten until it satisfied her. Thus my readers, as well as myself, owe Priscilla a great debt.

"Good Hope"   S. E. Morison
Northeast Harbor, Maine
15 May 1974

Contents

The Great Explorers

❋ I ❋

English Ships and Seamen

1490-1600

Design, Build, and Rigging

Before embarking with Cabot and his successors on their important North Atlantic voyages, my readers will wish to know what sort of a ship they used, how they built and rigged her, and what manner of men sailed her. To cover these topics with any degree of accuracy is a difficult if not impossible task. Records of English shipbuilding, design, rig, and handling for the closing years of the fifteenth century are very scarce. The situation respecting French ships is clearer, owing to the researches of Mollat, Bernard, and others; and we can also learn much from Frederic C. Lane's magistral works on Venetian shipping.

The ships which the English, French, and other northern explorers had at their disposition around 1500 were the result of centuries of trial and error. The English, leaving the basket-like curragh to the Irish, adopted the Scandinavian knarr, which made an excellent coastwise freighter but took in too much water for offshore work.

The next development, completed by 1200, was the *cog*, or *cogge* (*coque* in French), invented in Germany or the Netherlands. One of the difficulties in marine research is that the same word means different things at different times. For instance, by 1600 *cog* had become *cock* or *cock-boat*, a ship's boat propelled by oars and sail; *hulk* became a ship without masts, and *barge* became a flatboat to carry coal, or the admiral's boat on a flagship.

The cog originally was a single-masted ship with one sail and a bank of oars to use to windward or in a calm, but it had four important advantages over the knarr. It was completely decked over, so that water

3

taken in from sky or sea flowed overboard instead of having to be pumped or bailed out. It had a rudder, hung to the sternpost by iron pintles and gudgeons, and a long hardwood tiller mortised to the rudder head, affording the helmsman good leverage, while the sterncastle protected him from the elements. It had flimsy, openwork "castles" forward and aft, which were detachable and expendable, together with what we would call a crow's nest atop the single mast, valuable both for a lookout station and for defense. It had a bowsprit, first used to stay the mast. Originally clinker-built like the knarr, the cog, owing largely to her stern rudder and big mainsail with "bonnet" attached, was a far better sailer and more efficient cargo carrier. Cogs, built in great numbers in the Hanseatic League seaports, ran the Scandinavian merchant fleet out of business, except for local trade in sheltered waters. A well-built cog was perfectly capable of crossing the Atlantic; I would choose her every time rather than a modern yacht of her size with a "self-bailing" cockpit and an open companionway ready to gobble up a following sea.

The next important development came in the early fifteenth century. A cog's hull, now carvel-built, lengthened, and provided with two more masts, became first the *hourque*, or hulk, then the *nef, nau*, or full-rigged ship. The first explorers of America used these because they had nothing better; and as a result of experience, they came to prefer the smaller ships, under 100 tuns, to the bigger. Thus, Columbus found his little *Niña* more serviceable than the big *Santa María*.

Methods of building were essentially the same in the Middle Ages as those described in Longfellow's *Building of the Ship*, and as practised in small-boat yards of England, France, Nova Scotia, and both American coasts down to 1945, when fibre-glass construction began to replace wood. Similar methods are still maintained today in other parts of the world. The builder first selects a "slip" at the head of tide, slightly inclined so the vessel will launch easily, and places big oak blocks evenly spaced to support her when built. Some small vessels were doubtless built by eye, but the larger ones, like those shown in the Hastings Manuscript, were carefully planned with compass and divider, the members "laid down" in a mould loft with chalk or charcoal, and templates of them made with thin pieces of light wood. The English builder, if he does not own an oak forest himself, arranges with another to take out the timber he wants. Oak is preferred, not only for its strength but because limbs growing from the trunk at different angles

Edward Fiennes, Earl of Lincoln, Lord High Admiral, 1550–54 and 1558–85, holding a dry-card mariner's compass. From painting by unknown artist. Courtesy Ashmolean Museum, Oxford.

make natural crooks for the ribs or frames, the knees, and the curved stem piece. Builders would carry a wagon-load of templates into the oak grove, match them against standing trees, cut down those they wanted, and shape them with ax and adze. England then grew plenty of oak.

Venice, as Frederic C. Lane has vividly described, possessed shipyards which had many of the elements of a modern assembly plant,

with gantry cranes and vehicles for bringing the component parts together. In comparison, the building yards of England and France seem
to have been small and simple. The oak keel is laid with the keelson
(the inside part of the keel) on top; all "scarfed and bolted straight
and strong." Into the keelson are mortised the ribs or frames. Cross-
beams tie them to the deck, and all must be adzed into shape. Pine is
preferred for side-planking and deck. These were designed to shed
water quickly by being given both sheer (fore-and-aft slope) and
camber (transverse slope). Iron is used for fastenings, but such timbers
as keel and stern piece are bolted by trunnels, long pegs of soft wood,
which will swell in the water and hold as fast as iron or copper. Spars
are almost invariably spruce fir, of which, surprisingly, there were
large stands in England and Scotland at this time. Parts under water
are covered with black tar or pitch, the best substance then known to
discourage the growth of weed and barnacles. Topsides are gaily
painted in longitudinal stripes of green, blue, yellow, and red.

Whether carvel- or clinker-built, topsides and decks had to be
caulked. Oakum (shredded fibers of hemp) was driven into the seams
and topped off with pitch locally distilled from pine tar or imported
from the Baltic. The musical ring of the caulking iron driving home
the precious stuff was evident in shipbuilding then as in the early
twentieth century; and if a laboring ship "spewed her oakum," it was
time for her crew to pray or abandon ship.

When the hull is complete, the launching takes place; that was always done with ceremony, as even today. A crowd of people attends
to see it done, and lend a hand if necessary; one could have seen just
such a community launching ceremony at St. Vincent, B.W.I., in
1969. If the vessel was not originally laid down on a cradle, one is now
built under her keel, resting on greased "ways," two stout wooden
rails leading down to water of sufficient depth, at high tide, to float
her. A priest says a few prayers, sprinkles the bows with holy water,
and pronounces her chosen name, usually that of a saint or an apostle
expected to look after her safety and welfare.* At the moment chosen

* In England and northern France "Saint" was not often prefixed to the name;
but, to familiar saints' names, the home or builder's port was added to distinguish
her; e.g. *Mary of Guildford, Anthoine de Bordeaux.* Sometimes a northern ship
had a nickname used instead of her real name: the ship *Sampson,* which started
off with John Rut in 1527, was also called *Dominus Vobiscum,* reflecting a justified popular verdict on her safety. After the Reformation, English ships were

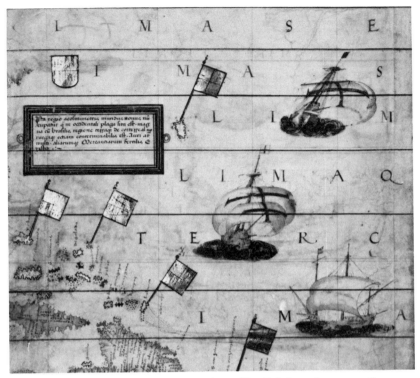

Long-course Portuguese ships from the Miller I Atlas of *c.* 1525. Courtesy Bibliothèque Nationale.

by the master shipwright, the "shores" which prevented the hull from toppling are knocked away by workmen with big mallets; and, if everything has been planned correctly,

> She starts,—she moves,—she seems to feel
> The thrill of life along her keel,

and she glides gracefully into her destined element, while the assembled multitude cheers.

After the hull is launched comes the ballasting, masting, and rigging.

Several important building and rigging innovations came about during the fifteenth century before Cabot set sail. Clinker-built gave way to

less often named after saints and angels, more often after qualities or things, such as *Delight, Aid, Sunshine, Mayflower;* and in the fifteenth century saints' names become less usual for French ships.

7

carvel-built, with flush, smooth planking, edges laid just close enough to one another to admit caulking. That made a much tighter ship for deep-sea work than those of earlier centuries. Spars and rigging, too, were fundamentally changed. Down to 1400 the cog and every other sailing type in northern waters was one-masted; but by 1500 all but the smallest had become three-masters: (1) the foremast, which went through the forecastle and might even be stepped on the stem-piece; (2) the mainmast, which carried the principal weight, always stepped on the keelson; (3) the mizzenmast, which thrust through the sterncastle and was stepped on the deck. Later, around mid-century, the high-steeved bowsprit, by supporting a square spritsail spread on a yard, acted as a fourth mast, and the "bonaventure" mizzen, stepped on the taffrail, a fifth. Fore and mainmast each carried a square lower course, also called foresail and mainsail. Note in all contemporary pictures of around 1500 how long the main yard and how big the mainsail appear to be in comparison with the ship; but ship pictures from 1544 on suggest that designers had realized the advantage of dividing the sail area and putting more of it into the topsails. The seaman of 1480–1550 counted on his main course to provide the drive, just as a modern yachtsman depends on his genoa jib and spinnaker.

For the variables in the North Atlantic, a more balanced rig was preferable. The mizzen sail, always lateen, i.e. triangular, was valuable chiefly on the wind, and to kick the stern around when tacking. Sails were no longer made of wool, but of flax woven at home, or cut out of canvas imported from Oleron or Dieppe. All rigging was made of hemp, mostly imported from the Baltic, and properly laid in a rope walk. Bridport in Dorsetshire had the reputation of making the best sails and cordage in England. Standing rigging, the shrouds which held the masts in place, was tarred down and secured to the bulwarks by lanyards running through deadeyes, a method that lasted for merchantmen well into the twentieth century. Cordage was comparatively costly. The royal household books for 1501 show that the rigging of two "berkes" cost £46 13s. 4d.

Pictures or models of northern ships of this period are rare; time has disposed of most *ex voto* models in churches, and the occasional carvings of vessels on seals, corbels, and capitals are foreshortened and usually represent the crew as big as the ship. The best representatives of what Cabot's *Mathew* and other early exploring ships looked like are those we have reproduced from the Hastings Manuscript. The single vessel (with oversize mariners) is entering the English Channel with a fair wind aft, and a sailor is sounding from the sterncastle, which seems odd. Probably the lead was cast from the bow, but the line coiled aft, enabling the men to sound without coming up into the wind each time. The ensign, a big burgee with the red cross of St. George on a white field, flares out bravely, and shields of the same design are displayed topside to warn all and sundry that this is an English ship, not to be fooled with. The mizzen is furled so as to facilitate sailing before the wind; there is no spritsail, although Spanish ships as early as Columbus's day had one, bent to a yard slung from the bowsprit. Note the big anchor, of exactly the same design as those still used in the twentieth century, with cable bent onto the ring, ready for lowering. Halyards, braces, and clewlines are indicated on the forecourse and mainsail; and the shrouds are well "rattled down" (crossed with sections of tarred rope), so that sailors can nip up to the crow's nest quickly. All she seems to lack is bonnets on the main course.

The other painting from the Hastings Manuscript, a harbor scene, is even more explicit. The two ships at the top, and perhaps the big one in the center, have just entered harbor and are about to strike sail and anchor. The one at lower right is moored to two anchors (the general practice), and either the current makes her lie stern to wind or the artist has made her flags blow the wrong way. The one at the left is being towed by her longboat to a position where she may safely make sail and beat out. At lower left is one of the primitive lighthouses of the period—an iron cresset on a pole, to hold a warning fire. The ships' tops are bristling with weapons. Rigging is detailed and correct, assuming that the loops hanging from main yards in the two bottom ships are buntlines and clewlines that the crew has not had time to haul taut and belay. Puzzling features are the thing like a brailed-up mizzen held by a sailor on the forecastle of the biggest ship, and the fact that all three under sail have their mizzens furled; one would suppose that they should have been set either for beating out or rounding into the wind to anchor. But we cannot expect—and seldom get—complete accuracy from artists in this era. They had a general idea of what a ship looked like but were not trying to paint portraits of individual vessels.

Late fifteenth-century ship heaving the lead when entering the English Channel. From the Hastings Manuscript. Courtesy J. Pierpont Morgan Library.

English shipping in the late fifteenth century. From the Hastings Manuscript of *c.* 1480. Courtesy J. Pierpont Morgan Library.

Other ship pictures which we may presume to be accurate are on Portuguese charts from about 1510. Two excellent ones are on the section of the "Miller I" of *c.* 1525, which we illustrate near the end of Chapter III below. The vessel at lower right is a much more sophisticated, blue-water type than those on the Hastings Manuscript, and may well be a delineation of the sea-going caravels that carried the Corte Real brothers and Fagundes to Newfoundland and Cape Breton. She is scudding before so strong a wind that the topsails and mizzen are furled. This sketch is remarkably accurate as to hull, profile, and rigging; the artist has depicted a fine, tall ship that any blue-water yachtsman would love to sail today. The vessel in the foreground is running free, her foresail and mainsail bellying to a fresh breeze. Portuguese cartographers, notably Ribero, loved to depict these ships in the trades, with their great square sails bellying like a modern balloon-spinnaker. Skeptical historians assert that such enormous mainsails, with bonnet and drabler (the second bonnet) lashed to the foot, are exaggerated; but I differ. We know from many sources that the *nef* or full-rigged ship carried a main yard as long as her over-all length and that the sail bent to it produced a surprising speed off the wind.

A *navicula* or little ship such as Cabot's *Mathew,* not less than fifty or over sixty feet long, would have had two decks, the main deck laid a few feet over the ballast, and the spar deck exposed to the elements; the head-room between them five feet or even less. On this main deck, against the bulwarks, were lashed the seamen's chests; here they slept, lapped in blankets or an old bit of sail, anywhere they chose; only the officers had bunks. These were in the after superstructure, the sterncastle, which also comprised the steerage. There the principal pieces of furniture were the tiller, shelves or lockers for charts, and traverse board, later superseded by a sea-journal kept on a slate. Here hung the half-hour glass, the ship's only timepiece; a boy was supposed to turn it every half hour (the origin of ships' bells which came later); if he forgot, he received from the bo'sun a few strokes of the "cat o'nine tails." Turning the glass not only served to keep the dead reckoning (as sailors still call navigation by time, distance, and direction), but at every eighth glass to call the new watch on deck.

Forward of the sterncastle, and between it and the forecastle, was the waist of the ship. Here were stowed the smaller ship's boats; the biggest one, the pinnace, or longboat, for which there was no room on

Long-course Portuguese ships of *c.* 1529 from the Ribero World Map
of that date. Reproduced from Nordenskjold's *Periplus*.

deck, had to be towed, and consequently was often lost in heavy
weather. In a rack around the masts or on the bulwarks were the belaying pins, of exactly the same design as in the twentieth century, to
secure running rigging. In the waist was a crude capstan for winding
in the hemp anchor cable by means of wooden pauls (handspikes) to
provide leverage.

The waist of the ship between forecastle and sterncastle was so near water level as to be constantly drenched. So a "waist-cloth," a long strip of canvas, was fitted to each side, to be lashed on to prevent too much water coming in, or to repel boarders. If noble or armigerous gentlemen were on board, they had their arms painted on the waist-cloths or attached their particular shields to them, a practice going back to Viking times. These purely decorative shields were called *pavesses*.

Tunnage in England and France at this period meant a ship's capacity in *tuns*, double-hogsheads in which they shipped wine. Usually this burthen was arrived at by a series of measurements which differed from one country to another. From this developed the modern standard for a maritime *ton* as 40 cubic feet.

I have often wondered how these ships of the early discoverers would have stood up in some of the strong gales and hurricanes described in Adlard Coles's classic *Heavy Weather Sailing*. Would they have hove-to and "laid a-hull" or "a-hold" as the boatswain ordered in *The Tempest?* Or would they have run before it under storm fore-sail or bare poles? We have almost no data to go on. Columbus on his homeward passage in *Niña* in 1493 logged a cyclonic storm so accurately that a modern meteorologist could map it, and the Admiral consistently drove the little caravel before it until he had no canvas left but a storm trysail with which to claw off the Rock of Sintra. One advantage those old ships had over modern yachts (too often designed for personal comfort rather than seaworthiness) is that they were really tight above and below, if the caulking had not been allowed to disintegrate. Their few hatches could be battened down watertight, they had no "self-bailing" cockpit to scoop up a big sea, and no companion-way ladder over which the salt water could flow like a young Niagara into the cabin.

An officer on the highest and driest part of a sixteenth-century ship, the sterncastle, "conned" (directed) the helmsman through a small hatch. I was amused to learn that Bernard Moitessier, who successfully rounded Cape Horn in a forty-foot ketch in the 1960's, approximated a sterncastle by building aft a metal cupola, the "pilot's post," from which he steered. But one place which prevented these old ships from keeping completely tight and dry was the open port where the long tiller joined the rudder head, and which had to be kept open to allow for the rudder's play. When she was running free in a blow, every big wave must have sloshed through this port and drenched the helmsman before flowing into the waist and out through a drain port.

In the seventeenth century high forecastles and sterncastles were abandoned in favor of flush-decked hulls with an uninterrupted sheer from bow to stern. Nineteenth-century steamships followed this basic deck plan, but the two high castles (now called superstructures) have been revived for small freighters. For it is more economical to have your cargo holds run all the way fore and aft, and put the people, the galley, ward-room, etc. topside. When I saw a small Norwegian freighter depart from the Magdalen Islands in September 1969, laden with frozen fish for Boston, the thought occurred to me that if you masted and rigged her, she would closely resemble the ships depicted in the Hastings Manuscript!

Comparing those and other vessels of the late fifteenth and early part of the sixteenth century with those shown in our picture of London River in 1600, it is clear that the principal modifications in the course of the century were (1) square spritsail and sometimes spritsail topsail on bowsprit; (2) square topsail on mizzen, and (3) much larger fore and main topsails in comparison with the lower courses. As topsails increased in area the courses, especially the mainsail, were reduced, and the yards shortened radically. These changes required smaller crews and made the ships both faster and handier. Finally, with greater depth of hold dry compartments could be built between ballast and lower deck for cargo, dry stores, and powder.

In the meantime a new category appears, the "bark," or "barque." This is identified as early as 1552 as a "little shyppe," and an Act of Parliament of 1585 distinguishes between owners and masters of "any Ship, Bark or Boat." Shakespeare, in *The Merchant of Venice* (III, iv), has Gratiano say:

> How like a younker or a prodigal
> The scarféd bark puts from her native bay,
> Hugg'd and embraced by the strumpet wind!

Throughout the sixteenth century *bark* usually meant a ship of under a hundred tuns' burthen, but I have seen mention of one or two slightly over a hundred tuns. The bark was rigged exactly like the ship —fore and mainmast square, mizzen lateen.

In the last third of the sixteenth century there emerges a type called the *flyboat, fliebote,* or *flute.* Sir Walter Raleigh's 140-tun *Roebuck,* named from his family crest, is an example. The name came from the Dutch *vlieboot,* originally one of the small boats used on the *Vlie,* or Sleeve, the channel leading to the Zuyder Zee; but the English flyboat could be anything from 20 to 150 tuns' burthen, and to the English "fly" denoted speed, not sleeve. The late sixteenth-century flyboat was a small three-master, rigged exactly like the bark but built to sail faster and carry less, and requiring a much smaller crew. She was larger than the pinnace. One was described in 1590 as built "to take and leave, when the skyrmish is to hote for him to tarry," meaning that her speed enabled her at will to engage, or break off. Several flyboats were used in the voyages to America under Gilbert and Raleigh.

The smallest sea-going type, called *galion* in French and *pinnace* in English, was a small, shoal-draft, and presumably fast vessel, very useful for exploring bays and the like. Frobisher's pinnace had a crew of only four men. Not completely decked over, these tiny vessels were liable, like a modern yacht, to be pooped and swamped by a heavy following sea, as happened to Gilbert's *Squirrel.* The best practice was to carry a prefabricated pinnace in the hold and assemble it ashore at the first convenient place in the New World. Since davits had not yet been invented, the largest ships' boats were often towed across the Atlantic when there was no room for them on deck. These were called longboats; or, as early as 1578, "gundalos." An account of Frobisher's third voyage says, "Towing our gondelo at stern, she did split therewith and so we were forced to cut her from the ship and lost her." For the same reason, lack of deck space, the smallest boats, called "shallops" (*chaloupes* in French), were often towed, and so lost. John White in his account of the 1590 voyage to Virginia notes on 25 March, "At midnight both our Shallops were sunke being towed at the ships stearne by the Boatswaines negligence." Always blame "Boats"!

John Norden's *Description of the Moste Famous City of London* (1600) shows a number of different small craft in the Thames above London Bridge, types which are occasionally mentioned in the voyages of discovery. At lower left are moored three *tilt-boats* and three more are being rowed along the other bank. These were rowing boats with a lightly built cabin covered by an awning. They were, in effect, water

Shipping in London above the Bridge, 1600. From Visscher's *Londonium* (1616), reproducing John Norden's *Description of the Moste Famous City of London,* 1600. Other small craft will be seen in the second half of this engraving, at the end of the chapter. Courtesy British Museum.

taxis in which Thames watermen rowed paying passengers from Greenwich or even Gravesend to the City. Sir Richard Grenville took a tiltboat to Virginia in 1585, and had himself grandly rowed about Pamlico Sound. Between "South" and "Warke" is a wherry, a type of rowboat persistent to our own day, with fixed thwarts and square slots for the oars. These too were taken overseas. A shallop is being rowed out to the one-masted wood boat over FLUVIUS, and I daresay that even some of the barges, here floating haystacks down from the upper river, were carried to America. In a country where there were very few wharves, slips, or quays, boat service was exceedingly important; and even more so on returning home. We shall find two instances in the Virginia voyages of vessels battered at sea, with beat-up crews, having to anchor in or even outside a harbor and wait for someone to send them a boat.

Getting Under Way

Weighing anchor was an occasion for a chantey; and a Lowland Scots writer of about 1548 records one that he heard on an English galeass— a big ship with three masts and a bank of long sweeps:

> Veyra, veyra, veyra, veyra
> Wind, I see him!
> pourbassa, pourbassa
> haul all and one (*bis*)
> haul hym up to us (*bis*)

Having properly catted, fished, and secured the anchor, let us hear our complaining Scot tell us how a ship got under way.

The master orders "two men above to the foretop to cut the rib-bands"—meaning the gaskets or stops on the furled foresail, "and let the foresail fall." Then, "haul out the bowline," the line secured to the leach (edge) of a square sail to keep it taut on the wind; for want of a jib these vessels had to depend on the foresail to head them off the wind and gather way. The foresail yard is hoisted home to this chantey:

> Ho, ho, ho—
> Pull a', pull a'
> bowline a', bowline a'
> darta, darta,
> hard out stiff (*bis*)
> before the wind, (*bis*)
> God send, God send
> Fair weather, fair weather,
> Many prizes, many prizes
> God fair [wind] send (*bis*)
> stow, stow,
> make fast and belay!

"Then the master cried and bade renze [rein, i.e. lash on] a bonnet, veer the trusses [parrels that bind the yards to the mast], now hoist!" The mariners then perform their most arduous job, hoisting the heavy main yard and sheeting home the main course, to this chantey:

> heisa, heisa
> vorsa, vorsa

wow, wow
one long draft (*bis*)
more might, more might
young blood, young blood
more mude, more mude
false flesh, false flesh
lie aback, lie aback
long swack, long swack
that, that, that, that
there, there, there, there
yellow hair, yellow hair
hips bare, hips bare
tell 'em all, tell 'em all
gallowsbirds all, gallowsbirds all
great and small, great and small
one an' all, one an' all
heist all, heist all

"Now make fast the tiers [halyards]. Then the master cryeth 'set your topsails, haul your topsail sheets veer your lifters [clewlines] and your topsail braces and hoist the topsail higher. Haul taut the topsail bowline. Hoist the mizzen and change it over to leeward. Sway the sheets on the belaying-pins, haul the braces to the yard.' Then the master cryeth to the helmsman, 'Mate, keep her full and by, a-luff. Come no higher, hold your tiller steady as you are, steer from tip of the helm thus and so.' Then, when the ship is tacked, the master cryeth, 'Boy to the top. Shake out the flag on the topmast, take in your topsails and furl them, pull down the point of the yard dagger-wise. Mariners, stand by your gear and the tackling of your sails, every quartermaster to his own station.' "

All this makes sense to anyone who has sailed a square-rigger, but even to old shellbacks some of it needs explanation. The purpose of trimming a yard "dagger-wise," later called "cockbilling," was to spill the wind out of the sail when maneuvering. Changing the mizzen from one tack to another required many hands because this lateen sail, on a long diagonal yard, had to be shifted around the mast whenever the ship came about. This *Complaynt of Scotlande* (1548) indicates that many methods, words, and commands which lasted right through the age of sail, were already in use in the reign of Henry VIII. With allowances for greater simplicity and less yelling on a small vessel, we may apply them to the reign of Henry VII, and imagine John Cabot's crew on the *Mathew* sounding off like those that the Scots "Complayner" heard on the English galeass.

Food, Cooking, and Clothing

At the forward end of the spar deck, partly protected by the forecastle, was the galley, an eighteenth-century term; in our era it was called the cook-box. On the smaller ships this was merely a hooded box placed athwartship and carrying several inches of sand or earth as a base for the fire. A few pots and pans and a supply of firewood sufficed to cook everything for the crew of a 50-tun ship. Native sloops in the West Indies and Arab dhows in the Persian Gulf have similar cooking arrangements today; all very well for smooth seas and fair weather, but not for the rain, fogs, and variables of the Western Ocean. Thus, on every merchant ship or fisherman designed for transatlantic work, the cook-box was built directly on top of the sand, shingle, or rock ballast forward, below the spar deck, and became the "cook-room." This allowed cooking in almost all weather. A Spaniard who boarded John Rut's ship *Mary of Guildford* in 1527 reported that she also had an oven for baking bread. Smoke from the cook-room fire first emerged through the hatches, but by 1571 some sort of "charley noble" or smoke-pipe had been devised, since we hear of Frobisher's *Aid* catching fire from a defective one.

Sebastian Cabot, in his "Ordinances . . . for the direction of the intended voyage to Cathay" via the Northeast Passage (1553), required "the steward and cooke of every ship" to present the captain weekly with an account of the expenditure of victuals "as wel flesh, fish, bisket, meate, or bread, as also of beere, wine, oyle or vinegar." Nobody thought of drinking water until the wine, beer, and cider gave out or spoiled, and in northern latitudes one could usually depend on refilling water butts from rain. The pickled beef and pork, packed in brine, were what English sailors since time immemorial have called "salt horse"; and the "bisket," their main breadstuff, they called "hardtack." It was purchased from bakeries that specialized in ship chandlery, but despite being stored in the driest part of the ship, it always became mouldy and maggotty before the end of a transatlantic round voyage. Ferdinand Columbus relates of his father's fourth voyage, "What with the heat and dampness, our ship biscuit had become so wormy that, God help me, I saw many who waited for darkness to eat the porridge made of it, that they might not see the maggots; and others were so used to eating them that they didn't even trouble to pick them out because they might lose their supper had they been so nice." "Stock-fish," sun-cured codfish from Newfoundland, soon replaced salt herring on the menu for fast days. Potatoes were a gift of the New World, and both coffee and tea came from the Indies; a couple of centuries elapsed before sailors could enjoy either. Spanish ships, and probably northern ships too, carried a supply of salted flour which, kneaded with water into rolls, could be baked in the hot ashes as a relief from the tooth-breaking "bisket."

For Frobisher's second voyage in 1577 we are fortunate to have not only the total amount of each foodstuff, but the way it was calculated: One pound of biscuit and one gallon of beer per man per diem, one pound of salt beef or pork per man on flesh days and one dried codfish for every four men on fast days, with oatmeal and rice if the fish gave out; a quarter-pound of butter and half a pound of cheese per man per day, honey for sweetening (sugar was still an expensive luxury); a hogshead of "sallet oyle" and a pipe of vinegar to last 120 men for three or four months. Considering that they were able to catch all the fresh cod and salmon, and shoot all the wild fowl and game that they wanted, once they had reached the New World, this suggests that English sailors in the reign of Elizabeth I ate hearty. They drank hearty, too, unless the beer went sour or its container leaked.

The mariner's standard costume, which he usually provided himself, was a gown made of coarse serge with a hood attached to protect the neck from wind and rain, loose "trews" (trousers), and "shipmen's hose" (long woolen stockings). From a John White painting we know that sailors' clothes were colorful—bright red or blue; or, if leather, buff. They had shoes, but most of the time went barefoot, as leather skids on a wet deck or spar. Petty officers might add to this simple costume a wide-sleeved belted jacket, with a dagger or knife in a scabbard. Masters and owners made no provision for foul- or cold-weather garb. Apart from Frobisher's ships, in which some mariners had up to six changes of clothing, there was no attempt until 1628, even in the Royal Navy, to provide seamen with spares. A writer to the Admiralty de-scribed changes as "necessary . . . for the preservation of health as to avoid nasty beastliness to which many of the men are subject by continual wearing of one suit of clothes." The Willoughby expedition of 1553 in search of the Northeast Passage carried a "slop-chest," so called because rough, cheap clothes were a specialty of Shropshire (abbreviated Salop). It was stocked, among other articles, with canvas breeches, doublets lined with cotton, petticoats (a short man's-coat worn under the doublet), and "rugg"—a coarse woolen cloth—"for sea gowns."

The hammock for sleeping, discovered by Columbus in 1492 in the Bahamas, was not introduced to the Royal Navy until 1596, but may have been used earlier in big merchant ships. Prior to the issue of hammocks, mariners slept any place they could find; bunks were provided only for officers and some petty officers.

The Sailor, His Wages and Division of Labor

In the early seventeenth century it became a literary fashion to describe the "character" of a lawyer, merchant, divine, etc. One such book, Richard Braithwait's *Whimzies, or New Cast of Characters* (1631), thus describes "A Sayler":

"He is an *Otter*, an *Amphibium* that lives both on Land and Water . . . His familiarity with death and danger, hath armed him with a kind of dissolute security against any encounter. The sea cannot roar more abroad, than hee within, fire him but with liquor . . . In a Tempest you shall heare him pray, but so amethodically, as it argues that hee is seldome vers'd in that practice. . . . Hee makes small or no choice of his pallet; he can sleepe as well on a Sacke of Pumice as a pillow of doune. He was never acquainted much with civilitie; the Sea has taught him other Rhetoricke. Hee is most constant to his shirt, and other his seldome wash'd linnen. Hee has been so long acquainted with the surges of the Sea, as too long a calme distempers him. He cannot speake low, the Sea talks so loud. . . . Hee can spin up a rope like a Spider, and downe againe like a lightning. The rope is his roade, the topmast his Beacon. . . . Death hee has seene in so many shapes, as it cannot amaze him."

The Laws of Oleron, the traditional laws of the sea, dictated the relative responsibilities of master, supercargo, and mariner, as well as sea discipline. We are informed, for instance, that "Yf the maister

Shipboard punishments for mutiny. From Olaus Magnus, *Historia de Gentibus Septentrionalibus*, 1555. One sailor's hand is impaled by a dagger to the mainmast, the one in the water is being keel-hauled, and the one aft is to be repeatedly dunked until almost drowned. Courtesy Harvard College Library.

smyte any of the maryners the maryner ought to abide the fyrst buffet, be it with fyste or flat with his hande. But if he smyte any more he may defend hym[self]."

Seamen in the Royal Navy during the reign of Henry VII were paid 1s. 3d. per week or 5s. per month on active service, and their food cost the government another shilling and a few pence weekly. The master touched 3s. 4d. per week, and the petty officers up to 1s. 8d. In the merchant marine the only figure so far noted is 10s. per month, for Frobisher's sailors. The "portage" or share system of compensating mariners—similar to the "lay" in American whalers and fishermen of the nineteenth century—was already obsolete in 1480, and money wages were the rule in the merchant marine, except in fishing vessels. Sailors were usually given some clothing by the owner, and received a bonus if they took the place of stevedores in unloading the vessel. Mariners had their own "Shipmen's gilds," corresponding to our unions, at Bristol, York, Hull, and elsewhere, to protect those that do business in great waters from being too much put upon by shipowners.

We have no hint as to how *Mathew*'s crew of eighteen divided their duties, except by comparison with Columbus's *Niña*, which had twenty-two men including the captain and the master-owner. *Niña*'s

roster shows, among the officers, a pilot—who took charge of navigation—a surgeon, and a marshal, an office that existed in English vessels
well into the seventeenth century. Captain John Smith wrote: "The
Marshall is to punish offenders and to see justice executed according to
directions; as ducking at the yards arme, haling under the keel, bound
to the capsterne or maine-mast with a bucket of shot about his necke,
setting in the bilbowes." We must never forget that in the great age of
discovery a sailor's life was rough, hard, and perilous. Punishments for
mutiny or refusing orders were cruel, and the punishment for inatten-
tion to his particular business was apt to be crashing a reef, broaching-
to, and death for all hands.

Mathew and every English or French vessel had two essential petty
officers, boatswain and carpenter. "Bo'sun" or "Boats" transmitted the
master's orders with the aid of his whistle, and was responsible for
the gear. He taught the boys how to tie knots, and the mysteries of
splicing, whipping, worming, and parceling the cordage. "Chips" the
carpenter and his mate performed all necessary repairs to the wooden
fabric and spars, and saw to it that topsides and decks were properly
caulked and the seams payed with pitch. Vessels larger than *Niña* or
Mathew carried a cooper to see that the casks of wine and barrels of
beer were kept in good condition, and that enough fresh water was
collected from rainstorms for cooking, or, at a pinch, drinking. *Niña*
shipped seven able seamen and seven gromets (the old name for ships'
boys) who would graduate to ordinary seamen after one voyage; one
of them doubled as the captain's servant. Most mariners in the age of
discovery preferred nimble young boys, despite their tendency toward
skylarking, to old salts who were always grousing and grumbling; but
they had to ship a fair proportion of able seamen to see that the work
got done and to teach the boys how to "hand, reef and steer." The
lowest rating of mariners was known as the "swabber," since it was his
duty to keep the ship clean; and a mop, when it goes to sea, still becomes a "swab."

Ballast and Bilgewater

One great problem on long voyages, especially if there were passengers,
was to keep the ship clean. All hold space not used for ships' stores and
cargo was filled with sand, shingle, or cobblestone ballast from the

beaches of the West Country; and two square, wooden box-like pumps led from the spar deck to the keelson to suck up bilge water. That did not consist entirely of leakage, but of urine, vomit, and various foul food-leavings that lazy sailors discharged into the ballast contrary to orders, under the cheerful belief that the pumps would take care of it. They did, to some extent; and a passenger on an English vessel sailing to the Mediterranean complained of the "foul stinkes" from the pump, against which he was so unfortunate as to sleep. Sebastian Cabot, remembering conditions afloat early in the century, enjoined the 1553 Muscovy fleet, "No liquor to be spilt on the balast, nor filthines to be left within boord; the cook room, and all other places to be kept cleane for the better health of the companie." Despite threats and punishments, the ballast and bilge usually became so disgusting and emitted such "pestilential funkes," that the ship had to be "rummaged" before returning home. That meant heaving her down on some convenient beach, throwing all ballast overboard so that the tide would cleanse it, scraping the horrible gunk off the inside of the hold, spraying it with vinegar, and replacing the ballast with clean stones, sand or shingle. Sir Richard Grenville's *Revenge* was being rummaged at Flores in the Azores when he sighted the Spanish fleet and had to get under way in a hurry.

Some seamen in this era realized what disgusting smells they and their ship produced. This is indicated by Martín Cortés's explanation of the St. Elmo's fire which appeared on masts and yards in tempests or whenever the air was supercharged with electricity. As Englished by Richard Eden, Martín attributed the ghostly "corposants" to "the fumes and smokes of theyr Shyppe, with the heate of men couched close and neare together in a narrowe place, and when a tempest ryseth the sayde smoke is thyckned, prest together or beaten down by the windes," and virtually explodes into fire!

Such conditions bred vermin; rats were an even greater bane to seamen in those days than in ours. The laws of the sea, and charter parties, prescribed that every ship carry one or more cats to keep the rats in order. There was no means of dealing with cockroaches and other vermin except stepping on them; but as transatlantic voyages became more numerous, a tradition developed that shipboard insects remained coy until they reached the warmer parts of the Atlantic, when they came out in force to enjoy the tropics, and the crew.

Navigation

All ships of this era wanted the wind to be on the quarter, or dead aft, to make best speed and least leeway. If the wind came "scant," i.e. dead ahead, or less than four or five compass points from their course, they were forced, if the sea were very rough, to lay-to; or, in a moderate sea, to beat to windward, which they called "traversing." This meant zig-zagging with the wind first on one side and then on the other. Sir Humfry Gilbert on his 1583 voyage, when trying to make St. John's, Newfoundland (latitude 47°33'47″ N), on a due west course, encountered "winde alwayes so scant" from west-northwest and west-southwest, "that our traverse was great," running south to latitude 41° and then north to 51°, missing the harbor he wanted but making northern Newfoundland. This meant that his fleet could not sail nearer the wind than five points—56 degrees.

Celestial navigation is another matter. Before the age of discovery, ships could coast along western Europe, the Mediterranean, and even West Africa with no more shipboard aids to navigation than the compass, a pair of dividers, and the "three L's"—lead, log, and lookout—and the log was not invented until around 1575. Transatlantic voyages stimulated masters and pilots to use celestial navigation to fix their approximate position, just as aviation stimulated scientists to invent quicker methods to get a "fix" than the old time-sight. We shall observe how assiduous Verrazzano, Cartier, Frobisher, and Davis were in taking "heights," i.e. latitudes, of places they discovered.

The art of navigation had been developed by 1497, so that we may assume Cabot, Verrazzano, and Cartier carried a crude, non-reflecting quadrant and a mariner's astrolabe to take altitudes. The only heavenly bodies that the average navigator knew how to use before the end of the sixteenth century were Polaris (the North Star) and the sun. All "rutters" or sailing directions included a crude design to indicate the correction to apply to the height of Polaris, according to the positions relative to it of the "guards"—the two outer stars of the Little Bear or Dipper. Declination tables for obtaining latitude from a meridional observation of the sun were already available. Neither method was accurate within a degree, when practised from a ship at sea; but, once ashore or in harbor, the navigator could get a reasonably good estimate of his latitude. He had no accurate method of obtaining longi-

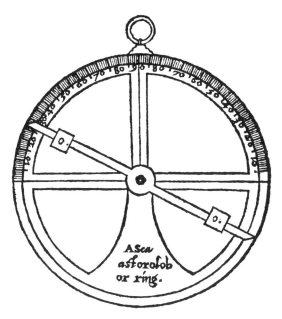

The mariner's astrolabe, or ring. From William Bourne's *A Regiment for the Sea*, 1574.

tude until "lunar distances" and the chronometer were invented in the eighteenth century. Navigators in the age of discovery simply guessed at a ship's speed and kept track of it in their sea journals. They did, however, know how to estimate speed "made good" when off course or beating to windward by a crude traverse board, or table. The rutters all charge the pilot to transfer data from traverse board, or table, to his "carde" (chart), a blank sheet of paper ruled for latitude and longitude. And he must "pricke the carde" for every noon or other estimated position.

The helmsman was directed by the officer on watch through a hatch or hole in the sterncastle deck, as the officer had the standard compass. That was a dry-card type on a pivot, floating in a bowl and enclosed in a waterproof binnacle which included a little whale-oil lamp. This, like similar binnacle lamps on nineteenth-century yachts, was always blowing out. On larger vessels, whose owners felt it a good investment, there was a second, steering compass just forward of the helmsman. Although ships of the period did a lot of rolling and pitching,

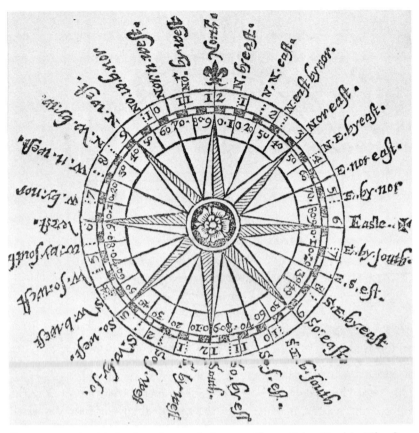

Compass card with both points and degrees. From John Davis's *The Seaman's Secrets*, 1594.

they were easy to keep on course if the sails were properly trimmed. As an aid to steering, prior to the invention of the wheel, a vertical beam called the whipstaff was riveted by one end to the deck, the middle loosely joined to the end of the tiller, and the top two or three feet used as a lever to pull it to starboard or larboard, as the port hand was called until the nineteenth century. This whipstaff did not become standard equipment in England until the second half of the sixteenth century, but the expert who constructed a model of Cartier's *La Grande Hermine* of 1525 gave her one.

The rutters (*routiers*), unofficial coast pilots of the period, were written primarily for finding one's way along European shores, but transatlantic voyagers were wise to have one on board for arrival and departure. Contrary to what most landsmen think, a shipmaster had a fairly easy time in blue water, where there were no obstacles; his troubles began when he arrived on soundings. That was when he snarled at his pilot, roared at the sailors, and aimed a kick at the ship's cat. Day and night he pored over his chart and his rutter, which might tell him from the depth of water, and the nature of the bottom, where he might be. Well did William Bourne, in his qualifications for a trans-atlantic captain, in 1574 write, "Also it behoueth him to be a good coaster, that is to say, *to knowe every place by the sight thereof.*" Fortunately an experienced seaman's memory of places he has passed but once, is phenomenal. The entire coast of western Europe is fraught with hazards to sailing vessels approaching from the sea; hazards which modern devices of lights, radio beacons, echo-sounders, etc. have miti-gated but not removed. Consider, for instance, the problem of a master entering St. George's Channel in thick or strong weather, bound for Bristol, Dublin, or Liverpool. On one side Fastnet and the Smalls await his ship with greedy fangs; on the other are the Scillies and the multi-tude of rocks between them and Lands End, Cornwall, including Seven Stones, where the big tanker *Torrey Canyon* came to grief in 1967, drenching the Cornish shores with black oil. Or, supposing he were a man of Devon seeking the sanctuary of Plymouth. He had to sail well south of his destination to avoid the Eddystone's *scopulos infames*, as Camden called them; but if he sailed too far south he might strike the equally dangerous Casquets off Alderney.

Or, the master mariner returning from Newfoundland, after picking up familiar landmarks—a church steeple, a clump of trees, an odd house—and about to enter his home port, might be forced to sea again by a radical change in the wind. In the English Channel gale of July 1953, a well-built ten-ton yacht meeting a big wind funnelling out of Cherbourg head-on, could not enter, even with the aid of her engine. She was blown across the Channel and foundered off the Isle of Wight.

In these narrow seas local knowledge and a judicious use of the lead were essential. The heavy leads (as shown in the Hastings Manuscript) had a socket "armed" (filled) with sticky tallow to pick up samples of the bottom; and from them, as well as the depth, the experienced pilot knew where he was. For instance, Master Jackman on Frobisher's 1578 voyage "sownded and had 70 faddems, oosy sand, whereby we judged us to be northwards of Scilly, and afterward sailed south east all that night." The ship rounded Lands End safely, and three days later "had sight of the Start, 5 leags off, God be praysed!" A rutter like Bourne's made a point of giving the character of the bottom ("white sand, soft worms, popplestones as big as beans, cockleshells," etc.) at every crucial point.

Not all master pilots were as smart as Jackman. The *Hopewell* from Newfoundland, bound for London in August 1587, "drawing neere the coast of England," sounded and found seventy fathom, but nobody could agree on interpreting what the lead brought up; so through "evil marinership were fain to dance the hay foure days together," running northeast, southeast, east and east-northeast. Finally they sighted Lundy in the Severn estuary, whence they shaped their course around Lands End to London. Dancing the hey or hay was an old country reel in which the boys and girls danced in serpentine fashion, like beating to windward.

Once within the chops (entrance) of the Channel, the careful pilot bound for London, ticked off the prominent headlands as he passed. These are described in the old chantey "Spanish Ladies":

> Now the first land we make it is calléd the Deadman
> Then Rams Head off Plymouth, Start, Portland and Wight;
> We sailed then by Beachy, by Fairlee and Dungeness
> Then bore straight away for the South Foreland Light.

Deadman was what sailors called Dodman Island, Cornwall; Start Point you had to round to make Dartmouth; Portland Bill is a conspicuous point which makes a bad tide-rip; St. Catherine's Point, Isle of Wight, and Beachy Head are perfect landmarks; Fairlee meant Fairlight Hill just east of Hastings, and Dungeness is the last prominent cape before reaching the South Foreland.

There were none but dim local lights along this coast in the sixteenth century, and very few buoys or other navigational aids. The French coast was better marked. Biggest lighthouse in Europe was the forty-eight-foot stone Tour de Cordouan at the mouth of the Gironde, first erected in the ninth century and rebuilt by the Black Prince; a tower so famous that it became a point of reference in John Cabot's voyage. There were also lighthouses at La Rochelle (lighted only in storms), at Dieppe, and perhaps seven other ports in Normandy and Brittany. But "practically nothing is known for certain about any English lighthouses between the Roman occupation and the middle of the seventeenth century except that a few primitive towers did exist," states the historian of the then unmarked Eddystone. One such is shown in our illustration from the Hastings Manuscript of 1480. These were erected and maintained by private individuals or coastal towns; a fire of bituminous coal or resinous wood furnished the light. They were undependable since the owners usually considered it a waste of fuel to light up on a clear or moonlit night, and when most needed they might be quenched by rain or snow.

In the narrow seas one could not ignore the danger of collision. No running lights were required until centuries later, but masters were recommended to keep a lighted "lanthorn" in a bucket to show if they were in danger of being run down. Want of artificial lights made it desirable to begin a transatlantic voyage near the moon's first quarter, in order to have moonlight to clear the Channel.

For the master of a vessel which had no auxiliary power, a knowledge of tides was a necessity, especially in the English Channel and Bristol Channel where tides run swift and high. If he knows their times, and the direction and force of the currents they create, tides are a boon to the knowledgeable sailor, and a terror to the ignorant. There were then no government or private tide tables, but every rutter taught the pilot how to compile his own. Based on the changeless fact that high water on the day of new moon comes at noon or midnight, you figure that it comes forty-eight minutes later every day thereafter. But only experience, or information handed down from the Middle Ages, could teach one the flow of the currents at danger points like Eddystone and Ushant.

In discussing navigational methods, one is apt to ignore the gap between the invention of a device and persuading owners to supply it or sailors to use it. For instance, the chronometer, which first enabled a navigator to get accurate longitude, was invented in 1750; but the royal French navy in 1833, with 250 ships, had only 44 chronometers. To assume that once an instrument is invented or a rutter or nautical almanac published, every offshore shipmaster is familiar with them, is a complete fallacy. The very simple mathematical calculations involved in obtaining latitude from a meridional observation of the sun were too much for most sailors in 1550, and are still too much for many sailors in the present century. I had the experience of teaching a good down-east sailing master to take accurate sights with a sextant; but he could never get through his head that there are only sixty, not one hundred minutes, to the degree, hence his results were all wrong. And another of the same breed once remarked, "I don't know nothin' about chronometers and ba-rometers, but I can find my way around!" No doubt he could; there is a certain *feel* for a ship and the sea, possessed by men like Columbus, Cartier, Frobisher, John Davis, and by thousands of humble shipmasters unknown to fame, which is as good or better than scientific navigation.

In general, the navigational methods in effect around 1500 lasted, with many refinements but no essential changes, until 1920–30. Then radio beams, timers, echo-finders, and the like were first installed on warships and big steamships, replacing the navigator's dependence on his own efforts with shipboard instruments. But, woe betide the master who neglects the traditional Three L's! Remember the *Andrea Doria!*

Shipboard Religion

Sailors in the age of discovery were highly sensible of the danger of their calling—and why not? John Cabot was lost with four ships and all hands, the Corte Real brothers were lost with two ships and all hands, Sir Humfry Gilbert's pinnace was "devoured and swallowed up of the sea" within sight of her consorts. They were conscious of being in a special sense in the hands of the Almighty, and so made a point of public prayers to remind God and the Virgin Mary, "Star of the Sea," that they counted on heavenly protection against the cruel elements. For the same reason, to avoid affronting God to the point of His becoming indifferent to a ship's fate, Sebastian Cabot charged "that no blaspheming of God, or detestable swearing be used . . . nor communication of ribaldrie filthy tales, or ungodly talke to be suffered in the company . . . neither dicing, carding, tabling nor other divelish games to be frequented, whereby ensueth not only povertie to the players, but also strif, variance, brauling . . . and provoking of God's most just wrath, and sworde of vengeance." Sebastian insists "that morning and evening prayer, with the common services appointed by the king's Majestie be read dayly by the chaplain or some other person learned," and "the Bible or paraphrases to be read devoutly and Christianly to God's honour, and for His grace to be obtained." As this indicates, every shipmaster provided himself with an Edward VI Book of Common Prayer. And the requirement of daily prayer lasted, as is shown by Captain John Smith's *Sea Grammar* of 1627, prescribing orisons and psalms at stated intervals. Similar injunctions against swearing and blasphemy are found in sailors' contracts in merchant marines right down to 1900.

Prior to Henry VIII's breach with Rome, English ships, and French ships later (unless owned by Protestants), probably followed the same ritual as did Columbus: a hymn, Our Father, and Hail Mary when changing the dawn watch; a little ditty each time the glass is turned; around sunset, when the first night watch is set, all hands repeating Our Father, Hail Mary, and the Creed, and singing the hymn *Salve Regina* to the Queen of Heaven. Frobisher held some sort of service at noontime; he records one day chasing Eskimo visitors off the ship at 11:00 a.m., "since we were to go to prayer."

Seamen were superstitious as well as religious, and still are. One must never sail on a Friday, because it was the day Our Lord was crucified. One must never lay a hatch cover upside down—goodness knows why. One must not destroy a printed page—it might belong to the Bible. In building a ship, a silver coin must be heeled below the mainmast. On the Isle of Man a burning brand had to be carried through every part of a new ship to drive out evil spirits. The ghost of an unbaptized infant buried at the foot of a tree whose wood was used to build a ship, would inhabit the vessel and bring her good fortune. This is the

> Sweet little cherub that sits up aloft
> To keep watch for the life of poor Jacke,

as wrote Charles Dibdin the sailor's poet.

Weapons, Sweeps, and Anchors

By mid-century, vessels built especially for war were designed differently from ordinary merchant ships, as you may see from our illustrations. But almost every merchant vessel mounted a few small cannon such as the lombard, which threw a stone cannon ball, and the smaller falconet, a swivel gun mounted on the bulwarks, which fired scrap metal. Verrazzano and Cartier, who sailed in kings' ships, probably

H.M.S. *Tegar*, 200 tuns, 100 "marrynars," and 20 "gonnars."

H M S *Lyon*, 140 tuns, 100 men. From the Anthony Roll of the Navy, 1545 Add. Mss. 22047. Both have dressed ship for a holiday. Courtesy British Museum.

carried larger ordnance; but the only weapon mentioned in any Cabot narrative is the crossbow. Every ship carried a stand of swords, cutlasses, and pikes to be used in case natives or enemies endeavored to take her by boarding. The difficulty in keeping gunpowder dry on a small ship in rough weather, and the danger of its exploding if placed near the galley fire to dry, made steel more popular with sailors than firearms; pike and crossbow did well enough against enemies who had nothing more lethal than bows and arrows.

Cannon were always mounted on the spar deck prior to 1501, when a certain Decharges of Brest had the wit to place guns below on the

Ship in Dover Harbor, *c.* 1530–37. The Cross of St. George, the men at arms, and tier of guns (with two stern-chasers sticking out beside the rudder) show that she is one of the smaller units of the Royal Navy. From Cottonian Aug. Mss. I. i. 23. Courtesy British Museum.

Ships on the Thames below London Bridge, 1600. From Visscher's *Londonium* (1616), copying John Norden's *Description of the Moste Famous City of London*, 1600. Courtesy British Museum.

main deck and to pierce ports for them to fire through. The earliest picture that I have seen to show gun ports is of the war vessel here illustrated, in a view of Dover *c.* 1530–37. Incidentally, this is one of the best ship-pictures of that period for accurate detail of sails, spars, and rigging. Note the halberdier on the forecastle and another in her waist, and an archer on the poop. The protection under the bowsprit with the head of a fox was known as the beak head, and supposedly had been copied from Mediterranean galleys which used it for ramming. After informal war began with Spain, every English ship carried heavy ordnance. In our picture of H.M.S. *Tegar*, in 1585, the gun ports are prominent.

All vessels the size of Cabot's *Mathew*, and larger ones too, were provided with long ash sweeps so that they could be propelled in a calm. And they could also be towed by their longboat.

Iron anchors, of a design unchanged for over four centuries, were stowed in the forecastle during a voyage, and a hemp cable bent onto the ring for use in harbor or alongshore. The Hastings Manuscript ship shows one very plainly. The tackles securing the anchor to the cathead and the sides of the ship were called *stoppers* and *shank-painters* as early as 1577, in the inventory of Frobisher's flagship *Aid*. Every transatlantic vessel carried at least four anchors; and as ships often had to moor in an open roadstead, breakwaters being scarce even in Europe, and forced to get under way in a hurry, they were apt to lose two or three in the course of a long voyage. Columbus was once left with only one anchor for two ships, so he had to "raft" them together, as members of the Cruising Club like to do.

Almost every transatlantic voyage ended at anchor. In the ports of London, Bristol, Le Havre, Rouen, Dieppe, and a few others, local authorities provided stone quays or jetties alongside which a ship could lay and discharge cargo; but in the New World every stop meant anchoring. The prudent captain, before entering an unknown harbor, would send in a boat to sound and test the holding ground; the harbor might turn out to have a bottom of hard stone or slippery eel grass over which an anchor would skid like a sled on snow. No wonder that the anchor became the symbol of hope (Hebrews vi. 19) and of admiralty.

Many improvements were made in English rigging and ship design during the sixteenth century, but the blue-water merchantmen of 1500 and 1600 were essentially similar. Greater changes came in the following century, owing (as Hakluyt predicted) to overseas trade's requiring faster and more seaworthy ships, and accommodation for passengers.

As Buckminster Fuller pointed out in his *Ideas and Integrities* (1963), the building of a ship that could harness the wind, and by "traversing" sail where her master wished, is one of the greatest and most admirable achievements of mankind. The building alone involved many techniques of the modern assembly plant, and to sail successfully overseas drew on astronomy, meteorology, and dynamics, as well as courage, resourcefulness, and sound common sense. All the world's great geographical discoveries were made with no other power than oar and sail. As Edouard Peisson remarked in his *L'Aigle de mer*, "Le voilier était à la mesure de l'homme. Il n'écrasait pas l'homme, mais l'attirait, le séduisait, le gardait." And it still delights us and fortifies us against a mechanized culture which reduces man to a moron.

The men who manned these ships, or sailed in them as passengers, were those who enlarged the scope of Europe to embrace the whole world. Would that we knew far more than we do about life on board their wooden vessels, their only homes for a large portion of their lives.

✻ II ✻

John Cabot's Voyages

1497-1498

Kepe then the sea that is the wall of England:
And then is England kept by Goddes hande.
—A LIBEL OF ENGLISH POLICIE, *c*. 1436.

Who Was John Cabot?

In view of his importance as the first discoverer of North America
since the Northmen's voyages almost five centuries earlier, and as the
man who gave England her American title, it is amazing how little we
know about John Cabot. But not for lack of trying. During the last
century and a half, research into his life and voyages has been both
intense and assiduous, with results disappointingly meager. No portrait
or personal description of him, no letter, no scrap of his handwriting,
not even a signature, has been found. His momentous first voyage cannot be definitely traced. His fate, on his second voyage, is not certainly
known. Part of the historical muddle is due to the fact that John's son
Sebastian, who may have accompanied him on the first voyage, showed
a notable lack of filial piety in claiming the discovery for himself;
and as John disappeared in 1498 and Sebastian became a great man,
people believed him and forgot his father. So, to put John Cabot
together again from the bits and pieces excavated from archives and
muniments is like trying to construct a big picture puzzle from one
per cent of the original pieces, few of which can be fitted together.
We have no sea journal by Cabot himself as we have for Columbus,
nor did any of his shipmates leave an account of the voyage. All the
evidence is hearsay, mostly at third hand, and by people who made

39

wild guesses. It is no wonder that scholars disagree about Cabot. One has to discard part of the scanty evidence to make sense out of the rest.

To begin with, Who was John Cabot?

An Italian certainly; a Genoese probably. The name, common on the European littoral in various forms such as Cabotto, Kaboto, Chiabotto, Bagoto, Cabuto, Savoto, etc.—sometimes corrupted by writers who did not hear it correctly, to Babate or Talbot—means simply "Coaster" —one who engages in coastal shipping. The Spanish ambassador at the Court of St. James's in 1498 called John "another Genoese like Colón," but nothing about his family has been found in the Genoese archives. Our first trace of him is in Venice when he became a naturalized citizen. The Venetian senate confirmed his citizenship in 1476, stating that he had been a resident of the Republic for fifteen years. He must, therefore, have been born not later than 1453, and probably earlier, even in 1451, the same year as Columbus. They might have been boys together in Genoa. John's father took him to Venice when he was not more than ten years old. Soncino, the Milanese envoy in London, calls John "a very good mariner" and "of a fine mind, greatly skilled in navigation." He must have been, to have done what he did. And he must have possessed uncommon courage to set forth with only one small ship. Even the Pilgrim Fathers started with two.

The first known fact on Cabot's sea-going activities was told by him to Soncino: "In former times he was at Mecca, whither spices are brought by caravans from distant countries." Those who brought them thither knew not where spices originated, but Cabot incorrectly inferred that they came from *northern* Asia.

John Cabot was already married and living in Venice in 1484; documents prove that he was there engaged in buying and selling real estate, and there was some dispute about his wife's dowry. Next, in the archives of Valencia, it appears that a Venetian called "Johan Cabot Montecalunya" resided in that Spanish seaport between 1490 and 1493. He tried to interest King Ferdinand the Catholic in building a jetty; the project fell through in March 1493 because "matching funds" were not forthcoming. It cannot be proved that this John Cabot with the strange suffix was our John, but he may well have been; and it does not strain one's imagination to assume that he happened to be in Barcelona at the time of Columbus's triumphal entry in April 1493, that he met the Admiral of the Ocean Sea and decided to do him one better, reaching the Indies by a shorter route. He sought support in Seville and Lisbon, but failed.

It then occurred to him that England, being at the end of the spice line and paying the highest prices, would be interested in finding a short, high-latitude route to the Indies. Spices, especially pepper, cloves, and nutmeg, were household necessities in that era, for want of refrigeration; a liberal use of them disguised the flavor of spoiled meat. So to England went Cabot, and England was the one country where he was likely to gain support. Henry VII, in turning down the proposition of the Columbus brothers, had missed his chance to be "first"; he was not going to miss it this time, particularly since Cabot offered to sail on "his own proper charges," so it would not cost the crown a penny. And it is certain that Cabot went there not later than 1495, because the Spanish ambassador wrote to King Ferdinand in January 1496 that "Uno como Colón" (a man like Columbus) was proposing to King Henry VII "another business like that of the Indies." In reply the Spanish sovereign ordered his ambassador to protest; but his excellency, if he got around to it, did not succeed. On 5 March 1496 Henry VII granted letters-patent to "our well beloved John Gabote, citizen of Venice, [and] to Lewes, Sebastian, and Santius, sonnes of the said John . . . full and free authoritie, leave, and power, to sayle to all partes, countreys, and seas, of the East, of the West, and of the North, under our banners and ensignes, with five ships . . . and as many mariners or men as they will have with them in the saide ships, upon their own proper costes and charges, to seeke out, discover, and finde, whatsoever iles, countreyes, regions or provinces of the heathen and infidelles, whatsoever they bee, and in what part of the world soever they be, whiche before this time have beene unknowen to all Christians." They may govern these newly found lands as the king's lieutenants, monopolize their produce and enter them duty free, paying to the crown "the fifth part of the Capitall gaine so gotten." And no one may visit these discoveries "without the licence of the foresayd John, his sonnes, and their deputies." These letters-patent follow the form of the *cartas de doacão* that the Portuguese kings had been granting to navigators who wished to be lords of any new country that they found. Since in those days you wrote your own ticket for royal letters-patent, Cabot probably obtained a copy of a Portuguese charter, altered it to suit his case, and paid a court scrivener to engross and

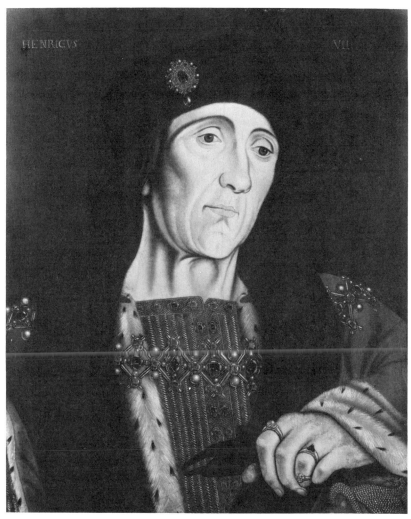

King Henry VII. By an unknown contemporary. Courtesy National Maritime Museum, Greenwich.

present it to Henry VII. And, as in the case of the Portuguese documents and of Columbus's contract with the Spanish sovereigns, nothing is said about a route to the Indies. Obviously a sovereign could not grant an ocean route, only the discoveries that the grantee might make while seeking it.

Bristol and the Transatlantic Passage

Bristol, where Cabot, his wife, and three sons settled shortly after they came to England in 1495, was the right place to gain local support. "Bristowe," as it was then pronounced and often spelled, is a truly extraordinary city. By making the most of its few natural advantages and surmounting every disadvantage, it had by 1400 become, and for four centuries remained, the second seaport in the kingdom. Bristol has never decayed. It welcomed the age of steam, built the first iron screw steamship *Great Britain* and hundreds of other steamships, created great industries out of its Spanish trade in sherry and its American trade in cacao and tobacco, survived some very severe bombing in World War II, and in 1969 enjoyed a trade not far short of £300 million per annum.

In the early Middle Ages, far-sighted Saxons chose a little peninsula between the junction of the Frome and Avon rivers, and there built a bridge and a town. Its original name, Brygstowe, means simply "Place of the Bridge." It lay eight miles from the Severn estuary, good insurance against surprise attack by pirates or other sea enemies. But the Avon, in comparison with the Thames below London, is difficult to navigate; a narrow, tortuous stream breaking through a rocky gorge up and down which tidal currents flow with tremendous force, the neaps having a rise and fall of twenty-one feet, and the springs forty feet, at Avonmouth. These are the highest tides in the world, excepting those in the upper Bay of Fundy; they rendered navigation between ocean and city both difficult and hazardous. In the last century an 800-ton steamship, running aground on the Horseshoe Bend at high water, rolled down the steep mud bank as the tide ebbed, and capsized. Just below the town the Avon is overlooked by green Brandon Hill, named for an otherwise unrecorded visit of St. Brendan. In 1497, there was an oratory on top dedicated to him; at the quatercentenary of John Cabot's voyage, this site was well chosen for the Cabot memorial tower, but the old name stuck. Men and boys of Bristol still play bowls there on spring and summer evenings, and several springs at the foot of St. Vincent's Rock, watered the Abbey of St. Augustine and the Carmelite Friary. Lower down the stream a hot well gushed out ten feet above the river at low water, but twenty-six feet below the high-tide level. This was drunk by homecoming sailors as a cure for

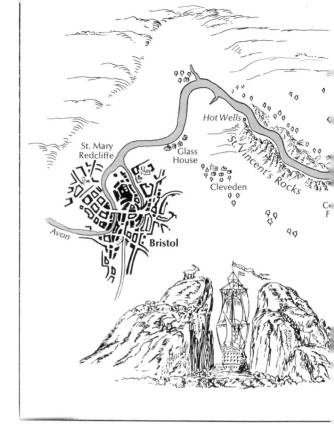

scurvy, and in the eighteenth century this Hotwell made Bristol a rival to nearby Bath. But that was long after Cabot's day.

The association with St. Brendan is not merely sentimental; at some time in the Middle Ages a group of Bristolians must have decided that if St. Brendan could make a voyage in a frail curragh, they could do better in stout wooden vessels built "shipshape and Bristol fashion," a phrase that went around the world. At any rate, that is what they did.

Two natural advantages Bristol possesses. It is the obvious outlet and shipping port for the Cotswold country, famous for sheep; and it lies about midway between Iceland and the Iberian Peninsula. Thus, by the twelfth century, there had grown up a profitable north-south trade of exporting woolens, some woven in Bristol, bringing back from Iceland stockfish (dried codfish), and from Spain and Portugal wine and olive oil—especially sherry, already called "Bristol milk." More wine and woad, the plant used to make a blue dye for woolens, came from Bordeaux and Bayonne in Gascony. The southern products were

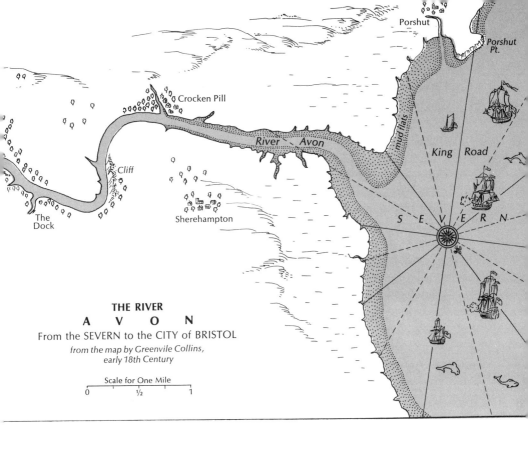

Porshut
Porshut
Pt.

Crocken Pill

River   Avon

mud flats

King   Road

Cliff

S   E   V   E   R   N

The
Dock

Sherehampton

THE RIVER
A   V   O   N
From the SEVERN to the CITY of BRISTOL
from the map by Greenvile Collins,
early 18th Century

Scale for One Mile
0   ½   1

mostly trans-shipped to Ireland, Wales, and Iceland; and the canny men of Bristol kept profits in their hands by building their own ships and manning them locally.

As early as the fourteenth century such prosperity descended on Bristol that, sensible of "every good and perfect thing" coming from God, the merchant-shipowners began to build superb churches. "Fairest and goodliest parish church in all England" (as Queen Elizabeth remarked) was St. Mary Redcliffe, built in a suburb on the left bank of the Avon where its noble spire could serve as a guide for any ship floating up on the flood tide. Here one may see the magnificent tomb of William Canynges (1400–1474), owner of ten ships and the first Englishman to be called a "merchant prince." Here also are buried John Jay who initiated an annual search for the elusive island of Hy-Brasil in 1480, and sheriff Richard Amerike, traditionally one of Cabot's backers and Bristol's nominee as the person after whom America was named—*not* Amerigo Vespucci, if you please!

The central part of Bristol in 1673. From Miller's Plan of Bristol, original in City Museum; facsimile by Waterlow & Sons Ltd., 1950. Courtesy City Archives of Bristol.

46

St. Mary's was not the only landmark for sailors; Bristol merchants in the fifteenth century built a church on Dundry Hill south of the town, and upon its square stone tower erected one of the primitive lighthouses of that era, burning coal in an iron brazier. As early as 1245, in order to make a second harbor right in their city, the Bristolians diverted the little Frome River from its lower course to St. Augustin's Marsh and built a stone quay ("The Key" on our map) against which sea-going vessels could safely moor when grounded at low tide. This became the principal place for ships to lade and discharge, although there was also a stone quay at St. Nicholas' Back, on the Avon below Bristol Bridge, and a custom house at each place. Right on "The Key" there was built in the thirteenth century—and beautifully rebuilt in 1470—the church of St. Stephen. Here, according to local tradition, the Cabots worshipped at the time of John's first voyage. That very likely is true; for in the nearby Marsh Street lived the "masters and mariners" who in 1445 founded a fraternity to support a priest and twelve poor old sailors, who should pray for their brethren "when passing and labouring on the Sea." St. Mary Redcliffe, however, claims the Cabots as parishioners after the voyage of 1497, when they became more affluent, and points to the rib of a cow-whale alleged to have been brought back from Newfoundland by John as a thank-offering. After his return he rented a house in St. Nicholas Street near the bridge, for £2 a year.

The 1480's and '90's, when the Cabots came to Bristol, were prosperous. During the last twenty years of the fifteenth century Bristol exported more cloth, imported more wine, and handled more dutiable goods than any other English provincial port. This little city, with a population not exceeding 10,000, imported from Gascony in 1480 816 tuns of wine and £2450 worth of woad, and exported 2192 "cloths" to Ireland, Spain, Portugal, and Gascony; a "cloth," by act of Parliament, was 24 yards long. But her Iceland trade had been in trouble for years, owing in part to sailors' brawls with the Icelanders and in part to the enterprise of the Hanseatic League in exploiting this unpleasantness.

Bristol was also the right place to arouse interest in spices. Everyone remembered how, forty years earlier, Robert Stormy, merchant of Bristol, had sent two ships to the Levant in the hope of opening a spice trade at the end of the caravan route, and how one was wrecked on the coast of Greece and the other "spoiled by the Janneys" (the Genoese), who did not want Bristol cutting in on their middleman's profit. To discover a short, northern route to the land of spices would make a fortune for Bristol, and for England.

Bristol also needed new fishing grounds or a new fishing base; Hy-Brasil might well do; and from 1480 on, every few years one, two or three vessels sailed from Bristol in the hope of locating it. One in 1480, commanded by Master Lloyd, reported to be "the most knowledgeable seaman in the whole of England," hunted for months for the elusive isle but found it not; two ships went on a similar mission in 1481; and from 1491 on, Bristol sent from two to four ships a year "in search of the island of Brazil and the Seven Cities," wrote Ayala the Spanish ambassador. English historians who have joined their Portuguese brethren in search of "firsts" are now arguing that Lloyd "must have" discovered Newfoundland in 1480 but forgot to note its location; and that all the others were trying to rediscover it. This argues a very low intelligence on the part of the mariners of Bristol, and also makes the king's patents and rewards to John Cabot senseless. No doubt, after Cabot's voyage, many Bristolians were saying "He found nothing but that old island which we discovered years ago."

Whilst Cabot's main object, and the king's in supporting him, was to discover a short ocean route to the Indies, he doubtless hoped to locate Hy-Brasil en route, just as Columbus counted on Antilia as a future staging point.

Whatever the reasons—timidity, dislike of the foreigner, or lack of funds—Cabot obtained but one vessel, a *navicula* (little ship) of fifty *toneles'* burthen, i.e. capable of carrying fifty tuns of wine. This was about the same as that of the *Niña* (60 tuns). Cabot's vessel probably spread the same sail plan as Columbus's sea-going caravels—squaresail on fore and main, lateen on mizzen, possibly a square main topsail. Her crew of eighteen included one Burgundian and a barber from Castiglione near Genoa—John did not intend to frighten the natives with a six weeks' beard! The rest we may presume to have been Englishmen.

The name of this ship, *Mathew*, so called in Toby's Chronicle of Bristol, has been challenged because Toby is under suspicion as a possible fabrication of Thomas Chatterton

. . . the marvellous boy,
The sleepless soul that perished in his pride,

the poet who supported himself by forgery. But William Adams's
"Pettie Chronicle," written in Bristol in 1625, states, "On the 24th of
June 1496"—his mistake for 1497—"was newfoundland fowend by
Bristol men in a ship called the *Mathew*."

Everything points to the fact that *Mathew* was a fast, able, and
weatherly craft. She performed a round transatlantic voyage of discovery in the astonishing time of eleven weeks, setting a record that
remained unbroken for almost a century. Quick to answer the helm she
had to be, to avoid crashing on a rocky headland when it suddenly
loomed up out of the fog; sea-kindly she had to be, to lay a-hull in
a heavy blow, with perhaps a small stormsail set, or run before it under
storm foresail. The model of her at the Bristol Museum, very carefully
worked out by local historians and based on the vessels depicted in the
Hastings Manuscript, is, in my opinion, excellent.

Mathew departed Bristol on her momentous voyage on or about 20
May. We do not know whether the city made a thing of it and the
rectors of St. Stephen and St. Mary Redcliffe blessed ship and crew; or
whether she slipped down the Avon with no other ceremony than
tender farewells by wives, sisters, and sweethearts. One can imagine
old codgers on the waterfront growling—There goes another voyage
to Brasil—God help the poor fools—there ain't no such island!—Why
do they think that furriner can find it when us men of Bristowe can't?

It was the spring of the year. Apple blossoms and the hawthorn were
out, and the sedgy banks of the lower Avon were white with great
drifts of *cochlearia officinalis*, which sailors called scurvy grass after
discovering that it was a better cure for scurvy than the water of the
Hotwell. Once safely around Horseshoe Bend, *Mathew* passed on the
port hand the village of Crockern Pill where lived a community of
river pilots and boatmen who made a living towing craft in a calm or
against headwinds. Bristol tradition affirms that a local pilot named
James George Ray accompanied Cabot. Possibly so; but it is more
likely that he piloted *Mathew* down river and went ashore at Avonmouth, where vast modern docks have enabled Bristol to keep her sea
supremacy.

Undoubtedly Cabot had pumped sundry master mariners of Bristol

Conjectural model of Cabot's navicula *Mathew* by Mr. N. Poole of Bristol.
Courtesy Bristol Art Gallery.

in the Iceland trade for information, and learned that in the spring of the year he would have more easterly winds than at any other season. April is now the best month for a westward passage. A westbound vessel on this northern route could expect an easterly wind on only a minority of days, but she would enjoy a good deal of due north and due south winds too, which *Mathew* could take on her beam. Once every so often—it happened last in the summer of 1958—a high-pressure system between Norway and Greenland produces a strong northeasterly in the region between latitudes 50° and 60° N, continuing from seven to twenty days. But as *Mathew* took 35 days Bristol to America, which means 32 or 33 days from Ireland to Newfoundland, she could not have enjoyed one of these lucky breaks. Nevertheless, thirty-three days land to land—exactly the same as on Columbus's first voyage although half the distance—was a good westward passage in latitudes north of 40°. Many, even in the last century, have taken two or three months to sail from England to North America. Peter Kalm in 1748 was delighted to have made Philadelphia in forty-one days from Gravesend; he noted that several vessels had taken fourteen to nineteen weeks for that passage.

Of *Mathew*'s Atlantic crossing we have provokingly few details. She sailed "north and then west," taking her departure around 22 May from Dursey Head, Ireland. That was a favorite point of departure for Atlantic voyages throughout the sixteenth century. This may have been because it was supposed to be the westernmost point of Ireland. It looks so as you approach from the south, and almost is; the Skelligs, the Blaskets, and Inishshark are only a few miles further west. The Irish coast between Dursey Head and Achill was reputed to be dangerous, and it behooved a prudent master to get sea room as soon as he rounded Fastnet. Day says that the wind blew from the east and northeast a good part of the way, but not all; and Soncino says that she "wandered about considerably"—a typical landlubber's interpretation of beating to windward. On the evening of the last day of May, a silver new moon hung in the western sky, and that moon would wax to full and wane to last quarter before *Mathew* made land. She enjoyed

Dursey Head and Bull Rock, Ireland. Photo in July 1969 by Captain H. K. Rigg of the Cruising Club of America.

smooth seas except for one gale two or three days before the landfall. Either on his outward or his homeward passage, Cabot noted a two-point (22½°) westerly variation of the compass.

Cabot's principle of navigation, the time-honored latitude sailing, is revealed by his latitude observations and by Soncino's statement that he kept the North Star on his starboard beam. Just as Columbus tried to sail due west along latitude 28° N, that of the Canary Islands, hoping to hit Cipangu; so Cabot tried sailing west on a high, short latitude, hoping to reach "Cathay," northern China. This crude method of navigation, later called running your westing—or easting—down, had been used even by Ulysses and by the Northmen without benefit of compass; uneducated sailing masters followed it up to within old men's memories. That explains why Cabot sailed northerly, around Fastnet and Cape Clear, to the west coast of Ireland and took his departure from Dursey Head, the northern entrance to Bantry Bay, at latitude 51°33′ N. He might have sailed further north to seek a slightly shorter crossing; but he may have caught a good easterly off Dursey and then decided to make his westing on that latitude. Another reason for taking off from Dursey Head was the reported position of Hy-Brasil, due west of it; he might pick that up en route and have a good laugh on Bristol's Brasil-searchers.

Since Cabot had the benefit of compass, quadrant, and traverse table, all of which the Norsemen lacked, he did not need to stick closely to his chosen latitude; he could always find it again if a westerly wind forced him north or south. Two or three days before landfall, says Day, i.e. on 21 or 22 June, there was a gale of wind; and it is interesting that Findlay, who wrote the old "seaman's Bible" on the North Atlantic in the nineteenth century, warns his readers that ships are frequently compelled to lie-to for two or three days in a northerly gale when approaching Newfoundland.

Nothing is said about fog or ice in any Cabotian source, but anyone who has sailed in those waters in early summer will agree that *Mathew* must have encountered plenty of each.

The Landfall, 24 June 1497

We may imagine that by the time *Mathew* ran into the gale her seamen were becoming restless, muttering if that other Genoese had made it in 33 days, why can't we? Didn't you hear the Old Man promise that our route would be shorter? And, when the tempest blew, say-

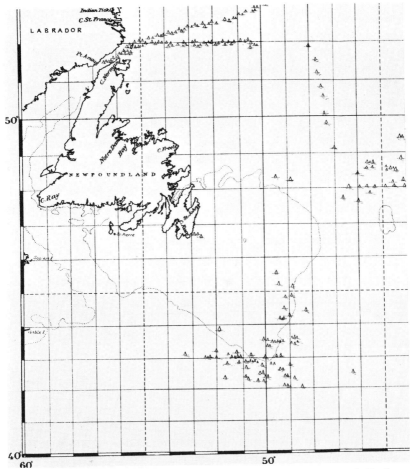

Icebergs and field ice off Newfoundland, July 1885. From Hugh Rodman *Report of Ice and Ice Movements in the North Atlantic Ocean* (1890). Note the dotted line indicating 100-fathom soundings. Inside of it are the Banks.

ing—this is it—we'll never get back to old Bristowe—and the more pious making vows to be performed at St. Mary Redcliffe if they ever did return.

What a pity that we have no exact account of the momentous land-fall! All we know is the inscription on Sebastian Cabot's Map of 1544, at the wrong place, that it happened at 5:00 a.m., 24 June. So let us supply a little imagination to bridge the few known facts.

After the gale the wind must have come off shore, blowing the fog away. Master Cabot makes all plain sail and shapes his course as near due west as possible. At nightfall 23 June, being an experienced mariner, he begins to *feel* "the loom of the land"—the odor of fir trees and other growing things floating out over the sea, low-hanging clouds, gannets, guillemots, and other non-pelagic birds flying and screaming. All that bright night—for it is never wholly dark in those lattitudes in June and they had a last-quarter moon—everyone keeps a sharp lookout, and the big bower anchor is unlashed and readied for use. Day breaks at three or four o'clock.

Now Cabot orders his little ship to shoot into the wind to check her headway, and lowers all sail, while the leadsman in the chains heaves the dipsy lead. It hits the bottom with a resounding thud—for the hundred-fathom line here approaches within twenty-two miles of the coast. "By the mark, eighty!" the sailor sings out, and with that reassuring depth of water under his keel, Cabot finds it unnecessary to lose time taking more soundings until he is close to land. Then comes the great moment. At 5:00 a.m. the rugged mass of Newfoundland's northern peninsula rises out of the sea, dead ahead, distant twelve to fifteen miles. Sailors are always delighted to make land in clear weather and early in the day, so that they may have plenty of daylight to work into a harbor. In the *Mathew*'s case, on a completely unknown coast, so early a landfall was particularly fortunate.

It is St. John the Baptist Day, 24 June, and Midsummer too; a date nobody was likely to forget, and a good omen for the rest of the voyage. A big island rose out of the sea fifteen miles to the northward. Cabot named it St. John's after the day; the French later called it *Belle Isle*, after an island off the Breton coast, and Belle Isle it still is.

The nearest rocky headland, as they approach, is framed in white foam from the ocean swells. Whether the day be fair or foul, breakers on that coast never cease beating in rhythmic strokes like an endless sword blade. It is the cape which the French later renamed Dégrat. Rising over 500 feet from sea level, it must have been sighted long before Cape Bauld (100 feet altitude), which marks the northernmost point of Newfoundland, appeared. The two capes, only one and a half miles apart, are on Quirpon Island, separated from the Newfoundland main by a narrow but navigable strait.

Mathew was now only five miles as the crow flies from L'Anse aux Meadows where Leif Ericsson had tried to establish a colony in 1001.

Cape Dégrat from the south. Belle Isle in the distance.

Capes Bauld and Dégrat from the north.

Cabot knew nothing of Leif's venture, and it probably would not have interested him if he had; but what an extraordinary coincidence! The first two Europeans to discover North America, half a millennium apart, hit that vast continent within a few miles of each other; and Jacques Cartier followed suit, 37 years after Cabot.

The master now starts his sheets, and with a fresh wind blowing off the land, skirts the coast to the southward, looking for a harbor. Why to the southward? Why not northabout, into the Strait of Belle Isle, considering that he was looking for a passage to Cathay? One may answer in one word—ice. Glance at the sketches of ice at the Strait of Belle Isle entrance in July 1885, by Lieutenant Hugh Rodman USN. Bergs and growlers enter the strait on the Labrador side, circulate within it, and pass out to sea on the Newfoundland side. Not very encouraging to Cabot! We don't know how thick the ice was in 1497, but in 1957 the eastern entrance to the strait was not open for shipping until 6/15 July (using both old and new style dates); and in 1964 it was not open until 13/22 July. Furthermore, "open" is now understood with respect to modern, high-powered shipping. Floating ice which any steamship could easily buck would have seemed forbidding to the master and crew of a little sailing vessel. Cabot naturally could not risk ending his voyage in a deep-freeze.

So, south he turned, to look for a harbor, and he had plenty to choose from: Quirpon (pronounced Carpoon) is the nearest, but the entrance is concealed and hard to find; Griquet (rhymes with cricket) Harbor, only four miles south of Cape Dégrat, comes next, and seems to me the likeliest spot. Wherever it was, John Cabot landed, formed a procession behind a ship's boy carrying a crozier, took formal possession for King Henry VII, and planted the banners of St. George for his sovereign, and of St. Mark as a reminiscence of Venice. Here too, at a quiet anchorage or ashore, he took a meridional altitude of the sun, and dawn and evening sights on Polaris, working them out as the approximate latitude of Dursey Head, Ireland, 51°33′ N. Considering that Cape Dégrat is on latitude 51°37′ N, and that Griquet Harbor is on latitude 51°33′, this must be considered one of the most accurate and successful bits of celestial navigation in the early era of discovery.

Any Cabot buff who reads the above will feel that I have assumed a lot—and I cheerfully plead guilty! Here it will be enough to say that

Quirpon Passage and Harbor (top) and Griquet Harbor (middle), where
Cabot probably first landed. Air view, summer of 1948, from 20,000
feet altitude. The dark areas are spruce forest. Courtesy Air Photo Division,
Canadian Government.

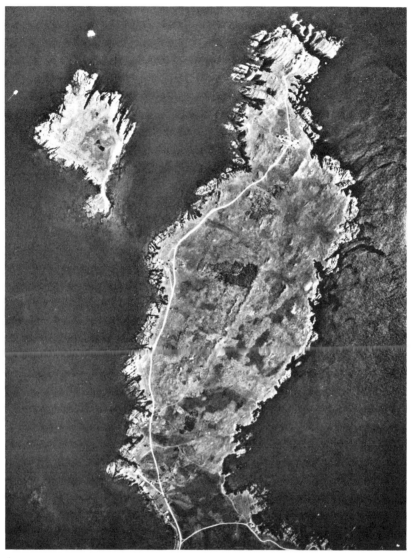

Cape Bonavista, Newfoundland. Taken 8 August 1965 from elevation of 8550 feet. Courtesy Air Photo Division, Canadian Government.

there is proof * that the "official" Canadian landfall on Cape Breton is wrong on two counts: (1) Cabot himself reported his landfall to

* The John Day letter, found in the Spanish archives at Simancas in 1956.

have been on the latitude of Dursey Head—51°33′ N; whilst the northernmost point of Cape Breton is latitude 47°02′ N. (2) In contrast to the inconstant winds, we must consider the constant factor of ocean depths. For any landfall south of Cape Bonavista, Newfoundland, *Mathew* would have had to cross the Grand Bank which extends some 220 miles east of the Avalon Peninsula, whilst the "Tail of the Bank" lies 250 miles southeast of Cape Race, with depths of twenty to forty-five fathom. This Grand Bank is a vast, balloon-like shoal embracing southeastern Newfoundland, with depths of twenty to eighty fathom, and a few isolated rocks that break in heavy weather. One may confidently assert that Cabot, like any experienced sailor, after striking soundings such as these, would have sailed as near due west as he could, feeling his way with frequent casts of the lead in dark or foggy weather, to the nearest point of land. A glance at the chart should convince any reasonable person that Cabot could not have sailed the five hundred or more miles from the eastern edge of the Bank to Cape Breton, missing Cape Race, Cape Pine, Cape St. Mary's, and Saint-Pierre. Also, for *Mathew* to have approached the coast far enough south to miss Cape Race and make first land on Cape Breton, one would have to assume that her navigator made a mistake of six degrees of latitude, 360 miles.

The Coastal Voyage

So, let us assume that Cape Dégrat was the 24 June landfall, and take *Mathew* on from there.

We learn from both Soncino and Day that Cabot went ashore shortly after his landfall to take possession. He saw no people, but observed signs of life such as snares and fish nets, and a stick painted red and pierced at both ends, probably a shuttle for weaving nets. He also noted dung which he supposed to mean that the natives kept cattle—moose or caribou were responsible. Why did Cabot never land again? Possibly because, with a small crew, he wished to avoid tangling with hostile natives; he admitted that he dared not explore inland further than the range of a crossbow from his ship. More likely, in my opinion, it was the mosquitoes. The rocky surface of eastern Newfoundland is full of small depressions which catch and hold the melting snow; swarms of mosquitoes breed therein and make life miser-

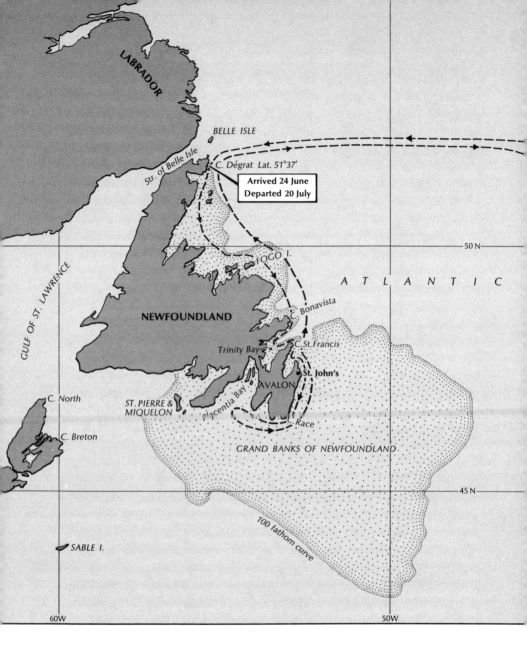

LABRADOR

BELLE ISLE

Str. of Belle Isle

C. Dégrat Lat. 51°37'

**Arrived 24 June
Departed 20 July**

50 N

FOGO I.

A T L A N T I C

GULF OF ST. LAWRENCE

NEWFOUNDLAND

C. Bonavista

Trinity Bay

C. St. Francis

St. John's

C. North

ST. PIERRE &
MIQUELON

AVALON

Placentia Bay

C. Breton

C. Race

GRAND BANKS OF NEWFOUNDLAND

45 N

100 fathom curve

SABLE I.

60W

50W

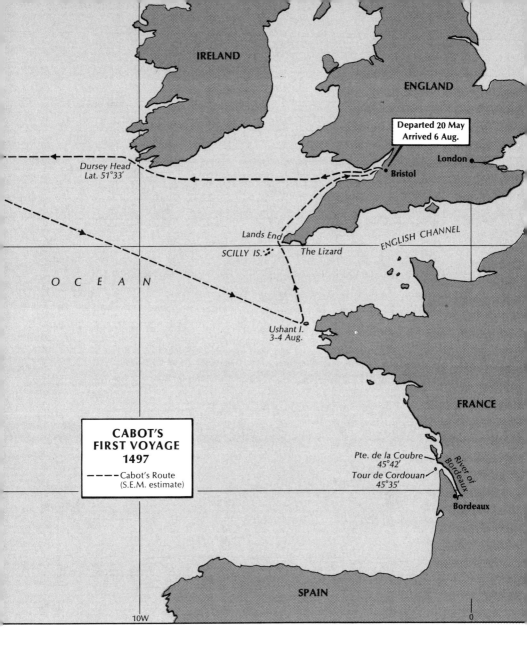

IRELAND

ENGLAND

Departed 20 May
Arrived 6 Aug.

London

Dursey Head
Lat. 51°33'

Bristol

Lands End

SCILLY IS.

The Lizard

ENGLISH CHANNEL

O C E A N

Ushant I.
3-4 Aug.

FRANCE

**CABOT'S
FIRST VOYAGE
1497**

— — — Cabot's Route
(S.E.M. estimate)

Pte. de la Coubre
45°42'

Tour de Cordouan
45°35'

River of Bordeaux

Bordeaux

SPAIN

10W

0

able for all but the most hardened "Newfies." So huge, hungry, and notorious are the Newfoundland mosquitoes that one authority, reading in the *Navigatio* of St. Brendan that the fathers were attacked by insects the size of chickens, adduced this as proof that the Saint had sailed to Newfoundland!

Jumping ahead four years, the Beothuk Indians whom Gaspar Corte Real kidnapped in Newfoundland and brought to Lisbon in 1501, possessed a broken gilt sword of Italian manufacture, and silver earrings "made in Venice." These can only have come from Cabot. They may have been relics of an otherwise unrecorded fight between him and the Beothuk on his second voyage in 1498, but it is more probable that they were left behind at the landing place and there picked up by the Indians. If it be objected that people do not ordinarily abandon such valuable possessions, one may answer that all sailors remember a shipmate who, after the vessel is under way, finds that he has left behind his camera, false teeth, or what not; won't the skipper please stop the ship so he can go look for them? Lescarbot tells of a shipmate who left his sword ashore in Nova Scotia and, going back for it, got lost himself and all but perished.

Contemporary informants tell us almost nothing about Cabot's coasting. Pasqualigo, the Venetian in London, says that he coasted 300 leagues—954 nautical miles—but this was pure guesswork, as Cabot had no means of measuring distance. *Mathew*, like every later voyager to Newfoundland, must have encountered fog. Lescarbot, in his passage to Port Royal with Poutrincourt in 1601, made land somewhere about St. John's on 23 June, and from that time on "fell to the fogs again, which (afar off) we might perceive to come and wrap us about, holding us continually prisoners three whole days for two days of fair weather that they permitted us. . . . Yea, even divers times we have seen ourselves a whole sennight continually in thick fogs, twice without any show of sun." It took them twelve days to sail from Saint-Pierre to Cape Breton.

Cabot took plenty of codfish simply by letting down and drawing up weighted baskets. He saw tall trees suitable for masts, and what appeared to be cultivated fields—probably blueberry bushes and other low shrubs. With typical discoverer's optimism, he reported the country to be temperate enough for growing logwood and silk. At one point he saw two *bultos* (big objects or figures), one chasing the other, but so far away that without benefit of telescope he could not tell whether they were men or beasts.

Here is how I think that he proceeded after taking possession at Griquet or some nearby harbor on 24 June 1497. Please keep in mind that this is all an iron-bound coast—cliffs against which the ocean swells perpetually dash, but with many harbor openings. Leaving Groais and Bell Islands to starboard, *Mathew* crosses White and Notre Dame Bays to Fogo, making a wide sweep to avoid the foul ground off that reef-girt island. Off Cape Freels she turns south, passes Cape Bonavista, and (possibly after looking into Trinity Bay) rounds high, cliffy, three-mile-long Baccalieu Island, so named by the Portuguese after the swarms of codfish that abound in these waters. From here on she has the benefit of moonlight; a new moon on 30 June, full moon 14 July. Possibly she investigates the completely land-locked harbor which today nourishes St. John's, the Newfoundland capital. She whips around Cape Spear, a typical high, rocky headland with sparse vegetation, and resumes a southerly course. She passes Cape Broyle, 570 feet elevation, and the lower Ferryland Head, keeping a few miles off shore to avoid breaking rocks and islets. About fifty miles south of Cape Spear she reaches Cape Race, a long, flat promontory of slate cliffs 100 to 150 feet above the ocean. This conspicuous headland is where windjammers and steamships, sailing as near as possible the great circle course from northern Europe, tried to make land before squaring away for Halifax, Boston, or New York; pilots used to call passing Cape Race "turning the corner." Cabot turned the corner too, and after investigating Trepassey Bay, steered west for 200-foot-high Cape Pine, eighteen miles distant from Cape Race. That would have been his furthest south—latitude 46° 37′ N—only forty-five to sixty-two miles north of the latitude of the mouth of the Gironde (45° 35′ to 45° 42′), which Day reported to have been Cabot's furthest south. And, since Cabot must have taken these latitude sights from *Mathew*'s deck in rough water, his estimate is not bad for the period. This "River of Bordeaux" latitude he undoubtedly knew from an earlier voyage, as the Tour de Cordouan lighthouse at the river mouth was one of the most famous seamarks in all Europe.

Cape St. Mary's, a 500-foot-high tableland, lies across the bay of the same name, about thirty miles west-northwest. It is the eastern promontory of Placentia Bay.

What Cabot Saw: Baccalieu Island and Grates Point; Cape St. Francis; Cape Broyle.

What Cabot Saw: Cape Race; Cape St. Mary's; Cape Pine. The whiteness on a cliff in the foreground (center picture), and the white specks over the sea, are thousands of gannets. The lighthouses are of course later additions to the scene.

All this time, *Mathew* has been on soundings. But, continuing west from Cape St. Mary's, she soon finds herself over the 100- to 170-fathom trough that starts near Argentina and stretches through Placentia Bay well out to sea. My guess is that Cabot, after making several casts of the lead and finding no bottom at 100 fathom, chose here to turn back. The land on Burin Peninsula, next to the westward, is low, flat, and generally invisible from a point fifteen miles west of Cape St. Mary's. The wind may have blown hard from the west—it generally does at that season. Keeping in mind that Cabot was primarily looking for a passage to the Indies, he would now have thought that he had found it. Regarding this voyage as a mere reconnaissance to prepare for a big expedition later, he decided to turn back.

John Day is positive that the *Mathew* returned to her original landfall before taking her departure for Bristol; and that makes sense, as doubling his course increased Cabot's knowledge of the coast and gave him, so he thought, an accurate latitude for running his easting down. On the return trip to Cape Dégrat he had time to look into harbors and bays which he had bypassed on the outward passage. He saw, says Pasqualigo, two islands that he had earlier missed: these could have been Great, Green, or Gull Islands off the Avalon Peninsula, or any two of a dozen islands further north; outlying islands are often sheathed in fog while the coast of Newfoundland itself is clear.

This coasting plan for Cabot is, of course, tentative; but the length of it—about 870 miles headland to headland (as I measure it on a modern chart)—fits a maximum cruise of twenty-six days, which no other hypothesis does, except the Cape Bonavista one. Still, there are several puzzling things about it. None of Cabot's reporters mentions fog, which he must have experienced. Nor do they refer to icebergs which he must have seen; they are most plentiful off the Newfoundland coast in July. I can only suggest that these omissions derive from the same motive as Eric's name Greenland for a country that is mostly rocks and ice; talk of fogbanks and icebergs would discourage further attempts to explore or exploit the "New Isle," as Henry VII named it. By 1502 the king was calling it "the newe founde lande" or "the Newfounded Island," and before long it became standardized as Newfoundland. With the English, once a thing is new, it always remains new, like Oxford's New College, and New York.

It is also odd that Cabot saw no Indians; but that fits Newfoundland rather than Nova Scotia. The Beothuk tribe which inhabited the big island were hunters and salmon fishermen, not particularly interested in the coast; but the Micmac of Nova Scotia, like the Abnaki of Maine, flocked to the shore in summer to fish and dig clams.

Another item that rings true is Cabot's report, through Pasqualigo, "that the tides are slack and do not flow as they do here" at Bristol. On the east and south coasts of Newfoundland the mean range is only 2.2 to 4.9 feet.

His Homeward Passage

Passing Cape Bonavista, Cape Freels, Fogo Island, and Cape St. John, Cabot picked up his landfall on Cape Dégrat and took his departure thence not later than 20 July, two days before a last-quarter moon. After a fast passage of fifteen days, *Mathew* made the Breton coast not later than 4 August. These calculations are based on Day's statement that *Mathew* crossed in fifteen days, made landfall in Brittany, and entered Bristol 6 August. The speed of this homeward passage is noteworthy, though not exceptional. Fifteen days was a passage which any yachtsman would be proud to make today; an average speed of about five knots. And this is calculated on the great circle course of 1720 nautical miles, without counting the dog-leg that *Mathew* must have made, at the instance of her sailors; for Day states that the mariners "confused" their captain and persuaded him to steer somewhat south of east, which explains why he missed England. Late July and August being a period of strong westerly winds in those latitudes, there is no reason to doubt Cabot's blue-ribband transatlantic passage. He had a new moon on 29 July, and it reached first quarter the day after his Brittany landfall. This we may assume to have been Ushant, which looms up conspicuously off the Breton coast; and, as *Mathew* is said to have been provisioned for a much longer voyage, Cabot had no reason to call at the nearest port.

Supposing she sighted Ushant at break of day 4 August, and that the brave westerly that brought her so far held good, she could have made Lands End—100 miles almost due north—at dusk, dodging the Longships and the Seven Stones; reached Lundy (80 miles more) by dawn, and on the 5th have begun picking up familiar landmarks in the Severn Estuary—the Welsh mountains, Flatholme and Steepholme, Denny

Island and Portishead. By evening she comes to an anchor in King Road off Avonmouth. There she had to await a fair tide to ascend the Avon, but messengers must have gone ahead on horseback to tell Bristol that the *Mathew* had returned with big news. If the wind fell or turned east, there were stout fellows with twelve-oared barges at the village of Crockern Pill inside the Avon entrance who could have passed her a line and towed her around Horseshoe Bend and through the narrow gorge of the Avon. Once past the site of the Clifton Suspension Bridge, the fair city bursts on her sight: green Brandon Hill looms up to port, and the tower of St. Mary Redcliffe appears dead ahead. She sails, or is towed, right up to the "Key," or the "Back," at Bristol Bridge. There she is met by wives, children, and sweethearts, and a delegation of the city fathers. It is 6 August 1497, a date of which we are certain.

Once customs formalities are over, friends greeted, and discovery of a "New Island" announced, John Cabot wastes no time in idle chatter. The same day he starts for London to see the king, tell his story, and claim his reward.

What Cabot thought he had found is less important than what he did find, but very interesting. Unfortunately the map that he brought home and showed to the king has long since disappeared. From his statement that he landed on *terra firma*, it is evident that he regarded northern Newfoundland as part of the Eurasian continent; and the Behaim globe of 1492 places "Cathay" in about the same latitude where Cabot thought he had hit the passage to China. But the language of his gift from Henry VII, "to hym that founde the new Isle," proves that Cabot regarded the major part of his discovery as insular, and that it was a *new* isle, not that tiresome old will o' the wisp Hy-Brasil, or the equally played-out Seven Cities. Obviously too, since Cabot had been given the right to "subdue, occupy and possesse" only "Isles, countryes, regions or provinces of the heathen and infidels . . . unknown to all Christians," and enjoy their "fruits, profits, gaines and commodities," he could not have made much out of a Hy-Brasil inhabited by Irish ghosts, or an Antilia with seven Portuguese cities. Newfoundland had to be new to be of any use to him or to the king. Now, the Avalon Peninsula looks like an island and almost is; most of the sixteenth-century maps show Newfoundland as an archipelago, to which its deep, narrow bays give credence; the Contarini-Roselli Map of 1506 which we have reproduced puts it at the tip end of a Chinese promontory called "Tungut Provincia Magna." As late as 1540, the commission of François-premier to Jacques Cartier defined Canada as *faisant un bout de l'Asie*.

The Contarini-Roselli Map of 1506 was evidently drawn from Portuguese sources, such as the Corte Real voyages. The Ruysch Map, which illustrated the Rome (1508) edition of Ptolemy, is more significant. Both Newfoundland and Greenland are eastern promontories of Asia, and the nomenclature is unique, as partly based on information derived from Cabot. *Terra Nova* is, of course, the English name for the "new isle," latinized; the "k" in *Baia de Rockas* suggests that Cabot appropriately called Notre Dame Bay the Bay of Rocks; *C. Glaciato* for Cape Bauld may record his finding ice and snow there on St. John's Day; and *Rio Grado* indicates that he investigated the mouth of the Gander River—but I do not claim that Gander is derived from Grado! South of that river are Baccalieu Island and the Cape of the Portuguese—Ruysch's concession to Cabot's rivals.

Mathew must have been quickly cleared at the Bristol custom house, for she brought back nothing except what was picked up at her one port of call. At any rate, Cabot lost no time in proceeding to London to lay his discoveries at the feet of the king. One of the main roads of England went from the West Country through Bristol to London; it was a narrow earth track some 130 statute miles in length, and the journey must have taken Cabot three days. He had no such impressive cavalcade as Columbus brought to Barcelona in 1493; no gold, no Indians, no parrots; there was only himself on a hired horse, accompanied perhaps by his three sons, and certainly by members of *Mathew*'s crew to corroborate his story. The road led through Chippenham, Marlborough, Hungerford, Newbury, Reading (where it crossed the Thames), Maidenhead, Colnbrook, and Brentford. The Cabot party pushed ahead as long as daylight lasted, spent two nights en route, probably at travelers' inns, reached London by the night of 9 August, and rode to Westminster to see the king next day.

Henry VII knew a good thing when he saw it and, for a Tudor, responded generously. The royal household books record that on 10–11 August 1497 the king gave £10 "to hym that founde the new

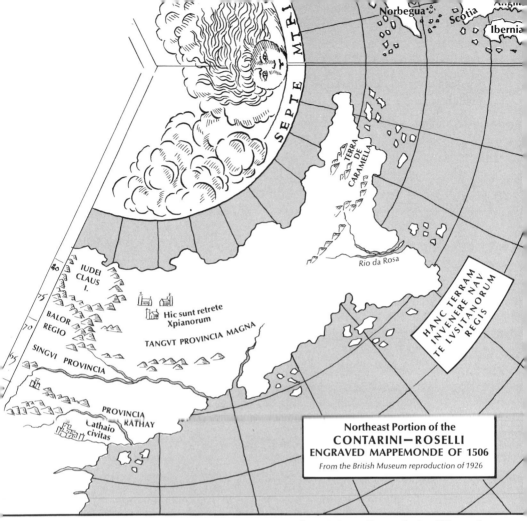

The lower legend means: "This Land found by sailors of the King of Portugal." "Terra de caramella" means Land of Ice, and here is on Greenland. This entire land mass is assumed to be China, and "Zippon" is just off this part of the map, on the same longitude as "Magna."

Isle," and the following January a "rewarde" of 66s. 8d. "to a Venysian," probably Sebastian, who always made a good impression. On 13 December 1497 he settled on his "welbiloved John Calbot of the parties of Venice" an annuity of £20, at the expense of the Bristol customs. Two months later he issued a warrant for payment of the same to "the said John Caboote," who had been unable to collect owing to lack of funds in the Bristol custom house. The last payment of this pension was made at some time during the twelvemonth following

Michaelmas 1498. The discoverer's name then disappears from the books. He had gone to "the undiscover'd country from whose bourn no traveler returns."

Cabot's Second Voyage

Cabot's first voyage made a brief sensation. He spent the £10 that the king gave him "to amuse himself," says Pasqualigo, and swaggered about Lombard Street in gay silken apparel. Soncino says that the common people "run after him like madmen," that he regarded himself as an admiral of princely rank, and promised to bestow islands on his Burgundian passenger and his Genoese barber.

Nobody recorded what the sailors thought about *Mathew*'s voyage.

Outline of a portion of the Ruysch Map of 1508. Against the double island in the middle, the legend states, demons assaulted ships near these islands, which were avoided but not without peril. "CATHAY" is around the corner to the southwest. From Henry Harrisse, *Terre Neuve*, p. 58.

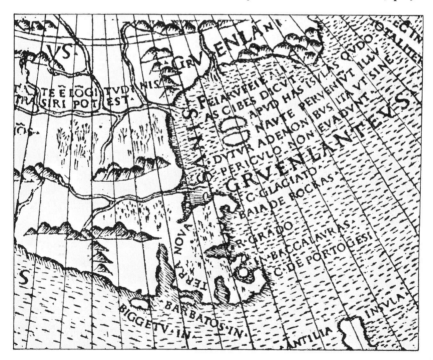

TERRA FIRMA
TERRITORIES
OF
GRAND CHAM

C. Dégrat

CATHAIA

Passage
to the
Indies

THE
"NEW ISLE"

•
Cambaluc
(Pekin)

SIANFU

Dotted line indicates
Martin Behaim's Asia

INDIA   ZAITUN

(Identified by Columbus
with Cuba)

Cabot's Idea of His First Voyage

We can imagine their telling unbelievable fish stories in Bristol, and grumbling about the fog, the chill, and the mosquitoes; grousing that they found no women because the Old Man never gave them shore liberty. They did confirm the discovery, says Soncino.

Cabot probably flitted between London and Bristol the rest of the summer and fall of 1497, engaged in preparations for his second voyage. It was a bad time to get royal assistance. Perkin Warbeck the pretender was still on the loose, supported by Cornishmen marching on London to protest against war taxes. The siege of Exeter by the rebels was not raised until the end of 1497. Nevertheless Henry VII found time to promote what we might call his race for the Indies. He did not intend to let Spain and Portugal get away with everything.

On 3 February 1498, Henry VII issued new letters-patent for the second Cabot voyage, granting "to our well beloved John Kaboto, Venician," power to impress six English ships of 200 tuns or under, together with their tackle and necessary gear, "and theym convey and lede to the londe and Iles of late founde by the seid John in oure name," paying at the rate of government charters. Cabot also had the right to enlist any English sailors who sign on willingly. Thus *"Messer Zoane,"* says Soncino, "proposes to keep along the coast from the place at which he touched, more and more towards the East, until he reaches an island which he calls *Cipango,* situated in the equinoctial region where he thinks all the spices of the world have their origin, as well as the jewels." There he will "form a colony"; i.e. set up a trading factory, by which means London will become "a more important mart for spices than Alexandria." The king provided, manned and victualed one ship, in which divers merchants of London ventured "small stocks." Merchants of Bristol freighted four more vessels laden with "course cloth, Caps, Laces, points and other trifles," supposed to be the proper trading truck for natives, and all five ships departed Bristol together at "the beginning of May" 1498.

As to who accompanied Master John, we are as much in the dark as on the first voyage. We know the names of but two shipmates: a Milanese cleric in London named Giovanni Antonio de Carbonariis, and a Spanish friar named Buil who had been a leading troublemaker on Columbus's second voyage. The Spanish ambassador on 25 July 1498 informed his royal master that Cabot had departed with five ships and a year's provisions, and that the ship in which Father Buil sailed had put into an Irish port in distress. The other four were expected home the following month. They never returned.

Thus, the only known facts of John Cabot's second voyage are that it departed Bristol in May 1498, that one ship returned shortly, and that Cabot and the other four ships were lost. His pension was paid for the last time, probably to his wife (not yet known to be a widow) within the twelvemonth following Michaelmas 1498. Polydore Vergil, a contemporary English historian, wrote somewhat flippantly that Cabot "found his new lands only in the ocean's bottom, to which he and his ship are thought to have sunk, since, after that voyage, he was never heard of more."

The rest is silence.

Juan de La Cosa's mappemonde dated 1500 shows a series of English royal standards planted along a coast which appears to stretch from the Labrador to Florida. A point usually identified as Cape Breton, but which may as well be Cape Bauld or Cape Race or Cape Cod, is named *Cavo de Yngleterra.* Stringing along to the westward are twelve names which make no sense and appear on no later map, and the inscription parallel to this coast reads, *mar descubierta por inglese* (sea discovered

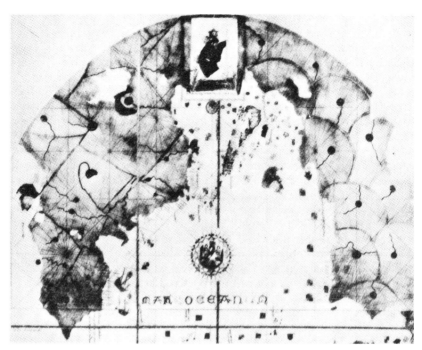

The Juan de La Cosa Mappemonde. The American part. Dated 1500, but certainly post-1505. The five flags on the northern coast are English.

by an Englishman). Certain historians consider this to be evidence that Cabot's second voyage ranged the coast of North America as far as Florida or even Venezuela, searching for a passage to Cathay. *But, if neither he nor any of his men returned, how did La Cosa get his facts?* Obviously, since the American half of this map has been post-dated at least five years, the English flags, if anything more than a whimsy, record a later voyage by the Bristol-Portuguese syndicate, to which we shall come in due course.

John Cabot and his four ships disappear without a trace. No report of them reached Europe. Anyone may guess whether they capsized and foundered in a black squall, crashed an iceberg at night, or piled up on a rocky coast. One remembers an old Irish proverb, "The waves have some mercy but the rocks have no mercy at all"; and God knows there are plenty of rocks both on and off the North American coast.

Nevertheless, John Cabot's first voyage was the herald and fore-runner to the English empire in North America. Like Columbus, he never learned the significance or value of his discoveries.

74

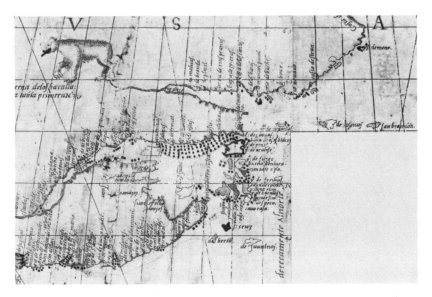

A section of Sebastian Cabot's 1544 Map (Yeux Ouvertes reproduction) compared with similar region on Nicolas Desliens's World Map of 1541 reversed. Photo of original in Sächsische Landesbibliothek, Dresden. Kindness of the Direktor, Dr. Burgemeister.

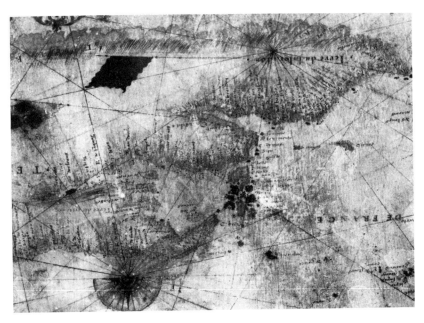

✳ III ✳

Voyages to the Labrador
and Newfoundland

1500-1536

João Fernandes, *Lavrador*

After the excitement over John Cabot's first voyage and his disappearance on his second, there came a distinct letdown in northern voyages to America. The quarter-century after 1500 is a dark period in the history of North American discovery, faintly and doubtfully illuminated by old maps. The brilliant success of the southern voyages turned men's minds away from the northern region of ice, snow, and fog; only the fishermen kept coming, as did a few hopeful searchers for a strait to China. Gold from Hispaniola was already pouring into Spain. In July 1499 one of Vasco da Gama's ships returned to Lisbon with the news that this great Portuguese captain had finally reached India by sea. Columbus sailed on his third voyage in 1498, discovered the South American continent, and opened the pearl fisheries. Vicente Yañez Pinzón for Spain, and Pedro Álvares Cabral for Portugal, bracketed the great country of Brazil in the same year, 1500. After that, who cared for codfish, mast trees, and icebergs?

As a literary wit remarked, America was discovered by accident, not wanted when found, and early explorations were directed to finding a way through or around it. Columbus's fourth voyage, starting in 1502, was a search for a strait from the Caribbean to the Indian Ocean; Cabot died seeking a strait through North America; and for the next eight decades all recorded voyages thither, except those of farmer Fernandes and fisherman Fagundes, were, first and foremost, searches for the elusive Northwest Passage to fabulous Cathay.

Two places in Europe remained committed to this quest—Terceira and Bristol. Terceira in the Azores by 1500 had become an intensively cultivated island, and the chief town, Angra, a favorite port of call for Portuguese caravels returning from Africa. Angra already had splendid churches in the Manueline Gothic style, and paved streets lined with stone mansions. One of these belonged to Pedro Maria de Barcelos, a second-generation landowner, founder of a noble family which endures to this day. One of his friends and neighbors was João Fernandes, a *lavrador*, or small landed proprietor, who farmed out his land while he went voyaging; and it was humble Fernandes rather than noble Barcelos who received letters-patent from King Manuel, dated 28 October 1499, to search for and discover islands in the Portuguese half of the world.

A descendant of Fernandes's partner, Dona Maria Isabel do Canto de Barcelos Coelho Borges, whom I met at Angra in 1939, reminded me of an old Virginian lady, living in the tradition of pre-Civil War. When I referred to her as Portuguese, she remarked firmly, "I am not a Portuguese. I am an Azorean." She had portraits of the last five or six kings of Portugal in her salon; and, on each stair landing, a sedan chair; for, as she explained, in her youth no lady went out on foot in Angra. She gave me to understand that her Barcelos ancestor was a very great person indeed; but as for João Fernandes, he was "a nobody—no one ever heard of him!"

Nevertheless, João Fernandes *lavrador* has left footprints on the sands of time, and although information on him is scarce enough, it is more than we have on his aristocratic partner. João visited England while Columbus was abroad, for the Bristol customs records show that he shipped goods thence to Lisbon in January 1493. In October 1499, as we have seen, he received the letters-patent from D. Manuel "to go in search of and discover certain Islands of our sphere of influence," and be captain thereof. Barcelos possibly financed and certainly accompanied the voyage that followed, but he is not mentioned in the document.

All we know about this Fernandes-Barcelos voyage is from legends on maps, starting with the Cantino dated 1502. From these we learn that the partners made Cape Farewell, Greenland, in the summer of 1500 and that, since João Fernandes gave the *aviso* (which I take to be the "Land, ho!"), they decided to call it *Tiera del Lavrador*, Land of the Husbandman. It was doubtless a great joke on board that a farmer first sighted land. Greenland had been so completely forgotten in southern Europe that it could be renamed after an Azorean! A century later, after Frobisher had tried to call it West England, geographers learned of the old Norse name, revived it, and shifted the name "Labrador" to the continental area of eastern Canada, which still bears it. There is no doubt, however, that the first Land of the Labrador was Greenland. *Cauo Larbradore* appears at Cape Farewell on the Oliveriana Map of the first decade of the century; the Munich-Portuguese chart, also reproduced here, tells that the Portuguese rediscovered it but did not land; and the Wolfenbüttel Map of 1527, in a scroll next to Greenland, states, "Because he who gave the *aviso* was a *labrador* of the Azores, they gave it that name."

Although it has been argued that the partners were primarily interested in finding the passage to Cathay that John Cabot had missed, the letters-patent of 1499 distinctly state that their main object was to discover an island or islands, over which Farmer John could be donatory captain. The probability is that D. Manuel, having heard of John Cabot's discovery of Newfoundland, and believing that it lay on the Portuguese side of the Line of Demarcation, wished to forestall the English by settling the New Isle. From his point of view, the English had no proper title to it. The partners' landfall was probably unintended, but if the Oliveriana Map records their voyage and not those of the Bristol syndicate, they continued to Newfoundland and the continent. More probably, discouraged by the amount of ice encountered, they gave up their quest for the time being; hoping, like Cabot, to do better another year.

Returning to Terceira empty-handed after a voyage which yielded nothing but a view of Greenland's Icy Mountains, João Fernandes heard the bad news that D. Manuel had conferred a grant similar to his but wider in scope on Gaspar Corte Real. Offended and disappointed, he proceeded to Bristol where he had trading connections, and joined two other Azoreans and three local merchants in a petition

to Henry VII for letters-patent, which were granted on 19 March
1501. Whether or not he accompanied the voyages that this Anglo-
Azorean syndicate made in 1501–2 we do not know. João disappears
from history after the granting of this patent.

Though soon forgotten, Fernandes is still commemorated in the
common speech of those northern regions, whose inhabitants invariably use the article when speaking of the country named after him.
They always say "The Labrador," never simply "Labrador." So, whenever you hear a fisherman speak of his "home in The Labrador," or a
seaman say, "I'm bound to The Labrador," pray give a kindly thought
to João Fernandes, the sea-going husbandman of Terceira.

Gaspar and Miguel Corte Real

Gaspar Corte Real was the youngest son of João Vaz Corte Real to
whom a pre-Columbian discovery of America, in company with Scol-
vus, Pining, Pothorst, and God knows who, is still officially credited
in Portugal. The Corte Real were a branch, probably illegitimate, of
the great Portuguese family of Da Costa and used their same punning
arms, six *costas* or ribs. They settled in the Algarve and honorably
served the Aviz dynasty. João Vaz Corte Real, chamberlain to the
Infante D. Fernando, showed such energy in obtaining colonists for
Terceira that the king made him captain of that island in 1474, and
within ten years added the island of São Jorge to his domain. He married a Spanish lady from Galicia after forcibly abducting her, and as
ruler in the Azores he had the reputation of being greedy, cruel, and
unjust. Dying in 1496, not greatly regretted, he left a family of three
sons: Vasco Annes, Miguel, and Gaspar. The eldest inherited his father's Azorean properties, but never visited the islands after his father's
death; the two younger, while maintaining the family connection with
the royal court, grew up in the Azores, already a veritable hothouse
for maritime discovery. And both lost their lives exploring the New
World.

Gaspar, the youngest son, born in Portugal about the year 1450,
served D. Manuel before that king's accession in 1481, and continued to
be a *fidalgo* (a gentleman of the court) while residing at Terceira to
look after his landed inheritance. Damião de Góis, in his *Crónica do
Felicissimo Rei D. Manuel*, described Gaspar as "valiant and adventur-

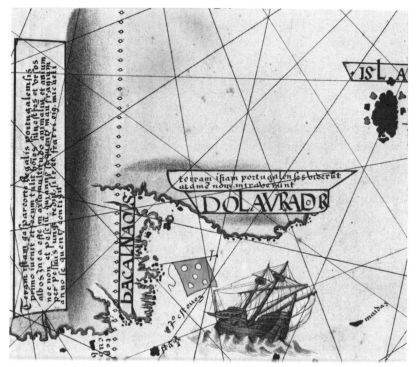

A section of the "Munich-Portuguese" Map. The legend on "Do Lavrador" (Greenland) reads: "This land the Portuguese sighted but entered it not." West of "Bacalnaos" (Newfoundland) the legend reads: "This land Gaspar Corte Real of Portugal first discovered and brought home men of the forest and white bears. Therein is a multitude of beasts, birds and fish. He was shipwrecked in the following year and never returned. His brother Michael next year went in search of him." From E. L. Stevenson's photographic facsimile.

ous and ambitious to win honor." Within a year of his father's death, he removed to Angra, as deputy captain of the island for his eldest brother, and on 12 May 1500 received an important donation patent from the king. In the preamble it states that Corte Real had already been on one voyage at his own expense, "to search out, discover and find . . . some islands and a mainland," and now wished to keep and govern whatever lands he might find on a subsequent voyage. Obviously a favorite of D. Manuel, Gaspar received unusually extensive privileges. He was guaranteed the property, jurisdiction, and trading monopoly of any lands he might discover for himself and his descendants. We know nothing of the earlier voyage, except that it was made at his own expense; he paid for this one too. Gaspar must have known about John Cabot's two voyages, yet was not dismayed by the Venetian's disappearance.

We have not the slightest hint as to the names, rigs, and burthens of the Corte Reals' ships. Since the brothers were men of means, they undoubtedly had the pick of the caravel fleet. This type, which the Portuguese had evolved for their voyages to the Western Islands and West Africa during the fifteenth century, was characterized by weatherliness. Owing partly to her lines, partly to her lateen rig on at least two of her three masts, the caravel could do better to windward than many a modern yacht. And weatherliness was the prime quality wanted in any vessel for North Atlantic discovery. The only certain item we have about Gaspar's outfit is that he received the privilege of drawing on the royal ship-biscuit bakery at Lisbon, and received 72½ quintals of hardtack in return for 7800 litres of country wheat.

More fortunate than Farmer Fernandes had been that very summer, Gaspar "discovered," says the chronicler, at about latitude 50° N, "a land that was very cool and with big trees," which he named *Terra Verde*. Newfoundland, undoubtedly.

Returning to Lisbon in the autumn of 1500, Gaspar obtained three ships, equipped them at his own expense, and departed in mid-May of 1501. His luck now ran out. Cantino, an Italian diplomat present at Lisbon when two of Gaspar's ships returned in October 1501, reports that the fleet had sailed due north for four months without seeing anything—obviously an exaggeration—ran into a huddle of icebergs, and a few days later into a field of pack-ice. They then sailed northwest and west for three months (but were away for only five!) and found a large and delightful country, well watered, covered with pines of mast-tree length, and "luscious and varied fruits." In the southern part of this *Terra Verde*, as they called Newfoundland, the Portuguese kidnapped fifty-seven Indians and brought them to the king at Lisbon. These were of the Beothuk tribe, who "live altogether by fishing and hunting animals, in which the land abounds, such as very large deer covered with extremely long hair, the skins of which they use for garments and also make houses and boats thereof. . . . Their manners and gestures are most gentle; they laugh considerably and manifest the greatest pleasure. . . . The women have small breasts and most beautiful bodies, and rather pleasant faces." To Cantino they appeared quite human, except for their costumes. "They go quite naked except for their privy parts, which they cover with a skin of the above-mentioned deer." Chronicler De Góis adds that the natives hunted, not with bow and arrow but with "pieces of wood burnt in the fire in place of spears, which when they throw them make wounds as if pointed with fine steel. . . . They live in rocky caves and thatched huts."

Although it is arguable that the Portuguese were the most thorough and successful European slave-traders of this or any other period, whether in Africa or America, they were not the only ones in that business. Columbus had shipped home thirty Indian slaves from Hispaniola in 1496, and many more followed; Ojeda began raiding the Bahamas for slaves in 1500. Everyone, including the early English and French voyagers, made a practice of "persuading" a few simple natives to sail home with them, as the best evidence that they had really discovered something, but few kidnapped for profit. The North American Indian slave trade never assumed the proportions of the African slave trade because the natives could not take it and would not endure it. In captivity or under forced labor they faded away. Pasqualigo, in his letter on Gaspar's voyage, said that the prospect of obtaining timber for masts and yards "and plenty of men slaves, fit for every kind of labor," was highly pleasing to D. Manuel, and evidence that "God is with his majesty."

After their first experiences with Europeans, the Beothuk retired to the interior. They were hunted like wild beasts and treated with the utmost cruelty both by the French and English settlers and eventually were exterminated.

The two ships of Gaspar Corte Real's expedition which reached Lisbon between 9 and 11 October 1501 reported that their commodore continued exploring southward, but Gaspar was never heard of again. He was lost, with all hands, and we have not the slightest hint of how it happened, any more than we have of John Cabot's fate.

It took more than shipwrecks to discourage maritime exploration in those days. In January 1502 D. Manuel assigned half the territory presumably discovered by Gaspar Corte Real to his next older brother, Miguel, who with two vessels embarked on a voyage toward Newfoundland in May. Again the flagship and all hands were lost. The other ship returned, but with no new knowledge.

The same Cantino who wrote about Gaspar's voyage caused to be made for his Lisbon master Ercole d'Este, Duke of Ferrara, a beautiful world map to illustrate the latest discoveries. This is still preserved in the Estense Library at Modena. Assuming that the American half of Juan de La Cosa's Mappemonde is no earlier than 1505, the Cantino Mappemonde, indubitably of 1502, becomes the first to incorporate the earliest voyages to the New World. Drafted in Lisbon, it expresses the Portuguese point of view, blithely ignoring the English voyages of Cabot and his followers, although Gaspar had found Cabot relics in Newfoundland. Against a deeply indented land studded with islands, west by south of a surprisingly accurate Greenland (here called "a point of Asia"), Cantino places the new *Terra del Rey de Portuguall*, and Portuguese flags are planted both there and on Greenland. The legend against the island states that it was discovered "by command of his most excellent majesty D. Manuel, King of Portugal, by Gaspar de Corte Real, a gentleman of the royal household, who sent thence a ship with both male and female natives, and stayed behind, but never returned. . . . There are many mast trees." The configuration suggests that Gaspar followed Cabot's course, ranging the coast from Cape Bauld to around Cape Race, breaking off near Placentia Bay.

When spring arrived in 1503 and Miguel Corte Real had not returned, the eldest brother, Vasco Annes, asked D. Manuel's permission to fit out ships and go in search of both his brothers. The king wisely refused his consent, on the ground that any such search would be useless.

Some day a lucky skindiver may come upon the wrecks of Cabot's ships, or the two Corte Real caravels that disappeared. Until then, their fate is a mystery.

All Gaspar's and Miguel's rights and privileges were transferred in 1506 to the surviving brother, Vasco Annes, and these were confirmed to his descendants by later kings over a period of seventy years. None of them did anything about Newfoundland, but the titular captaincy of the *Terra del Rey de Portuguall* remained hereditary in the family until 1578, when Manuel Corte Real, last in the male line, fell in battle fighting the Moors by the side of D. Sebastian, last Portuguese king of the house of Aviz.

The Anglo-Azorean Syndicate and Sebastian Cabot

João Fernandes *lavrador*, after his Greenland voyage of 1500—fruitless except for transferring his name to a vast territory—proceeded to England, obviously to shake off Corte Real competition. At Bristol he joined two other Azoreans, Francisco Fernandes (possibly his brother) and João Gonsalves, and two English merchants named Thomas Ashhurst and John Thomas, in a petition to Henry VII for a grant. Letters-patent were granted the same day, 19 March 1501. Unusually comprehensive, they authorized the partners "to sail and transport themselves . . . under our banners and ensigns" to any part of the world, and take possession for the crown of any place inhabited by "heathens and infidels" still "unknown to all Christians"; to colonize and govern such place and punish malefactors, notably those "who shall rape and violate against their will or otherwise any women of the islands or countries aforesaid." (This concern for the chastity of native women is unique.) The partners will enjoy a trade monopoly for ten years, subject to the royal customs; each and every one of them to be "Admirals in the same parts"—i.e. to exercise admiralty jurisdiction over their colony; and their heirs may inherit these overseas possessions. Apparently the king's lawyers regarded his two earlier grants to the Cabots as having lapsed, or, more likely, the syndicate bought off Sebastian and his brothers.

Whatever voyages these five partners organized have left precious little trace. On 26 September 1502 royal pensions of £10 a year were conferred upon "Fraunceys Fernandus and John Guidisalvus, squiers, in consideracion of the true service which they have doon to us to oure singler pleasure as Capitaignes into the newe founde land." But Fernandes the *lavrador* received nothing; he must have died, possibly on the voyage. On 9 December of the same year, Franceys and John, together with Hugh Elyot and Thomas Ashhurst, received fresh letters-patent. This looks as if the partners had made a reconnaissance in 1501 or 1502, and claimed to be on the track of the Northwest Passage; the king encouraged them in order to resist Portuguese claims and to continue searching for *the* strait. They may well have entered some northern strait where they certainly would have been stopped by ice; no practicable Northwest Passage for a sailing vessel has ever been found.

In my opinion, the highly controversial Oliveriana Map at Pésaro, of which the northwestern corner is reproduced at the end of this chapter, reflects the voyage of this Anglo-Azorean syndicate, as well as that of João Fernandes. The eastern promontory with the mountains, representing Greenland, contains six names that appear on no other map, together with *Cavo Larbradore* commemorating Farmer John. Next westward is a peninsula surely meant for Newfoundland, as it has the Portuguese names *bacalaos, del Marco, de la spera* (Cape Spear), and *Terra de Corte* [Real]. Finally, the western land mass which has but one legend, *costa fermoza* ("handsome coast"), vague as La Cosa's "Coast Discovered by the English," may well represent an extension of one of the Anglo-Azorean voyages to the North American mainland. This beautiful and little-known mappemonde, probably made in Florence for one of the Medici, as the Cantino had been for Ercole d'Este, cannot be dated earlier than 1504 or later than 1510. So it is not impossible that the cartographer gathered facts about the Anglo-Azorean voyages that have since been lost; the appearance of their former shipmate's nickname Labrador, both on Greenland and on a non-existent island replacing the mythical Antilia, as good as proves it. And the mysterious coast on the La Cosa chart may also be a record of the same voyages.

The rest of the evidence is from the household books of Henry VII, proving that he thought well of the Anglo-Azorean mariners. He gave £5 on 2 January 1502 to "men of bristoll that founde th' isle," tips to "a mariner that brought haukes" and "an other that brought an Egle"; and £20 in September to "the merchauntes of bristoll that have bene in the newe founde launde." In August or September 1505 the king gave £5 "to Portyngales that brought popyngais & catts of the mountayne with other stuf to the King's grace," and tipped a man 13s. 4d. for bringing said "wylde catts & popyngays of the New-found Island" to the king's grace at Richmond. Even more interesting gifts to Henry VII from overseas were three "men taken in the Newe Found Ileland" that the partners brought home. They were seen by Robert Fabyan the London chronicler, in 1502. These, the first Indians ever to be taken to England, were "clothid in beastys skinnys and ete Rawe Flesh," had the manners of "bruyt bestis," and spoke an unintelligible language. But they soon became civilized. Two years later Fabyan saw them in Westminster Palace, dressed like la-di-da English courtiers; but he couldn't get a word out of them.

The "Portyngales" who brought the wildcats and popinjays to Henry VII presumably were Fernandes and Gonsalves. "Popinjay" was then the common English name for a parrot, but here it must mean some noisy northern bird with bright plumage, such as the blue jay or the pileated woodpecker. A priest "that goith to the new Ilande" was given £2 in April 1504; this, as well as the popinjay entry over a year later, indicates that a third voyage of the Anglo-Azorean syndicate took place in the summer of 1504, and a fourth in 1505. Robert Thorne of Bristol and Seville claimed in 1527 that his father Nicholas, and Hugh Elyot, were the real discoverers of Newfoundland, but nobody has taken that claim seriously.

Thus the efforts of the Bristol syndicate, although persistently pursued for three or four years, seem to have had no result, not even attracting English fishermen to the Grand Bank. From maps of Newfoundland for the next quarter-century one would conclude that nobody but the Portuguese had explored these northern coasts.

Sebastian Cabot's supposed voyage in search of a Northwest Passage belongs in the doubtful class. We are still dependent on the accounts of sixteenth-century historians such as Peter Martyr, Gómara, and Ramusio, who built him up as *the* discoverer of North America. Sebastian, a pleasant and plausible fellow, impressed the great men of his day and, as *piloto mayor* of Spain (1518) who licensed all the deep-sea pilots, became one of them. As early as 1505, Henry VII granted an annuity of £10 to "our well-beloved Sebastian Caboot Venycian" in consideration of his "diligent service and attendaunce." What service could that young man have then done for the king?

Peter Martyr, the Italian humanist at the Spanish court who wrote the first history of the New World, stated that Cabot had often been his guest; and from Sebastian's lips he repeated an amusing tale. The codfish in Newfoundland, he said, swim up to shore in thick shoals to feed on the fallen leaves of certain tall trees overhanging the sea. Bears lie in ambush ashore, and when the codfish are busy feeding, they rush into the water, holding hands as it were, and surround the school of fish. Each bear then grabs a cod, which struggles to get free; the water is churned up, but in the end every little bear gets his codfish. As for the voyage, Peter Martyr and Gómara say that in 1508 Sebastian (then aged about twenty-six) fitted out two vessels with a crew of three hundred "at his own expense," sailed first to latitude 55° N, where, discouraged by great masses of ice, he turned south, passed "the Land of the Baccalai" (Newfoundland) and sailed as far as the latitude of Cuba. A certain "gentleman of Mantua" who claimed to have talked with Sebastian, reported to Ramusio, editor of the earliest published collection of voyages, that Cabot's search for the Northwest Passage took place in 1496; and in a later volume Ramusio said that Cabot had attained latitude 67°30′ on 11 June of an unspecified year; the sea was open and he could have sailed right on to China, but the master and crew compelled him to return. Gómara's *Historia General* (1552) says that Sebastian took three hundred men in two ships and sailed to latitude 58° N; Thevet in his *Singularitez de France Antarctique* adds that all three hundred were landed so far north that they died of cold in July. Despite these wildly contradictory yarns, virtually every historian or commentator on the New World prior to 1830 accepted Sebastian at his own valuation as a great navigator, discoverer, and chart-maker.

Not every contemporary did so. In 1521, when he was trying to whip up support for a five-ship fleet "to be prepared towardes the Newefound Iland," Henry VIII asked the advice of the governors of two important London guilds, the Drapers and the Mercers. They turned the proposal down in an amusingly ill-spelled document:

> We thynk it were to sore aventour to joperd five shipps with men & goodes unto the said Iland uppon the singuler trust of one man, callyd as we understond, Sebastyan, whiche Sebastyan, as we heresay, *was never in that land hym self*, all [even] if he makes reporte of many thinges as he hath heard his Father and other men speke in tymes past." They further observe, "That if the said Sebastyan had bene there and were as connyng a man in & for thoos parties as any man myght be," he would be in but one of the five ships, and could not control the others. They clinch this argument with an "old proverbe among maryners": "He sayls not surely that salys by an other mannys compas."

Methinks these worthy citizens of London had Sebastian's number! As a fifteen-year-old boy Sebastian may, as he asserted, have accompanied his father on the voyage of 1497, and he may have tried to find the Northwest Passage in 1508; several English historians accept this. The only voyage that Sebastian Cabot certainly commanded was one in 1525–28 under the king of Spain, which was supposed to follow

Magellan around the world. It got no further than the River Plate, and the voyage ended in disaster; but Sebastian landed on his feet as usual. He served under the kings of Spain and of England, receiving pay or pensions from both; and he also offered to sell his knowledge and services to the Venetian Republic. He took care to cultivate the "right people," especially those who were writing about voyages and discoveries; and so built himself up as to become the indispensable man to lead, or at least to advise, any new enterprise. In late life, Sebastian Cabot had his portrait painted. It shows an impressive old gentleman with a white forked beard, spreading a pair of dividers across the Arctic regions of a globe. Lest there be any doubt of who it was, he had a Latin inscription painted in the corner stating it to be the portrait of "Sebastian Cabot, Englishman, son of John Cabot, Venetian knight, first discoverer of Newfoundland under Henry VII, King of England." The Latin leaves it uncertain whether Sebastian intended to give his father credit or claim the discovery for himself; but he did give John a knighthood that he never had, so let us give him the benefit of the doubt.

One cannot help liking Sebastian. He was a genial and cheerful liar, devoted (insofar as it helped him) to the cause of oceanic discovery. See him at the age of seventy-four in 1556, pleasantly depicted by Stephen Borough, master of the pinnace *Serchthrift*, about to depart on a northeastern voyage of discovery:

> The 27 being Munday, the right Worshipfull Sebastian Ca-
> bota came aboord our Pinnasse at Gravesende, accompanied
> with divers Gentlemen, and Gentlewomen, who after that
> they had viewed our Pinnesse, and tasted of such cheere as we
> could make them aboord, they went on shore, giving to our
> mariners right liberall rewards: and the good olde Gentleman
> Master Cabota gave to the poore most liberall almes, wishing
> them to pray for the good fortune, and prosperous successe of
> the *Serchthrift*, our Pinnesse. And then at the sign of the
> Christopher, hee and his friends banketted, and made me, and
> them that were in the company great cheere; and for very joy
> that he had to see the towardnes of our intended discovery,
> he entred into the dance himself, amongst the rest of the young
> and lusty company: which being ended, hee and his friends de-
> parted most gently, commending us to the governance of al-
> mighty God.

Perhaps this caper at Gravesend proved too much for the old man. Philip II, when he came to England in 1557, tried to have his pension of 250 marks (about £166) annuled, and did; but Queen Mary (bless

Sebastian Cabot in his old age. From a copy of the original painting (since destroyed) made for the Massachusetts Historical Society in 1838. Translation of the inscription: "Portrait of Sebastian Cabot, Englishman, son of John Cabot, knight of Venice, First Discoverer of Newfoundland under Henry VII King of England." Courtesy Massachusetts Historical Society.

her for that!) restored it three days later. Even as he lay dying the old joker could still tell a good story. Richard Eden reported, "Sebastian Cabot on his death bed tolde me that he had acquired 'the knowledge of the longitude . . . by divine revelation.'" Eden concluded "that

THREE EARLY MAPS OF NEWFOUNDLAND'S EAST COAST
COMPARED WITH THE MODERN MAP (tilted 45°)

MODERN MAP (Shown tilted)

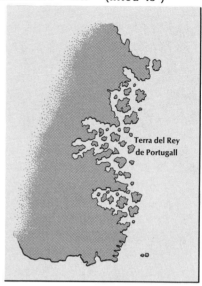

CANTINO, 1502

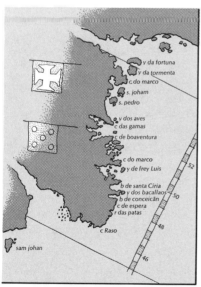

REINEL, 1505

MILLER No. 1, 1525

90

the good olde man, in that extreme age," was "somewhat doted, and had not yet even in the article of death, utterly shaken off all worldlye vayne glorie." In the late autumn of 1557 his pension payments stopped; and this, as in the case of his father almost sixty years earlier, is the only evidence we have of Sebastian's death. We know not the date, nor his burial place; nor was his will recorded.

Fishermen and Newfoundland Cartography, 1502–1524

The next quarter-century was an era of Portuguese supremacy in exploration of the north, and of other nations gradually getting on to the wonderful fishing to be had there.

Exactly how early the European fishermen resorted to the Grand Bank and the coastal waters of Newfoundland to take the cod we do not know, for fishermen leave few records, and their ordinary comings and goings were not noted. Judge Prowse, the historian of Newfoundland, asserted that West Country English were fishing off Newfoundland as early as 1498, but that is pure conjecture; he assumes that people rushed over to make a killing as soon as they heard Cabot's codfish stories. English fishermen are notoriously conservative, and I doubt whether any would have risked that long voyage until they had heard that the French and Portuguese were making apostolic hauls in American waters.

Although the Anglo-Azorean expeditions of 1501–5 may have done some fishing, the letters-patent point to exploration as their prime objective. And the earliest positive date we have for a French (Breton or Norman) fishing voyage is 1504. There were enough Portuguese doing it by 1506 to justify the king's clapping a 10 per cent import duty on their catch—the first European attempt to protect home industries from American competition!

After the Anglo-Azorean tentatives just noticed, prior to the voyage of Fagundes, we have only cartographic evidence about what was going on in northern waters. These early maps tell us a good deal. Suppose we tilt a modern map of Newfoundland about 40 degrees eastward so that the coast appears to run almost due north and south, and compare with it the delineations of the same coast on three old maps which took no account of compass variations, reducing them to the same scale. This will indicate a gradual unfolding and correction of the coastline, and a Portuguese nomenclature which, at least on the most conspicuous landmarks, endures to our day.

The first is the Cantino Mappemonde of 1502, still preserved in the Biblioteca Estense at Modena. The "Terra del Rey de Portuguall" (Newfoundland), the part we have reproduced, is placed much too far east in order to get it on the Portuguese side of the Line of Demarcation, which runs through the grove of pine trees. The west coast is vague, since nobody knew anything about it; but the east and south coasts indicate that Gaspar Corte Real had sent home an accurate chart of the points, bays, and islands from the Strait of Belle Isle to Placentia Bay. Newfoundland is out of scale, lengthwise, being twice as long as Ireland and longer than Great Britain. The label on it reads (in translation), "This land was discovered by order of the very high and excellent prince, King of Portugal D. Manuel, and the man who discovered it was Gaspar de Corte Real, gentleman of the court of said King; he who discovered it sent [home] a ship with . . . men and women who belonged to that land, and he [went off] with the other ship and never returned but was lost, and he [found] many mast [trees]."

The next outline of Newfoundland is on the Pedro Reinel Map, formerly (and perhaps still) in the State Library of Munich. Here the big island is not named but two Portuguese flags are planted thereon, and it occupies the same relative position (lat. 46° to 50° N) as on the Cantino Map. Although the date generally assigned to this Reinel Map is 1504/5, it cannot be earlier than 1521, as it incorporates some of the discoveries of João Alvares Fagundes, whom we shall consider shortly. Our third map, known as the Miller No. I, in the Bibliothèque Nationale, is (in my opinion) not earlier than 1525. Here Newfoundland is called *Terra Corte Regalis*, and Nova Scotia, *Terra Frigida*.

Note a little north of center on the three old maps, a deep bay containing three harbors. Comparing this with the modern map, it is evidently meant for Notre Dame and White Bays rolled into one, and the Reinel Map shows the two St. Barbe Islands as *y dos panes* (of the shields)—probably a reference to their peculiar rocks. Proceeding northward, we pass the high and conspicuous Grois or Gray Islands (*S. Pedro* and *S. Johan* on the Reinel) and reach the northern peninsula of Newfoundland. This peninsula, with an indentation meant for St.

Lunaire Bay, ends (on the Cantino) at Quirpon Island where Capes Bauld and Dégrat are situated.

West and north of these capes all the early maps show the Strait of Belle Isle, but it fades out in such a way as to suggest that the Portuguese navigators supposed it to be just another fjord. And the west coast of Newfoundland is always conventionalized as a straight line, half-moon, or series of scallops, proving it to have been as yet undiscovered.

Equally significant evidence of Portuguese supremacy on the outer Newfoundland coast are names which have lasted to the present, through corrupted English or French versions. Beginning at the southeast corner of Newfoundland, we have *c. raso* (shaved) which thereafter, and for all future time, will be Cape Race. About halfway from this cape to St. John's, the Miller I Map has *R. fremoso* (beautiful); this has become Fermeuse Harbor. Just south of St. John's Harbor (which Miller I already calls *Rio de Sam Joham*) is *c. de espera* (hope), now Cape Spear. Around Cape St. Francis, Conception Bay opens up; this is found, in various spellings, on all the early maps.

Off the next cape northward lies *y do baccalhao* or *y dos baccalaos*, celebrating the codfish that swarm about; this now is stabilized as Baccalieu Island. On the other side of Trinity Bay, which almost makes the Avalon Peninsula an island, is *C. de boa ventura*, the modern Cape Bonavista. Bonavista Bay is easily identifiable on the early maps by its depth; north of it every old map shows an *y do frey luis*, commemorating an otherwise unknown Fr. Luís, probably a ship's chaplain. The now forgotten friar's name has gone ashore and become Cape Freels; the island was either Stinkard (now renamed Cabot!) or Gull Island.

Next north of Cape Freels is Cape Fogo on the island of that name; we first find it as *y do fogo* (of the fire) on Miller I. Possibly some passing navigator saw a forest fire there. The name *Sam Joham*, attached to Groais Island in these early charts, has gone ashore, like that of Fr. Luís, and become Cape St. John. That takes us to Cape Bauld, which the Reinel and other early charts appropriately call *C. do Marco* (of the landmark); and off it lies *I. de la Fortuna* (Belle Isle), which Alonso de Santa Cruz says should rather be called the Isle of Ill Fortune, since a Portuguese fleet was wrecked there in the time of the Corte Reals.

An impressive record indeed of the Portuguese impact on Newfoundland, and of the growing importance of the Grand Bank fisheries. Local fishermen all along the Lusitanian coast must have been appalled by the competition when the first overseas vessels returned from the Grand Bank fairly bulging with enormous codfish all ready to cure; they obtained the 1506 protective tariff against what is nowadays called "dumping" of cheap goods.

It is a curious fact, yet unexplained, that around 1534–35, when Jacques Cartier sailed through the Strait of Belle Isle into the Gulf of St. Lawrence, mapmakers began to break up Newfoundland into five or more big islands separated by straits. It is as if they decided that since Cartier found the bay north of Cape Bauld to be a strait, all other deep bays must be straits too. Although a few Portuguese charts held out against that tendency, it was not until 1607 that the Stockholm Chart by James Hall shows Newfoundland properly, as a rough equilateral triangle, with no strait through it.

João Alvares Fagundes

At Viana do Castelo, a Portuguese fishing town near the Galician border, there lived a shipowner named João Alvares Fagundes, who took a keen interest in Codfish Land. In 1520, if not earlier, he made a voyage along the south coast of Newfoundland and into the Gulf of St. Lawrence, "apart from the land which the Corte Reals found to the northward." He named the principal places that he discovered, and we can identify most of them. *Isla de Pitigoen* means Penguin Island, for the "penguin" of that era was not the antarctic bird now so named, but the great auk, which also could not fly. The English were calling this Penguin Island as early as 1536; Lancaster, writing his account of Newfoundland for Hakluyt forty years later, said that the birds were so plentiful and helpless that you could lay your ship alongside the rocks at high water, drop a gangplank ashore, and drive as many waddling auks on board as you wanted. The fishermen used them for bait, and the Beothuk Indians made a cake out of their fat with wild strawberries. The island is still called Penguin, but the great auk has been extinct for over a century.

Fagundes's next discovery he called the Archipelago of the *onze mil virgenes*. He meant St. Pierre, Miquelon, and the numerous islets between them and the coast of Newfoundland. The story of St. Ursula, princess of Cornwall, and her eleven thousand sea-going virgins, who toured the waters of Europe for years but were murdered by the Huns at Cologne, was one of the most popular legends of the Middle Ages; and whenever an explorer found an extensive group of small islands he was apt to give them this name. Columbus so called the archipelago now known as the Virgin Islands of the United States and of Great Britain; and there is another group off the coast of Argentina. But this particular name of the Virgins was not honored by the French, except for Virgin Cove at Miquelon. On the early Portuguese maps, such as the Miller I which we have reproduced, they appear as a diagrammatic cluster of islets.

Fagundes mentioned an island called *Santa Cruz* "at the foot of the Banks," which may possibly have been Sable Island, and *Santa Ana*, which was "seen and not approached." Both appear on several early maps; St. Ann's became an overseas rival to Hy-Brasil. West of the Isle of Penguins he noted an island that he named after Saints John and Peter. This is probably the beautiful, rugged island later named after the Apostle Paul. It lies 130 miles due west from Penguin Island and 15 miles northeast of Cape North.

Upon returning from this voyage, Fagundes put all these facts into a petition to the king of Portugal for a captaincy, similar to those already granted to many navigators, pointing out that these places had not been discovered by the Corte Real brothers. D. Manuel complied, granting to Fagundes on 22 May 1521 complete property rights, jurisdiction, and privileges over this region—even to setting up soap factories! We do not know how or from what this enterprising Portuguese proposed to make soap, but he acutely observed that it would save time and labor for fishermen to cure their catch ashore instead of sailing every cargo the long distance to Lisbon or Viana; and, a century before the English, he set up a permanent shore establishment. Colonists were obtained in his native Minho and he even sent a ship to the Azores to recruit families who hoped to better themselves in the New World. They crossed the Atlantic in the summer, as early as 1521 or as late as 1525, and settled on a "beautiful harbor" on Cape Breton Island, which Fagundes called the Island of St. John. The harbor undoubtedly was Ingonish, which has everything that fishermen want: two bays, each with a protected harbor, and in each a sand beach where they

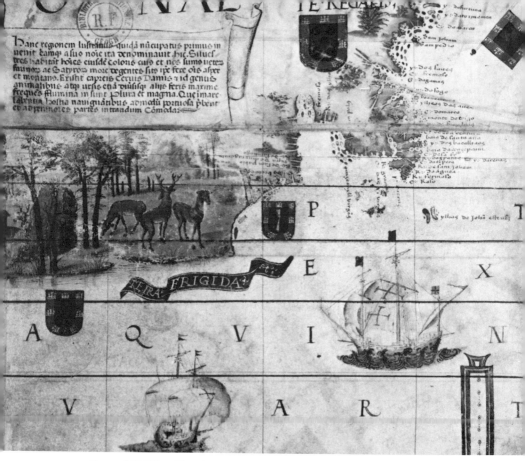

Part of "Miller I" Atlas world map. Courtesy Bibliothèque Nationale.

can draw up their shallops and a level area where they can cure the catch. No other place on Cape Breton has these advantages.

After a year or eighteen months at Ingonish, difficulties arose. As usual, the Indians turned hostile when they realized that the Europeans intended to stay instead of merely calling to fish and trade. Breton fishermen, from whom this island received its permanent name, cut the Portuguese fishing lines and destroyed their houses. Fagundes sailed along the coast of Nova Scotia, looking for a better spot, inadvertently discovering and mapping the Bay of Fundy. But his little colony could not continue without help from home, which it did not get. By 1526, perhaps before, this earliest (save the Norsemen's) of many vain attempts of Europeans to set up a colony in North America no longer existed.

Jean Alfonce, Roberval's chief pilot for his voyage of 1541–42, wrote an epilogue to these efforts in his *Voyages avantureux* (1559, but written 1544) when discussing Cape Breton Island: "Formerly the Portuguese sought to settle the land which lies the lowest, but the natives of the country put an end to the attempt and killed all those who came there."

The earliest cartographical record of Fagundes's voyages is on the so-called Miller I World Atlas at the Bibliothèque Nationale, by Jorge Reinel, of which we have reproduced the Newfoundland-Cape Breton sector. It shows no land connection between Cape Breton and Florida, proving that the map-maker knew nothing about the voyages of Verrazzano and Gomez in 1524–25; but it is clearly post-Fagundes. Note the archipelago of the 11,000 virgins, the southern entrance to this Gulf which Fagundes did not penetrate, and the uncharted back side of Newfoundland. Especially significant is the nomenclature of Cape Breton, *c. do bretoēs, R. de sam pablo, terra de mynta gente,* and *R. de saluago,* the last two being tributes to the natives. Below a herd of deer grazing on the future Nova Scotia appears the legend *Terra Frigida.* Reinel's Latin inscription records the discovery by Gaspar Corte Real, whose name is given to Newfoundland, and the nomenclature is purely Portuguese. The native Beothuk—whom other discoverers called "reds" from their lavish use of red ochre—are "of the same color as us," and "live like the ancient fauns and satyrs." Wild animals are listed but, strangely, no fish. South-southeast of Cape Race are the *ylhas de Johā Esteves,* shaped like two sausages. These, which one finds on earlier Portuguese maps, had been discovered by a fisherman from whom they were named, but could not again be located— more flyaway islands. This Miller I Atlas, a masterpiece of early Portuguese cartographical art, is also notable for its accurate drawings of animals and of ships. The two vessels on the part here depicted, barely one-twelfth of the whole, have already been discussed in Chapter I.

Whilst Reinel does not mention Fagundes by name, Diogo Homem's map of 1568 calls Cape Breton, *Cap Fagundo,* places Micmac Indian names along the outer coast, and inserts other names, none of which endured, along the Nova Scotian shore. Homem's definite delineation of the Bay of Fundy, with Grand Manan at its mouth, proves that either Fagundes or another Portuguese discovered that rough arm of the sea

The two harbors at Ingonish.

West coast of St. Paul Island.

where spring tides run up to sixty feet; and the cartographer's suggestion that he reached Penobscot Bay is supported by two French sources.

Posterity has been unkind to Fagundes. By 1600 his name had disappeared from North American geography. His countrymen long continued to come for fish, and their place names still remind us that these valiant seamen of a small nation helped to open up a new Western World.

Robert Thorne's Letter and John Rut's Voyage

The accession of Henry VIII in 1509 marks a notable falling off of interest by the English government and people in the New World. Postponing a discussion of the reasons, we shall here tell the brief and inglorious stories of English voyages, other than fishing trips, to Newfoundland and other northern regions during the half-century after Cabot's. The only ones known are the voyages of John Rut (1527) and Richard Hore (1536).

Robert Thorne of Bristol instigated Rut's voyage. This remarkable man, a precursor of Richard Hakluyt, was the son of Nicholas Thorne, who, with Hugh Elyot, had been a member of the Anglo-Azorean exploring syndicate of 1501–2. After representing the Admiralty at Bristol, Robert Thorne prospered as a merchant and resided in Seville, whence in 1527 he wrote "A Declaration of the Indies" to Henry VIII, and a "Booke" supporting the same, for Edward Lee, the king's ambassador to Charles V. "God and nature," he remarked, "both provided to your Grace . . . this Realme of England, and set it in so fruitful a place" as to be "free from foreign conquest," one cause being "that it is compassed with the Sea." Portugal and Spain had monopolized more than a fair share of the fruitful parts of the earth by sailing west, east, and south. Here "now rest to be discovered the sayd North parts, the which it seems to mee, is onely your charge and duety." And to Lee he made the astonishing suggestion that, there being "no land uninhabitable, nor sea innavigable," nothing prevented "sayling Northward and passing the Pole," then dropping down to the Equator on the other side of the world, so halving the distance sailed by Spaniards and Portuguese to the riches of Asia. He pointed out that in summer "perpetuall clereness of the day without any darkeness of the night" would help make this route safer than those of the king's rivals, which were fraught with "dangers or darkenesse." And to Lee he sent a world chart of his own making, with a latitude and longitude grid, to prove his point. Thus Thorne anticipated two leading airplane and submarine routes of our own day.

Henry VIII reacted promptly by setting up a voyage to discover the Northwest Passage. (His naval advisers evidently dissuaded him from trying the North Pole.) A fleet of "two fayre shippes," *Sampson* (nicknamed *Dominus Vobiscum*), commanded by Master Grube, and *Mary of Guildford*, John Rut, master, "well manned and vitailed, having in them divers connyng men," was quickly organized. Both were merchant ships owned by the crown; *Mary* (160 tuns, built 1524) had been employed by Henry VIII to fetch wine from Bordeaux for the royal household. Of Master Grube nothing seems to be known; but John Rut, of Ratcliffe, had served the king in war and peace for many years. The preparations acquired such fame that Lord Edward Howard, son of the Duke of Norfolk and an unemployed Captain R.N., begged Cardinal Wolsey "for the bittyr passion of Krist" to get him a berth and so relieve him from "as wretchyd a lyffe as ever dyd jentylman"; but he did not get it. Canon Albert de Prato of St. Paul's, "a great mathematician and a man indued with wealth, did much advance the action, and went therein himselfe in person." Under Grube's command they sailed from London River 20 May 1527, and from Plymouth 10 June, "to seke strange regions."

Rut's own letter states that he took final departure from the Scilly Isles, and on 1 July parted from Grube in "a marvailous great storme." Neither he nor anyone else saw *Sampson* again. On 21 July *Mary* made "Cape de Bas," Newfoundland, and entered a nearby harbor in latitude 52° N. No Cape de Bas appears on any known map; but as the Scillies are at latitude 50° N, and John Rut probably followed the time-honored latitude sailing; and as he rounded a big iceberg when returning to the same port in late July, it must have been north of Cape Bauld, Newfoundland (51°38′ N); probably near Battle Harbor, Labrador, at 52°15′ N. Rut's description of the place as having "many small Ilands," a "great fresh River going up farre into the mayne Land" fits that region best.

Master Rut evidently had no relish for northern exploration. According to his letter of 3 August to the king, he sailed only as far north as latitude 53°, that of Hawke Bay, Labrador. "There we found many great Ilands of Ice and deepe water, we found no sounding" (an obvious excuse, as that entire coast is on soundings), "and then we durst go no further to the Northward for feare of more Ice." So he "cast about to the Southward," took a sounding of 160 fathoms, which must have been at least twenty miles out, made land again at latitude 52° N, and, after passing a big iceberg, put in again at Cape de Bas. Tarrying ten days to water, and finding "all wildernesse . . . and no natural ground but all mosse and no inhabitation," only "footing of divers great beasts," he continued south, and on 3 August entered the harbor of St. John's. There he found ten fishing vessels: seven Norman, two Portuguese, and one Breton. Writing the same day to the king, he said he intended to return to Cape de Bas to look for *Sampson;* but whether he did or not we do not know.

What we do know is where he went next. *Mary of Guildford* ranged the coasts of Cape Breton and "Norumbega"—Nova Scotia and New England—frequently landing men to report on "the state of those unknown regions." And then she turned up in the West Indies.

A Spanish captain named Gines Navarro was loading cassava at Mona Island between Hispaniola and Puerto Rico, when a foreign ship of about 250 tuns' burthen sailed in and spoke him. The officers said they were Englishmen, that the vessel belonged to their king, and that when searching for a passage to "discover the land of the Great Khan," they had lost their consort. After various improbable adventures (such as entering a sea of hot water), they had sailed south along the coast that Ayllón had discovered, and now proposed to pick up a cargo of dyewood in Puerto Rico. Captain Navarro, entertained on board the English ship, reported that she had a crew of seventy, including artisans and shipbuilders with complete tool kits.

Spaniards reported the same ship—always unnamed—when she anchored off the Ozama River, the harbor of Santo Domingo, on 25 November 1527. The captain sent a boat ashore to ask permission to enter the harbor and obtain water and provisions. The authorities consented and sent out Diego Mendez, *alguacil mayor* of Hispaniola, with a harbor pilot to bring her in; but in the morning, when she lay just outside the bar waiting for a fair breeze, a trigger-happy commander of the fort fired a stone cannonball which made a near-miss. Master Rut, smelling "Spanish treachery," sent the alguacil and the pilot ashore and promptly made sail.

Oviedo, historian of the Indies, here picks up the story. Confirming

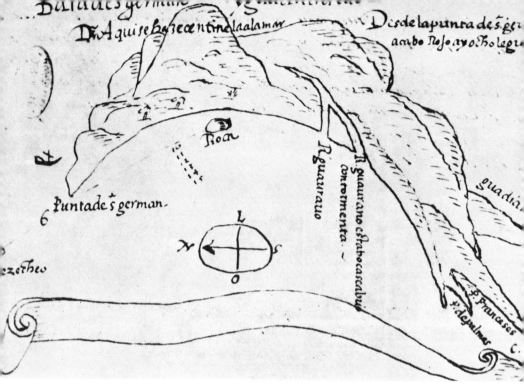

San Germán Bay, Puerto Rico. From the ms. *Derrotero* of Juan de Es-
calante de Mendoza, 1575, Real Academia de la Historia, Madrid. The
soundings show the approach to the original town of San Germán, which
by 1575 had been moved to its present site; at the time of Rut's visit, it
lay a short distance inland. The ship indicates the *Aguada*, a river of sweet
water which had been in use since 1493. To the south is Cape Rojo, the
southwestern point of Puerto Rico, and Guayanilla Bay, where Sir Richard
Grenville built a fort in 1585. Courtesy of Mr. Aurelio Tió.

the fact that the English ship was frightened away by a cannon shot, he
says that she crossed the Mona Passage and entered the Bay of San
Germán, Puerto Rico, now known as Añasco Bay. The town of San
Germán had been moved inland for protection from pirates, but not
far, so Rut was able to visit it and assure the alcalde that he had no intention to plunder, only to obtain provisions. These were furnished
and, in addition, he bought some *estano de baxilla,* tableware made of
marcasite from a nearby mine which, unlike those in Frobisher Bay,
yielded a profitable amount of silver. The ship departed in peace, her
conduct considered to be remarkably good manners for an Englishman,
or any foreigner, in the Antilles. *Mary of Guildford* was back in Eng-

land by the spring of 1528; and that autumn, still captained by John Rut, she sailed to Bordeaux to buy wine for the king's household.

Although Henry VIII bestowed an annuity of £20 on John Rut, it must be admitted that his voyage was a complete failure compared with the French voyages which preceded and followed his. Rut found nothing new, and left no trace on the nomenclature of the New World. Grube's ship had been lost with all hands; and Rut's, missing two chances (Strait of Belle Isle and Cabot Strait) to enter the Gulf of St. Lawrence ahead of Cartier, sailed south on what was little more than a pleasure cruise to the West Indies. Robert Thorne died in 1527; he did not suffer the mortification of learning about the frustration of his great design for superpolar sailing.

Master Hore's Tourist Cruise

Tourist cruises, with the pious excuse of a pilgrimage to Rome, the Holy Land, or some famous foreign shrine, were no innovation in the sixteenth century. For instance, in 1446, the cog *Anne* of Bristol carried to Joppa 160 pilgrims, who decided (fortunately for themselves) to return home overland; the cog on her homeward passage, laden with spiceries, crashed on the shores of Greece and lost all hands. Her owner, with another ship, then took fifty pilgrims to Santiago de Compostello. English curiosity about foreign countries was whetted by such books as Sanseverino's *Viaggio in Terra Santa* of 1458. But a pleasure trip to the New World was an innovation—much as if Thomas Cook or American Express were to set up an air trip to the moon—as they probably will do within a few years.

By 1536 Newfoundland was so well known that one Richard Hore, citizen and leather merchant of London, chartered two ships, *Trinity* and *William*, for the double purpose of catching codfish and giving certain gentlemen of London a pleasure voyage. This first tourist cruise in American history ended in misery, starvation, and even cannibalism.

Hakluyt, who traveled 200 miles to interview a survivor, says that Hore's "perswasions tooke such effect" that he signed on no fewer than "six score persons, whereof thirty were gentlemen." After attending mass at Gravesend they set sail near the end of April 1536. *Trinity* apparently was lost, but the *William* (which Hakluyt misnames *Minion*) passed Cape Race, and two months after leaving England

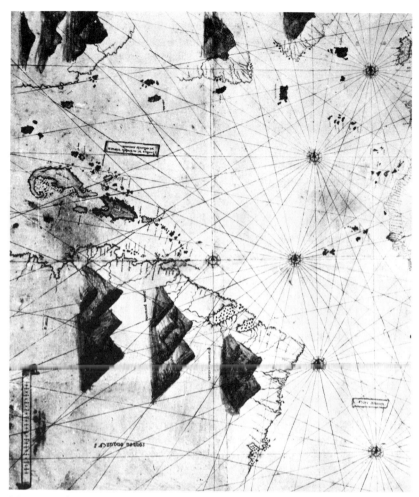

New World half of the Oliveriana Map, Pésaro. Giraudon enlargement of film kindly given me by Sr. Zicari, head of the Oliveriana Library, Pésaro.

anchored at Penguin Island, off the south coast of Newfoundland. There they killed a large number of "the foules" (the great auk) as well as "bears both black and white." Master Hore entered a small harbor on the adjacent Newfoundland coast and anchored. Provisions ran short even though they robbed an osprey's nest of the fish she brought to her young. The passengers first resorted to "raw herbes and rootes in the fields and deserts" and then took to cannibalism. Master Hore preached a sermon denouncing such ungodly and inhuman practice, and was rewarded by the arrival of a French ship "well furnished with vittaile" which the Englishmen promptly captured and "spoiled." By that time some of the tourists had died of starvation, and others had been killed and eaten. The survivors sailed for home, seeing "mighty Ilands of yce in the Summer season," and arrived at St. Ives, Cornwall, near the end of October 1536. One is glad to hear that Henry VIII compensated the Frenchmen; but why, in Heaven's name, could not the Englishmen have supported life from sea-fowl and fish?

That they did "make" (i.e. cure) codfish is evident from a lawsuit instituted by the owner of the *William* against Hore, complaining that the charterer defrauded him of his share of the fish. Next year, 1537, Master Hore procured another English vessel, named *Valentine*, sailed to Lisbon, and there shipped not only a cargo of salt and wine but a number of Portuguese passengers for London. Instead of taking them to their destination, he anchored at a small outport near Cardiff and tried to extort money from them. For that he was called to account by the lord lieutenant of the county, and subsequently he was sued by the crew of *Valentine* for £280. Master Hore seems to have been a rascal, and the gory details told by Hakluyt are credible.

Hore's voyage put an end to the tourist business, as far as the New World was concerned, for at least two centuries.

✳ IV ✳

The French Maritime Background

1453-1590

"Les français sont puissant sur mer, ils ont puissance partout
et s'accroissent toujours en nombre."
—PORTUGUESE AMBASSADOR TO D. JOÃO III, 17 FEBRUARY 1538

Emerging Normandy

In 1500 it was anyone's guess which European power would dominate
North America. Eliminating Spain and Portugal, both of whom had
little energy left for these supposedly poor and chilly regions of the
New World, we have France and England; and anyone estimating their
relative power in 1550 would have bet on France. She had sixfold
the population of England, double that of the Iberian peninsula, 50 per
cent more than the whole of Italy. France had a greater extent of
ocean-facing territory, as many or more seaports than England, an
equally enterprising maritime population, far greater wealth, and,
until her civil wars broke out, a government as much interested in
maritime affairs as that of the Tudors.

Why, then, did France not annex all America north of Florida? The
following chapters will provide part of the answer. In this we shall
briefly examine the maritime conditions and situation of France in the

* This chapter should be considered a supplement, insofar as France is concerned,
to Chapter I above, where the data on building, manning, and rigging English
ships, conditions of seafaring, etc., apply generally to France as well.

106

Jean Jolivet's two Norman ships and a galley from his map of Normandy, 1525. Courtesy Bibliothèque Nationale.

sixteenth century, especially preceding her first great voyages of discovery, those of Verrazzano in 1524 and of Cartier starting ten years later.

Maritime France, so far as northern voyages are concerned, consists of the ancient provinces of Normandy, Brittany, Saintonge, and Guienne. Mediterranean France participated very slightly in transatlantic discovery and trade.

Normandy, above all, is the center of maritime France; it has been ever since Rollo the Ganger and his merry men from Scandinavia took over in the ninth century. As far back as the twelfth century the Arab geographer Edrisi wrote, "Dieppe is a town where they build ships and a harbor whence maritime expeditions depart." When Béthencourt wanted colonists for the Canaries in the early part of the fifteenth century, he found them in Normandy. Dieppe lay right on the sea, in a perfect position to become at once the fulcrum for water traffic with England and the Netherlands and a leading center of the North Sea herring fishery. It was near enough to the mouth of the Seine to profit by exchanges with Rouen and Paris, and to vend its products through the center of France. In the Middle Ages, the Seine was to France what the Mississippi and the St. Lawrence later became to the United States and Canada: an axis of penetration. The Seine was navigable for small craft for many miles above Paris; a short carry took one to the head-waters of the Loire, and another to the Rhône; thus, salt herring directly from Dieppe figured at the breakfast tables of the popes at Avignon.

The end of the Hundred Years' War in 1453 found Normandy a devastated region. Under English occupation, Dieppe and Rouen had to live without their back country, farms were deserted, at least one-third of the population had evacuated, all maritime pursuits were feeble or dead. Almost complete anarchy prevailed on the narrow seas in the last decade of the fifteenth century, to such an extent that the king of France required his subjects before putting to sea, to sign a bond not to attack friendly craft. Honfleur had to fortify her main street leading to the sea, as defense against pirates; and no wonder, since our old friends Pining and Pothorst chased a convoy of twenty-five French *hourques* laden with salt for Danzig, selectively captured one that was charged with Madeira wine, and threatened to land and plunder every northern French seaport.

Normandy vegetated for about twenty-five years, after which so remarkable a revival set in that by 1503 bad times were forgotten. Profitable traffic with England and the Baltic was restored. In 1504 we have the first record of a Norman fishing vessel on the Grand Bank of Newfoundland, and in 1508–10 *La Pensée* of Dieppe and *La Jacquette* of Pléneuf were there; between the two dates, a third Norman vessel landed seven Indian slaves in Rouen from "Terra Nova." But the herring fishery in the North Sea was so profitable to Dieppe that she did not become really interested in the North American codfishery for several years.

D. João III, king of Portugal, complained to the king of France in 1510 that French ships had captured three hundred Portuguese sail in the last ten years. Jean Fleury, corsair of Dieppe, intercepted and spoiled a Spanish treasure fleet in 1523. But it would be a mistake to assume that Normandy's new prosperity came from piracy. Rouen was sending her locally woven cloth to Spain and the Mediterranean, in competition with the English clothiers; her *bonnetries*—hats and bonnets for gentlemen and ladies—found a ready sale in England where both sexes preferred French fashions to English. Instead of filching logwood and spices from homeward-bound Spanish and Portuguese ships, the Dieppois now cut their own logwood in Brazil; and Paris, formerly at the end of a lengthy land spice line, obtained her spices by sea via Rouen. A great churchman of Paris who wanted a pair of parrots, sent for them to Fécamp where a ship was just in from Brazil; Paris epicures who preferred smoked salmon from Scotland to their own from the Loire, could buy it at Rouen. The only European church or museum of the sixteenth century which has carvings or paintings showing natives of Brazil is Saint-Jacques at Dieppe, and natives of Brazil were the sensation of a fête given there to honor King Henri II.

The most important maritime section of Normandy was *le Pays de Caux*, which extends from the mouth of the Seine to that of the Somme, including Rouen, Dieppe, Fécamp, and Le Havre. This Pays de Caux resembles a big rounded cake of chalk, on the edge of which *le bon Dieu* with a giant cleaver made harbors; consequently they are short but deep—Dieppe means deep. A shipmaster sailing eastward up-channel might be tempted to put in at Fécamp, which had an excellent little harbor right on the sea, more conveniently situated for trans-shipments to the Seine. And Fécamp had a famous place of pilgrimage, an abbey with a magnificent church as big as Notre-Dame de Paris, and a monastic distillery which claimed to have given birth to the liqueur Bénédictine, distilled from aromatic plants growing on top of the chalk cliffs. Incidentally, Fécamp is one of the last strongholds of the French codfishery; it imported 22,000 tons of cured cod as late as 1961.

If in search of big business, the shipmaster would have been well advised to sail a few more leagues eastward to Dieppe. The excellent little harbor there owes its existence to the River Arques breaking through chalk to the sea and conveniently depositing silt outside the harbor on the modern *plage*. The river itself gave easy access for barges to the Forest of Arques, source of ship timber, and the mouth of the harbor was protected by a jetty, as early as the fifteenth century. Burghers of Dieppe maintained a primitive coal-fire lighthouse there, which made a range for entering with a second light mounted at Le Pollet, the suburb on the right bank of the Arques. Thus, with any northerly or westerly wind, and at any time of day or night, a sailing

A 1970 view of Fécamp harbor. The entrance is under the drawbridge to the right.

ship could nip into Dieppe, close-haul her sheets, and in fifteen minutes moor at the quai (later named Henri IV) right under the windows of the big merchants' establishments. There, within a quarter-mile, a ship-master could find everything he wanted: *douanes*, merchants, factors, building and repair yards, ship's charts and instruments, taverns, *filles*. For these and other reasons, this little place rose in the sixteenth century to surpass other Norman ports such as Harfleur and Honfleur.

Dieppe never eclipsed Rouen, despite the difficult access to that river city. Although the navigation of the Seine is more hazardous than that of the English Avon, and even dangerous when a tidal bore, the *mascaret*, sweeps up the river unexpectedly, hundreds of the little ships of the sixteenth century made the long passage from Havre de Grâce to Rouen with no other power than oar and sail. With a ten-knot current, three tides at least were required to make it either way, and you would see a whole fleet, like the *fragatas* of the Tagus a few years ago, strike sail and anchor when the ebb tide began, and wait until the flood set in. Pilots were available at Quillebeuf and Caudebec. There the Abbey of Sainte-Wandrille had the right to tax every passing ship in return for contributing to her safety by marking the edges of the mudflats (*battures*) with *balises* (perches). Ships of 100 to 120 tuns' burthen could easily get up to Rouen, where there were not enough quays to accommodate the traffic; vessels once discharged were ordered by the city council in 1520 to haul out into the stream, under penalty of having their lines cast off by the police.

Rouen was a great city, by sixteenth-century standards. Owing to its bridge, the lowest on the Seine, Rouen became the head of deep-sea navigation, where everything had to be transferred to small craft for

A plan of Dieppe in 1853, not very different from that of 1553. The Jetée de l'Est was the original jetty, where the fourteenth-century *phare* was located. From Eugène Chapus, *Dieppe et ses environs*, 1853.

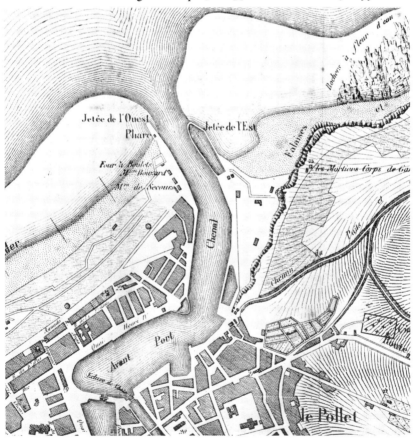

Dieppe and Environs, 1970: Harbor and quai Henri IV. Jean Ango's villa at Varengeville.

Rouen in 1526. Compiled from the manuscript album *Livre des fontaines de Rouen* of that date at the Bibliothèque Municipale, for an exhibition in 1845. The album pictures every church and almost every house in Rouen. Photo-Ellebé, Rouen.

passage to Paris or beyond; and a great deal of it was. In many respects Rouen was the French Bristol, with the additional advantage of being seaport to the capital. It lay up a difficult tidal river, it attracted foreign merchants (at Rouen, an Italian and a Spanish colony), the merchants built luxurious town houses and comfortable country manor-houses, and provided funds for magnificent churches—Rouen's cathedral, Saint-Ouen, and Saint-Maclou rival Bristol's cathedral and St. Mary Redcliffe. Finally, both towns have risen from their ashes. After terrific bombing in World War II they have repaired damage, rebuilt quays, shipyards, and dockyards, and Rouen is now the fourth port in France for tonnage.

Le Havre owes its existence as a great port to the interest of François-premier in creating a new deep-water naval harbor at the mouth of the Seine to replace silted-out Harfleur; no more could a "fleet majestical, holding due course for Harfleur," get into the harbor. On the site of a little fishing village on deep water, a long jetty was begun in 1517; quays and another jetty followed, and within three years the largest ships could moor there in safety. Nothing like this was ever done by the Tudors for any English port.

Norman shipmasters went to sea in the first half of the century better provided with printed and instrumental aids to navigation than (so far as we know) did any English captain prior to Frobisher. Pierre Garcie's *Routier* dates from 1483, and went through eighteen printings at Rouen before 1511.

In Chapter I we mentioned some of the difficulties that English ships experienced when approaching home ports after an Atlantic crossing. Those of the French were no less. *Haute Normandie*, extending from the Cherbourg Peninsula to the Seine, including the ports of Barfleur, Arromanches, and Honfleur, is very difficult to make out accurately from the sea, as the Anglo-American liberators of France found in 1944. A seemingly endless white cliff, with few church towers or other landmarks, confused mariners seeking the mouth of the Seine, which the Garcie rutter warned them not to enter at low water, owing to the numerous shoals and sand banks. For the Bretons, Ushant stretched out its ugly fangs and those with destination Saint-Malo not only had to avoid the Channel Islands and Les Minquiers but to thread the many off-shore reefs and rocky islands, like Cézambre, where the rise and fall of tide is almost equal to that of the Avon leading to Bristol.

Dieppe and Rouen were as famous as the cities of Flanders and Italy for great bourgeois families. Rouen boasted of three in particular—the Dufour, the Le Pelletier, and the Ango. The Dufours came from Geneva and had connections in Lyons; they were primarily drapers. The Le Pelletiers, who came from Provence, were merchants in almost "anything you can name or mention"; they so prospered that by 1550 some sixteen manors and châteaux in the Pays de Caux were theirs, and a few ships as well. They had connections with the Italian banker Bonacorso Rucellai, supporter of Verrazzano, and lent money to Charles VIII. The family that interests us most, however, is the Ango. Jean Ango, father and son, belonged to an old bourgeois family of Rouen and divided their time and interest between Rouen and Dieppe. The elder—known by popular acclaim as Le vicomte de Dieppe—financed a pioneer voyage to Newfoundland and was busily engaged in trade with the eastern Mediterranean, the British Isles, and the Low Countries; he helped to finance Verrazzano and Cartier. Ango owned great ships, small ships, and fishing vessels. His house flag, a Turkish crescent, adopted no doubt because of his Levantine interests (as did the nineteenth-century Boston families who traded with Smyrna), is flying from the mainmast of one of the Testu ships which we reproduce here, and the Norman cartographer Desceliers, whom Ango patronized, spread his crescent flag over the north of Canada as if he owned that too. In twenty years, 1520–40, his ships captured prizes worth a million ducats. The Portuguese condemned several Ango ships for trading with their possessions, and he retaliated by blockading Lisbon on his own account, with the approval of Admiral Chabot de Brion. François-premier did him the honor of visiting him at his manor at Varengeville. Under Henri II he fell out of favor, and in 1549, charged with withholding from the crown its due share of privateering profits, he was imprisoned and died soon after, a broken man. His family spent the next fifty years trying to recover his property.

Without the aid of Jean Ango, a veritable Renaissance merchant-prince, it is doubtful whether the voyages of Jacques Cartier would have been possible.

Dieppe by mid-sixteenth century had become a maritime metropolis where men not only built ships which established new trade routes, not only bought and sold seaborne merchandise, but studied cosmography, astronomy, and navigation. The proof of this is the appearance between 1542 and 1560 of a series of remarkable maps drafted by the Dieppe cartographers Roze, Desliens, Desceliers, and Vallard.* These Norman map-makers obtained their data fresh, at quayside, from master pilots such as Jacques Cartier, and produced charts of the northern regions equal to those of the Portuguese for accuracy and beauty. Why they did not undertake to chart Verrazzano's voyage we do not know; possibly the Florentine brothers refused to give out information so that Girolamo could keep it for his own purposes. Jacques Cartier, however, was generous with his information, which, incidentally, was more exact than that of any earlier navigator because he had broken out of the fish-and-salt class and learned all that Dieppe captains and Rouen rutters and instrument-makers had to teach.

The mariner's calling was as highly esteemed in Normandy and Brittany as that of the churchman, the physician, and the barrister. Jean Parmentier of Rouen, in his poem on the Marvels of God and the Dignity of Man, points out that to qualify as master pilot you need more time and training than to win a doctor's degree at a university:

* See reproductions in Chapter VIII below.

WESTERN FRANCE AND THE ENGLISH CHANNEL IN THE SIXTEENTH CENTURY

London
Thames R.
Portsmouth
I. of Wight
Exeter
Plymouth
Dartmouth
Portland Bill
Dodman Pt.
Lands
End
Falmouth
Start Pt.
50
SCILLY IS.
The Lizard
Dart R.

NORTH
SEA
Str. of Dover
Calais
Boulogne
ENGLISH CHANNEL
Dieppe
Fécamp
C. de la Hague
Casquets
Cherbourg
Harfleur
Le Havre
Honfleur
Rouen
CHANNEL IS.
Caen
PAYS DE CAUX
NORMANDY
Seine R.
Arques R.
ILE DE
FRAN
Pa

Ushant I.
(Ouessant)
Brest
Landerneau
Le Conquet
Pt. du Raz
48
Quimper
BRITTANY
C. Fréhel
Ft. La Latte
St. Malo
Granville
Mt. St. Michel

BELLE ISLE
Nantes
Loire R.
Tours

I. de Yeu
VENDÉE
ILE DE RÉ
La Rochelle
AUNIS
46
BAY OF
ILE D'OLÉRON
Brouage
Cognac
Charente R.
Pte. de la Coubre
SAINTONGE
DORDOGNE
Tour de Cordouan
BISCAY
Gironde R.

Bordeaux
Garonne R.
44
GASCONY

Scale of Nautical Miles
0   50   100

SPAIN
West 0 East

Or pour certain on tient qu'ung bon pillote,
Ung marinier qui tout son cas bien note,
Bien entendu et bien exercité,
Est plus longtemps pour entendre sa note,
Parfaictement qu'il ne s'en faille iote,
Qu'ung docteur n'est en l'université.

Brittany

Brittany's geography differed greatly from that of Normandy. The ancient Armorica has the same sea outlook as the Norman duchy, only more so; in situation, Brittany is to Normandy what Portugal is to Spain. In geology, however, Brittany is very different from Normandy, between Caen and Cherbourg. Like the coasts of Maine and the Maritime Provinces, Brittany was solid rock underneath, with "drowned" river valleys which became tidal estuaries such as the Rance, leading from Saint-Malo to Dinan. But the prescience of the sea-going monk St. Malo (his real name was MacLaw or Maclou, a disciple of his contemporary St. Brendan) in founding this city on a rocky neck thrusting seaward made it unnecessary for Breton mariners to grapple with the tidal currents of the Rance. For all that, the rocks, reefs, and islets of Saint-Malo Bay make the town difficult of access; but it has always made its main business the training of mariners, and it is the last Breton harbor to send fishing vessels (now diesel-powered) to the Grand Bank.

Today, pastures as green as Normandy's come down to the edge of the Breton cliffs, but in the sixteenth century most of these grew only gorse and other wild stuff; and although Brittany lost less than Normandy in the Hundred Years' War, she had less to lose. As in Scandinavia, rural poverty made for maritime enterprise; and in the revival of the early sixteenth century we find Breton ships doing a large part of the French carrying trade. The aptitude of their crews in the New World fishing is proved by the large number of Breton pilots employed on Norman fishing craft. Saint-Malo seems to have prospered in good times and bad. Brest, which did not become *le boulevard de la marine* until after Louis XIV had built it up in the seventeenth century, was eclipsed by two little ports—Landernan, up river, and Le Conquet behind Ushant, a favorite port of call for north-south traders, or those coming from across the Atlantic in urgent need of water and provisions. And there were at least a dozen other tiny ports like Quimper and Paimpol where small vessels were built to take part in fishing or the carrying trade. Lower Brittany too. had her axis of penetration— the Loire, flowing down past Nantes from the fat provinces of Anjou, Maine, Touraine, and the Orléanais.

"The permanent presence of Bretons in Norman ports is a prime factor," states the historian Mollat. They brought in woad for the Rouen and Paris dye-pots, wine and wheat from Gascony, and, above all, salt. Lower Brittany was the northernmost European country where salt could be made economically from ocean water; and in western Europe mineral salts had not yet been exploited. Enormous amounts of salt were used for seasoning and for preserving essential foodstuffs, and prior to the age of refrigeration all salt had to be supplied by evaporation from seawater. Brittany here had an advantage over Normandy, because when the duchy became part of France, through the marriage of its last duchess to Charles VIII, the French king agreed to exempt Bretons from the *gabelle*, the French salt tax. At that time Portuguese salt-pans at Aveiro and Setubal produced the best and purest salt, but they were too far away for imports, unless in small quantities for table use. The same applied even more strongly to Cadiz Bay, another major source of sea salt. Breton vessels mostly loaded at the salt-pans of the *marais* of Guienne, or at their own in Bouin, Brouage, and elsewhere. This copious, steady suppy of largely untaxed salt helps to explain the pre-eminence of the French in Newfoundland fisheries during the middle of the sixteenth century.

La Rochelle

The Biscayan coast of France south of the Loire is marshy, with long beaches open to the sea, and no harbor until you reach L'Ile de Ré. Behind that island rises the remarkable city of La Rochelle. One is now out of Brittany, in the old province of Aunis, or Saintonge, which be- came an eminent maritime region of France. Samuel de Champlain, her great captain-explorer of the next century, was born at the little salt-pan center, Brouage, in 1570, and in his writings described himself as *Xaintongeois*. Nobody has explained why La Rochelle (founded in the eleventh century) was placed where it is, fifteen miles north of the nearest navigable river, the Charente, and twice as far from the

Gironde mouth, gateway to rival Bordeaux. The harbor of La Rochelle is well protected, but only little streams suitable for small boats flow into it, and the salt marshes press in so close that the town lacked room for expansion. Only one road led out of it and that was impassable after a prolonged rain or during a high spring tide. The back country, too, was not fertile. It produced a white Aunis wine, and Cognac lies up the Charente; but there was nothing comparable to the vineyards of Bordeaux. Nevertheless, La Rochelle prospered, and in the late Middle Ages it became a semi-independent commune, like the city-states of Italy.

The real reason why this seaport flourished was the character of the people. A grim, determined race like the Scots, they found Calvinism to their liking and embraced the Reformed Religion with exceptional ardor. The Huguenot synod there in 1571 drew up a famous Confession of Faith, and in the religious wars La Rochelle successfully withstood a siege by the Catholic League in 1573. Since the city had become the chief Protestant stronghold in France, Cardinal Richelieu besieged and captured it in 1628. The siege reduced the population from 26,000 to 5000, most of those lost having died of starvation; but La Rochelle rose again. Years later, the Protestant cause was further damaged by the revocation of Henri IV's tolerant Edict of Nantes, and La Rochelle lost many of her most industrious citizens—hence New Rochelle, New York. Yet the city never gave up; in 1891 the construction of a new ship harbor, La Pallice, to handle big vessels, saved her foreign commerce, just as Avonmouth saved Bristol.

The merchants of La Rochelle, even before they went Calvinist, showed a great aptitude for finance. Whilst the oldest marine insurance policies issued in England are dated 1547, and they by Italian bankers, the Rochelais capitalists were insuring wine cargoes as early as 1489; and in 1563 no fewer than forty-five merchants of La Rochelle combined to underwrite two local vessels and one Portuguese for European voyages, at premiums of 7 and 8 per cent. Incidentally, I have found no instance of any transatlantic voyage, fishing or otherwise, being insured in the sixteenth century. They were considered much too risky.

By 1523 it is possible to name several fishing vessels from La Rochelle that were fishing on the Newfoundland Banks—*Marie*, *Catherine*, and *Marguerita*. And it is a good measure of Rochelais enterprise that Cartier, discovering (as he thought) the Gulf of St. Lawrence

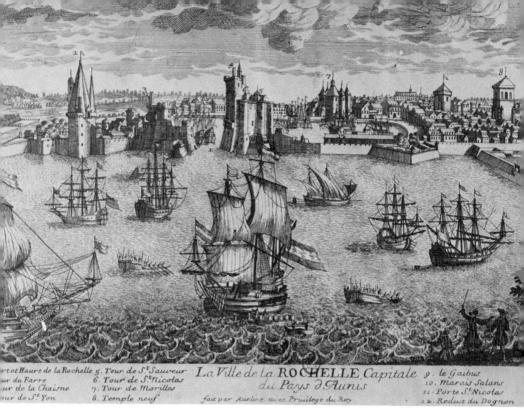

in June 1534, found a fishing vessel from La Rochelle there ahead of him. Never, in this or any other century, did the Rochelais take back wind from anyone.

The historians of La Rochelle have not done justice to her fishing interests; but certain facts stand out on the sharing of expenses and profits. The industry was organized on the share or "lay" system, like almost all coastal fishing in England, France, and North America down to the twentieth century. A document of 1523–24 indicates that one-third of the profits of a voyage, in fish and fish-oil, went to the crew; but out of that they had to pay the master or pilot. The rest went to the owners, except for a *pot de vin*, a tip, to the fishermen, at signing on. This for the "dry" fishing; for the "wet," the crew only got one-quarter of the profits, probably because "wet" took less time and two trips could be made a year.

As for quantity, the statistics collected by the local historians are impressive though contradictory. Departures from La Rochelle for Newfoundland or the Banks start with five in 1523 and jump to forty-nine in 1559, an average of over ten annually for the twenty-six years covered by this table. Another table gives one hundred departures from La Rochelle for Terre-Neuve in the years 1534–65. Whichever is correct, it is evident that La Rochelle was one of the leading overseas fishing ports of France, and that this led directly to its heavy participation in the settlement of, and trade with, Canada. Roberval, as we shall see, fitted out and sailed from La Rochelle in 1542, and his celebrated pilot, Jean Alfonce, was a Rochelais.

Bordeaux and the Gironde

Jacques Bernard has rescued Bordeaux from the imputation of earlier French historians to the effect that the Bordelais did nothing but grow grapes and drink wine, leaving ships and shipping to others. But he does not deny that wine was the basis of the region's prosperity. By constant care and applied intelligence, the Bordelais transformed a region of poor soil and marginal agriculture into one where the vineyards yielded a quality of wine which all the world then wanted; it still does. Claret, as the English called the red wine of Bordeaux, became a favorite during their domination of Guienne and Gascony. The Falstaffs and Fluellens preferred the stronger sack from Spain, but your English country gentleman or merchant drank claret, or *vin d'Aunis* or German hock on the rare occasions when he wanted white wine. Only in the eighteenth century did the English merchant prefer port wine to claret.

Owing to the value of the medieval wine trade, the Cordouan lighthouse at the mouth of the Gironde, begun under Charlemagne and rebuilt by the Black Prince under the English occupation, became the biggest and most famous in Europe. We have already seen how John Cabot used it as a point of reference; he had doubtless sailed up and down the "river of Bordeaux" as he called it, many times. No spot in Europe, not even the Eddystone, needed a lighthouse more; Cordouan was surrounded by *battures,* sand or mud flats, like those later encountered by the French in the St. Lawrence.

Your typical Bordeaux shipbuilder in the sixteenth century was not a specialist. Primarily he was a peasant, owner of vineyards or of meadow and tillage, who took to shipbuilding as a seasonal occupation when farming did not require all his time. He always figured on getting his boats finished by Michaelmas, so as not to interfere with the vintage. Similarly, the eastern Maine farmers, many of whom this writer knew in his youth, took to shipbuilding and boat-building in the fall, as soon as their crops were gathered into the barn, and enough salt fish or pickled mackerel was "made" to last the family through the winter.

Bordeaux ship-carpenters had so good a reputation that English vessels needing repairs tried to plan their voyages to lay over there; and Bordeaux as a wine metropolis was a very pleasant place at which to linger. Most of the vessels built there were under 80 tuns' burthen; a bill of sale of 1515 gives the specifications of a 35-tunner; 35 *pieds* (11–12 meters) on the keel, 14 *pieds* beam. All vessels destined for the sea were completely decked over, with castles forward and aft. The sail plan of the *Marie Johan* in 1493, described as a *nabiu* (navire) of eighty tuns, has four masts (two of them lateen-rigged mizzens), a main course with three bonnets, a fore course with two bonnets, and a square main topsail. Fifty years later, one always finds a square spritsail under the bowsprit.

Shipbuilding

Had we been fifteenth-century sailors we would probably have been able to tell a French-built from an English-built ship at a glance. From the records one can see no difference between the hulls and rigging of French vessels and those we have described in England. Norman shipbuilding underwent a tremendous expansion after 1520, most of it owing to the demands of transatlantic commerce. For the New World was a graveyard of ships; count up the wrecks we have mentioned from Cabot's down, add the fishermen and unrecorded others who foundered off Newfoundland, and you will realize that never in the history of merchant navies, not even after the ravages of World War II, has there been so great a need of replacement shipping as in the years 1530–1600. By the latter date, western Europeans had learned many lessons in safety, both in sailing and construction, and the casualty rate began to fall. There is one difference between the French and the English: although Dieppe and Bordeaux obtained their oak locally (Dieppe from the Arques forest, Bordeaux from the Dordogne), and used largely local pine or beech for planking, they imported almost every-

The Cordouan lighthouse. From an engraving of 1612. Courtesy Musée de la Marine, Paris.

thing else: tar and pitch from the Pyrenees or the Baltic (Danzig was already an entrepôt for naval stores in 1500), cordage from England, anchors and other ironwork from Bilbao. The English, however, imported canvas sailcloth from Dieppe, which probably obtained her supply from the Baltic.

In general the French shipbuilders seem to have gone through the same evolution as that of the Low Countries and England. First the one-masted *cogge*, then the three-masted *houlke* which, with certain refinements, became the *nef, nau, vaisseau,* or ship. Dieppe shipbuilders may not have invented the carvel type of construction, but with them it had completely superseded clinker-built by 1500; whilst in England, John Davis (over the objections of his shipmates) took a "clincher" pinnace with him to the Arctic regions in 1587, and sailed her home. The medium-size ship, under one hundred tuns, was called *barque* in

France, *bark* in England; the smallest, without which no overseas expedition was complete, *galion* in France, *pinnace* in England. To add to the confusion, France had at least ten other types of vessels which we cannot now identify; and the *galion* grew and grew until it became equal to the Spanish galleon of 1588.

Practical seamen preferred small ships to big ones for overseas exploration; but certain merchant-shipbuilders built them of five hundred tuns up, not only for prestige but because the big ones could be converted to naval vessels or powerful corsairs. For instance, the royal French navy bought Harfleur-built *L'Hermine* of 500 tuns in 1517; *La Louise*, 780 tuns, flagship of Admiral Louis Malet de Graville, came from Dieppe; and, most extraordinary, between 1521 and 1527, at a little place near Le Havre, there was built *La Grande Françoise*, which had five masts and measured 1500 tuns. She even had a built-in chapel, ballroom, and tennis court, like a modern cruise ship! For six years *La Grande Françoise* resisted every effort to launch her; finally a tempest threw her on her beam ends and she had to be scrapped. This leviathan was much bigger than the pride of the Tudor navy, *Harry Grace à Dieu*, or Scotland's *Great Michael*, built in 1511, which cost £30,000, and, manned by three hundred sailors, was said to be capable of carrying one thousand soldiers.

Inauguration of the Grand Bank Fishery

Neither Dieppe nor any other French port had trading relations with Iceland in the Middle Ages; their famous *pêcheurs d'Islande*, immortalized by Pierre Loti, belong to later centuries. The reason is obvious— smoked and pickled herring of the North Sea and English Channel had saturated the French market. Hence it is not to be expected that Normans and Bretons would flock to the Grand Bank as soon as Cabot's news reached France of the plenty of codfish there, nor did they. The first authentic records of any French ship on the Newfoundland Banks are those of Jean Denys of Honfleur in 1504, who fished between Cape Bonavista and the Strait of Belle Isle, and Thomas Aubert in the *Pensée* of Dieppe, belonging to Jean Ango, two years later.

Once they had found this new source of fish, the French lost no time in exploiting it. In 1507 a Norman vessel brought from Newfoundland to Rouen an extra cargo of seven *sauvages;* they must have been

French *nefs* of 1555. From the Guillaume le Testu album in the Bibliothèque des Forces Armées, Paris. Note the *pavesses* (shields of gentlemen on board) on the waistcloths and along the poop on the one; and the house flag of Jean Ango on the other. Photo Giraudon.

Beothuk Indians. We know of an early Breton fishing voyage by *La Jacquette* of Dahouët (who sold her stockfish at Rouen) because of a shipboard brawl that led to trouble. The master, Guillaume Dobel, aged twenty-two, alleged that she was carrying too much sail. He qualified Skipper Picart as an *idiot*, and Quartermaster Garroche as a *veau*, apparently a serious insult, like *cochon* today. Garroche dropped the tiller, roared up to the quarterdeck in a menacing posture, and collected a sock in the jaw from Dobel, who then drew a dagger and chased him overboard. They tried to rescue him, using their small towed boat, but he drowned. Dobel made the best restitution he could to the widow Garroche (apparently by marrying her!); influence was brought to bear, and on the ground that he was a good mariner and a valuable citizen in peace and war he received a pardon from the king.

Another human touch is in Elegy XI of the poet Jean Doublet, who flourished in mid-sixteenth century. He writes on the age-old theme of a sailor's mother watching in vain for his return. *La bonne mère* burns candles to the saints to promote her son's return, watches every ship that comes in, hoping it be his, and queries every returning mariner for news of her dear boy.

We have indubitable evidence that these intrepid fishermen were accustomed to make two fishing trips annually to the Grand Bank. The first set out in late January or early February and, braving the winter westerlies of the North Atlantic, returned as soon as their holds were full; then discharged, started off again in April or May, and were home in September. This, of course, was the "wet" fishing, which required no call at a Newfoundland harbor. Saint-Malo set aside a rocky section of the shore called *Le Sillon* for curing the fish, as early as 1519.

Shipboard prayers, superstitions, and customs of the sea were similar in France to those in England. One difference I have noted is that the mainmast at Bordeaux, and presumably elsewhere, had a symbolic value, so that a religious ceremony took place when it was stepped.

Salt fish were sold wholesale in France by the thousand; and from ancient custom, a thousand fish meant twelve hundred. In 1515 Michel Le Bail, Breton merchant, sells 17,500 salt codfish to the local merchants at Rouen; and thenceforth no year passes without a record of one or more *terre-neuviens* discharging stockfish at Fécamp, Dieppe, or Rouen. By 1529 Normandy is re-exporting it to England. The

French Newfoundland fishery had become big business; sun-cured *morue* were pushing *hareng salé* hard in the salt-fish market, and Rouen had become the distributing center of it for the interior of France. Cured codfish, if properly cooked, is tastier than pickled herring and easier to handle. One can throw it about and stack it like cordwood, whilst herring has to be contained in a barrel full of brine. It was a great day for Rouen in 1542 when no fewer than sixty vessels departed the same day for the Grand Bank of Newfoundland.

This new transatlantic business, as well as earlier logwood traffic with Brazil, attracted to Rouen a group of Italian bankers; and in the sixteenth century, as in the twentieth, local prosperity was signaled by the need of credit and bankers moving in. To what good purpose these Italians came to Rouen and Dieppe we shall see in the next chapter.

Although the French seaports had every possible advantage for Atlantic exploration that the English had; although the French crown gave its merchant marine more support and encouragement than the Tudors ever did, there is one English asset which the French lacked— a Hakluyt. That English compiler of voyages not only published everything he could find on his own nation's voyages; he translated Verrazzano's report long before it was available in French, and even rescued the original accounts of two Cartier voyages from oblivion.

The fact is that seafaring was a central activity in England, a peripheral one in France. England had but one land frontier, with Scotland; whilst France had the House of Hapsburg on two fronts, the German Empire in the center, and Savoy in the southeast. The French kings from Louis XI through Henri II were far from indifferent to seaports and mariners, but their series of wars with the Empire and Spain made the army their chief concern. Then came the religious wars; and by the time they were over and Henri IV had brought internal peace to France, it was too late for his country to become the great North American power. His predecessors had ignored what Verrazzano found; he had to make do with what Cartier explored.

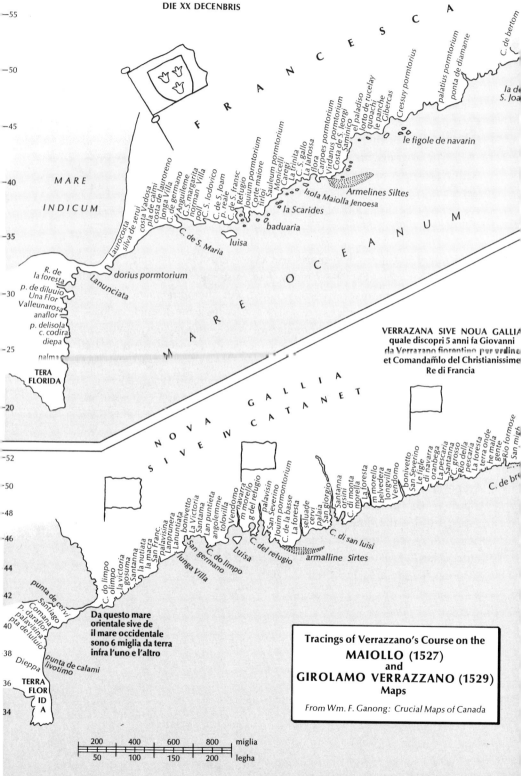

−60

−55

−50

−45

−40

−35

−30

−25

−20

−55

−52

−50

−48

−46

44

42

40

38

36

34

VESCONTE DE MAIOLLO CONPOSUY
HANC CARTAM IN JANUA ANNO DÑY 1527
DIE XX DECENBRIS

F R A N C E S C A

C. de bertom

palatius pormtorius
ponta de diamante

la de
S. Joa

Cressuy pormtorius

el paladiso
orto de rucelay
quoachi
le panche
Gibercas

le figole de navarin

Carpoes pormtorium
Virdanus pormtorium
Costa de S. leorgi
Saminico

Iouium pormtorium
Sauleum pormtorium
Careßi
La trinita
C. S. gallo
La lartossa
flora

Moncelli

Armelines Siltes

Isola Maiolla Jenoesa

la Scarides

costa Vadosa
pla de calmi
costa de laturoreno
longa Villa
C. de germano
Anguileme
G. S. margarita
norman Villa
poli
C. S. lodovico
C. de S. Joam
p. reale
C. de S. fransc
Refugio
Corte maiore

baduaria

MARE

INDICUM

Laurocosta
silva de serui

C. de S. Maria

luisa

R. de
la foresta

dorius pormtorium

Lanunciata

p. de diluuio
Una Flor
Valleunarosa
anaflor

p. delisola
c. codira
diepa

nalma

TERA
FLORIDA

M A R E   O C E A N U M

VERRAZANA SIVE NOUA GALLIA
quale discopri 5 anni fa Giovanni
da Verrazano fiorentino per ordine
et Comandamlo del Christianissime
Re di Francia

N O V A   G A L L I A
S I V E   I V   C A T A N E T

Rio formose
San migh

C. de bre

terra onde
he mala
gente

la foresta
pescaria
C. delia
rio della
C. grosso
Santanna
La pescaria
oranbega
di navarra
San Severino
bonivetto

Vendomo
longuilla
belvedera
m morello
La moresta
C. di monta
morella
otsimi
Santanna
San giorgio

C. di san luisi

Santanna
Iouim pormontorium
San Severino
Palavisin
m morello
Vendomo
navarra

C. del refugio

C. de la basse

La foresta
cervi
seluade
palaia

armalline Sirtes

Luisa

C. do limpo

San germano

lunga Villa

bonivetto
tolovilla
Lan puntieta
angolemme
La Victoria
Santama
Lanpruner
Lanuntiata
San Franc.
la macra
la nutiata
Santanna
la victoria
gosuma

C. do limpo
olimpo

punta de cer vi.
Santiago
Comano
P. Garaflor
palavisna
pta de lululo

Dieppa

punta de calami
livotimo

TERRA
FLOR
ID
A

Da questo mare
orientale sive de
il mare occidentale
sono 6 miglia da terra
infra l'uno e l'altro

Tracings of Verrazzano's Course on the
MAIOLLO (1527)
and
GIROLAMO VERRAZZANO (1529)
Maps

From Wm. F. Ganong: Crucial Maps of Canada

200   400   600   800   miglia
50   100   150   200   legha

* V *

The Voyages of Verrazzano

1524-1528

François-premier and the Search for a Northern Strait

While others were trying to make something out of Codfish Land and Cape Breton, mighty events were unrolling in the southern half of the hemisphere. Hernando Cortés won a Mexican empire for Spain in 1521. Ferdinand Magellan relentlessly pursued the greatest recorded voyage of all time. Victim of an ill-conceived amphibious attack, Magellan left his bones at Mactan in the Philippines, but his valiant subordinate Juan Sebastián de Elcano carried on around the world. On September 1522 his ship *Victoria*, sole survivor of the five with which Magellan started, anchored at Seville, carrying home but eighteen of the 239 men who had set forth three years earlier. The first printed account of this circumnavigation, *De Moluccis Insulis* by Maximilian of Transylvania, appeared at Rome in November 1523 and at Cologne in January 1524; and, just as the first voyage of Columbus sparked off that of John Cabot, so Elcano's stimulated two attempts by major powers to find a better western route to Asia than the tempestuous Strait of Magellan.

François d'Angoulême, who succeeded his cousin Louis XII in 1515, ordered the first. François-premier, as he is generally called, dissipated a

129

Posthumous portrait bust of Verrazzano. Courtesy Samuel H. Kress Collection, National Gallery of Art, Washington, D. C.

good part of his energy on love affairs, and the major share of his revenue in fighting the Emperor Charles V; but he was not indifferent to things of the sea. By marrying his cousin Claude, daughter of Louis XII and of Anne, Duchess of Brittany, he united that province of ships and sailors to the French crown, and, at one stroke, doubled the maritime potential of his kingdom. And for his Norman duchy he began the fortification and reconstruction of Havre de Grace in 1516. The Queen Mother, Louise de Savoie, took such a keen interest in Magellan's voyage that Antonio Pigafetta, the Italian gentleman who made the complete circuit, visited her at court in 1523 and presented her with "certain things from the other hemisphere."

François-premier, one year younger than Henry VIII, resembled in many respects his English cousin, whom he met formally on the Field of the Cloth of Gold in 1520. Both were handsome, gallant, and courageous; both were arbitrary, arrogant, and intolerant; both patronized arts and letters. The French king differed from the English monarch in nourishing a strong pro-Italian bias. He invited Leonardo da Vinci, Cellini, Solario, and Primaticcio to his court; for army generals he chose a Pallavicini and a Montecuccoli; he had Italian ministers, bankers, mistresses, and chefs de cuisine; and, since the Spanish sovereigns had patronized an Italian navigator named Colombo, and Henry VII supported another named Caboto, the king of France must have one, too. Hence Verrazzano.

Spanish and Portuguese explorers, having covered the entire east coast of the Americas from Florida to Patagonia, could find no strait north of Magellan's; so the only two stretches left to investigate were Florida-Newfoundland and Labrador-Greenland. On every map of the New World hitherto drafted—always excepting Juan de La Cosa's and possibly the Egerton—Newfoundland floated aloof in the North Atlantic, or became a northern promontory of Asia. Between it and Florida lay a region extending over some thirteen degrees of latitude and covering the coast of the future United States from Maine to Georgia. Nobody yet knew anything about it, since nobody who crossed by the northern route, and returned, had pushed further south or west than the Bay of Fundy. Surely here, if anywhere, not in the frozen north which the English and Portuguese had failed to penetrate, would be found *the* Strait. Even better, one might find an open sea,

François Ier, roi de France. Attributed to François Clouet. Musée du Louvre. Photo Giraudon.

which ships from western Europe could romp through to "the happy shores of Cathay," as Verrazzano called the coast of China.

Such was the opinion of a group of Italian bankers resident in Lyons, center of the French silk industry. They anticipated high profits from a discovery which would greatly lower the freight on silk. With royal patronage and approval they appointed as commander a master mariner of their own group, Giovanni da Verrazzano. One of the Lyons merchants, Bonacorso Rucellai, was not only a relative of the sea-going Florentine, but the banker for Jean Ango, the leading merchant-ship-owner of Rouen and Dieppe. Another, named Guadagni, was father or brother to Verrazzano's wife. The Guadagni were a leading Florentine family, banished in 1434; they settled at Lyons and became immensely wealthy. These Florentine bankers and merchants of Lyons formed a syndicate and, in March 1523, sent sums of money to some of their

Giovanni da Verrazzano. Late sixteenth-century copy of an earlier Florentine portrait. Courtesy of the Sig. Sindaco, municipio di Prato.

"De Guadagnis, Citizen of Florence," brother or father of Verrazzano's wife. Portrait Medal in Musée de Lyon. Photo Camponogara.

friends in Rouen to outfit the overseas expedition. Verrazzano also had a commission from François-premier, but it has not survived.

The Oliveriana Map (now at Pésaro), which we reproduced in part in Chapter III above, may also have encouraged Verrazzano's search for a northern strait. As this map gives every indication of having been made in Florence for a princely individual, it is possible that Verrazzano, as a Florentine, had an opportunity to study it.

Giovanni da Verrazzano, Gentleman Explorer

In Tuscany, thirty miles south of Florence, one enters the Chianti country and a Tuscan landscape that has hardly changed since the painters of the *cinquecento* used it for backgrounds. Sparkling streams and rivers, bordered by conical hills, whose slopes are planted with vines almost to the summits; each hill-top crowned with a villa or a castle. By no means the least of these is the Castello Verrazzano, ancestral home of that noble family, whose arms are a six-pointed star.

It is a real castle with two stone towers for defense, but in the sixteenth century modern rooms were built, and a detached chapel, and a fish pond. Long has it been "comfortably accepted" (to quote Dr. Lawrence C. Wroth) that our Giovanni was born here in 1485. A recent French biographer denies this, giving Giovanni a new pair of parents, Alessandro da Verrazzano and Giovanna De Guadagni, and a Lyons birthplace. This is indignantly denied by everyone in the Chianti country, and ascribed to French chauvinism! Castello Verrazzano near Greve is indubitably the ancestral home, and as Giovanni and his brother were always referred to as Florentines, there is no sense quarreling whether they were born here or in the Florentine community of Lyons.

"This valiant gentleman," as Ramusio called him, differed from other heroes of northern exploration in that he was well born and well educated. All contemporary documents refer to him as such; some even call him a nobleman.

The Castello Verrazzano, Greve in Chianti. From a photo taken prior to recent "restoration." Courtesy Signor Carlo Baldini of Greve.

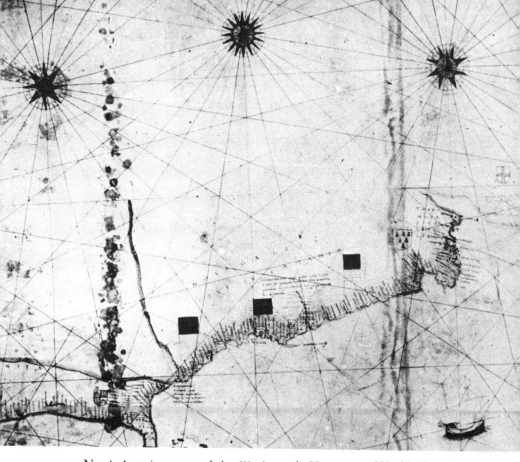

North American part of the Girolamo da Verrazzano World Map of 1529. Vatican Library. Note east shore of Pacific Ocean north and east of Florida. The three blacked-out flags are French; the arms of Brittany are north of Cape Breton, and the arms of England on the Labrador. The ship probably meant for *La Dauphine* is in the southeast corner. Photo by Giraudon.

If born in France, he was sent to Florence for his education, for the language of his Letter on the voyage of discovery and its literary allusions indicate that he received an upper-class Renaissance education. It also reveals that he knew more mathematics than most gentlemen of his time—or of ours.

The earliest actual fact that we know about him is that on attaining his majority, about 1506–7, he removed to Dieppe, in order to pursue a maritime career. A gossipy annalist of Dieppe, writing nearly three centuries later, stated that "Jean Verason," presumably our man, sailed in Ango's *La Pensée* to Newfoundland in 1508. In any case, the allusions to Carthage, Damascus, and the Saracens in the famous Letter prove that Verrazzano made voyages to the Levant, and there are hints that he was friendly with Magellan at Seville before the great circumnavigator's departure in 1517. A gentleman navigator, yes; but thoroughly professional.

None of the existing portraits of Verrazzano are contemporary with him, but as they all derive from one by Zocchi painted in his lifetime or shortly after, they may be assumed to be roughly correct. All show him with strong, confident features, black or dark brown hair, heavily bearded and mustachioed, with a prominent Roman nose; a thoroughly attractive and impressive figure.

By 1523, when he had attained the age of thirty-eight, Verrazzano had an impeccable maritime record, and as an Italian he appealed to the king. In the sixteenth century there was no hard-and-fast line between official voyages and privately financed voyages. Verrazzano borrowed *La Dauphine*, a ship of the royal French navy, and reported to the French king; but the Florentine bankers of Lyons and Rouen supplied most of the funds as well as the second ship, *La Normande*, which did not go far. *La Dauphine*, built in the new royal dockyard of Le Havre in 1519, was named after the dauphin François, heir to the throne, for whose birth the year before the great bell at Rouen tolled for twenty-four hours. She measured one hundred tuns and carried a crew of fifty; this was twice the burthen of Cabot's *Mathew*, and almost thrice the number of his crew. She probably flew the royal ensign of azure sprinkled with gold fleurs-de-lys. *La Normande* was a merchant ship chartered by the Lyons bankers from Jean Ango. The vessel we have reproduced here as her possible portrait is depicted on Girolamo da Verrazzano's map, sailing west along the route he took, and one may hazard the guess that Girolamo meant her to represent Giovanni's ship *

The outfitting took place at Dieppe, probably under the eyes of Jean

---

* One may object that the ship on the chart does not seem big enough for a 100-tunner; for what Norman ships of that burthen then looked like, see those reproduced in Chapter IV from a contemporary map of Normandy.

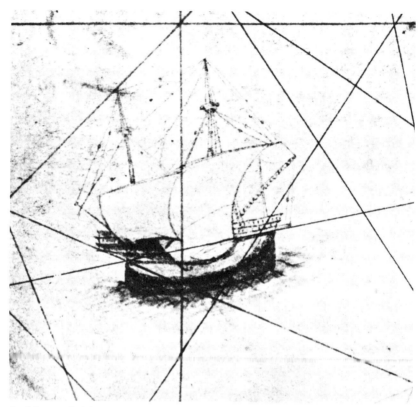

A ship, probably *La Dauphine*. From the Vatican Verrazzano Map. This ship is sailing on a course from Madeira to Florida, and is the right burthen. Note the furled mizzen, as she is running free.

Ango, who owned *La Normande*. Spies reported to D. João III of Portugal that French mischief was afoot; this Florentine boasts that he is going "to discover Cathay," but his real objective may be a raid on Brazil. Be on your guard, Your Majesty!

Verrazzano should have had a fleet of four ships, but a tempest in the autumn of 1523 disposed of two, and only *La Normande* and *La Dauphine* were left. They put in for refuge at a Breton port, and after repairs started south in company, taking a number of prizes off the coast of Spain. For reasons unexplained, probably because she had to escort the prizes to France, *La Normande* peeled off, and *La Dauphine* alone continued to America.

We have not the name of a single shipmate of Verrazzano's, except that of his brother Girolamo, the map-maker. Giovanni, even less generous than Columbus in giving credit to subordinates, does not mention a single person in his official Letter to François-premier, and he refers to the crew as *la turba marittima*—the maritime mob. They had good reason to dislike him, as *La Dauphine* almost always anchored in an uncomfortable roadstead, and they had shore liberty but once in the entire voyage.

Before sailing, Verrazzano made his will: "Le noble homme Jehan Verrassenne, capitaine des navires esquippez pour un voiage des Indes," named brother Girolamo his heir and made him co-executor with Rucellai, his banker cousin. And in his official letter to François-premier he made the object of the expedition perfectly clear: "My intention on this voyage was to reach Cataia and the extreme eastern coast of Asia, not expecting to find such a barrier of new land as I did find; and, if I did find such a land, I estimated that it would not lack a strait to penetrate to the Eastern Ocean"—i.e. the Pacific.

We have no hint as to what navigational instruments Verrazzano had at his disposal. That he took a keen interest in scientific navigation is indicated by his keeping a day book or journal (which has not survived), and by making an honest effort to determine longitude. His latitudes, more accurate than any prior to Cartier's, suggest that he was not confined to Columbus's imperfect instruments, the triangular wooden quadrant, with its tiddly plumb-bob on a thread, and the mariner's astrolabe; that he had at least one of the newly invented *balestilas*, or cross-staffs. But we cannot be certain, for it took a long time for new inventions to be adopted by sailors. The Ribero World Map of 1529, made subsequent to the voyages of Verrazzano, Gomez, and Ayllón, illustrates the quadrant and astrolabe, but no cross-staff.

From Deserta to the "Isthmus"

Verrazzano's plan for his ocean crossing ran parallel to that of Columbus in 1492; but instead of dropping down to latitude 28°N and the Canaries, he chose to take off from Las Desertas in the Madeira group at latitude 32°30'N. French corsairs had already been preying on the Spanish treasure fleets, Spanish warships were looking for prowling Frenchmen, and Verrazzano obviously wished to avoid hostile confrontations in order to carry out his mission. The Madeiras were Portuguese.

On 17 January 1524 *La Dauphine* said farewell to the Old World. The latitude the Captain chose for the crossing lay well above the normal range of easterly trade winds, but for about three weeks *La Dauphine* enjoyed them: "Sailing with a zephyr blowing east-southeast with sweet and gentle mildness," as he puts it in his Letter. Like Columbus, Verrazzano appreciated the beauty of smooth seas and prosperous winds, and on the northerly edge of the trades he had them at their best.

On 24 February he ran out of luck, and encountered as sharp and severe a tempest as he or his shipmates had ever experienced. "With the divine help and merciful assistance of Almighty God and the soundness of our ship, accompanied with the good hap of her fortunate name, we were delivered," wrote Verrazzano. He altered course to west by north, and then turned west on latitude 34°N. Thus he made landfall on or about 1 March 1524 at or near Cape Fear, which is on latitude 33°50'47"N; Verrazzano said it was on 34°, "like Carthage and Damascus." Near enough—Damascus is on 33°30'.* Note that this navigator, like Cabot, compared latitudes of his discoveries with known points in Europe, which meant something to those who read his report.

Cape Fear, southernmost of North Carolina's three capes (Fear, Lookout, and Hatteras), is a long alluvial promontory where the Cape Fear River has been depositing detritus for many millennia. The tip is formed by Bald Island, a tract of still unspoiled dunes and wet marsh where birds, fish, and turtle breed, and a live-oak forest grows, and the Frying Pan Shoals extend some fifteen miles farther out to sea. Verrazzano did not tarry, as he wished to explore the coast between there and Florida before turning northward. His distances are difficult to follow on the map, because every unit is "50 leagues" (about 110 nautical miles).**

So, from her landfall, *La Dauphine* sailed south for "fifty leagues,"

---

* But what did Verrazzano mean by Carthage? Nobody then knew the exact site of Rome's ancient rival, but many thought it was Tripoli, which is on 32°54' N.
** I assume that Verrazzano used the French *petite lieue marine*, equivalent to between 2.2 and 2.31 English nautical miles (see note to Chapter VI below); but his brother Girolamo's map has a scale showing four Italian miles to the league, which must have been the same league that Columbus used, equaling 3.18 nautical miles.

then turned north again "in order not to meet with the Spaniards." Since she had not found any "convenient harbor whereby to come a-land," the turning point must have been short of Charleston; on Girolamo da Verrazzano's map this point is called *Dieppa*, after *La Dauphine*'s home port. Returning to the place of her landfall, she anchored well off shore, probably in the lee of Cape Fear. Unlike other mariners of the period, Verrazzano liked anchoring in an open roadstead, provided he found good holding ground. However, he sent a boat ashore on or near Cape Fear, and briefly consorted with a group of natives who "came harde to the Sea side, seeming to rejoyce very much at the sight of us; and, marveiling greatly at our apparel, shape and whiteness, showed us by sundry signs where we might most commodiously come a-land with our boat, offering us also of their victuals to eat."

Verrazzano here describes their manners and customs "as farre as we could have notice thereof":

> These people go altogether naked except only that they cover their privy parts with certain skins of beasts like unto martens, which they fasten onto a narrow girdle made of grass, very artificially [i.e. artfully] wrought, hanged about with tails of divers other beasts, which round about their bodies hang dangling down to their knees. Some of them wear garlands of birds' feathers. The people are of color russet, and not much unlike the Saracens; their hair black, thick, and not very long, which they tie together in a knot behind, and wear it like a tail. They are well featured in their limbs, of mean [average] stature, and commonly somewhat bigger than we; broad breasted, strong arms, their legs and other parts of their bodies well fashioned, and they are disfigured in nothing, saving that they have somewhat broad visages, and yet not all of them; for we saw many of them well favoured, having black and great eyes, with a cheerful and steady look, not strong of body, yet sharp-witted, nimble and great runners, as far as we could learn by experience; and in those two last qualities they are like to them of the uttermost parts of China.

This reference to China indicates that Verrazzano was familiar with *The Book of Ser Marco Polo*.

Continuing some distance northward, the Frenchmen again landed, noted sand dunes fronting the upland palmettos, and bay bushes and cypresses "which yield most sweet savours, far from the shore"—even a hundred leagues out. So he named this land *Selva di Lauri* (Forest of

Laurels), and *Campo di Cedri* (Field of Cedars). Like Columbus, Verrazzano had a genius for giving newly discovered places beautiful and appropriate names; but, unlike those given by Columbus, few of his names stuck. Unless an explorer is shortly followed by others, or by colonists of his nation, his names are quickly forgotten.

As laurel and cedar grow all along the coasts of Georgia and South Carolina, we cannot identify these places. Strange that neither the Florentine, nor the Englishmen who came here in 1585–90, mentioned the yucca palm, with its spiky fronds and great clusters of white blossoms. Possibly it did not grow that far north in the sixteenth century.

Continuing north-northeasterly, *La Dauphine* anchored again in an open roadstead and sent a boat ashore. Here is how Hakluyt translates Verrazzano's story of the encounter:

> While we rode on that coast, partly because it had no harbor, and for that we wanted water, we sent our boat ashore with 25 men; where, by reason of great and continual waves that beat against the shore, being an open coast without succour, none of our men could possibly go ashore without losing our boat. We saw there many people, which came unto the shore, making divers signs of friendship, and showing that they were content we should come a-land, and by trial we found them to be very courteous and gentle, as your majesty shall understand by the success. To the intent we might send them of our things, which the Indians commonly desire and esteem, as sheets of paper, glasses, bells and such trifles, we sent a young man, one of our mariners, ashore, who swimming towards them, cast the things upon the shore. Seeking afterwards to return, he was with such violence of the waves beaten upon the shore, that he was so bruised that he lay there almost dead, which the Indians perceiving, ran to catch him, and drawing him out, they carried him a little way off from the sea.

The young man, fearing to be killed, "cried out piteously," but these Indians had no sinister intention. They laid him down at the foot of a sand dune to dry in the sun, and beheld him "with great admiration, marveling at the whiteness of his flesh." They then stripped him down and "made him warm at a great fire," which caused his shipmates to expect him to be roasted and eaten.

> The young man having recovered his strength, and having stayed awhile with them, showed them by signs that he was

The Bailly Globe, 1530, with "Sea of Verrazzano" showing the Verrazzano concept of North America. About half actual size. Courtesy J. Pierpont Morgan Library, New York.

desirous to return to the ship; and they with great love clapping him fast about with many embracings, accompanying him unto the sea; and, to put him in more assurance, leaving him alone they went unto a high ground and stood there, beholding him, until he was entered into the boat. This young man observed, as we did also, that these are of color inclining to black, as the other were; with their flesh very shining, of mean stature, handsome visage, and delicate limbs, and of very little strength; but of prompt wit. Farther we observed not.

This spot Verrazzano named *Annunziata* because the day was 25 March, the feast of the Annunciation of the Virgin. It must have been on the Outer, or Carolina, Banks between Capes Lookout and Hatteras, or a few miles north of Hatteras. According to his own marginal note, Verrazzano here committed his great geographical error. He found "an isthmus a mile in width and about 200 long, in which, from the ship, we could see *el mare orientale* [the Pacific Ocean], halfway between West and North"; i.e. northwesterly. This sea, he says, "is the same which flows around the shores of India, China and Cataya. . . ." To this isthmus the discoverer gave the name *Verrazzania*, and the entire land discovered was called *Francesca* after King François.

This passage has attracted a good deal of scorn to the Florentine mariner, but without justice. You may sail for twenty miles south and twenty miles north of Cape Hatteras without seeing the mainland from the deck or mast of a small sailing ship. We flew Verrazzano's route on a beautiful June day with high visibility at an altitude of two hundred feet, and for fifty miles could see no land west of the Banks. Even from the modern motor road, which (spliced out with car ferries) extends along the Banks, the far shore is commonly invisible. Verrazzano is, however, open to two criticisms. (1) In view of his preference for open roadsteads, why did he not anchor off one of the inlets and send in a boat to explore? These inlets are always shifting, but we cannot imagine that there were none in 1524, since the flow of fresh water always breaks out new ones when an old one closes. Sir Walter Raleigh's colonists found at least three in the 1580's with two fathom of water in each. (2) Verrazzano must have been familiar with a similar topography, on a smaller scale, in the Venetian lagoon; but there you can almost always see foothills from outside the Lido.

The Letter continues: "We sailed along this isthmus," i.e. the Outer Banks, "in continual hope of finding some strait or northern promon-

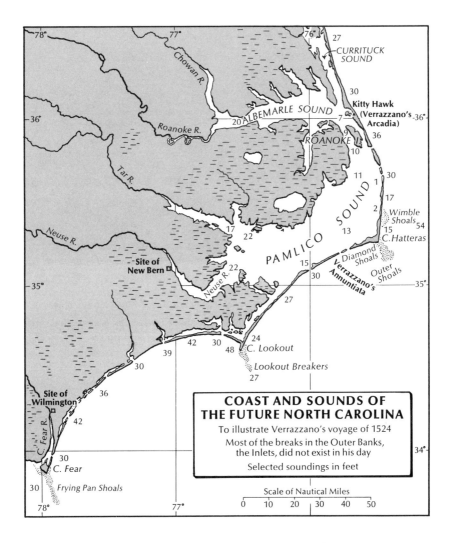

**COAST AND SOUNDS OF
THE FUTURE NORTH CAROLINA**

To illustrate Verrazzano's voyage of 1524

Most of the breaks in the Outer Banks,
the Inlets, did not exist in his day

Selected soundings in feet

Scale of Nautical Miles

0   10   20   30   40   50

tory at which the land would come to an end, in order to penetrate to
quelli felici liti del Catay" —those happy shores of Cathay.

Rather pathetic, is it not? Verrazzano and his shipmates straining
their eyes to find a bold, northward-looking promontory like Cape St.
Vincent or Finisterre, which *La Dauphine* could whip around in a
jiffy, and everyone on board would shout and yell, and the musicians
would strike up the *Vexilla Regis*, knowing that they had found the
long-sought Passage to India.

Verrazzano's "Pacific Ocean." The "Sea of Verrazzano" seen over the Carolina Outer Banks, each side of Cape Hatteras.

Thus Verrazzano assumed that he had sighted the Pacific Ocean across an isthmus much narrower than that of Panama! This tremendous error was perpetuated for a century or more by his brother Girolamo and the Italian cartographer Maiollo. Their world maps give North America a narrow waist around North Carolina, with the Pacific Ocean flowing over some 40 per cent of the area of the future United States. A good example is the Bailly Globe of 1530, which we have reproduced here.

Et in Arcadia Ego

The next place where *La Dauphine* called, after the usual "fifty-league" sail from Annunziata, "appeared to be much more beautiful [than the other Outer Banks] and full of very tall trees." "We named it *Archadia* owing to the beauty of the trees," recalling the Arcady of ancient Greece.

The Arcadian concept, an ideal landscape inhabited by simple, virtuous people, is derived from Virgil. In his *Eclogues* (x) he has the lovesick Gallus say, "Arcadians, you will sing my frantic love for Phyllis to your mountains, you alone who know how to sing; for you have cool springs, soft meadows, and groves. Among you I shall grow old, now that an insane love enchains me, and in the forest amidst the dens of wild beasts carve the story of my loves on the tender bark of trees: *crescent illae, crescetis amores;* as they grow, so shall my loves." Virgil's story took a new lease on life in Jacopo Sannazzaro's fifteenth-century novel *Arcadia*. This opens with a tribute to the tall, spreading trees that grow wild on mountains, especially to the grove "of such uncommon and extreme beauty," which flourishes on the summit of Mount Parthenius in Arcadia. If not Virgil, Sannazzaro's novel, so popular as to be printed at least fifteen times before *La Dauphine* set sail, must have inspired Verrazzano to call this fair land after the fabulous province of ancient Peloponnesus.

After flying along the entire coast from Cape Fear River to Barnegat, New Jersey, in search of a hilly section with big trees, I have no hesitation in locating Verrazzano's Arcadia at Kitty Hawk, North Carolina, the scene of the Wright brothers' pioneer flights in 1900–1903. Kill Devil Hill, Kitty Hawk, although but 91 feet in elevation, is the highest natural eminence except Cape Henry (105 feet) on the coast be-

Arcadian landscape on Miller I Atlas. Courtesy Bibliothèque Nationale.

tween Florida and the Navesink Highlands. Already bare in the Wrights' day, as in ours, it was undoubtedly heavily wooded in Verrazzano's. Near by, under a high dune of tawny sand now called Engagement Hill, there is still a heavy forest growth of pine, live oak, red oak, bay, laurel, holly, and dogwood. Undoubtedly this was the most beautiful spot—to European eyes—that Verrazzano encountered on his voyage prior to New York Bay, and it is no wonder that he called there and spent three days, despite the lack of a harbor.

Moreover, Girolamo Verrazzano's map, immediately east of a misspelled Annuntiata, places *Lamàcra*—a misspelled L'Arcadia—and there are a dozen place names between it and New York Bay.

The doings of the Frenchmen were anything but Arcadian. Here is Verrazzano's account of a kidnapping:

> That we might have some knowledge thereof, we sent 20 men a land, which entered into the country about two leagues, and they found that the people were fled to the woods for fear. They saw only one old woman with a young maid of 18 or 20

Site of Verrazzano's Arcadia. Kill Devil Hill, Kitty Hawk, with the nearby forest, in June 1970.

years old, which, seeing our company, hid themselves in the grass for fear; the old woman carried two infants on her shoulders, and behind her neck a child of 8 years old; the young woman was laden likewise with as many. But when our men came unto them, the women cried out; the old woman made signs that the men were fled unto the woods as soon as they saw us; to quiet them and to win their favor, our men gave them such victuals as they had with them to eat, which the old woman received thankfully; but the young woman disdained them all, and threw them disdainfully on the ground. They took a child from the old woman to bring into France, and, going about to take the young woman (which was very beautiful and of tall stature), they could not possibly, for the great outcries that she made, bring her to the sea, and especially having great woods to pass through, and being far from the ship, we purposed to leave her behind, bearing away the child only.

Loud screaming, woman's first line of defense, here worked very well; but one would like to know what became of the poor child, snatched from his Arcadian people at a tender age.

"In Arcadia," continued Verrazzano, "we found a man who came to the shore to see what [manner of men] we were. . . . He was handsome, naked, his hair fastened in a knot, and of an olive color." Approaching near a group of twenty Frenchmen, he thrust toward them "a burning stick, as if to offer us fire." This must have been a lighted tobacco pipe, and the poor fellow was simply making a friendly gesture, offering the intruders a pipe of peace. They, having neither seen nor heard of tobacco, took his intentions to be hostile and fired a blank shot from a musket. At that the Indian "trembled all over with fright" and "remained as if thunderstruck, and, like a friar, pointing a finger at sky, ship and sea as if he were invoking a blessing on us."

Verrazzano describes the dugout canoes which the Indians constructed by burning out the interior of a hardwood log, and wild grapevines that climb trees "as they do in Lombardy"; "roses, violets, lilies, and many sorts of herbs, and sweet and odoriferous flowers, different from ours." The Indians wore leaves for clothing, and lived mostly by fishing and fowling; but they offered him pulse (beans) "differing in color and taste from ours, of good and pleasant taste." *La Dauphine* remained in Arcadia for three days around 10 April, anchoring, as usual, off shore; and the captain states that he would have stayed longer but for the absence of a harbor.

Arcadia is one of three place names of Verrazzano's which have survived, but later map-makers continually moved it eastward until it became *L'Acadie*, the French name for Nova Scotia, New Brunswick, and part of Maine. Verrazzano must have been very bored, as he sailed northward, to find the same long, thin, sandy islands fronting lagoons, with only two breaks—the Virginia Capes and the Delaware Capes. He missed these entrances to Chesapeake and Delaware bays, which he surely would have explored as possible straits to Cathay. Prudently avoiding shoal water, he evidently sailed *La Dauphine* so far out to sea that these great bays were not visible.

After Barnegat, New Jersey, he closed the shore and began observing places more to his liking. He anchored every night off shore; named one promontory *Bonivet*, after the grand admiral of France; and a river *Vendôme*, after Charles de Bourbon, duc de Vendôme; but it is impossible to locate these from his vague directions. A coast "green with forests" which he called *Lorraine*, after one of the titles of Jean Cardinal Guise, was probably New Jersey.

Verrazzano was the first North American explorer to name places newly discovered after personalities and beloved spots at home. His predecessors generally confined themselves to descriptive names, such as codfish, grapes, boldness, or flatness, adding a few saints' names appropriate to the date of the landfall. The Florentine set a precedent which most of his successors honored; Cartier, for instance, used some of the same names, and a few of them have survived.

One thing is certain: *La Dauphine* was favored by extraordinarily good luck in weather. To sail along the coast from South Carolina to New York, in the turbulent spring of the year, and anchor off shore without mishap, is an exploit that any merchant captain under sail, and some steamship masters too, might well envy. The United States Coast Guard estimates that there are six hundred wrecks off the Carolina Outer Banks. On the *National Geographic*'s map of them, the names of known wrecks in historic times are so close together as to seem continuous. When Verrazzano's Letter was published in 1841, many a practical seaman said, "It cannot be—the fellow is a fraud and a fake!" But there the record is, in black and white, from an honest captain; and who are we to deny it? But for his tragic end, we might conclude Verrazzano to have been especially favored by the gods of the sea and the winds.

Four personages of the French court, for whom Verrazzano named places on the American coast: François le Dauphin; Louise de Savoie, duchesse d'Angoulême and Queen Mother; la duchesse de Vendôme, née d'Alençon; le seigneur de Bonnivet, amiral de France. From Gower, ed., *Three Hundred French Portraits*, 1875; Moreau-Nélaton, *Les Clouet et leurs Émules;* and Originals in Dêpot des Étampes, Bibliothèque Nationale.

Angoulême and Refugio

"In space of 100 leagues sailing," continues Verrazzano, "we found a very pleasant place, situated amongst certain little steep hills; from amidst the which hills there ran down into the sea a great stream of water, which within the mouth was very deep, and from the sea to the mouth of same, with the tide, which we found to rise 8 foot, any great vessel laden may pass up."

This description well fits New York Bay; the hills, the first he had seen since Kitty Hawk, might have been the Navesink Highlands, Staten Island, or Brooklyn Heights. The day was 17 April, *La Dauphine* sailed gently before a soft southwest wind, and New York Bay never looked fairer than on this very first day when European eyes gazed upon it.

The rest of Verrazzano's brief account indicates that he anchored in the Narrows, now renamed after him and spanned by the Verrazzano Bridge:

> But because we rode at anchor in a place well fenced from the wind, we would not venture ourselves without knowledge of the place, and we passed up with our boat only into the said river, and saw the country very well peopled. The people are almost like unto the others, and clad with feathers of fowls of divers colors. They came towards us very cheerfully, making great shouts of admiration, showing us where we might come to land most safely with our boat. We entered up the said river into the land about half a league, where it made a most pleasant lake about 3 leagues in compass; on the which they rowed from the one side to the other, to the number of 30 of their small boats, wherein were many people, which passed from one shore to the other to come and see us. And behold, upon the sudden (as it is wont to fall out in sailing) a contrary flaw of wind coming from the sea, we were enforced to return to our ship, leaving this land, to our great discontentment for the great commodity and pleasantness thereof, which we suppose is not without some riches, all the hills showing mineral matters in them.

Verrazzano showed good judgment in weighing anchor and standing out to sea, rather than risk dragging ashore in the Narrows. But we wish he could have spent more than one day at the site of the future city, and not confined himself to this brief description of it and the feather-clad natives. His short boat tour indicates that he regarded the

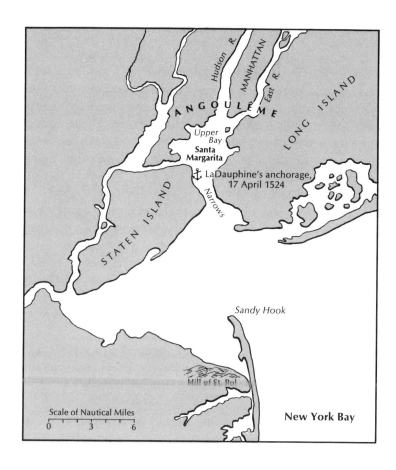

The following text labels appear on the map: Hudson R., MANHATTAN, East R., LONG ISLAND, ANGOULÊME, Upper Bay, Santa Margarita, LaDauphine's anchorage, 17 April 1524, STATEN ISLAND, Narrows, Sandy Hook, Hill of St. Pol., Scale of Nautical Miles, 0 3 6, New York Bay

Narrows as part of the river, and that the "pleasant lake" about ten miles in circumference was the Upper Bay. Of the Hudson River he viewed only the mouth; and if he noticed the East River he probably figured that it flowed from the same source as the "Great" (Hudson) River, verdant Manhattan Island dividing the river's lower course so that it emptied into the sea by two mouths. He named this part of the country *Angoulême*, the title of François-premier before he became king, and the bay *Santa Margarita* in honor of the king's sister, Marguerite, duchesse d'Alençon, who (he explains), "surpassed every other woman for modesty and intelligence." (She is best known as the authoress of the *Heptaméron*, which she wrote after she had become queen of Navarre.) He also named a promontory *Alençon* after her, somewhere on the Jersey coast.

"We weighed anchor," continues the Letter," and sailed toward the East, for so the coast trended, and always for 80 leagues,* being in the sight thereof, we discovered an island in the form of a triangle, distant from the mainland 10 leagues, about the bigness of the Island of the Rhodes. It was full of hills covered with trees, well peopled, for we saw fires all along the coast. We gave it the name of your Majesty's mother, not staying there by reason of the weather being contrary." From the fact that *La Dauphine* immediately scudded into Narragansett Bay to escape foul weather making up, it is clear that this triangular island, which recalled Rhodes to Verrazzano, and which he named *Luisa* after the Queen Mother, was Block Island. The French later called it *Claudia* after the queen of France, and the Dutch renamed it after one of the navigators in the early seventeenth century.

Here, inadvertently and astonishingly, Verrazzano named a future State of the Union. Roger Williams, founder of the colony and state to which Block Island has always belonged, wrote a letter in 1637 dated "at Aquednetick, now called by us Rode Island." On 13 March 1644 the colonial assembly declared, "Aquethneck shall be henceforth called the Ile of Rhods or Rhod-Island." And in 1663 the name Rhode Island was applied to the colony. Roger Williams, a well-read gentleman and scholar, must have brought to New England a copy of either edition of Hakluyt which contains a translation of Verrazzano's Letter, and interpreted his island "about the bignesse of the Ilande of the Rodes, . . . full of hilles, covered with trees" as Aquidneck. That is the big island in Narragansett Bay, the future seat of Newport; and its shape does resemble that of Rhodes in the Aegean. Thus, the smallest state of the Union owes her name to Roger Williams's mistaken notion of the island which Verrazzano compared to Rhodes!

The natives who flocked around *La Dauphine* in canoes as she anchored a few miles outside Narragansett Bay on a hard, boulder-strewn bottom were so friendly that Verrazzano (doubtless to the joy of his crew) decided to make an exception to his practice of mooring in the open. Piloted by an Indian he sailed *La Dauphine* into the bay. Leaving the future Point Judith and Beaver Tail to port, he noted the little rocky islands now called The Dumplings as a suitable place for a coast-defense fort; the American patriots of 1775 agreed

---

* I.e. 176 miles, if I have the right factor for the French league, and that is not far off. From the Narrows outside Long Island to Block Island is about 150 nautical miles.

Verrazzano's *Petra Viva*. The Dumpling Rocks off Conanicut Island,
Brenton Point in the background. Photo of about 1885, courtesy Mr. Wm.
King Covell.

with him and fortified the biggest islet. Verrazzano punningly named
this cluster of rocks *Petra Viva* after the wife of Antonio Gondi, one
of his banker promoters; her maiden name was Marie-Catherine de
Pierre-Vive. The native pilots conducted *La Dauphine* to a completely
sheltered anchorage, the present Newport Harbor, behind the highest
point of Aquidneck. There he spent a fortnight palavering with the
natives—but he never did hear about a Portuguese, Miguel Corte Real,
having been their chief only thirteen years earlier.

These Indians were the Wampanoag, whose domain extended over
the eastern side of Narragansett Bay and southeastern Massachusetts.
They had lately taken Aquidneck from the Narragansett tribe and
were apprehensive about a comeback. This in part accounts for their
friendliness to the Frenchmen and, almost a century later, to the Pilgrim Fathers.

Verrazzano's description of the Wampanoag corresponds closely to
what Roger Williams later wrote about them. They came on board
fearlessly after the Captain had caused a few "bells and glasses and
many toys" to be tossed into their canoes. Among the visitors were
two "kings," one about forty and the other about twenty years old.
Each was clothed in a deerskin artistically embroidered with dyed por-

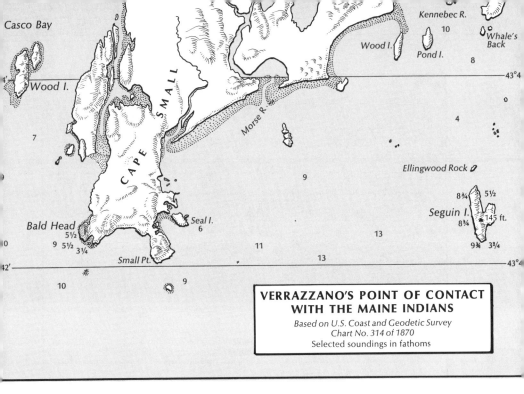

Wood I.

Kennebec R.

Wood I.   Pond I.   10   Whale's Back

8

43°4

CAPE SMALL

Morse R.

0

7

4

9

Ellingwood Rock

13

8¾   5½

Seguin I.   145 ft.

8¾

9¾   3¾

Bald Head

5½

9   5½

3¼

Seal I.

6

11

Small Pt.

13

42'

43°4

10

9

VERRAZZANO'S POINT OF CONTACT WITH THE MAINE INDIANS

Based on U.S. Coast and Geodetic Survey
Chart No. 314 of 1870
Selected soundings in fathoms

cupine quills, and, as an emblem of office, "a large chain garnished with divers stones of sundry colors." "This is the goodliest people, and of the fairest conditions, that we have found in this our voyage," wrote Verrazzano; "they exceed us in bigness," are comely, "with long black hair, which they are very careful to trim"; their eyes are "black and quick," and their color, various shades of "brasse." Their bodies are well proportioned, "as appertaineth to any handsome man." The women, too, are "very handsome and well favored," and "as well mannered and continent as any women of good education. They are all naked, save their privy parts, which they cover with a deer's skin, branched or embroidered, as the men use." Some "wear on their arms very rich skins of leopards." They use elaborate head-dressings "like unto the women of Egypt and Syria," and ornaments made of their own hair hang down on both sides of their breasts. "When they are married, men as well as women wear divers toys, according to the usage of Asiatics." For "toys" we should read trinkets or gewgaws; and for leopard skins, those of wildcats or lynxes.

Verrazzano particularly noted the Wampanoags' most valued possessions, "plates of wrought copper, which they esteem more than gold."

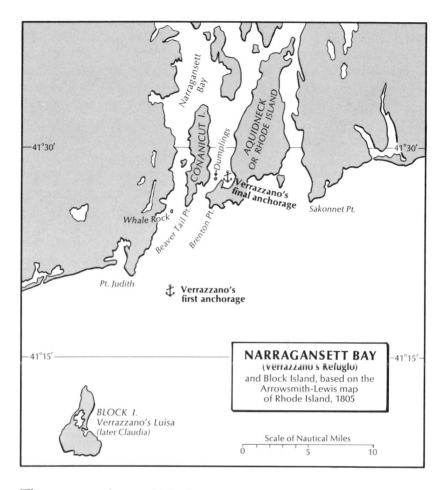

Map labels:
Narragansett Bay
CONANICUT I.
AQUIDNECK OR RHODE ISLAND
Dumplings
—41°30'—
41°30'—
Verrazzano's final anchorage
Sakonnet Pt.
Whale Rock
Beaver Tail Pt.
Brenton Pt.
Pt. Judith
Verrazzano's first anchorage
—41°15'—
41°15'—
BLOCK I.
Verrazzano's Luisa
(later Claudia)

NARRAGANSETT BAY
(Verrazzano's Refugio)
and Block Island, based on the
Arrowsmith-Lewis map
of Rhode Island, 1805

Scale of Nautical Miles
0   5   10

These copper plates, which they obtained by trade from tribes of the Great Lakes region, were the native jewelry; they were mistaken for early Norse on the Indian remains which Longfellow celebrated as "The Skeleton in Armor." The bells which Verrazzano gave them, and which he says they "esteemed most" after copper, were tiny spherical hawks' bells, which Columbus found to be greatly prized by natives of the Caribbean; and the blue crystal beads next in favor were no doubt Venetian. These were used as earrings or necklaces. Strangely enough, the Wampanoag had no use for cloth—peltry suited them better—nor did they want iron or steel implements to replace their stone axes.

The one disappointing thing about these natives, from the crew's point of view, was the men's concern for the chastity of their women. Every day, when anchored in the future Newport Harbor, "The people repaired to see our ship, bringing their wives with them, whereof they are very jealous." While they came on board and stayed "a good space," their poor wives had to sit stolidly in canoes. If it was a royal visit, the queen and her ladies stayed in a canoe at Goat Island "while the king abode a long space in our ship, . . . viewing with great admiration all the furniture," and demanding to know its use. "He took likewise great pleasure in beholding our apparel, and in tasting our meats, and so courteously taking his leave departed." Landing on the island, "The king drawing his bow, and running up and down with his gentlemen, made much sport to gratify our men."

During the fifteen days that *La Dauphine* tarried in Newport Harbor, parties of sailors explored the interior for some thirty miles. They noted plains near the present Pawtucket, fertile soil, and woods of oak and walnut; they flushed game such as "luzernes" (lynxes) and deer, which the Indians took in nets or shot with flint and jasper arrowheads; they admired the native houses covered with mats, and the cornfields; and they undoubtedly found means to frolic with Indian girls when their lords and masters were away hunting.

Verrazzano also wrote that the Wampanoag were "very pitiful and charitable towards their neighbors, . . . make great lamentations in their adversity," and at their death "use mourning, mixed with singing, which continueth for a long space." These prolonged bouts of mourning were a characteristic of the Algonkin and other Indian nations of the northeast. Roger Williams recorded that Wampanoag families went into mourning for "something a quarter, halfe, yea a whole yeere," during which time they considered it "a prophane thing" to play, or "to paint themselves for beauty." As bad as English court mourning in the reign of Queen Victoria!

Following Cabot's practice of noting comparative latitudes, Verrazzano adds, "This land is situated in the parallel of Rome, in 41 degrees and 2 terces"; i.e. 41°40′ N. The center of Newport is on 41°30′ N, and the Vatican is on 41°54′ N. This proves, even better than his earlier comparison of his landfall with Damascus, that the Captain was a competent celestial navigator. He must have "taken" the sun and Polaris frequently and averaged them; Rome's latitude he could have obtained from any printed Ptolemy or rutter.

This fortnight at the site of Newport must have been the most enjoyable part of the voyage, from the point of view of *La Dauphine*'s sailors.

Maine—"Land of Bad People"

On 5 or 6 May, *La Dauphine* resumed her voyage eastward, passing Sakonnet Point, which Verrazzano named *Jovium Promontorium* after his friends, the Giovio family of Como. The Captain sailed through Vineyard Sound, Nantucket Sound, and Pollock Rip (which daunted the *Mayflower* in 1620) rather than around Martha's Vineyard and Nantucket. The treacherous shoals where, in spots, there was only three feet of water, he called *Armellini*, possibly by way of a crack at Francesco Cardinal Armellino, a prelate much disliked for his avarice and his success at collecting papal taxes. Next, the ship rounded *un eminente promontorio*, which Verrazzano named *Pallavisino* after Pallavicini, one of the king's Italian generals. This must have been Cape Cod; *eminente* means "outstanding," which that Cape certainly is.

Stretching across Massachusetts Bay, *La Dauphine* hit the coast of Maine at or near Casco Bay. Verrazzano described the land as fair, open, and bare, with high mountains (the White Mountains) visible far inland. But the Abnaki natives, although they looked like the Wampanoag, were "of such crudity and evil manners, so barbarous, that despite all the signs we could make, we could never converse with them. They are clothed in peltry of bear, lynx, 'sea wolves' and other beasts. Their food, as far as we could perceive, often entering their dwellings, we suppose to be obtained by hunting and fishing, and of certain fruits, a kind of wild root." These were ground-nuts, which the early settlers of New England found to be a good substitute for bread.

Wherever the crew came ashore, these Indians raised loud warwhoops, shot at them with arrows, and fled into the forest. But they consented to trade meagerly with a French boat crew from a rocky cliff on the seashore, letting down in a basket on a line "what it pleased them to give us . . . taking nothing but knives, fishhooks, and tools to cut withall." The latitude of the place where this happened, says Verrazzano, was 43°40′ N, and the only two spots in that area whence one could let down a basket on a line into a small boat are Seguin Island

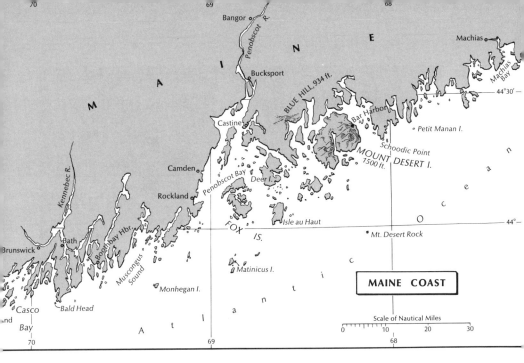

(latitude 43°42′) and Bald Head, at the tip of Cape Small (latitude 43°43′ N), the eastern entrance to Casco Bay. Both are cliffy and steep-to; Bald Head is the more probable place, as it is on the mainland. What displeased the Frenchmen more than the awkward method of trading were the Indians' uncouth manners; at parting they used "all signs of discourtesy and disdain, as was possible for any brute creature to invent, such as exhibiting their bare behinds and laughing immoderately." One can well picture this scene—glowering Frenchmen in the boat, braves exhibiting bare buttocks, little boys urinating, and men, women, and children raising just such an unholy clamor of whoops, laughs, shouts, and yells as only Indians could make. Since North American natives were usually friendly to the first Europeans they encountered, and hostile only after being abused or cheated, this attitude of the Abnaki suggests an earlier visit by foreigners raiding the Maine coast for slaves. However that may be, Verrazzano gave this coast a bad name, *Terra Onde di Mala Gente* (Land of Bad People), as it is called on his brother's map.

La Dauphine continued northeasterly along the Maine coast, counting in the space of fifty leagues some thirty-two islands "lying all near the land, being small and pleasant to the view, high, and having many turnings and windings between them, making many fair harbors and

Isabeau d'Albret, vicomtesse de Rohan. Portrait by Clouet in Musée Municipal de Lille. Photo by Giraudon. Courtesy of the Musée and of Professor Michel Mollat.

channels, as they do in the gulf of Venice in Illyria and Dalmatia." A very apt comparison: the Dalmatian coast always reminds one of Maine, and Maine of Dalmatia.

May on the Maine coast is a joy to all seamen—when the fog does not roll in. Verrazzano not only admired the excellent harbors but appreciated the beauty of this region—white fleecy clouds, turquoise sea flashing in the sunlight, islands where the shad-bush flings out masses of white blossoms among somber evergreens. He named the three biggest islands that he passed after three young princesses at the French court—*le tre figlie di Navarra*, "the three daughters of Navarre." These were Anne, Isabeau, and Catherine, daughters of Jean, duc d'Albret, and Catherine de Foix, queen of Navarre. They were then between fifteen and eighteen years old, celebrated for their beauty, and as orphans spent much time at the French court. The islands thus honored were Monhegan, Isle au Haut, and Mount Desert. These stand out above all others as one sails wide along that coast, and all have a natural beauty worthy to be compared to that of the lovely daughters of Navarre.

Here Verrazzano added another word to American nomenclature. Near the Daughters of Navarre, on his brother's Vatican map, appears *Oranbega*. This is obviously Norumbega, which in the Abnaki language means a stretch of quiet water between two falls or rapids. That fits in well with the spot on the Penobscot River which later writers magnified into the capital of a region. Its appearance on the Verrazzano

Monhegan Island. Photo by Augustus Phillips.

Mount Desert Island, from Mount Desert Rock. Photo by Augustus Phillips.

map is puzzling; his brother's relations with the Abnaki were brief and brusque, yet it is the only native Indian name on the map. After the voyage, map-makers and writers began to expand Norumbega to cover the entire region between the Hudson and the St. Lawrence, complete with a rich and noble city of the same name on the Penobscot River, and in the first printing of Verrazzano's Letter, by Ramusio, it is captioned as "Della Terra de Norumbega."

La Dauphine now ran into easterly winds and had to beat to windward, making good an east-northeast course. This neatly covered the rest of Maine. After sailing for 150 leagues, missing the Bay of Fundy and most of the future Nova Scotia, she "approached the land that in times past was discovered by the British, which is in fifty degrees." There, says Verrazzano, "Having spent all our naval stores and victuals, and having discovered 700 leagues and more of new country, we topped off with water and wood and decided to return to France." In view of his remarkable accuracy in taking latitudes, we may conclude that Verrazzano sailed along the east coast of Newfoundland and took his departure from Cape Fogo or Funk Island (latitude 49°50'). Both his brother's and the Maiollo map cover Newfoundland. They use the old Portuguese place names instead of applying new French ones, suggesting that they had a Portuguese chart on board and claimed no new discovery.

The ship made a speedy passage, a little more than two weeks, and had safely anchored at Dieppe by 8 July 1524, the day that Verrazzano dated his Letter to François-premier. It concludes with the gallant Captain's prayer that God and his majesty may help him to bring this initial step to a perfect end, so that, in the holy words of the evangelist (Romans ix. 18), *in omnem terram exivit sonus eorum*, . . . "Their sound went into all the earth, and their words unto the ends of the world."

End of the Voyage, and of Giovanni

Near the end of his Letter Verrazzano makes some interesting observations on the longitude of his discovery. He states that if a degree on the equator is 62.5 miles (as he was using Italian miles of 1480 meters, or 1619 yards, this was an underestimate), a degree of longitude at latitude 34° N, upon which he endeavored to cross the Atlantic, is fifty-two miles. He and his officers kept careful estimates of distance, making daily meridian elevations of the sun, and decided that they had sailed 4800 miles, land to land. This, divided by fifty-two, assured Verrazzano that *La Dauphine* had crossed 92 degrees of longitude. But the true difference in longitude between Deserta and Cape Fear is about 61.5 degrees! This 50 per cent overestimate was due in part to the Captain's underestimate of the length of the degree, and in part to exaggerating the speed of his ship. Columbus erred similarly; any sailor will condone a mistake of that nature.

Nevertheless, this miscalculation enabled Verrazzano to state emphatically what his predecessors had said less firmly, that the coast between Florida and Newfoundland belonged to a completely New World. It might, he admitted, be joined to northern Europe in the Arctic regions, but the land he had coasted was no promontory of Asia, as many map-makers had depicted it, and would long go on doing. This insistence on the newness of the New World cancels Verrazzano's earlier mistake about the false isthmus. Unfortunately, Ramusio omitted this from his early version of the Letter, so it did not circulate. Verrazzano and Cartier were not the last navigators to look for

"Cathay" just around the corner. Frobisher, as we shall see, thought that the north side of his bay in Baffin Island was part of Asia. As late as 1638, when Jean Nicolet was sent as envoy to the Winnebago tribe, he provided himself with an embroidered robe of Chinese damask, just in case he should meet Chinese mandarins!

Verrazzano sounded a note of reasoned optimism. Although he had not found the Northern Strait and had written it off as non-existent in those latitudes, he had discovered a vast continental mass which could be of immense value to France. He hoped to be allowed to follow it up. Unfortunately for France, he returned at the very worst time for organizing a second voyage. François-premier, preparing to resume his interminable war against Charles V and to carry it into Italy, gave the discoverer an audience at Lyons and, in a moment of enthusiasm, allotted him four ships for a second voyage; but he decided that they were needed for coastal defense and canceled the order. His Italian campaign ended disastrously in the battle of Pavia on 26 February 1525; the king lost his army and for a year his freedom, and would have lost his throne but for the sagacious regency of his mother, Louise of Savoy. Nor did Verrazzano impress his banker supporters; the samples of drugs, gold ore, and "aromatic liquors" that he brought home proved to be spurious or worthless, and the bankers were not interested in a long view of future values. They missed the chance to obtain Manhattan Island for even less than the traditional $24 worth of goods.

The discoverer, after considering (it was rumored) and rejecting good offers from Henry VIII and D. João III of Portugal to enter their service, turned for support to Jean Ango of Dieppe and Philippe de Chabot, sieur de Brion and admiral of France. Giovanni received the command, and the right to one-sixth of the profits. In the spring of 1527 the fleet sailed from Dieppe. Off the Cape Verde Islands one ship separated in a gale and the sailors of the two others mutinied, insisting on returning home; but as they knew nothing of navigation, Verrazzano fooled them, nipped across the Atlantic Narrows to Brazil, cut and loaded a cargo of logwood, and returned to Dieppe in mid-September of the same year. The fourth vessel eventually made the Brazilian coast and she too loaded logwood. This "Brazil wood," in great demand for dyeing cloth, sold well to the clothiers of Rouen.

Verrazzano had never renounced his ambition to find a new strait through the Americas. The dyewood profits suggested to him and his backers a means of combining exploration with profit—seek the strait in a region where, if you failed to find it, you could cut a cargo of logwood. Accordingly they arranged a third voyage, consisting of two or three ships, with Verrazzano's flag in *La Flamengue* of Fécamp. They departed Dieppe in the spring of 1528. Our sole knowledge of what happened on this voyage, which ended fatally for the Captain, is derived from a few words in Ramusio's collection of voyages, and a poem by Giulio Giovio, nephew and disciple of the humanist Paolo Giovio. Girolamo the map-maker, who survived, told the tragic tale to both Giovii, and Giulio wrote of it in a long narrative, *Storia Poetica*.

This fleet crossed the Atlantic by a route slightly north of Columbus's. First raising the coast of Florida, Verrazzano sailed to the Bahamas and then shaped a course for the Isthmus of Darien, intending probably to investigate the Gulf of Darien for a possible strait. En route he changed his mind and followed the chain of the Lesser Antilles. There he made the mistake of anchoring well off shore, as he customarily did. Unfortunately, the island where he chose to call—probably Guadeloupe—was inhabited by no gentle tribe of Indians, but by ferocious, man-eating Caribs. The Verrazzano brothers rowed shoreward in the ship's boat. A crowd of natives waited at the water's edge, licking their chops at the prospect of a human lunch; but the French as yet knew nought of this nation of cannibals. Giovanni innocently waded ashore along while Girolamo and the boat's crew plied their oars far enough off the beach to avoid the breakers. The Caribs, expert at murder, overpowered and killed the great navigator, then cut up and ate his still quivering body whilst his brother looked on helplessly, seeing the "sand ruddy with fraternal blood." The ships were anchored too far off shore to render gunfire support.

Questo infelice fine hebbe questo valente gentilhuomo, wrote Ramusio. "To so miserable an end came this valiant gentleman."

From subsequent lawsuits we know that *La Flamengue* continued her voyage to Brazil, and in March 1529 brought back a cargo of logwood to Brittany. Girolamo, after finishing his chart showing the 1524 voyage, sailed back to Brazil in 1529 as master of the ship *La Bonne Aventure* of Le Havre.

Verrazzano may have opened for France a lucrative trade with Brazil, but the results of his voyage along the North American coast were largely negative. The "Isthmus" and "Sea" of Verrazzano, his only positive contributions, turned out to be pure fantasies—but they influenced North American cartography for over a century. By reporting the absence of any strait between Florida and Nova Scotia, he turned the exploratory efforts of France and England northward; Jacques Cartier took up the quest where Verrazzano left off, and Frobisher continued it, further north. Neither discovered "the happy shores of Cathay," but empire followed in their wakes, whilst France completely ignored that of *La Dauphine*, which subtended a land of riches immeasurable—the Carolinas, Virginia, New York, New England. But it was not Verrazzano's fault that the French government remained indifferent to the opportunities that he opened.

There is no blinking the fact that Verrazzano missed many important places, and that he was singularly incurious. His habit of avoiding harbors caused him to miss great bays such as the Chesapeake, the Delaware, and the Hudson estuary, leaving them for the English, Dutch, and Swedes to explore and colonize in the following century. His failure to take a good look at the mouth of the Hudson River is perhaps the greatest opportunity missed by any North American explorer. But no sailor will blame him for missing things, since most of them have done so themselves. The great Captain Cook missed Sydney Harbor. Drake and all the Spanish navigators missed the Golden Gate and San Francisco Bay, which were discovered by an overland expedition. Why, even Des Barres's Royal Navy team of surveyors in 1770 missed Northeast Harbor, Maine!

Let us, however, judge Verrazzano by what he tried to do, rather than by what he accomplished. If he failed to find the strait "to the happy shores of Cathay," it was because it was not there; his attainable vision of a New France stretching from Newfoundland to Florida faded because king and country were not interested. His greatest ambition, as his brother told Ramusio, had been to people the regions he discovered with French colonists, to introduce European plants and domestic animals, and to bring the "poor, rough and ignorant people" of North America to Christianity. When one contemplates the fate of the North American Indians, one cannot be very enthusiastic over these benevolent gestures of European pioneers; but at least they tried.

✳ VI ✳

Cartier's First Voyage

1534

Now brothers, for the icebergs
   Of frozen Labrador
Floating spectral in the moonshine
   Along the low, black shore,
Where like snow the gannet's feathers
   On Bradore's rocks are shed
And the noisy murre are flying
   Like black scuds overhead.

J. G. WHITTIER "THE FISHERMAN"

Le Maître-Pilote Jacques Cartier

In southern Normandy near the border of Brittany there stands out the remarkable island and abbey of Mont-Saint-Michel. Of old it could be reached only by sea at high water or over the sands at low water; a dangerous procedure because the flood tide roars in with the speed of a galloping horse, overwhelming any man or beast it overtakes. The monastery, built in the Dark Ages and rebuilt or enlarged by the piety of Norman dukes and French kings, has been a place of pilgrimage for a thousand years. Pilgrims still go there to pray, make vows, and be shrived; tourists come to admire the site and the architecture—and also to consume omelettes *chez* Madame Poulard *aînée*. Madame and her rival daughter-in-law are long since gone; but (judging from what their successors did for us) at any hour a fire of crackling thorns will be kindled on an open hearth, eggs broken into a heavy iron skillet, and a delicious omelette produced.

Since omelettes are a traditional delicacy of Mont-Saint-Michel, we

Saint-Malo from Saint-Servan, by Louis Garneray, *c.* 1820. Musée de Saint-Malo. Photo Philippot.

permit ourselves to imagine that they figured in the hospitality afforded to François-premier at a moment when the history of France in the New World began. The king, performing a pilgrimage in 1532 in company with his son the Dauphin, was received by the very magnificent Jean Le Veneur de Tilliers, abbot of Mont-Saint-Michel, grand almoner of France, bishop and count of Lisieux. He there presented to the king a relative of the abbey's treasurer, Jacques Cartier by name, master mariner of nearby Saint-Malo. This man, said the bishop, in consideration of his voyages to Newfoundland and Brazil, is capable of commanding ships "to discover new lands in the New World" for France; and if the king would consent so to employ him, the bishop promised to furnish chaplains for the voyage, and even contribute to the cost.

François-premier did consent, Cartier sailed, and Canada was born. But many voyages had to be performed and many false starts made before the fleur-de-lys could be firmly planted on the Rock of Quebec by Samuel de Champlain.

The first obstacle was the bull of Pope Alexander VI dividing the New World between Spain and Portugal. Clement VII, pope in 1532, was a Medici and an ally of François-premier against Charles V; one of the king's sons, the future Henri II, married the pope's niece Catherine de' Medici. That made it easy, when king, pope, and Bishop Le Veneur met at Marseilles to celebrate this union in 1533, to persuade the Holy Father to declare that the Alexandrine edict applied only to lands already discovered, not to those later found by other sovereigns. Thus François-premier had the green light from the Vatican, and passed the word to Jacques Cartier.

Who was this master mariner of Saint-Malo, destined to become the founder of New France? We know a little more about him than we do of Verrazzano, and far more than we do of John Cabot. He was born in 1491, at "the ancient town of Saint-Malo, thrust out like a buttress into the sea, strange and grim of aspect, breathing war from its walls and battlements of ragged stone, a stronghold of privateers, the home of a race whose intractable and defiant independence neither time nor change has subdued." Thus Francis Parkman happily described this ancient seaport and the Bretons. After a destructive bombardment in 1944 the town rose from its ashes, and was rebuilt in the old style with Breton granite, gray with flecks of gold.

Cartier in legal documents is called a bourgeois. Born to a respectable family of mariners, he improved his social status in 1520 by marrying Catherine des Granches, of a leading Malouin ship-owning family. For aught we know they were a faithful and loving couple, but they had no children. His good name in Saint-Malo is proved by its frequent appearance in baptismal registers, as godfather or witness. And we have more than the bishop's word that he had made voyages to Newfoundland and Brazil. In his narratives of the Canadian voyages he makes several allusions to the people and products of Brazil, and in Newfoundland he seemed to be at home.

We do not really know what Cartier looked like. The portrait with which the public is most familiar, showing a stern-visaged man looking glumly out to sea, was painted by a Russian artist in 1839 for the city of Saint-Malo. It might as well have been labeled "Dostoevski Communing with his Soul." Other portraits have been "discovered" or

Sketch by M. Dan Lailler, Conservateur du Musée de Saint-Malo, of an early portrait of Cartier. Owned privately.

produced by obliging antique dealers of Paris from time to time, but none can reasonably be accepted as genuine. The Desceliers-Harleian Map of 1542, here reproduced, shows on the Gaspé peninsula a cloaked figure, featureless except for a forked beard, handing something to a man with a huge pointed nose, behind whom a horse team harrows a patch of ground outside a French-style farmhouse. The one we have used, from a sketch by M. Dan Lailler, is not strictly contemporary, but nearly so; and I believe it to be a portrait of the navigator in his old age.

Since no contemporary has left us a word on Cartier's personality, it has to be inferred from such sources as we have. They indicate that Champlain's later description of the character of "a good and perfect navigator" applies to him:

> Above all to be a good man, fearing God, not allowing His sacred name to be blasphemed on board his ship, . . . and careful to have prayers said morning and evening. . . . He had better not be a delicate eater or drinker, otherwise he will be frequently upset by changes of climate and food. . . . Be continually on his guard against scurvy, and be provided with remedies against it. He should be robust and alert, have good sea-legs and be indefatigable . . . so that whatever accident may befall he can keep the deck and in a strong voice order everyone to do his duty. He must not be above lending a hand to the work himself, to make the seamen more prompt in their attention. . . .
> He should be pleasant and affable in conversation, absolute

Section of the Harleian-Desceliers-Dauphin Map of 1542, with alleged portrait of Cartier. Courtesy British Museum; photo Giraudon.

in his commands, not too ready to talk with shipmates, except
the officers; otherwise he might be despised. He should punish
ill-doers severely, and reward good men, gratifying them from
time to time with a pat on the back, praising them but not
overdoing it, so as to give no occasion for envy—that gangrene
which corrupts the body and if not promptly quenched leads
to faction and conspiracy among the crew. . . . He should
never let himself be overcome by wine, for if an officer or
seaman becomes a drunkard it is dangerous to entrust him with
responsibility; he might be sleeping like a pig when an accident occurs . . . and be the cause of loss of the vessel. . . .
He should turn night into day, watch the greater part of the
night, always sleep clothed so as to be ready to come on deck
promptly if anything happens. He must keep a private compass below and consult it frequently to see if the ship is on
her course. . . . He must be . . . cognizant of everything
concerning ship handling, especially of making sail. He should
take care to have good food and drink for his voyage, and
such as will not spoil, to have good dry bins to keep bread or
hardtack; and, especially for long voyages, to take too much
rather than too little. . . . He must be a good economist in
issuing rations, giving each man reasonably what he needs,
otherwise dissatisfaction will be created, . . . and entrust the
distribution of victuals to a good and faithful steward, not a
drunkard but a good manager; for a careful man in this office
is above all price.

Considering that Cartier made three voyages of discovery in dangerous and hitherto unknown waters without losing a ship; that he entered
and departed some fifty undiscovered harbors without serious mishap;
that the only sailors he lost were victims of an epidemic ashore, and
that he performed everything that a good seaman could for king and
country, we may assume that he conformed to these rules later dictated
by his great sucessor Champlain. They were as applicable in the following centuries as in the sixteenth; in fact, a modern naval officer or
master of a merchant ship would do well to heed them today.

Fishermen from Saint-Malo and other Breton ports, as we have seen
in earlier chapters, were already doing well on the Grand Bank and
inshore. Cartier must have sailed in one or more of these vessels; possibly the one which discovered that the Strait of Belle Isle led to a
great gulf. For, in the court order organizing Cartier's first voyage, he
is authorized to sail "beyond the strait of the Baye des Chasteaulx,"
the earliest name of the Strait of Belle Isle.

Cartier's title, in all these documents pertaining to his first voyage, is

"Capitaine et Pilote pour le Roy." This means that he was captain by the king's command, but a master pilot by experience. In all European languages *pilot* then had two meanings: (1) a local river or harbor pilot who guided ships in and out, as today; and (2) a seagoing officer, corresponding roughly to first mate, next under the captain and master. He took charge of navigation, kept the reckoning, and usually (unless the master insisted on taking charge) ordered making and taking in of sail. Cartier was the second kind of pilot, and in his American voyages he took on the responsibilities of captain and master as well. Moreover, in all three fleets he was senior captain, what we would call commodore.

Cartier's First Voyage Gets Under Way

Even in want of any surviving copy of Cartier's royal commission, we can infer from the narratives of his voyage that his main charge was to find a passage to China; and his second, to discover sources of precious metals. Verrazzano had insisted (without adequate evidence) that these were to be found in northern regions. Preparations for the first voyage were not too easy. The king's treasurer for his navy granted Cartier on 18 March 1534 the sum of 6000 livres tournois (roughly equivalent to the same number of gold francs) for the equipment, provisioning, and seamen's wages of "certain ships . . . which should in company with and under the command of Jacques Cartier make the voyage from this kingdom to *Terres Neufves*, to discover certain isles and countries where there is said to be found a vast quantity of gold and other rich things." And in a local court order of next day, he is described as *"Maistre Jacques Cartier, capitaine et pilote pour le Roy*, in charge of voyaging and going *aux Terres Neuffves*, beyond the strait of the *baye des Chasteaulx*." Terres Neuffves in this instance means all lands to be newly discovered in that region.

As Columbus had wryly observed, royal orders are not promptly obeyed in outports; and the merchants of Saint-Malo, fearing a scarcity of hands for their fishing vessels, were so successful in preventing mariners from signing on with Cartier that he had to persuade the *procureur* of Saint-Malo to clap an embargo on the Banks fishing vessels until such time as the "Captain and pilot for the king" had obtained a full complement. That did it; and on 20 April 1534 Cartier was able to sail from Saint-Malo in command of two ships, each of "about" sixty tuns' burthen and each manned by a crew of sixty-one men. This means that they were of about the same burthen as Verrazzano's *La Dauphine*. Regrettably, no record of their names or those of their officers has survived.

The voyage began with a ceremony at Saint-Malo. Charles de Mouy, vice-admiral of France, swore in the captain and crew, in the presence of wives, sweethearts, and parents, "well and loyally to conduct themselves in the service of the king and under command of the said Cartier." The two vessels sailed 20 April under a first-quarter moon—good for clearing the English Channel—and on 10 May, in the dark of the moon, made landfall on Cape Bonavista, Newfoundland—an Atlantic passage of only twenty days. Cartier must have been favored by a rare prolonged burst of easterly wind. It is evident that he was using the old method of latitude sailing, and to a known objective. For the latitude of Saint-Malo is 48°39′ N, and that of Cape Bonavista, 48°42′. Cartier's *Première Relation* of this voyage called it 48°30′—near enough; any yacht navigator of today would be pleased to do as well. Cape Bonavista had obviously become a favorite landfall of French fishermen.

Nevertheless, Cartier ran risks in arriving so early in the year. The 10th of May (19 May in our calendar) is a bad time for ice on the east coast of Newfoundland, and he encountered plenty of it—so much indeed that he found it necessary to enter "un havre nonmé *saincte Katherine*" five leagues to the southeast. Distance and bearing are correct for the harbor now called Catalina, a snug little port where the English later established a flourishing fishing village. Here the two ships tarried for ten days, making repairs; the fast ocean passage must have been rough on sails, spars, and tackle.

On 21 May when the wind came west, blowing away icebergs that were hammering the coast, and the new moon had passed its first quarter, "We departed the said harbor," says Cartier's *Première Relation*. He shaped a northerly course to *L'Isle des Ouaisseaulx* (Isle of Birds), as he named it, 80 miles distant. For reasons obvious to the nose it became *Puanto* (stinking) island on the Testu map of 1555, and is Funk Island today. This islet, hardly more than a rock, lies 32 miles northnortheast of Cape Freels, the nearest land. As Cartier doubtless remembered from his earlier visit, it was covered with nesting birds, under a feathered umbrella of thousands more, flying and screaming. The big-gest species, unable to fly, was the great auk, the original penguin, which Cartier called *apponatz*. His crew in half an hour killed enough to fill two boats. They ate some fresh, and salted down ten or twelve barrels for future consumption. In addition they saw multitudes of birds that they called *godez* (either the murre or the razorbill auk) and the snow-white *margaulx* (gannet) "which bite even as dogs" when one disturbs their nests. The Beothuk Indians used to paddle their canoes to Funk Island for the sake of great auk meat, and it is said that bears swam from Cape Freels to gorge themselves on wild fowl. Cartier's ships met a swimming bear on 24 May after they had left the island, "as big as a cow and white as a swan." The men took to their boats and killed this enterprising polar bear; "its flesh was as good and delicate to eat as that of a two-year-old steer." Sebastian Cabot had set the fashion for bear stories about Newfoundland.

From Funk the two ships stretched northwest some 140 miles, and on the day of full moon, 27 May, made Cape Bauld, which Cartier calls *Dégrat;* this is the first appearance of the name of Cabot's probable landfall. Cartier observed that the cape was on an island with two good harbors—*Karpont* (now Quirpon) and *L'Anse Dégrat*—on the eastern side of Quirpon Island. How strange that three distinguished dis-coverers, Leif Ericsson, John Cabot, and Jacques Cartier, were drawn to this remote and lonely spot at intervals of five hundred years and more! Cartier well observes that Quirpon Harbor may be entered from the east or the west, and that the western entrance is the better; he gives the latitude as 51°30′ N, which is almost correct, the eastern entrance being only five miles north of that.

Cartier or one of his men must have climbed 500-foot-high Cape Dégrat, since he writes that from it one sees clearly two *Belles Iles* "which are near Cap Rouge," well to the southward. He could not have meant the present Belle Isle, which lies 18 miles *north* of Cape Dégrat, and was not so named until after Cartier's day, but two "fair islands," the pair now known as The Gray, or Grey, Islands, Groais and Bell. The former, a high island, could easily have been seen from Cape Dégrat. The real Belle Isle, Cartier never mentions, outward or homeward; but it is so named and described in *La Cosmographie* of Jean Alfonce, Roberval's pilot.

South Shore of The Labrador

Cartier was delayed several days at Quirpon by contrary winds and ice. During the first week of June, sailing west by north from Cape Bauld, he passed two islands to port. These must have been the bigger Sacred Island, which in the eleventh century screened Leif Ericsson's settlement from the sea, and Schooner Island. This he well describes as flat, low, and appearing to merge with the mainland; he named it *Saincte Katherine*, after his wife's patron saint. Then, sailing fifteen miles due north across the Strait of Belle Isle, he entered *le hable des Chasteaulx*, Labrador, already so named by French fishermen and still called Château Bay. The island at the entrance, with a sheer cliff of vertical columns of basaltic rock two hundred feet high, and a flat top like the glacis of a castle, gave the harbor its name. The official Sailing Directions for Newfoundland dismisses Château Bay thus: "Little grass grows in the vicinity but moss is plentiful and there is considerable cranberry growth. Mosquitoes and flies are troublesome in summer." The back country here is to the last degree rocky and barren, but the harbor is excellent and in the colonial era it rivaled Blanc Sablon as a fishing rendezvous. Considered to be the key to the northern fisheries, it was fortified in the eighteenth century by both the French and British.

As Cartier turned southwest up the Strait of Belle Isle to follow the mountainous south coast of the Labrador, he began the most difficult, as well as the least profitable, leg of his voyage. The entire north coast of the Gulf, as far as the Bay of Seven Islands, is studded with outlying islets and reefs; and these waters are opaque, unlike those of the Caribbean where one can see bottom through six fathom or more of water. Cartier, however, had threaded all the murmurous passes of the sea into iron-bound Brittany, and he sailed so carefully that not once on this voyage did either of his ships touch bottom.

Steering southwesterly through the Strait of Belle Isle, Cartier named two small harbors *des Buttes* (of the knolls) and *de la Baleine* (of the whale). The first, now Black Bay, with two conspicuous hillocks, is recommended by the Sailing Directions as a temporary summer anchorage only; the second, now Red Bay, with red granite cliffs and

Château Island, Château Bay, Labrador.

marked by a 550-foot hill with white boulders on top, was formerly
a favorite anchorage for fishing vessels. It was here that Dr. Wilfred
Grenfell founded his first Labrador hospital. Alas, there was not a sailing fisherman to be seen in the entire Gulf of St. Lawrence when we
flew around it in 1969. But there were still plenty of icebergs.

Thirty-five miles further, Cartier reached the harbor of Blanc Sablon,
already named by French fishermen and still so called today. Cartier
well describes it as "a *conche* [shell] where there is no shelter from the
south or southeast," to which he might have added the southwest. At
the head of it is a gray sandy beach and dunes, which when sunstruck
look white. Despite its exposed anchorage and being closed in by ice
from December to mid-May, Blanc Sablon became a famous fishing
port. The fishermen liked the beach, where they could haul up their
boats, and the dunes, on which they dried their catch; sheltered anchorage for their ships lay around the corner.

Lying off Blanc Sablon to the south-southwest, says Cartier, are two
islands which he calls *Bouays* and *des Ouaisseaulx;* they are now Isle au
Bois and Greenly Island. On Greenly, marked by two hillocks, Cartier

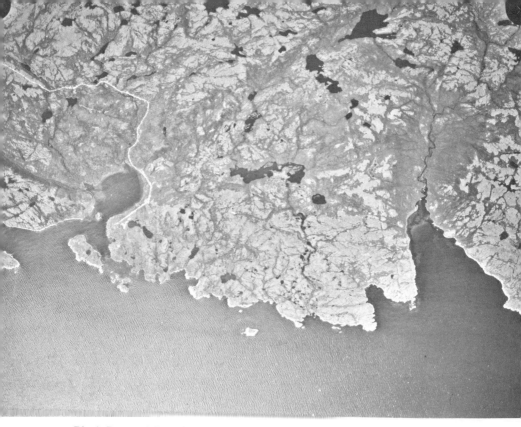

Black Bay and Red Bay, Labrador. Cartier's *Port des Buttes* and *Port de la Baleine*. Taken 26 August 1967 from elevation of 30,000 feet. The dark areas are dwarf spruce; light areas, bare rock. Courtesy Air Photo Division, Canadian Government.

first encountered great flocks of puffin, which he describes as having red beaks and feet, and nesting in holes in the ground like conys. Multitudes still nest there, now that Greenly has become a Canadian bird sanctuary. The French named this bird *perroquet* (parakeet) because of its parrot-like beak, and a little island around Long Point is so named. Greenly Island figures in the history of aviation, because in April 1928 three aviators, Fitzmaurice, Koehl, and Von Huenefeld, one Irish and two German, attempting a transatlantic flight from Dublin in the W-33L *Bremen*, made an emergency landing there. It was the first east-west crossing by air, and took 36½ hours. Although the *Bremen* was smashed, the aviators survived. Floyd Bennett died on a flight to rescue them from Greenly.

Cartier, passing island-studded Bradore Bay and safely threading

Greenly Island off Blanc Sablon.

The beach that gave Blanc Sablon its name.

The natural rock road from Blanc Sablon village to the harbor.

another archipelago with the aid of alert masthead lookouts, entered on 10 June a harbor that he named after Brest in Brittany. There the two ships took on wood and water. This was the harbor now named Bonne Esperance, which the Sailing Directions for the Gulf of St. Lawrence describe as "excellent." Cartier took the sun and recorded the latitude as 51°55'. This was not one of his best efforts—about thirty miles out.

Next day, 11 June, was St. Barnabas's day, which in the Julian calendar was the longest of the year, and it was also the day of new moon. English children used to sing:

> Barnaby bright—
> Longest day and shortest night.

Cartier, after hearing mass, organized a boat party and had himself rowed westward, discovering innumerable islands which he called *Toutes Isles*. The crew spent the night on one, where they found and cooked fresh eider ducks' eggs; these were also greatly relished by Canadians in the nineteenth century.

On 12 June, the boat party having returned, the ships resumed their voyage, and at twilight entered a good harbor which Cartier named *Saint-Antoine*, it being the feast of that much-tempted saint. He investigated another harbor a mile distant, which he called *Saint-Servan* after the old town adjoining Saint-Malo. One league southwest of Saint-Servan he landed on "an islet round as an oven" and set up a cross with the arms of France. Saint-Antoine has been identified by H. F. Lewis as the now unnamed space between Dog Islands and the mainland, Saint-Servan as Rocky Bay, and the islet as the present Le Boulet. Lewis found there a cairn of stones which may well have been a base to Cartier's cross.

Two leagues beyond (assuming that *dix* of the narrative is a mistake for *deux*), they entered a bay—either the Shekatika (now renamed Jacques Cartier) or St. Augustine River, which they named *Rivière Saint-Jacques*, after their Captain's patron saint. Here they took many salmon. In the offing, becalmed, they saw the only ship encountered on this voyage: a big fishing craft from La Rochelle, whose seamen (said Cartier) did not know where they were; a remark perhaps dictated by annoyance over his being second on the scene. But he sent his long boats to tow the vessel into a nearby harbor. The Rochelais joined

Dog Island and Le Boulet, "round as an oven," where Cartier set up the Cross.

Lobster and Rocky Bays.

Cartier, and in company sailed to one of the several harbors in the St. Augustine estuary, probably the one now named Cumberland, which the Captain named after himself, *Havre de Jacques-Cartier.* He observed that it was "one of the best harbors in the world"—an exaggeration, of course; but the official *Sailing Directions* concede it to be "one of the best harbors along this coast." At that point, apparently, the fishermen parted company and sailed home, with a good fare of fish, it is to be hoped.

Cartier in his *Première Relation* is very uncomplimentary about this land. "Were the soil as good as the harbors, it would be fine; but this [coast] should not be called *Terre Neuve*, being composed of stones and frightful rocks and uneven places; for on this entire northern coast I saw not one cartload of earth, though I landed in many places. Except for Blanc Sablon there is nothing but moss and stunted shrubs. To conclude, I am inclined to regard this land as the one God gave to Cain."

Such candor about a newly discovered country, well justified in this case, is very rare among discoverers. For most, a scrawny wood is a noble forest, every stretch of open country the richest soil in the world, every glittering stone a precious gem. Even Cartier, as we shall see, was seduced into the belief that he had discovered diamonds. Audubon, who called this a "poor, rugged, miserable country," endorsed Cartier's description. The desolation is the same today: granite hills smoothed by a glacier, stunted spruce in the valleys the only green, and all extending northward as far as the eye can see.

The natives, whom Cartier had met somewhere between Blanc Sablon and Rocky Bay, he describes thus: "The men are well enough formed but untamed and savage. They wear their hair bound on top of their heads like a fistful of twisted hay, sticking into it a pin or something and adding some birds' feathers. They are clothed in peltry, men and women alike, but the women shape theirs more to their figures and gird their waists. They paint themselves with tan colors. They have boats in which they go to sea made of birch bark, and from which they catch a great quantity of seal. Since seeing them I have ascertained that they are not natives of this place, but come from warmer regions to take seal and other things to eat."

From this brief description, and the vocabulary which he added to the *Première Relation,* some ethnologists conclude that these were an Iroquoian tribe from the St. Lawrence valley; others identify them as the Newfoundland Beothuk, who are known to have been great seal hunters. Seal-bone heaps are as common along the Newfoundland coast as clamshell heaps in Maine.

West Coast of Newfoundland

Returning to New Brest (Bonne Esperance Harbor), Cartier caused mass to be held on Sunday, 14 June, and next day shaped a new course to explore the west coast of Newfoundland. Nobody knows why he made this radical change of course instead of continuing right on to "Cathay." A change of wind, perhaps, or mere curiosity to discover the back side of Newfoundland, which all earlier maps had left blank.

Sailing south twenty leagues (46 nautical miles), he came into his first Newfoundland thick o'fog. It lifted in time to sight a cape where there was a long, low point and behind it one small hill and a big one; so he named it *Cap Double*. This may easily be identified as Point Rich; the profile in Captain Cook's chart of 1770 shows the two hills very clearly.

After spending the night in a small harbor near by, Cartier's fleet on 16 June sailed southwest by south thirty-five leagues (80 miles) along a range of mountains that he named *Monts des Granches* because one of them resembled a barn—*grange* in French. It does look like a huge stone barn as you pass it today. The mountains, now called the Long Range, have an even altitude of some 2500 feet. In the evening the Captain observed a break in the coastline and approached a promontory, which he called *Cap Pointu*. He described it as rugged on top but pointed where it enters the sea, and to the north of it, a flat islet. This cape is the modern Cow Head, and the islet is now Stearing Island. He spent the night in a very beautiful harbor just south of the point, now St. Paul's Bay and Inlet.

On 17 June a northeast gale blew up. They clewed up the mainsail, housed the topmasts, and scudded southwesterly until the following morning, when they found themselves off a bay "full of round islands like dovecotes, and for this reason gave them the name *Coulombiers*" and the bay, *Sainct Jullian*. This was the beautiful Bay of Islands, opening between two gray, rocky headlands covered with spruce trees. Two or three islets, with a little imagination, may be compared to dovecotes.

High Land of S! John

Sketch of the scenery from Ferolle Pt. to Point Rich (Cartier's *Cap Double*). From Captain James Cook's Chart of Newfoundland, 1770.

From here southward the scenery becomes more spectacular, a high, bold coast with reddish cliffs and waterfalls cascading directly into the sea. Cartier noticed 1255-foot-high Bear Head and named it *Cap Royal*. Off that cape, on a twenty-fathom bank marked on the modern chart, his men found the best fishing of the entire voyage; in

St. Paul's Inlet.

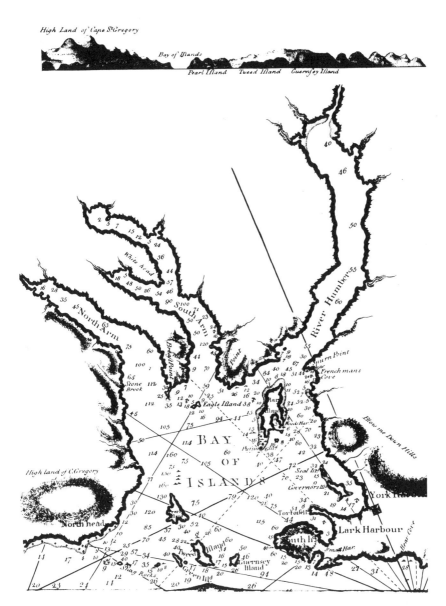

Bay of Islands (Cartier's *St. Julian*), from C. Gregory to Bear Head
(*Cap Royal*). Capt. Cook's Chart of Newfoundland, 1770.

187

Cape St. George (Cartier's *Cap de Latte*), Newfoundland. Note the castle-like point. Photo by Dr. Paul Sheldon, 1970.

Fort La Latte, Brittany, from Cap Fréhel.

Fort La Latte, close-up.

less than an hour, while waiting for the other ship to catch up, they pulled in more than a hundred *grosses morues*, big codfish.

The next prominent point, off which lay a low island at a distance of a mile and a half, Cartier called *Cap de Latte*, after Fort La Latte near Saint-Malo, with which he was familiar. The Breton fort is a medieval castle on a lonely promontory. The ruins, when first I saw them in 1913, might well have inspired the last act of Wagner's *Tristan und Isolde;* but the fort has since been restored. Cartier's Cap de Latte is magnificent, and so sheer as to suggest castle walls rising directly from the edge of the sea, as they do in the Breton fort. The English changed the name to Cape St. George; and the low island which Cartier noticed is now named Red, from the color of the rocks.

"The next day, the 18th of the said month" (June), states the *Première Relation,* "the wind blew strong and contrary so we returned to find shelter," and put into a great bay between Bear Head and Cape St. George, now called Port au Port. The latitude he gives as 48°30', which is correct for Cape St. George. A boat party sent ahead to explore reported so much foul ground that Cartier decided not to enter: a sound decision and a good instance of the care with which our *maître-pilote* reconnoitered a new harbor. One could not risk being entangled in foul ground or suffer the inconvenience of being embayed by a wind blowing directly into a narrow entrance. The current Sailing Directions give a forbidding picture of the rocks and shoals within this entrance; the only secure anchorage is in Head Harbor, twelve miles above Fox Island, which Cartier noted but did not name, and Fox Island is six miles inside the entrance. Probably the boat party penetrated that far and reported adversely to their commander.

Accordingly they put out to sea, shaping a westerly course. From 19 to 26 June they had contrary winds and stormy weather and did not sight land again until "the day of St. John," when they sighted Cape Anguille—which Cartier accordingly named *Cap Sainct Jehan.* Even with a full moon, it was too risky to close the coast and seek a harbor; and actually there was none. Codroy, now an active little port, had to be made snug by a breakwater.

Cape Anguille, briefly glimpsed through the mist, was the last point of Newfoundland that Cartier sighted on this voyage until he turned homeward. He had found nothing but fish "to write home about" on the west coast of Newfoundland. Presently he would discover islands and harbors to arouse his enthusiasm.

The Magdalen Islands
Bird Island (Cartier's *Ile de Margaulx*). The white dots in the air are gannets, and so are the white places on the cliffs.

Ile de Brion.

Beach connecting two parts of the Magdalen Islands.

Brion, Magdalen, and Prince Edward Islands

From Cap Saint-Jean on 25 June, Cartier sailed west-northwest close hauled in "foul weather, overcast and blowy," and in the evening he hove-to. The two ships made sail again at midnight, when the wind shifted to northwest as it usually does after an easterly gale. A southwest traverse on 26 June brought them to "three islets, two of them as steep as a wall, so that you cannot climb up." These are the Bird Rocks; the biggest is 105 feet high and less than a quarter-mile long. Cartier named them *Isles de Margaulx* after the gannets which, together with auks, murres, puffins, and kittiwakes, were "as thick ashore as a meadow with grass." Or, as Captain Charles Leigh described them half a century later, "as thicke as stones lie on a paved street." Even after four centuries of indiscriminate slaughter they still do; the gannets sit so close as to look like icing on a cake, and their whiteness renders these rocks visible seven miles away on a moonlit night. Cartier's men landed on the biggest islet and killed more than a thousand murre and great auk; in an hour they could have filled thirty boats with birds had they wished.

"Five leagues west from the said islets," says Cartier, "was another island, . . . about two leagues long and as wide. We spent the night there to take on wood and water. . . . This island has the best land that we have seen; one *arpent* of it is worth more than the whole of Newfoundland. We found it full of beautiful trees, meadows, fields of wild wheat and pease in flower as fair and abundant as I ever saw in Brittany, and appearing to have been sowed by farmers. There are plenty of gooseberries, strawberries and roses of Provins, parsley, and other good sweet-smelling herbs. And around this island, several big beasts, big as oxen, with two teeth in their mouth like the elephant, and which live in the sea"—the walrus. "We also saw bears and foxes." The island he named *L'Ile de Bryon* after his supporter, Philippe de Chabot, seigneur de Brion and admiral of France. Cartier's description seems ecstatic for an island only one mile by five; but he did not exaggerate— much. A French writer who visited the island about 1878 wrote: "Brion has lost its air of terrestrial paradise. Its great trees have disappeared. . . . Its incarnadine roses are dead, suffocated by the bitter kisses of the north wind. But the island's soil has preserved its fertility;

Southern part of the Magdalen Islands in 1969.

Entry Island, Magdalen Group. The red cliffs with huge white blotches make it an ideal landmark for fishermen.

its meadows are famous throughout the Gulf of St. Lawrence. . . .
The cattle pastured there are superb, and the sheep of Brion meet the
requirements of our most finicky Canadian butchers at Eastertide."
When we visited Brion Island in 1969, it was about half open-pasturage
and half spruce forest; nobody appeared to be living there but the
lighthouse keeper, and no cattle were visible.

At this point Cartier interjects in his *Première Relation*, "I rather
think, from what I have observed, that there exists a passage between
Newfoundland and the Land of the Bretons; if so, it would be a great
time and distance saver if this voyage [to China] succeeds." Of course
there was such a passage—Cabot Strait between Cape Ray and Cape
Breton; and why Cartier did not investigate it before returning home
is a puzzle.

"Four leagues from the said island to the west-southwest," says
Cartier, "there is a *terre firme* which appears to be an island, surrounded by sand islands. It has a fair cape which we called *Cap du
Daulphin*, as it marks the beginning of good land." This name, the
title of the king's eldest son, has since been attached to the eastern
point of the Magdalen Islands. Cartier did not name these islands
because he considered them to be mainland. He sounded the eight-
mile channel between Brion Island and Cape Dauphin and found
"fine sandy bottom and even depth." The modern chart agrees. "We
struck sail and lay-to" for the night, says Cartier, because he wished
to gain a more ample acquaintance with these waters.

"On the 27th of the said month of June" with a full moon, "we
ranged this land, which runs east-northeast—west-southwest, and
seems to consist of sand dunes. . . . We could not go thither or land,
because the wind made up from off shore," which made it too difficult
for a rowing boat. Next day, 28 June, having apparently lain at hull
all night, he resumed his sail along the Magdalens, noting a cape of
bright red earth (Hospital Point, Grindstone Island) which he named
Cap Saint-Pierre, it being the feast of Saints Peter and Paul. He observed the sand bars, the numerous lagoons, and the curve of the coast.

The Magdalen group is a curious chain of islets, each with a fairly
high hill, and most of them connected by sand causeways which every
big gale threatens to wash away; over the centuries it has been the
scene of very many wrecks. The English captain George Drake
in 1593 found the harbors occupied by Bretons from Saint-Malo and

Basque whalers from Saint-Jean de Luz, and when Leigh tried to obtain a footing there he was repulsed by two hundred French and three hundred Indians. After the expulsion of the Acadians from Nova Scotia, they effected a permanent settlement on the Magdalens, and their descendants are still there. Admiral Sir Isaac Coffin R.N., a native of Nantucket, received a grant of the islands from the crown as a reward for saving his frigate under their lee during a furious gale, when conveying Lord Dorchester to Quebec in 1786. He established a feudal tenure and made a good thing out of the dues. His heirs were bought out by Quebec and, owing to the rich cod and other fisheries in the surrounding waters, which have given them the name *le royaume des poissons* among the French, the islands in 1969 boasted a population of over 10,000, have a lively export trade in frozen cod fillets, and are beginning to attract tourists.

Noting the 300-foot-high Southwest Cape on Amherst Island, Cartier sailed west, and, eight miles beyond, observed a high, pointed rock, which he named *Allezay*, an old French word having something to do with an anvil. Later the French called it *Corps-Mort*, which the English translated as *The Deadman*. Tom Moore, in a poem that he wrote about it when sailing by in 1804, explains the name. A shadowy bark, wraith of a wreck on the "cold and pitiless Labrador,"

> To Deadman's Isle, in the eye of the blast,
> To Deadman's Isle she speeds her fast,
> By skeleton shapes her sails are furl'd,
> And the hand that steers is not of this world!

Cartier seems to have been fascinated by this group of islands, which he evidently regarded as mainland until his return from the second voyage in 1536. This is borne out by the Desceliers Harleian Map of 1542 (which we have reproduced) showing *C. de Daulphyn* on a mainland near *Yle de brion* and *isles de Margaux*—the Bird Rocks.

On 29 June, with wind south by west, Cartier left these waters, ran west all night, and next day at sunset sighted what appeared to be two islands. These were the heights of land on Prince Edward Island around New London Bay. He reached this big fertile island at about its middle and coasted northwest to a "very beautiful cape" which he named *Cap d'Orléans* after Charles, duc d'Orléans, youngest son of the king. This was probably Cape Kildare. "All this land is low and uniform," wrote Cartier, "the fairest one could possibly see, and full of

Allezay, The Deadman.

Cap des Sauvages, Cape North, P.E.I.

View on the north shore of Prince Edward Island. Courtesy Canadian
Government Travel Bureau.

fine trees and meadows; but we could find no harbor there," only
shoals and rocks. They landed several times from their boats and entered a beautiful but shallow river, "where we saw the savages' boats,
and for that reason called it *rifvière de Barraques.*" This figures conspicuously on the Harleian Map, in a shape that suggests Malpeque
Bay. Sailing as he did, from point to point, Cartier never realized that
Prince Edward was an island, although Gomez and probably Fagundes
had done so before him. He did, however, have the good sense to put
out to sea when an easterly wind blew up, making that coast a lee shore.
Clawing off on the starboard tack, he cleared the land safely, and at
10 a.m. on 1 July sighted the cape he had just named d'Orléans and
another, seven leagues north by east, which he named *Cap de Sauvages,*
because an Indian appeared on the shore, making friendly gestures. Although the distance is exaggerated, the course is almost correct, and

this "wild men's cape," as Hakluyt translated it, must have been Cape North of Prince Edward Island; Cartier observed the dangerous shoal off it on which the sea was boiling. Apparently he rounded the cape and coasted for about thirty miles toward Egmont Bay without finding a harbor, landing in four places "to see the trees, which are marvellously beautiful and sweet smelling; and we found them to be cedar, yew, pine, white elm, ash, willow, and several others unknown to us." The open country he found "very fair and full of pease, white and red gooseberries, strawberries, raspberries, and wild wheat like rye, which looks as if it had been sowed and cultivated"—Leif Ericsson's lyme grass again. "It is the most temperate land that one could ask for, and of great heat; and there are many turtledoves, wood-pigeons, and other birds; only good harbors are wanting." This is a fair description of that part of Prince Edward Island, now intensively cultivated by the industrious inhabitants. As Cartier observed, there is nothing more de-

John Rotz's "Boke of Idrographie," 1542, folios 23–24. Rotz had information of Cartier's first voyage only, as proved by Cape Gaspé being joined to Anticosti, and the Magdalen and Prince Edward Islands being joined to the mainland. The V-shaped bay on the west is the Penobscot. Courtesy Map Division, Public Archives of Canada.

lightful than sailing along a wooded coast in the early summer, close
enough to hear bird-song and smell the green herbage.

Gaspé

Sighting the cliffy Richibucto Head ten miles across Northumberland
Strait on 2 July, Cartier crossed the strait with a last-quarter moon,
turning northward as the land opened up, and discovered the present
Miramichi Bay. He named it *Baye Sainct Lunaire* after a Breton saint
whose festival fell on the first of the month, and which also was the
title of his patron, the abbot of Mont-Saint-Michel. Sending his longboats into this bay, outlet of a famous salmon river, he observed its
triangular shape, but the boats reported so many rocks and shoals that
he did not attempt to bring in his ships. Ten leagues off shore, he says,
the depth was twenty fathom—exactly what the modern chart gives
on a line ten miles from each cape.

Foul weather and strong wind that night (2–3 July) forced the two
ships to heave-to off the coast, but on the morning of the third the
wind came fair and they rounded North Point on Miscou Island, the
southern entrance to Chaleur Bay, and entered that bay. Cartier, who
named it, waxed more enthusiastic over this beautiful sun-drenched
bay, with its warm air and water, than over any other place discovered
on this voyage. He admired the land and the spruce trees, tall enough
to mast a ship of three hundred tuns. These amenities must have been
a joy to his sailors after experiencing the ice and fog of the eastern
Gulf. Cartier reported the climate to be more temperate than that of
Spain, the soil rich, "fairest you could see anywhere," the flora like
that of Brion Island and the waters teeming with salmon.

As at the northern entrance to Chaleur Bay, mountains were visible
to the north, and one could see no land at the head of the bay. Cartier
hoped that he had found a strait like that of Belle Isle, which would
lead him to *the* passage to China. For that reason, he said, he named
the present north point on Miscou Island *Cap d'Esperance*. The latitude at midbay, he said, was 47°30′, half a degree short of correct;
and here he attempts a longitude, 73° W. But as usual he does not tell
us what prime meridian he counted from. The head of this bay is
68°45′ W of Paris, but Cartier more probably counted from Saint-
Malo, which would be a few degrees less, or Ferro, which would have

made the correct longitude 50°25′ W. Thus he was no better at guessing longitude than Verrazzano. Both navigators, like Columbus, hopefully placed America on the globe much nearer to Asia than it really is.

The rich soil, teeming fisheries, and warm climate (temperature often passing 90°F. in summer) have made Chaleur Bay one of the most thickly populated parts of the Gulf littoral. All along the northern shore are farms of uniform shape and size—so many *arpents*—which were parceled out to *habitants* in the colonial era; a neat little house near the shore, vegetable garden, hayfield, and pasture behind it in that order, and usually ending in a woodlot. Cartier on 4 July put in at a little harbor that he named *Conche Sainct Martin*, it being the feast of the translation of the relics of St. Martin of Tours. Cartier always called an open, shell-shaped harbor like Blanc Sablon, a *conche* (shell). St. Martin is now Port Daniel, seat of a huge wood-pulp mill. And there the ships rested for eight days, part of which was taken up with exploring the bay in one or more longboats.

The village of Paspebiac, whose inhabitants were nicknamed "Paspy Jacks," used to be the Canadian headquarters of the famous Jersey firm of Robin & Cie. In the 1870's they were exporting $300,000 worth of fish annually to the Mediterranean, Brazil, and the West Indies, and schooners from Cape Ann took home as much more. "The annual yield of the Bay of Chaleur is estimated at 26,000 quintal (each 112 pounds) of dry codfish, 600 quintal of haddock, 3000 barrels of herring, 300 barrels of salmon, and 15,000 gallons of codliver oil," states the standard guidebook of 1875. "The fisheries, the bay and gulf are valued at $800,000 a year, and employ 1500 sail and 18,000 men. . . ."

On 6 July, somewhere on the north shore of Chaleur Bay, probably near the site of Paspebiac village, Cartier had his first meeting with the Micmac tribe. This first encounter was not encouraging. Two fleets of forty to fifty canoes, loaded with natives, approached from the south shore of the bay, and a large number landed close to the French boat, yelling their loudest and brandishing peltry on sticks—a sure sign that European fishermen had been there before. "We having only the one boat," wrote Cartier, "did not care to land there but rowed toward the other lot, still at sea. They [of the first fleet], seeing that we fled, manned two of their biggest canoes to catch up with us, joined five others of the second fleet, then at sea, and came alongside our boat, dancing and making divers signs of joy and of wanting our friendship. . . . Not trusting them, we made signs to them to sheer off, which they didn't like, but paddled with such great strength that with their seven canoes they completely surrounded our boat. So, since they wouldn't obey our signs, we shot over their heads two *passevolans*," small pivot-guns mounted on the gunwale. The natives retired momentarily but returned, and the Frenchmen had to hurl two *lanses à feu* among them before they could frighten off the importunate visitors. They obviously meant well, and the next encounter may be said to have inaugurated three centuries of friendship between French Canada and the Micmac.

That came next day, 7 July. Nine canoes full of savages appeared at the mouth of Port Daniel, the paddlers making a hideous racket but again displaying peltry for sale. "We made them signs that we wished them no harm," wrote Cartier, "and sent two men ashore to deal with them, bringing knives and other cutlery, and a red cap to give their chief." Some Indians then landed, and a profitable traffic took place, the natives dancing, making amicable gestures such as pouring seawater over their heads, and selling the very clothes off their backs—furs, of course.

On 8 July, Cartier resumed his exploration of Chaleur Bay by boat. It was now the dark of the moon, but at that season the nights are always luminous if there is no fog. They rowed, he says, 25 leagues (80 miles) up to the head of it, and that is nearly accurate. On the morning of the 10th "We had cognizance of the end of said bay, which gave us grief and displeasure," he writes. The magnificent scenery at that point, the mountains at the mouth of the Restigouche, were no compensation for finding this bay a dead-end instead of a passage to China. Upon turning back, at the site of the present Carleton behind Tracadigash Point, the boats encountered some three hundred Micmac men, women, and children, who brought them strips of broiled seal meat on wooden platters; the French responded with gifts of "hatchets, knives, paternoster beads, and other merchandise." This started a brisk trade of peltry "and what else they had." The women came freely to the French, rubbing their arms—a friendly gesture—selling the furs they wore, and retiring completely naked. Cartier remarked that these *sauvages* were nomads who lived largely on fish, that they were ripe for conversion. Near by were fields of "wild wheat with a head like barley and a seed like oats"—lyme grass again—ripe berries, sweet-smelling white and red roses, and a pond full of salmon. He recorded the words that the savages used for hatchet and knife, which gave proof that they were of the Micmac nation.

With regret at leaving the warmth, both human and climatic, of Chaleur Bay, Cartier on 12 July resumed his search for Cathay, under the new moon. He sailed east along the coast "some 18 leagues" to *Cap de Pratto* where "we found a wonderful range of tide, little depth, and a very high sea. We found it best to hug the shore between the said cape and an island about one league to the eastward, and there we dropped anchors for the night." Although this is a matter of controversy, I believe that Cap de Pratto (Cap du Pré on the Desceliers Map of 1546) is the present White Head, or Cap Percé, where in Cartier's time there may have been enough open grass to be called a meadow; and that the island was Bonaventure, with 250-foot red cliffs. Between this and the main is an anchorage in fifteen fathom which the modern Sailing Directions recommend, except in bad weather. But why did not Cartier mention the extraordinary Ile Percé, with its natural arch? For the simple reason that the sea had not yet broken through the soft sandstone isthmus that connected that island with the point; one may also conjecture that the famous hole or tunnel had not yet been pierced. Early in the nineteenth century Ile Percé had two holes, but one collapsed in 1843.

These now peaceful shores have echoed cannon fire many times in the past. Sir William Phips dropped in on his way to Quebec in 1690, and burned all the houses and churches on Cap Percé and Bonaventure Island. Hovenden Walker, in 1711, cut out two French ships from the roadstead where Cartier anchored, but in the great storm of 22 August three of his own ships were wrecked and all hands were lost. Local tradition insists that a phantom ship crowded with men in uniforms of the old régime appears off shore in foggy calms, crashes on the cliffs, and disappears. The last scene of violence, apart from wrecks, was in 1776, when H.M.S. *Wolf* and *Diligence* sank two American privateers off Ile Percé.

Cartier's fleet now encountered a spell of foul weather; the ships set forth but could make no progress. This is a place where the north and the south winds meet and make either a calm or a disturbance. He anchored in the outer roadstead for two days while his boats explored

Mouth of Miramichi Bay.

Cap Percé and Bonaventure Island.

View in Gaspé Bay. Courtesy Canadian Government Travel Bureau.

the spectacularly beautiful Gaspé * Bay, then selected Gaspé Harbor near the head of the bay and tarried there from 16 to 25 July.

Cartier here made a new and important contact with a party of about two hundred Huron Indians in forty canoes—who with their chief, Donnaconna, were on a mackerel fishing trip—from the site of Quebec. As they seemed friendly like the Micmac, he let them paddle close to the ships, and issued the usual trading truck of cheap knives, combs, and glass beads. These people, wrote Cartier, "could well be called savages, for they are the poorest people that can be in the world; all their possessions, apart from the canoes and fishing nets, were not worth five sous." They wore nothing but a G-string and a few furs that they threw over their shoulders like scarfs. Unlike the natives encountered before, their heads were shaved "except for a topknot that they leave as long as a horse's tail, which they bind and tie to their heads in a knot with strips of leather"—the scalp lock. They eat both fish and meat almost raw, and their only huts are their canoes, reversed. Naturally, as this was a summer fishing party, the natives brought noth- with them but bare necessities.

On St. Mary Magdalen's day, 22 July, the French rowed ashore to where the natives had assembled and mingled with them, dancing and singing. Prudently, the Indians had sent all their young girls away ex- cept two or three; to each of them the Captain gave a little tin hawk's bell, which so delighted the damsels that they rubbed his arms and chest, their mode of expressing appreciation. Suddenly Cartier was al- most overwhelmed by twenty more girls rushing out of the forest whither their menfolk had banished them, all trying at once to massage him and earn a bell; and he amiably gave one to each. One assumes that French sailors followed the girls back into the discreet thickets where they could celebrate the Magdalen's day appropriately if not sacerdo- tally.

Cartier noted a kind of wild grain "like the pease of Brazil" that they ate in lieu of bread and called *kagaigo*—this probably was maize—and plums which they dried for winter use and called *honnesta;* both are Huron words. "They will never eat anything with a salty taste," he says, and "they are wonderful thieves, filching anything they can lay hold of."

---

* This name, of Micmac origin, was first used by Champlain in 1603 in the form *Gachepé*. Cartier consistently used a form of *Honguedo*, the Huron name for the region.

On 24 July the master pilot caused a cross thirty feet tall to be raised on a point of this harbor, inscribed VIVE LE ROY DE FRANCE, and attached to it a carved panel displaying three fleurs-de-lys, the arms of François-premier. The Indians followed this proceeding with interest. As soon as the cross was set up, the sailors knelt and with joined hands adored it, making signs toward Heaven that their redemption lay aloft. The Huron obviously could not make much sense out of the doctrine of the redemption, but they did gather that this was a formal taking possession. Their chief, Donnaconna (of whom we shall hear more), came on board dressed in an old black bearskin and conveyed by signs that this was his country and nobody should erect a cross without his permission. But he was placated by gifts, and acquired such confidence in Cartier that he allowed him to carry off two of his teen-age sons, Domagaya and Taignoaguy, on the promise that they would be returned. The boys were promptly dressed European fashion, in shirts, livery jackets, red hats, and brass necklaces, which pleased them greatly; their cast-off furs were bestowed on their friends who stayed behind. Next day some thirty Indians came out in canoes to say goodbye.

Political reasons explain Donnaconna's desire to make friends with the visitors. His tribe, which dominated the St. Lawrence River from Quebec down, was being pressed hard by the Etchemin of Maine, and he needed a powerful ally.

Anticosti and Home

Departing Gaspé Bay 25 July, the day of full moon, Cartier rounded Cape Gaspé and ran into a wall of fog. Skirting the fogbank, he sighted the great island of Anticosti. Assuming that the part he saw of it was a peninsula jutting out from Gaspé, Cartier did not attempt to penetrate the fogbank but steered for the island's nearest point, and made it on the 27th. He then ranged the southeast coast of the big island and named East Cape *Cap Saint-Louis* because it was the feast of a local Breton saint of that name. He gives its position as latitude 49° 15′ N, longitude 63° 30′ W. The latitude is correct within five miles, and the longitude was not too bad; East Cape is 61° 40′ west of Greenwich—but no Frenchman for centuries would use the Greenwich meridian, and Cartier never tells us which meridian he used: Ferro, Saint-Malo, or Paris. Cartier was a fairly good guesser at longitude, for the first half of the sixteenth century, but no more.

Cartier's *Cap St. Louis*, East Cape, Anticosti.

Cap Rabast, Anticosti. Off here Cartier turned back on his first voyage.

Anticosti, an island singularly devoid of charm—except to salmon fishermen—is now almost completely covered with spruce forest and peat bog; but Cartier found the south coast "flat, and the most bare of timber of any place we have seen, with beautiful fields and marvellously green meadows." From its position in the mouth of the great river, and its fringe of reefs, Anticosti is a menace to navigation. "This hideous wilderness," wrote George Warburton in 1846, "has been the grave of hundreds, by . . . starvation. Washed ashore from maimed and sinking ships . . . they drag their chilled and battered limbs up the rough rocks"—but there is no shelter, no food, and if not frozen by the winter cold they are eaten by immense swarms of black flies and mosquitoes. Five stout fellows of Sir William Phips's invading Yankee army, sole survivors of a ship wrecked there in 1690, built themselves a skiff and rowed all the way to Boston, the passage taking forty-four days. I heartily agree with a modern yachtsman, Oliver Green, who observed, "The sight of land is usually welcome, but this had an eerie look. . . . It seemed to have remained since the creation and had certainly never given any welcome to man."

On Wednesday, 29 July, the two ships rounded Cap Saint-Louis and ranged the northern coast of Anticosti, naming Table Head as they passed after Anne de Montmorency, grand constable of France. They sounded some twenty miles off shore and found clean bottom at 100 and 150 fathom—which agrees with the modern chart. Incidentally, this proves that Cartier carried good long dipsey lead lines. On 1 August the highlands of southern Quebec were sighted across *le Détroit de Saint-Pierre* (St. Peter Strait). They made such slow progress along the coast against head winds and the strong ebb current that Cartier ordered both longboats manned to row ahead and investigate a prominent Anticostian cape. The Captain's boat, when trying to benefit from counter-currents near shore, struck a rock "which was immediately cleared by dint of the whole crew jumping overboard to shove her afloat." Good evidence of a loyal crew, as the last thing a sailor cares to do is to go over the side in cold water; one hopes that the Captain issued a tot of brandy to all hands after the salvage. Even with thirteen oars manned, the longboats could make no progress, so they were left ashore under guard while Cartier and a dozen men scrambled along the rocks to the cape, which on his second voyage he named *Rabast*. Having ascertained it to be the narrowest part of the strait, and that the Anticosti shore fell off thence to the southwestward, they returned to the longboats and rowed to the ships. These, though under sail, had drifted over twelve miles to leeward of the spot where the boats had been hoisted out.

Once back on board, Cartier summoned "all captains, pilots, masters and *compagnons* [gentlemen volunteers]" to his cabin to consult them "as to the best to be done." After everyone had had his say, they decided. "Considering that heavy downstream winds had set in, and that the tidal currents were so strong that they did nothing but lose ground, and that it was impossible to gain beyond this season; and also that tempests begin at this season in Newfoundland, that we were even now very far [from home] and knew not what dangers lay ahead; it was high time either to turn back or to stay right there; and moreover, if a succession of east winds caught us, we might be forced to stay. These opinions, once taken, we decided, almost unanimously, to return [to France]."

A very sensible decision, and it was just like Cartier to take the others into his confidence and solicit their views. Very few captains did that, especially in the age of discovery. This conference took place on 1 August 1534, in the Détroit de Saint-Pierre, which has been renamed Jacques Cartier Passage.

So, homeward turned the two ships on 2 August, the day of the moon's last quarter. Thenceforth and until Wednesday 5 August, a prosperous gale of wind blew them eastward at high speed. They paused only once, at Natashquan Point, where they received on board a party of Montagnais Indians engaged in fishing for a certain Captain Thiennot, whose ships were lying in Natashquan harbor. Cartier apparently knew Thiennot, as he named the cape after him; that name has vanished from the maps but there are still some famous codfishing banks a few miles off the point. After passing Cape Whittle on 8 August, Cartier steered due east for the west coast of Newfoundland and made it between Cow Head and Point Rich. When the wind blew up furiously from the east-northeast, they sailed north to Blanc Sablon, spent six days there, and with a first-quarter moon on 15 August, after hearing mass, made sail for the homeward passage. On that, as on the outward one, Cartier is reticent. Mid-passage they were "tost and turmoyled three days long with great stormes coming from the East," as Hakluyt's translation tells it; but "with the help of God we suffered and endured it," says Cartier, "and arrived at the haven of

Limoïlou. The farmhouse, the well, the nearby cross (with M. Lailler and Mrs. Morison), and close-up of the Cartier arms.

September iceberg on Cartier's route. Photo by James F. Nields, 1969.

Some of Cartier's *Toutes Iles.*

Saint-Malo whence we had departed, on the 5th day of September"
1534, only three weeks from Blanc Sablon.

Since Jacques Cartier probably regarded this voyage only as a reconnaissance, he had every reason to be pleased with himself. In the
space of five months he had sailed completely around the Gulf of St.
Lawrence and, although no passage to Cathay had miraculously opened
up, he had a good idea where to start looking for one—in St. Peter
Strait—next time. He had discovered the beginning of the great axis
of penetration of the North American continent. This was the Gulf
and River of St. Lawrence and the Great Lakes, which French explorers in the next century would follow west to the Dakotas and down the
Mississippi to the Gulf of Mexico.

This first voyage enhanced Cartier's status at Saint-Malo. He adopted
a coat of arms, and had it carved on the entrance gate of a farm that
he acquired outside Saint-Malo. Since his town house has long since
disappeared, and his ships have crumbled to dust, this farm, still named
Limoïlou, and still a working farm, brings us closer to the great Captain than any other place short of Canada. Located in the parish of
Saint-Ideuc, it is within sight of the sea, and near enough to Saint-Malo
for the Captain to ride there in an hour's time. A short distance away is
a cross-roads with a typical Breton granite cross, where he is said to
have prayed before his last two voyages; and in the nearby village
of Rotheneuf is a tiny chapel where he worshipped when spending
a Sunday or saint's day at Limoïlou. Like many another sailor, Cartier loved the land, and between voyages as in old age he spent all
the time he could at Limoïlou.*

Cartier's sailors spread stories that enhanced his popularity. They had
lived off the fat of the land—auk meat, salmon, and other fresh fish,
goose eggs, and wild strawberries. The savages were gentle and kind,
and their Captain was not only an expert mariner but a just man, who
gave them opportunities to enhance their pay by trading knickknacks
for peltry. They were ready to sign on for a new voyage under Maître-
Pilote Cartier, and soon they had their opportunity.

* Also spelled *Limoelou;* pronounced as a four-syllable word. I am deeply indebted
to M. Dan Lailler, conservateur du Musée de Saint-Malo, for his sympathetic and
intelligent guidance there, and wish him well in his efforts to have Limoïlou classi-
fied a *monument historique.*

☀ VII ☀
Cartier's Second Voyage
1535-1536

En un bon vaisseau il n'y a à craindre que la terre et le feu.
SAMUEL DE CHAMPLAIN

To Sea with Royal and Episcopal Blessing

Did Cartier go to court and talk with the king? We do not know, but his friends and supporters lost no time in providing him with the means and the authority to make a second voyage of discovery and exploration. He arrived home on 5 September 1534, and as early as 30 October 1534 received a commission from his patron, Philippe Chabot de Brion, who uses his full titles: "Compte de Buranczoys et de Charny, baron d'Aspremont, de Paigny et de Mirebeau, seigneur de Beaumont et de Fontaine-franczose, admiral de France, Bretaigne et Guyenne, governeur et lieutenant-général pour le Roy en Bourgougne, aussi lieutenant-général pour monseigneur le Daulphin ou governement de Normandie."

The recipient, described as "le capitaine et pillote maistre Jacques Cartier de Sainct-Malo," is

> by royal command, to conduct, lead and employ three ships
> equipped and victualed for fifteen months, for the perfection
> of the navigation of lands by you already begun, to discover
> beyond *les Terres Neufves;* and on this voyage to endeavor
> to do and accomplish that which it has pleased the said Lord
> King to command and order you to do. For the equipment

212

thereof you will buy or charter ships at such price as people of means know to be reasonable, and such as you think good and proper for the said navigation. For these ships you will engage the number of pilots, masters and mariners as you think to be requisite and necessary for the accomplishment of this voyage. . . . We give you power and special command over the total charge and expense of these ships, the voyage and navigation, both out and home. We order and command all the said pilots, masters, gentlemen, mariners, and others who will sail in the said ships to obey and follow you in the service of the King . . . under pain of suitable punishment if disobedient.

Cartier, despite his popularity at Saint-Malo, had the same trouble as before in obtaining a full complement, and for much the same reason. Most of the available seamen owed money to shipowning merchants and were prevented by them from signing on for a non-fishing voyage. Of expenses, the king contributed only 3000 livres tournois; the rest was probably furnished by Cartier's local friends and supporters. The master pilot did, however, obtain three ships from the royal French navy, whose names we know, as well as those of their officers.

Here was what we might call Capitaine Jacques Cartier's task organization:

LA GRANDE HERMINE, *nef générale* (flagship), 100 to 120 tuns and 12 guns; Thomas Fromont, master. Several *compagnons* (gentlemen volunteers) such as the dauphin's cupbearer Claude de Pontbriand, as well as the two Hurons, Domagaya and Taignoagny, sailed in her.

LA PETITE HERMINE, about 60 tuns and 4 guns; Macé Jalobert, captain and pilot; Guillaume le Maryé, master.

L'ÉMERILLON, galion of about 40 tuns and 2 guns; Guillaume Le Breton, captain and pilot, Jacques Maingard, master.

Total complement, 112 officers and men.

Hermine (weasel) had a special significance for Brittany; *hermine enchaînée* was an important part of the arms of Anne de Bretagne, queen of Louis XII. The little one, formerly called *Courlieu* (the curlew) was renamed for this voyage. *Émerillon* means a merlin, or sparrowhawk. Both "weasels" were larger than the two ships Cartier sailed on his first voyage, but *L'Émerillon* was smaller than either, a *galion*, what the English called a pinnace. Galions at that era were not big, lumbering warships like the Spanish galleons in the Armada of 1588, but small maneuverable vessels which carried oars as well as sails

La Grande Hermine sailing past Saint-Malo. Rendering by Commandant Denoix for his full-sized model of her, built for Expo 67.

and had a one-to-four or one-to five ratio of beam to length as compared with one-to-three for the *nef*, the standard three-masted ship. The French employed them extensively for coastal voyages and Grand Bank fishing. Cartier agreed with what Columbus learned from *Niña*, that a small, handy ship is the most suitable for coastal exploration and equally capable of crossing the ocean. Henceforth we shall find no fleet for northern discovery complete without one.

The only models I have seen of *L'Émerillon* are inaccurate, but Commandant Denoix of the French navy, the leading authority on French ships of the sixteenth century, designed a full-sized one of *La Grande Hermine* for the Montreal exposition of 1967 which, in my opinion, is correct. There are cabins for officers and gentlemen volunteers in the sterncastle. Petty officers bedded down in the forecastle, and the men shared the 'tween decks (headroom four feet or less) with the cooking arrangements, and even some of the smaller cattle and poultry. However, most of them were Bretons who lived in one-room, dirt-floor *chaumières* with a cow or goat, so they probably didn't mind.

About two-thirds of the 112 names on the *rôle d'équipage* indicate that Cartier had a home-town crew. No fewer than twelve were his relatives. Captain Jalobert of *La Petite Hermine* was the son of Catherine Cartier's sister, and the masters of the other two were her nephews or cousins. There were seven carpenters—very necessary for repairing hull and gear; a barber who doubled as surgeon, an apothecary, corresponding to our modern pharmacist's mate, and a trumpeter. The last was a required rating on sea-going vessels for at least two hundred years. With a "noise of trumpets" passing ships were hailed, boats recalled, the men summoned to general quarters, or the watch changed. And there is evidence in the *Brief recit* that other musical instruments were shipped, and an informal orchestra organized to amuse both sailors and natives. The rest of the crews, whose names do not appear on the list, were probably gromets, or ship's boys, the lowest rating in European merchant marines.

Two men on the crew list were entitled "Dom," and mass was said on board; but, as on the first voyage, this may have been a *messe blanche*, and it seems significant that Cartier refused baptism to the Huron chief Donnaconna on the ground that he had nobody competent to do it, and that he directed divine service himself. These *doms* were probably bachelors of arts, who, like Portuguese kings, were so entitled in that century.

The objects of this voyage, as stated in Cartier's commission and in a royal order to pay him 3000 livres tournois, were *descouvrir outtre les Terres Neufves* (explore beyond Newfoundland) *pour aller descouvrir certaines terres longtaines* (to discover certain far-away countries). There was to be no fooling around with straits north of the Labrador, or with isthmuses reported by Verrazzano. Neither missionary efforts nor gold nor precious stones are mentioned; but every discoverer expected to play apostle to the Indians, and to find quantities of gold, silver, and gems. Apparently the two Huron boys had not told anyone in France about the marvelous Kingdom of Saguenay, which Cartier hoped to be the first to exploit.

On Whitsunday, 16 May 1535, the Captain and every crew member confessed and received holy communion in the cathedral of Saint-Malo, and the bishop blessed all hands, and their ships and mission.

Retracing First Voyage

We are fortunate to know about this voyage from Cartier's own *Brief recit*, printed at Paris in 1545.

The "second voyage made by wish and command of the Most Christian King of France, François-premier, for the achievement of discovery of western lands parallel to the territories of the said prince," began on 19 May 1535, with a moon two days past full. That being the time of Cabot's departure in 1497, Cartier should have enjoyed a prosperous crossing. Up to a point he did; but on 26 May, foul weather and contrary winds set in, tossing them about for a full month; and on 25 June each of the three ships lost sight of the other two. After fifty days at sea, the flagship sighted Funk Island on 7 July. It made an excellent landfall in the fog; screaming sea-fowl (as I have observed in the Bay of Fundy) are as good as a modern diaphone to warn mariners of their approach to land. The men gathered two boatloads of great auk here, as Breton sailors relished their meat.

Without calling at any Newfoundland harbor, the Captain shaped a course for Blanc Sablon, arriving 15 July, again under a full moon. Eleven more days elapsed before the two smaller ships turned up. Necessary repairs and loading wood and water took three days more, so it was not until 29 July at break of day that the voyage of exploration really began.

The three vessels romped up the Strait of Belle Isle with an east wind, and were not much bothered by icebergs. Unless the Indians had thrown it down, Cartier had the gratification of seeing the cross he had erected on the little island "round as an oven," but he did not tarry. After two or three days, sailing right through the luminous nights, they reached "two islands further off shore than the others, which we named *les ysles sainct Guillaume*." It was the feast of St. William, bishop of Brieux. Cartier's description fits Great Mecatina Island and several offshore islets which stand out conspicuously from the mainland. Whittier, in "The Fisherman," writes:

> Hurrah! for Meccatina
> And its mountains bare and brown!

We found no cheer in this high, gray granite island, with its sparse vegetation; nor did Cartier.

Cormorant Rocks and Cape Whittle.

Mont-Saint-Pierre, Gaspé Peninsula, Notre Dame range in distance.

The westward voyage continued at a good pace; Cartier well described the coast as "bordered by islands, all cut-up and rocky, with no good land or wood, save in a few valleys." Islands which he named in passing *ysles saincte Martre*, after St. Martha whose feast was on 29 July; must certainly have been the Harrington Islands. Centuries before they acquired that English name they were called, in Alfonce's *La Cosmographie* (1544), *les isles de la Demoiselle*, obviously in memory of Marguerite de La Roque, whom Roberval marooned there in the summer of 1542 (see Chapter VIII). Next came *Les ysles sainct Germain*, the Cormorant Rocks off Cape Whittle, named on 30 July after Saint-German l'Auxerrois, since it was the vigil of his feast. Others, such as the St. Mary group, Cartier noted but did not name. The islands here are so numerous, and so confusing even with a modern chart in hand, that it is a wonder that none of the Captain's three ships struck; but he had the benefit of a waxing moon.

After spending a night hove-to off Cape Whittle, the fleet resumed course west by south on the last day of July. The land became low and fair, covered with tall spruce trees, in sharp contrast to the "land of Cain" to the eastward; but there is no such contrast today. Recognizing Cape Thiennot, named on his previous voyage after a French fisherman, and with clear weather and a fair wind, Cartier ventured to sail westward all night. He then turned for shelter to a "neat little harbor" which he named *Saint-Nicolas;* the date, 7 August, was correct for a local St. Nicholas of Brittany. With the Captain's accurate description, Lewis has identified it as Mascanin Bay. Cartier raised "a big wooden cross" on the nearest island as a landmark to help other vessels enter. "One must bring this cross bearing northeast, then head for it and leave it on the starboard hand; and, avoiding the shoals, anchor in the said harbor in four fathom." At Saint-Nicolas he tarried until Sunday, 8 August.

With a waxing moon, Cartier crossed the channel to Cap Rabast on Anticosti, which again he found to be harborless and unattractive. He then returned to the mainland and entered a harbor well protected by two islands (Sainte-Geneviève and Hunting), which he named *La baye sainct Laurins*. The day, 10 August, was the feast of St. Lawrence, the Roman martyr who was grilled alive. Here is the first appearance of the name which Cartier's successors applied to the great gulf, to the mighty river that he discovered, and to the mountain range northward. Never, since the Roman empire, have two local names received such a vast extension as Canada and St. Lawrence.

On 13 August, the day of full moon, Cartier again crossed obliquely the strait that he had named Saint-Pierre (now renamed after him), and doubled West Point, Anticosti. Now recognizing it to be an island, and on the vigil of "Our Lady's Day of August," he named it *L'Isle de l'Assomption*. He then turned southwest across Gaspé Passage to the mainland, which he called by its Huron name, *Honguedo*. His aiming point must have been the highest peak (altitude 4160 feet) of the range now officially called Monts Jacques Cartier; he named these "marvellously high mountains" *Les Monts Notre Dame*. For some twenty miles he sailed along that beautiful coast where every few miles a fertile river valley bursts through the mountain chain to the shore, and on 17 August turned north, having sighted mountains on the Quebec shore. Upon arriving at the Bay of Seven Islands, Cartier consulted his two captive savages, who well knew the country from there to Quebec. They informed him that "this was the beginning of the Saguenay and inhabited country, and that thence came the red copper that they called *caignetdaze*," an Iroquoian name for any metal other than gold. And the great river they had just crossed where it is sixty miles wide, was "the great river of Hochelaga and *chemyn de Canada*."

Thus, almost inadvertently, Canada entered the stream of history.

Le Chemyn de Canada

The *Brief recit* reflects Cartier's excitement over being at the gates of the fabulous Kingdom of Saguenay, which the two Huron boys were already building to the status of a northern Peru. As they further asserted, he was at the mouth of "the grand river of Hochelaga . . . which, always narrowing, leads to Canada, where one finds fresh water in the said river, which comes from such a distance that no man has been to the end, so far as they had heard say; and no other passage was there except for boats."

Unwilling as yet to trust the young savages, Cartier insisted on sailing eastward along the coast between Seven Islands and Saint-Laurent to make certain that the way to Saguenay and Canada did not lie there. This took him four days, 18–21 August, with the moon waning to last quarter. All they saw were the barren Mingan Islands and the Moisie

(PROVINCE OF QUÉBEC)

66   64   62   60

2

(Moisie R.)

18-21 Aug. 1535

B. St. Laurins
10 Aug. 1535

St. Nicolas
(Mascanin Bay)
7 Aug. 1535

C. Thiennot

(C. Whittle)

0   Baie des Sept Isles

(Mingan Is.)

(Hunting I.)

Détroit de St. Pierre

Natashquan Pt.)

Is. St. Germain
(Cormorant Rks.)

(West Pt.)   C. Rabast

× Cartier
turned back
2 Aug. 1534

(R. St. Lawrence)

I. DE L'ASSOMPTION
(ANTICOSTI I.)

C. de Montmorency
(Table Head)

Mont St. Pierre
14 Aug. 1535

(Salt Lake Bay)

C. St. Louis
(East Cape)

HONGUEDO
(GASPÉ PENINSULA)

(South Pt.)

Gaspé Hbr. and Bay
16-25 July 1534

Gulf of St. Lawrence

(C. Gaspé)
15 July 1534

C. Pratto
(White Hd.)

(Percé)
(I. Bonaventure)

Conche St. Martin
(Port Daniel)

(Tracadigash Pt.)
10 July 1534

Paspébiac Pt.
6 July 1534

I. de Margaulx
(Bird Rocks)

Ile de Bryon
1 June 1536

8

Baie de Chaleur

C. Espérance
(Miscou I.)

Cap du Dauphin

(MAGDALEN I.)
(Grindstone I.)

B. St. Lunaire (Miramichi Bay)
2 July 1534

Allezay
(Deadman I.)

C. St. Pierre

(St. Paul I.)

C. des Sauvages
(North Pt.)

C. de Lorraine
(C. St. Lawrence)

C. St. Paul
(C. North)

(Richibucto Hd.)

Cap d'Orleans (Kildare)

R. des Barraques
(Malpecque B.)

(Ingonish)

(Egmont Bay)

(Scutari I.)

46

(PRINCE EDWARD I.)

(CAPE BRETON)

(Northumberland Strait)

(C. Breton)

(Bay of Fundy)

(NOVA SCOTIA)

66   64   62   60

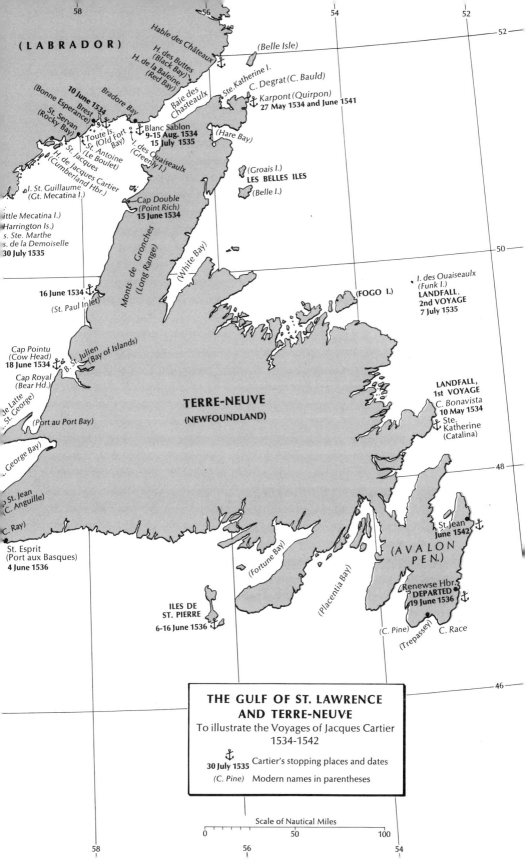

THE GULF OF ST. LAWRENCE
AND TERRE-NEUVE
To illustrate the Voyages of Jacques Cartier
1534-1542

⚓ 30 July 1535   Cartier's stopping places and dates

(C. Pine)   Modern names in parentheses

Scale of Nautical Miles

0 ——— 50 ——— 100

Entrance to Bay of Seven Islands.

The Moisie River. Cartier thought this might be the strait to China.

River, up which they made a boat trip to make sure that it was not *le chemyn de Canada*. This beautiful river, flowing like a miniature Saguenay between high, wooded, rocky banks, with frequent rapids where you may see bears fishing for salmon, was not named by Cartier. At the entrance his boat party marveled over the walruses, which they described as "fish with the shape of horses, which spend the night ashore and the day in the sea." "And as soon as we were convinced that we had ranged the entire coast," wrote Cartier, "and that there was no passage [to China,] we returned to our ships which were at the said *Sept Isles* where there are good anchorages in 18 and 20 fathom, sandy bottom."

Indeed there are. The modern chart agrees; one can almost see the spots where the two *Hermines* and *L'Émerillon* dropped their hooks. Sept Iles is now humming with activity, since it has become the shipping point for iron ore which comes by railway from the mines of Knob Lake, 350 miles to the northward. Six, not seven, high and wooded islands protect this bay from the sea, but Cartier's name, Seven Islands, has stuck. In the nineteenth century it became a famous rendezvous for fishermen, and the title of a romantic poem by Whittier. The Yankee skipper of fishing schooner *Breeze* falls in love with one of the twin daughters of a French Canadian family on the Bay. Her parents forbid the match; but the night before *Breeze* sails the skipper finds the girl, as he thinks, on board. She turns out to be the other twin and such a termagant that on his next summer's visit the skipper hopes to "turn her in," as it were, for the girl he loves. But she, alas, had died of a broken heart.

This site of blighted love lies many miles beyond Cartier's furthest western stop on his first voyage; and, although it was now later in the year than that day in 1534 when he decided to go home, he had no intention of turning back.

The Captain, concluding that his Huron passengers were speaking the truth, decided to continue up the main stream, which he calls the *La Grande Rivière* or *La Rivière de Hochelaga*. On 24 August, states the *Brief recit*, "we made sail and stood along the coast." They passed Egg Island off Pointe-aux-Anglais—a name commemorating the worst shipwreck in Canadian history, that of eight out of fifty-five ships in the invading fleet of Admiral Sir Hovenden Walker in 1711; almost nine hundred men were drowned. The Coast Pilot still warns ships of the foul ground between here and Pointe des Monts, and the modern chart calls

The Bic Islands, Cartier's *Iles St. Jean.*

Old Bic Harbor.

the reach between that point and Cap Chat on the Gaspé shore the most dangerous part of the lower river for sailing vessels. Here tides from the Gulf meet the river current, and a two-knot or more set during the flood runs due south cross-river, tending to throw ships onto the Gaspé shore. "Vessels inward bound should not attempt to take advantage of westward currents sometimes found close inshore with rising tide," warns the modern chart. Domagaya and Taignoagny, their navigational experience limited to the birch-bark canoe, may have tried to persuade their captain to do just that, but Cartier refused to take the risk. He probably anchored east of Pointe des Monts in sixteen fathom until the current or the wind turned. The middle of the river here, and for many miles upstream, is two hundred fathom deep. He passed and described, but did not name, the Manikuagan River which flows into the St. Lawrence between two headlands, one high and the other low, and fringed by dangerous shoals.

On 29 August, the day after new moon, the three ships anchored behind "three flat islands, which stand right out in the stream." These Bic Islands—Bic, Bicquette, and what is now a mere reef—Cartier named *Ysleaux sainct Jehan* because it was 29 August, "the day of the decapitation of the said saint"—John the Baptist. That name did not stick—there were already too many St. John capes, islands, and bays. The Captain's statement that his chosen harbor dries out on the ebb, that the rise and fall of tide is two fathom, and that the best anchorage is "to the south of an islet, near another islet," well fits Old Bic Harbor. He also observed Barnaby Island, six miles eastward, so long and narrow that it looks like a breakwater. Next day they reached the mouth of the Saguenay.

In Parkman's vivid prose, "To ascend this great river, and tempt the hazards of its intricate navigation with no better pilots than the two young Indians . . . was a venture of no light risk. But skill or fortune prevailed; and, on the first of September the voyagers reached in safety the gorge of the gloomy Saguenay with its towering cliffs and sullen depth of waters." Cartier called it "a very deep and rapid river, which is the . . . *chemyn du royaume et terre du Saguenay*, as our men of Canada have told us." Off its mouth lies a very dangerous part of the St. Lawrence, with a sandbank in midstream, tide-rips, currents up to seven knots, and a narrow entrance between shoals. But the fleet weathered it safely and anchored off the site of Tadoussac. Here, four

Mouth of the Saguenay, Tadoussac, Red Island and reefs.

The Saguenay, a few miles above Tadoussac.

canoes of Hurons on a fishing party "from Canada" (Quebec) were so frightened by the sight of the ships that only one came near enough to be hailed by Domagaya, who named and identified himself, and persuaded them to board. "This river," noted Cartier, "flows between high mountains of bare rock, which nevertheless support a vast quantity of trees of various kinds, which grow on said bare rock as if on good soil; we saw a tree suitable for masting a ship of 30 tuns, and as green as it could be, growing out of a rock without a trace of earth." Spruce trees apparently growing out of solid rock are a common sight along the shores of Maine and the Maritime Provinces; it is odd that Cartier had not noticed one before. The tree actually seeds itself in a small accumulation of dead needles, but can only survive by thrusting a root into a crevice leading to water and better nourishment.

On 2 September, leaving the Saguenay for future exploration, Cartier got his three vessels under way "pour faire le chemin vers Canada." The tide was running swift over Red Islet Bank, with (he correctly noted) "a depth of only two or three fathom" and a bottom of boulders as big as hogsheads; *L'Émerillon* was only saved from grounding by the other ships' sending boats to tow her clear.

Five leagues up-river the fleet reached a long island in midstream (on their return named *Ile aux Lièvres*, Hare Island) and the Captain decided to anchor there to await flood tide. Steamships are still advised so to do if they wish to avoid wasting fuel bucking the current. Cartier notes that his fleet tried sailing upstream, made no progress, and, finding no bottom at 120 fathom a bowshot from shore, returned to Hare Island "where we anchored in 35 fathom with fine holding ground." One can see that spot on the modern chart, a mile or two west of Hare Passage. Cartier's ships must have carried cables at least a hundred fathom long to anchor in so great a depth. The business of getting in that length of sodden hemp rope, several inches in diameter, must have been the most back-breaking of all tasks for the mariners.

Upon leaving this Hare Island anchorage on 3 September, Cartier was too busy admiring a school of beluga, or white whale "with head like a greyhound," to notice Murray Bay and Pointe au Pic. The beluga is still caught in those waters, largely for its edible inner skin, which is marketed under the Eskimo name, muktuk. Not until the 6th could the fleet make *L'Ile aux Coudres*, so named by Cartier because his men found there a grove of trees bearing hazel nuts "bigger and of better

Hare Island, Cartier's *Ile aux Lièvres*.

Baie de Saint-Paul.

Cartier's anchorage off *Ile d'Orléans* or *de Bacchus*.

228

flavor than ours" in France. They anchored between the island and the mouth of Baie Saint-Paul; saw an "inestimable number" of snapping turtles and more beluga. The currents, up to five knots on the modern chart, reminded him of the Gironde at Bordeaux.

On 7 September, "jour Nostre-Dame," says the *Brief recit* (it was the vigil of her birthday), "after hearing mass, we left the said isle to go up the said river, and we came to fourteen islands." This archipelago begins with Goose Island and extends to Madame Island; there are more than fourteen if you count the islets. These "mark the beginning of the land and province of Canada."

They did indeed. Cartier had really arrived.

Stadaconé—Quebec

After a hard pull upstream, all ships manning their sweeps, they anchored the same day between the north shore and "a great island," where were camped a great number of natives engaged in fishing. Cartier landed with a large company, including his Huron guides, who convinced their fellow tribesmen, after an initial panic, that the Frenchmen were not to be feared. These jolly Hurons "made good cheer, dancing and making several 'talks'; and some of the chief men came to see our boats, bringing us a heap of eels and other fish, with two or three loads of maize, the bread that they live on here, and several big melons." This delegation bearing gifts was followed by another of both sexes. They were "well received" by Cartier, who regaled them with "what he had" and gave them little gifts of slight value, "with which they were well content." Cartier found the island richly wooded, with such masses of wild grapevines clinging to the trees that he named it *Ile de Bacchus*. Thinking perhaps that this would not go well at home, he renamed it *Ile d'Orléans*, after Charles, duc d'Orléans, son of François-premier.

Next day, 8 September, "The seigneur of Canada, named Donnaconna, whose title was Agouhanna," came on board *La Grande Hermine* with a suite of sixteen warriors, in twelve canoes. After talking with his two sons, whom he had not seen for over a year, and learning of the good usage they had received in France, Donnaconna asked Cartier to extend his bare arms to be kissed and wrapped around his neck "which is their way of greeting in that country." The English called this "colling." As soon as he had performed the ceremony (not too pleasant, as the Indians were well greased), Cartier treated the delegation to bread and wine, "with which they were much pleased." He then manned his ships' boats to explore upstream with the flood tide and find a good harbor. After passing the mouth of the Montmorency River—without noting the waterfall—there burst on them a magnificent view—again, no comment. A high scarped promontory thrust between the Great River and its tributary the St. Charles; and at its foot nestled a dirty, squalid native village called Stadaconé. This promontory was the great Rock of Quebec, now fraught with historic memories—Samuel de Champlain, Bishop Laval and Count Frontenac, Montcalm and Wolfe, the death of General Montgomery, Sir Wilfrid Laurier, Mackenzie King, and the Quebec Conference which gave the signals for victory in September 1944. For Cartier, however, a good anchorage was the only subject of immediate interest; and, exploring in *Grande Hermine*'s longboat, he found "at a forking of the waters, fair and pleasant, where there is a little river [the St. Charles] which he named *Sainte-Croix*, and a harbor with a bar and two or three fathom, which we found suitable for placing our ships in safety." Upon his return the people of Stadaconé flocked to the waterside, a leading man gave a "preachment"—a typical Indian talk, while the women danced and sang, standing in water up to their knees. Cartier distributed a few trinkets; and, as his men rowed him back to the flagship downstream, they could hear the people singing miles away. This was indeed the golden age of race relations in North America.

With a good eye to geography, Cartier realized that Stadaconé was the focal point of the Great River. On 14 September he brought all three ships up from Ile d'Orléans, preceded by Donnaconna, and twenty-five canoe-loads of subjects. Two days later he warped *Grande* and *Petite Hermine* into the fork of the two rivers, anchoring at spots which he had sounded and buoyed, and where they would ground out at low water. *L'Émerillon*, the little pinnace, he anchored in the roadstead right under the Rock of Quebec, ready to take him upstream. As soon as the *Hermines* were moored, canoes full of Indians swarmed about them, and Donnaconna with his two boys and members of his council boarded.

Domagaya and Taignoagny, who had promised to pilot the French up-river to Hochelaga, now began to sulk and stall, and Cartier soon

found out what ailed them. Their father did not wish Cartier to go to
Hochelaga. The chief there, also a Huron, claimed dominion over
Donnaconna, who did not relish the relationship; but their respective
positions would be reversed if the chief of Stadaconé could gain such
powerful allies as the French, with their ships, firearms, and iron tools.
He feared that if Cartier reached Hochelaga he would be persuaded by
the chief there to be his ally, not Donnaconna's. Taignoagny told
Cartier that his father was displeased with the projected visit to Hochelaga and would not let him serve as pilot; the Captain answered that he
was determined to push on, and would make it worth while for the lad
to accompany him. But he failed to move him.

Donnaconna now tried another tack. Inviting Cartier ashore, he
made a speech and then presented the Captain with his niece, a little
girl of ten or twelve years, and two younger boys, one his own son.
Taignoagny explained that these were a gift to dissuade him from going to Hochelaga. Cartier answered that, in that case, he would have to
return them. Domagaya then took up the dialogue, declared that
Donnaconna made these gifts out of pure affection and that he, Domagaya, would pilot the pinnace. Two swords and two brass wash basins
were then presented to the chief, at whose request a salute of twelve
guns was fired from the flagship. Consternation among the natives!
"They howled and yelled so loud you would have thought that hell
had broken loose," says the *Brief recit*.

Next day, 18 September, with the moon at last quarter, Donnaconna
emptied his bag of tricks. Three medicine men dressed as devils—
blackened faces, long horns, and dogskin pelts—paddled out and
around the flagship, one making a harangue. Presently Taignoagny
and Domagaya came on board crying *Jesus! Maria! Jacques Cartier!*
and explained that their god, *Cudouagny* by name, was warning the
Frenchmen by means of these black-faced actors that there would be
so much ice and snow up-river that they would all perish. Cartier and
his men laughed them off and said that their priests had consulted
Jesus, who predicted fair weather! Donnaconna then affected to regard
the whole thing as a joke, and the day ended pleasantly with more
dancing, singing, and shouting of *Ho! Ho! Ho!* Cartier decided that
the two boys were a choice pair of rogues who would probably try
to run him aground if taken as pilots, and that he would dispense with
their services.

MER DES ETILLES:

TROPIQVE DE CANCER:

LA MER OCCEANE:

MER DESPAIGNE:

MER DE FRANCE:

CANADA

ISLAND

QVE: LA TERRE DV LABOVREVR.

orth America in the Desceliers Mappemonde of 1546. The top is south; e bottom, north. Photo of original in John Rylands Library, Manchester, England. Courtesy, Map Division, Public Archives of Canada.

Everything was fair at this season around the Rock of Quebec. Cartier admired the trees, the cornfields, the wild grapes; and he might well have called it a day and gone into winter quarters. Ambition, curiosity, and a sense of duty to his king forced him on.

Hochelaga

So, on 19 September 1535, *L'Émerillon* made sail and started upstream with the flood tide and a last-quarter moon, towing the two longboats of the bigger ships. Cartier and several gentlemen volunteers were on board, together with Captain Jalobert of *La Petite Hermine*, who came to help Le Breton and Maingard. They did a very good job getting the pinnace upstream and down without mishap, for this was the most difficult part of the entire voyage. Fortunately, the river was nearing its annual low, which meant that the currents were at least strength; but, even so, there must have been many times when the crew of the pinnace had to man their sweeps to make progress or keep her from grounding.

Passing between wooded shores festooned with wild grape, and encampments of friendly Indians who approached to trade; and hearing the song of the blackbird, the thrush, and (as they imagined) the nightingale, the expedition in one day proceeded about thirty-two miles, to a place the Indians called *Achelacy*. This has been identified as the modern Notre-Dame de Pontneuf. Here a local chief came on board, warned them against the rapids ahead, and presented Cartier with another little girl, eight or nine years old. There is no blinking the fact that these Indians, like primitive tribes in other parts of the world, considered the gift of a fresh young virgin to be a compliment to a distinguished visitor, and that Cartier accepted them as such. The little girl previously presented by Donnaconna ran away, complaining that she had been abused by the ship's boys when their captain was absent. Captured and returned, she was taken to France, where she and all but one of the other Indian children died.

It took the pinnace nine days to get seventy-three miles up the great river, "without losing a day or an hour," states the *Brief recit*. First, and without benefit of pilot, she had to get through the Richelieu Rapids, where the ebb current runs 5½ knots in a channel less than a quarter-mile wide, between *battures*, banks of boulder-covered shale, bare at low water. After these rapids came five channels, even narrower, but with less swift currents. Cartier must have anchored during the ebb, sent his boats ahead to sound, and proceeded during the flood. It became a little easier after passing the site of Trois Rivières at the mouth of the St. Maurice. On 28 September (having made an average of only 8.2 miles a day), the pinnace arrived at the outlet of Lac Saint-Pierre, a widening of the river twenty miles long. This lake is very shoal; *L'Émerillon*'s leadsmen found no depth greater than two fathom.

After more or less feeling their way across Lac Saint-Pierre, the Frenchmen were puzzled how to get on, for the St. Lawrence flows into this lake by five different channels separated by islands. Anchoring the pinnace, Cartier explored the islands with his boats, incidentally encountering a friendly group of five savages. One of them, when the boat grounded, picked up the Captain in his arms and carried him ashore "as if he had been a six-year-old child." These natives were hunting muskrat, of which they had accumulated a great number, and gave Cartier all he and his men wanted to eat; the French found them good. The Indians also indicated which channel to follow to Hochelaga, and said it would be a three-day journey. It took Cartier exactly that; the distance is sixty-five nautical miles.

The Captain wisely decided to leave *L'Émerillon* moored at the west end of Lac Saint-Pierre, and to proceed upstream in the longboats. He provisioned them with as many dry and liquid stores as they could hold, and, accompanied by masters Le Breton and Jalobert, four gentlemen volunteers,* and twenty-eight sailors to do the work, set forth on 29 September, with the new moon two days old. The longboats, each manned by seven oarsmen (three to each side and a coxswain), pushed along in perfect weather, trading knives and other trifles for fish, with the natives encountered en route.

On 2 October the boats arrived before Hochelaga, the present Montreal. This was a more impressive place than Stadaconé, Quebec. More than a thousand natives came to the edge of the river to greet the

---

* These four, who deserve mention as members of the first European party to reach Montreal, were Claude du Pontbriand, *eschanson* (cupbearer) to the dauphin; Charles de La Pommeraye, nephew to a canon of the cathedral of Saint-Malo; Jean Guyon, seigneur de Thaumetz; and Jean Poullet of Dol, who probably edited for publication the *Brief recit*. It is a curious coincidence that Pontbriand's father was seigneur de Montréal (Gers), a little place just east of the Landes, as well as governor of the château de Bergerac, Cyrano's home.

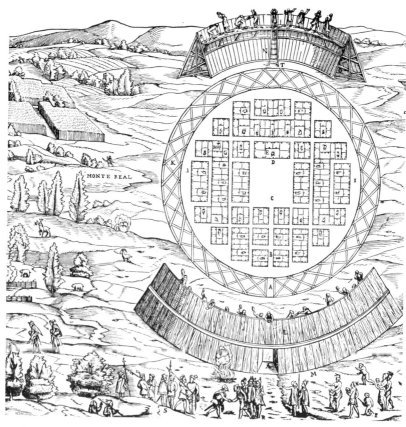

Ramusio's plan of Hochelaga. Courtesy Harvard College Library.

Ramusio's key, translated, is as follows:
A Gate to City of Hochelaga
B Principal street, which goes to the Plaza
C The plaza
D House of the king Agouhana
E Courtyard of said royal house, and his fire
F One of the ten streets of the City
G One of the private houses
H Courtyard with fire, where the kitchen is
I Space between the houses and the City, where one can go around it
K The palisade, made of boards around the City in lieu of wall
L Palisades outside the City
M Space outside the city circuit (Cartier greeting the Agouhana)
N Palisade behind the city circuit
O, P Gallery where men stand to defend the City
Q Space between one palisade and the other
R Indian men, women and children outside the City to see the Frenchmen

S Frenchmen who enter the City, and who take the hands of the Indians who
   come outside the City to see and caress them.
T Ladder to the platform

The main thing wrong with this picture is the boards; they should have
been logs and poles with the bark on, erected vertically. This way of constructing a fort was universal among the Iroquois tribes.

Frenchmen. They bore gifts, especially corn bread, of which "They
threw so much into the boats that it seemed to fall from the air."
When Cartier and his chosen companions landed, the people crowded
in and the women brought their children for him to touch. This spot
may confidently be identified as the beginning of the Sainte-Marie
sault, which runs five knots on the ebb. Opposite is L'Ile Saint-Hélène,
site of the famous Expo 67, and the river is now crossed at that point
by a bridge named for Jacques Cartier. All night these Hurons "remained on the river bank, keeping fires burning, dancing, and calling
out *aguyase*, which is their term for a joyful welcome."

Between a conspicuous hill and the river were well cultivated cornfields and a wooden citadel such as Eastern Indians generally built for
defense. The Hurons who dwelt here, and the name of whose
Agouhana (chief) we do not know, were in a far more vulnerable position than Donnaconna's subjects, being situated on one of the favorite
warpaths of the Five Nations. The picture-plan of Hochelaga, which
we owe to Ramusio's curiosity, must have been based on a sketch or
description brought home by Cartier, whose *Brief recit* agrees with it
perfectly. Hochelaga citadel was situated some three miles from the
river bank, partly on the present grounds of McGill University, but
mostly southeast of them.

On Sunday, 3 October, Cartier donned his dress cloak and, with his
gentlemen and twenty sailors armed with pikes, marched through a
beautiful oak grove to a point where he was greeted by a head man and
several Indians. They passed open fields where maize was ripening,
and reached the citadel, overshadowed by a hill which the Captain
named *Mont Royal*. This eventually became *Montréal*. His description,
which Ramusio's picture follows closely, states that the town was protected, not only by a wooden wall but by two redoubts, "garnished with

rocks and stones, for defense and protection." Inside the wall the town contained some fifty bark and wood dwellings, each with several rooms, an open fireplace in the middle, and lofts where braided sheaves of corn were hung for winter provision. He even gives us a recipe for the corn bread with which the French were showered on arrival: the maize is brayed in a mortar, mixed with water into dough, and separated into cakes which are cooked on a hot stone and covered with hot pebbles. They also smoked fish and eels for winter use. The Frenchmen disliked the Huron food, not because of the dirt but for absence of salt. Cartier describes their most precious possession as *esnoguy*, or white wampum, beads made from shells of river clams, which they used as currency. These clams were obtained by planting in the river the dead bodies of criminals or enemies, with buttocks and thighs cut. The clams worked into these incisions and were pulled off when the bodies were withdrawn.

The Frenchmen were conducted into the central plaza, where the women flocked around to touch and stroke them. A bark mat was brought in for the guests to sit on, and the "chief lord of the country, whom they call in their language *Agouhana*" was carried in by ten braves on a deerskin litter. A partly paralyzed man of about fifty years of age, his rank was displayed by a red headband of porcupine quills. This he presented to Cartier after the Captain had obliged by rubbing the royal arms and legs. Numerous blind and crippled Indians then came to be touched; "One would think that God had come down there to cure them!" wrote Cartier. He read the opening words of the Gospel according to St. John—*In principio erat verbum*—making the sign of the cross "and prayed God to give them knowledge of our holy faith and of the passion of Our Lord." He capped this by reading the gospel account of the passion in John xviii and xix. It is difficult to imagine what the Hurons got out of this, but at least they were impressed; and after the Captain had distributed gifts and let the children scramble for handfuls of pewter rings and little tin representations of *agnus Dei*, they evinced "a marvellous joy." Finally, Cartier caused his trumpets and other musical instruments to sound off, which put the people in ecstasies.

Now the Captain and his party climbed to the top of Mont Royal, where they were rewarded by a magnificent view—the Laurentians on the north, outspurs of the Green Mountains and the Adirondacks to the south, and the Great River flowing through the picture from west to east like a long band of silver. To his dismay, Cartier saw, just above the point where he had left the boats, a series of rapids which no boat bigger than a canoe could pass. These were the Lachine rapids around which Canada eventually built a canal. In the *Brief recit* he simply calls them "a *sault* of water, the most impetuous one could possibly see." Tradition states that Cartier named these sardonically *La Chine*, as the nearest he was able to get to China; but they were so named by Robert Cavelier de La Salle, who had a seigneurie there in the next century, and the sarcasm is his.

Before leaving the site of Montreal, Cartier acquired from the local Indians a second installment of what we may call the Saguenay dream. After a canoe journey up the Great River, one would reach another river flowing from the west—the Ottawa, obviously. This waters the Kingdom of Saguenay, inhabited by "bad people" armed to the teeth, armored in wood, tough fighters; but a country rich in precious metals. That concept the Hochelaga Indians conveyed by touching Cartier's silver whistle chain and a sailor's gilt dagger handle, pointing northwesterly and crying *Saguenay! Saguenay!* The Hurons, like Verrazzano's Wampanoags, wore copper ornaments, and when Cartier asked if these too were products of Saguenay they answered truthfully, "No," and pointed west to the Hiawathan "Land of Gitche Gumee" —Lake Superior.

After this excursion the Frenchmen returned to their boats, some being carried piggyback by obliging natives, as shown in Ramusio's picture of Hochelaga. Cartier had sailed or rowed almost a thousand miles from the open ocean; enough for one voyage.

The current being favorable, and the moon waxing daily, they took off at once in their boats and reached their pinnace in Lac Saint-Pierre on 4 October. Next day they made sail in *L'Émerillon* and started downstream for "the province of Canada," explored the lower reaches of the St. Maurice, one of the Three Rivers which give that town its name. On Monday 11 October, the day of full moon, the pinnace joined her consorts at "the port of Sainte-Croix," the mouth of the St. Charles, at Quebec.

Here the sailors of the two *Hermines* had built a fort on the shore, close to where they lay, constructed of vertical logs and mounted with ships' guns so as to cover all possible approaches. Donnaconna, evi-

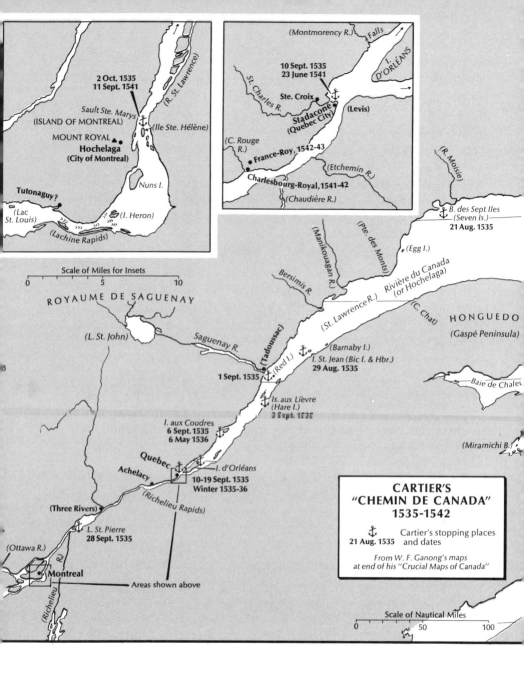

2 Oct. 1535
11 Sept. 1541

Sault Ste. Marys
(ISLAND OF MONTREAL)
(Ile Ste. Hélène)

MOUNT ROYAL ▲▲ ●
Hochelaga
(City of Montreal)

(R. St. Lawrence)

Nuns I.

Tutonaguy?

(Lac
St. Louis)
(I. Heron)

(Lachine Rapids)

(Montmorency R.) Falls

I. D'ORLÉANS

10 Sept. 1535
23 June 1541

St. Charles R.

Ste. Croix

Stadacone (Levis)
(Quebec City)

(C. Rouge
R.)
● **France-Roy, 1542-43**

(Etchemin R.)

Charlesbourg-Royal, 1541-42

(Chaudière R.)

Scale of Miles for Insets
0   5   10

(R. Moisie)

ROYAUME DE SAGUENAY

(Manikouagan R.)

Bersimis R.

(pte. des Monts)

Rivière du Canada
(or Hochelaga)

⚓ B. des Sept Iles
(Seven Is.)
21 Aug. 1535

● (Egg I.)

(St. Lawrence R.)

(C. Chat)

HONGUEDO

(Gaspé Peninsula)

(L. St. John)

Saguenay R.

(Tadoussac)

(Red I.) ⚓
● (Barnaby I.)
I. St. Jean (Bic I. & Hbr.)
29 Aug. 1535

1 Sept. 1535

Baie de Chaleu

⚓ Is. aux Lièvre
(Hare I.)
3 Sept. 1535

I. aux Coudres
6 Sept. 1535
6 May 1536

(Miramichi B.)

Quebec
Achelacy
I. d'Orléans
10-19 Sept. 1535
Winter 1535-36

(Three Rivers) ●

(Richelieu Rapids)

L. St. Pierre
28 Sept. 1535

(Ottawa R.)

● **Montreal**

Areas shown above

CARTIER'S
"CHEMIN DE CANADA"
1535-1542

⚓
21 Aug. 1535   Cartier's stopping places
and dates

*From W. F. Ganong's maps
at end of his "Crucial Maps of Canada"*

Scale of Nautical Miles
0   50   100

240

dently convinced that he had better not try any more funny business, invited Cartier "to visit him the following day at Canada," i.e. Stadaconé. After the usual song-and-dance and presentation of gifts—Cartier must have had barrels of small wares—the chief showed the Captain some scalps of his enemies, whom he called *Toudamans*, which his braves had obtained that summer. This was in revenge for one of his fishing parties in the Gaspé having been ambushed two years before, and all but five out of two hundred people slaughtered. Whether these Toudamans were Micmac, Etchemin, or Seneca is disputed; but it does not much matter since, apart from the Iroquois confederation, every North American Indian tribe was in a perpetual state of war with its neighbors.

First Winter in Canada

Exactly when Cartier decided to spend the winter of 1535–36 in Canada he does not say; but he must have done so before he returned to Stadaconé, for it was then too late to depart. It would have taken him a least another month to reach the open sea, and he did not care to risk a winter passage of the Atlantic. Also, he wished to experience a Canadian winter. And that he did!

It was now October, the fairest season of the year in that northern region. All along the Great River and on every side of Stadaconé the fall foliage was at its height, and the hunter's moon was full. There is nothing more superb in nature than this autumnal pageant in Canada. Yellow birch leaves, brilliant scarlet, gold, and crimson maple, bronze ash and walnut, flash their colors against a background of green conifers, of which alone the larch, or hackmatack, turns its needles to gold before snow falls. During the halcyon days of autumn the colors are reflected in the river; then a line gale strips the leaves from the branches and, when the wind drops, they float on the calm water like a stippled painting. Cartier never mentioned this; but neither (to my knowledge) did any of his successors refer to autumn foliage prior to the romantic eighteenth century. Could the sight of this splendor have been repulsive to men used to the muted colors of the European autumn? One remembers the story of Matthew Arnold's being taken to see fall foliage near Boston and exclaiming, "I say! Are your trees infected with some sort of *disease?*"

Cartier and his men, oblivious to the beauties of nature, prepared for winter, strengthening their fort, bringing in great stacks of firewood, and salting down fish and game. Cartier compiled for his *Brief recit* a sort of gazetteer of the St. Lawrence which must have been very useful to his successors. He included several pages on the manners and customs of his savage hosts, at whose habit of going almost naked in the dead of winter, except for moccasins and leggings, he never failed to marvel. One custom rather shocked him, although it must have pleased his men; nubile girls were placed in a common brothel, where all men of any age could take their pleasure, and no girl could leave until she had hooked a fellow to marry her; but as a Huron could have two or three wives, the girls really had a chance. If they failed to secure a husband, they became community drudges. Cartier wrote that he and his friends visited several of these establishments "and found these houses as full of girls as schoolrooms in France were of boys." The same *maisons de plaisir* served as gambling houses, where the men, using a crude dice game, staked their all, even to their G-strings, and emerged naked as their mothers bore them.

Cartier also made the earliest recorded mention of tobacco in these northern parts. The natives carried in a pouch the sun-dried leaves of a plant that they called *kiyekta*, crumbled them into powder which they crammed into a pipe made of baked clay with a reed stem, lit it with a live coal, and alternately sucked in and blew out great clouds of smoke. "They say it keeps them warm and in good health, and never go abroad without it." The Frenchmen tried a few drags from a lighted pipe but found the smoke too hot to bear, "like powdered pepper."

The most favorable impression of the Gulf and River that Cartier carried away was the vast number and variety of fish, fowl, and game, especially the fish, in which "this river is the most abundant in all varieties that in the memory of man have been seen or heard of." He mentions twelve varieties, as well as seal, walrus, porpoise, and beluga. Canadian economy was long based on fish and fur.

From mid-November 1535 to mid-April 1536 the French fleet lay frozen solid at the mouth of the St. Charles, under the Rock of Quebec. Ice was over two fathom thick in the river, and snow four feet deep ashore. "All our beverages," says the *Brief recit*, "froze in their casks. And on board our ships, below hatches as on deck, lay four fingers' breadth of ice." To add to their discomfort, scurvy broke out, first among the Huron of Stadaconé and then among the French. Considering the plentiful game, fish, fruit, and berries that Cartier boasts about, it seems strange that either race should have been so afflicted; but the symptoms that Cartier relates are unmistakable—teeth falling out, gums rotting, swollen limbs, acute pain. By mid-February, "out of the 110 men that we were, not ten were well enough to help the others, a thing pitiful to see"; in addition, some fifty savages had died. Cartier put on a brave front to conceal his plight from the natives when only three or four of his men were still healthy, making a great noise behind the fort's palisade as if scores of hearty fellows were brawling. Then, "God in His holy grace took pity on us, and sent us knowledge of a remedy." This happened after Cartier had made a vow to go on pilgrimage to Rocomadour, and staged a service of intercession to Our Lady; if she heard, she chose a strange instrument for the cure.

Domagaya, who had suffered a bad case of scurvy, came to the fort for a friendly call, and appeared to be cured. What had healed him? The juice and concoction from a certain tree which he called *annedda*. He sent two women with Cartier to gather it. "They brought back from the forest nine or ten branches and showed us how to grind the bark and boil it in water, then drink the potion every other day and apply the residue as a poultice to swollen and infected legs." The sailors gagged at something new, said they'd rather die than drink that stuff; but a few bold fellows tried it, felt better at once, and after two or three days were completely cured. This miraculous tree, a specimen of the common arborvitae (*Thuja occidentalis*) was pulled to pieces by the Frenchmen, and every leaf and piece of bark consumed in a week by sailors frantic for relief. Even some who had suffered for five or six years from *la vérole* (syphilis) said they were cured of that! Cartier, before he left Stadaconé, dug up some young arborvitae which were successfully transplanted in the royal garden at Fontainebleau. He remarked that if all the doctors of Louvain and Montpellier (the leading medical schools of western Europe) had been there with all the drugs of Alexandria, "They could not have done as much in a year as this tree did in a week." Everyone who took it recovered, leaving the total company at eighty-five men.

After the turn of the year, Donnaconna and some of his pals went off on a hunting expedition on snowshoes and were gone two months. They returned with several score natives whom the French had not seen before, causing Cartier to suspect that the chief was plotting to overwhelm and massacre the French. On the contrary, Donnaconna was bringing in what modern politicians would call "mattress voters" to support him in the forthcoming election! A strong faction of the local Hurons wished to depose him in favor of a brave named Agona; but the temporary voters, from a village called Sitadin on the Beauport shore, were for him. Taignoagny even suggested that Cartier seize candidate Agona and carry him to France. But the Captain, as he admits, had already made up his mind to take Donnaconna to France.

A clever spinner of tall tales, Donnaconna embroidered on the fancied wealth of that mythical Kingdom of Saguenay, which (he said) could be approached either by the Saguenay River or the Ottawa. He had been there himself! It had immense quantities of gold, rubies, and other valuable things; the people were as white as Frenchmen and went clothed in woolens. Cartier did not realize that Indians were not only great liars and story-tellers but yes-men, eager to please. They noticed that the Frenchmen's eyes sparkled and fingers twitched when gold was mentioned, so Donnaconna let Cartier have it. The Captain even swallowed a yarn that his host had been in a land of pygmies who were unipeds (like Thorfinn Karlsevni's alleged murderer), and in another region where the people had no anus, hence subsisted on liquids which they could void as urine.

Donnaconna paid heavily for his fun. Cartier decided to kidnap him so that he could tell François-premier convincingly about the wonders of Saguenay. For this outrage—a violation of his royal instructions— Cartier executed a ruse as carefully planned as a bank robbery. With no sense of inconsistency, he set Holyrood day (3 May), the feast of the Holy Cross, for the treacherous act. After raising a wooden cross with a Latin inscription and the arms of France as an excuse for important tribesmen to attend, a band of well-rehearsed sailors seized and bound the chief, his two sons, and two leading subjects, and whisked them on board ship. The others, alarmed by gunshots, "scampered off like sheep before a wolf, some across the river and some to the forest, each for himself." All night on the river bank they "cried and howled like wolves" for their beloved chief, but Cartier was implacable. In all he carried to France ten natives, including the little girls and boys given to him as gifts. Not one ever returned to Canada.

Donnaconna's subjects were somewhat appeased by the chief showing himself to be alive, and by Cartier's promising to return him in "ten or twelve moons," loaded with gifts after seeing the king. Also he presented the hull of *La Petite Hermine* to the intruders from Sitadin who wanted it to extract the iron. He abandoned her as the least valuable of his fleet, because after the epidemic he had only enough men to handle two vessels; but he saved her sails and other gear for which the natives had no use. After a final exchange of gifts, *La Grande Hermine* and *L'Émerillon* set sail for France on 6 May 1536.

The river was so high and swift as to be dangerous, so Cartier anchored behind Ile aux Coudres until 16 May when the spring floods abated, and he had a new moon. He then anchored off Ile aux Lièvres (Hare Island), so named because his men snared a large number of hares. Next day a strong east wind blew up-river and they had to return to the Ile aux Coudres anchorage. Wind came fair on 21 May, and they sailed downstream through the passage between Anticosti and the Gaspé Peninsula, which had been solid with fog on the first voyage, "passed cap de Pratto, beginning of the Baie de Chaleur," carried on day and night "because the wind was both full and fair" and the moon was waxing. On the 24th they sighted Brion Island. This, the *Brief recit* explains, "was just what we wanted to shorten our route." Cartier wished to try the strait between Cape Breton and Newfoundland which Fagundes had discovered, but the French, apparently, had never used. It has subsequently been named for John Cabot, who never saw it.

On 25 May, Ascension Day, they sailed ten miles to East Island of the Magdalen group, found no good anchorage, so returned to Brion Island and there remained until 1 June, enjoying the beautiful groves and meadows seen on the first voyage. They then sailed around the Magdalens, ascertaining that they were islands indeed; and, sighting mountains above the horizon to the southeastward, steered for them. These were on Cape Breton Island. Cartier named the northwestern point, now Cape St. Lawrence, *Cap de Lorraine* after an important cardinal of the house of Guise-Lorraine. He noted the strong shoreward set of current against which mariners are warned today. Cape North, the next promontory, he named *Cap de Sainct Paoul*. On 4 June he sighted Newfoundland, and entered a harbor named *Sainct Esprit* because it was Whitsunday. This must have been Port aux Basques, about seven miles east of Cape Ray. There they rode until the 6th, when they coasted eastward to *Les Iles de Saint-Pierre*, a

Cross on Ile aux Coudres, looking toward the north shore of the river.
Courtesy Canadian Government Travel Bureau.

name which had replaced the Portuguese Eleven Thousand Virgins.
This was the only place that Cartier visited on his voyages which is
still under French sovereignty. There on St. Barnaby's day, 11 June,
they met the first ships encountered on this long voyage—fishermen
from Brittany and other parts of France.

Sailing from Saint-Pierre 16 June, Cartier rounded Cape Race, Newfoundland, and entered Renewse Harbor (which he calls *Rougnouse*),
to top off with wood and water. This place served French fishermen as
a second-hand boat exchange. Since shore fishing was done mostly
from small boats, it was convenient to pick up *chaloupes* in Newfoundland and turn them in before returning home, rather than encumber the
deck and risk losing the lot in a storm. Cartier left behind one of his.

From Renewse, *La Grande Hermine* and *L'Émerillon* took their
departure on 19 June, the day after new moon. Favored by fine weather

and fair westerlies, they crossed the Atlantic in three weeks, reaching Saint-Malo on 15 July "by grace of the Creator, praying him at the close of our voyage to grant us his grace for paradise hereafter."

So ended the second and most profitable of Cartier's voyages, lasting fourteen months. Having already located the entrance, he now opened up the greatest water route for penetrating North America. He had made an intelligent estimate of the resources of Canada, both natural and human, despite considerable exaggeration on the mineral side. Whilst some of his actions with respect to the "savages" were dishonorable, he did his best, according to his lights, to establish friendship with the Huron up and down the Great River, an indispensable preliminary to French settlement. And on his third voyage he made a serious attempt to found a colony.

Tip end of Cape Breton Island; Cape North, Cartier's *Cap de Saint-Paul*, in background. Courtesy Canadian Government Travel Bureau.

✳ VIII ✳
The Search for Saguenay
1538-1543

Preparations for Cartier's Third Voyage

On 16 July 1536, Capitaine et Maître-Pilote Jacques Cartier brought *La Grande Hermine* and *L'Émerillon* safely through the many rocks and other hazards of Saint-Malo Bay and into L'Anse de Mer Bonne, the harbor. He had lost some twenty-five shipmates, victims of scurvy; but, partly to balance, he brought to France ten Hurons—Chief Donnaconna, his two unstable sons, two little girls, two little boys, and three adults. None ever saw their own country again. By the time Cartier set sail on his third voyage, all had died except one ten-year-old girl, and what became of her we know not. Domagaya and Taignoagny merged into the Paris underworld and came to no good; but Donnaconna enjoyed four years of glorious life as publicity agent for the mythical Kingdom of Saguenay. Cartier brought him to court where he was baptized, given a pension, and eventually a Christian burial.

François-premier regarded Saguenay as a means of re-establishing the balance of power in his favor. Apart from England there were only three great powers in western Europe—France, Spain, and Portugal; and England apparently had forgotten about John Cabot's discovery. Spain drew immense wealth from the mines of Mexico and Peru and financed her wars against France with American gold. Portugal waxed rich from her slave and spice trade with Africa and the Moluccas. Now, at an easy distance north of the Great River of Canada, lay another horn of plenty waiting to be emptied by France. Donnaconna, noting the king's interest in spices, added clove, nutmeg, and pepper to the products of Saguenay, and besides repeating the stories of unipeds and anus-less people, invented more yarns, with which the king loved to regale his friends. For instance, Saguenay grew oranges and pomegranates, and nourished a race of men who had wings instead of arms and flew like bats from tree to tree. To one skeptic the king replied testily that Donnaconna never varied in his stories and, under pain of death for blasphemy, had even sworn to their truth before a notary

Marguerite, reine de Navarre. By François Clouet. Courtesy Dépôt des Gravures, Bibliothèque Nationale.

public! Moreover, Cartier brought back and showed to the king some sparkling rocks which he believed to contain diamonds, and some iron pyrites—"fool's gold"—as samples of the mineral wealth of Canada.

So, a third voyage to Canada there must be—this time with no hope of getting through to China, but of conquering (like a northern Cortés or Pizarro) the curious, fabulous, glorious Kingdom of Saguenay.

That took time. Cartier's third voyage did not begin until almost five years after his return from the second. For two years the delay was due to a fresh war between France and Spain, which ended in the Treaty of Nice, June 1538. Preparations then began; but they were so elaborate and encountered so many diplomatic difficulties that three more years elapsed before the third voyage took off.

What was Cartier doing in the meantime?

Apparently he was fairly well off. He owned a small house and garden in Saint-Malo and the farm at Limoïlou. The king made him a gift of his former flagship, *La Grande Hermine*, and the Spanish ambassador complained that he used her to capture and pillage Portuguese and Spanish ships. Cartier had something to do with the attempt of Lord Gerald Fitzgerald to become king of Ireland, which failed, like all enterprises of that nature. An English spy at Rouen reported that the defeated Fitzgerald had arrived at Saint-Malo in March 1540 "conducted by sea by one Jackes Carter pylot of St. Mallow," but French historians believe that all Jacques did was to show Gerald the honors when he came ashore. Cartier probably fulfilled a vow made during the scurvy epidemic to make a pilgrimage to the famous shrine of Rocamadour. The early navigators, starting with Columbus, were always getting themselves involved in these pious journeys as a fair return to Our Lady for bringing them safe home.

It is a mark of the long neglect by France of Canada and of Cartier, that, of his third voyage and the first of Roberval, there have survived only the English translations of the sea-journals, summarized in Hakluyt. These abbreviated accounts have been augmented in the present century by the discovery of scores of documents in French and foreign archives on the preparations. We know ten times as much about the preliminaries as we do of the voyages themselves.

Not long after the Treaty of Nice, a few inconclusive preparations were made. The king repaid Cartier 3500 livres tournois (about $700 in gold) for expenses of his second voyage, plus 100 l.t. more for his care of the *gens saulvaiges*, the Hurons he brought home. And the royal archives preserve a detailed list of what Cartier, in September 1538, considered necessary to establish a colony on the banks of the Great River, as a base from which to discover Saguenay. He wants at least six ships with full crews, and 120 extra mariners to man boats for exploring rivers, and to remain in Canada. He wants forty *arquebuziers* (musketeers), thirty carpenters (both ship carpenters and sawyers), and ten master masons. He should also have from three to twelve each of tile-makers, charcoal burners, blacksmiths, metallurgists, vine-dressers, and farmers; barbers and apothecaries "who know about herbs"; jewelers who know precious stones and metals; tailors, cobblers, ropemakers, gunners, and priests; a total of 274. They should be provided with clothes and victuals to last two years, allowing five livres per man per month. Knocked-down boats to be assembled in Canada are wanted for exploring rivers; naval stores for repair and caulking of the ships; and one thousand francs a month for the people's payroll until the expedition starts. Also, a variety of seeds, domestic animals, and poultry should be taken to make the colony partly self-supporting. Quantities of iron and tile, and materials to build a water mill and a windmill, were a "must."

François-premier probably took one look at this and exclaimed, in effect, "Sacré nom d'un nom! trop cher!" Anyway, he paid no attention to Cartier for more than two years. Then, in August 1540, he alarmed the courts of Spain and Portugal by inviting all and sundry of his subjects to go, as the Spanish ambassador wrote to Charles V, to *las tierras nuevas*. On 17 October of the same year, the king issued a new commission to "*nostre cher et bien amé* Jacques Cartier, who having discovered the great country of the lands of *Canada* and *Ochelaga*, constituting a westward point of Asia," is to return thither "and to Saguenay if he can find it . . . to mingle with their people and live among them, the better to fulfil our aforesaid intention to do something agreeable to God." To that end, having confidence in the said Cartier's "good sense, capability, loyalty, prudence, courage, great diligence and good experience," the king appoints him Captain-General and master pilot of all ships embarked in said enterprise, and commander of all who engage therein. He may break up the "already old and obsolete" galion *L'Émerillon* to repair other ships. Royal officials in the north and west of France are ordered to let him recruit fifty convicts from the prisons, provided they had not been condemned for heresy, lèse majesté, or counterfeiting coins.

This permission to recruit convicts may mean that Cartier's popularity had waned at Saint-Malo, or merely that the word had gone around the waterfront that Canada was a lonely, frigid place which gave you nothing but scurvy. From a sailor's point of view there was far more fun and profit to be had in a fishing voyage to the Grand Bank, with a chance to trade with the Indians for valuable furs. Actually, twenty-four French ships went a-fishing to Newfoundland that very year. Similarly, after Columbus's first voyage, everybody wanted to go to the Indies; but after his second voyage nobody wanted to go, and Spain had to rake the jails to obtain settlers for Hispaniola. It is difficult for Americans, north or south, to accept the fact that for a century after Columbus's discovery, the ordinary sort of European had to be bribed, drugged, or beaten to go out to this "land of promise," unless to fish.

Roberval and Diplomatic Snooping

In January 1541 François-premier put a new face on his Canadian enterprise by placing Roberval over Cartier. Offspring of the high nobility, Jean-François de La Roque, sieur de Roberval and of a dozen other feudal fiefs, was the offspring of a royal ambassador who came from Provence and a noblewoman of Picardy. Born in or about 1500, a decade after Cartier, he had been a soldier in the Italian wars, a courtier, a friend of the poet Clément Marot, and, like that poet, a Protestant. Marot dedicated to Roberval two of his worst poems. Both men had to flee from the persecutions of 1525; but Roberval soon returned to court, protected by the king and his sister Marguerite de Navarre, authoress of the Heptaméron. Nobody knows why this Protestant nobleman, who had never been to sea, should have been promoted over Cartier.

Roberval's royal commission of 15 January 1541, more than twice as long as Cartier's, made him lieutenant-general, chief, commander, and captain of the said enterprise, including both ships and people; and conferred on him viceregal powers. The king gave him complete authority over the new lands, and over every Frenchman who went thither, with the privilege of granting lands in feudal tenure to gentlemen volunteers. Cartier became definitely a subordinate; his authority henceforth could be exerted only when Roberval was not around. Happily for the Captain, he almost never was.

At the same time, paradoxically, the enterprise entrusted to this Protestant gentleman now received a distinctly Catholic missionary flavor. Nobody before had said much or done anything about converting Canadians; Cartier had missed one opportunity, and only three of the ten natives he brought home were even baptized. But his new commission put conversion of the heathen on a par with discovering Saguenay; Roberval's is even more explicit. From now on the enterprise, on paper though not in fact, is fraught with apostolic zeal to bring thousands of *les sauvages* to embrace the Catholic faith. The obvious reason for all this beating of the religious drum was to placate the new pope, Paul III. At Rome, Emperor Charles V was again invoking the bulls of Alexander VI that divided the New World between Spain and Portugal; and the pope was no longer the complaisant Clement VII. François-premier cannily estimated that if he made a great noise about adding thousands of souls to the Catholic fold, the pope would not interfere. And probably the only reason the pope did not is that his nuncio at Paris informed him that the king had determined to send this expedition whether Rome liked it or not. To a Spanish grandee who remonstrated, François-premier replied with a phrase that made the rounds of Europe: "That the sun shone for him as for others, and he would like very much to see Adam's will to learn how he divided up the world!"

The king's earlier invitation to all and sundry of his subjects to emigrate to *les terres neufves* soon set every rumor mill a-grinding and all diplomatic bees a-buzzing. "Stop Cartier" letters fly to and fro like the diplomatic cables of 1939 on stopping Hitler. Spanish and Portuguese spies infest Paris and the seaports, seeking out and passing along to their sovereigns alarming information as to the scope of the expedition. The Emperor Charles V needs to know how many ships are involved, when they will sail, and what is their destination (maybe Canada is just a blind—may they not intend to raid Brazil or West Africa?). One report says there will be three fleets of forty sail each! The Emperor tries to stir up his brother-in-law João III of Portugal, who has an equal interest to keep the French out of Brazil and the codfish country. D. João replies he cannot be bothered; but he did send a fleet to defend Malagueta (the future Liberia) and lost it en route. More to the point, D. João sent a special envoy to the court of France, a lusty young man, the former lover of the duchesse d'Estampes, now the royal mistress, with valuable presents for her, in order to obtain knowledge of her bedroom confidences from the king. João III is not one of the most famous kings of Portugal, but he certainly had sense; to the Spanish ambassador who at Christmastide 1541 brought up the matter of a combined fleet to stop Cartier, he replied that he cared to hear no more of the subject; suppose he and the king of Spain did equip a fleet, it would have little effect, "since the ocean is vast," and the French destination unknown, "so there was no certainty where to encounter them."

The cardinal archbishop of Toledo, originally an advocate of a preventive war against Cartier, now advises the king to forget him; the French will find nothing of value up north, will get sick of it and go home—as indeed happened. His Eminence of Seville points out that Canada is too remote from New Spain to become a base for piracy. The Spanish ambassador at Paris consults Orontius Finus, a celebrated cosmographer, who assures him that the French can never get through to the Pacific via Canada, as the Emperor Charles V feared they might Even the English, quiescent about America for years, take notice; Henry VIII's ambassador writes from Paris, "The French king sendythe certayne shippes to seeke the trayde of spicerey by a shorter waye than the portingallez doth use with a nombre of fyve or six hundred fotemen intending to passe by *mare glasearum*. Theire pilate ys one Jacquez Cartier a britton." Just what Robert Thorne had recommended, and what Frobisher and Davis would attempt. Charles V orders several key points in the Antilles to be fortified, stations 150 musketeers at Nombre de Dios, fifty each at the Havana and San Juan de Puerto Rico, and a hundred at Santo Domingo, to protect those towns from being plundered by Cartier! He is so apprehensive as to send two caravels to search for Cartier in the summer of 1541; both vessels crossed the Atlantic and sailed from Newfoundland to Florida without finding hide or hair of the French. In November 1541 the Spanish ambassador to France learns that Cartier had been seen in Newfoundland, icebound, and that Roberval intends to plunder the West Indies before joining him. Even after the entire French enterprise had been liquidated, Charles V caused a number of Spanish fishermen who had met the explorers in Newfoundland to be interrogated at Fuenterabbia, and only then did he feel secure in his American possessions.

Cartier's Third Voyage

Captain-General Cartier, as we should now style him, was ready to sail in April 1541; Roberval, arriving on the 21st, found five ships riding at anchor in the harbor of Saint-Malo. Crew, colonists, and animals were on board, yards crossed, and sails bent. The squadron consisted, first, of two gifts from the king to Cartier, his old flagship *La Grande Hermine* under a new master (Thomas Fromont having died in Canada), and the sprightly pinnace *L'Émerillon*, Macé Jalobert, master. Cartier evidently liked *L'Émerillon* too well to break her up. In addition, he had ships *Saint-Brieuc* and *Saint-Georges* and a third whose name we do not know. According to a Spanish spy's report written from Saint-Malo in the same month of April, Cartier and Roberval had a combined fleet of ten sail. The total complement, according to the spy, was 400 mariners and twenty master pilots, obviously an exaggeration.

Cartier himself had recruited only twenty colonists from the jails, but on 19 May there marched into Saint-Malo a gang of chained convicts secured by Roberval. These were of both sexes ranging in age from eighteen to forty-five, who had been condemned for everything from homicide to "stealing bronze to make bells." For romantic interest there was an eighteen-year-old Manon Lescaut, engaged to prisoner Gay, who insisted on accompanying her fiancé; and five "persons of quality" —a mint master who had juggled the currency, a man who had beaten up a royal prince's maître d'hotel, a fugitive from justice, and two murderers. Roberval turned all these over to Cartier because he was not ready to sail himself and did not wish to pay for their keep until he did. So, not only were 'tween decks congested with convicts but the spar decks were uncomfortably crowded with horses, cattle, swine, sheep, goats, and poultry.

The Spanish spy took a very dim view of the alleged 150 members of the nobility and gentry who were supposed to accompany Cartier. Apart from Pierre du Plessis, sieur de Savonnières, they were a sorry lot, and no more than twenty-five "so-called gentlemen" actually

sailed. That may well be; but Roberval recruited many for his squadron, and Cartier's brother-in-law the vicomte de Beaupré certainly
went with him.

On 19 May Cartier made his will, describing himself as *capitaine &
maistre pillote du Roy ès Terres Neuffves . . . bourgeois en Saint-
Malo*, and leaving to his wife Catherine all his property, including the
Limoïlou farm and a "petite maison et jardin derrière" in Saint-Malo.
Next day he is on record as quelling a street brawl over money between his trumpeter Pierre and a local cobbler. The trumpeter drew a
sword on his adversary, whose wife slapped Pierre in the face. Cartier
broke it up, but the trumpeter's brother-in-law, a carpenter, grabbed
the cobbler by the hair, threw him down, and punched him, "and
would have done more but for the said Cartier."

Roberval now informed Cartier that he was not yet ready to sail,
having received neither artillery nor ammunition nor other important
supplies. But he ordered Cartier to get going. This the Malouin was
only too glad to do, for there is nothing more exasperating than being
delayed when one is ready for sea. What happened to Roberval we
shall see in due course; we may now follow Cartier to Canada for the
third and last time.

The fleet of five departed Saint-Malo 23 May 1541, with a two-day
new moon. Although but three days later in the season than John
Cabot's start, they had a very rough crossing, with not thirty hours of
fair wind; and all but one other vessel parted from flagship *La Grande
Hermine*. Water ran short, and goats and swine had to be given cider
to survive. It took the flagship a month to make the familiar Quirpon
Harbor behind Cape Dégrat, Newfoundland. Cartier spent some time
there, awaiting the rest of his fleet, taking on wood and water, and
buying or borrowing bread and wine and *chaloupes* from the French
fishing vessels he found there. The fishermen were loath to part with
their *chaloupes*, but Cartier had lost several small boats during the
crossing and had to have replacements.

We have no details of the passage between Quirpon and Stadaconé
(Quebec), where the fleet anchored 23 August 1541, three months out.
The Huron received Cartier with the usual "show of joy." Agona,
who had taken Donnaconna's place, seemed not displeased with the
news that his predecessor had died. He placed his leather coronet
edged with wampum on the Captain-General's head, gave him two

wampum bracelets, and subjected him to the usual "colling," or embrace. Cartier lied about the other deportees, asserting that they stayed in France "as great Lords, and were married." His intuition told him that all was not well between the two races—and no wonder! Hence he decided not to seat his colony at Stadaconé.

Leaving his ships at the St. Charles anchorage near Quebec, Cartier took two boats and had himself rowed eight or nine miles upstream, past the mouth of the Chaudière, to the present Cap Rouge. There, on a spot he had observed on his previous voyage, he decided to settle, and so brought up all five ships. The convicts and other colonists were landed, the cattle which had survived three months on shipboard were turned loose, earth broken for a kitchen garden, and seeds of cabbage, turnip, and lettuce planted. The men also began collecting quartz crystals ("diamonds") and iron pyrites ("gold"). Ships *Saint-Brieuc* and *Saint-Georges* were dispatched home on 2 September under charge of Macé Jalobert and Cartier's great-nephew Etienne Noël. They made a fast passage, arriving Saint-Malo 3 October 1541, and Jalobert proceeded directly to Paris to bedazzle the court with his samples of spurious mineral wealth.

The Captain-General now directed the building of a palisaded and fortified settlement. This he named Charlesbourg-Royal after Charles, duc d'Orléans, son of the king; and he also built a fort on the falaise overlooking Charlesbourg, as additional protection.

Cartier's idea in settling on Cap Rouge rather than at Stadaconé was to establish a base for discovering Saguenay that was not cheek-by-jowl with the Huron capital. Moreover, it was nearer the Ottawa River which he had been lead to believe was one of the two routes to Saguenay. He felt that the Indians were not so cordial as they had been at his departure; and he was right. American natives, usually friendly and hospitable to newcomers from Europe, inevitably turned hostile when they learned that their visitors intended to settle. Furthermore, Cartier and his men had not given the Huron uniformly good usage; he had kidnapped several, including their chief, and some of his young men (according to Jean Alfonce who had it straight from Donnaconna in France) made a practice of helping themselves to any poor savage's possessions that took their fancy, and trying their sword blades on the natives' limbs.

Having set everyone to work at Charlesbourg-Royal, and leaving his

Charles, duc d'Orléans. For whom Ile d'Orléans and Charlesbourg-Royal were named. Portrait by François Clouet. From Gower, ed., Clouet's *French Portraits*.

brother-in-law the vicomte de Beaupré as governor, Cartier took the longboats with sundry "gentlemen, masters and pilots" to make a Saguenay reconnaissance. They departed 7 September with a moon two days full and called on the "Lord of Hochelay" (Achelacy, near Pontneuf), by whom the French had been well received on the previous voyage. Cartier presented the chief, on unfriendly terms with the Stadaconé Hurons, with a "cloake of Paris red" trimmed with "yellow and white buttons of tinne and small belles." The chief consented to receive into his household two French boys to learn his language— Domagaya and Taignoagny having proved wanting as interpreters. This new method of bridging the language gap became standard in Canada throughout the colonial period. What became of the French lads we do not know; presumably Cartier took them home next year.

On 11 September, within sight of Mont Royal and Hochelaga,

Cartier's boats reached the first *sault*, Sainte-Marie, which had blocked his way in 1535. Leaving one boat ashore, he double-banked the other but could do nothing against the current, so returned to the first boat (which he had left near the site of the modern Jacques Cartier Bridge) and followed an Indian portage along shore. This led him to a village of friendly natives called Tutonaguy, where he obtained four young men as guides to Saguenay. These lads led him to another village situated on the north bank of the Lachine rapids, which fall forty-two feet in two miles. The boys made him a sort of map with sticks, but told him that there was another big *sault* to pass; meaning, no doubt, the Long Sault. And here Cartier quit. It was as near Saguenay as he ever got. It seems strange that the natives did not direct him up the Ottawa River—but perhaps they were trying to put him off.

Returning downstream to Charlesbourg-Royal, Cartier missed the chief of Achelacy, who had gone to Stadaconé to confer with Agona; and when the Frenchmen arrived at their new settlement they were apprised by Beaupré that things looked ominous. The Hurons no longer made friendly visits or peddled fish and game, but prowled about in a sinister manner; it seemed likely that Agona was organizing a concerted attack to wipe out the colony. If so, he did not plan it well, and most of the French escaped. These savages now realized what all other North American natives learned sooner or later, that co-existence with Europeans meant death for them. If you accepted the palefaces, they tilled, built, shot, and pillaged you out of land, game, possessions, house, and home. If you attacked and succeeded in wiping them out, others came back with more ships and greater fire power. Had some Indian genius invented the sea-going ship and gunpowder by 1500, native empires might have withstood predatory Europeans for centuries, just as Japan did. But their inveterate defect, lack of organization, would probably have been their undoing.

Hakluyt's, the one surviving narrative of Cartier's third voyage, abruptly ends with his return to Charlesbourg-Royal. All we know of what happened there in the winter of 1541–42 comes from bits of gossip picked up when the sailors reached home. The Indians attacked, killing first some carpenters who were out cutting wood, and more than thirty-five people all told. It would be interesting to know how the colonists took this, but not a word has survived. Scurvy broke out but was cured by the magic arborvitae. The impression one gets is one of general misery and of Cartier's growing conviction that he had insufficient manpower both to protect his base and go in search of Saguenay. Roberval never having turned up, Cartier assumed that he had been lost at sea and that the game was up.

At any rate, Cartier raised camp in early June 1542, and with his three remaining ships (*La Grande Hermine*, *L'Émerillon*, and the nameless one) carrying all surviving colonists and (according to gossip) eleven barrels of "gold," a basket of "precious stones such as rubies and diamonds," and seven barrels of "silver," he entered the harbor of St. John's, Newfoundland, before the end of the month.

And there, lying at anchor, as pretty as you please, were Roberval's three big ships!

Cartier Meets Roberval and Goes Home

And what had the king's Lieutenant-General and Governor for Canada been doing all this time? It took him the better part of a year after Cartier's departure to get going. He sold one of his estates to raise the wind, but that was not enough to pay all the "land sharks" to whom he owed money; so, desperately, he armed his ships and practised piracy in the English Channel, capturing several Portuguese and English merchantmen. Henry VIII complained vigorously through his ambassador at Paris, who wrote back that François-premier (tongue in cheek) professed to be profoundly shocked and threatened to hang Roberval. Nothing, of course, was done; and on 16 April 1542, almost one year after Cartier, Roberval sailed. He commanded three new merchant ships that he had bought at Honfleur, named *Marye* of Saint-Malo (nicknamed *Lechefraye*) of 80–100 tuns, *Sainte-Anne* (80 tuns), and *Vallentyne* of Jumièges, 92–100 tuns. Alonce de Civille, the leading Italian merchant-shipowner of Rouen, largely financed Roberval's expedition and guaranteed the cost of these ships.

According to the Spanish spy, Roberval embarked three hundred soldiers, sixty masons and carpenters, ten priests, three physicians, and ten barbers. This is doubtless an exaggeration, but his ships were well armed and provisioned. Each carried knocked-down *charretes*, the two-wheeled carts of the period, two mills, and a quantity of ironware.

Marye, *Sainte-Anne*, and *Vallentyne* sailed from La Rochelle 16 April 1542, with a new moon. After spending several days anchored under the lee of the Breton Belle-Ile awaiting a fair wind, they put to sea, enjoyed an easy crossing, and anchored in St. John's Harbor, Newfoundland, on 7 June 1542. Twenty-seven fishing vessels were already there. Roberval had engaged as pilot, Jean Alfonce, evidently experienced in latitude sailing. Belle-Ile, off Quiberon Bay, is on latitude 47°23'; St. John's, on 47°34' N.

A few days later, Cartier's three ships entered the harbor of St. John's, Newfoundland. Although the Captain-General now came legally under the orders of the Lieutenant-General, he refused to admit it. When his efforts to persuade Roberval to give up and go home failed, and the younger man ordered him to return to Canada, Cartier refused, and the following night "stole privily away" with his three ships and set a course for Saint-Malo, where he arrived about mid-October, 1542.

This flight home looks like a black mark on Jacques Cartier's record; another instance of desertion at sea, too common in that century. He rightly warned Roberval that it would be impossible for the French to defend themselves at Charlesbourg-Royal; but he refused to assist his legal commander, who was determined to try. Roberval ascribed it to Cartier's "ambition" to cash in on the "diamonds." On the other hand, Roberval's failure to join him earlier had caused Cartier to assume that the Lieutenant-General was never coming, and he had made up his mind to return to France. This had been announced to his passengers and crew, who probably would have mutinied rather than spend another winter in Canada. In any case, Cartier's reputation at home did not suffer. The Malouins, obviously glad to have their sailors safe home, treated the Captain as their most prominent citizen; the government consulted him on maritime matters, and the *Brief recit* of his second voyage was published in 1545. He never received a patent of nobility for his efforts, to be sure; but neither did any other early navigator, not even Columbus; and the king repaid almost all that he was out of pocket for the voyage, as well as presenting him with *La Grande Hermine* and *L'Émerillon*.

"The good captain must know his ship, and have sailed in her, whence he will learn the trim that she demands, and the speed she can make according to the strength of the winds, and what leeway she makes with the wind abeam, or hove-to with only the topsail or main course set, so as not to labor. . . ." So wrote Samuel de Champlain

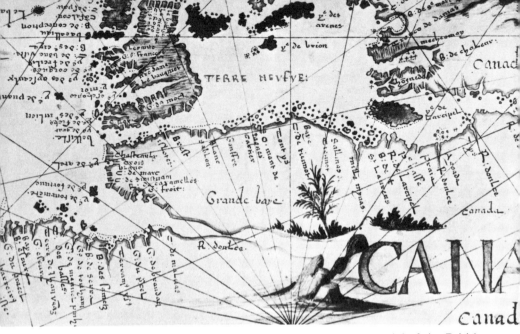

West Canadian part of Desceliers Planisphere, 1550. Original in British Museum, Add. Mss. 24.065. Courtesy of Map Division, Public Archives of Canada.

after thirty-eight years' experience at sea. Cartier, after two transatlantic voyages in *La Grande Hermine* and *L'Émerillon,* must have known them as well as any master ever knew any ship; and he now owned both, a royal gift. The pinnace he appropriately renamed *Canadie,* and both vessels were employed in the merchant marine, under other masters. Considering their performance in 1535–36 and 1540–41, they belong in the maritime hall of fame along with *Mathew, La Dauphine, Santa Maria,* and *Vittoria.*

Among the numerous entries in local church records of Cartier's apparently favorite recreation, attending baptisms, there is one which suggests that his last years were anything but sad. The name of Jacques Cartier "avec d'aultres bons biberons" (with other good drinkers), appears as a witness. This allows one to imagine old Master-Pilot Cartier as a jolly *bon-viveur* spending his time between farm, town and tavern, and perhaps visiting his relative at Mont-Saint-Michel to eat an omelette with him and the abbot. He had a neat little house and garden on the rue de Buhen in Saint-Malo, and enjoyed his farm at Limoïlou. Jacques doubtless regaled young Malouins with tales of storms, rapids, savages, and the fabulous Kingdom of Saguenay which he would certainly have

East Canadian part of same map. Top is south.

found had he been given more time, and thus made every Breton sailor richer than a conquistador of Mexico. Around 1550 he entertained in the town house some distinguished visitors—André Thevet the sea-going monk, a Swedish navigator named Bayarni, and the aged Sebastian Cabot. What would we not give for a tape-recording of their conversations! Cabot seems to have held the floor, as usual, telling about a voyage to Florida that he never made.

Jacques Cartier died at Saint-Malo from an epidemic then raging, on 1 September 1557, aged 66. His wife survived him by several years. Although the English Hakluyt did more for his reputation than any Frenchman, his compatriots both in France and Canada have more than made up for his neglect during the last hundred years. Rightly so, for Cartier ranks among the most expert seamen and careful explorers in the era of discovery.

The Valiant Demoiselle

Roberval's official narrative of this voyage, like Cartier's, is known only through Hakluyt's translation, but we have another valuable source in *La Cosmographie* written by his pilot Jean Alfonce. According to him, Roberval (whom he refers to as "the General") spent about three weeks at St. John's after Cartier's departure, and entered the Gulf of St. Lawrence by the Strait of Belle Isle.

The atmosphere in Roberval's ships, apart from the barnyard odors of the cattle, sheep, swine, and horses, was one of youth and gaiety. Most of the gentlemen volunteers, and all the lady colonists, had embarked with him. Jacques Cartier doubtless displayed some of his "gold" and "diamonds" before parting from Roberval at St. John's; thus the General's ladies and gentlemen continued the voyage with high expectations of profit as well as fun. Monsieur de Roberval had royal authority to grant fiefs in Canada; wouldn't it be nice to own a piece of land which included a mine of gold or diamonds? A few of these passengers of noble blood are named in Roberval's narration; Paul d'Aussilon, seigneur de Sauveterre; Nicholas de Lépinay, seigneur de Neufville-sur-la-Wault; a son of Jacques de Frotté, president of the parlement de Paris; the sieurs de Noirefontaine and La Vasseur de Coutances; the sieur de Longueval, a cousin of the General.

A master mariner likes a cheerful atmosphere among his passengers; but one couple in the flagship were too gay for Roberval. His own niece or cousin, a damsel named Marguerite de La Roque, was accompanied by her old nurse, a Norman peasant named Damienne, and—as it later appeared—by her lover. Damienne played the classic maid's part in covering up her mistress's gallantry; but on a crowded ship the dalliance of lovers could not forever escape notice. When brought to Roberval's attention, his Calvinist principles were so outraged that he marooned Marguerite and Damienne. The place of their exile was one of the Harrington Islands, which Cartier had passed and named St. Marthe on an earlier voyage. Roberval set the two women ashore with a few provisions and arquebuses for defense, and left them to their fate.

With despair they saw the ships weigh anchor, make sail, and depart; but see! What is this? A man swimming ashore! This was the gallant, whom Roberval intended to keep on board as prisoner but had not got around to putting in irons. He leaped overboard during the confusion of the ship's getting under way, and swam ashore bringing two more guns and a supply of ammunition.

With such an expert swimmer for companion, Marguerite fared well enough for a time. Until winter set in, the lovers lived an idyllic life. The gentleman built a cabin for his mistress and her maid, chopped

The Harrington Islands.

wood, caught fish, and shot wild fowl; but before winter ended, he died. Marguerite, unable to dig a grave in the frozen ground, guarded his body in the cabin until spring, to protect it from wild animals.

In the ninth month of exile a child was born to her and promptly died. Another winter passed, and Damienne died, leaving Marguerite alone. The intrepid demoiselle gathered enough food to keep alive and defended herself not only against the bears (she killed three, one "white as an egg"), but against spirits of another world. Demoniac voices shrieked about her cabin, howled the louder when she fired a gun, but were stilled when she read passages from a New Testament which she had brought ashore.

It seems incredible that she survived, but the evidence that she did is conclusive. In the early spring of 1544, after she had been two years and five months on the island, smoke from her fire was observed by passing French fishermen. They landed, found Marguerite emaciated and in rags; but, more charitable than Roberval, gave her passage back to France. She returned to her home at Montron in Picardy, became a schoolmistress, and told her story to Jean Alfonce. He in turn told it to Marguerite, queen of Navarre, sister of François-premier, and patroness of Roberval; and she, in turn, used it as Nouvelle No. LXVII in her famous Heptaméron. Marguerite proved the Pauline doctrine that "God hath chosen the weak things of the world, to confound the

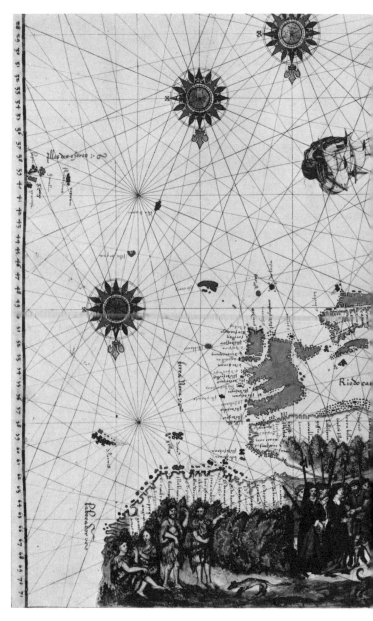

North American section of Nicholas Vallard Map, 1547. (The

op of this map is south.) Courtesy Henry E. Huntington Library.

things which are mighty" (1 Corinthians i.27). This poor, weak woman on a desert island protected the corpse of her man against wild beasts and exorcised the powers of darkness by reading the Word of God; and God saw to it that she survived. Thus Marguerite was presented to the public by this intelligent Protestant queen as a shining example to womankind.

France-Roy and Search for Saguenay

Cartier, before sailing for home from St. John's, must have left with Roberval's pilot Alfonce his own sailing directions for Canada. The Roberval fleet departed St. John's at the end of June 1542, passed through the Strait of Belle Isle, and a few days later marooned poor Marguerite. They then sailed up-river, passed Stadaconé without stopping, and toward the end of July came to an anchor off Cartier's Charlesbourg-Royal at the mouth of the River Rouge.

According to Spanish spies, Roberval had hundreds on board—585 men and women. Even if you cut this down to 150 (which is my guess), he had plenty of people to build a fortified camp, and he had time to plant vegetable seeds to provide vitamins for winter diet. Cartier's Charlesbourg-Royal, which possibly had been taken apart by the Huron, is not mentioned; and, disdaining Cartier's names, Roberval renamed this place *France-Roy*, and the river *France-Prime*. The site of the *habitation*, he says, was "upon an high mountain," probably the spot where Cartier had his lookout post; but "there was also at the foote of the mountaine another lodging" with "a great Towre of two stories high," used largely for storage. The main building on the hill, enclosed by a palisade, had towers from which an enemy's approach could be observed, barracks for the soldiers, a central building with hall, kitchen, and offices; places for everyone to sleep, one or more mills for grinding corn, and an outdoor oven.

The general appearance of this building we may infer from Champlain's drawing of the *habitation* built by him and Poutrincourt at Port Royal in 1605; or still better, by visiting that beautifully restored building at Lower Granville a few miles from Annapolis Royal, Nova Scotia.

Nicholas Vallard's Map of 1547 is probably as near as we can get to a contemporary picture of France-Roy. The number of ladies, gentle-

Restored Port Royal *Habitation* of 1605. Courtesy Canadian Government Travel Bureau.

men, and soldiers indicates that this depicts Roberval's company, not Cartier's The bearded figure pointing to the natives must be intended for Roberval, and the little stockade armed with cannon, which the artist had to make small for lack of room, was the defense.

On 14 September, Roberval sent home two of his ships, commanded by Paul d'Aussilon, who had been tried for killing a sailor, and acquitted. His object was to carry news of the voyage to the king, inquire what the experts thought of Cartier's gold and diamonds, and bring out more supplies next year.

The trees shed their brilliant leaves. Dark November days followed, and then the brief Indian summer—St. Martin's summer it was called in Europe—when the winds were hushed and the sun shone bright and all nature seemed to be taking a deep breath before winter set in. Then drear December, snow and more snow; one could not venture out without *raquettes*, as the French called the savages' snowshoes. There were clear, cold days when ice in the river sent chords of unearthly harp music ringing in one's ears. At night the northern lights threw up white and rosy flashes almost to the zenith, and only Orion and the Bear and a few other constellations reminded the French that they were on the same globe as Paris. Apparently the kitchen gardens did not yield much, as everyone went on short rations for the winter; each mess—five to eight people—had two loaves of bread for breakfast, bacon and half a pound of butter for dinner, and half a pound of beef, with beans, for supper. Wednesday, Friday, and Saturday were fast days when they had nothing but dried or fresh codfish, porpoise meat, and beans. The Indians helped them by bringing "great store of *aloses*" (shad); but this must have been in the spring shad-run. We would dearly love to know more about that winter at France-Roy. Did the gentlemen and ladies organize theatricals, or something like *l'ordre du bon temps* which kept everyone cheerful at Port Royal more than a half-century later? Did the men go hunting on snowshoes? Or did they mope by the fire, complaining and begging Roberval to take them home? We simply do not know. Not one person brought overseas by Cartier and Roberval, unless an obscure mariner, ever cared to return to Canada.

Although Cartier must have warned Roberval of the winter disease and told him about the arborvitae cure, the colony suffered greatly from scurvy, and "about fifty people" died. Roberval kept strict discipline; men and women were flogged, others put in irons, and one man hanged for theft, "by which means they lived in quiet." There is no reason to accuse the General of undue severity. As Columbus found in Hispaniola, and the English learned at Jamestown, a colony consisting of all sorts and conditions of people, planted in a remote country, must have strict discipline to survive.

So far as we can learn from the meager records, the Indians never attacked France-Roy; it had more formidable defenses than Charlesbourg-Royal, as they doubtless observed. Yet, all in all, it must have been a very unhappy winter for the French.

The river ice began to break up in April, but it was not until

6 June, when the white birch was shaking out its tender green leaves
and the shad-bush gleamed white among the stately conifers, that Roberval began his search for the Kingdom of Saguenay. Probably he had
waited for the river current to abate. An upstream expedition set forth
in eight boats carrying seventy people, leaving thirty behind at France-
Roy. The numbers indicate that Roberval had lost more than fifty
from scurvy and other causes. He left as deputy governor one Sieur de
Royeze, but most of the gentlemen volunteers accompanied him upstream. After one boat had been wrecked and eight men drowned,
Roberval turned back, at the Lachine rapids.

Here the one existing narrative of Roberval's voyage breaks off; we
have to carry on as best we can with that of his chief pilot. Jean Alfonce probably explored the Saguenay River while Roberval was
up the St. Lawrence. In his *La Cosmographie* he had this to say about
it: "The entrance is between two high mountains. The point of the
Saguenay is a white rock" (actually it is a light-colored clay) "and the
entrance of the said Saguenay is at 48°20′, and it is only a quarter of a
league wide." That measure is accurate, and Alfonce's latitude is less
than twelve miles out. He adds that the mouth is difficult and dangerous to enter, as the river current meeting the tide "makes a terrible
raz"—the Breton word for a violent tidal current. "Inside the entrance,"
he continues, "the river widens after two or three leagues, and begins
to take on the characer of an arm of the sea, for which reason I estimate
that this sea leads to the Pacific Ocean or even to *la mer du Cattay*."
There he leaves us flat. It seems probable that Alfonce, using one of
Roberval's long boats, rowed up the Saguenay and turned back short
of the Chicoutimi rapids which, had he seen them, would have taught
him (as the Lachine did Cartier), that this was no arm of the sea. His
own map shows Lac Saint-Jean, from which the river issues; but he
may simply have been told about it by the natives.

Although Roberval had written to the king asking for a relief expedition, he decided some time in the summer not to await it but to
abandon France-Roy and return to France. We have no record of the
time of his departure. It was probably at the end of July, as he had arrived in France by 11 September 1543. On that date he ordered the
sale of *Sainte-Anne* and the other unnamed ship which had brought
him home. The only explanation of this decision is on one of Desceliers's
maps, where there is an inscription stating, "It was impossible to trade

Title page of *L'Heptaméron*, 1560 edition. Courtesy Harvard College Library.

with the people of that country because of their austerity, the intemperate climate of said country, and the slight profit."

So ended this valiant French enterprise, and so died the dream of the rich, glorious Kingdom of Saguenay, a new Mexico in the Laurentian wilds. Saguenay lasted for over a century on maps, even one dated 1677, then quietly disappeared, except as the name of the river. For the Kingdom had never been anything but an *ignis fatuus*, a will-o'-the-wisp, with no basis in fact, not even in Indian folklore; it was simply a collection of tall tales made up to fool the French. Since nothing in history is too foolish to be wholly discarded, the Kingdom of Saguenay has been revived in recent years both as a tourist attraction and to support the theory that Norsemen, Irishmen, "Quii," and whatnot were wandering about the interior of North America in the Middle Ages.

François-premier died in 1547. His son and successor Henri II cared nothing for American exploration, and before his death France fell into the religious wars that exhausted the energy of her adventurous sons. Roberval, a cousin of Diane de Poitiers, the king's mistress, frequented the court of Henri II and received a royal concession to search for and exploit mines of iron or precious metals. Herein, too, he failed. The former Lieutenant-General for the king in Canada was killed in a religious riot in Paris in 1561.

These efforts were not entirely wasted. For half a century Canada was left to her native inhabitants (which was all to their good), but Cartier's voyages brought about a revolution in North American cartography. Not only French maps, but those of the Spaniards, the Portuguese, and Sebastian Cabot show in detail the Gulf of St. Lawrence, the Great River of Canada, and the Lachine rapids beyond which no European had penetrated.

Many, many years elapsed before any French expedition comparable with Cartier's and Roberval's came in this direction; for Canada had, as it were, been laughed off the map. As all things in France end in jest, so here; it became a popular saying, applied to everything that glittered and was not gold, or sparkled and was not diamond; *C'est un diamant du Canada!*

✳ IX ✳

Queen Elizabeth and
Her Master Mariners

The glittering fleece that he doth bring, in value sure is more
Than Jason's was, or Alcides fruite, whereof was made such store . . .
And bringes home treasure to his land, and doth enrich the same,
And courage gives to noble heartes, to seek for flight of fame.

THOMAS ELLIS'S POEM TO FROBISHER.

Gloriana

The age of Elizabeth, in which English genius burned brightly in almost every aspect of life, now reached its acme. Shakespeare's "happy
breed of men," living on a "precious stone set in the silver sea," awakened to a feeling of exuberant life. They reached high achievement in
arts and letters, in music and in science, in exploration and warfare,
such as few people had attained since ancient Greece. This was an age
when the scholar, the divine, and the man of action were often one and
the same person; for the Elizabethans well knew that life is empty
without religion, that the tree of knowledge bears no fruit unless
rooted in love, and that learning purchased at the expense of life and
liberty is a sorry bargain. Man in those days was not ashamed to own
himself an animal, nor so base as to quench the divine spark that made
him something better; but above all he exulted in the fact that he was
a man, "What a piece of work is a man!" declaims Hamlet. "How
noble in reason! how infinite in faculty! in form, in moving, how express and admirable! in action how like an angel! in apprehension how
like a god! the beauty of the world! the paragon of animals!" Christopher Marlowe's Tamburlaine declares that Nature

274

Queen Elizabeth the First. From a portrait by an unknown artist. Courtesy of Trustees of National Maritime Museum, Greenwich.

Doth teach us all to have aspiring minds;
Our souls, whose faculties can comprehend
The wondrous architecture of the world,
And measure every wandering planet's course,
Still climbing after knowledge infinite,
And always moving as the restless spheres
Will us to wear ourselves and never rest.

Which is about what has happened to us in the present century.

Queen Elizabeth, in her forty-fifth year in 1578, had not lost her charm for men; and twenty years on the throne had taught her statecraft in the school of experience. She was excommunicated by the pope in 1570, and in *de facto* war even before the declared war with Spain, whose ambassador financed an unsuccessful plot to assassinate her. Elizabeth found security only in the hearts of her subjects. They rendered to their queen a love and loyalty that no English monarch had yet received or would receive for centuries to come. "Gloriana," as the poets named her, called the wisest men in the kingdom to her council, but she was wiser than some and shrewder than any. More than any European prince she encouraged with her patronage and supported from her privy purse the overseas voyages of her subjects. She had a "good liking" to all, not only Frobisher's, and showed her approval both of Drake's circumnavigation and of his despoiling a Spanish treasure ship by knighting him on the deck of the *Golden Hind* when he returned in November 1580. In this queen England found her identity.

All England in her reign was insecure. Unfriendly Scotland lay on her northern border; hostile Spain, Portugal, and often France confronted her on the Continent. She stood constantly on the verge of disaster at the hands of Spain, just as she has been twice in our times on the edge of bitter defeat at the hands of Germany; but then as now she came through gloriously. Everyone knew that once Spain got rid of Elizabeth, the fires of Smithfield would be relighted and the Reformed Religion stamped out in a series of St. Bartholomew massacres. Then as now, her first line of defense was the Royal Navy, with its merchant auxiliaries; ships and sailors were the main factors that enabled England to break through her encompassing enemies.

Elizabeth had a genius for compromise, but she remained uncompromisingly Protestant in religion, refusing offers of marriage from several Catholic princes. Her Protestantism enhanced the insecurity and isolation of her realm, but stimulated national pride. Englishmen now felt a spiritual urge to adventure, and expansion; it was their duty to see that American savages got the Gospel straight and pure, and that Protestant colonies were planted in the New World to counterbalance the overwhelming power of Spain.

Enter Gilbert and Frobisher

The English record of northern voyaging in 1575–1600 is a series of glorious failures which left experience as a foundation for the English colonies of the seventeenth century. With Martin Frobisher, in 1576 a thirty-seven-year-old mariner of abounding courage though with a shady past, English discovery comes full circle. Muscovy Company, Morocco, West Africa, West Indies, and now back to the Northwest Passage, the short cut to the Indies that inspired John Cabot. Neither then, nor for centuries, could the English get that concept out of their heads; and only when the objective was shifted from gold and spices to exploration was the goal finally reached in 1905, by a Norwegian, Roald Amundsen in *Gjøa*.

Mariners and cosmographers of at least four nations had been working on the Passage to Cathay idea for some eighty years, starting with John Cabot's first voyage. John Dee's German friend Gemma Frisius had produced a map calling the Passage *Fretum Trium Fratrum*. At the Pacific end, Spaniards produced a mythical Strait of Anian through North America to the Atlantic; Drake searched for it on his circumnavigation. Antonio Urdaneta, a Spanish friar, claimed to have sailed through it from west to east; and Humfry Gilbert adduced these "facts" and many more, in his *Discourse*, to prove that the passage existed and was practicable. Everybody said you could do it from east to west, but who would try? Martin Frobisher would, and did.

First, however, a word on Humfry Gilbert, born to a Devonshire family of substance in 1537. In a petition that he made to Elizabeth I in 1565, Humfry began, "Whereas of longe tyme, there hath bin nothinge saide or donne concerning the discoviringe of a passage by the Northe to go to Cataia, & all other east parts of the worlde," he wishes "to make tryall thereof" at his "owne costes & charges." He only asks for a monopoly of trade through the Passage for his lifetime, and a 25 per cent cut of the customs duties all goods brought through it to England. Anthony Jenkinson of the Muscovy Company, disillusioned with the Northeast Passage and impatient over the meager results of trade with Russia and Persia, joined Gilbert in petitioning the Queen for Northwest Passage privileges. Next year, during his leaves from fighting in Ireland, Sir Humfry wrote *A Discourse of a Discoverie for a New Passage to Cataia*. Although it was not printed for ten years, this tract made a great impact on English opinion. Gilbert threw in quotations from ancient and modern writers to show that "any man of our country that will give the attempt, may with small danger passe to Cataia . . . and all other places in the East, in much shorter time than either the Spaniard or the Portingale doth." His appended map (here reproduced) makes it deceptively easy: Choose a wide passage between "Baccalaos" and "Canada," and you enter an immense sea which will lead you by the fabled Strait of Anian to Quivira and the Sierra Nevada (known from the Spaniards), where you are on the edge of the Pacific and a short sail from Japan, China, and the Moluccas. Gorgeous prospects are painted of the rich commodities England could obtain by this route: "Gold, silver, precious stones, cloth of gold, silks . . . grocery wares"—which last, in that era, meant spices, sugar, raisins, and other foreign products.

In the matter of export, he holds out hope that the shortness of the passage will enable England to vend her products in the Far East far cheaper than the Spaniards can sell theirs. And he holds forth the possibility of settling the Strait with "such needie people of our Countrie, which now trouble the common welth, and through want here at home, are inforced to commit outragious offences, whereby they are dayly consumed with the Gallows." Gilbert concludes with a fine flourish: "That he is not worthie to live at all, that for feare, or daunger of death, shunneth his countrey service, and his own honour, seeing death is inevitable, and the fame of vertue immortall."

Gilbert's *Discourse* was published in 1576 as promotion literature for a company that had been formed to send Martin Frobisher to discover the Northwest Passage.

Frobisher, coeval with Humfry Gilbert, belonged to a very different breed. He was a dour Yorkshireman, not a jolly man of Devon; a professional sailor rather than a part-time writer and soldier; a man incapable of writing a good letter, but of speaking very expressively: on one occasion, we are told he "swore no smale oathes," including "God's wounds!" One of three children born to a family of country gentry in Pontefract, Yorkshire, near the end of 1539, he and his rela-

Martin Frobisher. From a portrait by an unknown artist, dated 1577.
Courtesy Bodleian Library, Oxford.

tives spelled the name some fifty different ways, but historians in desperation have settled on *Frobisher*. His father having died, his mother
sent him at an early age to be raised by her brother Sir John York of
London, a merchant adventurer in African voyages. Martin did not
take to letters; all his life he spelled even more abominably than the
nobility, and so phonetically that we may be sure he talked with a
rough North Country accent. Sir John, observing that his nephew was
a lad "of great spirit and bould courage and naturall hardnes of body,"
got him a berth on the almost completely fatal Wyndham expedition
of 1553 to West Africa; Martin, aged fourteen, was one of the survivors. After fighting in Ireland, where he probably met Gilbert, he
shipped on John Lok's African voyage of 1562. The captain left him
as a hostage with the Portuguese, who imprisoned him at their Mina
fortress for several months and then shipped him home. Apparently the
lad did not enjoy this stretch in jail, as he next figures in a scheme to
capture the Mina; and when that failed he became captain of a privateer
which brought in both French and Spanish prizes. The first were legitimate since England was then at war with France, but the second got
him into trouble, since the Queen was not yet ready to break with
Spain. He then became a professional sea-rover, accepting commissions
from French rebels and the Prince of Orange, or anyone, and for a
time doing very well. But, on account of having seized a London merchant's cargo of wines, he enjoyed another short stretch in jail, this
time in England. There are records of Frobisher's being involved in a
dozen enterprises of questionable legality down to the year that he
signed on for the series of voyages that made him famous.

The contemporary full-length portrait of Frobisher grasping a
petronel or horse-pistol in his right hand suggests that he was not a
person to be trifled with. For seamanship, courage, and experience, no
man could have been better qualified than Frobisher for the voyages
he now undertook; no earlier voyage of discovery was so well
equipped, and few were so unfortunate.

Martin Frobisher's First Voyage, 1576

Martin had been dreaming of this for fifteen years, and he was now
only thirty-seven years old. As shipmate George Best wrote of Frobisher, he was "persuaded of a new and nearer passage to Cataya, than

by Cape d'buona Speranza, which the Portugallas yeerley use. He began first with himselfe to devise, and then with his friends to conferre, and layde a playne platte unto them, that that voyage was not onely possible by the Northwest, but also as he coulde prove, easie to bee performed."

And who were these friends? Advocates, of course, of the Northwest Passage—Sir Humfry Gilbert, merchant-shipowner Michael Lok, Stephen and William Borough, and, most important, the famous John Dee, who had brains, and Ambrose Dudley Earl of Warwick, who had money. The noble earl brought Frobisher's project to the notice of Lord Treasurer Burleigh; and it was he and Michael Lok who "perceavinge the corrage and knowinge the aptnes of Martine Furbusher" persuaded the Muscovy Company to relinquish their yet unused right to northwestern exploration, to a group of merchant adventurers of London. These included, principally, Michael Lok, Sir Thomas Gresham founder of the Royal Exchange, and two others who subscribed £100 each; five who put in £50 each, and a number who paid £25 each; total, £875. That proved to be not nearly enough, and Lok had to pay the balance, some £739. The same group organized the Company of Cathay for Frobisher's second voyage, but for the first they were only a partnership.

The task organization was as follows:—

Bark GABRIEL, 15–30 tuns,* Christopher Hall, master, specially built for this voyage at a cost of £152, including the pinnace. Crew of 18, including George Best.

Bark MICHAEL, 20–25 tuns, Owen Gryffyn, master, purchased all equipped for £120. Crew of 17.

Pinnace, unnamed, 7–10 tuns, 4 men.

The "tackeling" for all three cost £172 extra.

Nobody has yet found even a crude sketch of any vessel of Frobisher's three fleets. Both participants on this first voyage are described as "barks," then a generic name for a small three-masted ship under 100 tuns. At the highest estimate neither *Gabriel* nor *Michael* had the burthen of Cabot's *Mathew*, Verrazzano's *Dauphine*, or Cartier's *La*

---

* Where I give two figures for tunnage, they are from different sources and there are intermediate estimates too.

Grande Hermine. Neither had room on board for the indispensable pinnace, even if knocked down and stowed below. Frobisher's pinnace had to sail on her own bottom, and she did not sail far.

More impressive than the ships was the equipment. Some £100 was paid to Humfrey Cole, the leading instrument-maker of London, for nautical instruments and books. The literature included two works by André Thevet: his *Cosmographie universelle*, just out, and *Singularitez de la France antarctique;* and Medina's *Arte de Naviguar*, one of the best available treatises on navigation. Strangely enough, Frobisher did not carry William Bourne's more recent *Regiment of the Sea* (1574). Probably more for amusement than anything else, he had a copy of Sir John Mandeville's famous book of whoppers. Also, for good measure, a "great" English Bible. This was probably the "Bishop's Bible" of 1572, whose title page includes a portrait of the Queen, useful to show the natives. Navigational instruments on board were impressive in number and quality. They included a cross-staff (also called Jacob's staff, jackstaff, and balestila), an instrument for taking celestial altitudes recently brought by John Dee from the Netherlands; a "ring of brasse" (mariner's astrolabe), and a regular astrolabe; but no quadrant. The cross-staff was more efficient than the wooden quadrant with its plumb-bob hanging by a silken thread, but both continued to be made and used for centuries. George Best records that Polaris was so faint in the high northern latitudes that you could not catch it in the peep-holes of an astrolabe. They found meridional altitudes of the sun with the cross-staff the best means of determining latitude.

There were no fewer than twenty "compasses of divers sorts," and eighteen half-hour sand glasses. The other instruments included an *armilla tolomei* (armillary sphere); a *horologium geometricum*, a sundial adjustable to any latitude; a *compassum meridianum*, a compass with an attachment for recording the sun's shadow at high noon, thus determining the variation at that point; and a *holometrium geometricum*, a version of the French surveying instrument called *holometre*. John Dee spent many days in the spring of 1576 on board *Gabriel* and *Michael* instructing the pilots in navigation, and in the use of these instruments. It is difficult to see what use the armillary sphere and the holometer could have been to Frobisher; but the rest, with declination tables from Medina and a traverse board, certainly helped him to obtain his remarkably accurate latitudes.

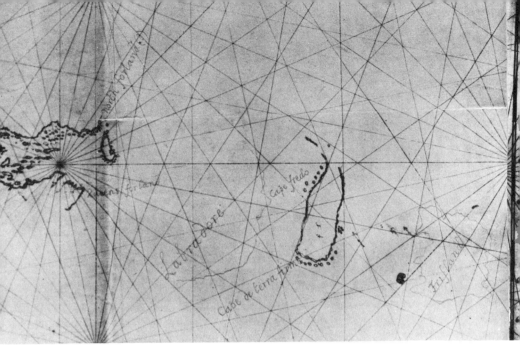

William Borough's Map furnished to Frobisher for his first voyage, and inspired by John Dee, who was responsible for the odd Greenland (western half only). The faint outlines and names were inserted by Frobisher on his first voyage, as well as the snub-nosed Greenland and Frobisher Bay. The arrows record his observations of compass variation. From the photo in Miller Christy, *Silver Map of the World* (1900), from the original in Hatfield House.

The most significant piece of Frobisher's equipment was a "carta of navigation . . . ruled playne," prepared especially for the expedition by William Borough the Muscovy Company commander. As one may see by our reproduction, Borough took a blank parchment, crossed and recrossed it with rhumb lines, dubbed in the British Isles and Norway (in the eastern half which we have not reproduced), and gave it to Frobisher to add what he found. He did just that, spotting in very faintly "Friesland," "Cape de terra firma" (at Cape Farewell), "Labradore," and "Cape fredo"; and, firmly, Greenland, his own strait, and Hall's Island. The arrows are Frobisher's record of compass variation; one of them, under his own strait, explains why it is oriented E-W instead of SE-NW. This is the kind of map-making which every explorer did, starting with Columbus; but Frobisher's is the only one prior to 1600 that is extant.

Frobisher's geographical contributions would have been more valuable had he not included in his sea-going library, and trusted, a copy of the Zeno brothers' fictitious voyages and map. These, as we have seen, made a sensation when printed at Venice a few years earlier. They even misled Mercator, who introduced Zeno features into his 1569 map, the best chart that Frobisher had on board. The English believed the Zeno map to be authentic, and it continued to befuddle northern navigators and cartographers for at least a century.

Besides books, charts, and instruments, we have a complete list of "furniture" for this voyage, including pots, pans, kettles, gridirons, and trivets for cooking over the open grates; grates rather than fire boxes, since Frobisher wisely brought "sea coal," guessing that firewood would be hard to come by in the north. The most expensive item, £13 18s., was for three hogsheads of aquavitae to give internal warmth when the external was wanting. For daily drink there were five tuns of beer which the Admiralty supplied for ten guineas. "Mr. Captayne Frobiser" paid an upholsterer £3 16s. 5d. for bedding. The other officers evidently supplied their own, and the common sailors, as usual, could expect no bed but a "soft plank," and brought their own blankets.

Frobisher was too sophisticated a navigator to depend on old-fashioned latitude sailing to attain his objective. Sailing 7 June 1576, he shaped a course well north of west. The ironical thing is that if he had followed the old system and taken his departure from northern Ireland at about 55° N, he could have followed the Labrador coast north for another five degrees, rounded Cape Chidley and entered Hudson Strait where no one had earlier penetrated. As it was, by deciding beforehand to hit the coast of America at around 63° N, he discovered only the dead-end Frobisher Bay; and when by accident he entered Hudson Strait on his third voyage, he had neither time nor inclination to press through.

Despite all these precautions and preparations, the fleet was fraught with misfortune from the start. It sailed 7 June from Ratcliff on the Thames, with a first-quarter moon. Off Deptford the pinnace collided with an anchored ship and had to be fitted with a new foresail and bowsprit. That done, they sailed past Greenwich, firing a royal salute, and in return receiving a gracious wave from Queen Elizabeth as she watched them from a window of the palace. She followed this up by sending "a Gentleman abbord of us, who declared that "her Majesty had good likings for our doings, and thanked us for it."

Foul winds forced the fleet to put in at Harwich and Yarmouth. Thence they had a good run to "St. Tronions" (St. Ninians) in the Shetlands, arrving 26 June. The wind now made up to a heavy gale that lasted eight days and proved too much for the pinnace. She disappeared, and her crew of four was never heard of again.

Christopher Hall's log indicates that *Gabriel* was a fast sailer, and that she enjoyed a prosperous wind from the Shetlands to Greenland. There were few four-hour watches in which she did not reel off nineteen or twenty knots; and in one, on 4 July, she made an average of seven. During the twenty-four hours between 7 June and noon on the 28th she made, by Hall's reckoning, 136 to 137 nautical miles before a "good gale," with forecourse, main topsail, and square spritsail set. On 1 July, "We had so much winde that we spooned * afore the sea Southwest 2 leagues." Hall's log indicates careful and skillful navigation, frequently working out compass variations from the new instrument.

On 11 July, in a full moon, the two ships sighted a land which Frobisher thought to be the mythical Friesland of that precious pair of fakers, the Zeno brothers. It was the east coast of Greenland. They could not even approach the shore because of pack-ice. Here, says Best, the master and men of bark *Michael*, "mistrusting the matter, conveyed themselves privilie away from him and returned home." *Michael* reached London 1 September where her cowardly master spread the lying excuse that *Gabriel* had been "cast awaye."

Far from it! Frobisher, after consulting his officers, decided to press on. Off or near Cape Farewell *Gabriel* ran into "an extreme storm which cast the ship flat on her syde"—on her beam ends as sailors usually express it. The water poured down an open hatchway, and she almost foundered; but "In this distress, when all the men in the ship had lost their courage, and did dispayre of lyfe," Frobisher "like himself with valiant courage" ran along the ship's exposed and almost horizontal topside, cutting or casting off lines and braces to relieve the pressure; he then ordered the mizzenmast to be cut away, and that

---

* To spoon, properly spoom, means to send your ship scudding before a heavy wind and sea. "Spoom her before the wind, you'll lose all else!" cries the jailer's daughter in John Fletcher's *Two Noble Kinsmen*, Act III, scene iv. Good advice!

righted her. But he forbade his men to sacrifice the mainmast, which they wanted to do.

This incident may well have inspired an outburst which George Chapman in one of his plays, *Byron's Conspiracy*, puts into the mouth of Chabot de Brion, Cartier's friend:

> Give me a spirit that on life's rough sea
> Loves t'have his sail filled with a lusty wind
> E'en till his sail-yards tremble, his masts crack,
> And his rapt ship runs on her side so low
> That she drinks water, and her keel plows air;
> There is no danger to the man that knows
> What life and death is: there's not any law
> Exceeds his knowledge; neither is it lawful
> That he should stoop to any other law.

Frobisher would certainly have agreed with the last four lines of this Elizabethan extravaganza; but like every other real sailor he preferred fair weather to foul, and calm seas to rough water. In his one recorded poem, Frobisher praises "An easie passage, void of loathsome toil." He never enjoyed such a one himself.

Gabriel, once righted, spoomed south before the wind until she could be pumped dry and a new mizzen rigged; she then turned westward and on 20 July, with a last-quarter moon, sighted what Christopher Hall first supposed to be Labrador, "a new land of marveilous great heith" with "a good store of Yce." This was Resolution Island off the southeastern cape of Baffin Island; Frobisher named it Queen Elizabeth's Foreland. Sailing north, he "descried another forlande, with a great gutte, bay, or passage, deviding as it were two mayne lands or continents asunder"—America and Asia. The Passage to Cathay! The ice parted and Frobisher "determined to make proof of this place, to see how farre that gutte had continuance . . . and so entred the same" on 21 July and sailed up it for some 150 miles. He persuaded himself that the high land to starboard was "the continente of Asia" and the equally lofty land crowned with glaciers on his port hand to be America. So he named that body of water "Frobishers Streytes, lyke as Magellanus at the Southwest ende of the Worlde, havying discovered the passage to the South Sea, . . . called the same straites Magellanes streightes."

Alas, Martin, this was no strait, and you were some thousands of miles from the South Sea; yet this dead-end sound or bight shall forever bear thy gallant name, as the real strait bears that of the noble Portuguese captain.

One calm day Frobisher had his men sound all around an iceberg, which fell apart while they were so engaged, making a terrifying noise "as if a great cliffe had fallen into the Sea." Returning to the mouth of the bay, they landed on an island which Frobisher named Hall after his competent sailing master Christopher Hall.* Here they began to see "sundry tokens" of people. Frobisher on 19 August climbed to the top of a hill and saw "a number of small things fleeting in the Sea a farre off, whyche he supposed to be Porposes, or Ceales, or some kinde of a strange fishe." They turned out to be Eskimo in kayaks. Elizabethans never called these natives Eskimo; that is a corruption of the Abnaki word for them, meaning "eaters of raw flesh," which the English and French colonists picked up in the next century. Frobisher and Davis referred to them simply as "the savages" or "the countrey people." Hall noted, "They be like to Tartars, with long blacke haire, broad faces, and flatte noses, and tawnie in colour, wearing Seale skinnes . . . the women are marked in the face with blewe streakes downe the cheekes, and round about the eies." That was, and still is, the fashionable beauty treatment for the females.

These Englishmen seem to have been as ill prepared as the Norsemen had been some five centuries earlier for dealing with the jolly but wily Eskimo. This group tried to cut Frobisher off from his boat, but he was too quick for them. By signs he invited a number on board, and cautiously bartered furs, fresh meat, and salmon for the usual trading truck. The natives showed that they were no strangers to European ships by doing gymnastic exercises in *Gabriel*'s rigging, proving that they were "verie strong of theyr armes, and nimble of their bodies."

One Eskimo who came on board was engaged, by sign language, to pilot *Gabriel* through the supposed Strait by paddling ahead in his kayak. Frobisher sent him ashore in one of his boats with a crew of five, whom he strictly enjoined to land the man at a good distance from his fellows and return on board at once. The first part of this order they carried out literally; but "their wilfulnesse was such" that they rowed to a point crowded with natives, hoping, sailor-like, to do some private trading. No Englishman ever saw them again. Frobisher waited for

* Hall's is now Loks Land, the north foreland to Frobisher Bay; but the islet off Loks is still called Hall.

them several days, tried without success to get his hands on some natives to force an exchange, but they eluded him, laughing contemptuously. Gunshots and trumpet blasts availed naught; the Eskimo simply folded their sealskin tents and stole away to the interior of Baffin Island.

Stefansson, who should know, insists that these actions of the Eskimo prove that they had had experience dealing with Europeans. In all probability, some vessels of the Newfoundland fishing fleet had sailed this far north, or missed the Strait of Belle Isle and made Baffin Island, and from them the Eskimo had learned to keep out of their clutches and to move inland if the Europeans became too obnoxious.

Frobisher was now on a spot. "Being thus maymed," he "dispayred how to procede furder on his voyage toward Cathay." Presently a fleet of kayaks approached the ship. Clearing for action by stretching canvas cloths across the open waist, covering the chain plates where an enemy might climb on board with canvas nailed to the ship's side, and shotting every gun, Frobisher succeeded in frustrating the probably intended attack. Next, having learned that the Eskimo loved bells, "He wrought a pretty pollicie" (strategy) by ringing a small one to make known "that he would give him the same that would come and fetch it." As the Eskimo still held off, he rang a louder bell, which attracted to the ship's side in his kayak the native who had agreed to be his pilot. The Captain, being a man of resource and of prodigious strength, "caught holde on the man's hand, and with his other hand caught holde on his wrest; and suddenly by mayn force of strength plucked both the man and his light bote out of the sea into the ship in a tryse." Frobisher gave the Eskimo to understand that he would be set free in exchange for the five Englishmen; but, although the man was given a chance to communicate with his fellows, they did nothing.

The loss of these five left *Gabriel* with only thirteen men and boys, "so tyred and sik with laboure of their hard voyage," that Frobisher decided to return home forthwith. First, however, he took formal possession of the land. Then he sent most of his reduced company ashore in relays to pick up what they could, "living or dead, stocke or stone," as souvenirs or tokens of possession. One brought from Hall's Islet a piece of coal-black stone which, by its weight, seemed to be metallic. This little lump of marcasite or iron pyrites set off a chain reaction in London.

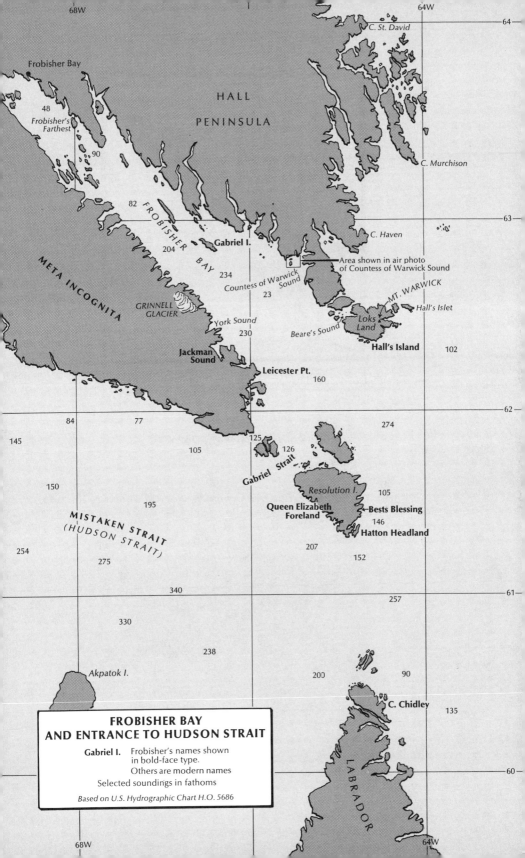

68W

64W

C. St. David

64

Frobisher Bay

HALL

48
*Frobisher's
Farthest*

90

PENINSULA

C. Murchison

82 F R O B I S H E R

Gabriel I.

204

B A Y

234

Countess of Warwick
Sound

23

63

C. Haven

Area shown in air photo
of Countess of Warwick Sound

MT. WARWICK

Hall's Islet

M E T A   I N C O G N I T A

*GRINNELL
GLACIER*

York Sound

230

Beare's Sound

Loks
Land

**Jackman
Sound**

Leicester Pt.

160

Hall's Island

102

84

77

62

145

105

274

125

126

Gabriel   **Strait**

Resolution I.

105

150

195

**Queen Elizabeth
Foreland**

Bests Blessing

146

Hatton Headland

M I S T A K E N   S T R A I T
(H U D S O N   S T R A I T)

254

275

207

152

340

257

61

330

238

Akpatok I.

200

90

C. Chidley

135

60

L A B R A D O R

**FROBISHER BAY
AND ENTRANCE TO HUDSON STRAIT**

Gabriel I.   Frobisher's names shown
in bold-face type.
Others are modern names
Selected soundings in fathoms

Based on U.S. Hydrographic Chart H.O. 5686

68W

64W

From Pedro de Medina *Regimento de Navigacion* (1964 reprint).

Shooting Polaris with cross-staff.

From Justin Winsor, *Narrative and Critical History of America*, II (1886).

Departing 26 August with the new moon, and continually enduring "extreme storms of weather but the wynde still in their favour homewards," *Gabriel* made the Orkneys a month later, Harwich on 2 October 1576, and London on the 9th. There they were "joyfully received with the great admiration of the people, bringing with them their strange man and his bote, which was such a wonder onto the whole city and to the rest of the realm that heard of yt." The Queen herself named the mainland they had found, *Meta Incognita*, the unknown bourne. It is still so called today.

The Eskimo died shortly of a pulmonary complaint.

Frobisher, confident that he had "discovered the passage to the South Sea," now submitted to supposed experts the "peace of a blacke stone" from Hall's Islet. Two different assayers declared it to be marcasite, the old name for iron pyrites, which undoubtedly it was; but a third, an Italian named Agnello, insisted it was gold ore, and in three trials produced a speck of gold dust. To skeptical Michael Lok, inquiring how he found gold after the others reported none, Agnello remarked, "*Bisogna sapere adulare la natura*"—nature needs a little coaxing! Possibly the Italian had been bribed; possibly he had "salted" the stone himself, a practice not unknown in the nineteenth-century gold rushes; but iron pyrites, though well deserving the name "fool's gold," do sometimes contain small quantities of the precious metal. A German mineralogist named Jonas Schultz supported Agnello's opinion, the word went around that Frobisher had discovered a real gold mine, and a firm conviction to that effect, which is what all England dearly wished to believe, spread through the city and the court. Another Saguenay!

☀ X ☀
Frobisher's Second and Third Voyages

1577-1578

Second Voyage Begins

O Frobusher! thy bruit and name
    shall be enrold in bookes,
That whosoever after comes
    and on thy labour lookes,
Shall muse and marvell at thyne actes,
    and greatnesse of thy minde.
I say no more, least some affirme
    I fanne thy face with winde.

THOMAS CHURCHYARD, "A WELCOME-HOME TO
MASTER MARTIN FROBISHER" (1578)

Optimism about gold and the expectation that "Frobisher's Strait" really was a strait, reigned so high that the Captain's original backers now joined with others to form the Company of Cathay. By receiving a charter from the crown (17 March 1577), this company became a respectable joint stock corporation. Meeting in London, the stockholders elected Michael Lok governor for life, and Frobisher "High admiral of all seas and waters, countries, lands and isles, as well of Cathay as of all other countries and places of new discovery." The precedent was Columbus's appointment as Admiral of the Ocean Sea and of the Indies. Queen Elizabeth subscribed £1000, several others paid up to a total of £4275, and Lok levied a 20 per cent assessment on the stockholders. The crown furnished a fine tall ship, the *Aid*, and both *Gabriel* and the recreant *Michael* of the previous voyage were available. George Best gives us the task organization as follows:—

"Generall of the whole Company": MARTIN FROBISHER

Ship AID, 200 tuns, Christopher Hall, master; also on board, the General's deputy George Best. Complement: 115 to 120, "whereof 30 or more were Gentlemen and Souldyers, the rest sufficient and tall Saylers." Among the gentlemen were members of the Carew, Stafford, Lee, Kinnersley, and Brackenbury families, and Dionyse Settle, who wrote one of the two extant accounts of this voyage.

Bark GABRIEL, 15–30 tuns, Edward Fenton, captain; William Smyth, master. Complement: 10 mariners, 3 soldiers, and about 5 more.

Bark MICHAEL, 25 tuns, Gilbert Yorke, captain; James Beare, master, who doubled as fleet surgeon. Complement: 10 mariners, 2 soldiers, and about 4 more.

Thirty of the ships' companies were miners, refiners, and other appropriate civilians. Also there were six criminals to be set ashore on "Friesland" (Greenland) to civilize the natives (!). Provisions included hardtack, flour, pickled beef and pork, dried peas and codfish, butter, cheese, oatmeal, rice, honey, "Sallet oyl," and vinegar. For drink, eighty tuns of beer (calculated to give every man one gallon a day for six months) and five tuns of sack and malmsey for the officers. For clothing there was a slop-chest of "wollinge clothe for jirkens, breche and hose, canvas and lynnenge clothe for dublets and sherts." The Company intended its men to eat hearty and dress warm. On the third voyage we find that some mariners owned five changes of clothing.

Among those on board *Aid* was a young man named John White, a member of the Painter-Stainers' Company of London, who would win posthumous fame centuries later as the artist of the first Virginia colony. Owing to him we have the first European pictures of the Eskimo.

Frobisher's orders from the Company of Cathay were, (1) to set his sappers and miners to work collecting "gold ore" on Hall's Island or elsewhere; (2), in one of the barks, to sail no more than 100 leagues up his "Strait," but not so long as to jeopardize returning home the same year; (3) to leave some of his company to winter on the Strait, with a pinnace and supplies; and (4) if no more promising ore were forthcoming, to send the flagship home and go on to China with the two barks.

The inventory of flagship *Aid*, which has survived in the Public Record Office, includes enough detail to enable a fairly accurate model to be constructed—if only someone would do it! Built for the Royal Navy prior to 1571, she was bought by the Company "of the Queenes

Majestie" in 1577 especially for Frobisher's second voyage. Stepping three masts and a bowsprit, she flew the St. George ensign (red cross on white field with arms of England at the crossing). She carried a square spritsail on bowsprit, spread lower courses and topsails on the foremast and mainmast, and a lateen mizzen; a mizzen topmast also is mentioned, on a short yard. All her blocks (still called "pulleys") were brass-bound with brass sheaves. Her "skyffe" shipped twelve oars and mounted Rotherhithe ironwork; her longboat, which she probably towed, had its own mast, sail, and windlass. On *Aid*'s deck were mounted a main capstan with iron "collor and paull" and four bars, and a fore capstan with two bars. She carried four great anchors complete with stoppers and shank painters, and three ordinary ones, and their cables were of twelve-inch hemp. There were many spare rodes and hawsers down to five-inch. The only items mentioned below deck are "a bed sted and a table in the captaines cabbine, the table broken."

Of brass ordnance, *Aid* mounted five minions and falcons; of cast-iron guns, 14 sacres, minions, and falcons. She was well furnished with iron and stone balls, crossbar shot and chain shot; and, in addition, whole racks and chests of calivers, long bows and arrows, partisans, pikes, and arrows tipped with "wilde fyer," presumably like Cartier's fire lances. Those who took the flagship's inventory judged her to be worth £838 16s. 8d., including the equipment.

The fleet weighed at Blackwall, London, 25 May 1577 with a first-quarter moon. It called at Harwich on the 28th to take on "certayne victualles," and tarried until the 30th. Frobisher there received orders from the Privy Council reminding him that his official complement, 120 persons, had been exceeded; he was reported to have shipped some fifty more. Tongue in cheek, the General put on the beach the six criminals designated to civilize Greenland, and enough other "proper men, whych with unwilling myndes departed," to bring the number down to 120. Hearing that the Queen was staying at the Essex seat of his supporter Ambrose Dudley, Earl of Warwick, Frobisher had the tact to call on her "with diverse resolute and forward gentlemen . . . to take their leaves." "Kissing her highness's hands" and receiving her "gracious countenance & comfortable words," they "departed towardes their charge." If anything were needed to increase Frobisher's resolution, this royal interview did. Whatever happened, he could not let his Queen down.

The fleet next called at the Orkneys on 7 June and traded old shoes and junk rope with the natives for fresh provisions. Departing with "a merrie winde by night," and a last-quarter moon, they steered west-northwest and soon lost sight of land. The wind turned scant and forced them to beat, or, as Best called it, to "traverse on the Seas." They spoke three sail of fishermen returning from Iceland and sent letters home by them. Twenty-six days of beating or lying-to followed, and they saw "many monsterous Fishe and strange Fowls." Then, "God favoured us with more prosperous windes," and a full moon on the last day of June. *Michael*, in the lead on 4 July, fired a gun and struck topsails as a signal she had sighted land. At 10 p.m. they "made the land perfect, and knew it to be Freeseland"; the latitude they found to be 60°30'. Greenland again, of course. Men on the becalmed flagship caught a "hollibut" big enough to feed all hands and to make some sick who overate. Twice Frobisher tried to land but could not get through the ice floes, and "having spent 4 days & nights sailing alongst this land, finding the coast subject to such bitter cold & continuall mistes," he decided to bear away for his own Strait. En route the fleet had to "lay a-hull" a couple of days, and *Michael* broke her "steerage" and lost a topmast. On 17 July, with a new moon, they made the North Foreland "otherwise called Halles Iland, and also the small Iland bearing the name of the saide Hall, whence the Ore was taken uppe." The latitude, says Best, was 62°30' N; correct. "Happie landfall" indeed!

Frobisher Bay Again

Frobisher and "goldfiners" landed on Hall's next day to look for more gold ore. They found a bit of marcasite no bigger than a nut, but collected a quantity of "Egges, Fowle, and a yong Seale." The flagship, in the meantime, spent most of the night dodging "monstrous and huge yce, comparable to great mountaines." They never could have escaped, wrote Dionyse Settle in his account of this voyage, "If God . . . had not provided for this Our extremitie a sufficient remedie, through the light of the night whereby wee might well discerne to flee from such imminent dangers, which we avoided" by tacking fourteen times in one four-hour watch. He credits master's mate Charles Jackman the temporary commander, and pilot Andrew Dyer, "men expert both in navigation, and other good qualities." Frobisher returned on board 19

Little Hall's Island, "Whence the Ore was taken uppe." Photo taken 31 August 1959 from 30,000 feet elevation. The white objects off shore are icebergs. Courtesy Air Photo Division, Canadian Government.

July 1577 "with good newes of great riches . . . in the bowels of those barren mountains." This brought "a sudden mutation" from black despair to extravagant delight. "We were all wrapt with joy, forgetting both where we were, and what we had suffered." The northwest wind having blown the icebergs out to sea, disclosed "a large entrance into the streight." In they sailed, and on the 20 July "founde out a faire Harborough for the shippe and barkes to ride in and named it after our Master's mate Jackman's Sound." This was on the southwest shore of Frobisher's Strait, which the Queen had named Meta Incognita. *Gabriel* nipped in behind Queen's Foreland, finding a strait that is still named after her. Frobisher still thought the eastern shore, part of Baffin Island, to be a far-thrusting cape of Asia.

The "Generall" now held a special service of thanksgiving for their safe arrival, praying "that by our Christian studie and endeavor, those barbarous people trained up in Paganrie and infidelitie, might be reduced to the knowledge of true religion, and to the hope of salvation in Christ our Redeemer." * He exhorted the ships' companies to obey

* In the silly controversy whether Virginia or Plymouth had the "first Thanksgiving," nobody has mentioned this, much the earliest English thanksgiving service on American soil that has been recorded.

Jackman Sound, Frobisher Bay, and part of Grinnell Glacier. Photo taken 2 September 1959 from elevation of 30,000 feet. Courtesy Air Photo Division, Canadian Government.

Part of Hall's Island (now Loks Land). Photo from elevation of 30,000 feet, 31 August 1959. "Mount Warwick," which Frobisher climbed and named, is almost in the middle. Courtesy Air Photo Division, Canadian Government.

Fenton, Yorke, and Best while he landed with Settle and some forty gentlemen and soldiers on the big Hall's Island, to explore and take possession of the supposed continent of Asia. The company erected "a Columne or Crosse of stones" on the highest hill of this island, planted an ensign, named the hill Mount Warwick after their noble patron, and, with noise of trumpet and "certain prayers" said on their knees, took possession in the name of the mighty princess Elizabeth, Queen of England, France and Ireland, Defender of the Faith.

After they had come down the hill, some Eskimo appeared and made signs of friendship; and each side sent two men to do a limited trade in "pinnes and pointes and such trifles." Frobisher and his partner, hoping to secure hostages to trade for the five sailors captured on the previous voyage, tried to grab two "salvagies," but the maneuver failed; the greasy Eskimo slipped out of their clutches, recovered their weapons, and chased the two Englishmen ignominiously back to their boat, Frobisher suffering an arrow wound in the buttock. One of his boatmen, Nicholas Conger, "being a Cornishman, and a good wrastler," grappled with an Eskimo and showed him "such a Cornishe tricke, that he made his sides ake . . . for a moneth after." All had to spend the night in the open, "keeping verie good watche and warde . . . upon harde cliffes of Snowe and Ice, both wet, cold and uncomfortable."

This was not the best way to "allure them to familiaritie" or get word of the five men abandoned the year before; nor did the next episode help. The landing force, rowing around the opposite side of Hall's Island, suddenly came upon a group of Eskimo who "fiercely assaulted our men with their bowes and arrows." The Englishmen replied with arquebuses whose reports so terrified the natives that they either fled to the hills or leaped off the rocks into the sea. We are fortunate to have a colored sketch of this scene, made on the spot by John White, to which we have referred before. In a ship's longboat containing seven or eight men, two are shooting at three Eskimo on a cliff, who reply with bows and arrows; one Englishman, an officer, is trying to fend off arrows with sword and target. The scenery is correct for Frobisher Bay, and the royal ensign on the boat is right for a Queen's ship. Note in the background a fleet of kayaks, angry natives, and sealskin tents; in the foreground, ice floes, and space filled up by depicting an Eskimo in his kayak.

Frobisher's men landed and managed to capture two women. One was so old and ugly that the sailors took her to be a witch, "had her buskins plucked off, to see if she were cloven footed." Disappointingly she had normal feet, so they let her go. The other, a young mother carrying a baby, they kept and brought on board. The Englishmen

John White's painting of the Eskimo mother and baby captured by Frobisher in 1577. Courtesy British Museum.

then "made a spoyle" of the Eskimo tents, where they found old clothes which must have belonged to the five missing men.

The rest of their stay in Frobisher's Strait that summer was devoted to two objects: recovering the five lost sailors and loading ore. A party of Eskimo conveyed by signs that three missing Englishmen were living up-country and wished to communicate. Frobisher gave them pen, ink, and paper to deliver to his shipmates, with a letter remarkable for its Biblical diction and patent sincerity:

> In the name of God in whom we all beleve, who, I trust, hath preserved your bodyes and souls amongst these Infidels, I commend me unto you. I will be glad to seeke by all meanes

you can devise, for your deliverance, eyther with force, or with any commodities within my Shippes, whiche I will not spare for your sakes, or anything else I can doe for you. I have aboord, of theyrs, a Man, a Woman, and a Childe, which I am contented to delyver for you, but the man which I carried away from hence the last yeare, is dead in ENGLAND. Moreover you may declare unto them, that if they deliver you not, I wyll not leave a manne alive in their Countrey. And thus, if one of you can come to speake with me, they shall have eyther the Man, Woman, or Childe in pawne for you. And thus unto God whom I trust you do serve, in hast I leave you, and to him we will dayly pray for you. This Tuesdaye morning the seaventh of August. Anno. 1577.

> Yours to the uttermost of my power,
>
> MARTIN FROBISHER.

John White's painting of the Eskimo captured by Frobisher in 1577. Courtesy British Museum.

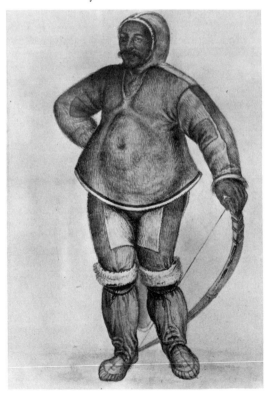

> I have sente you by these bearers, Penne, Incke, and Paper,
> to write back unto me agayne, if personally you can not come
> to certifye me of your estate.

No word, no reply came, and the mystery of the Englishmen's fate lay hidden for nigh three centuries. Around 1862 it was solved when an American explorer named Charles F. Hall stayed for two years in Frobisher Bay, mingling with the Eskimo and learning their language. An ancient woman named Ookijoxy Ninoo, and other old people, told him this story. Long, long ago, *kodlunas* (white men) came to their country in three successive years; first year two ships, second year three ships, third year a great many ships (Frobisher's three visits, almost exactly). Five Englishmen, captured by the Innuit (as these Eskimo called themselves), went to the island now called Kodlunarn (White Men's Island), dug a sloping trench in the rock close to the water's edge, built a boat with timber that Frobisher had left behind, and sailed away, only to perish from the cold.

What an amazing example of the reliability of oral tradition among primitive, unlettered people! We can now see what happened. The Eskimo kept the five Englishmen prisoner until after Frobisher's final departure in 1578. Then, either because they had no further use for them, or from feelings of compassion, the hosts turned them loose. The wretched men went to the island where Frobisher had abandoned plenty of materials, built a boat, put to sea, and perished.

Hall, and in 1943 my late friend Dr. Alexander Forbes, visited Kodlunarn Island and found trenches where Frobisher dug out "ore" on his third voyage, the dock they excavated to help loading, and where the five Englishmen probably built their boat, and foundations of the Englishmen's houses, together with fragments of brick, glass, and iron. On our reproduction of Forbes's air photograph, the rectangular loading dock is conspicuous on the east side facing the mainland, and off it the fleet anchored. West of the dock can be seen one of the deeper trenches where they excavated "ore," and, in the center of the island, a little round thing marks the stone foundations of the house that Frobisher built on his next voyage.

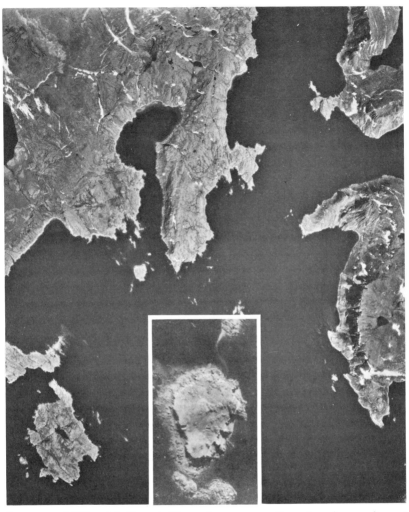

Countess of Warwick Sound. Photo from 30,000 feet elevation, 4 August 1959. Courtesy Air Photo Division, Canadian Government. Insert: Low-altitude photo of Kodlunarn Island (800 feet long), taken by Alexander Forbes in 1943.

Conclusion of Second Voyage

A find that aroused almost as much interest as the female captive was that of a dead narwhal on the shore. George Best, who made a sketch of it, called it a sea unicorn, and described it as about twelve feet long, "havyng a horne of two yardes long, growing out of the snoute or nostrels . . . wreathed and strayte, like in fashion to a Taper made of waxe." The horn they took home and presented to the Queen, who kept it in her wardrobe, handy for bringing out to exhibit "as a Jewel," and to stimulate the art of bawdy conversation that she is said to have loved.

"Having now got a woman captive for the comforte of our man," wrote Best, the two were brought together, surrounded by a circle of Englishmen curious to see what would happen. The Eskimo behaved with exemplary dignity and, although forced to bunk together on the voyage home, "did never use as man and wife." Best marveled at their modesty: "The man would never shift himselfe, except he had first caused the woman to depart out of his Cabin, and they both were most shamefast, least anye of their privie parts should bee discovered, eyther of themselves, or any other body."

John White depicted the Eskimo man twice, and the woman with her baby peeking out of her hood. Both are done in watercolor and in great detail, showing the hair on the sealskin, exquisite needlework on jacket, boots and breeches, and narrow fur edgings. Since these Eskimo had worked out a way of life suited to their boreal environment and available food, their fashions did not change; not only Hall but Amundsen in 1905 found them wearing the same styles as those of 1577, including the dorsal flap to the jacket—a very useful appendage when you had to sit on ice or frozen ground.

Having secured these hostages, Frobisher concentrated on obtaining a quantity of "ore" to take home. On an island (the modern Kodlunarn) which he named *Anne Warwick* after the Countess, he dug out some 200 tons of worthless rock and stowed it in the three ships. Other interchanges with the "craftie villains" led to nothing, but the captured Eskimo showed them how to harness the dogs to sleds. Settle concluded that here "there is nothing fitte, or profitable for the use of man" except the supposed minerals "couched within the bowels of the earth."

George Best's narwhal. From his *True Discourse*. Courtesy Harvard College Library.

By 21 August, when the holds of the three ships were crammed with supposed gold ore, and a first-quarter moon hung in the sky, it seemed "good time to leave." Nature gave warning by surrounding the ships with fresh ice every night. Next day "We plucked downe oure tentes" on Anne Warwick Island, and after lighting bonfires, marching with ensigns displayed, and firing a volley in honor of the Countess, the company departed for home. They took meridional latitude sights daily from the sun with the cross-staff, says Best; and of Polaris too.

On 17 September, approaching England cautiously with frequent casts of the lead, and lighted by a first-quarter moon, the fleet made Lands End. The flagship put in at Padstowe roads in Cornwall, then at Milford Haven in Wales, and finally at Bristol. *Gabriel*, too, made Bristol, whilst *Michael* sailed northabout to Yarmouth. And so ended Frobisher's second voyage to his "Streightes" and the Meta Incognita.

At Bristol the three Eskimo made a great sensation; a local chronicler described how the man put on an exhibition shoot in the Back (the upper harbor), carrying his kayak to the shore and hitting ducks on the wing with his spear.

Fortunately, there happened to be living at Bristol, Lucas de Heere, a refugee artist from the Low Countries. He produced, for the French edition of Dionyse Settle's account of Frobisher's second voyage, the picture that we have reproduced. The Eskimo hunter, like those of other primitive tribes, used a throwing-stick to enhance the speed and deadliness of his spear. He is shown both bringing his kayak to the shore and using this weapon; a dead duck lies in the water, and other fowl are trying to escape. The woman and her baby are interested observers. In the background, instead of Bristol, De Heere has depicted what he supposed to be a native Eskimo scene, complete with dog har-

Lucas de Heere's drawing of the Eskimo's demonstration at Bristol, with a native background. Note the spearthrower, the kayaks, the dogsled, and the sealskin tent. From Dionyse Settle's *True Report* (1577). Courtesy British Museum.

nessed to sled. He exhibits the usual European inability to depict Indian or Eskimo faces correctly; John White was the exception.

Although the English catered to these captives by feeding them raw meat and not trying to replace their sealskin clothing with wool, they died within a month.

Part of the supposed "ewer" (as the English often spelled "ore") was landed at Bristol, where Jonas Schultz built a "furnace" to smelt it next the house of Sir William Winter, an investor in this voyage to the tune of £500. The other part was smelted at Dartford on the Thames where a rival German "expert," known as "Doctor" Burcot or Burchard, took charge. This plant cost the Company of Cathay £1105.

On one occasion, it is said, Frobisher became so furious with Jonas's double-talk that he pulled a dagger on him when attending the Bristol furnace "naked," but no harm was done.

Third Voyage

The second voyage cost the Cathay Company some £6410; and as only £2500 had been subscribed before sailing, the 200 tons of "ore" brought home just *had* to be pay dirt. Remembering how the Paris assayers had shown up Cartier's worthless gold and diamonds thirty-five years earlier, one wonders whether the two Germans employed by the Company were corrupt or just plain stupid. Their final estimate accepted by the Cathay Company was this: one ton of Meta Incognita ore yielded gold worth £7 15s., and silver valued at £16, at a cost of £10 for refining. Since this meant a profit of £5 per ton, the Cathay Company cheerfully accepted it as correct and proceeded to organize an ambitious third voyage for 1578. Sixteen persons subscribed £6952 10s. to finance it, the Queen giving more than half. The Warwicks stuck by Frobisher, and the names of Knollys, Suffolk, Pembroke, Sydney, and Walsingham appear on the list; all subscribers except Michael Lok were of the nobility and gentry. Canny merchants kept "hands off."

Mariners and soldiers were paid 10s. per month; officers as high as £6 13s. 4d.

The task organization, from Best and other sources, was as follows:

Captain General: Martin Frobisher

AID: "Admirall" (flagship), 200 tuns, Frobisher, captain; Charles Jackman, master.

THOMAS ALLEN (vice admiral), Gilbert Yorke, captain; one Gibbes, master; Robert Davis, master's mate; Christopher Hall, chief pilot.

JUDITH, rear admiral, Frobisher's lieutenant general, Edward Fenton, captain

ANNE FRANCES, George Best, captain; John Gray, master

HOPEWELL, Henry Carew, captain; Andrew Dyer, master

BEARE of Leicester, property of Michael Lok, Richard Philpot, captain

THOMAS of Ipswich, William Tanfield, captain; Cox, master

EMANUELL of Exeter (also called ARANELL or ARMONELL), Courtney, captain

FRANCES of Fowey, Moyles, captain

Buss MOONE of Fowey, Upcot, captain; John Lakes, master

Buss EMMANUELL of Bridgewater, commonly called "The Buss of Bridgewater," Newton, captain; James Leech, master

SALAMON or SALAMANDER of Weymouth, Thomas (or Hugh) Randall, captain

Bark DENNIS or DIONYSE, Kendall, captain

Bark GABRIEL, Edward Harvey, captain; William Smyth, master

Bark MICHAEL, Kinnersley, captain

Frobisher's instructions from the Company ordered him to depart not later than 1 May. He may call at "Fryzeland" en route to Countess of Warwick's Sound. He will put men to work on the Countess's island, look for other mines and minerals and search for the lost men with his two barks. He must keep a written record of all metal, ore, etc. removed from the country and pack them "in apte and peculiar boxes." When he has accumulated 800 or more tons, the fleet may sail for home. But he is to provide for forty able seamen, shipwrights, and carpenters, thirty soldiers, and thirty "pyoners with sufficient vittalle for 18 monthes" to be left behind at Meta Incognita under Captain Fenton, together with ship *Judith* and the two old barks. Absolutely nothing is said about pursuing the northern waters further west; in their greed for gold, the adventurers seem to have forgotten about that passage to Cathay. Miners were requisitioned from Cornish towns which, as few real miners accepted, impressed anyone they could lay hands on. Poor devils, they had a rough time at sea and ashore, and many died before returning home.

Now in command of a fleet of fifteen sail, Frobisher felt obliged to issue a set of general orders: No swearing, dice, card-playing, or filthy communications to be allowed; serve God twice daily "with the ordinary service" according to the Church of England. The Admiral to lead the fleet, and none to part further than a mile from her. Each ship to speak the Admiral every evening between seven and eight o'clock to receive night orders from chief pilot Hall. If weather grows thick or wind contrary, forcing *Aid* to tack or lay at hull, she shall fire one or two guns, and the *Thomas Allen* and *Judith* must reply in kind. When sailing in a fog, every ship to "keepe a reasonable noyse with Trumpet, Drumme or otherwise." If any ship "lose company by force of weather," she must rendezvous at "Freeseland" or the Strait. If attacked by an enemy, four designated ships "shall attend upon" *Aid* and *Thomas Allen*.

Frobisher obviously knew how to conduct a fleet, although he asked too much to expect a sailing vessel to keep station within a mile. Even steamships found that difficult in World War II convoys.

In November 1577 Francis Drake's fleet, including the *Golden Hind* in which he circumnavigated the globe, sailed from Plymouth. The court and the public expected much less of Drake than they did of Frobisher, who must later have wished that he had shipped with his great contemporary. That opportunity would come later.

Frobisher's fleet, collected from ports as far apart as Yarmouth and Bristol, assembled at Harwich, sailed 31 May 1578 with a last-quarter moon and shaped a course through the English Channel. Just before taking their departure from that favorite jumping-off place, Dursey Head, Ireland, they spoke a derelict vessel manned by "poore menne of Bristowe" who had been "spoyled" by French pirates. Most of the crew, wounded, had been left on board with nothing to sustain them but "olives and stinking water." Frobisher (wrote Best), "who well understandeth the office of a Souldioure, and an Englishman, and knoweth well what the necessity of the sea meaneth . . . relieved them with Surgerie and salves, to heale their hurts, and with meate and drinke to comfort their pining hartes."

First stop, as usual, was the east coast of Greenland. Frobisher, seeing signs of people, had himself rowed ashore, but by the time he landed the Eskimo had fled, leaving some forty dogs to guard their possessions. The Englishmen captured two puppies which, if they survived the voyage, were the first huskies to reach England. The Captain General, imagining that he and his were the first "Christians that ever set foote upon that ground," took possession of Greenland in the name of their Queen, and even named it "West England."

On 20 June the fleet "having a fayre and large wind" and a full moon, departed for Frobisher's Strait. *Salamander* bumped a whale which "thereat made a great and ugly noise" and stopped her dead in

A fair June day in Frobisher Bay. From foot of Grinnell Glacier looking toward Baffin Island. U. S. Navy Photo of 20 June 1946.

the water. Approaching the coast in the dark of the moon, they sighted on 2 July Queen's Foreland (now Resolution Island) off the southern entrance to the Strait, and there their troubles began.

That summer of 1578 was abnormally cold and stormy. Frobisher's Strait was "combred with Ise," "enclosing us, as it were, within the pales of a Parke," and those little ships, like the mammoth tanker that made the Northwest Passage in 1969, had to watch for a passage through the floes and among the bergs, "looking everie houre for death . . . our ships so troubled and tossed among the yce." *Judith* and *Michael* disappeared and were given up for lost; actually they had nipped ahead to Countess of Warwick Sound, where the rest later joined them. Bark *Dennis*, "being but a weake shippe & brused afore among the yce," was so damaged that she came apart and sank within sight of her consorts "which so abashed the whole fleete, that we thought verily we should have tasted of the same sauce." They manned their boats in time and despite the icy obstacles rescued every man jack of her crew. Those men were mariners, no doubt about it.

While the fleet lay "compassed . . . on every side with Ise," there arose a "sodaine and terrible tempest" from the southeastward, which worsened the ice problem and prevented all but four ships (*Anne Frances, Moone, Frances* of Fowey, and *Gabriel*) from recovering sea room. Some set sail to take advantage of every opening, others took in sail and drifted, others anchored to the lee side of a big berg; all buttressed their topsides with old junk, spars, fenders, spare spars, and even bedding to protect them "from the outragious sway and strokes of the said Ise." As extra precaution, mariners stood by with poles, pikes, oars, and three-inch plank to sheer off threatening floes and bergs. Some ships were so squeezed as to be "heaved up" a foot or more, resulting in bent and broken knees and beams. George Best commended the captains for encouragement of the men, and the "poore Miners unacquainted with such extremities," who toiled "to the everlasting renowne of our nation."

After two days and nights of extreme peril, the wind veered to northwest, "which did not only disperse and dryve forthe the Ise before them, but also gave them libertie of more scope and Sea roome." The fleet, rejoining the four sail which earlier had sought safety at sea, spent several days off shore, effecting repairs and hoping (in vain so it turned out) that sun and offshore wind would melt the ice.

The "Mistaken Straits"

Alas, more woe lay ahead.

On 7 July, Frobisher, with twelve of his fifteen sail, again closed the shore. The General, making South or Queen Elizabeth's Foreland on 7 July in a snowstorm, judged it to be Hall's Island, the North Foreland, and so left it on the starboard hand. When the sun came out and a meridional altitude was taken from the flagship's deck, the resulting latitude, 62° 10′ N, proved that *Aid* was on the wrong side of Queen Elizabeth's Foreland. She was sailing up what Frobisher called "the Mistaken Straites." After another great explorer had resolutely sailed through, these would be named Hudson Strait.

High summer in Frobisher Bay, 1864. Meta Incognita and Grinnell Glacier in background. From C. F. Hall, *Arctic Researches* (1866).

For twenty days the fleet sailed cautiously up Hudson Strait, with a waxing moon, which for most of the time was shrouded in fog. The currents were so strong as to turn a ship around "after the manner of a whirlepoole." Captain Yorke of *Thomas Allen*, with chief pilot Christopher Hall on board, and *Anne Frances* commanded by the narrator George Best, peeled off and sought the open sea. There they ran into another press of ice so thick that the men made plans to save themselves in boats and on hatch covers. The rest of the fleet, "following the course of the Generall whyche ledde them the waye, passed up above 60 leagues within the sayd doubtfull and supposed straytes, having alwayes a fayre continente uppon their starreboorde syde, and a continuance still of an open Sea before them."

After he had realized his mistake, Frobisher looked for an opening on the north that would connect with his own "strait." When he had given up hope of that, he debated whether to sail on, in the expectation that this would prove to be *the* passage to "the ritch Countrey of Cataya" (since he had observed that the flood tide ran three hours to the ebb tide's one, indicating a great body of water to the westward); or return to fulfill his duty of gathering ore. Duty won; but in the meantime some of Frobisher's men landed on the shore of the Ungava

Peninsula, found it to be far better stocked with fauna and flora than Meta Incognita, and did a little trading with the local Eskimo.

It was no small task to get out of Hudson Strait, with its headwinds, baffling currents, and a "furious overfall" (tide rip) at the entrance, which one could hear roaring afar off, like the tide race at London Bridge. Frobisher at times had to anchor in more than 100 fathom, bending two long cables together, and on other occasions sailed over rocky reefs with only six inches to spare. When all seemed lost, the men would cry out, "Lorde, now helpe or never; nowe Lorde looke down from Heaven and save us sinners, or else oure safetie commeth too late!" Then, "at the very pintch one prosperous breath of winde" would waft them past the threatened danger. Nobody in Frobisher's fleet doubted the efficacy of prayer, or that he owed his life to the compassionate help of His Divine Majesty.

By 24 July the fleet again united in harbor, except for *Gabriel* which had just got through the strait named after her on "the backside and Western point of the Queen's Foreland." There are two entrances to Frobisher Bay behind this big cluster of islands. Captain Bob Bartlett in 1942 conned schooner *Morrissey* through the narrower, to the admiration of Alexander Forbes. "Next morning," wrote Dr. Forbes, "we entered our first ice floes, a picture of rare and thrilling beauty, the ice pans either of clear blue or snow white, in strong contrast against the calm water." But Frobisher's men had neither taste nor time to admire the beauty of this scene. Buss *Emmanuell* reported ice so thick and dangerous that, despite all efforts to sheer off the floes, she was holed in many places and could only be kept afloat by pumping 250 strokes an hour. Sailors and even some officers now "beganne privily to murmure against the Generall" for his "wilful manner of proceeding," saying that they had better seek a safe harbor in the Queen's Foreland, or go home; and they would rather stand their chance of being hanged in England for mutiny, than freeze to death. Master Frobisher would hear none of it. He determined to return to his port in Countess of Warwick Sound, and load up.

A Summer's Ore-Gathering

While Frobisher lay to seaward of the Foreland, still debating what to do, "There arose a sodaine and terrible tempest," making the headland

Frobisher Bay.
Photos by Alexander Forbes, July–August 1942. Meta Incognita, from
Frobisher Bay. Delano Bay, on southwest shore. *Morrissey* at anchor
among the islands. Courtesy of Dr. Forbes's heirs.

a lee shore and driving back the ice which had floated seaward. Every ship inside Frobisher Bay furled her sails and drifted; *Anne Frances, Moone,* and *Thomas* "plyed oute to Seawarde, holding it for better policie and safetie to seeke Sea roome." The General and others managed to weather the Foreland and get inside the Bay. Before all did, on 26 July, came "an horrible snowe," which "laye a foote thicke upon the hatches," and "did so wette thorowe oure poore Marriners clothes, that he that hadde five or sixe shifte of apparell, hadde scarce one drie threede to his backe." And many now fell sick.

Once inside the bay named after him, Frobisher rallied his fleet, "and where he saw the Ise never so little open, he gat in at one gappe, and out at another." Dr. Forbes described the same procedure in the *Morrissey* exactly 364 years later. The lookout picks the open lanes and cons the ship; and if ice closes in she rams the pans with a terrific crunch and opens a new lead. *Morrissey*, however, was a specially built vessel, bigger than any of Frobisher's, sheathed with ice-resisting greenhart, and having a powerful auxiliary engine. The best method that Frobisher's vessels could apply to clear a lane was to hook onto one ice floe with two anchors, and with all sail set push it ahead to butt other ice floes out of the way.

"The 28 day" of July, wrote Ellis, "we passed the dangers, by day light. Then night falling on the face of the earth" (it was the dark of the moon), they hove-to "in the cleare, till the chearefull light of the day had chased away the noysome darknesse of the night: at which time wee set forward towards our wished port; and by the 30 day we obteined our expected desire." In Countess of Warwick Sound they found riding at anchor behind Kodlunarn Island, Fenton's *Judith* and bark *Michael*, "which brought no small joy unto our Generall, and great consolation to the hevie heartes of those wearied wightes." The fleet chaplain, Master Wolfal, now conducted a service of thanksgiving. George Best praised this parson for having left a pleasant country parish, "a good honest woman to wife, and verie towardly Children," to save pagan souls and minister to the mariners. *Judith* and *Michael* had been in constant danger for the month of July, often so encompassed by ice that the men could walk ashore or from one vessel to another, and shot seals on the ice to eke out their rations. On one berg, estimated to be half a mile in circumference and 1200 feet high, the water fell down in "sundry streames." They only survived by hooking anchors to the leeward side of these monsters, or by driving a sizable floe before them to crush another.

Troubles with ice were far from ended. Frobisher had not been two hours at anchor, on 30 July, when big ice floes began driving toward the flagship. *Aid* hastily weighed, but the ice struck her before the anchor could be catted, and it drove one fluke right through the bows of the ship, under water. The people had to pump and bail all night; next day they heeled her until the hole came out of water, and covered it with a sheet of lead.

Frobisher, after appointing an advisory council of his captains, began mining on Anne Warwick (Kodlunarn) Island on 1 August. He drew up a set of remarkable sanitary regulations for these operations: 1. No washing of hands or clothes in the spring set aside for drinking water. 2. "Easement" only to be permitted "under the cliffes where the Sea maye washe the same awaye." 3. No garbage to be cast overboard from the ships. In view of what we are struggling with today, these regulations appear highly significant; on pollution problems, Frobisher was almost four centuries ahead of his time. Houses were erected ashore, and everyone not specially employed was put to work digging up the worthless rock from long trenches. Ships occupied the rectangular dock dug the previous voyage, so they could load easily. Gentlemen set the example to "the inferiour sorte" in these futile labors.

"Mining," as they called it, was not confined to this tiny island. As the rocks there were very hard and difficult to break up with no better tool than a pickaxe, Frobisher sent the smaller ships and pinnaces along the shores of his Strait looking for similar marcasite or iron pyrites that would be easier to dig out and load. One mine was named after the Countess of Sussex—Frances, daughter of Sir William Sydney of Penshurst and founder of Sydney Sussex College, Cambridge. The others were called Beare's Sound, Queen's Foreland, Dyer's Passage, Fenton's Fortune, and Winter's Furnace. Out of 1350 ton of so-called ore loaded in thirteen ships for the return passage, only 65 tons came from Kodlunarn Island. George Best in his *True Discourse* (1578) had a crude map of the "Straights," indicating the other mines; all they produced was equally worthless. Best's general conception of the area, based on the Zeno brothers' map, he and Frobisher later rejected.

Gabriel and the three ships which had sought sea-room joined within a week. When the entire fleet had assembled, except *Thomas* of Ips-

Sir Martin Frobisher. Posthumous portrait by the Dutch engraver Crispin de Passe, *c.* 1595. Courtesy of Trustees of National Maritime Museum, Greenwich.

wich, Captain Tanfield (who, "compelled by what furie I know not," said Ellis, had sneaked off home), Frobisher held a council to decide future action. He had already planned to return shortly with such ore as could be collected in a few weeks, and to leave behind, under Captain Fenton, three ships and a hundred men to accumulate a quantity for shipping home next year. Many objected. If this be summer, with water freezing nightly in the Strait, what would winter be? How could any man or ship survive? Captain Best of the *Anne Frances,* to whom we owe this account, denounced any cut-and-run plan as dishonorable; he would have none of it, and urged everyone to search for a better harbor. He was allowed to do just that, and on the outer shore of Resolution Island found a harbor with such a "plentie of blacke Ore" (marcasite) "that it might reasonably suffise all the golde gluttons of the worlde." Reporting this to Frobisher on 9 August, Best was honored by having the place named "Best's Blessing." Captain Fenton, too, undeterred by "the cruell nipping stormes of the raging winter" or "the savagenesse of the people," wished to remain, and a hundred men including Master Wolfal volunteered to stay with him, desirous "to have profited their countrie."

Either at this conference, or when Best was absent, Frobisher and the other captains decided to cancel the wintering plan. Lucky for all that they did! Among the decisive factors were the "many straunge Meteors"—the aurora borealis which are particularly brilliant and blinding as seen from Frobisher Bay. The General took them to be a warning to leave.

"Nowe, whilest the Marriners were romaging theyr Shyppes," continues Best, "the Miners followed their laboure, for getting togither of sufficient quantitie of Ore," and the carpenters assembled *Anne Frances*'s prefabricated pinnace. In her Captain Best, Captain Upcot of *Moone*, and a crew of twenty-eight went on an exploring expedition, starting 19 August with a full moon. They "shot up about 40 leagues within the straites," named a big island after bark *Gabriel* and met another pinnace from the *Thomas Allen* whose crew was excavating supposed gold ore from the Countess of Sussex Mine. Eskimo occasionally appeared but were too wary to be spoken to, much less kidnapped.

The stone house intended for Captain Fenton's winter residence on Kodlunarn Island was finished, in order to "prove against the nexte yere, whether the snowe could overwhelme it, the frosts breake uppe, or the people dismember the same." To "allure and entice" the Eskimo "against other years," Frobisher garnished it "with many kinds of trifles," such as dolls on foot and horseback, besides fresh bread "for them to see and taste." Hopefully, he made a winter sowing of grain and peas. The Captain-General made a final exploration of Hall's Island in his pinnace, and returned to Countess Anne's sound. On 22 August his company "plucked downe" their tents ashore, built bonfires at the highest point of Kodlunarn Island, marched about with ensign displayed and trumpets sounding, and fired a farewell volley "in honour of the right Honourable Lady Anne, Countesse of Warwicke, whose name it beareth." Master Wolfal offered a mass on shore, and on the last day of August, in the dark of the moon, Frobisher left his Strait for the last time.

Homeward Bound

Their toils and troubles were not yet over. Frobisher set a fleet rendezvous at Beare's Sound between Hall's Island and the mainland, as he wanted to top off some ships' cargoes there with ore. At a time when men were ashore or in boats transferring stone from beach to ship, there made up the most "outragious tempest" of the voyage, "beating on our ships with such vehement rigor, that anchor and cable availed naught; for we were driven on rockes and Islandes of yce." Not one ship escaped without damage or loss of ground tackle and boats. Many men, caught ashore by the sudden storm, were lucky to board any ship when their own had been blown out to sea. Frobisher himself, going ashore in the prefabricated pinnace to pick up some of his men, almost lost his life. "Chips" warned him that she was held together only by nails, since oaken knees had not been provided by the builders and none could be cut in the Strait; but he insisted on taking her ashore for want of anything better, since the alternative was to leave his mariners stranded in that barren land with no provisions. Upon being rowed back, the pinnace leaked so badly that the General ordered the rowers to hasten to the nearest ship, *Gabriel*. He had barely stepped on board when the boat fell apart and sank. So Frobisher returned to England in *Gabriel*.

At last, on 2 September 1578, they dropped the desolate shores of Hall's Island and Meta Incognita, never to return. The passage home was boisterous. *Aid* cracked her main yard and was pooped by a following sea. The ships were unable to keep together, and the barks were so "pestered with men" from other ships that provisions ran short. Whether from exposure, ship fever, or from what cause we know not, men died almost daily. Thomas Ellis, with unusual compassion, mentions every death by name, thus: "The 7th, God called to his mercy George Yong, myner." Altogether about forty members of the fleet never reached home alive.

The most memorable incident of the homeward passage was the pretended discovery of a new island by the buss *Emmanuell*, familiarly known as "the Busse of Bridgewater." After an almost miraculous escape from shipwreck in the "outragious tempest" of 1 September, she raised "Frisland" (Greenland) on the 8th, and departed two days later, steering southeast. At 1100 she fell in with a hitherto unknown island at latitude 52°30′ N. Sailing along the coast for twenty-eight hours, the captain observed two harbors and much ice, of which they were never free. But the land looked fruitful, full of woods and open meadows. Passenger Thomas Wiers in the buss, a man of vast imagination, told this to Hakluyt.

The "Island of Buss," as they named this phantom, became a favorite of cosmographers who wanted something to fill vacant spaces southeast of Greenland. It acquired a shape, a toponymy, and a wreath of whales and walruses, although nobody could ever locate it. As late as 1675 John Seller's *Atlas Maritimus* places it on latitude 57°30′ N, "not yet fully discovered." Even after a century of searching had failed to locate Buss, the cartographers, loath to give it up, introduced a "Sunken Land of Buss" which, like Hy-Brasil, hung on into the nineteenth century.

Almost all the way home the wind blew "large" and fair for England. *Gabriel* lay off the Scillies on the day of full moon, 24 September, an ocean passage of twenty-two days; the other twelve made port by the first of October. Most of their worthless cargoes were shipped to Bristol or London where Schultz, Burcot, and perhaps other "experts" got to work on the sacks of rock. Best and Sellman rushed into print with their narratives of the third voyage before a final report had been made. In the meantime there was wrangling and jangling among the seamen for their pay, and adventurers demanded their money. Thomas Allen, owner of the like-named ship, wrote to Walsingham on 8 December 1578 begging him for funds to pay off her crew: "Crystmas beynge so nere, every man cryyeth out for money!"

Attempts to smelt precious metal out of the 1350 tons of rock that Frobisher brought home went on for five years. The Company turned from one expert to another in the vain hope of finding "pay dirt," assessing the stockholders some £9270 for the heavy expenses. Michael Lok, furious, drew up a list of "The Abuses of Captayne Furbusher against the Company." The ore brought home on the first voyage was full of gold, but on the next two, instead of getting more of the same, Frobisher had loaded up with "not one stoane therof." His refusal to let the men winter at Countess of Warwick's island was due to jealousy of Fenton. He should have sent the two barks ahead to find the passage to Cathay. He wasted supplies and provisions, and allowed his officers to pilfer them. Men in the *Aid* died from being forced to eat "evill fishe" four days in the week, and "all the way homewards they drank nothing but water." Horrible, horrible! Lok even held the exploration of Hudson Strait against Frobisher. "Arrogant in his governement . . . and imperious in his doeings," the General drew a dagger against Captain Fenton, and raised "sclannderous reportes against Mr. Lok," author of this bill of complaints. Frobisher replied that Michael Lok was "a bankrupt knave" who had "cozened" the Company out of £3000 without investing one groat; Lok replied that he had ventured £2600 of his own money, and that the assayers should be punished for their false reports on the ore, as well as Frobisher for his conduct of the expedition. In the end, the Company of Cathay went broke; and (wrote the historian Camden in his *Annals*) the stones, "when neither Gold, Silver, nor any other metall could be drawne" from them, "we saw them throwne away to repayre the high-wayes."

To so inglorious an end came this great enterprise.

Conclusion

Frobisher's revised ideas of his geographical discoveries may presumably be represented by the interesting world map in George Best's *True Discourse* of 1578. "Frobussher's Straights," covering a greater area than the Great Lakes, end in the Pacific where the "Straight of Anian" feeds into them. "Cathaia" is now relegated to its true position instead of extending into Baffin Island; Meta Incognita, instead of being the south side of Frobisher Bay, is divided into six islands and a four-part *Terra Sep-ten-triona-lis* (Greenland apparently represents the *ten* section) balances *Terra Australis*.

When everyone had to admit that the ore was worthless, recriminations such as those that we have quoted passed back and forth. Sellman, Lok's agent on board the flagship, probably produced most of the "scandell" about Frobisher; for, by his own account, Sellman intervened twice in disciplinary matters in which he had no business, and was promptly slapped down by the General.

In view of their objectives, all three voyages, which cost the stockholders about £20,160, were complete failures; and there is no use try-

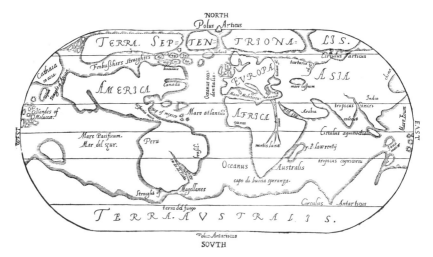

George Best's map of the world in his *True Discourse* (1578). Courtesy
Harvard College Library.

ing to blame anyone except the "goldfinders" for their dishonest or incompetent reports on the ore. Why could not the Company of Cathay
have imported French assayers, who had showed up Cartier's gold and
diamonds? Why did the English fiddle around with it for five years?
Possibly mere stupidity; but one suspects skulduggery—investors trying to hold back the truth so they could unload.

Frobisher's reputation declined, as it were, with the market; but for
a year or more it remained very high. Shipmates Best, Settle, and Ellis
praised his conduct of the voyage in their printed accounts. The Queen
gave him a gold chain. Besides Thomas Churchyard, one stanza of
whose poem we have quoted at the head of this chapter, several bards
unknown to fame contributed poetical effusions to Ellis's *True Report*.
John Kirkham, for instance, called Frobisher "a martial Knight," whom
"no chaunces dire could dismay, no doubt could daunt his hart." "He
ventred not to knowen coastes, nor lands devoid of feare," but sought
boreal lands of storms and snow and "mightie mountaines huge of cold
congealed yce."

> A Hector stout he is on land, Ulysses on the seas,
> Whose painfull pilgrimage hath brought unto his countrie ease.

All this adulation was based on the conviction that Frobisher "the way
to golden Fleece to Britane had made plaine." When it became clear

322

that he had brought home nothing more valuable than paving stones, his reputation fell under a cloud.

Frobisher's petition to the Queen in 1579 for financial relief or employment was not answered. His old bark *Gabriel* for which (as McFee wrote), "Frobisher seems to have had an affection more durable than any woman could command," was knocked down by the Cathay Company's creditors for a mere £80, and Martin was too poor to cover that bid. Of necessity, he took up his former occupation of piracy or privateering. Once more in the money, he subscribed £300 toward a projected expedition in 1582, hopefully financed in part by still affluent members of the Company of Cathay, to reach those "happy shores" via the Cape of Good Hope. Frobisher was to have commanded it, but when the adventurers placed his former lieutenant Edward Fenton, whom he detested, next in command, he gave it up. Fenton sailed in May 1582 but mismanaged things badly and got no further than Brazil.

Although Frobisher did not participate in the Virginia voyages, he highly approved of them; as may be seen by his prefatory poem in Sir George Peckham's *True Report* of Sir Humfry Gilbert's exploits.

> A pleasant ayre, a sweete and firtell soil,
>   A certain gaine, a never dying praise:
> An easie passage, voide of loathsome toile,
> Found out by some, and knowen to me the waies,
>   All this is there, then who will refraine to trie:
>   That loves to live abroad, or dreads to die.

In 1585 Frobisher obtained the highly honorable command of vice-admiral in Drake's expedition against the Spanish West Indies, and fought both well and profitably. When the *felicissima armada* threatened to invade England, the Lord High Admiral, Howard of Effingham, gave him command of the Channel fleet. After Lord Henry Seymour had relieved him from that command, Frobisher was given sixty-gun galleon *Triumph*, biggest ship in the Royal Navy. After covering himself with glory, twice beating off four great Spanish galleasses in the fight off Portland Bill, he was rewarded by knighthood, and by being given command of a division of fighting ships under Lord Howard.

After the Spanish defeat there broke out an altercation between Frobisher and Drake because Sir Francis tried to keep for himself and his own sailors the entire prize money from the Spanish galleon *San*

Charles Howard of Effingham, Lord High Admiral, 1585–1618. By D. My-
tens. Courtesy of Trustees of National Maritime Museum, Greenwich.

Luís, leaving none for the ships and men who had covered him and so made that capture possible. Sir Martin declared that Sir Francis behaved in the battle "like a cowardly knave or a traitor—I rest doubtful which!" The hero Drake "thinketh to cozen us of our shares of 15,000 ducats, but we will have our shares, or I will make him spend the best blood in his belly!" After the dispute had been adjudicated by the privy council, Sir Martin was awarded £4979 as his share of the prize money—a small fortune for that era.

Next summer Sir Martin commanded a task force of five naval vessels which captured two Spanish treasure ships off the Azores. He repeated this exploit in 1592; and two years later commanded an amphibious operation in support of Sir John Norris to expel the Spanish garrison from Brest. For his conduct there he received a complimentary letter from the Queen.

In his last letter, a report to the Lord High Admiral, Sir Martin told about the assault on the fort named Crozon ("Croydon" was the nearest he could get) on 7 November 1594. "It was tyme for us to goa through with it," he said, as a Spanish relief force was advancing. He and Sir John personally led the assault; they took the fort and put all Spaniards to the sword, but Frobisher received a bullet in his leg. Provisions running short (as usually they did in the Queen's navy), the victors had to sail home or starve, and the mariners vowed they would not leave without Sir Martin. En route the infected wound festered, and on 22 November 1594, aged fifty-five, the gallant seaman, already old by standards of the time, died at Plymouth. His body was taken to London and buried at St. Giles's, Cripplegate.

Frobisher's first wife having died shortly after his return from the Arctic in 1578, he married Dame Dorothy Widmerpole, daughter of Lord Wentworth, and she survived him. They lived as country gentry in Altofts, Yorkshire, where he became a considerable landowner. His first wife bore him a son who predeceased him, and a spendthrift nephew inherited the fortune that Sir Martin had accumulated from prize money.

Frobisher's character was based on simplicity and integrity. Every shipmate except Fenton and Lok's man Sellman paid high tribute to him, praising his humanity in dealing with his own men and the poor natives. He suffered, no doubt, from lack of learning, and of the courtly manners which make Raleigh and Gilbert so attractive to romantic historians. Reading between the lines of his shipmates' narratives, it is clear that the old sea-dog was impatient, irascible, and incapable of concealing his rage when once aroused, as it always was by injustice. But he was endowed with "a singular faculty for leadership." He "had in him not only greatness, but a human quality which made men curse him and love him, grumble at him and toil for him," wrote McFee, an old sailor himself. Sir Martin was a sailor's sailor of the same breed as John Paul Jones, Collingwood, and the Perrys. For my part, I conclude that Frobisher was a very great seaman indeed, that his courage and resource enabled him and his ships to survive adversities of ice and weather which would have ruined anyone else, and that he fully deserves his reputation as one of the English mariners who paved the way for England's greatness.

It was tyme for us to goa through with it. That sentence in the last letter that he wrote is typical of Frobisher. What he undertook he went through with; no turning back like Gilbert, no sliding off like John Rut to something easy and pleasant.

Futile as they were, unsuccessful in immediate results, we would not erase those three voyages from the roll of maritime history. There were high moments, when all men of the fleet pitched in to protect one another from the ice, "to the everlasting renowne of our nation." No higher quality of seamanship and devotion to duty has been shown anywhere than among the officers, the "paynefull Mariners" and the "poore Miners" embarked in those sailing vessels, all so small, weak and comfortless in comparison with the giant icebreakers of our day. England and her offspring have every reason to cherish the records of the "late voyages of discoverie . . . under the conduct of Martin Frobisher, General." If nothing else, they taught England to "goa through with it" to glory, dominion, and empire.

The Northern Voyages of John Davis

1585-1587

I desire that it may please his divine Majestie to shew us such mercifull favour that we may rather proceed then otherwise; or if it be his wil, that our mortall being shal now take an ende, I rather desire that it may be in proceeding then in returning.

JOHN DAVIS'S SPEECH TO HIS MEN OFF THE STRAIT OF MAGELLAN.

John Davis, Master Mariner

The reader must have concluded by this time that the story of English voyages is one of repeated failure; and that in a sense is correct. No amount of hero-worship can conceal the plain fact that the voyages of John Rut, Martin Frobisher, and Humfry Gilbert were failures, if we compare their objectives with the results. And before we take up another failure, which stemmed from Gilbert's, that of his half-brother Raleigh's first Virginia colony, we must take a look at the series of searches for the Northwest Passage by John Davis. They at least eliminated one dead end, and indicated where a successful search might begin.

Failure and success are not absolutes, and the historian should attempt to understand the one as well as the other. Of overseas expeditions, only one like John Cabot's second, lost with all hands, may be accounted a complete failure. Cartier failed to find the "passage to Cathay," but he vastly increased European knowledge of North American geography. Frobisher, with his pitiful cargoes of worthless rock, at least turned the gold-seekers away from northern regions. Sir Humfry Gilbert blew to a high flame the torch of colonization which Richard Hakluyt had lit, and at his death it passed to Walter Raleigh. And now comes John Davis, with three voyages in fruitless search of the Northwest Passage. Why bother with him? Because his voyages are highly interesting in themselves, and because he "lighted Baffin into his bay," whence the first successful traverse of the Northwest Passage started in 1903. And also because his gallantry, persistence, and enthusiasm are examples to sailors and space explorers for all time to come.

John Davis was born to a yeoman family at Sandridge Barton, a farm on the right bank of the Dart, near Stoke Gabriel, where he was baptized in October 1543. Sandridge Barton is as unchanged as Cartier's Limoïlou farm in Brittany. At the end of a narrow, steep lane bordered by hawthorne hedges, one comes upon a cluster of buildings, now a dairy farm, overlooking a bend in the Dart. The farmer's house is not more than two centuries old; but the stone-walled fowl house and cow barn might have been there in Davis's lifetime. A typical Dart valley farm, it is all uphill and down dale, the only level spots being the house and a notable feature which dates from even before 1500. This is a great hollow elm embracing a well of sweet water, which keeps cool in the hottest weather. Davis's biographer imagines him paddling and fishing salmon with the Gilbert boys, and rowing downstream to wonder at the sea-going ships anchored off Dartmouth; but the distance socially and also in miles, between their respective houses, renders that improbable. They certainly became intimate in the late 1570's after Davis had qualified as a master mariner. He married Faith, daughter of a neighboring magnate, Sir John Fulford; this raised him in the social scale and allied him with the Gilberts, but the marriage was not happy. During one of Davis's voyages, Faith took a lover, one Milbourne, who had her husband clapped into jail on a trumped-up charge after his return, and the eminent navigator had to use influence to get free.

The earliest definite fact that we know about Davis subsequent to his christening, is at the age of thirty-six when, apparently, he had retired to Sandridge Barton after a successful career as a privateersman and shipmaster. The Gilberts now interested him in undertaking a fresh search for the elusive Northwest Passage. Davis and Adrian Gilbert (Humfry's younger brother) called on John Dee the philosopher at his Mortlake home in October 1579 to talk it over, and again in June of the following year. In January of 1583, wrote Dee, he met Secretary Walsingham, Adrian Gilbert, and John Davis at Mortlake. "And so

Sandridge Barton: The farm and a view of the Dart with the great elm.

talk was begone of the North-west Straights discovery." In March these four, together with Thomas Hudson (probably an uncle of Henry), Sir George Barnes, a leading director of the Muscovy Company, and a member of the Towerson family noted for African voyages, held a colloquy on this subject. Dee argued that there were five passages from Europe to Cathay—the two that Spain and Portugal had pre-empted, the Northeast which the Muscovy Company had in vain pursued, the route right over the Pole (as Thorne had advocated fifty years earlier), and the Northwest. The last two, he thought, were worth looking into.

Thus it came about that in February 1585, when Queen Elizabeth granted a patent to Adrian Gilbert and associates, they were empowered to sail "Northwestward, Northeastward or Northward," using as many ships, barks, and pinnaces as they chose. They were given a monopoly of trade with any newly discovered region, and, if they elected to plant a colony on its shores, they would enjoy the same governmental powers as had earlier been conferred on Adrian's brother Sir Humfry.

It was under this authority that Davis made three voyages, which enlarged English knowledge of the Arctic but brought nothing profitable to him.

Since by this time very little money was available in the Gilbert and Davis families, the partners appealed for funds to "divers worshipful merchants of London." Of these, the principal was William Sanderson, who had married a niece of the Gilbert and Raleigh brothers, and signaled his interest in them and maritime affairs by naming his first three sons Raleigh, Cavendish, and Drake. Sanderson was a noted merchant adventurer, who had traded to all European countries and acted as Sir Walter Raleigh's business manager—he once had to raise £16,000 in a hurry to keep Sir Walter out of jail. He also made, or helped others to make, celestial and terrestrial globes; that pursuit probably explains his interest in and knowledge of Davis. For it was Sanderson who persuaded the associates to appoint "one Mr. John Davis, a man well grounded in the principles of the arte of navigation, for Captaine and chief Pilot of the exploit."

This language, as well as the lack of earlier records about Davis, suggests that he was not too well known in 1585. But there is no doubt that the partners made the right choice. No portrait of John Davis, or description of his person, has yet been found; no research into the life of this great seaman has been done for over a century. As one who has "lived" with him vicariously for several years, I may be privileged to imagine him as a strong man, bearded, with brown hair, blue eyes, and a serene gaze not easily ruffled. A man with a strong feeling of loyalty both to his supporters, headed by the Queen, and to his officers and men. Toward the natives he entertained liberal and benevolent feelings which, on occasion, were sorely strained. He never made any money, and his little patrimony was largely spent on the Arctic voyages which brought him nothing but fame, and little of that. He was never knighted or given any other honors, and after his death memory of him faded. But for Hakluyt, we would know little or nothing about Davis today.

Although Davis's *Seaman's Secrets* did not come out until his northern voyages were over, we may assume that the instruments of navigation he there described were being tried out in 1585–87. He says that the minimum equipment necessary for a skillful seaman consists of the compass, cross-staff, and chart, as the astrolabe and quadrant have proved to be "very uncertaine for Sea observations." Columbus and many others would have agreed heartily! He tells in detail how to use the cross-staff and his own backstaff to obtain latitude from sun or Pole Star. He improved the old traverse-board by compiling a "Traverse-Booke," and Hakluyt printed one for his third voyage. It is in the form of the standard nineteenth-century ship's log or journal; column one for courses, with the time spent on each; column two for calculated distance made good in each watch; column three for meridional observations of the sun; column four for wind direction, and a fifth for "the Discourse," what we would call "Remarks."

First Voyage, 1585

There were no Gilbertian delays to any of John Davis's voyages. He received the royal patent in February 1585 and was ready to sail in June. We are fortunate to have an account of this first voyage by a participant named John Janes, nephew "to the worshipfull M. William Sanderson," who shipped as supercargo. Here is the task organization as he gives it:

CAPTAIN AND CHIEF PILOT, JOHN DAVIS

Bark SUNNESHINE of London, 50 tuns, 23 people. John Davis, captain; William Eston, master; Richard Pope, master's mate; John Janes, "marchant." The roll includes a gunner, a boatswain, a carpenter, eleven mariners, one boy, and the inevitable four-piece orchestra. No Elizabethan voyage of discovery could do without that.

Bark MOONESHINE of Dartmouth, 35 tuns, 19 people. William Bruton, captain; John Ellis, master; "the rest mariners."

Thus the total complement was forty-two—a very modest expedition compared with Frobisher's and Gilbert's. But the sailors were picked men, as stout-hearted as their captain.

Departing Dartmouth 7 June 1585 with a moon approaching last quarter, they ran into the usual westerly winds, put into Channel harbors thrice, and only got clear of the Scillies on the 28th. Their first important event, on 19 July, was to hear "a great whirling and brustling of a tyde" and a "mighty great roaring of the Sea"; a terrifying sound in a fog so thick that neither bark could see the other. Davis, Janes, and Eston put out in a boat, and "did perceive that all the roaring which we heard, was caused onely by rouling of this yce together." Next day "the fogge brake up" and with a full moon they raised the east coast of Greenland "which was the most deformed rocky and mountainous land that ever we saw." Snowy mountain tops stood up above the clouds, and there was a league of ice to break through before reaching shore. Greenland acquired a new name from Captain Davis: "Land of Desolation." Markham, who knew somewhat of this coast, identifies the spot as Cape Discord.* Efforts to push through the ice to the shore came to naught, and the cold so took it out of the men that the captain increased their rations. For breakfast, every mess of five would rate half a pound of hard-bread and a "kan"—a pint-size mug—"of beere." No tea, no coffee, nothing hot for Arctic voyagers in those days.

Making no further effort to explore the east coast, Davis turned south, doubled Cape Farewell without seeing it, and sailed northwesterly until 29 July when he sighted land to the northeastward. He found the latitude to be 64° 15′ N; a good instance of his expertise at

---

* This name has disappeared from the map, but I find it in T. G. Bradford, *Illustrated Atlas of the U.S.* (1844). Apparently it is now called Cape Wallace, lat. about 60° 40′.

taking and working out a sight, as Bowditch gives 64°11'. He had hit the entrance to the complex of fjords which had been the Norsemen's Western Settlement, and is now Godthaab. Davis named it Gilbert Sound.

The Englishmen's relations here with the Eskimo, who had moved in on the Northmen about a century earlier, were not altogether happy but very amusing. They announced their presence, after Davis, Eston, and Janes had showed themselves on a rocky island, by making a "lamentable noyse . . . with great outcryes and skreechings" like "the howling of wolves." The Captain's boat party converged on this island with a similar party from *Mooneshine*, which included the four-man orchestra. These, after landing, played while the captains and sailors danced. Ten Eskimo kayaks now approached, and when their paddlers landed "we allured them by friendly embracings and signes of curtesie." This approach not seeming to work, master Ellis of the smaller bark, as a self-appointed expert in race relations, alternately struck his breast and pointed at the sun, gestures which he believed would break the social ice, which they did. After depositing caps, stockings, and gloves on the ground as gifts, the Englishmen country-danced and played themselves into their boats and called it a day. What a pity that Davis did not have an artist like John White to depict this scene—fiddlers fiddling, mariners capering, and grinning Eskimo as audience.

After this overture it was easy to persuade the Eskimo to trade. The English bought five kayaks and "their clothes from their backs," for they appreciated the fine sealskin garments and boots tailored by Eskimo women and perfectly adapted to their habitat. Janes observed the dwarf willows and evergreens of Greenland, and a profusion of yellow flowers "like primroses."

On 1 August, with a fair wind, the two barks crossed the strait that would be named after their captain and made land in latitude 66°40', with no ice visible. They named it Exeter Sound, from the city that had supported Davis, and the two forelands after Sir Edward Dyer and Sir Francis Walsingham. At Totnes roadstead—named after a town up the Dart which had provided money for the voyage—and "under Mount Raleigh" four "white bears of a monstrous bignesse" were killed. Time has been kind to Davis's names, as a glance at the modern map will indicate; and his latitude is correct for Cape Walsingham.

This was the furthest north for Davis's first voyage. He amiably in-

George Clifford, Earl of Cumberland. Miniature by Nicholas Hilliard. Courtesy of Trustees of National Maritime Museum, Greenwich.

creased rations—for a mess of five men, four pounds of hard-bread daily, twelve wine quarts of beer, and six Newfoundland codfish on fast days; on flesh days, when bear meat helped out the salt beef, a gill of dried pease. But he had to cut down on their butter and cheese.

Sunneshine and *Mooneshine* made sail and departed Exeter Sound 8 August. They doubled the southernmost cape of the Peninsula on the 11th, naming it Cape of God's Mercy (God has been dropped from the name today), and entered a deep sound, hoping it would prove to be the Passage. Davis named it after George Clifford, Earl of Cumberland, a privateer owner and sailor in the war with Spain, perhaps an investor in this voyage.

They sailed some 180 miles into Cumberland Sound, and it is not

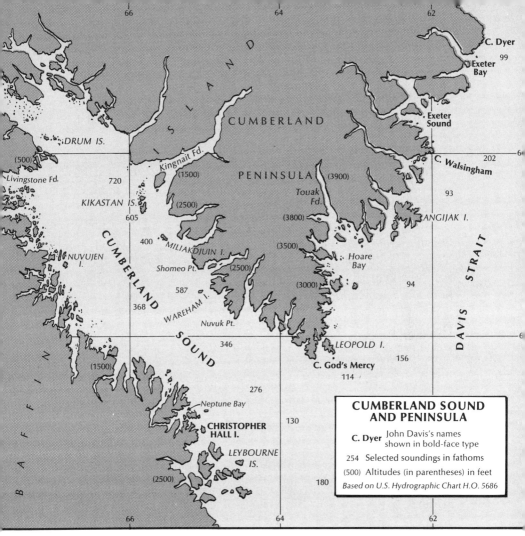

The map shows labels:

C. Dyer
99
Exeter Bay
Exeter Sound
CUMBERLAND
DRUM IS.
C. Walsingham
202
(500)
Kingnait Fd.
Livingstone Fd.
720
(1500)
PENINSULA
(3900)
93
KIKASTAN IS.
(2500)
Touak Fd.
605
(3800)
ANGIJAK I.
400
MILIAKDJUIN I.
(3500)
NUVUJEN I.
Shomeo Pt.
(2500)
Hoare Bay
587
(3000)
94
368
WAREHAM I.
Nuvuk Pt.
(1500)
346
LEOPOLD I.
156
C. God's Mercy
114
276
Neptune Bay
130
CHRISTOPHER HALL I.
LEYBOURNE IS.
(2500)
180

STRAIT
DAVIS
BAFFIN

CUMBERLAND SOUND AND PENINSULA

C. Dyer — John Davis's names shown in bold-face type
254 — Selected soundings in fathoms
(500) — Altitudes (in parentheses) in feet
Based on U.S. Hydrographic Chart H.O. 5686

surprising that Davis thought this was "it." The further he sailed, the deeper the water. "Hard aboord the shoare" among islands (either the Miliakdjuin or the Kikastan group) he found no bottom at 330 fathom. No wonder, for the modern chart gives no bottom at 400 fathom off the Miliakdjuins and 485 to 605 fathom off the Kikastans. Other signs, too, convinced Davis that he was on the right course for Cathay; whales were sighted swimming from that direction, and tidal currents were swift and powerful. But, as with every other Northwesterman for three centuries, he did not press far enough to see. On arriving among islands at the head of Cumberland Sound, on 20 August, the day of full moon, the wind turned northwest. After discussion with Captain Bruton, the two masters, and the narrator Janes, Davis decided to start home. It was indeed high time, if they did not wish to be frozen in for the winter, with provisions for only six months. But Davis always regretted that he had turned back, and to Cumberland Sound he returned in 1587.

The Eskimo, doubtless remembering Frobisher's kidnapping, kept out of sight, but the Englishmen found ashore a pack of their huskies, two sleds, one of wood and the other of whalebone, and some Eskimo children's toys, including a miniature kayak.

After anchoring in a harbor on the south coast of Cumberland Sound, *Mooneshine* and *Sunneshine* cleared for England on 24 August. They picked up the "Land of Desolation" (Greenland) on 10 September, "thinking to goe on shoare, but we cold get never a good harborough," sighted England after a fast passage of two weeks, and on 30 September anchored off Dartmouth. How good those green hills of Devon must have looked! Adrian Gilbert and the whole clan warmly welcomed and encouraged Davis, who now heard what Raleigh was doing to fulfill Gilbert's plans.

Davis had enjoyed very good luck, compared with Frobisher, as it happened to be a warm summer. Even Cumberland Sound was "altogether void of any pester of ice."

Second Voyage, 1586

Captain John Davis, with the unquenchable optimism of Elizabethan mariners, now wrote to Sir Francis Walsingham about Cumberland Sound: "The northwest passage is a matter nothing doubtful, but at any tyme almost to be passed, the sea navigable, voyd of yse, the ayre tolerable and the waters very depe." The faithful merchants renewed their support, and on 7 May, with a new moon, began "The second voyage attempted by Master John Davis . . . for the discoverie of the Northwest Passage, in Anno 1586." He now had a fleet of four: ship *Mermayd* of 120 tuns, chartered by the adventurers for £100 a month, the same barks *Sunneshine* and *Mooneshine* as on the first voyage, and a ten-tun pinnace, the *North Starre*, "provided to be our scout for this discovery." A second pinnace, broken down, was carried in the ship. The total investment amounted to £1175, of which Exeter merchants contributed £475, those of Totnes £375, and London only £162 10s. Whatever the worshipful Mr. Sanderson gave is not known; but as Davis reported to him, it must have been considerable.

On 7 June, one month out, *Sunneshine* and *North Starre* broke off in pursuance of instructions to investigate the "straight over the Pole" route. We shall come back to them later.

This was a slow-sailing fleet. Not until 15 June did they raise the coast of Greenland, "mightily pestered with yce and snow, so that there was no hope of landing." The pack-ice that year extended from 30 to 150 miles off shore. Davis gives the latitude as 60° N, which is right for Cape Farewell, and even attempts to name its longitude—47° W of London. That was about three degrees off—a remarkably close longitude guess for the sixteenth century. Obviously he had been keeping accurate dead reckoning with his chip log and traverse table.

His next latitude after doubling Cape Farewell, 64° N, is exactly right for Gilbert Sound (Godthaab) and the complex of fjords behind it. The ships were not even anchored before swarms of Eskimo came out in kayaks, welcoming their musical friends of last year with embraces and gifts. Next day the Englishmen landed their knocked-down pinnace on a convenient island in the Norsemen's old bailiwick and began to assemble it. The Eskimo, forty to a hundred kayaks at a time, visited the men at their labor, bringing fish, fowl, hides, and white hares. Other Englishmen explored inland over "a plaine champion countrey" where the Norsemen had pastured their cattle. Davis with some of his men visited an Eskimo village, challenged the natives to a jumping contest, and "from leaping they went to wrestling; we found them strong and nimble, and to have skil in wrestling, for they cast some of our men that were good wrestlers."

On 4 July the pinnace was launched, with the help of forty natives shoving and hauling; and they held another wrestling match. The same day the master of *Mermayd*, on an excursion in search of firewood, uncovered what must have been the grave of Christian Norsemen, "having a crosse laid over them," since the Eskimo here were all "idolaters." "These people," concluded Davis, "are very simple in their conversation, but marvellous theevish, especially for iron." They began "to shew their vile nature" by cutting ships' cables to get the anchors. They cut away *Mooneshine*'s skiff and stole objects from the decks, to such an extent that Davis was persuaded to fire two cannon shots "which strange noice did sore amaze them, so that with speed they departed." Next day they were back, bearing propitiatory gifts but light-fingered as ever; and when prevented from boarding the ships, they threw big stones onto their decks with slings. The mariners, furious, told their Captain that that was his fault—"lenity and friendly using of them gave them stomacke to mischiefe." Better fire a broadside as a good example; but Davis "desired them to be content," i.e. tolerant; his visit was too short to convert the natives or "make them know their evils."

Following another visit on board, in which gifts were presented, the Eskimo treated *Mooneshine* to another barrage of stones, one of which hit the boatswain. Captain Davis then lost his temper, manned an armed boat, and pursued the kayaks. The natives escaped, just as they had from Frobisher's men, because no boat rowed by Europeans could ever catch a one-man kayak.

On 11 July five Eskimo came on board "to make a new truce." The Englishmen retained one as hostage for the stolen anchor, but did not wait long enough to get it back. "Within one houre that he came aboord, the winde came fayre, whereupon we weyed and set saile, and so brought the fellow with us." Davis, finding that this Eskimo "could not indure the cold" at sea, gave him a "new sute of frize after the English fashion . . . of which he was very joyfull." He lent a hand in sailing, and "became a pleasant companion among us." But he did not survive the voyage.

Sailing on 17 July, with moon in last quarter, *Mermayd* and *Mooneshine* fell in with an enormous iceberg, so big that the pinnace was sent to see if it were not land; it must have been more than one big berg as they "coasted this mighty masse of yce" for almost two weeks, their sails, shrouds, and lines becoming sheathed with ice. The men "through this extremity began to grow sicke and feeble," and respectfully urged Davis, for his own sake as well as theirs and their families, to return home. Davis compromised; *Mermayd* "not so convenient and nimble as a smaller bark, especially in such desperate hazzards," he consented to send home with about half the company, and to proceed with *Mooneshine* and the pinnace.

On 1 August, at latitude 66°33'—which is nearly accurate for the site of the present village of Inugsugtsusok—"and in longitude from the Meridian of London 70 degrees" (really 53°45' W), they "discovered the land." There they graved (cleaned the bottom of) *Mooneshine* and stowed some of *Mermayd*'s provisions in her. The Eskimo were friendly, but "a flie which is called Atuskyte . . . did sting grievously."

Leaving *Mermayd* at this spot to begin her homeward passage, Davis in *Mooneshine*, on 12 August, crossed the strait that would be named after him. Two days later he made the Cumberland Peninsula, Baffin Island, where he had been the year before. The crossing he estimated to be 210 miles, which is nearly correct, and the latitude 66° 19', which is less than twenty miles out. Now, turning south, he passed "a very faire promontory in latitude 65°, having no land on the South." This was almost the correct latitude for Cape of God's Mercy, which Davis had named on his previous voyage. Why did he not recognize it? Davis now makes an interesting obervation which proves him to have been a careful navigator. From noon to noon, 18–19 August, "by precise ordinary care"—meaning dead reckoning, and using the chip log, "We had sailed 15 leagues South by west, yet by art and more exact observation, we found our course to be Southwest," proving the existence of a westward-running current. This means that he was taking meridional altitudes of the sun, and probably dawn and dusk sights of Polaris, with the backstaff that he had invented.

On 19 August at 6 p.m., just as those in the little bark thought they were hot on the trail to China, it began to snow. Davis hove-to all night and, when morning broke fair, turned shoreward and found a fine landlocked harbor in which to spend the night. This must have been either on Resolution Island or Hall's Island. The Captain climbed a hill to look for a possible passage, but saw only islands. How tired he must have been of seeing nothing but one archipelago after another!

Mooneshine now coasted south until 28 August when, according to Davis's calculations, they were in latitude 56° off the Labrador. They had missed the entrance to Hudson Strait, which would have led to something worth while, though considerably short of China. They called at "a very faire harbour" up which they sailed, and which we can identify from Davis's latitude as Jack Lane Bay; the inlet has been named Davis in his honor. He reported the trees and the wild fowl, "of the partridge and fezant we killed a great store with bowe and ar-rowes." Englishmen of that era were expert archers both with long bow and crossbow, and they used arrows in preference to bullets for shooting birds.

After riding out a couple of storms, Davis left this pleasant spot of the Labrador coast on 1 September, continuing south. On the 3rd at 54° 30'—which is just right for Cut Throat Tickle and Run By Guess

Island—they dropped a kedge anchor to fish, and made an apostolic haul of cod, "the largest and best fed fish that ever I sawe," wrote Davis, and "divers fishermen" with him agreed. They were at the northern entrance to Hamilton Inlet, the appearance of which gave Davis "a perfect hope of the passage," and he was eager to explore it; but a strong west wind blowing directly out of the inlet prevented.

On 4 September in a good roadstead "among great store of Isles" off Cape Porcupine and the Norsemen's Wonder Strands, Davis anchored and hauled in a "mightie store" of codfish. Wishing to save for his homeward passage the fish that they could not eat at once, he sent some men ashore, probably on the Wonder Strands at Trunmore Bay, to split and cure them on flakes. That detained them several days. On the morning of 6 September five young sailors, having rowed ashore to uncover the fish, were suddenly attacked by "the brutish people of this countrey," as Davis calls them, "who lay secretly lurking in the wood." The Captain promptly rendered gunfire support to the young men, who were fighting desperately with their backs to the sea. He slipped cables, sailed shoreward under foresail, and discharged two volleys of musketry "at the noyse whereof they fled." But two young seamen had been killed by arrows and two were badly wounded; the fifth, with an arrow through his arm, escaped by swimming.

That evening "It pleased God farther to increase our sorrowes" by blowing up "a mighty tempestuous storme" which lasted four days. The direction of the gale, north-northeast, put *Mooneshine* on a lee shore with the pleasant prospect of dragging her anchor and grounding on the Wonder Strands "among these Canibals for theyr pray." Davis cut down his top-hamper almost to bare poles, yet the windage caused the cable of his sheet-anchor to part. "In this deepe distresse the mightie mercie of God, when hope was past, gave us succor, and sent us a fayre lee." The wind suddenly backed to the westward—"so we recovered our anker again, and newe mored our shippe." They had been held "by an olde junke," * a single strand of the other cable; another proof of divine protection.

On 11 September, with a fair west-northwest wind, Davis departed the inhospitable Wonder Strands, "shaping our course for England." They arrived somewhere in the West Country at the beginning of October.

* The original meaning of "junk" is old rope; the naval accounts of Henry VII distinguish "old jonkes" from "hausers."

Now let us see what happened to the other half of this fruitless second voyage—bark *Sunneshine*, Richard Pope, master, with sixteen men, and pinnace *North Starre* with about ten men. They sailed with Captain Davis, took their departure from Dursey Head the same day (11 May 1586), and at latitude 60° N, by agreement, broke off to seek a passage between Greenland and Iceland up to latitude 80° N, "if land did not let us." Their plan was to prove Robert Thorne's and John Dee's scheme of sailing right over the North Pole.

No land prevented them, but ice did. They called first at Iceland, departed 16 June, and it took them three weeks to reach Greenland, which "was very high, and it looked very blew." As usual the pack-ice prevented them from landing. Ten days later they recognized a place which Captain Davis the year before had named "Land of Desolation," presumably Cape Discord. Again, plenty pack-ice and no possible landing. This indicates that master Pope gave up his polar quest before even crossing the Arctic Circle, and decided instead to nip around to Gilbert Sound (Godthaab) on the west coast, which Davis had fixed as a rendezvous. There *Sunneshine* and *North Starre* arrived on 3 August, weeks after Davis had departed. They tarried for twenty days. Although the local Eskimo at first exhibited only unfriendly and threatening attitudes (Davis having kidnapped one of them), they gradually warmed up. The English did a good trade in sealskin, bringing home 500 whole ones and 140 half-skins. "Divers times," says purser Morgan of *Sunneshine*, who wrote this narrative, "they did weave us on shore to play with them at the foot-ball, and some of our company went on shore to play with them, and our men did cast them downe as soon as they did come to strike the ball."

This first recorded international football match did not resemble anything known as football today. It must have been the English medieval village game, in which two goals were set up as much as a mile apart, and the contestants, of any number provided both sides were equal, tried to kick, butt, or throw the ball through the other side's goal. Apparently the Eskimo had a similar game but had not learned how to ward off a tackle.

On 30 August, Pope anchored in a harbor south of Gilbert's Sound. There the English had an unnecessary scuffle with the natives over a kayak which they had bought, but tried to turn in when it proved to be leaky. Bows and arrows were the weapons on both sides. Casualties were three Eskimo killed and several wounded, and one Englishman wounded. Having thus undone most of the good that Davis had done for race relations at this point, *Sunneshine* "departed from Gilberts sound for England" on the last day of August, and dropped Greenland under the horizon on 2 September.

The third day out, at night, "We lost sight of the *North Starre* our pinnesse in a very great storme," and lay a-hull for a full day hoping to sight her. But she was never heard of again. We have already observed the high mortality among pinnaces—Frobisher's and Gilbert's. The trouble with this type was its want of a complete, watertight deck, making it liable to be pooped and swamped by a heavy following sea.

Sunneshine reached Dartmouth 4 October and continued through the English Channel and up the Thames to Ratcliff, "in safety God be thanked," on 6 October.

The indefatigable John Davis, according to his report on 14 October 1586 to William Sanderson, seems to have been very pleased with himself after a voyage which had really been a failure. He is certain that the Northwest Passage "must be in one of four places, or els not at all." "This voyage may be performed without further charge, nay, with certaine profit to the adventurers." He is ready to sell his portion of Sandridge, the family estate, to "see an end of these businesses."

Never is there "an end of these businesses," even today.

Third Voyage, 1587

John Davis must have been very plausible and impressive, since Adrian Gilbert, Sanderson, and other supporters now backed him for a third voyage as "Chiefe Captaine & Pilot generall, for the discoverie of a passage to the Isles of the Molucca, or the coast of China, in the yeere 1587."

His task force consisted of the old *Sunneshine* of London, 50 tuns, a Dartmouth bark named *Elizabeth* (burthen unknown), and a small "clincher" (clinker-built pinnace) named *Ellen*, or *Helene*, of London, Captain Pierson. Janes and the Captain were very doubtful of taking a clincher on so long a voyage; "neverthelesse we put our trust in God," and all three sailed from Dartmouth on 19 May, a week after full moon. The clincher made a bad start, breaking her tiller first night out. Nevertheless, says Janes, "we went forward, hoping that a hard beginning would make a good ending." And so it did.

This time they had fair northeasterly winds to clear the Channel and Scilly. One week out, *Sunneshine* sprang a leak, pumped 500 strokes a watch, but located and stopped it by shifting the ballast until the hole came out of water, while the other two vessels waited, hove-to. On the 28th *Elizabeth* for eighteen hours towed the *Ellen* "which was so much bragged of by the owners report before we came out of England, but at Sea she was like a cart drawn by oxen. Sometimes we towed her because she could not saile in a head wind." A bad handicap to the fleet's speed.

A near-mutiny broke out because some of the sailors had been promised a profitable fishing voyage and wanted to sail to the Banks right away; but "after much talke and many threatenings they were content to bring us to the land." Davis, in the column of his "Traverse-Booke" for remarks, indicates that he was constantly working out "true course"—i.e. course made good, "drawn from divers traverses." For instance, seventy-two hours' sailing 2–5 June, with wind west-south-west, he made good 135 miles "W. by S., Southerly," indicating that in mid-ocean with presumably a heavy sea, all three (the clincher sometimes under tow) made good a course better than five points on the wind. Davis did not embrace this opportunity to make better northing and westing because he was bound for the west coast of Greenland and did not care to risk bumping into ice off Cape Farewell.

On 7 June wind shifted to the southeastern quadrant, and even the despised clincher could keep up. On the 14th, moon almost full, they sighted high land, and on the 16th, "being in the latitude of 64° through God's helpe we came to an anker among many low islands." This was already familiar Godthaab, Greenland, which Davis had named Gilbert's Sound. His latitude was correct: Bowditch gives that of Godthaab's flagstaff as 64°10'36". The Eskimo "came presently to us after the old maner, with crying *Ilyuoute*, and shewing us Seales skinnes." This slogan apparently meant "I have no knife, so let us talk."

The first job there was to assemble a second pinnace which had been brought knocked-down in the *Elizabeth*. After Davis had made the mistake of capturing "a very strong lusty young fellow" as a hostage for good behavior, the natives started stripping the planking off the new pinnace as fast as the strakes were nailed in place, "onely for the love of the iron in the boords." *Sunneshine*'s gunner fired a blank shot to make them desist, but they scampered off with their spoil to another island. Captain Davis decided that under these circumstances there was no use trying to assemble the pinnace; he had her knocked down again and stowed on board *Elizabeth* for use in fishing. William Bruton, master of *Sunneshine*, informed his captain that "the good ship which we must all hazard our lives in" was leaking 300 strokes an hour while riding at anchor. "This disquieted us all greatly." No wonder! Davis, typically, "determined rather to end his life with credite then to returne with infamie and disgrace," and so inspired his shipmates that they "purposed to live and die together, and committed ourselves to the ship." Since the crew of leaky *Sunneshine* as well as that of *Elizabeth* preferred to continue their voyage fishing instead of exploring, and were likely to be mutinous and useless if denied, Davis generously released them, and on 21 June "departed from this coast, our two barks for their fishing voyage, and my self in the pinnesse for the discovery."

The main purpose of this voyage being to explore the northern part of Davis Strait, which later became Baffin Bay, the Captain set a northerly course, along the west coast of Greenland. Clincher *Ellen* crossed the Arctic Circle, and on the 24th arrived at latitude 67°40' off the modern Nordrestromfjord. That day and the next they had profitable trucking with Eskimo who paddled thirty miles off shore to get the white men's "pinnes, needles, bracelets, nailes, knives, bels, looking glasses and other small trifles," in return for "salmon peale" (grilse), caplin, wild fowl, and seal skins. "For these last 4 dayes the weather hath beene extreame hot and very calme, the Sun being 5 degrees above the horizon at midnight," recorded Davis in his "Discourse," and he noted that the compass variation was 28° W.

On 30 June, day of full moon, after "we took the heigth and found ourselves in 72°12'," Davis continued to the site of the modern Upernavik, where an 850-foot cliff rises sheer from the sea. The latitude is 72°46', and this was Davis's furthest north. He named the place "Hope Sanderson" in honor of his backer; and a good hope it proved to be, as the Northwest Passage starts across Baffin Bay, in Lancaster Sound.

Sanderson's Hope disappeared from the map in the last century, but it was well known as such when the explorer Sherard Osborn arrived on Midsummer Day 1850. "We hauled-in for the land," he wrote. "Passing into a channel, some four miles in width, we found ourselves running past the remarkable and lofty cliffs of "Sanderson his Hope." . . . The Hope's lofty crest pierced through the clouds which drove athwart its breast. . . . Under its lee, the water was a sheet of foam and spray, from the fierce gusts which swept down ravine and over headland; and against the base of the rocks, flights of wild fowl marked a spot famous amongst arctic voyagers." Elisha Kent Kane followed Osborn a few years later and left us a good illustration of it.

Davis now turned west, and soon encountered the long north-south pack-ice which blocks the middle of Baffin Bay the year round, melting a little every summer and gathering more ice every winter. With a north wind blowing, he could not hope to "double it out by the North" (nor, had he tried, could he have found any end); so he coasted the mass southerly. On 6 July, seeing a gap in the ice which apparently led to clear water, Davis "put our barke with oares through," found himself in a pool surrounded by towering icebergs, and was glad to get out alive.

Not until 16 July could the clincher double the southern tip of this pack-ice. Then, after two days of fog, Davis sighted the mountains on Baffin Island, just north of Exeter Sound, where he had named a hill Mount Raleigh on the first voyage. By midnight they were "athwart the Streights," as Davis hopefully called the dead-end Cumberland Sound. Doubling Cape of God's Mercy, *Ellen* sailed up Cumberland Sound 150 to 180 miles, and on 23 July anchored "among many Isles in the bottom of the gulfe, naming the same *The Eerle of Cumberlands Isles*," and noting a 30-degree westerly variation of the compass. On the 24th Davis "set saile, departing from the place, and Shaping our Course southeast to recover the Maine Ocean againe."

Becalmed on the 25th, "the weather marvellous extreme hot," master Bruton and several mariners went ashore "to course dogs"—the first hint that Davis had with him a few couple of hounds. They had not been let ashore earlier for fear of the Eskimo huskies, with the result that they were so soft and fat from eating codfish "that they were scarce able to run." Here is the most comic episode of the voyage —musicians blowing horns, sailors trying to "sic" the hounds onto a fox or hare, all hands shouting "tally-ho!" and cracking whips, and the overfed hounds waddling a short distance then lying down with their tongues lolling out. The Englishmen, furious at being robbed of their sport, had to call off the hunt, unsuccessful as their quest for the Northwest Passage.

On 29 July *Ellen* cleared Cumberland Sound, under a full moon,

Sanderson's Hope, almost three centuries later. From Elisha Kent Kane, *Arctic Explorations* (1856).

and on the 30th passed the mouth of an "Inlet which lay between 63 and 62 degrees of latitude, which we called *Lumlie's Inlet*." It was named after John, Baron Lumley, high steward of the University of Oxford and an important person at Queen Elizabeth's court. At that of her successor, James I, he became unpopular because he boasted too much about his ancestors; the king is said to have cut off one such harangue with, "Stop mon! thou need'st no more: now I learn that Adam's surname was Lumley!"

Lumley's Inlet must have been Frobisher Bay; the reason that Davis did not recognize it as such was that the map-makers, confused by the false Zeno chart, had driven Frobisher's discovery right through southern Greenland. Passing a headland (the southern tip of Meta Incognita or of Resolution Island) which he named Warwick's Foreland, Davis's *Ellen* fell into an "overfall" or tide-rip, "lothsomly crying like the rage of the waters under London bridge," and had the curious but alarming experience of racing an iceberg caught in the same current. It was a fair wind, and the clincher bent on every sail, but the iceberg won.

Between 31 July and 1 August she "passed by a very great gulfe, the water whirling and roaring as it were the meetings of tydes." Why

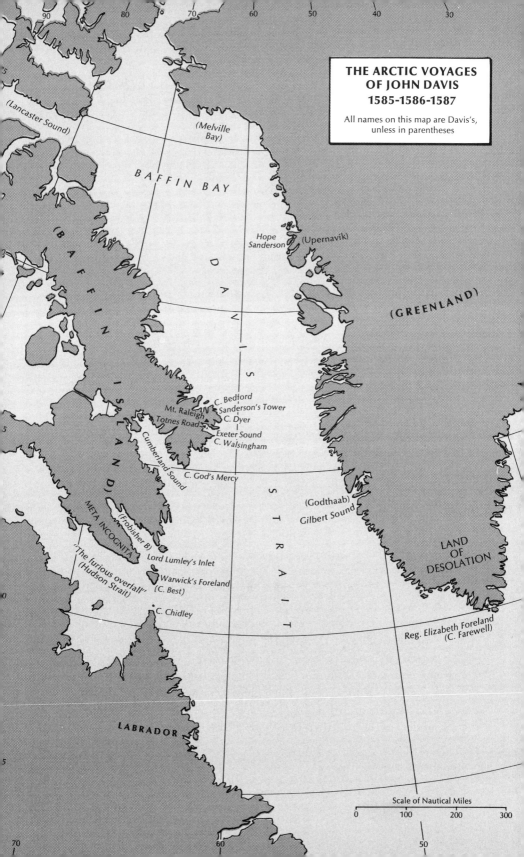

did Davis not explore it? This was Hudson Strait, which would not, to be sure, have led to Cathay but to a valuable bay. Possibly "ice" is the answer, for *Ellen* had to coast "a banke of ice which was driven out at the mouth of this gulfe" before reaching the northernmost point of the Labrador. This cape, whose latitude Davis gives correctly as 60°26′ N, he named *Chidleis* after his friend, an old Devon master mariner, Captain Chudleigh. Cape Chidley it still is today.

The Captain had set a rendezvous with his barks on the Labrador coast between latitudes 54° and 53°, where they were then supposed to be fishing. He therefore ranged the Labrador as he had done the previous year, looking for the errant vessels. A "frisking gale at the west-northwest" blew up on 10 August. Next day he sighted five deer on an island that he named Darcie's after John, Baron Darcy of Chiche, father-in-law of Lord Lumley. Assuming Davis's latitude 54°32′ to have been correct, this was White Cockade or Brig Harbor Island at the northern entrance to Hamilton Inlet, where he had anchored the year before. The presence of game gave these Englishmen another chance for a hunt with their lazy hounds. The fat mutts, apparently having been put on short rations, now condescended to provide a little sport; they coursed the deer twice around the island—imagine the yapping and yelling and tooting of horns!—only to have their quarry take to the sea and escape to the next island. "One of them was as big as a good prettie Cow, and very fat, their feete as big as Ox feet," observed Janes. He did shoot a gray hare, small consolation for losing the deer.

Finding neither bark nor any "marke, token or beacon" which they might have set up, Davis sailed as far south as Château Bay, the famous fishing rendezvous on the Strait of Belle Isle. Thence, on 15 August, with a new moon "we shaped our course for England, in God's name," without even stopping to take on wood and water. Two days later they were chased by a Basque vessel on the Grand Bank, but escaped. "After much variable weather and change of windes we arrived the 15 of September in Dartmouth, anno 1587, giving thanks to God for our safe arrival." *Elizabeth* and *Sunneshine* had already arrived, their holds crammed with stockfish. This big haul convinced the dwellers on the Dart that the Newfoundland fishery was really profitable.

To Sanderson in London, Davis wrote on the 16th, "Yesterday . . . I landed all wearie therefore I pray you pardon my shortnesse. . . .

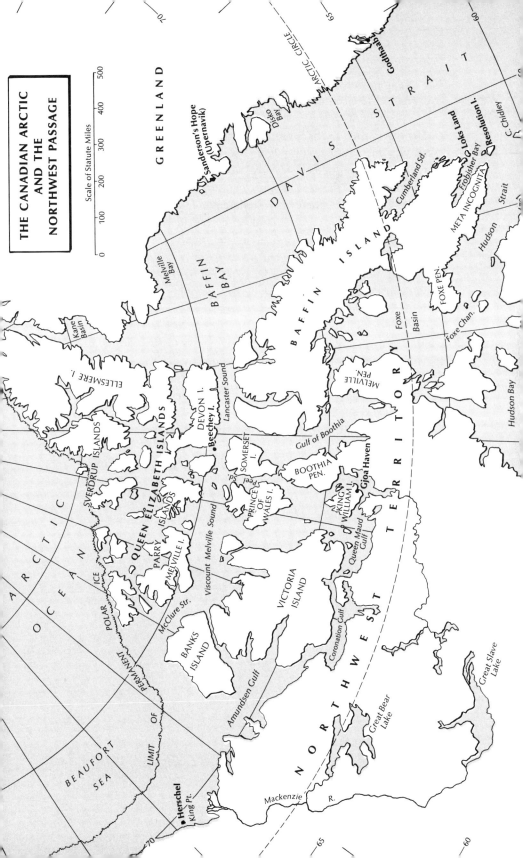

THE CANADIAN ARCTIC
AND THE
NORTHWEST PASSAGE

Scale of Statute Miles
0   100   200   300   400   500

GREENLAND

ARCTIC CIRCLE

Godthaab

DAVIS STRAIT

Sanderson's Hope
(Upernavik)

Disko Bay

Loks Land
Frobisher Bay
Resolution I.
C. Chidley

META INCOGNITA

Hudson Strait

Melville Bay

BAFFIN BAY

Cumberland Sd.

FOXE PEN.

Kane Basin

ELLESMERE I.

SVERDRUP ISLANDS

QUEEN ELIZABETH ISLANDS

PARRY ISLANDS

DEVON I.

Beechey I.

Lancaster Sound

SOMERSET I.

Peel Sd.

PRINCE OF WALES I.

Gulf of Boothia

BOOTHIA PEN.

Gjoa Haven

KING WILLIAM I.

MELVILLE PEN.

Foxe Basin

Foxe Chan.

Hudson Bay

BAFFIN ISLAND

NORTHWEST TERRITORY

MELVILLE I.

McClure Str.

Viscount Melville Sound

VICTORIA ISLAND

Queen Maud Gulf

Coronation Gulf

ARCTIC OCEAN

ICE

POLAR

LIMIT OF PERMANENT

BANKS ISLAND

Amundsen Gulf

Great Bear Lake

Great Slave Lake

BEAUFORT SEA

Herschel I.
King Pt.

Mackenzie   R.

70

65

60

The passage is most probable, the execution easie." It was a remarkable voyage to have been made in the tiny, slow-sailing pinnace *Ellen.*

Janes's account in the 1589 edition of Hakluyt suggested to the king of Denmark that he had better assert his prior rights to Greenland (assuming his succession to King Olaf Tryggvason), or some other power would get it. Accordingly, Greenland has been under Danish sovereignty since the seventeenth century, and the Danes have dealt with the Eskimo humanely and intelligently.

No more just, courageous, and wise seaman than Davis ever sailed under the Cross of St. George. Humane, modest, a good but not stiff disciplinarian, and so intelligent a navigator as to invent new instruments and methods, he should be regarded as the greatest of not only the Devon group but of all Elizabethan mariners. It is too bad that his skills and aptitudes were wasted on an enterprise, seeking the Northwest Passage, as impossible a goal for that age as a landing on the moon would have been in 1900. Nevertheless, just as Cartier on his first voyage found the key to a major water route to penetrate the continent; so Davis, by reaching Sanderson's Hope (Upernavik) at latitude 72°46′ N, had unwittingly found the key to the Northwest Passage. Almost directly across Baffin Bay, west-northwest from Sanderson's Hope, lies the entrance to Lancaster Sound where the actual Northwest Passage begins. Less fortunate than Jacques Cartier, John Davis had many more adventures at sea before being killed by Japanese pirates in 1605 at the age of fifty-five.

✳ XII ✳

Christopher Columbus

The African Background

On 12 October 1492, when the little fleet of Christopher Columbus raised a Bahamian island that he named San Salvador, neither he nor anyone else guessed that this would be an historic date. Even Columbus, who regarded himself as a child of destiny, thought he had merely found an outlying island to "the Indies." Had his entire fleet been wrecked, nobody would have been the wiser, and in all probability America would not have been discovered until 1500 when Pedro Álvares Cabral, on his way to the real India, sighted a mountain near the coast of Brazil. Thus, the entire history of Europeans in America stems from Columbus's First Voyage. The Northmen's discovery of Newfoundland almost five centuries earlier proved to be dead-end. Pre-Columbian Portuguese, Welsh, Irish, English, and Venetian voyages to America are modern-made myths, phantoms which left not one footprint on the sands of time. But Columbus's First Voyage proved to be the avant-garde for thousands of hidalgos who, weary of sustaining their haughty pride in poverty, were ready to hurl themselves on the New World in search of gold and glory.

Columbus's discovery led within a year to the first permanent European colony in America, in Hispaniola; and he himself made three more voyages of discovery, as well as sparking off those of Ojeda, Juan de La Cosa, the younger Pinzón, Vespucci, both Cabots, Magella 1, and countless others. Not only the northern voyages, starting with John Cabot's of 1497, which are related earlier on but the southern voyages of discovery now to be described, and Spain's vast empire stretching from Florida to Patagonia and out to the Philippines, stem from the First Voyage of that intrepid mariner and practical dreamer Christopher Columbus, Admiral of the Ocean Sea.*

Just as these southern voyages flow from Columbus's First, of 1492, so that was an indirect result of Portuguese voyages south along the west coast of Africa and out to the Madeiras and Azores. This had been going on since about 1430, when the Infante Dom Henrique (Prince Henry the Navigator) established himself at Sagres near Cape St. Vincent "where endeth land and where beginneth sea," as the great Portuguese poet Camoëns described it. There, a natural place for ships on all north-south routes to anchor, he set up a sort of information service where shipmasters might consult the latest charts and pick up useful data about wind and currents. This was no "naval academy" or "astronomical observatory" as some of the Infante's more enthusiastic biographers have maintained, but he did encourage the bolder navigators and reward new discoveries out of his royal revenues, with such success that his nephew D. Afonso V and great-nephew D. João II, kings of Portugal, carried on the good work after his death in 1460.

It took some time before D. Henrique could persuade anyone to round Cabo de Não ** on the western bulge of Africa, because of two superstitions: that one would never get back against the prevailing northerlies, and that anyone who persisted would run into boiling hot water at the Equator. Finally Gil Eanes, a Portuguese captain, rounded this cape in 1434 and found that the reputed terrors of the southern ocean did not exist, and that with a new type of ship, the

* Since ancient times Ocean had been regarded as one and indivisible.
** In English called Cape Nun, and subject of a punning verse:

> Quem passar o Cabo de Não
> Ou voltará ou não.

> When old Cape Nun heaves into sight
> Turn back, me lad, or else—good night!

It was, apparently, the next cape after the better known Bojador.

caravel, one could beat to windward and get back. Within a few years ships had gone far enough along West Africa to trade for black slaves and gold dust, and the Portuguese had erected a fortified trading factory on Arguin Island near latitude 20° N. By 1460, when the Infante died, his caravels had passed the site of Dakar and were within hailing distance of Sierra Leone, only ten degrees above the Equator.

It is still a matter of controversy whether or not D. Henrique consciously sought India by circumnavigating Africa. The Pope did indeed grant Portugal in 1455 exclusive jurisdiction over the coast of Guinea "and past that southern shore all the way to the Indians": but did he mean the real India or only the "Hither India" of Prester John? That mythical Christian potentate was supposed to hold sway somewhere in western Asia or northern Africa. The substance behind this legend was Ethiopia; but in European imagination Prester John was a more wealthy and powerful monarch than any of their own princes. Contact with him was ardently desired in order to kindle a Christian backfire against the infidel Turk. Columbus once thought he was hot on the trail of Prester John in Cuba!

For almost a decade after Prince Henry's death the Portuguese made no great progress southward, except to settle the Cape Verde Islands. Then, in 1469, D. Afonso V gave a Lisbon merchant named Fernão Gomes the monopoly of trading with the Guinea coast, on condition that he explore a hundred leagues farther every year. And there is no doubt that by this time the crown was seeking a southern sea route to India. Gomes's vessels promptly swung around the bulge and opened up the richest part of West Africa: the Gold and Ivory Coasts and Malagueta, where a variety of pepper almost as hot as the East Indian was found. By 1474, when his monopoly expired, Fernão Gomes had sent ships clean across the Gulf of Guinea and reached the island of Fernando Po on latitude 3°30′ N, where the African coast again turns southward.

In this African exploration the Portuguese developed a type of small sailing ship that they named *caravella*, the caravel. We know little of its hull design or construction, which, combined with its lateen sail plan, enabled the caravel to sail closer to the wind and faster than any square-rigger. This capability enabled a mariner to go as far as he pleased along the African coast, with assurance that he could get back. A long reach on the starboard tack, which the Portuguese called *a volta do mar largo*, would take her from the Canaries or the west coast of Africa to the Azores, where she could replenish at the port of Angra in Terceira and catch a good slant for Lisbon.

This long hitch off soundings taught the Portuguese mariners confidence and led to the development of celestial navigation—shooting the sun or the North Star with astrolabe or quadrant, applying declination and working out your latitude. Land-based European geographers already knew how to calculate latitude by observation of sun and North Star, but to introduce those methods on board ship took time. Most master mariners and pilots of that era were illiterate, and for them the application of declination to altitude was an insoluble problem. Whether or not D. Henrique held "refresher courses" for pilots in Sagres, the fact is that by 1484, when Diogo Cão discovered the mouth of the Congo, Portuguese ships carried charts with a latitude grid, and Portuguese pilots had built up such a reputation that all organizers of Spanish, English, and French voyages of discovery sought to engage one for their ships.

All, that is, except Columbus. But he himself had been trained in the Portuguese service for years before beginning his great voyage.

Enter Columbus

Christopher Columbus was born Cristoforo Colombo, in or near the city of Genoa some time between 25 August and the end of October 1451. He was son and grandson to woolen weavers who had been living in various towns of the Genoese Republic for at least three generations. His long face, tall stature, ruddy complexion, and red hair suggest a considerable share of "barbarian" rather than "Latin" blood, but do not prove anything; and he himself was conscious only of his Genoese origin. There is no more reason to doubt that Christopher Columbus was a Genoa-born Catholic, steadfast in his faith and proud of his native city, than to doubt that Abraham Lincoln was born in Hardin, Kentucky, in 1809, of British stock.

This is not to say that Columbus was an Italian in the modern sense. The people of proud Genoa, *Genova la Superba*, have always held themselves apart from (and superior to) other Italians. In the *majorat*

Christopher Columbus in middle age. Courtesy Museo Giovio, Como.

or entail of his estate that Columbus executed before departing on his Third Voyage to the New World, he charged his heirs "always to work for the honor, welfare and increase of the city of Genoa," and there to maintain a house for some member of the Colombo family, "so that he can live there honorably and have foot and root in that city as a native thereof . . . *because from it I came and in it I was born.*" And, "being as I was born in Genoa," his executors shall accumulate a fund in the Bank of St. George at Genoa, that "noble and powerful city by the sea."

Every contemporary Spaniard or Portuguese who wrote about Columbus and his discoveries calls him Genoese. Four contemporary Genoese chroniclers claim him as a compatriot. Every early map on which his nationality is recorded describes him as Genoese or *Ligur*, a citizen of the Ligurian Republic. Nobody in his lifetime, or for three centuries after, had any doubt about his origin or birthplace.

Nevertheless, by presenting far-fetched hypotheses as proved, and innuendoes as facts, by attacking authentic documents as false, and by fabricating others, Columbus has been presented as Castilian, Catalan, Corsican, Majorcan, Portuguese, French, German, English, Irish, Greek, Armenian, Polish, and Russian. And now, American! A Scandinavian writer named Thorwald Brynidsen has "proved" that the discoverer was a native North American, a descendant of the eleventh-century Norse colony. He built himself a Viking ship, sailed her to Spain, changed his name to Colón, and set forth to rediscover Vinland!

Enough of these fantasies.

Giovanni Colombo, the Discoverer's paternal grandfather, was a weaver, his son Domenico, a master weaver; hired a house just inside the Porta dell' Olivella, the eastern gate of Genoa. About 1445 he married Susanna Fontanarossa, daughter of another local weaver. She brought Domenico a small dowry, and he obtained a respectable municipal appointment as warder of the Olivella gate. In this house, near the gate, in a quarter so rebuilt that the site cannot now be definitely fixed, Cristoforo was born in the late summer or early fall of 1451.

Thus Columbus's forty-first birthday fell during his first great voyage of discovery. Very likely he did not remember the exact date, since boys and girls then celebrated the feast day of their patron saint rather than their own birthday. On 25 June, the feast of Saint Christopher, young Cristoforo would have made a point of attending Mass with his mother, and then would have received a little pocket money and a glass of wine from his father.

The story of Saint Christopher,* familiar to every child in the Middle Ages, made Columbus's baptismal name far more significant to him than his patronymic. Christopher was a great hulk of a pagan who,

---

* Recently and regrettably demoted from saintly status by the Vatican.

hearing of Christ, went forth in search of Him. A holy hermit said, "Perhaps Our Lord will show Himself to you if you fast and pray." "Fast I cannot," said Christopher, "and how to pray I know not; ask me something easier." So the hermit said, "Knowest thou that river without a bridge which can only be crossed at great peril of drowning?" "I do," said Christopher. "Very well, do thou who art so tall and strong take up thine abode by the hither bank, and assist poor travelers to cross; that will be very agreeable to Our Lord, and mayhap He will show Himself to thee." So Christopher built himself a cabin by the river bank and, with the aid of a tree trunk as staff, carried wayfarers across on his broad shoulders.

One night the big fellow was asleep in his cabin when he heard a child's voice cry, "Christopher! come and set me across!" Out he came, staff in hand, and took the infant on his shoulders. But as he waded through the river the child's weight increased so that it became almost intolerable, and he had to call forth all his strength to avoid falling and to reach the other bank. "Well now, my little fellow," said he, "thou hast put me in great danger, for thy burden waxed so great that had I borne the whole world on my back, it could have weighed no more than thou." "Marvel not, Christopher," replied the child, "for thou hast borne upon thy back the whole world and Him who created it. I am the Christ whom thou servest in doing good; and as proof of my words, plant that staff near thy cabin, and tomorrow it shall be covered with flowers and fruit." The saint did as he was bid, and found his staff next day transformed into a beautiful date palm.

This story would certainly have gone home to the boy who became the man we know as Columbus. He conceived it his destiny to carry the word of that Holy Child across the ocean to countries steeped in heathen darkness. Many years elapsed and countless discouragements were surmounted before anyone would afford him means to take up the burden. Once assumed, it often became intolerable, and often he staggered under it; but never did he set it down until his appointed work was done.

In 1455, when Christopher was four years old, his parents removed to a house with a courtyard and garden near the Porta Sant' Andrea. His next younger brother, Bartholomew, the future *Adelantado*, was then about two years old. His youngest brother, Giacomo or Diego, seems to have been Christopher's junior by seventeen years. Christopher felt for him the affection that an older brother often does for the baby of the family. He took him on his Second Voyage, and after ascertaining the young man to be an indifferent seaman and a bad administrator, helped him to obtain holy orders and made futile efforts to procure a bishopric for him.

Domenico Colombo, the father of these three boys, was a master clothier (to use the old English term) who owned one or more looms, bought his own wool, sold the finished cloth, and taught apprentice boys their trade. As a citizen of Genoa and member of the local clothiers' gild, he had a respectable position in the middle class. A fairly vivid personality emerges from the dry records. He made promises that he was unable to fulfill, bought goods for which he could not pay, and started unprofitable sidelines such as selling cheese and wine instead of sticking to his loom. Although a poor provider for his family, Domenico must have been a popular and plausible sort of fellow to obtain property on credit and to be appointed on committees of his gild. He was the kind of father who would shut up shop when trade was poor and take the boys fishing; and the sort of wine seller who was his own best customer.

For years the records tell us nothing of the Colombos. By March 1470 Domenico had removed to nearby Savona with his family and looms. He also retailed wine; on 31 October of that year, son Cristoforo, "over 19 years of age," acknowledged a debt of 48 Genoese pounds for wines delivered to him and his father. He lived at Savona long enough to make two fast friends in the upper class:—Michele de Cuneo, who accompanied him on the Second Voyage, and Bartolomeo Fieschi, who on the Fourth Voyage shared the famous rescue voyage from Jamaica to Haiti.

Domenico died about 1496, but was not forgotten; for Christopher and his brother Bartholomew named their new capital, Santo Domingo, after the patron saint of their father.

Such are the facts that we have of the life of Christopher Columbus to the age of twenty-two, and of his family. Since this boy was father to the man of recorded history, we may assume that he was a proud and sensitive lad, faithful to his religious duties, following a hereditary calling in order to help support his parents, but eager for adventure, mystically assured of a high mission and a noble destiny.

The absence of Italian in his preserved writings, except for a stray word or phrase, is a great talking point of the *Colón Español* and *Colom Català* sects. The earliest bit of his writing that has been preserved, a postil (marginal note) dated 1481 on one of his books, is in bad Spanish mingled with Portuguese; all his letters, even those to Genoese friends and to the Bank of St. George, are in Spanish. None of the authors to whom he alludes wrote in Italian; the *Divine Comedy*, ever beautiful where Dante describes the sea, apparently he knew not.

Actually the lack of Italian in Columbus's writings is good evidence of his Genoese birth. The Genoese dialect of his day, even more than in ours (when a Genoese speaking it in a trial at Rome around 1910 had to have an Italian interpreter), was very different from Tuscan or classical Italian; possibly even more so than the Venetian and Neapolitan dialects. It was essentially a language of common speech, rarely written. A poor boy of Genoa would not have known Italian, unless he learned it at school. Christopher undoubtedly left home almost if not completely illiterate, and when he finally learned to read and write, used the Castilian language because it was that of his new associates. Many thousands of peasant Italian emigrants have done just that. Arriving in their New World home illiterate, they learn to read and write in English, Spanish, or Portuguese according to the country of their residence, and eventually forget the dialect they were brought up to speak.

A careful analysis of Columbus's writings has been made by the most eminent Spanish philologist of the last hundred years, Ramón Menéndez Pidal. The Discoverer, he reports, did not write Jewish-Spanish or Italian-Spanish, but Portuguese-Spanish. To the end of his life he wrote Castilian with Portuguese spellings, indicating that he spoke Portuguese first. During the decade he lived at Lisbon, Castilian was a widely favored language among the educated classes of Portugal into which Columbus married; even Camoëns used that language for his sonnets. So an ambitious young man would naturally have chosen the more literary and widely expanded language.

What effect if any did Christopher's residence of some twenty-two years on Genoese territory have on his future career? Genoa was certainly the place to give any active lad a hankering for sea adventure. The Ligurian Republic bathes in the sea, spreads her arms to embrace it, looks southward to a clean horizon. The *libeccio* (southwest wind) blows in fresh from the Mediterranean and gives the terraced hills above the coast sufficient moisture for tilth, vineyard, and pasture. Shipbuilding went on in little coves and harbors all along the shore. Great galleys and carracks were constantly clearing for and arriving from the Aegean, the Levant, and North Africa. Genoa cherished traditions of navigators like the Vivaldi who sought the ocean route to India by way of Africa as early as 1291, and of Malocello, one of the discoverers of the Canaries. Genoa had a noted school of mapmakers who supplied portolan charts to half the Mediterranean, and who helped the Portuguese to chart their new African possessions. One may picture young Christopher looking wistfully out on the harbor from his parents' house while he worked at a loathed trade. Here, too, he may even have conceived his grand enterprise; for the achievements of a great man are often but the fulfillment of youthful dreams.

Such speculations are for the poet or novelist, not the historian. All we now know and all we shall probably ever know of Columbus's life to the age of twenty-two is that he helped his parents at Genoa and Savona in their respectable trade of weaving woolens, and that he had little or no schooling. Yet his youth was neither so hard nor his life so bitter as to cause him to forsake allegiance to "that noble and powerful city by the sea."

Early Years at Sea

Cristoforo grew up in a community where every healthy boy went sailing whenever he could. Fishing trips, out with the evening land breeze to net sardines by the light of flaring torches and race the fleet home at dawn. Maybe a run over to Corsica and back; seeing the points of a high, jagged island shoulder up over the horizon, watching them run together into one island, and the white specks on the shore become houses. You anchor in a strange harbor where the men jabber in a weird dialect, and the girls seem so much more beautiful and outgoing than those of your home town. Most of Genoa's commerce went by sea; and it would have been natural for Domenico to send Cristoforo along the coast in a little lateen-rigged packet to sell his cloth, and buy wool, wine, and cheese. Coastwise experience is not to be despised. Whoever can cope with a sudden squall off the mountains near home is half prepared to meet a storm at sea.

In a letter to the Spanish Sovereigns written from Hispaniola in

January 1495, Columbus describes a trip across the Mediterranean on board a Genoese ship chartered by King René of Anjou for his short war with the king of Aragon. That could have happened between October 1470 and March 1472. His next recorded voyage was in a Genoese ship named *Roxana* in 1474, to help the city's trading factory on Chios defend itself against the Turks. The valuable product of Chios was the lentisk, from which they extracted gum mastic (*Pistacia lenticus*), a base for varnish; and twice on his First Voyage Columbus inaccurately designated a local tree, the gumbo limbo, as the lentisk, "which I have seen in the island of Chios." He may have made another voyage to Chios in 1475. On these trips, Christopher learned to "hand, reef and steer," to estimate distances by eye, to make sail, let go and weigh anchors properly, and other elements of seamanship. He learned seamanship the old way, the hard way, and the best way, in the school of experience. As yet illiterate, he could not navigate and thus rate an officer's billet.

Not long after returning from Chios, Columbus joined a fleet that played into the hands of destiny by casting him up on the shore of Portugal. In May 1476, Genoa organized a big convoy to protect a quantity of Chian mastic being shipped to Lisbon, England, and Flanders. One ship, named *Bechalla*, owned by Luis Centurione of Genoa and manned largely by men of Savona, took young Christopher on as foremast hand. On 13 August, off the coast of Portugal near Lagos, the convoy was suddenly attacked by a Franco-Portuguese war fleet commanded by a famous naval hero, Guillaume de Casenove. The Genoese proved no easy prey. All day the battle raged, and by night-fall seven ships, including *Bechalla*, had gone down and the surviving vessels were glad to sheer off and seek the nearest friendly port. When *Bechalla* sank, Columbus leaped into the sea, grasped a sweep that floated free, and by pushing it ahead of him and resting when exhausted (for he had been wounded in the battle), he managed to reach the shore, over six miles distant. The people of Lagos treated the survivors kindly and passed Columbus on to Lisbon, where someone of the local Genoese colony took him in and cured his wounds. His host may have been his younger brother Bartholomew, who had already established a small chart-making business in Lisbon.

Christopher was in luck to fall on his feet in Portugal. At the age of twenty-five, chance had brought him to the European center for blue-

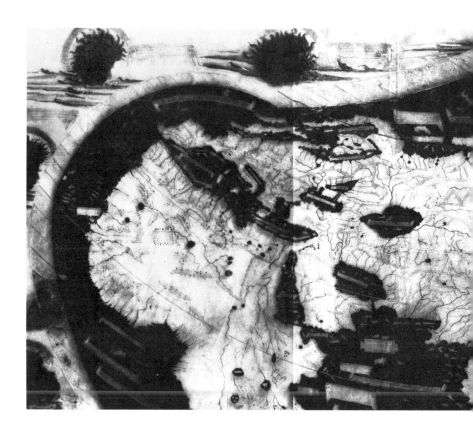

water voyaging and overseas discovery. He was among people who could teach him all he wanted to learn: Portuguese, Castilian, and Latin; mathematics and astronomy for celestial navigation. He already knew all the basic seamanship that a common sailor could pick up.

And he had plenty more on a northern voyage. His son Ferdinand wrote that among his father's notes he found a statement that in February 1477 he sailed a hundred leagues north of Iceland, to which island "which is as big as England, come the English, especially of Bristol, with their merchandise." And he adds that in this particular winter season the sea was not frozen, and the range of tides ran up to fifty feet. This statement has aroused no end of controversy. But the

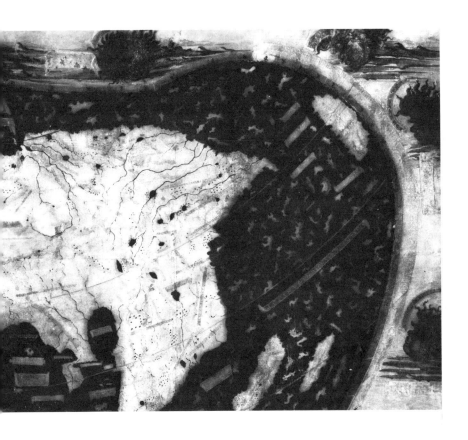

Henricus Martellus Germanus world map of 1492. Courtesy Beinecke Collection, Yale University.

winter of 1476–77 was unusually mild, so that this Portuguese ship could have sailed beyond Iceland to Jan Mayen Land in latitude 70°50′ N. If, however, Columbus actually did make this voyage, did he land in Iceland and pick up data on the Northmen's explorations of the eleventh century? Son Ferdinand's statement is full of inaccuracies —the latitude he gives for Iceland is more than ten degrees out, and the spring range of tides at Reykjavik is only thirteen feet, not fifty. And even if the ship did land in Iceland, would this young mariner have attended a saga-reading party (in translation) and have heard about Vinland? Not likely. In any case, there was nothing in the Greenland-Vinland story of polar bears, walrus ivory, and white falcons to interest a young seaman already dreaming of an ocean route to the fabulous Indies of gems, spices, and precious metals.

More important to him was something he saw at Galway, going or coming: two boats drifting ashore containing "a man and a woman of extraordinary appearance," both dead. These probably were flatfaced Lapps or Finns who had escaped from a sinking ship; but Christopher and the Irish assumed that they were Chinese, "blown across." As for tides, Professor Ruddock of the University of London has a plausible explanation. She found record of a Bristol ship trading in 1481 with the friary of La Rábida where (as we shall see) Columbus became intimate. The Bristolians told the monks about the tremendous tides on the Avon, and they somehow applied this to the Arctic Ocean when Ferdinand, much later, picked up the story of the Iceland voyage.

We find Christopher at sea again in the summer of 1478 as captain of a Portuguese ship which Centurione, his former employer, had chartered to buy sugar in Madeira. This Genoese merchant provided the young captain with so little money that Funchal merchants refused to deliver, and he sailed empty-handed to his old home. Next year Christopher, at twenty-eight years a master mariner, contracted an advantageous marriage with Dona Filipa de Perestrelo e Moniz, daughter of Bartolomeu Perestrelo, hereditary captain of Porto Santo in the Madeira group, and a contemporary of the Infante D. Henrique. The young couple shortly went to live in Porto Santo where their only son, Diego (later the second admiral and viceroy), was born, and where Dona Filipa's mother placed at Christopher's disposal the charts and journals of her seagoing husband. Not long after the birth of this, their one and only child, the Columbus couple moved to Funchal, Madeira.

In 1481 D. Afonso V died and was succeeded by his son D. João "the Complete Prince." Young (aged 26), energetic, wise and learned, ruthless and ambitious, D. João II equaled any monarch of his age. Just before his accession, a long and fruitless war with Castile had been concluded by the Treaty of Alcáçovas. In this Spain recognized Portugal's exclusive rights to the African coast and islands south of the Canaries, which Spain retained. D. João, who had formerly managed the crown monopoly of the African trade, determined to build a castle or fortified trading factory on the Gold Coast, strong enough to beat off any European rival, and to keep the natives in order. A fleet of eleven vessels was fitted out at Lisbon, soldiers, stonemasons, and other artisans were engaged, and late in 1481 it set sail from Lisbon under the command of Diogo d'Azambuja. On the Gold Coast the men worked hard and well that winter, erecting a great stone castle of medieval design, complete with turrets, moat, chapel, warehouse, and market court; and a garrison was left in charge. São Jorge da Mina (St. George of the Mine), as this castle was named, upheld Portuguese sovereignty and protected her trade on the Gold Coast for centuries. The site and the ruins today are called Cape Coast Castle.

Columbus either took part in Azambuja's expedition or, more probably, made a voyage to São Jorge da Mina in 1482–83 or 1483–84, as officer of a trading expedition. West Africa deeply impressed the young mariner. In the journal of his First Voyage to America he frequently compares people and products of "The Indies" with those of Guinea; he expected to find a *mina* in Hispaniola, and his Third Voyage had particular reference to the supposed latitude of Sierra Leone. The experience of a passage to the Gold Coast and back, in company with Portuguese pilots, must greatly have improved his seamanship, although it may be doubted whether it gave him any competence in celestial navigation.

Christovão Colom, as he was called in Portugal, learned many useful things from his Portuguese shipmates, the world's finest mariners of that era: how to handle a caravel in head wind and sea, how to claw off a lee shore, what kind of sea stores to take on a long voyage and how to stow them, and what sort of trading truck is wanted by primitive people. Every voyage that he sailed under the flag of Portugal made it more likely that he would succeed in the great enterprise that was already in his brain. Above all, he learned from the Portuguese confidence that, with a good ship under him and with God's assistance, the boundaries of the known world might be indefinitely enlarged; that the Age of Discovery had only just begun. From his own experiences he had learned that the ancients did not know everything; despite their denials the Torrid Zone was habitable.

By 1484, when he returned from Guinea voyaging, Columbus was ready to make an amazing proposition to the king of Portugal.

✷ XIII ✷

His "Enterprise of the Indies"

Columbus's Great Idea

Columbus's "Enterprise of the Indies," *Empresa de las Indias,* as he called it, and to the furthering of which he devoted all his time and energy from about 1483 on, was simple enough. It was to discover a short sea route to the Indies * instead of thrusting along the African coast as the Portuguese were doing. He also hoped to pick up en route some island or archipelago which would be a useful staging area; but the be-all and end-all was to rediscover eastern Asia by sailing west from Europe or Africa. He expected to set up a factory or trading post, like Chios or La Mina, on some island off the Asiatic coast, where European goods could be exchanged for the fragrant and glittering wares of the Orient much more cheaply than by trans-Asia caravans with their endless middlemen and successive mark-ups.

Exactly when Columbus conceived this momentous plan, or had it planted in his brain, is still a mystery. It may have come silently, like the grace of God, or in a rush and tumult of emotional conviction, or from observing, in Lisbon, the painful effort of the Portuguese to

---

* "The Indies," as the term was then used in Europe, included China, Japan, the Ryukyus, the Spice Islands, Indonesia, Thailand, and everything between them and India proper.

approach the Orient by sailing around Africa. All educated men of western Europe knew that the world was a sphere; all observant sailors knew that its surface was curved, from seeing ships hull-down. Columbus never had to argue the rotundity of the earth. When he had learned enough Latin to read ancient and medieval cosmographers, he ascertained that Aristotle was reported to have written that you could cross the Ocean from Spain to the Indies *paucis diebus*, in comparatively few days; and Strabo recorded that certain Greeks or Romans had even tried it but returned empty-handed, "through want of resolution and scarcity of provisions." He picked up from two famous medieval books, Pierre d'Ailly's *Imago Mundi* and Pope Pius II's *Historia Rerum Ubique Gestarum*, numerous guesses about the narrowness of the Ocean; and fortunately we have his own copies of these works, amply underlined, and their margins filled with his postils. He combed the Bible and ancient literature for quotations that might apply to his enterprise, such as Psalm lxxi (or lxxii) 8, "He shall have dominion also from sea to sea, and from the river unto the ends of the earth." He cherished the prophecy in Seneca's *Medea*—"An age will come after many years when the Ocean will loose the chains of things, and a huge land lie revealed; when Tethys will disclose new worlds and Thule no more be the ultimate."

Against this passage in Columbus's own copy of Seneca his son Ferdinand wrote this proud annotation:

This prophecy was fulfilled by my father the Admiral, in the year 1492.

The first trace we have of any outside influence on Columbus forming his great idea is the Toscanelli correspondence, his earliest known scholarly backing. Paolo dal Pozzo Toscanelli was a leading Florentine physician in an era when the best astronomers and cosmographers were apt to be medicos, since they alone acquired enough mathematics to be men of science. Toscanelli had become what nowadays is called a "pen pal" of a canon of Lisbon Cathedral named Fernão Martins, to whom he conveyed the idea that the Ocean between Spain and the Indies was much narrower than anyone else supposed. Martins passed this on to the king, D. Afonso V, who invited the Florentine to develop his views in a letter; and that Toscanelli did. Dated 25 June 1474, a copy of this "Toscanelli Letter" in Columbus's hands became his principal exhibit when arguing for a narrow Atlantic. In brief, it says

that Paul the Physician is pleased to hear that the King of Portugal is interested in finding a shorter sea route to "the land of spices" than the one his mariners are seeking via Africa. Quinsay (modern Hang-chow), capital of the Chinese province of Mangi, is about 5000 nautical miles due west of Lisbon. An alternate, and shorter, route to the Orient goes by way of Antilia to the "noble island of Cipangu"—

Seville in the early XVI century, by Sanchez Coelho. Courtesy Museo de América, Madrid.

Marco Polo's name for Japan, where the temples and royal palaces are roofed with massy gold. At some time not later than 1481 (Toscanelli died in May 1482), Columbus was shown a copy of this letter, became greatly excited over such exalted backing for his ideas, and wrote to Florence, asking for more. Toscanelli replied by sending a copy of his earlier letter, with a chart (long since lost) to illustrate his notion of the Ocean's width, and a covering letter praising the young mariner's "great and noble ambition to pass over to where the spices grow."

By this time Columbus had learned enough Latin to read ancient and medieval authors who speculated on the length of the land and width of the Ocean. The result of his studies was to arrive at an extraordinary perversion of the truth. The distance from the Canaries to Japan via Antilia, which Toscanelli estimated at 3000 nautical miles (and Columbus whittled down to 2400) is actually about 10,000 miles between their respective meridians, measured on latitude 28° N. Toscanelli's Canaries-to-Quinsay route of 5000 miles (reduced by Columbus to 3550) is actually about 11,766 nautical miles by air.

How did he arrive at this colossal miscalculation, upon which his great voyage of discovery was based? Through several basic errors: reducing the length of a degree of longitude by one-quarter, stretching Ptolemy's estimate of the length of the Eurasian continent (Cape St. Vincent to eastern Asia) from 180° to 225°, adding another 28° for the discoveries of Marco Polo, plus 30° for his reputed distance from the east coast of China to the east coast of Japan, and saving another nine degrees of westing by starting his Ocean crossing from the outermost Canary Island * That left only 68 degrees of Ocean to cross before hitting Japan; still too much for Columbus. The medieval calculators used too long a degree of longitude, he argued; he proposed to cross on latitude 28° N where the degree (he thought) measured but 40 nautical miles; thus he would have only 60 × 40 or 2400 miles of open water to cover. In other words, his figures placed Japan in relation to Spain about where the West Indies actually are. That is why those islands were given the name *Las Indias* and their inhabitants called *Indios*, Japan then being reckoned as part of "The Indies." And a Nuremberg geographer named Martin Behaim in the Portuguese service compiled in 1492 a globe (a tracing from which we reproduce) that showed a close correlation with what Toscanelli had written.

TRANSOCEANIC DISTANCES IN NAUTICAL MILES

	Toscanelli	Behaim	Columbus	Actual Airline
Canaries to Cipangu (Japan)	3000	3080	2400	10,600
Canaries to Quinsay (Hangchow)	5000	4440	3550	11,766

* Columbus owned a copy (still in the Biblioteca Colombina, Seville) of the 1485 edition of Marco Polo, who placed Japan some 1500 miles east of the coast of China, thus shortening the projected ocean passage.

Columbus's calculations were illogical, but his mind never followed the rules of logic. He *knew* he could make it, and had to put the mileage low in order to attract support.

Another colossal miscalculation of his was the relative proportion of land to water on the globe. Modern measurements divide our planet's surface into 30 per cent land and 70 per cent water,* but Columbus more than reversed this figure by insisting on the medieval notion (based on 2 Esdras vi. 42, "Six parts hast Thou dried up") that water covered less than 15 per cent. Very comforting, if true!

Dealing with Princes

Columbus in 1484, subsequent to his voyage or voyages to Guinea, received a hearing from D. João II. The leading Portuguese historian of this reign, João de Barros, recorded that *Christovão Colom*, "Of Genoese nation, a man expert, eloquent and good Latinist," requested the king to "give him some vessels to go and discover the Isle Cypango by this Western Ocean." D. João referred Christopher to a newly appointed maritime advisory committee. They dismissed him politely but firmly, considering his plan "as vain, simply founded on imagination, or things like that Isle Cypango of Marco Polo." For most learned men at that era regarded *The Book of Ser Marco Polo* as pure fiction, and Cipangu-Japan as a mythical island in a class with Hy-Brasil and Antilia. They felt that the length of the proposed voyage had been fantastically underestimated.

Columbus and D. João parted friends, and were to see each other twice again. But, for the present, there was nothing for him in Lisbon. His wife Dona Filipa had already died. Brother Bartholomew, first convert to the Enterprise of the Indies, then took off for England and France, to promote it.

About the middle of 1485 Columbus and his little son Diego took passage on a merchant ship for Spain and disembarked at a sleepy little seaport called Palos de la Frontera because of its nearness to the Portuguese frontier. Although he probably chose that port to enter Spain for no better reason than having been offered free passage to it by the skipper, it turned out to be as lucky as swimming ashore at Lagos nine years earlier. When his ship rounded the promontory

* Peter J. Herring (ed.), *Deep Oceans*, p. 13. In the Northern Hemisphere the proportion is 40–60; in the Southern, 19–81.

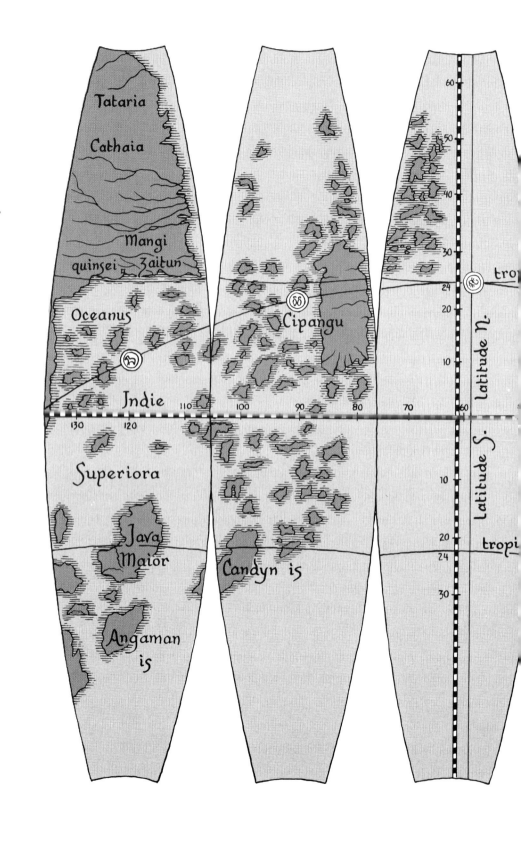

Tataria

Cathaia

Mangi

quinsei   Zaitun

Oceanus

Indie

Cipangu

Superiora

Java
Maior

Candyn is

Angaman
is

tropi

Latitude N.

Latitude S.

tropi

60

50

40

30

24

20

10

110

100

90

80

70

60

130

120

10

20

24

30

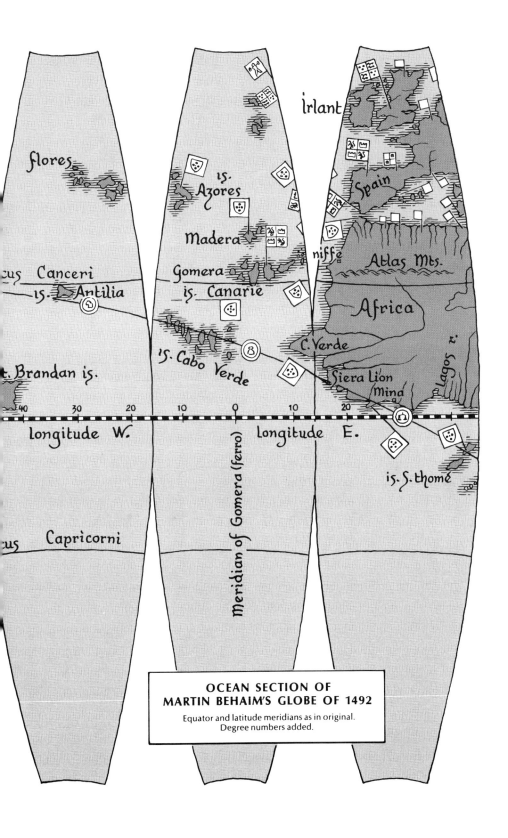

Irlant

flores

is. Azores

Madera

Gomera

niffe

Atlas Mts.

cus Canceri

_is. Antilia

is. Canarie

Africa

Spain

t. Brandan is.

'S. Cabo Verde

C. Verde

Siera Lion
Mina

Lagos r.

40   30   20   10   0   10   20

longitude W.   longitude E.

is. S. thome

Meridian of Gomera (ferro)

cus Capricorni

**OCEAN SECTION OF
MARTIN BEHAIM'S GLOBE OF 1492**

Equator and latitude meridians as in original.
Degree numbers added.

where the Rio Tinto joins the Saltés, Columbus noted the conspicuous buildings of La Rábida, a friary of the Franciscan order which took more interest in discovery than did any other branch of the church. Franciscan missionaries had been to China around 1320 and others were eager to return. For the present, Columbus, puzzled what to do with little Diego while he tramped about Spain seeking support, remembered that Franciscans often maintained boarding schools in connection with their friaries. Over a quarter-century later, a physician who happened to be present testified that father and son made the long, dusty walk from Palos to La Rábida, that Christopher asked for bread and a cup of water for the boy, and then got into conversation with Antonio de Marchena, a highly intelligent Franciscan who happened to be visiting. Columbus not only arranged for Diego's admission as a boarder but convinced Marchena, an astronomer of repute, that he "had something"; and Marchena gave him a letter of introduction to the Duke of Medina Sidonia. Columbus called at the ducal castle and was referred to a kinsman, the Count of Medina Celi, who owned a merchant fleet based at Puerto Santa Maria near Cadiz. This nobleman (later promoted duke) declared himself ready to provide Columbus "with three or four well equipped caravels," for he asked no more, "but felt that the Enterprise of the Indies was too great for a mere subject to take over; that the Genoese must see the Queen.

As Pierre Chaunu observes, La Rábida became a key to the Christian expansion that flowed from Columbus's voyage, as Palos and the caravels were the keys to immediate success. For Palos, a nursery of Spanish blue-water mariners, lay so close to the Portuguese frontier that an exchange of caravel designs was easy. Without La Rábida and Palos, there would have been no Voyage of Discovery, at least not in 1492.

Columbus now proceeded to the royal city of Cordova. Arriving in January 1486, he missed the Catholic Sovereigns, but tarried to await the Queen's return, and her pleasure.

In the meantime he made a pleasant connection with a pretty peasant girl. At Cordova there was a colony of Genoese, one of them an apothecary, and apothecary shops in those days were informal meeting places for physicians and amateur scientists. Columbus naturally dropped in at his compatriot's shop and there became acquainted with one Diego de Harana, who frequented it. Diego invited him to his house, where he met a twenty-year-old cousin of the Haranas, Beatriz Enriquez. She became Columbus's mistress and in 1488 bore him his second son, Ferdinand. The undoubted fact that Columbus never married Beatriz has troubled his more pious biographers, and judging from certain provisions for her in his will, it troubled his conscience too; but nobody at the time seems to have held it against him. A second marriage with a peasant's daughter would have been unsuitable for one who intended to become a nobleman and an admiral. The Harana family were pleased with the connection; at least two of them later served under Columbus, and the friendship between them and his legitimate descendants continued for two or three generations.

On May Day 1486, almost a year from the time he first set foot in Spain, Columbus was received by the Queen in the Alcazar of Cordova. *Isabel la Católica* (Isabella in English) was one of the ablest European sovereigns in an age of strong kings. She had an intuitive faculty for choosing men, and for timing. Close to Columbus in age, she had blue eyes and auburn hair resembling his, and she shared his religious mysticism. Her marriage with Ferdinand of Aragon had united all "the Spains" excepting Portugal (to whose royal family she was allied) and the remnant of the Moorish caliphate of Cordova, which she had resolved to conquer. Some spark of understanding evidently passed between Christopher and Isabella at their first meeting, and although she turned down his enterprise more than once, he found that he could count on her in the end. On this occasion she appointed a special commission under her confessor Hernando de Talavera to examine the Enterprise of the Indies and recommend whether it should be accepted or rejected.

The most unhappy period in Columbus's life extended over the next six years. He had to sustain a continual battle against prejudice, contumely, and sheer indifference. A proud, sensitive man who *knew* that his project would open fresh paths to wealth and for the advancement of Christ's kingdom, he had to endure clownish witticisms and crackpot jests by ignorant courtiers, to be treated like a beggar; even at times to suffer want. Hardest of all, he learned by experience the meaning of the phrase *cosas de España*, the endemic procrastination of Spaniards. In later years he often alluded bitterly to these experiences and contrasted the enormous wealth and power his

Isabella of Castile. Flemish school. Original in Windsor Castle. Courtesy, Keeper of H.M. Paintings, Windsor Castle.

Ferdinand of Aragon. Flemish School. Original in Windsor Castle. Courtesy,
Keeper of H.M. Paintings, Windsor Castle.

discoveries had conferred on Spain to his own protracted efforts to obtain a fair hearing, and later to secure his just rights.

Even in our day we have known men of great strength of character who felt inspired by God in the pursuit of some ideal goal, who exasperated people who held other views, and were almost impossible to fight against. You can argue your head off against people like that, but they always come up with a fresh argument.

The Talavera commission, meeting at Salamanca around Christmastide 1486, could not agree. Its deliberations have been distorted by Washington Irving and other writers into a debate as to whether the world was round or flat. Actually, we know nothing definite about the arguments, but we may be certain that since the commission consisted of men of learning, the sphericity of the earth never came into question. At least one member, Diego de Deza, favored the Great Enterprise; and it was doubtless due to his influence, or Talavera's, that early in 1487 Columbus received a retaining fee of 12,000 maravedis a year, the pay of an able seaman, enough to support a man of his simple tastes.*

Christmas of 1487 passed without any report from the Talavera commission. So, early in 1488, Columbus wrote to D. João II of Portugal, requesting another hearing and asking for a safe-conduct from arrest for his unpaid bills in Lisbon. The King replied promptly and most cordially, urging Columbus to come immediately, and promising protection. The probable reason for this sudden and flattering change of attitude was that Bartholomew Dias, embarked on one more Portuguese attempt to reach the Indies by rounding Africa, had been gone seven months and nothing had yet been heard from him.

For want of funds, Christopher delayed leaving for Lisbon, and before he and his brother Bartholomew (who had remained there) could "do business" with the King, Dias returned. The Columbus brothers were present in December 1488 when his three caravels sailed

---

* To convey the equivalent of Spanish currency of this era, I have tried to state the gold content in U. S. coinage before we went off the gold standard. Thus, 12,000 maravedis equaled about $83 in gold of 1934. Whatever way you figure it, a maravedi was less than a cent in specie value, but its purchasing power was much greater. Twelve maravedis a day were allowed by the crown for feeding each seaman in the navy. A bushel of wheat in 1493 cost 73 maravedis. Sancho Panza's wages from Don Quixote were 26 maravedis a day and found, much better pay than that of Columbus's gromets.

proudly up the Tagus. Dias had rounded the southernmost cape of Africa—the Cape of Good Hope as the King named it—and sailed well up the east coast, when the men mutinied and forced him to turn back. But he had discovered a sea route to India. That ended D. João's interest in Columbus. Why now invest money in a doubtful West-to-the-Orient project?

Around New Year's 1489 the Columbus brothers decided on a plan of action. Christopher returned to Spain where he still hoped for support from the slow-moving Talavera commission, while Bartholomew sold his chart-making business and embarked on a long journey to persuade some other prince to support the Great Enterprise. Henry VII of England, first to be approached, turned him down flat. Bartholomew then proceeded to France, where Anne de Beaujeu, sister to King Charles VIII, befriended him and employed him to make charts for her at Fontainebleau. Through her, Bartholomew became friendly with the French king, but never obtained any real prospect of his support.

Success always seemed to be just around the corner, but in 1489 Christopher still had three years to wait before obtaining anything definite. We know very little of how he passed the time, except that he not only sold books but did purposeful reading in works on cosmography that he found in the libraries of monasteries where he received hospitality. Some of these books have been preserved in his son Ferdinand's Biblioteca Colombina at the Cathedral of Seville, and Columbus's marginal notes, especially in Pierre d'Ailly's *Imago Mundi* (3 vols., Louvain, 1480–83) and Pius II's *Historia Rerum Ubique Gestarum* (1477), are most revealing. For instance, these from Pierre d'Ailly:

> The end of the habitable earth toward the Orient and the end of the habitable earth toward the Occident are near enough, and between them is a small sea.
>
> Between the end of Spain and the beginning of India is no great width.
>
> An arm of the sea extends between India and Spain.
>
> India is near Spain.
>
> Aristotle [says] between the end of Spain and the beginning of India is a small sea navigable in a few days. . . . Esdras

[says] six parts [of the globe] are habitable and the seventh is covered with water. Observe that the blessed Ambrose and Austin and many others considered Esdras a prophet.

The end of Spain and the beginning of India are not far distant but close, and it is evident *that this sea is navigable in a few days with a fair wind*.

The Queen took notice of his return to Castile by giving him an open letter to all local officials, ordering them to feed and lodge him en route to court, which was then being held in a fortified camp outside the Moorish city of Baza, under siege by the Spanish army. There is some indication that Columbus joined the army as a volunteer while waiting for an answer.

Late in 1490 the Talavera commission issued an unfavorable report. The experts advised the Queen that the West-to-the-Orient project "rested on weak foundations"; that its attainment seemed "uncertain and impossible to any educated person"; that the proposed voyage to Asia would require three years' time, even if the ship returned, which was doubtful; that the Ocean was infinitely larger than Columbus supposed, and much of it unnavigable. And finally, God would never have allowed any uninhabited land of real value to be concealed from His people for so many centuries! But one must admit that most of the commission's arguments were sound. Suppose that no America existed, no ship of that era, however resolute her master and crew, or frugal in provision, could have made a 10,000-mile non-stop voyage from Spain to Japan. Magellan's voyage would prove that.

Apparently a complete stand-off. Columbus knew he could do it; the experts were certain he could not. It needed something as powerful as feminine intuition to break the deadlock. The Queen did give Columbus fresh hope. He could apply again, said she, when the war with the Moors was over. He waited almost another year and then decided to leave Spain and join his brother in France. Calling at the La Rábida friary near Palos to pick up son Diego, now about ten years old, he was persuaded by the prior, Father Juan Pérez, to give the Queen another chance, and he wrote to her to that effect. She replied by summoning Columbus to court and sent him some money to buy decent clothing and a mule.

Columbus always found more friends and supporters among priests than among laymen. They seemed to understand him better, since his

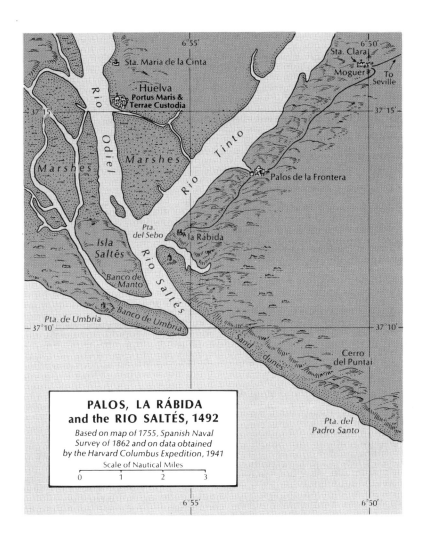

thoughts, deeds, and aspirations were permeated with religious faith. He was more particular than many clergymen in saying daily the Divine Office of the church—prime, tierce, sext, none, and compline; and seldom missed an opportunity to hear Mass. He had a fine presence and an innate dignity that impressed people of whatever estate, and although he never spoke perfect hidalgo Castilian, it was not expected that he should as Genoa-born and a former resident of Portugal.

Isabella Takes Him On

At about Christmastime 1491 Columbus again appeared at court, then being held in the fortified camp of Santa Fe during the final siege of Granada. The Royal Council reviewed the findings of a new commission. Although the exact details are not known, it seems probable that the commission, reading the Queen's mind, recommended that Columbus be allowed to try, but the Council rejected it because of the price he asked. For this extraordinary man, despite poverty, delay, and discouragement, had actually raised his demands. In 1485 he had been willing to sail west for Medina Celi on an expense-account basis without any particular honors or emoluments. Now he demanded not only the title of Admiral, but also that he be made governor and viceroy of any new lands he might discover, that both titles be hereditary in his family, and that he and his heirs be given a 10 per cent cut on the trade. He had suffered so many insults and outrages during his long residence in Spain that—by San Fernando!—he would not glorify Spain for nothing. If the Sovereigns would grant him, contingent on his success, such rank, titles, and property that he and his issue could hold up their heads with the Spanish nobility, well and good; but no more bargaining. Take it, Your Majesties, or leave it.

Leave it they did, in January 1492, immediately after the fall of Granada. Ferdinand and Isabella told him this at an audience which the King, at least, intended to be final. Columbus saddled his mule, packed the saddlebags with his charts and other exhibits, and started for Seville with his faithful friend Juan Pérez, intending to take ship for France and join Bartholomew in a fresh appeal to Charles VIII.

Just as, in Oriental bargaining, a storekeeper will often run after a departing customer to accept his last offer, so it happened here. Luis de Santangel, keeper of King Ferdinand's privy purse, called on the Queen the very day that Columbus left Santa Fe and urged her to meet Columbus's terms. The expedition, he pointed out, would not cost as much as a week's entertainment of a foreign prince. This Genoese asked for honors and emoluments only in the event of success; and they would be a small price to pay for the discovery of new islands and a western route to the Indies. The Queen jumped at this, her really last chance. She even proposed to pledge her crown jewels for the expenses, but Santangel said that would not be necessary; he would find the funds, and did. A messenger overtook Columbus at a village four miles from Santa Fe, and brought him back.

Although the voyage was now decided upon in principle, there were plenty more *cosas de España* to be endured, and it was not until April 1492 that the contracts between Columbus and the Sovereigns, the Capitulations as they are generally called, were signed and sealed. Therein the Sovereigns, in consideration that Cristóbal Colón (as Columbus was now called in Spain) is setting forth "to discover and acquire certain islands and mainlands in the Ocean Sea," promise him to be Admiral thereof, and Viceroy and Governor of lands that he may discover. He shall have 10 per cent of all gold, gems, spices, or other merchandise produced or obtained by trade within those domains, tax free; he shall have the right to invest in one-eighth of any ship going thither; and these offices and emoluments will be enjoyed by his heirs and successors forever. The Sovereigns also issued to him a brief passport in Latin, stating that they were sending him with three caravels "toward the regions of India" (*ad partes Indie*) and three identical letters of introduction, one to the "Grand Khan" (the Chinese emperor) and the other two with a blank space so that the proper title of any other prince could be inserted.

To us, accustomed to the power of Asiatic countries, it seems impossibly naïve for a European to expect to land somewhere on the coast of China or Japan with fewer than one hundred men, and "take over." But Europe was then grossly ignorant of the Far East; the Portuguese had had no difficulty in dealing with black kings in Africa, so why should not Columbus do the same thing in Asia? Moreover, the establishment that Columbus had in mind was not what we think of as a colony, but a *factoria, feitoria,* or factory, long familiar to Europeans. This was something more than a trading post; an extension of sovereignty for commercial purposes. It might be armed, if located in a relatively savage region like São Jorge da Mina on the Gold Coast; or it might be a peaceful extraterritorial settlement such as the Hanseatic League's steelyard in London and the Merchants Adventurers' factory in Amsterdam. The 1492 globe of Martin Behaim, who shared Columbus's geographical ideas, shows an archipelago south of Japan, corresponding to the Ryukyus. Supposing the Ocean had been as narrow as Columbus estimated, and no American barrier, he might have fetched up on an island like Okinawa and there set up an entrepôt between China and the West, both for commerce and conversion. That was what eventually happened at Manila.

Preparing for the First Voyage

Practical details came next. For good reasons, it was decided to fit out the fleet and recruit the men at Palos, the same little port in the Niebla district of Andalusia, where Columbus had first set foot in Spain. There he had made friends of the Pinzón family, leading ship-owners and master mariners who had built caravels like those of nearby Portugal, and who enjoyed the confidence of local sailors. Palos, moreover, had committed some municipal misdemeanor for which the Queen conveniently fined her two well-equipped caravels. Columbus, with his friend Fray Juan Pérez, made a public appearance in the Church of St. George, Palos, on 23 May 1492, while a notary read the royal order. It so happened that a ship from Galicia, owned and captained by Juan de La Cosa, then lay in port. Columbus chartered her as his flagship, making a fleet of three.

This *Santa Maria,* the most famous of Columbus's ships, left her bones on a reef off Hispaniola, and no picture or model of her has survived; but several conjectural models have been made, and at least three full-size "replicas" have been constructed in Spain. The original *Santa Maria* was probably of about 100 tuns' burthen, which meant that her cargo capacity was 100 tuns (double hogsheads) of wine. Her rig, the conventional one for a *nao,* or ship, called for a mainmast taller than her length; the main yard, as long as the keel, spread an immense square sail (the main course), counted on to do most of the driving. Above the main course a short yard spread a tiny main topsail, The foremast, much shorter than the main, carried but one square sail. The mizzen mast, stepped on the high poop, carried a lateen sail, and under the bowsprit hung a square spritsail, which performed rather inefficiently the function of a modern jib.

Here, as near as we can state it after the careful researches of the late Alice Gould and Admiral Julio Guillén y Tato, and of the Admiral's former subordinate Juan Maria Martínez-Hidalgo, is the task organization of Columbus's First Voyage of Discovery. This little fleet with the great destiny had no official name—so at long last let us give it one:—

LA ARMADA DE INDIA, 1492.
CAPITÁN GENERAL: CRISTOBAL COLON

SANTA MARIA, *nao* (ship) of *c.* 100 tuns' burthen, *c.* 85 feet overall.
Captain: Columbus. Master and owner, Juan de La Cosa. Pilot, Peralonso Niño. *Alguacil* (marshal), Diego de Harana. *Escribano* (scribe, secretary), Rodrigo de Escobedo. Interpreter, Luis de Torres. Surgeon, Juan Sánchez. Seven petty officers, captain's steward and page, 11 able seamen, 10 *grumetes.** Total, 40.

PINTA, *caravela redonda* (square-rigged caravel) of *c.* 60 tuns, *c.* 69 feet overall.
Captain: Martín Alonso Pinzón. Owner and able seaman, Cristóbal Quintero. Master, Francisco Martín Pinzón. Pilot, Cristóbal García Sarmiento. Marshal, Juan Reynal. Surgeon, Maestro Diego. Two petty officers, 10 able seamen, 8 gromets. Total, 27.

NIÑA, caravel of *c.* 50 tuns, *c.* 55 feet overall.
Captain: Vicente Yáñez Pinzón. Master and owner, Juan Niño. Pilot, Sancho Ruiz de Gama. Surgeon, Maestre Alonso. Marshal, Diego Lorenzo. Two petty officers, 8 able seamen, 6 gromets. Total, 21.

Allowing for three more people whose names have not been found, the fleet's grand total was about 90 men and boys.

Compared with other recorded task organizations in the era of discovery, this one was exceedingly modest. Only John Cabot's and Verrazzano's single-ship expeditions were smaller.

Regarding the crew, two qualities stand out: homogeneity and good health. The only foreigners on board were Columbus, one other Genoese, one Venetian, and one Portuguese; and not one man died at sea—an extraordinary record as we shall see in comparison with later voyages. The only casualties were the men left behind in Haiti. In contrast to later Spanish voyages such as Magellan's and Loaysa's, there were no priests and few "idlers" (as sailors used to call everyone who did no physical work); each captain was allowed but one page or servant.

* "Gromets," in Elizabethan English; these were either young landsmen who had never been to sea before so not entitled to be called *marineros*, or ship's boys, or apprentice seamen.

Señor Martínez-Hidalgo's model of *Santa Maria*. Note especially, the tiny size of the topsail, foresail, and spritsail compared with that of the main course. Courtesy of Señor Martínez-Hidalgo, Maritime Museum, Barcelona.

A Spanish ship in those days had an official name, usually that of a saint, and a nickname which the sailors used; theirs for *Santa Maria* was *La Gallega*, "The Galician." One of the two caravels provided by the town of Palos took her name *Santa Clara* from a local saint, but is better known by her nickname *Niña*, so given because she belonged to the Niño family of Palos. *Niña* was Columbus's favorite. She carried him safely home from his First Voyage, took him to western Cuba and back to Spain on the Second, and made another voyage to Hispaniola. At the start she was rigged with three lateen sails like a Portuguese caravel, but in the Canaries Columbus had her rerigged

Stern view of Señor Martínez-Hidalgo's model of *Santa Maria*. The jars under the *toldilla* were to keep fish or meat fresh. Note the "round tuck" at the stern. Courtesy of Señor Martínez-Hidalgo, Maritime Museum, Barcelona.

square like her two companions, because square sails are much handier than lateen rig when running before the wind. *Pinta*, also a locally built caravel, was a little larger than *Niña*, and square-rigged from the first. Her real name we do not know; *Pinta* was probably derived from a former owner named Pinto. She was a smart sailer; the New World was first sighted from her deck, and she made first home.

All three were fastened mostly with wooden trunnels or pins such as one sees in the frames of colonial houses; iron fastenings were used only in key spots. They carried inside stone ballast. Their sides were painted gay colors above the waterline and, below it, payed with pitch to discourage barnacles and teredos (ship worms). Crosses and heraldic devices were emblazoned on the sails, and the ships carried a variety of brightly colored flags to be flown on entering and leaving port. Queen Isabella's royal ensign, quartering the castles and lions of Castile and Leon, streamed from the main truck, and on the foremast flew the banner of the expedition: a green cross on a white field with a crown on each arm—a concession to Aragon. All three vessels carried a little crude artillery, to repel pirates or other unwelcome boarders, but they were in no sense combatant ships, and carried neither soldiers nor gunners.

Columbus as a foreigner could never have recruited officers and men without the enthusiastic support of the three leading shipping families of Palos—Pinzón, Niño, and Quintero. Martín Alonso Pinzón commanded *Pinta* and took his younger brother Francisco along as master, a rank that corresponds roughly to the modern first mate. Another brother, Vicente Yáñez Pinzón, commanded *Niña*, and Vicente Yáñez became a discoverer in his own right. *Niña*'s master-owner was Juan Niño; his brother Peralonso Niño, who piloted *Santa Maria*, also became an explorer. La Cosa remained on board the flagship as master. Each vessel had a pilot, a very important rank as he was supposed to take charge of deep-sea navigation.[*] Each carried a surgeon. Among the "idlers" were certain specialists—Luis de Torres, a converted Jew who knew Arabic (Columbus thought that this would enable him to converse with Chinese and Japanese); Rodrigo Sánchez, the royal comptroller, whose main duty was to see that the crown got its share of any gold acquired; and Pedro Gutiérrez, formerly butler of the king's dais, who shipped as chief steward. Diego

[*] On Spanish ships the order of precedence was captain, pilot, *escribano* (secretary or scribe), and master.

de Harana, a cousin of Columbus's mistress, served as *alguacil*, marshal of the fleet, corresponding to the old naval rating of master-at-arms.

Almost all the enlisted men were from the Niebla or the cities of Andalusia: Seville, Cordova, and Jerez de la Frontera. Each seaman received about the equivalent of $7.00 in gold per month, the petty officers twice that, and the boys about $4.60.

It is not true that an Englishman and an Irishman were on board, but there is foundation for the jailbird tradition. Three local lads who had been sentenced to life imprisonment for helping a condemned murderer to break jail were set free in return for shipping with Columbus; they turned out to be trustworthy and sailed with him on later voyages, as did a considerable number of the others. In general, Columbus's crews were made up of sound, capable men and boys from the locality, with members of three leading families in key positions. Encouraged by an ancient pilot, who was sure he had just missed the Indies on a Portuguese voyage westward forty years earlier, these *hombres* overcame a mariner's natural conservatism in the hope of winning glory, gold, and adventure. Those who survived won plenty of the first two, and all shared in one of the greatest adventures of all time—Columbus's First Voyage.

✳ XIV ✳

Columbus's First Voyage of Discovery

August-October 1492

Columbus the Man

Although there exists no contemporary portrait of Christopher Columbus, we are fortunate to have descriptions of his appearance, personality, and character from several men who knew him: his son Ferdinand who lived with him many years, Oviedo the official historian of the Indies who witnessed his triumphal return in 1493, and Bishop Las Casas, who met him in 1500 in Hispaniola, and whose father and uncle had been Columbus's shipmates. All three agree that the Admiral was more than middling tall, long-visaged, blue-eyed, with bright red hair which turned gray early; impressive in port and countenance, exuding authority, "worthy of all reverence." Usually pleasant and affable, he became irascible when crossed; and when moved to rebuke sailors, instead of culling obscenities from the choice assortment of seagoing profanity, he uttered no other oath than "By San Fernando!" and no reprimand except "May God take you!" Persistent to the point of stubbornness, and so confident of being right that Las Casas said he seemed to know the world as if it were his own chamber, Columbus believed that God willed him to discover this short route to the Indies, therefore he must succeed; anything else discovered en route should be considered a divine gift to him and to Spain. He daily read the Divine

Office like a priest, observed faithfully all church festivals, cultivated the company of ecclesiastics, headed every letter with a little cross, and often concluded with the prayer

Jesus et Maria   Jesus and Mary
Sint nobis in via   Be with us on the way.

Confident of being God's instrument, Columbus met the hardships of the sea with stoic endurance. Yet he also had a keen business sense, and planned to establish solidly his rank, titles, and fortune for generations to come. To maintain communication with the Catholic Sovereigns, he saw to it that one or both sons became pages at court, to defend his interests. It is rare that in the twentieth century we can find any descendant of a sixteenth-century discoverer, but Columbus's descendants through his son D. Diego are now numerous and include people of high rank such as the Dukes of Alba and of Veragua.

Columbus's character, tempered in the fire of adversity, did not come out pure steel. A proud and sensitive man, he never forgot the jeers of witless courtiers at his enterprise; and too often, after his triumphal return, he would say, "What a fool you were not to believe me!" Or, "I did it, despite your bad advice!" Thus he got men's backs up, and they did all they could to pull him down, or otherwise bedevil him. They succeeded only too well.

But in this bright August of 1492 his fortunes were at young flood, and that tide in his affairs carried him to a New World.

From Palos to San Salvador

The fleet was ready for sea on 2 August 1492. Every man and boy confessed his sins, received absolution, and received communion at the Church of St. George in Palos. The Captain General (as we should call Columbus at this juncture) went on board *Santa Maria* in the small hours of Friday the third, and at break of day made signal to get under way. Before the sun rose, all three vessels were floating down the Rio Tinto on the morning ebb, with sails hanging limp from their yards, the men pulling on long ash sweeps to maintain steerageway. As they swung into the Saltés and passed La Rábida close aboard, they could hear the friars chanting the ancient hymn *Iam lucis orto sidere* with its haunting refrain, *Et nunc et in perpetuum*, "Evermore and evermore."

This fleet of high promise, destined radically to affect world history, sailed parallel to a very different fleet of misery and woe. On the very same tide there dropped down the Saltés the last vessel carrying the Jews whom Ferdinand and Isabella had expelled from Spain; 2 August was their deadline; anyone who remained thereafter was to be executed unless he embraced Christianity. Thousands of pitiful refugees, carrying what few household goods they could stow in the crowded ships, were bound for the more tolerant lands of Islam, or for the Netherlands, the only Christian country which would receive them. Columbus has left no word of pity for this persecuted people; he even expressed the wish to exclude them from the lands that he discovered. But, had there been a new prophet of Israel, he might have pointed out the Columbian fleet to his wretched compatriots on that August morning, as the ships which in due time would lead the way to a new life for the Jewish exiles.

The Captain General's simple, seaman-like plan for the voyage ensured its success. He would carefully avoid the boisterous head winds, monstrous seas, and dark unbridled waters of the North Atlantic which had already baffled Portuguese would-be discoverers thrusting westward. Instead, he would run south before the northerlies prevailing off Spain and North Africa to the Canary Islands and there make, as it were, a right-angle turn. For he had observed on his African voyages that winter winds in the latitude of the Canaries blew from the east. Moreover, the mean latitude of the Canaries 28° N, he believed would cut Japan, and also pass the spot where several maps of the period located the mythical isle of Antilia, which would make a good break. Thus, he proposed to reach the Indies by the same traditional "latitude sailing" practised by northern seamen even before the invention of the compass.

On the first leg of the voyage, *Pinta*'s rudder jumped its gudgeons, so Columbus decided to send her into Las Palmas for repairs while *Santa Maria* and *Niña* went to Gomera, westernmost of the conquered Canary Islands. There he sent men ashore to fill water casks, buy breadstuffs and cheese, and salt down native beef. He then sailed to Las Palmas to superintend *Pinta*'s repairs and with her returned to Gomera. By 2 September all three ships were anchored off San Sebastián, the port of Gomera. Columbus there met Doña Beatriz de Peraza y Bobadilla, widow of the former captain of the island, a beautiful lady still under thirty. He is said by a shipmate to have fallen deeply in love with her; nonetheless, he did not tarry. Additional ship's stores were quickly hoisted on board and struck below, and on 6 September 1492 the fleet weighed anchor for the last time in the Old World. It had still another island to pass, lofty Ferro, or Hierro. Owing to calms and variables, Ferro and the 12,000-foot peak of Tenerife were in sight until the ninth, but by nightfall that day every trace of land had sunk below the eastern horizon, and the three vessels were alone on an uncharted ocean. The Captain General himself gave out the course: "West; nothing to the north, nothing to the south."

How were those vessels navigated? * Celestial navigation was then in its infancy, but rough estimates of latitude could be made from the height of the North Star above the horizon and its relation to the two outer stars (the Guards) of the Little Bear, or Little Dipper. A meridian altitude of the sun, corrected by the sun's declination, for which tables had long been provided, also produced latitude. But the instruments of observation—a wood or brass quadrant and the seaman's astrolabe—were so crude, and the movement of a ship threw them off to such an extent, that most navigators took their latitude sights ashore. Columbus relied almost completely on "dead reckoning," which means plotting your course and position on a chart from the three elements of direction, time, and speed.

The direction he had from one or more compasses, which were similar to the dry-card type used in small craft until recently. His had a circular card graduated to the 32 points (N, N by E, NNE, NE by N, NE, and so on), with a lodestone under the north point. It was mounted on a pin and enclosed in a binnacle with gimbals so it could swing freely with the motion of the ship. Columbus's standard compass was mounted on the poop deck under observation of the officer of the watch. The helmsman, who steered with a heavy tiller attached directly to the rudder head, operated from the main deck below, and could see very little ahead. *Santa Maria* may have had another compass for him to steer by, but in the two caravels he was conned by the officer of the deck through a hatch, and kept his course steady by the feel of the helm. On a sailing vessel you can do that; it would be impossible in a power craft.

Time on the vessels of that day was measured by a half-hour glass

* For more details on navigation methods of that era, see pp. 26–38, above.

which hung from a beam, so the sand could flow freely from the upper to the lower half. As soon as all the sand had come down a ship's boy turned the glass, and the officer of the deck recorded it by making a stroke on a slate. Eight glasses made a watch; the modern ship's bells were originally a means of marking the glasses. This half-hour-glass time could be corrected daily in fair weather, since local noon came when the sun bore due south. Columbus did this every week or so.

Speed long remained the most variable of these three elements. Columbus had no chip log or other method of measuring the speed of his vessels. He or the officer of the watch merely estimated it. Captain J. W. McElroy, by carefully checking Columbus's Journal of his First Voyage, ascertained that he made an average 9 per cent overestimate of distance. This did not prevent his finding the way home, because the mistake was constant, and time and course were correct. It only resulted in Columbus's placing the islands of his discovery further west than they really were.

Even after making the proper reduction for this overestimate, the speed of Columbus's vessels is surprising. Ships of that day were expected to make 3 to 5 knots in a light breeze, up to 9½ in a strong, fair gale, and at times to be capable of 12 knots. In October 1492 for five consecutive days, the Columbus fleet made an average of 142 miles per day, and the best day's run, 182 miles, averaged almost 8 knots. On the homeward passage, in February 1493, *Niña* and *Pinta* covered 198 miles one day, and at times hit it up to 11 knots. Any yachtsman today would be proud to make such records. Improvements in sailing vessels since 1492 have been more in comfort than in speed. Square-riggers of around 1500 actually could sail closer on the wind than their descendants of 1900, because they had much less standing rigging to prevent the yards' being braced sharp up; the mainmast, a stout and not very tall tree, needed much less support than the masts of later centuries.

One reason Columbus always wanted two or more vessels was to have someone to rescue survivors in case of sinking. But he made an unusual record for that era by never losing a ship at sea, unless we count the *Santa Maria*'s grounding without loss of life. Comforts and conveniences were almost totally lacking. Cooking was done over a bed of sand in a wooden firebox protected from the wind by a hood, and tucked under the forecastle. The diet, a monotonous one of salt meat, hardtack, lentils, and beans, was washed down by red wine, and when that gave out, by water which often went bad in the casks. Only the captains had cabins with bunks; others slept where they could, in their clothes.

On 9 September 1492, the day he dropped the last land below the horizon, Columbus decided to keep a true reckoning of the course for his own use, and a false one to give out to his people so that they would not be frightened at sailing so far from land. But, owing to his overestimate of speed, the "false" reckoning was more nearly correct than the "true"!

During the first ten days (9 to 18 September), the easterly trade wind blew steadily, and the fleet made 1163 nautical miles westward. This was the honeymoon of the voyage. *Que era plazer grande el gusto de las mañanas*—"What a delight was the savor of the mornings!"—wrote Columbus in his Journal. That entry speaks to the heart of anyone who has sailed in the trades. It recalls the dawn, kindling both clouds and sails rose-color, the smell of dew drying on a wooden deck, and (a pleasure Columbus never knew) the first cup of coffee. This feeling is beautifully expressed by my old friend Dr. Frederick Fraley in his poem "The Morning Watch"—

> Wide waste of waters, dim receding stars,
> The breeeze of dawn that barely fills the sail. . . .
> Creak of the rigging, gently furrowed wave
> Under the bows that answer to the swell,
> Set sails, wet deck, breath of the salty air
> And clear resounding stroke of brazen bell.
> "Our little life is rounded with a sleep."
> Strangers and sojourners we are with Thee,
> But, we who sail the reaches of the deep
> Feel of its might, know its serenity,
> Look for the sun in measured course to keep
> Appointment with the morning watch at sea.

Succinctly is the beauty of sailing expressed in a stanza (i. 19) of Camoëns' *Lusiads:*—

> Já no largo Oceano navegavam
> As inquietas ondas apartando;
> Os ventos brandamente respiravam,
> Das naos as velas concavas inchando:
> Da branca escuma os mares se mostravam . . .

"Now in broad ocean navigating / the restless waves parting, / the winds softly blowing, / concave sails filling, / the white foam of their waves following. . . ."

Since Columbus's ships were sailing near the northern limit of the northeast trades, where the wind first strikes the water, he found a smooth sea; and the air (he remarked in his Journal), was "like April in Andalusia, the only thing wanting was to hear the song of the nightingale." But there were plenty of other birds following the ships: the little Mother Carey's chickens dabbling for plankton in the bow waves and the wake; the boatswain bird, so called (as old seamen used to say) because it carries a marlinspike in its tail; the man-of-war or frigate bird, "thou ship of the air that never furl'st thy sails," as Walt Whitman wrote; and when the fleet passed beyond the range of these birds, big Jaeger gulls gave it a call.

On 16 September the fleet first entered a field of sargassum (gulf-weed) and found that it was no hindrance to navigation. "Saw plenty weed" became an almost daily notation in Columbus's Journal. The gulfweed bothered him much less than observing a westerly variation of the compass, for in European waters the variation at this era was easterly

Ten days out from Ferro, the fleet temporarily ran into an area of variable winds and rain. It had reached the point on Columbus's chart where the fabled island of Antilia should have been, and all hands expected to sight land. The Captain General ordered the deep-sea lead to be hove, and spliced together his two 100-fathom lines for that purpose. Naturally he found no bottom—the ocean there is about 2300 fathom deep! Ordinary seamen who, on the tenth day of the northeast trades, were beginning to wonder whether they could ever beat back home, were cheered by the change of wind. They were never bothered by fear of "falling off the edge of the world"—that is just one of the many old wives' tales about this voyage.

Only 234 miles were made good during the next five days. During this spell of moderate weather it was easy to converse from ship to ship. In the middle of one of these colloquies, a seaman of *Pinta* gave the "Land Ho!" and everyone thought he saw an island against the setting sun. Columbus fell on his knees to thank God, ordered *Gloria in Excelsis Deo* to be sung by all, and set a course for the island. But at dawn no island was visible, for none was there. A cloudbank above the western horizon, a common phenomenon at sea, had deceived all hands. Columbus refused to beat about looking for this island because, he said, "His object was to reach the Indies, and if he had delayed, it would not have made sense."

The trade wind now returned moderately, and during the six days, 26 September to 1 October, the fleet made only 382 miles. Under these circumstances the people began to mutter and grumble. Three weeks was probably more than they had ever been beyond sight of land. They were all getting on each other's nerves, as happens even nowadays on a long voyage to a known destination. Grievances, real or imaginary, were blown up; cliques were formed; fist fights had to be broken up by the alguacil, the master-at-arms. Every minute Spain grew further away, and what lay ahead? Probably nothing, except in the eye of that cursed Genoese. Let's make him turn back, or throw him overboard!

On the first day of October the wind increased, rain fell in torrents, replenishing the water casks, and in five days (2 to 6 October) the fleet made 710 miles. On the sixth, when they had passed longitude 65° W and actually lay directly north of Puerto Rico, Martín Alonso Pinzón shot his agile *Pinta* under the flagship's stern and shouted, "Alter course, sir, to southwest by west . . . Japan!" Columbus did not understand whether Martín Alonso meant that he thought they had missed Japan and should steer southwest by west for China, or that Japan lay in that direction; but he knew and Pinzón knew that the fleet had sailed more than the 2400 miles which, according to their calculations, lay between the Canaries and Japan. Naturally Columbus was uneasy, but he held to the west course magnetic, which, owing to the variation for which he did not allow, was about west by south, true.

On 7 October, when *Niña* made another false landfall, great flocks of birds passed over the ships, flying west-southwest; this was the autumn migration from eastern North America to the West Indies. Columbus decided that he had better follow Pinzón and the birds rather than his chart, and changed course accordingly that very evening. A very good guess, for this was his shortest route to the nearest land. Every night the men were heartened by seeing against the moon (full on 5 October) flocks of birds flying their way. But mutiny once more reared its ugly head. Even by Columbus's phony reckoning which he gave out, they had sailed much further west than anyone

The "White Cliffs" first sighted by Columbus. David Crofoot photo.

had expected. Enough of this nonsense, sailing west to nowhere; let the Captain General turn back or else—! Columbus, says the record, "cheered them as best he could, holding out good hope of the advantages they might gain; and he added, it was useless to complain, *since he had come to go to the Indies, and so had to continue until he found them, with the help of Our Lord.*"

How typical of Columbus's determination! Yet even he, conscious of divine guidance, could not have kept on indefinitely without the support of his captains and officers. According to one account, Martín Alonso Pinzón cheered him by shouting, *Adelante! Adelante!* which the poet Joaquin Miller translated, "Sail on! Sail on!" But, according to Oviedo, one of the earliest historians who talked with the participants, it was Columbus who persuaded the Pinzóns to sail on, with the promise that if land were not found within three days he would turn back. This promise was made on 9 October. Next day the trade wind blew fresher, sending the fleet along at 7 knots, and on the 10th the fleet made a record day's run. On the 11th the wind continued to blow hard, with a heavy following sea. Now signs of land, such as branches of trees with green leaves and even flowers, became so frequent that the people were content with their commander's decision, and the mutinous mutterings died out in keen anticipation of making a landfall in the Indies.

As the sun set under a clear horizon 11 October, the northeast trade breezed up to gale force, and the three ships tore along at 9 knots. Columbus refused to shorten sail, signaled everyone to keep a par-

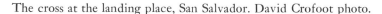

The cross at the landing place, San Salvador. David Crofoot photo.

ticularly sharp watch, and offered extra rewards for first landfall in addition to the year's pay promised by the Sovereigns. That night of destiny was clear and beautiful with a late-rising moon, but the sea was the roughest of the entire passage. The men were tense and expectant, the officers testy and anxious, Columbus serene in the confidence that presently God would reveal to him the promised Indies.

At 10:00 p.m., an hour before moonrise, Columbus and a seaman, also simultaneously, thought they saw a light "like a little wax candle rising and falling." Others said they saw it too, but most did not; and after a few minutes it disappeared. Volumes have been written to explain what this light was or might have been. It may well have been a mere illusion created by over-tense watchfulness. But Mrs. Ruth Malvin, a long-time resident of San Salvador, believes it to have been a bonfire lighted by natives living on cliffs or hills on the windward side, to keep sand fleas out of their cabins; and this is the best rational explanation yet made. She had fires lighted on High Cay and other places, and when some 28 miles out to sea could see light "rising and falling" just as Columbus said.

The little light does not cause Columbus to alter his course. His ships rush on, pitching, rolling, and throwing spray, white foam at their bows and wakes reflecting the moon. *Pinta* is perhaps half a mile in the lead, *Santa Maria* on her port quarter, *Niña* on the other side. Now one, now another forges ahead. With the fourth glass of the night watch, the last sands are running out of an era that began with the dawn of history. Not since the birth of Christ has there been a night so full of meaning for the human race.

At 2:00 a.m. 12 October, Rodrigo de Triana, lookout on *Pinta*, sees something like a white cliff shining in the moonlight and sings out, *Tierra! tierra!* "Land! land!" Captain Pinzón verifies the landfall, fires a gun as agreed, and shortens sail to allow the flagship to catch up. As *Santa Maria* approaches, Columbus shouts across the rushing waters, "Señor Martín Alonso, you *did* find land! Five thousand maravedis for you as a bonus!"

Land it was this time; gray clay cliffs, white in the moonlight, on the windward side of a little island of the Bahama group. The fleet would have crashed had it held course, but these men were no fools to pile up on a lee shore. Columbus ordered sail to be shortened and the fleet to jog off and on until daylight. At dawn they made full sail, passed the southern point of the island, and sought an opening on the west coast through the barrier reef. Before noon they found it, sailed into a shallow bay, and anchored in the lee of the land, in five fathoms.

Here on a gleaming beach of white coral occurred the famous first landing of Columbus. The commander (now by general consent called Admiral) went ashore in the flagship's longboat displaying the royal standard of Castile, accompanied by the two Captains Pinzón in their boats, flying the banner of the expedition—a green crowned cross on a white field. "And, all having rendered thanks to Our Lord, kneeling on the ground, embracing it with tears of joy for the immeasurable mercy of having reached it, the Admiral rose and gave this island the name *San Salvador*"—Holy Saviour.

❊ XV ❊

The Greater Antilles

12 October 1492 – 15 March 1493

South to Cuba

The first natives encountered on Guanahaní (their own name for this island) fled to the jungle when they saw three winged monsters approaching; but curiosity proved too much for them, and when they saw strangely dressed human beings coming ashore, they approached timidly, with propitiatory gifts. Columbus, of course, had to believe that he was in the Indies, so he named these people "Indians," and Indians the native inhabitants of the Americas have become in all European languages.

These were of the Taino branch of the Arawak language group. Within the previous century they had wrested the Bahamas and most of Cuba from the more primitive Siboney. They grew corn, yams, and other roots for food; they knew how to make cassava bread, to spin and weave cotton, and to make pottery. The Spaniards observed with wonder their fine physique and almost complete nakedness, and noted with keen interest that some wore, suspended from the nose, little pendants of pure gold. The guilelessness and generosity of these children of nature—"They invite you to share anything that they possess, and show as much love as if their hearts went with it," wrote Columbus—their ignorance of money and of iron, and their nudity, suggested to every educated European that these people were hold-overs from the Golden Age. Peter Martyr, the court historian, wrote that "They seem to live in that golden world of the which old writers speak so much, wherein men lived simply and innocently without enforcement of laws, without quarreling, judges and libels, content only to satisfy nature."

Columbus would much rather have encountered sophisticated Orien-tals than "noble savages," but as usual he made the best of the situation. He observed "how easy it would be to convert these people—and to make them work for us." In other words, to enslave them in return for saving their souls. Every Spaniard seems to have concluded from the tales of mariners who returned from this voyage that no white man need do a hand's turn of work in the New World; God had provided docile natives to labor for the lords of creation.

For two days Columbus explored San Salvador. It was a pretty island then, with a heavy covering of tropical hardwood; but the Admiral knew full well that, interesting as the discovery of an island inhabited by Golden Age natives might be, he must take home certain evidence of Japan or China, or plenty of gold and spices, to prove his voyage a success. The natives indicated by sign language that scores of islands lay to the west and south; it seemed to the Admiral that these must be those shown on his chart, lying south of Cipangu; and that if they did not lead him to golden Japan, they would prove to be stepping-stones to China.

So, detaining six Indians as guides, Columbus weighed anchors on the afternoon of 14 October. That day he discovered another island which he named *Santa Maria de la Concepción*; the English prosaically re-named it Rum Cay. This is still one of the prettiest Bahamian islands; hilly, well timbered, free of development blight. Today it has only about one hundred inhabitants clustered in a small village ambitiously called Port Nelson. The island has no roads, and a virgin forest covers it.

The natives here proved to be similar to those on San Salvador and were equally pleased with the Admiral's gifts of red caps, glass beads, and hawks' bells. These were little spherical bells about the diameter of a quarter-dollar or shilling, which were attached to the birds used in falconry; they had the pleasant tinkle of a miniature sleighbell, and the natives loved them. Indians would paddle out to the flagship wagging their fingers and saying, *Chuq! chuq!* meaning, "More hawks'

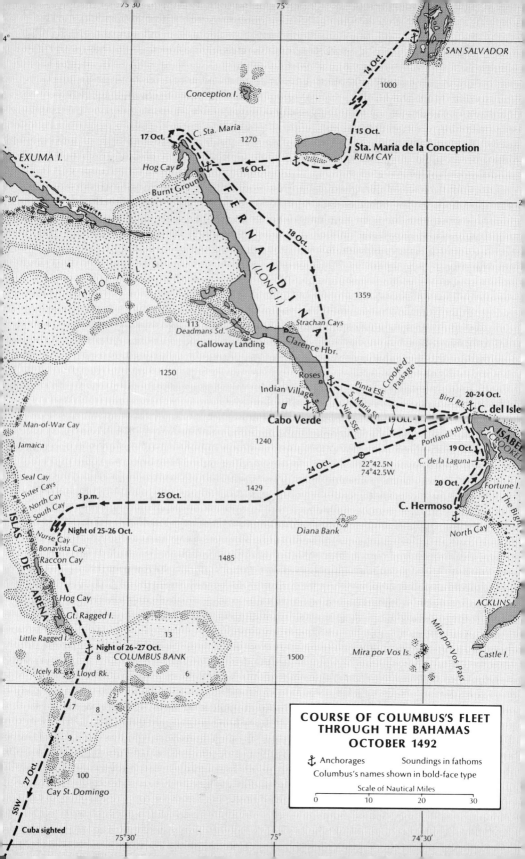

COURSE OF COLUMBUS'S FLEET
THROUGH THE BAHAMAS
OCTOBER 1492

⚓ Anchorages   Soundings in fathoms
Columbus's names shown in bold-face type

Scale of Nautical Miles
0   10   20   30

Columbus's *Maravilloso Puerto*, Santa Maria Harbor, Long Island. David Crofoot photo.

bells, please!" Lace points, which were metal tips for the laces then used to fasten men's clothing, brass tambourine jingles, and Venetian glass beads were also favorites.

The Admiral's native guides, eager to please, kept assuring him by signs that in the next island there would be plenty of gold; but each one in succession—Long, Crooked, and Fortune—proved to be no different from San Salvador. Each was jungle-covered, inhabited by friendly natives who had no gold except for a few ornaments which they had obtained elsewhere. Where they got them he could never make out, because of the language barrier; Torres, the interpreter, found his Arabic completely useless. The Spaniards observed, and Columbus noted, the first maize or Indian corn ever seen by a European, the first hammocks, woven from native cotton, and the first yams and sweet potatoes; also, a tree that he estimated correctly would prove to be good dye-wood. But no sign of gold except on the natives' persons.

As the Admiral and his Indian guides came to understand each other better, he heard about a big island that they called *Colba* (Cuba), and made up his mind that it must be either Japan or a part of China. So to Colba he must go, and the Indians took him there by their usual canoe route, so laid out as to be the shortest possible jump over blue water.

First they sailed due west from Rum Cay to the northern end of Long Island, which they could see from the mastheads. *Fernandina*, as Columbus named Long Island, he described as very green, level, and fertile, and the natives friendly. He anchored off a village, and next day (17 October) investigated a *maravilloso puerto*—a marvelous harbor. Entering by a high bluff, he found it big enough to hold a hundred ships, "if it were deep, and clean bottom, and deep at the entrance," which unfortunately it was not. This description perfectly fits Santa Maria Harbor just east of the cape of that name. You enter it around high limestone cliffs, where there is now a small lighthouse, and it has water enough for small craft, but is much too shoal for a caravel or any other seagoing vessel.

While a shore party filled water casks from a well (one that is still used, since fresh water is scarce in the Bahamas), Columbus, in his own words, "walked among some trees, which were the most beautiful thing to see that ever I had seen, viewing as much verdure in so great a development as in the month of May in Andalusia, and all the trees were as different from ours as day from night, and so the fruits, the herbage, the rocks, and all things." This is a good example of his rapturous descriptions of scenery, flora, and natives, in which he stands out from all other discoverers and explorers of that era.

Sailing to the south end of Long Island on the 18th, Columbus decided to cross the Crooked Island Passage, now an important sea route to Cuba. Next day he ordered his ships to fan out on an easterly course so they would not miss the next island—Crooked Island, which he named *Isabela* after the Queen. Here again he writes about the scenery

Crooked Island, Portland Harbor and Bird Rock.

ecstatically, and even notes the "fair and sweet smell of flowers or trees from the land . . . sweetest in the world." As we hove-to in the lee of this land in 1940, the land breeze similarly favored us with delicious odors.

Finding much to admire but nothing to detain him at Crooked and Fortune islands, Columbus sailed back across Crooked Island Passage to the line of cays at the southeast edge of the Great Bahama Bank. On 27 October, from an anchorage off Ragged Island, the fleet made a fast sail with a fresh northeast wind to a big island which the Indians pointed out as "Colba." And on the morning of 28 October they entered a Cuban harbor easily identified as Bahia Bariay. It is marked by a beautiful mountain now called La Teta de Bariay, which Columbus said had "on its summit another peak like a pretty little mosque." He had never seen so beautiful a harbor—trees all fair and green and different from ours, some with bright flowers and some heavy with fruit, and the air full of birdsong. But where was the evidence of Japan? Where were the gold-roofed temples, dragon-mouthed bronze cannon? Where were the lords and ladies in gold-stiffened brocade?

Next day the three ships sailed westward along the many-harbored coast of Oriente Province of Cuba, hoping every moment to meet a welcoming fleet of Chinese junks. They anchored in Puerto Gibara, and there remained for twelve days, except for a brief jaunt westward to Punta Cobarrubia and back.

The interpreters shipped at San Salvador assured local Indians that the strangers in the white-winged monsters were good people, with plenty of trading truck, so Columbus's Cuban relations were pleasant and peaceful. The natives told him that plenty of gold could be found at *Cubanacan* (mid-Cuba) in the interior. The Admiral, mistaking this word for *El Gran Can*, the Great Khan, sent an "embassy" up country to present his letter of introduction to the Chinese emperor; he remained in Puerto Gibara to oversee the beaching and graving of his ships. Luis de Torres the Arabic scholar took charge of this diplomatic mission, and beside him trudged Rodrigo de Jerez, a seaman who had once met a black king in Guinea and so was thought to know the proper way to address pagan royalty. They carried the diplomatic portfolio (Latin passport and royal letter of credence to the Grand Khan), strings of glass beads to buy food, and a gift suitable for royalty. The embassy tramped up the valley of the Cacoyuguin River, past fields cultivated with corn, beans, and sweet potatoes, to what they hoped would be Cambaluk, the imperial city of Cathay. Alas, it turned out to be a village of about fifty palm-thatched huts, on the site of the present town of Holguin. The two Spaniards, regarded as having come from above, were feasted by the local cacique while the populace swarmed up to kiss their feet and present simple gifts. Rodrigo the sailor loved it—he had never had it so good in Africa—but Torres, expecting a reception by mandarins in a stone-built capital of ten thousand houses, felt badly let down.

Yet, on their way back to the harbor, the embassy made a discovery which would have more far-reaching results than any possible treaty. They met "many people who were going to their villages, both women and men, with a firebrand in the hand and herbs to drink the smoke thereof, as they are accustomed." You have guessed it, reader; this was the first European contact with tobacco smokers. The Tainos used it in the form of cigars which they called *tobacos*. A walking party, such as the embassy encountered, would carry a large cigar and at every halt light it from a firebrand; everyone then took three or four "drags" of the smoke through his nostrils; after this refreshment the march resumed, small boys keeping the firebrand alight until the next stop. Not long after Spaniards settled in the New World, they tried smoking tobacco and liked it, and through them its use spread rapidly through Europe, Asia, and Africa.

Columbus, in the meantime, totted up his dead reckoning and figured that he was right where China began. He decided that Cuba was the "Province of Mangi," a name which the imaginative maps of China that he had seen located on a peninsula at the southeast corner of the Celestial Empire. The Admiral also tried to shoot the North Star with his primitive quadrant. But he picked the wrong star—Alfirk of the constellation Cepheus—which on that November evening hung directly over Polaris. Thus he found Cuba to be on latitude 42° N, that of Cape Cod! Of course he knew this to be wrong, since he had sailed across on 28° N; and in his Letter to the Sovereigns he corrected the latitude of northern Cuba to 26°, still 5 degrees too high.

Here the Admiral began to collect specimens which he hoped would convince people that he was at least on the fringe of Asia. There was a shrub which smelled something like cinnamon and so must be cinnamon; the gumbo-limbo, supposedly an Asiatic form of the gum mastic that he had seen in Chios; and a small inedible nut, now called *nogal del pais*, he identified as the big coconut mentioned by Marco Polo. Coconut palms are such a feature of the Caribbean coast today that we forget that they, like the banana, were introduced later. The men dug up some roots which Sánchez the surgeon pronounced to be Chinese rhubarb, a valuable drug imported into Europe, but it turned out to be something quite different, not even as valuable as the humble pieplant.

As yet, no gold. When the Spaniards asked for gold, the Cubans always waved them on to some other place. According to them, there was an island called Babeque where the people gathered gold on the beach by candlelight and hammered it into bars. This choice piece of misinformation brought about the first rift in the Spanish high command. Without asking the Admiral's permission, Martín Alonso Pinzón took off in *Pinta*, hoping to be the first to reach Babeque. He called at

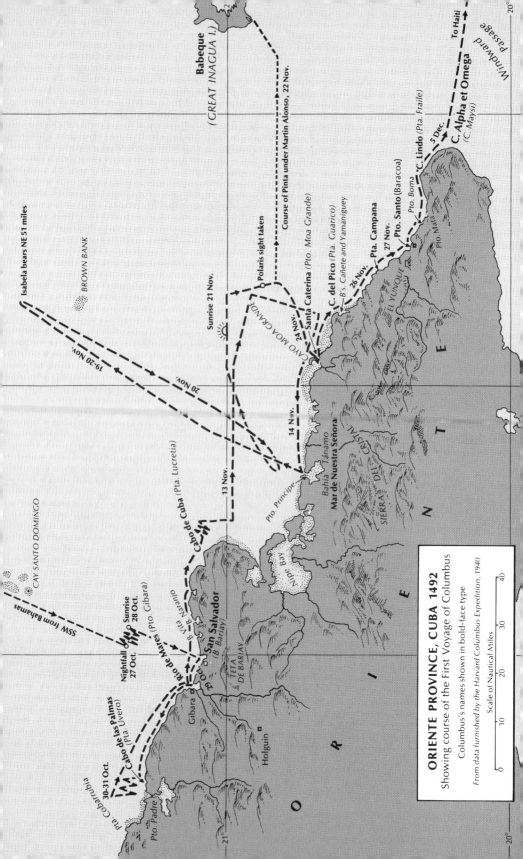

ORIENTE PROVINCE, CUBA 1492

Showing course of the First Voyage of Columbus

Columbus's names shown in bold-face type

From data furnished by the Harvard Columbus Expedition, 1940

Scale of Nautical Miles

0   10   20   30   40

Babeque
(GREAT INAGUA I.)

BROWN BANK

Isabela bears NE 51 miles

Course of Pinta under Martin Alonso, 22 Nov.

Polaris sight taken

Sunrise 21 Nov.

19-20 Nov.

20 Nov.

14 Nov.

13 Nov.

CAYO MOA GRANDE

Santa Caterina (Pto. Moa Grande)

C. del Pico (Pta. Guarico)

B's. Cañete and Yamaniguey

24 Nov.

26 Nov. Pta. Campana

27 Nov. Pto. Santo (Baracoa)

Pto. Boma

Pto. Mata

C. Lindo (Pta. Fraile)

5 Dec.

C. Alpha et Omega
(C. Maysí)

To Haiti

Windward passage

EL YUNQUE

O   R   I   E   N   T   E

SIERRA DEL CRISTAL

Bahía Tánamo

Mar de Nuestra Señora

Pto. Principe

Cabo de Cuba (Pta. Lucretia)

CAY SANTO DOMINGO

SSW from Bahamas

Sunrise 28 Oct.

Nightfall 27 Oct.

Río de Mares (Pto. Gibara)

Vita Naranjo

San Salvador
(B. Bariay)

TETA DE BARIAY

Gibara

N De Bay

N De Bay

Cabo de las Palmas
(Pta. Uvero)

30-31 Oct.

Pta. Covarrubia

Pto. Padre

Holguin

O   R   I   E   N   T   E

Great Inagua Island, which lay in the general direction indicated by the Indians, and, needless to say, found no gold by candle or any other light.

The Admiral in *Santa Maria* with *Niña* sailed eastward along the superb coast of Oriente Province. Noble mountains rise directly from the sea, but every few miles there is a river whose mouth makes a good land-locked harbor. He called at Bahía Tánamo, entered its bottleneck entrance, and within noted little wooded islands running up "like diamond points," and others flat-topped "like tables." You can see them all today. He put in at Puerto Cayo Moa, where you have to pick an opening through the breakers but then find yourself, as Columbus said, in "a lagoon in which all the ships of Spain could lie and be safe." The peculiar charm of this harbor, so calm between lofty mountains and the barrier of foaming reefs, was noted by Columbus in words that are not in the least exaggerated. He had an eye, too, for practical matters; when the men rowed him inside the river mouth, he observed on the mountain slopes pine trees which he said would make timber for the Spanish navy. The descendants of those pines, when we passed that way, were being sawed at a mill run by a mountain stream, whose distant roar Columbus heard on a Sunday in November 1492.

On he sailed, with a breeze that fortunately came from the west, noting nine little harbors, behind which leafy valleys ran up into the lofty sierra. He passed the anvil-shaped mountain El Yunque, landmark for Baracoa, a harbor which Columbus well described as round "like a little porringer." Here the Spaniards pitched their first settlement in Cuba in 1512; but Baracoa afforded no gold, and the fleet passed on as soon as the wind turned fair. At sunrise 5 December it was off Cape Maisí, easternmost point of Cuba. Identifying this as the eastern extremity of Asia, corresponding to Cape St. Vincent, the western extremity of Europe, Columbus named it Cape Alpha and Omega, where East ends and West begins. He later remarked that if you had the time and strength, you could walk from here around the back of the world, to Spain!

Hispaniola

The fleet now crossed the Windward Passage, and at nightfall arrived off the Haitian harbor of San Nicolás, so named by Columbus be-

Moustique Bay, where Columbus named Hispaniola. David Crofoot photo.

cause he entered it on 6 December, the feast day of that favorite saint of children. It is still St. Nicolas Môle. His Indian guides promised that gold would be found on this great island, the home of their ancestors, and they were right. This island saved Columbus's reputation, for had he returned home with no more "evidence" than hitherto he had obtained, people would have said, "This Genoese has found a few islands inhabited by gentle natives of the Golden Age, but as for their being the Indies—pooh!"

And what beauty! I sailed the same waters in January 1939, deck passenger on a chaloupe of the Haitian Coast Guard. The shores were lined with bayahonde and other great tropical trees which Columbus mistook for clove and nutmeg. At night the Southern Cross was poised like a great kite over the headland that Columbus named *Cabo del Estrella* (Cape of the Star); and in the northern sky the Great Bear stood up on his tail.

A fair breeze took *Santa Maria* and *Niña* into Moustique Bay, where easterly winds detained them for five days. Here the Admiral, "seeing

412

the grandeur and beauty of this island and its resemblance to the land of Spain," named it *La Isla Española*—the Spanish Isle. His seamen captured a young and beautiful girl wearing only a golden nose plug, and brought her on board. She indicated that she would gladly stay with the boys, but the Admiral "sent her ashore very honorably," decently clad in slopchest clothing and bedecked with jingles and hawks' bells. This move proved to be good for public relations, as the damsel was a cacique's daughter. Next day nine Spaniards ashore were conducted to a big village of a thousand people and given everything they wanted—food, drink, girls, and parrots.

On 15 December *Santa Maria* and *Niña* beat up the Tortuga Channel to the mouth of Trois Rivières, a clear mountain stream that flows through a valley that Columbus well named the Valley of Paradise. Next day, when the fleet lay off a beach, some five hundred people came down accompanied by their youthful cacique, who made the Admiral a state visit. Bedecked with gold jewelry, he dined alone with the Admiral in his cabin and behaved with royal poise and dignity. Dinner over, Columbus had the cacique piped over the side in naval style and given a twenty-one-gun salute. Again the thought passed through his mind that these people were ripe for exploitation—"very cowardly," and "fit to be ordered about and made to work, to sow, and do aught else that may be needed." A wonderful opportunity, he observed, for his Sovereigns, whose subjects were not notably fond of hard work!

At sunrise 20 December the ships were off Acul Bay, the beauty of which was so striking that the Admiral ran out of adjectives describing it in his Journal; declared that all "ancient mariners" on board would bear him out. In 23 years at sea he had never seen so perfect a harbor as the one here, landlocked so completely that even in a blow one's anchor cable does not stretch taut. The high mountains part to reveal a conical peak at the head of the valley, which since 1806 has been crowned by the stone citadel of Henri Christophe, king of Haiti. Here the natives of 1492 were in an even more pristine state of innocence than elsewhere; the women, completely naked, had "very pretty bodies," and no male jealousy prevented their offering themselves freely. Moreover, these natives appeared to have plenty of gold.

During the night of 22–23 December and the following morning, about a thousand people came out in canoes to visit *Santa Maria*, and

Acul Bay. David Crofoot photo.

some five hundred more swam out, although she anchored more than three miles from the nearest shore. A messenger now arrived from Guacanagarí, the cacique of Marien (the northwestern part of Haiti), and a more important potentate than the one entertained a few days earlier. Guacanagarí sent the Admiral a magnificent belt with a solid-gold buckle, and invited him to call. He needed no second invitation, since everyone assured him that the gold mines were in that direction, the central part of the island called Cibao, which suggested Cipangu, Japan. So, before sunrise on 24 December, *Santa Maria* and *Niña* departed Acul Bay, all hands planning to spend a merry Christmas at the court of the cacique, who might even turn out to be the emperor of Japan!

Fate decreed otherwise. With a contrary wind, the two vessels were unable to cover the few miles between Acul and Guacanagarí's capital on Caracol Bay by daylight. At 11:00 p.m., when the watch was changed, *Niña* and *Santa Maria* were becalmed east of Cape Haitien,

414

inside the Limonade Pass to the barrier reef. Everyone on board was exhausted from the previous all-night entertainment of the natives; and as the water was calm, with only a slight ground swell and no wind, a feeling of complete security—the most dangerous delusion a seaman can entertain—stole over the flagship. Even the Admiral retired to get his first sleep in forty-eight hours; the helmsman gave the big tiller to a small boy and joined the rest of the watch in slumber.

Just as midnight ushered in Christmas Day, *Santa Maria* settled on a coral reef so gently that nobody awoke with the shock. The boy helmsman, feeling the rudder ground, sang out; the Admiral came first on deck, followed by Master Juan de La Cosa and all hands. As the bow only had grounded, Columbus saw a good chance to get her off stern first, and ordered La Cosa and a boat's crew to run an anchor out astern. Instead of obeying orders, they rowed to *Niña*, which had passed well outside the reef. Captain Pinzón refused to receive them, and sent a boat of his own ship.

But an hour had been wasted, owing to La Cosa's cowardice or insubordination, and that doomed *Santa Maria*. The ground swell drove her higher and higher up the reef, and coral heads punched holes in her bottom. As the hull seemed to be filling with water, Columbus ordered abandon ship, hoping that daylight would make it easier to float her. Guacanagarí and his subjects worked hard with the Spaniards to get her off after daybreak, but it was too late. All they could salvage were the equipment, stores, and trading truck, which the Indians faithfully guarded without (so the Admiral recorded) purloining so much as a lace point.

The Admiral tried to figure out what this apparently disastrous accident meant. Presently he had it: God intended him to start a colony at that point, with *Santa Maria*'s crew. Guacanagarí begged him to do so, as he wanted help against enemies elsewhere on the island. The Spaniards fell over each other to volunteer, because signs of gold were now so plentiful that they were confident of making their fortunes. So Columbus gave orders to erect a fortified camp ashore and named it *Villa de la Navidad* (Town of the Nativity) in honor of the day of disaster, which he fondly thought God had turned to his advantage.

Navidad, first attempt by Europeans since the Northmen to establish themselves in the New World, was quickly built, largely out of *Santa Maria*'s timbers. It was probably located on the sandspit now called

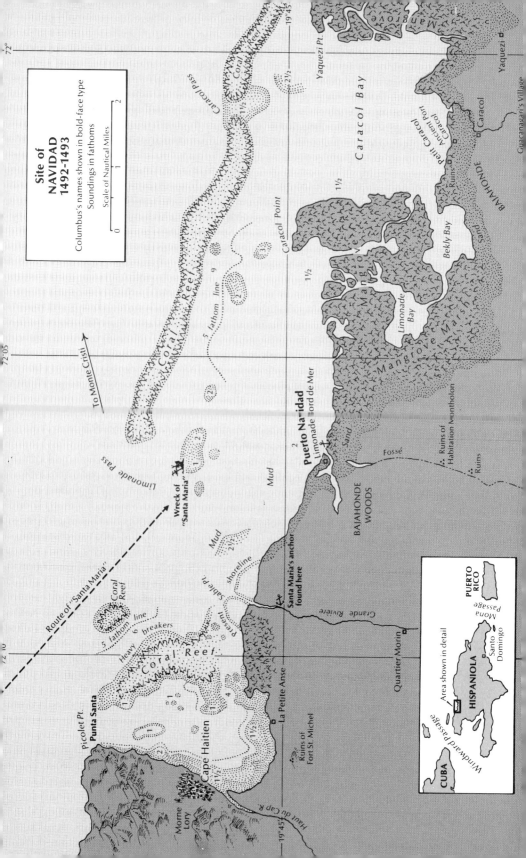

Site of
NAVIDAD
1492-1493

Columbus's names shown in bold-face type

Soundings in fathoms

Scale of Nautical Miles

0   1   2

CUBA

HISPANIOLA

PUERTO RICO

Santo Domingo

Mona Passage

Windward Passage

Area shown in detail

Caracol Bay

Yaquezi Pt.

Yaquezi

Guacanagari's Village

Caracol

Ruins

Caracol

Archienu Port

Petit Caracol

BAJAHONDE

Sand

Bekly Bay

Mangroves

Limonade Bay

Mangrove Marsh

Ruins of Habitation Meuntholon

Ruins

Fossé

Coral Reef

Coral Reef

Caracol pass

2½

1½

1½

1½

Caracol Point

3

9

5 fathom line

2

2

To Monte Cristi

Coral Reef

Limonade pass

2½

2

Wreck of "Santa Maria"

1

2

Mud

Sand

Puerto Na-idad

Limonade Jord de Mer

2

BAJAHONDE WOODS

Santa Maria's anchor found here

Grande Riviere

Quartier Morin

Route of "Santa Maria"

Picolet Pt.

Punta Santa

Coral Reef

5 fathom line

6 breakers

Heavy breakers

Coral Reef

1

1

4

1

1½

Present shoreline

Sable Pt.

Mud

Mud

2½

La Petite Anse

Ruins of Fort St. Michel

Cape Haitien

Morne Lory

1

2

1½

Haut du Cap R.

72°

72°05′

19°45′

19°45′

72°

72°05′

Limonade Bord-de-Mer, off which there is good anchorage. Sixteen men from the flagship and five from *Niña* volunteered to stay behind, under command of Columbus's Cordovan friend Diego de Harana. The Admiral gave them a share of his provisions, most of the trading truck, and the flagship's boat. They were instructed to explore the country with a view to finding a permanent settlement, to trade for gold, and to treat the natives kindly.

Columbus was now certain that he had found the Indies.

On the day after New Year's 1493, Guacanagarí and Columbus held a farewell party. *Niña* fired cannon balls through what was left of the hull of *Santa Maria* to impress the natives, and the cacique feasted all hands. After final expressions of mutual love and esteem, the allies parted and the Admiral went on board *Niña*, to return home in her. At sunrise 4 January she set sail, and the homeward passage began.

Homeward Passage

Two days later, Columbus sighted *Pinta* sailing in a contrary direction, down-wind. Martín Alonso came on board and gave a fairly convincing account of his doings during the last three weeks. He had called at the Great Inagua, ascertained that the yarn about picking up gold by candlelight was a myth, then sailed along the coast of Hispaniola and anchored in Puerto Blanco. There a shore party penetrated the Cibao and found plently of gold. Pinzón had heard of the flagship's wreck by Indian "grapevine," and so sailed back to lend the Admiral a hand. Columbus, pleased to have company on the voyage home, decided to let bygones be bygones.

While waiting for a fair wind to double Monte Cristi peninsula, with its tent-like promontory behind which he anchored, Columbus explored by boat the lower course of the Rio Yaque del Norte and found gold nuggets as large as lentils. Even today there is gold in that river valley; the country women pan it out laboriously, and when they have enough to fill a turkey quill, they use it to pay for their shopping.

At midnight 8 January, *Niña* and *Pinta* resumed their homeward passage. Passing along the coast of Hispaniola, they looked in at *Puerto Plata* (so named by Columbus on account of silver clouds over the mountains) and anchored near the mouth of Samaná Bay. There, at a place still called *Punta de las Flechas*, the Spaniards encountered the

Monte Cristi, which Columbus compared to a great Moorish tent.

first natives who were not pleased to meet them, and who were armed with bows and arrows. These were a branch of the Tainos called Ciguayos, who in self-defense against raiding Caribs had adopted their weapons. By dint of catching one Ciguayo, treating him well and sending him ashore with an assortment of red cloth and trinkets, the rest were appeased, and a brisk if somewhat cautious trade was conducted. Also, one or two were persuaded to join the native contingent bound for Spain.

On Wednesday, 18 January, three hours before daybreak, the caravels sailed from Samaná Bay. A rough, tough voyage lay ahead. This homeward passage was a far greater test of Columbus's seamanship and ability to handle men than anything he had hitherto undertaken. With the greatest geographical discovery of all time locked in his breast, knowing that it would be of no use to anybody unless delivered, the Admiral had to fight the elements and human weakness for his survival.

The west wind with which they took off soon petered out, easterly trade winds returned, and the caravels sailed as best they could, close-hauled on the starboard tack. Modern sailing craft can sail as close to the wind as four points (45 degrees) or, if very smart racers in smooth water, even closer. *Niña* and *Pinta* would lay up to five points (56 degrees) if the sea was smooth, but under ordinary conditions could not do better than six points (67½ degrees); and *Pinta* was slow on the wind, owing to a sprung mizzenmast. This meant, in practice, that if it blew from the southeast, the caravels could steer ENE; with a due east wind the best course toward Spain of which they were capable was NNE; and if it backed to NE (as the trade wind often does), the Admiral had to bring them about on the port tack and steer ESE.

In this manner *Niña* and *Pinta* continued through January of 1493, reaching further north and edging a little closer to Spain. As they were near the northern limit of the trades, the sea was smooth, and providentially the wind held and blew them across the horse latitudes, as seamen used to call the calms between latitudes 30° and 33° N. They crossed the Sargasso Sea, having the rare and beautiful experience of sailing with a fresh wind across an undulating meadow of gulfweed, under a full moon. Boatswain birds, boobies, and the fork-tailed frigate bird were flying about; and one day the sea abounded in tunnies, which the Admiral (making the only humorous remark recorded in his writings) said he expected to end in the Duke of Cadiz's tunny factory at Cadiz. That name caused the seamen to lick their lips in anticipation of seeing again the Cadiz girls, famous through Europe for their saucy beauty and salty wit.

During this uneventful part of the voyage the Admiral took time and pains to write a report on his impressions to Ferdinand and Isabella. Of the natives he writes, "In their islands I have so far found no human monstrosities" (as everyone expected from John de Mandeville). "On the contrary . . . good looks are esteemed; nor are they blacks, as in Guinea, but with flowing hair." A glowing account of their products follows—gum mastic as in Chios, spices, cotton, aloes, slaves.

> All go naked, men and women, as their mothers bore them, except that some women cover one place only with the leaf of a plant or with a net of cotton which they make for that. Although they are well-built people of handsome stature, they are wonderfully timorous. They have no other arms than arms of canes, and they dare not make use of these. . . . After they have been reassured and have lost this fear, they are artless and so free with all they possess, that no one would believe it with-

out having seen it. Of anything they have, if you ask them for it, they never say no; rather they invite the person to share it, and show as much love as if they were giving their hearts; they are content with whatever little thing of whatever kind may be given to them. I forbade that they should be given things so worthless as pieces of broken crockery and broken glass, and ends of straps, although when they were able to get them, they thought they had the best jewel in the world; thus it was ascertained that a sailor for a strap received gold to the weight of two and half *castellanos*,* and others much more for other things which were worth much less; yea, for new *blancas*,** for them they would give all that they had, although it might be two or three castellanos' weight of gold or an *arrova* † or two of spun cotton. . . . They believe very firmly that I, with these ships and people, came from the sky . . . and this does not result from their being ignorant, for they are of a very keen intelligence and men who navigate all those seas.

He particularly admired their dugout *canoas* (here that word enters European language) "made of a single log," carrying up to seventy or eighty men. His description of the scenery and the flora are ecstatic, and not exaggerated, except that he identified very ordinary and useless plants as spices or rare drugs.

Without knowing it, Columbus had followed the best sailing directions for reaching home quickly. Had he tried to sail straight across to Spain (as he did in 1496), he would have had to beat to windward most of the way; but this long northerly leg took him up to the latitude of Bermuda into the zone of rough, strong westerlies.

On the last day of January the wind swung into the west, and four days later, when the Admiral figured by a simple "eye sight" of the North Star that he had reached the latitude of Cape St. Vincent (and actually was on that of Gibraltar), he set the course due east, 90 degrees. Owing to compass variation, this worked out as about 80 degrees true, right for picking up the Azores. The weather now turned cold and a fresh gale made up. During four days the caravels made an average run of 150 miles, and at times attained a speed of 11 knots.

When any sailing yacht the length of *Niña* and *Pinta* hits it up to

---

* $7.50 in gold.
** A copper coin worth half a maravedi, a fraction of a cent.
† A weight equivalent to 25 lbs., or 11½ kilos.

11 or 12 knots today, you have something to talk about; and these
caravels were having the finest kind of sailing. They were running
before a fresh gale over deep blue, white-crested water. On they sped
through bright, sunny days and nights brilliant with Orion and other
familiar constellations that seemed to be beckoning them home. It is
hard for any sailor to be sorry for Columbus, in spite of his later
misfortunes; he enjoyed such glorious sailing weather on almost every
voyage. But he had some very tough experiences, and one of the worst
was about to come.

The westerly gale died down by nightfall 7 February, and for two
days the caravels had light variables and made little progress. On the
ninth they were able to square away again eastward. Next day the
pilots and captains held a ship-to-ship discussion of their position.
Everyone, including Columbus, thought they were much further south
than they actually were, and all except the Admiral put them on the
meridian of the eastern Azores; but Columbus estimated correctly
that they were almost due south of Flores, and decided to call at one
of the Azores, if possible.

He very nearly didn't make it. The two caravels were sailing into
an area of dirty weather in one of the coldest and most blustery winters on record—a winter in which hundreds of vessels went down,
scores crashed ashore, ships lay windbound at Lisbon for months, and
the harbor of Genoa froze over. The center of an area of very low
pressure was passing north of the Azores with southwest to west winds
of full gale strength, and the caravels had to pass through three
weather fronts.

Niña, stripped down to bare poles, on 12 February scudded before
the wind, laboring heavily. The wind moderated slightly next morning, then increased, and the little caravel ran into frightful seas. The
elongated isobaric system brought opposite winds very close to one
another, and the resulting cross seas formed dangerous pyramidical
waves that broke over the caravels from stem to stern. With only her
reefed main course set, and the yard slung low, *Niña* sailed in a general northeasterly direction, while the Admiral and Captain Pinzón
took turns as officer of the deck, watching every wave to warn the
helmsman below. One mistake by either, and she would have broached-
to, rolled over and sunk, and *Pinta* could never have rescued survivors
in such a sea.

The following night, 13–14 February, the two caravels lost sight of each other and never met again that side of Spain. We have no record of how *Pinta* fared, but *Niña*'s crew almost gave up hope on St. Valentine's Day. Thrice, officers and men drew lots for one to go on a pilgrimage to some famous shrine if they were saved; but the wind only blew harder. Then all made a vow "to go in procession in their shirts" to the first shrine of the Virgin they might encounter. The wind then began to abate. Columbus afterward admitted that he was as frightened as anyone. Desperate lest both ships and all hands perish, at the height of the gale he wrote on a parchment an abstract of his journal of the voyage, wrapped it in waxed cloth, headed it up in a cask, and hove it overboard in the hope that someone might pick up the true story of his discovery. The cask never was recovered but sundry faked-up versions of the Admiral's "Secrete Log Boke" are still being offered to credulous collectors.

Shortly after sunrise 15 February, land was sighted dead ahead. Columbus correctly guessed that it was one of the Azores, he dared not guess which. The wind then whipped into the east, and three days elapsed before *Niña* was able to come up to this island and anchor. The Admiral sent his boat ashore and ascertained that it was Santa Maria, southernmost of the group. He anchored near a village called Nossa Senhora dos Anjos (Our Lady of the Angels), where a little church was dedicated to the Virgin, who had appeared surrounded by angels to a local fisherman. Anjos was an answer to prayer, and the proper place for the crew to fulfill their vow made at the height of the storm.

There then took place what, in retrospect, seems really comic. Here were men bursting with the greatest piece of news in centuries, a discovery that would confer untold benefits on all Europeans; yet, how were they, and it, received? While saying their prayers in the chapel, clad only in their shirts (as a sign of penitence), half the crew was set upon by "the whole town" and thrown into jail. The Portuguese captain of the island suspected that they had been on an illicit voyage to West Africa! He even rowed out, hoping to capture Columbus and the few members of *Niña*'s crew who had stayed on board, intending to make their pilgrimage later. The Admiral refused to receive him and threatened to shoot up the town and carry off hostages if his people were not released. Before the captain could make up his mind, another storm blew up. *Niña*'s cables parted, and she was blown almost to São Miguel and back. And she did well to get back, because only three seamen and the Indians were left on board to help the Admiral and the skipper. By the time *Niña* returned, the Portuguese captain, having grilled the captured sailors and discovered no evidence of poaching on royal preserves, surrendered them and furnished the entire crew with much-needed fresh provisions.

Columbus resumed his homeward voyage on 24 February 1493. The distance to his desired landfall, Cape St. Vincent, was only 800 miles, which should have required only a week's sail in the prevailing north wind. But this piece of ocean in winter is a place where low-pressure areas hang around and make trouble for sailors, and the winter of 1493 was unusually foul. Another tempest overtook *Niña* about 250 miles from Santa Maria and stayed with her all the way, giving her an even worse beating than did the storm west of the Azores.

Two days out from Santa Maria, trouble began. The wind shifted to southeast, forcing *Niña* to change course to ENE. Next day both wind and sea made up, and for three days more they were blown off their course. On the night of 2 March the warm front of the circular storm hit *Niña*, the wind changed to southwest, and she was able to sail her course; but that same night the cold front overtook her with a violent squall which split the main course and blew the furled foresail and mizzen out of their gaskets, whipping them to ragged ribbons. Columbus did the only thing he could do, forge ahead under bare poles. *Niña* pitched and rolled frightfully in cross seas and the wind made another shift, to northwest, on 3 March. This was the backlash of the cyclone, worse than the forelash. As the dark winter afternoon waned, anxiety became intense. Columbus and the pilots knew by dead reckoning that they were driving right onto the ironbound coast of Portugal, and that only a miracle could prevent a fatal crash against the cliffs.

Shortly after six o'clock, when the sun set, the crisis came. Lightning flashed overhead, and great seas broke aboard from both sides. The wind blew so strong it "seemed to raise the caravel into the air." Fortunately, it was the night of full moon, which sent enough light through the clouds so that at seven o'clock land was sighted dead ahead, distant perhaps five miles. Columbus then performed the difficult maneuver, well known to every old-time seaman, of "clawing off" a lee shore. The coast ran north and south, the wind blew from the northwest, so they set one little square foresail that had been saved intact, wore ship in a smother of foam, and shaped a course south, parallel to the coast, with wind on the starboard quarter. No wonder *Niña* became the Admiral's favorite vessel, to stand all that beating and respond to this difficult maneuver without broaching.

When day broke on 4 March, Columbus recognized prominent Cabo da Roca that juts into the ocean from the mountains of Sintra, just north of the entrance to the Tagus. With only one square sail between him and utter destruction, the Admiral naturally elected to enter the Tagus and call at Lisbon to refit, rather than attempt to continue around Cape St. Vincent to Spain. He well knew that he was taking a great risk in placing himself in the power of D. João II, the monarch who had turned him down twice; but his first consideration was to get word of his discovery to Spain. So, after sunrise, *Niña* whipped around Cabo da Roca, passed Cascais where the fishermen were amazed to see so tiny a vessel coming in from the sea, crossed the smoking bar at the river mouth, and by nine o'clock anchored off Belém, the outer port of Lisbon.

To be safely anchored in a snug harbor after long tossing at sea gave the sailors a wonderful feeling of relief, but the Admiral and his battered crew still had plenty to worry about. *Niña* would have to be refitted before proceeding to Spain, and would the Portuguese allow it? And what had happened to *Pinta?*

The first Portuguese gesture was not assuring. Moored near *Niña* was a large warship, the name of whose master was Bartholomew Dias —not, apparently, the discoverer of the Cape of Good Hope. Dias came over in an armed boat and ordered Columbus to report on board and give an account of himself. The Admiral stood on his dignity and refused; but he showed his credentials, which satisfied both Dias and his captain. Columbus had already sent a letter to D. João II asking permission to enter Lisbon, and on 8 March a nobleman brought the answer, which not only granted his request—ordering that *Niña* be supplied with all she needed—but invited the Admiral to visit the king at his country residence. Columbus decided he had better accept, although he feared lest visiting the King of Portugal before reporting to the Queen of Castile would offend her—as indeed it did. So, selecting two or three followers and some of the healthiest of his captive Indians, Columbus landed at Lisbon and chartered a train of mules to take himself and his suite up-country. Pity the poor Indians who, after their terrible buffeting at sea, must now suffer the rigors of muleback transport along the narrow, muddy roads of Portugal! It took them two days to make the thirty-mile journey to the monastery of Santa Maria das Virtudes, where the King was then staying.

D. João II received Columbus with unexpected graciousness, but his court chronicler tells us that he was really furious with the Admiral and suspected that the new discoveries had been made in a region where Portugal had prior rights. Courtiers urged the King to have this boastful upstart discreetly assassinated, as he had recently disposed of an annoying brother-in-law. Fortunately, he refused. And the King had to admit that his Indian guests looked very different from any Africans he had ever seen or heard of. Two of them made a rough chart of the Antilles with beans, convincing the King, who smote his breast and cried out, "Why did I let slip such a wonderful chance?"

On 11 March Columbus and his suite departed, escorted by a troop of cavaliers, and made a detour to call on the Queen of Portugal at the Convent of Santo António da Castanheira. The Admiral was so sore from his muleback cruise that on reaching the Tagus he chartered a boat to take him down-river to *Niña*. During his absence she had been fitted with a new suit of sails and running rigging, and had taken on fresh provisions, wood, water, and wine. She was now ready for the last leg of the voyage, all her crew were on board, and on the following morning, 13 March, the gallant little caravel weighed anchor from Lisbon.

Strange to relate, *Pinta* was following her, not far astern. She had missed the Azores, thus escaping the worst of the tempests that swept over *Niña*, and about the end of February made Bayona near Vigo in northwest Spain. Here Martín Alonso Pinzón attempted to beat Columbus home with the great news. He sent a message across Spain to Ferdinand and Isabella at Barcelona, announcing his arrival and begging permission to come himself and tell them about the voyage. The Sovereigns sent back word that they preferred to hear the news from Columbus himself. *Pinta* then sailed from Bayona for Palos.

Niña wore ship around Cape St. Vincent at daybreak 14 March and passed the beach where Columbus had swum ashore after the sea fight seventeen years earlier. At midday 15 March she crossed the bar of the Saltés and dropped anchor off Palos. *Pinta* followed on the same tide.

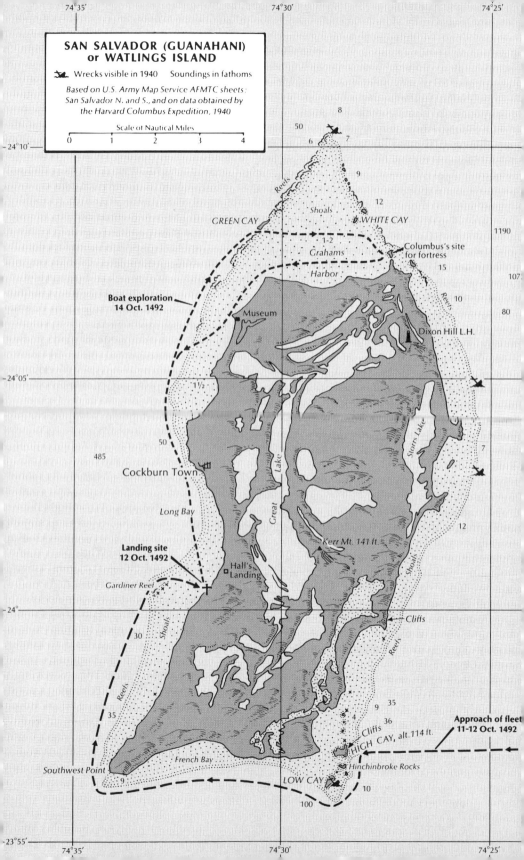

SAN SALVADOR (GUANAHANI) or WATLINGS ISLAND

✈ Wrecks visible in 1940   Soundings in fathoms

Based on U.S. Army Map Service AFMTC sheets: San Salvador N. and S., and on data obtained by the Harvard Columbus Expedition, 1940

Scale of Nautical Miles

0   1   2   3   4

74°35'   74°30'   74°25'

24°10'

8

50

6   7

9

12

Reefs

GREEN CAY   Shoals   ● WHITE CAY

1-2   Columbus's site for fortress

Grahams   15

Harbor   Reefs   10

Boat exploration 14 Oct. 1492

● Museum   Dixon Hill L.H.

24°05'

1½

50

Lake

Storrs Lake

485

Cockburn Town   ⌂

Great

Long Bay   Kerr Mt. 141 ft. ▲   12

Landing site 12 Oct. 1492

Hall's Landing

Gardiner Reef   ✝

24°

Cliffs

30   Shoals

Reefs

Reefs

35   35

9

4   36

35   Cliffs

Approach of fleet 11-12 Oct. 1492

HIGH CAY, alt. 114 ft.

Southwest Point   Hinchinbroke Rocks

French Bay

9   LOW CAY   10

100

23°55'

74°35'   74°30'   74°25'

1190

107

80

7

12

The sight of *Niña* already there, snugged down as if she had been at home a month, finished Martín Alonso Pinzón. Older than Columbus, ill from the hardships of the voyage, mortified by his snub from the Sovereigns, he could bear no more. He went directly to his country house near Palos, took to his bed, and died within the month.

So ended, 224 days after it began, the greatest recorded voyage in history. Here is Columbus's final prophecy in his Letter to the Sovereigns: —

> So, since our Redeemer has given this victory to our most illustrious King and Queen, and to their famous realms, in so great a matter, for this all Christendom ought to feel joyful and make celebrations and give solemn thanks to the Holy Trinity with many solemn prayers for the great exaltation which it will have, in the turning of so many peoples to our holy faith, and afterwards for material benefits, since not only Spain but all Christians will hence have refreshment and profit.

✳ XVI ✳

Triumph and Tragedy

March 1493-April 1494

Hour of Triumph

Columbus had already sent a copy of his official report on the voyage from Lisbon to Barcelona. Fearing lest it miscarry or be impounded by D. João II, he now sent another copy to the Sovereigns by official courier, and a third to the municipality at Cordova. Before proceeding to Seville to await the reply, he fulfilled his vows at the local church and spent two weeks with Fray Juan Pérez and other friends at La Rábida. On Palm Sunday, 31 March, he entered Seville in time to take part in the traditional ceremonies of Holy Week.

Holy Week in Seville, with its alternation of humility and pride, penance and pardon, death and victory, seemed at once a symbol and a fitting conclusion to this great adventure. The daily processions of the brotherhoods with their gorgeously bedecked statues of saints, the ancient ceremonies in the Cathedral—rending of the temple veil, knocking at the great door, candles on the great *tenebrario* extinguished until but one remained, the washing of feet on Maundy Thursday, the supreme Passion on Good Friday when one heard the clacking of the *matraca* in place of cheerful bells, the consecration of the paschal candle, and the supreme ecstasy of Easter morn—all that moved Columbus as no worldly honors could, and strengthened his conviction that his own toils and triumphs fitted the framework of the Passion. And it was pleasant to receive the congratulations of old friends who "always knew he would make it," to be presented to noblemen and bishops, and to have choice young *caballeros* introduced by their fathers in order to plead with Señor Almirante to take them to the Indies, where they would do anything he asked. (They meant, anything but work!)

What the Indian captives thought of it all we know not.

On or shortly after Easter Sunday, 7 April, the Admiral's cup of happiness overflowed upon receipt of a letter from Ferdinand and Isabella, addressed to "Don Cristóbal Colón, their Admiral of the Ocean Sea, Viceroy and Governor of the Islands that he hath discovered in the Indies." These were the exact titles they had promised him if he did reach the Indies, and the use of them indicated that they believed he had. They expressed pleasure at his achievements, commanded him to attend court, and "Inasmuch as we will that that which you have commenced with the aid of God be continued and furthered," ordered preparations for a second voyage to be started immediately.

Sweet words! Columbus promptly drafted a report for the Sovereigns on how Hispaniola should be colonized. As chance entries in his Journal prove, he had been thinking this over for several months. The result was a modification of the trading-factory idea with which he had begun his First Voyage. He now proposed to recruit two thousand settlers who would be required to build houses in a designated town in return for a license to trade for gold with the natives. Each must return to the town at stated intervals and hand over his gold for smelting to an official who would deduct the Sovereigns' fifth, the Admiral's tenth, and another tax to support the church. There should be a closed season on gold-hunting in order to ensure that the settlers would take time to grow crops. Foreigners, Jews, infidels, and heretics must be kept out of the Indies, but priests should be sent there to convert the natives.

Columbus had already realized from his contact with the Tainos that their wants were few and easily met, so that they could not be expected to flock to the beach to sell gold, as did the natives of Africa. To do much business, Spaniards would have to work the interior of Hispaniola and perhaps other islands too. But, in the interest of fiscal control, everyone must check in at a trading factory on the coast, and all transatlantic traffic must go through Cadiz.

After sending this report ahead by courier, the Admiral purchased clothes suitable for his rank, and organized a cavalcade, including a few of his officers and servants, and six long-suffering Indians in native dress, carrying parrots in cages. At Cordova the municipality gave him a reception, and he met his mistress Beatriz and picked up his two sons to join him. They arrived at Barcelona around 20 April 1493. As he entered the hall of the Alcazar where the Sovereigns held court, his dignity, gray hair, and noble countenance tanned by eight months at sea made the learned men present compare him to a Roman senator. As he advanced to the throne to make obeisance, Ferdinand and Isabella arose; and when he knelt to kiss hands, they bade him rise, and seated him on the Queen's right. The Indians were presented, the gold artifacts and samples of alleged rare spices were examined, a multitude of questions asked and answered; then all adjourned to the chapel where *Te Deum* was chanted. It was observed that at the last line, "O Lord, in Thee have I trusted, let me never be confounded," tears were streaming down the Admiral's face.

Columbus at this point could have had anything he wanted—castle in Spain, title, pension, or endowment. It would have been well for him had he then taken his profits and retired with honor, leaving to others the responsibility of colonization. But he was not that kind of a man. Had he been, this great voyage would never have taken place. He must see that the islands he discovered were settled by Christians; he must put the gold trade on a proper footing, and start conversion of the natives; he must meet the Grand Khan or some Oriental potentate of higher rank than Guacanagarí. The rights already granted to him, incident to his offices of Admiral and Viceroy, promised to be far more lucrative than any estate in Spain; and so they would have been, had the crown respected them. Moreover, he was in good health, full of energy, in the prime of life (aged forty-one), and he regarded the work for which God had appointed him to be just begun.

His sense of a divine mission also appears in the curious Graeco-Latin signature he now adopted, and of which no contemporary explanation exists. In the entail of his property he describes it as "an X [by which he probably meant a Greek chi] with an S over it and an

M with a Roman A over it and over that an S, and then a Greek Y [by which he probably meant a capital upsilon] with an S over it, preserving the relation of the lines and points." The way he wrote it is as follows:

. S .

S . A . S

X . M . Y

: Xpo FERENS

Many attempts have been made to solve the riddle. My suggestion is that the initials stand for *Servus Sum Altissimi Salvatoris, Christoû Mariae Yιοû* (Servant am I of the Most High Saviour, Christ Son of Mary). The last line, *Xpo Ferens,** is a Graeco-Latin form of *Christopher*, emphasizing his most cherished mission, to carry Christianity to lands beyond the sea. Even on such brief chits as have survived, he signed himself *Xpo* FERENS, the Christ Bearer.**

Columbus tarried at court over Whitsuntide, Trinity Sunday, and Corpus Christi. The King and Queen and Infante Don Juan having graciously consented to act as godparents, six Indians were baptized. The first in rank, kinsman to Guacanagarí, they christened "Ferdinand of Aragon"; another, "Don Juan of Castile"; while the clever interpreter was named "Don Diego." Don Juan attached himself to the royal household and died within two years; the other five returned with the Admiral to the New World.

These christenings expressed good intentions of the Sovereigns and of Columbus toward the natives, but in the Indies themselves, human greed had to be satisfied first, and forced labor exterminated almost the entire native population of Hispaniola within half a century. But the Indians unwittingly had their revenge on Europeans through *Treponema pallida*, the spirochete of syphilis, which the conquerors contracted in the Indies and brought back to Spain. The first recorded outbreak of syphilis in Europe took place in 1494 among the soldiers of a French army which marched to Naples and back. Bishop Las Casas, who admired Columbus, loved the Indians, and spent a large

---

* This is not to be read "Expo" but "Christo," the letters Chi Rho being a common Greek abbreviation of *Christ.*

** Sometimes he signed himself "El Virrey"; and on one occasion, "Virrey de Asia."

part of his life in a vain effort to protect them, states in his *Apologetica Historia* of around 1530 that the disease was transmitted to the French army by Spanish women who were infected by the Indians brought to Barcelona by Columbus. He adds that, from repeated questioning of the natives of Hispaniola, he believed the disease to be one of long standing in the New World; so long, indeed, that the natives did not suffer greatly from it. Among Europeans, however, syphilis promptly assumed the most hideous and malignant forms, with many fatalities, just as measles and smallpox affected the Indians when introduced by Europeans. It seems, therefore, probable that the Indians whom Columbus brought to Barcelona were so joyfully and briskly entertained by the women of the town as to infect these women, who either infected Spanish volunteers in the army of Charles VIII or accompanied that army as camp followers.

This subject is controversial; but it appears to me that Las Casas was correct. *Niña's* crew for the return voyage cannot have contracted syphilis, for all were healthy and able to work the ship up to the moment of landing; Columbus more than once remarked on it with amazement, since on African voyages sailors were expected to sicken and die. Medical authorities assure me that it would have been almost impossible for a man infected with syphilis to make a tough voyage of two months without becoming very sick indeed. As for those in *Pinta*, a Spanish surgeon named Ruy Díaz de Isla, in his book on the disease printed at Seville in 1539, stated that the spirochete infected "a pilot of Palos called Pinzón," and implies that he attended him. It will be remembered that three Pinzóns shipped in *Pinta*, and that Martín Alonso, the captain, died shortly after her arrival; but Díaz de Isla admits that the disease also spread from Barcelona. It became a terrible plague in Europe and among the Spanish colonists of Hispaniola. They used a local Indian remedy, decoctions of guiacum or lignum vitae. This had no therapeutic effect whatsoever, but people, both natives and Europeans, thought it to be a sovereign cure.

Although Columbus tarried several weeks in Barcelona, he did not simply bask in the sunshine of royalty. He looked after their interests, and his own. The Sovereigns' letters patent granting him a coat of arms gave him the singular privilege of quartering the royal arms of Spain, the castle of Castile and lion of Leon, with an archipelago and five anchors, the symbol of admiralty. At the same time the rights and privileges granted him conditionally at Granada the previous April were confirmed. He and his heirs "now and forever" were to be styled Admiral of the Ocean Sea and Viceroy and Governor of "the said islands and mainland that you have found and discovered." As Viceroy he could appoint and remove all officials in the Indies and have complete civil and criminal jurisdiction; as Admiral he would have jurisdiction over all who sailed the ocean west and south of a line from the Azores to the Cape Verdes. Admiralty jurisdiction meant that he or his deputies could handle all disputes among fishermen or merchant mariners in American waters and try all cases of mutiny, piracy, barratry, and the like. It did not imply command of a fleet, or flag rank in the navy, but nonetheless was a very high and honorable distinction.

The Admiral also worked for the Sovereigns. His famous Letter on the voyage was printed at Barcelona, in Spanish, about the time that he arrived. A Latin translation, dated 29 April, appeared shortly after in Rome. The object of this prompt publication was not so much to spread the news but to obtain papal confirmation of the lands newly discovered, as the public law of Europe then required. The Sovereigns depended on Columbus to prove that his discoveries were outside jurisdiction previously granted to the king of Portugal. Pope Alexander VI, a Spanish Borgia who owed his election to Ferdinand and Isabella, let them practically "write their own ticket" in a series of papal bulls. The third and most important, dated 4 May 1493, drew a line of demarcation along the meridian one hundred leagues (318 nautical miles) west of the Azores. All undiscovered lands east of it would belong to Portugal; all west of it, to Spain.

Columbus undoubtedly suggested this line, because he believed that compass variation changed from east to west, and that the boisterous winds of Europe gave way to the gentle trades, on or about that meridian of longitude. According to Bishop Las Casas, it was an entomological boundary as well. He observed that seamen and passengers departing from Spain were tortured by lice and fleas until they reached a hundred leagues west of the Azores, when the insects began to disappear; but upon the return passage they emerged from hiding at the same longitude "in great and disturbing numbers!" A later form of this myth described insect life as disappearing at the Equator. Readers of *Don Quixote* will remember how, in that famous voyage in the enchanted bark, the Knight of the Rueful Countenance bids Sancho Panza search himself for vermin, in order to ascertain whether or not they have passed the Line.

Nevertheless, the line of demarcation set up by the Pope was not enforced. Portugal protested, and as the hostility of D. João II would have jeopardized their communications, Ferdinand and Isabella in the Treaty of Tordesillas (1494) consented to push the line to the meridian 370 leagues (roughly 1175 miles) west of the Cape Verde Islands. From that new division of the world, Portugal derived her title to Brazil and her claim to Newfoundland.

During the three months that Columbus resided at Barcelona, news of his discovery spread wide, by means of epistles from Italian residents in Spain, and from the printed Letter in many translations. But the news traveled very slowly beyond the Alps. The learned men of Nuremberg, center of geographical study in northern Europe, were ignorant of it as late as July 1493, and brother Bartholomew, living near Paris, did not hear of it in time to join the Admiral's Second Voyage.

Judging from the letters and chronicles, the items in the news that aroused the most attention were gold, the naked natives, and the opportunity to convert them. Columbus had stressed all three in his Letter, as well as opening a new trade route to China. Europe was then so short of specie that any gold strike made a universal appeal, as it would today. Fashions in 1493 required women to be heavily clothed from head to foot, so that a community where the natives wore less than a bikini for full dress was news indeed, besides suggesting the state of innocence before Adam's fall. And as Europe had an uneasy conscience at letting Christianity fall back before the Turks, this opportunity to gain souls and redress the balance aroused agreeable anticipation. Of the real significance of the discovery for Europe's future there was not one hint in contemporary comment, nor did anyone venture to suggest that Seneca's prophecy of a vast continent had been fulfilled.

Columbus's assertion that he really had reached the Indies was accepted by the Spanish Sovereigns and the Pope, but not by everyone. Peter Martyr d'Anghiera, an Italian humanist at the Spanish court, wrote to a correspondent that the size of the globe seemed to indicate that Columbus could not have reached Asia, and in November 1493 he described the Admiral in a letter to Cardinal Sforza as "Novi Orbis Repertor," "Discoverer of a New World." To him, as to other contemporaries, New World did not mean a separate, undiscovered continent, but land unknown to Ptolemy; a group of islands adjacent to the Malay Peninsula would be a New World. That is exactly the conclusion reached by Columbus himself in 1498, and by Amerigo Vespucci a little later. But Amerigo got the credit, as we shall see.

Columbus's Second Voyage

We must never forget that Columbus made three more voyages to America, any one of which would entitle him to top rank as a navigator. The Second Voyage, of 1493–94, Spain's follow-up to the First, employed a big fleet, and also set up the first European colony in America that survived. But it was also important for discovery—the Lesser Antilles, the Virgin Islands, Puerto Rico, the south coast of Cuba, and Jamaica.

Within a month of his arrival from the First Voyage, he agreed with the Sovereigns to lead a second expedition for further discovery, and to establish a colony in Hispaniola. They gave him full latitude as to means in their instructions issued 29 May 1493. Prime objective was to be the conversion of the natives, for which purpose six priests were assigned to the fleet, and the Admiral must see to it that the Indians are "treated very well and lovingly." Hundreds of laymen were to be recruited for the second declared objective: the establishment of a colony. Whilst in 1492 it required the utmost persuasiveness to induce any but the very young and adventurous to ship with Columbus, now the Admiral was embarrassed by the number of volunteers. Both his fame and public expectations were at their zenith; anticipation of finding gold and valuable spices was high; thousands of men and boys were eager to go with him, hoping to make their fortunes and, in any event, to have fun. Finally, the Admiral was charged to explore Cuba, in the hope that it might be a peninsula of Asia leading to the golden cities of Cathay.

In June 1493, accompanied by five of the six baptized Indians and his younger brother Diego, Christopher Columbus set forth from Barcelona. After passing through Madrid and Toledo, he took the pilgrims' road to Guadalupe in the Estremadura, passing through

Trujillo where a thirteen-year-old boy named Francisco Pizarro, future conqueror of Peru, was then engaged in caring for his father's herd of swine. Columbus prayed long and fervently before the famous Virgin of Guadalupe, and the monks asked him to name an island after her. En route to Seville, he passed through the little town of Medellin where a small boy named Hernándo Cortés must have seen him go by.

Columbus arrived at Cadiz, where the Second Voyage was mounted, in early July. Juan de Fonseca, archdeacon of Seville, had done an excellent job of organizing this fleet. He had bought or chartered seventeen vessels, victualed them for a round voyage of six months, recruited at least 1200 sailors, soldiers, and colonists, and collected the necessary seeds, plants, domestic animals, tools, and implements to plant a colony. Citizens of Jerez furnished wheat at 73 maravedis a bushel (about fifteen cents in gold value). Others were paid to grind it into flour and bake ship biscuit—the "hardtack" that formed the staple diet of sailors almost to our own day. Cattle and swine were slaughtered and pickled in brine. Wine, purchased by the pipe, should have been delivered in stout new oaken casks. Columbus complained bitterly that many of the casks were secondhand and let so much wine leak out that Spaniards in Hispaniola for months endured the incredible hardship of drinking only water! One curious element in the expedition was a cavalry troop of twenty lancers who sold their blooded barbs in Cadiz, purchased some sorry hacks, and lived high on the difference; but the substitutes proved good enough to terrorize the natives of Hispaniola.

Unfortunately the records do not allow us to compile a task organization of this fleet, unsurpassed even by Magellan's. The flagship, named *Santa Maria* (like that of the First Voyage) and nicknamed *Mariagalante*, was considerably bigger than her namesake; say 200 tuns' burthen. Two other *naos* were called *Colina* and *La Gallega*. There were about ten square-rigged caravels including gallant *Niña* of the First Voyage, at least two lateen-rigged caravels, and some small Cantabrian barques for shoal-water exploration. The Pinzón family was conspicuously absent, but four members of the Niño family of Moguer participated. Most of the sailors were from that region. Everyone was on the royal payroll except about two hundred gentlemen volunteers; no women were allowed.

On 25 September 1493, a bright autumn day with a light offshore breeze, "This fleet so united and handsome," as Columbus called it, departed white-walled Cadiz. Every vessel flew the royal standard of Castile. Every captain dressed his ship with brightly colored banners, and waistcloths emblazoned with the arms of gentlemen volunteers were stretched between forecastle and poop. A number of big sea-going Venetian galleys which happened to be in Cadiz harbor escorted the fleet to the open sea amid music of trumpets and harps and the firing of cannon.

On 2 October the fleet made the Grand Canary, and on the fifth called at Gomera, home of Doña Beatriz de Peraza y Bobadilla, lady captain of the island. Columbus, according to his shipmate Cuneo, had become *tincto d'amore* ("dyed with love") for her on his previous visit, and she now received his fleet with salvos of cannon and fire-works. But if Beatriz expected to play Circe to this Ulysses, she was disappointed. Columbus tarried but a few days and spent most of his time topping off the vessels with water, provisions, and livestock. She would indeed have been a very proper wife for the now "Very Mag-nificent Don Cristóbal Colón, Almirante del Mar Océano, Virrey de las Indias." Probably, however, as a practical young widow, she did not want a sailor for her second husband, but a man who would stay at home and look after her and her small boy.

The fleet ran into the usual Canary Islands calms and took its final departure from Ferro on 12 October 1493, first anniversary of the discovery of America. The course set by the Admiral was west by south. He planned to shorten the ocean passage and make discoveries in the Lesser Antilles. The captive Indians had told him that Matinino (Martinique) and Charis (Dominica) of the Lesser Antilles were the nearest islands to Spain, and he figured the course to them correctly, within half a compass point.

Sailing before the trades in a square-rigger is a sailor's dream of the good life at sea. You settle down to the pleasant ritual, undisturbed by shifts of wind and changes of weather; and this ocean crossing seems to have been pure joy for everyone who loved the sea. There is the constant play of light and color on the bellying square sails (gold at sunset, silver in moonlight, black in starlight, white as the clouds them-selves at noon). The sea, flecked with whitecaps, is of a gorgeous deep blue, the schools of flying fish spring like a flash of silver from the bow wave. And on this Second Voyage there were seventeen ships in company, so that from the high-pooped flagship one could see white sails all around the horizon. Every day the faster vessels romped ahead, racing one another, but toward sundown each closed *Maria-galante* within hailing distance so that the Admiral could give night orders. As darkness fell, every ship lit her stern lantern or kindled light-wood in an iron cresset. Throughout the night, during which the trade wind blew full and steady, each tried to keep her assigned station, as in a modern convoy. Every half hour the voices of the ships' boys announced the turning of the glass. Just before 7:00 a.m., when the morning watch came on duty, a priest on board the flagship celebrated what was called a "dry Mass," in which he went through the motions but did not consecrate the sacred elements lest the ship's motion cause them to be dropped or spilled. On the other vessels the men watched for the elevation of the host, a signal to kneel and cross themselves. Then a hymn was sung, the glass turned, the watch relieved, and every ship cracked on sail to race the others during the daylight hours.

A thunder squall on St. Simon's Eve (26 October) split a number of sails and lighted ghostly "corposants" on the tips of masts and yards. All the rest of the outward passage, the ships enjoyed fair wind and made the 2500 nautical miles from Ferro to Dominica in 21 days, an average speed of about 5 knots. On All Saints' Day, 1 November 1493, the Admiral was so confident of making land within three days that he issued an extra allowance of water. As an experienced seaman he knew land was near at sundown, 2 November, by clouds gathering over the horizon ahead. That night he shortened sail lest his fleet over-run the land before moonrise, which came shortly before dawn. An anxious night it must have been, young men imagining that they saw lights or heard breakers, leadsmen heaving the deep-sea lead and sing-ing out, "No bottom!" At five in the morning of Sunday, 3 Novem-ber, just as the first faint gray of dawn appeared in the east, a lookout in *Mariagalante* sees a dark cone blotting out a small section of the star-studded horizon ahead. He sings out, *Albricias! Que tenemos tierra!* ("The reward! For we have land!") The cry of *Tierra! Tierra!* passes from ship to ship; all is bustle and excitement, and the Admiral sum-mons all hands to prayer on the quarterdeck, where they sing *Salve Regina* and other hymns "very devotedly, giving thanks to God for

The Grand Carbet waterfall, Guadeloupe. Just as Columbus saw it in 1493, plunging from the clouds. David Crofoot photo.

so short and safe a voyage." Only 21 to 22 days land to land, one-third less than the First Voyage, and a marked contrast to later southern voyages of discovery.

From Dominica to Navidad

Columbus named the island of his landfall Dominica, and this Sabbath-day island still is, in my opinion, the most beautiful of all the Carib-bees. With no other aid then his captive Indians' advice, he had hit the Antilles at the exact spot recommended by official sailing directions for the next four centuries! For here the passage between the islands is clear, with no dangerous reefs to avoid; and once inside the Carib-bean you can count on fair winds whether bound for Venezuela and the Spanish Main or Vera Cruz and Mexico, or the Leeward Islands, Puerto Rico, Hispaniola, and Cuba.

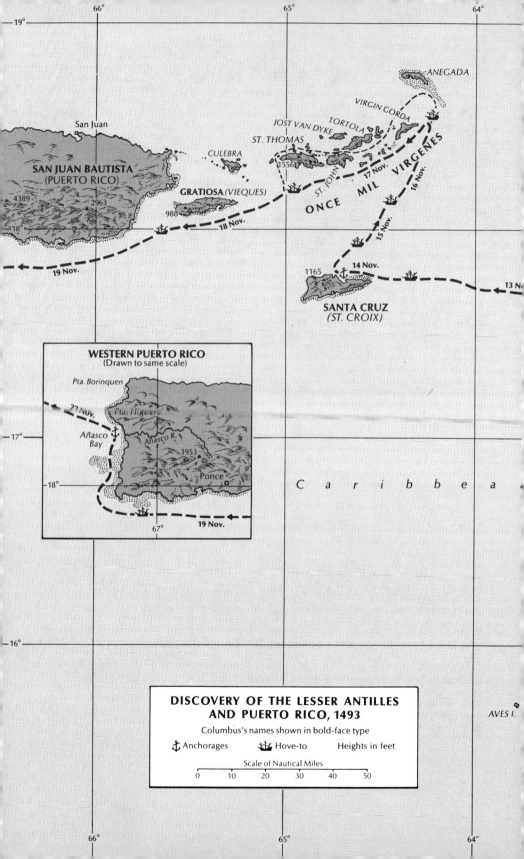

66°   65°   64°

19°

ANEGADA

VIRGIN GORDA

TORTOLA

JOST VAN DYKE

ST. THOMAS

San Juan

CULEBRA

17 Nov.

SAN JUAN BAUTISTA
(PUERTO RICO)

1556

16 Nov.

ONCE   MIL   VIRGENES

4389

2963

GRATIOSA (VIEQUES)

ST. JOHN

15 Nov.

988

18 Nov.

18°

1165

14 Nov.

13 Nov.

19 Nov.

SANTA CRUZ
(ST. CROIX)

WESTERN PUERTO RICO
(Drawn to same scale)

Pta. Borinquen

22 Nov.

Pta. Higuero

17°

Añasco
Bay

Añasco R.

3953

18°

Ponce

C   a   r   i   b   b   e   a

67°

19 Nov.

16°

DISCOVERY OF THE LESSER ANTILLES
AND PUERTO RICO, 1493

Columbus's names shown in bold-face type

⚓ Anchorages   Hove-to   Heights in feet

Scale of Nautical Miles

0   10   20   30   40   50

AVES I.

66°   65°   64°

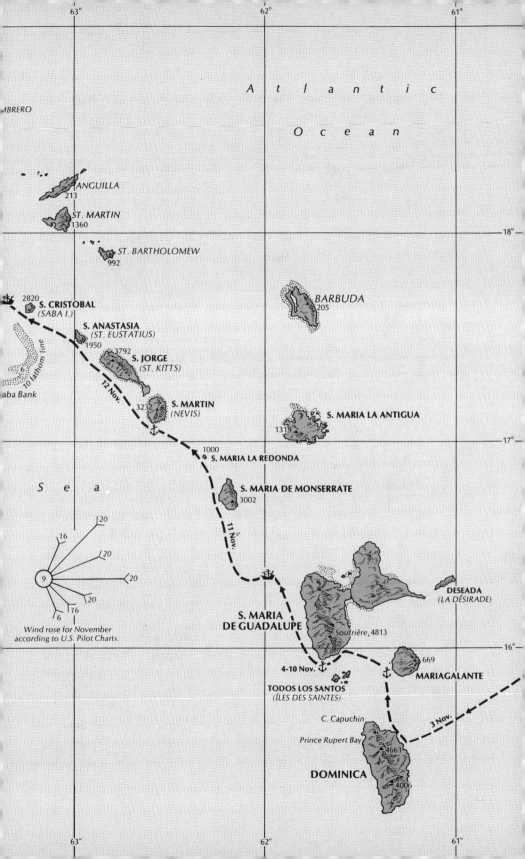

Atlantic

Ocean

MBRERO

ANGUILLA
213

ST. MARTIN
1360

ST. BARTHOLOMEW
992

BARBUDA
205

2820 **S. CRISTOBAL**
(SABA I.)

S. ANASTASIA
(ST. EUSTATIUS)
1950

3792

S. JORGE
(ST. KITTS)

12 Nov.

323 **S. MARTIN**
(NEVIS)

S. MARIA LA ANTIGUA
1319

10 fathom line

6

aba Bank

1000
S. MARIA LA REDONDA

S. MARIA DE MONSERRATE
3002

S   e   a

11 Nov.

20

16

20

20

9

20

20

16
6

Wind rose for November
according to U.S. Pilot Charts.

DESEADA
(LA DÉSIRADE)

S. MARIA
DE GUADALUPE

Soufrière, 4813

4-10 Nov.

669

MARIAGALANTE

TODOS LOS SANTOS
(ÎLES DES SAINTES)

3 Nov.

C. Capuchin

Prince Rupert Bay

4661

DOMINICA

4006

63°

62°

61°

18°

17°

16°

As the light increased on 3 November and the fleet sped westward, they sighted a round, flat island which Columbus named *Mariagalante* as a tribute to his flagship, and a group of islands which he called *Todos los Santos* for the feast of All Saints just passed. (French since the seventeenth century, they are still Mariegalante and Les Saintes.) Columbus anchored on the lee side of the first-named, went ashore with his banners, and formally took possession for Spain. In the meantime, a high island was sighted to the westward, and as Mariagalante offered little of interest, Columbus ordered anchors aweigh and shaped his course thither. This was the big kidney-shaped island which he named *Santa Maria de Guadalupe*, as he had promised the monks to do. (Guadeloupe, as the French called it, is now their oldest colony; it became a sugar island so valuable that the British in 1763 seriously thought of swapping all Canada for it.) As the fleet approached this island, they saw the strange and beautiful sight of a high waterfall, slender as a silver thread, which appeared to plunge out of the clouds hanging over the mountains. The vessels anchored under the southern slope of the island's 5000-foot volcano, in a sheltered bay now called Grande Anse, and there remained five or six days.

Columbus did not intend to stay more than one night, but his first shore party lost itself in the dense tropical rain forest. Since the natives here were the dreaded man-eating Caribs, these men were lucky to be located by one of four search parties of fifty men each. In the course of their wanderings, the searching Spaniards learned a good deal about the manners and customs of the Caribs, the tribe from which the word "cannibal" is derived. In huts deserted by the natives they found human limbs and cuts of human flesh partly consumed, as well as emasculated boys who were being fattened to provide the main dish for a feast, and girl captives used to produce babies for the hors d'œuvre. Two boys and "twelve very beautiful plump girls from fifteen to sixteen years old" were picked up by the Spaniards. These girls, who had been captured by the Caribs in a raid on Hispaniola, were useful as interpreters, and doubtless in other ways too.

From Guadeloupe on, the fleet enjoyed a spectacular sail along the leeward (western) coasts of the Lesser Antilles, with a quartering or beam wind. Each island is a mountain peak rising 3000 to 5000 feet from the Caribbean. Depths from a few hundred yards off each shore are deepest sapphire, whilst the shoals vary from brilliant emerald to a luminous golden yellow. At dawn the next island ahead is a vague

boriquen
las Virgines
Circulo cancro
s xpobal s de lanieve
S cruz
cnidi la gorda S martin
s: mjª de monsera
S: mjª de guadalupe
s: mª galante
domjnjca
asencion
el falcon
las agulas
mayo los hermanos
pªyna
boca del drago

**THE LESSER ANTILLES ON
JUAN DE LA COSA'S MAP**

shadow, a dark shape against the celestial sphere. With the increase of
light, and upon one's own swift approach, the land takes form, substance, and color. One can watch the sun kindle the mountain pinnacles to flame, the forested slopes turning from gray to green, and
finally to a blue a few shades lighter than the sea. As the wind makes
up during the forenoon watch, it forms a cloud over each island, and
if you are off the leeward coast by noon, you are apt to be becalmed
under the heights; that happened to Columbus at Guadeloupe. The sea
then becomes a gently undulating mirror, reflecting the colors of the
land and broken only by flights of flying fish and leaping dolphins.
But the calm never lasts long. The wind springs up again, the island is
left astern, and you gaze back at it, fascinated, as showers lash the
forested slopes and the clouds turn orange with the declining sun.

And if the western horizon is clear, the sun as it dips below sends up a brilliant emerald flash.

Even more than most sailors, Columbus was devoted to the Virgin Mary, and for several days he named almost every island after one or another of her shrines. Some of his names were later transferred to other islands, but from the famous chart by Juan de La Cosa, the Admiral's shipmate on this voyage, we may trace the fleet's course with some confidence. Next after Guadeloupe it passed an island that Columbus named *Santa Maria de Monserrate* after a famous monastery near Barcelona; it is still called Montserrat, and is famous for the Irish brogue of the natives, black or white, inherited from Oliver Cromwell's captives with whom the English peopled it in the seventeenth century. Next came a tiny round island, *Santa Maria la Redonda;* this has never been settled, although a crazy American once claimed to be king of it. To windward Columbus saw but did not visit a large island which he named *Santa Maria la Antigua*, after a famous painting of the Virgin in Seville Cathedral. During the night of 11–12 November the fleet lay at anchor in the lee of an island which the Admiral named *San Martín* because it was the vigil of the feast of St. Martin of Tours. This was probably Nevis and not the present Franco-Dutch island of Saint-Martin or Sint-Maarten, which was too far off his course for

Les Saintes.

St. Eustatius.

Columbus to have visited or even seen. Originally, Nevis was *Santa Maria de las Nieves*, St. Mary of the Snow, so called from the pretty story that Santa Maria Maggiore in Rome was built on the Esquiline because the Virgin indicated the proper site by causing snow to fall there in August.

Next to the modern Nevis is the present St. Christopher (abbreviated St. Kitts), which Columbus traditionally named after his own patron saint because the shape of the mountain resembled a giant carrying someone pick-a-back. That answers better to the next island, St. Eustatius, but it is anybody's guess how to apply some of the northern names on Juan de La Cosa's map.*

The night of 12–13 November was spent by the fleet hove-to off

* As Mauricio Obregón has said, names on discoverers' maps are nomads. A good instance is the wandering of *Arcadia* from North Carolina to Nova Scotia (see p. 151, above).

Scene of the first fight. Salt River Bay, St. Croix. David Crofoot photo.

the northern end of the island chain. That must indeed have been a brave sight. Seventeen vessels under short sail, slowly drifting to leeward, lights from the stern lanterns of the big ships and the iron cressets of the smaller vessels reflected in the water. At break of day each vessel makes sail and scurries to the flagship for orders. The Admiral sets a course almost due west, to an island whose direction his Indian guides pointed out and called *Ayay*.

The island, which the Admiral called *Santa Cruz*, and for which we now use the French form St. Croix, is the first future United States territory discovered by Columbus. Unlike the heavily forested islands that they had passed, St. Croix was intensively cultivated by its Carib inhabitants and looked like a great garden as they skirted its northern coast. Missing the future Christiansted Harbor, owing to the outer reef barrier, they anchored off a small estuary now called Salt River Bay. And here the Spanish mariners had their first fight with American natives.

446

At noon 14 November, Columbus sent an armed boat with twenty-five men toward a small village at the head of this harbor. The inhabitants fled, but as the boat returned, a Carib canoe suddenly came around the point. The paddlers at first were stupefied by the sight of the great ships, but presently recovered their senses; and although they numbered only four men and two women, picked up their bows and arrows and let fly, wounding two Spaniards, one mortally. Columbus's boat rammed and upset the dugout; but the Caribs swam to a rock where they fought like demons until overcome and taken. A horde of natives in warpaint now ran down to the shore, eager for revenge, but they had no weapons that could reach the ships.

This skirmish at Salt River Bay gave the Spaniards a healthy respect for the Carib nation, which in general they left alone, visiting their islands only with strong armed parties. Probably the first Carib in history to be subdued was a "very beautiful girl," one of the canoe party, captured in the fight by Michele de Cuneo, Columbus's boyhood friend, and presented to him by the Admiral as a slave. "Having taken her into my cabin," wrote Cuneo, "she being naked according to their custom, I conceived a desire to take pleasure." She gave him a

Sir Francis Drake Channel, Virgin Islands.

severe working-over with her fingernails, he "thrashed her well" with
a rope's end, and she raised "unheard-of screams," but "finally we
came to an agreement in such manner that I can tell you that she
seemed to have been brought up in a school of harlots."

Columbus did not care to tarry at St. Croix, lest the Caribs bring up
reinforcements. Having already noted the rounded tops of a number
of islands over the northern horizon, he decided to investigate them.
As the ships approached, more and more islands appeared. The Admiral appropriately named them *Las Once Mil Vírgenes*, after the
11,000 seagoing virgins from Cornwall who, according to legend,
were martyred by the Huns at Cologne after a long and pleasant
yachting cruise.

To explore these Virgin Islands the Admiral used the smaller
caravels and Cantabrian barques. He sent them through the easterly
passage to look at Anegada, after which they squared away down
the channel later named after Sir Francis Drake, with high, handsome
islands on either hand. The sailors marveled at the dazzling colors of
some of the rocks and at the pink coral beaches. In the meantime,
Mariagalante and the larger vessels sailed in deep water south of the
two larger islands, St. John and St. Thomas. On the morning of
18 November the fleet again united west of St. Thomas. That day
they raised an island which Columbus named *Gratiosa*, after the noble
mother of his friend Alessandro Geraldini, who had entertained him
in his days of poverty. Unfortunately that name, recording filial piety
and a deep friendship, has been replaced by Vieques, or Crab Island.

After another night hove-to, the fleet made the south coast of a big
island which the natives called *Boriquén* or *Borinquen;* the Admiral
named it for St. John the Baptist. All day 19 November Columbus's
fleet sailed along the mountainous southern coast of Puerto Rico, and
on the morning of the 20th rounded its southwest point, Cabo Rojo,
and steered northwest "on a bowline," looking for a good passage
through the reefs which protect the first twenty miles of the island's
west coast.* Finally the reefs ceased to mask the land, and the fleet
sailed in deep water right up to the land, in what is now Añasco Bay.

---

* Before seeing the island, I mistakenly followed earlier historians in stating that
Columbus landed in the nearest harbor, Boqueron Bay. A glance at the chart
should satisfy anyone that no good sailor would risk his fleet working through
so narrow an unexplored channel.

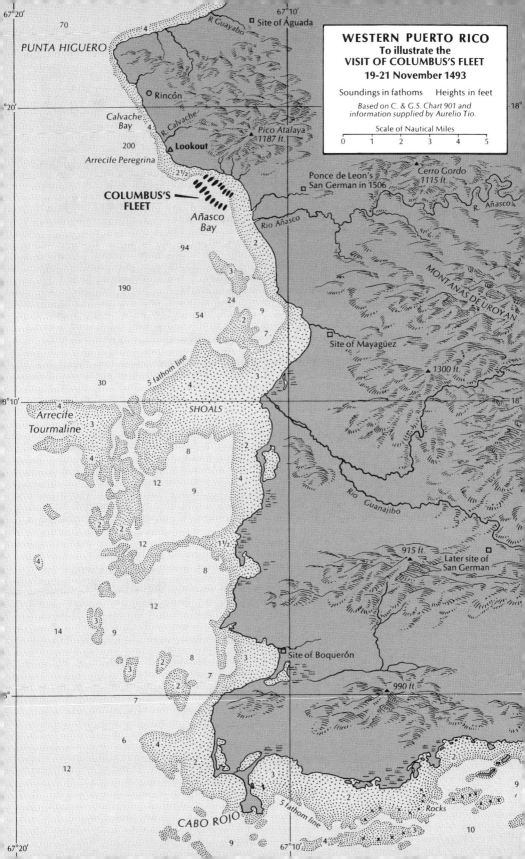

67°20'   70   67°10'   □ Site of Águada
PUNTA HIGUERO   R Guayabo

18°20'   ○ Rincón

Calvache   4   R. Calvache
Bay   ▲ Lookout   Pico Atalaya
200   1187 ft.
Arrecife Peregrina   2½   Ponce de Leon's   Cerro Gordo
                                    San German in 1506   1115 ft.
COLUMBUS'S   □   ▲
FLEET   R. Añasco
        Añasco
        Bay   Rio Añasco
            94   2
190   MONTAÑAS DE UROYAN
        3
            24   9
        54   2
            7   Site of Mayagüez
                        □
            3   1300 ft.
30   5 fathom line   4   ▲
18°10'   4   SHOALS
Arrecife   3
Tourmaline   8   2
        4   4
        12   9
        2   1½
            8
    12   915 ft.   Later site of
                    ▲   San German
14   9
    8   3   □ Site of Boquerón
    7
    2   990 ft.
3°   7   ▲
    6   4
    12   2   Rio Guanajibo
    3
    1   Rocks   9
CABO ROJO   5 fathom line   10
    9   67°10'   4

WESTERN PUERTO RICO
To illustrate the
VISIT OF COLUMBUS'S FLEET
19-21 November 1493

Soundings in fathoms   Heights in feet

*Based on C. & G.S. Chart 901 and
information supplied by Aurelio Tio.*

Scale of Nautical Miles
0   1   2   3   4   5

Lookout Mound, Ensenada de Calvache.

It was a perfect place for watering a large fleet, as not only the big Rio Añasco rising in the mountains empties here, but a dozen other smaller streams of sweet water gave every vessel an opportunity to replenish her casks.

This area was heavily populated by Indians, but when the Spaniards visited a big village they found it completely empty. This branch of the Arawak lived in constant terror of raids from the eastern half of the island by Caribs and (as son Ferdinand noted) maintained a continual watch at a natural lookout on the shore whence they could be warned of an approaching fleet of war canoes. Sight of the Columbus fleet must have convinced them that the Caribs had grown wings, and they all fled to the mountains.

One of the Admiral's shipmates on this voyage, Ponce de León, decided that Borinquen would do nicely for him, and early in the next century conquered it, as we shall see in due course.

From Puerto Rico the fleet crossed the Mona Passage, and at eventide 22 November made landfall on Cape Engaño, Hispaniola. An Indian whom Columbus had picked up at Samaná Bay in January came out and directed the fleet to his home village. He was set ashore, well provided with trading truck, in the hope of mitigating the fears of the suspicious Indians there. Apparently that worked, as a number of Ciguayos visited the ships and traded. The sailor wounded in the fight at St. Croix, who had since died, was here given Christian burial.

Columbus now ranged a coast that he had already discovered coming home. On the evening of 27 November the fleet anchored outside the pass to Caracol Bay. In view of what had happened on the last Christmas Eve, the Admiral refused to enter in the dark. Flares were lighted and cannon fired, but no answer came from the shore. Late at night a canoe approached, manned by Indians calling *Almirante! Almirante!* and, when Columbus came on deck, they presented him with gifts from Guacanagarí. They assured him that the Spaniards at Navidad were all right—except that a few had died:—some understatement! "Diego Colón," the Indian interpreter, got the truth out of them, a tale so horrible that Columbus at first refused to believe it.

The Spaniards at Navidad had acted without restraint or reason. Two of the leaders, including Gutiérrez the crown official, formed a gang and roamed the island looking for more gold and women than Guacanagarí was able or willing to supply. They fell afoul of Caonabó, cacique of Maguana in the center of Hispaniola, a chief of stouter stuff than the feeble and complacent cacique of Marien. He killed the Gutiérrez gang and then marched on Navidad to wipe out the source of trouble. Only ten men were left under Diego de Harana to guard the fort. Caonabó disposed of them easily, hunting down and slaughtering every Spaniard who took to the bush. Thus ended the honeymoon between Christians and natives.

Columbus's immediate problem was to choose a site for his trading-post colony. Dr. Chanca, the fleet surgeon, ruled out the swampy shores of Caracol Bay where the natives were friendly, and Cape Haitien seemed far from the gold-bearing Cibao. So the Admiral decided to turn eastward in search of a good harbor. Sailing against the trades and westward-flowing current meant a long, tedious beat to windward, and it took the fleet 25 days to make good about 32 miles. Frequent shifting of sail and constant wetting with salt spray wore sailors down, exasperated the colonists, and killed a large part of the livestock. On 2 January 1494, when the fleet anchored in the lee of a peninsula that afforded shelter from the east wind, Columbus decided to pitch his city there and then. Although named Isabela after the Queen, this settlement was founded under an evil star.

Here for the time being discovery ended, as happiness had already ended for Columbus when he learned the fate of Navidad. Yet he must have derived great satisfaction from this voyage to Hispaniola. He had safely conducted across the Atlantic seventeen vessels, many of them very small, made a perfect landfall, and continued through a chain of uncharted islands with no accident serious enough to be recorded. He had discovered some twenty large islands and over two-score small ones upon which the eyes of no European had ever rested. Over the greatest fleet that had yet crossed the Atlantic, bearing 1200 seamen, colonists, and men-at-arms, he had kept discipline during a voyage that lasted fourteen weeks. In a region inhabited by man-eating Caribs he had avoided conflict save for one brief skirmish, and lost but a single man. Plenty of trouble was awaiting the Admiral when he left the deck of *Mariagalante* for dry land and exchanged the function of captain general for that of viceroy. The turn in his fortunes was sharp, and it came quickly. In years to come, when suffering in body from arthritis and in mind from the ingratitude of princes, Columbus must have sought consolation in the memory of those bright November days of 1493, the fleet gaily coasting along the lofty, verdure-clad Antilles with tradewind clouds piling up over the summits and rainbows bridging their deep-cleft valleys; of nights spent hove-to with his gallant ships all about, stars of incredible brightness overhead, and hearty voices joining in the evening hymn to the Blessed Virgin.

Evil Days at Isabela

Isabela was founded as a trading post, the only type of colony with which Columbus was familiar. Even as such the site was ill chosen, like so many of the first European colonies in America; for instance, Roanoke Island, Virginia, and St. Croix Island on the river of that name in Maine. Isabela had no proper harbor, only a roadstead open to the north and west, and no fresh water either. But Columbus was in a hurry to get his men ashore and send most of the ships home. He had wasted a month looking for a site which the Navidad garrison should have found, and the gold nuggets which they might have collected were not there. He must start trading quickly and produce something valuable to please his Sovereigns.

All the colonists and some of the seamen landed here. A town was laid out in classic form (for nothing less than a miniature Cadiz would suit the Admiral), with church and governor's palace fronting a square plaza—the pattern repeated wherever Spaniards settled in the New World. Men were put to work felling trees, cutting coral stone, and digging a canal to bring water from the nearest river, and some two hundred wattled huts were built as temporary housing. But insufficient wine and provisions had been brought over. Workers fell ill of malaria or from drinking well water and eating strange fish, although Dr. Chanca tried every new species on a dog before he would let any Christian touch it. Columbus, impatient to get things done, drafted some of the gentlemen volunteers for the hard labor, which caused great indignation; they had come out to fight or gather gold, not to do menial work. If they refused, they got no rations, and that was considered an abominable way to treat a Castilian hidalgo.

Many, however, were appeased by an early opportunity to gather gold. Isabela had been founded but four days when the Admiral organized an armed party to explore the Cibao and find the alleged mine. It was commanded by Alonso de Ojeda, an agile, handsome Andalusian who had attracted the Queen's attention and favor by the singular feat of pirouetting on a beam that projected from the Giralda, a tower 200 feet above the street in Seville.

With a score of Spaniards and native guides, Ojeda penetrated the great central valley of Hispaniola, the Vega Real, and reached the foothills of the Cordillera Setentrional in the Cibao. There he obtained three great gold nuggets, one with metal enough for a fifty-dollar gold piece. Within two weeks, on 20 January, he was back at Isabela bringing the first good news for many weeks. "All of us made merry," wrote Cuneo, "not caring any longer about spicery, but only for this blessed gold."

The Admiral feared that if he sent the ships home with nothing more than what Ojeda brought in, people might make nasty remarks about his line of samples—as they did. Yet he had to risk it, since the crews of seventeen ships were accumulating pay and eating up food, several hundred men were sick, Dr. Chanca had run out of drugs, and there were barely enough Spanish provisions left to see the fleet home.

So, retaining only *Mariagalante, Gallega, Niña,* and two smaller caravels, he dispatched the other twelve vessels under command of flag captain Antonio de Torres. Pierre Chaunu regards this eastward voyage of Torres as in a class with the Admiral's, for he not only made a record unbroken for centuries—35 days Isabela to Cadiz—but carried a real cargo. Thus Torres inaugurated the *carrera de Indias,* the regular trade between Spain and the West Indies. It is true that what Torres brought home was so-called cinnamon, only it tasted like bad ginger; strong pepper, but not with the flavor of Malayan pepper; wood said to be sandalwood, only it wasn't, not speaking of the 60 parrots and 26 Indian slaves; but gold to the value of 30,000 ducats sweetened the lot.

Antonio de Torres's fleet made Cadiz on 7 March 1494. As brother to the governess of Infante Don Juan, he had access to the Sovereigns and so was entrusted by Columbus with the outline of a report to present to them orally. This "Torres Memorandum" is a proof of Columbus's common-sense views on colonization. If he failed as a colonial administrator, it was not from odd ideas but from inability to control lazy and rough hidalgos who hated him as a foreigner. Las Casas wrote that the Archangel Gabriel would have been hard put to govern people as greedy, selfish, and egotistical as the early settlers of Hispaniola.

The gist of the Torres Memorandum was an appeal for more of everything—men, munitions, Spanish food and wine, tools, livestock, clothes, and shoes. Logistic supply in America was a major problem for all European pioneers; it will be remembered how the first English settlers in Virginia rotted and starved for want of their native bread, beef, and beer in a country abounding with maize, game, and good water; and how the French in Canada, a country teeming with fish, fowl, and venison, were always on the verge of starvation by spring.

Ferdinand and Isabella felt that most of their Viceroy's requests were reasonable. The only thing that the Queen rejected was his suggestion to build up a profitable export of Carib and other native slaves. Slavery was so taken for granted in those days, both by Europeans and Moslems (some of whom still practice it), that Columbus never gave a thought to the morality of this proposal. If he had, he would doubtless have reflected that the Indians enslaved each other, so why should we not enslave them, particularly if we convert them too, and save their souls? The Admiral concluded his memorandum by a generous tribute to Dr. Chanca and other subordinates, asked to have their salaries raised, and recommended that the two hundred gentlemen volunteers be placed on the royal payroll so that they could be controlled by him.

About a month after sending the fleet home under Torres, Columbus organized and in person led a reconnaissance in force of the interior, first of those overland marches of Spaniards in armor which set the pattern followed by Balboa, Cortés, Pizarro, and De Soto. In military formation with drums beating, trumpets sounding, and banners displayed, several hundred men set off from Isabela on 12 March 1494. Crossing the Cordillera Setentrional by a pass which Columbus named *El Puerto de los Hidalgos* after his gentlemen trailmakers, they soon came in view of a spacious valley "so fresh, so green, so open, of such color and altogether so full of beauty," wrote Las Casas, that "the Admiral, who was profoundly moved by all these things, gave great thanks to God and named it Vega Real," the Royal Plain. Guided by friendly Indians, they pushed up the northern slope of the cordillera to a mesa overlooking a bend of the Rio Janico, where Columbus left fifty men under Mosén Margarit to construct a rough earthen fort. "On that trip," wrote Cuneo, "we spent twenty-nine days with terrible weather, bad food, and worse drink; nevertheless, out of covetousness for that gold, we all kept strong and lusty."

Those left behind at Isabela were neither lusty nor strong. They had found no gold to compensate for living and working in that unhealthy spot. Almost the last of the Spanish provisions were spent. Discontent was rife, mutiny was seething, several troublemakers were in irons, and as a precaution Columbus placed all arms and munitions on board his flagship with brother Diego in command.

To raise morale and get rid of the troublemakers, he now planned a second reconnaissance in force under Ojeda, consisting of four hundred men with orders to march to Santo Tomás, relieve the garrison, and then explore the country and live off the natives. This was one of Columbus's worst decisions. He instructed Ojeda to do the Indians no harm, reminding him that the Sovereigns desired their salvation even more than their gold; but the first thing that Ojeda did was to cut off the ears of a native who stole some old clothes, and to send the cacique whom he considered responsible in chains to Isabela. Ojeda then relieved Margarit, who with some four hundred men roamed the Vega Real extorting gold from the natives, exhausting their food supplies, carrying off boys as slaves and young girls as concubines.

Before there was time for Columbus to learn of these doings, he had departed to explore Cuba, leaving his younger brother in charge at Isabela. That, too, was a mistake. Diego Colón, "a virtuous person, very discreet, peaceable and simple," was incapable of raising the morale of the colonists, much less of controlling people like Ojeda and Margarit. But Columbus felt that there was no one else in the colony whom he could trust.

✴ XVII ✴

Jamaica, Cuba, and Rebellion

1494-1496

Jamaica and the South Coast of Cuba

Between voyages, Columbus decided that Cuba must be the Chinese province of Mangi, the name which Marco Polo gave to all South China; and as the Sovereigns had ordered him to look into it, Columbus lost no time resuming his congenial role of discoverer. *Niña* served as flagship; the other two vessels that accompanied her were lateen-rigged caravels *San Juan* and *Cardera*. They are described as "much smaller" than *Niña* and carried crews of only fourteen to sixteen as compared with her twenty-eight to thirty. For officers, Columbus had one of the Niños, Pedro de Terreros, and several other veterans of his First Voyage. Fortunately for history, his gossipy friend Michele de Cuneo shipped as passenger, and Juan de La Cosa the chartmaker as able seaman. "Diego Colón," the best of the Indian converts, came along as interpreter, as did one of the priests.

The three caravels sailed from Isabela 24 April 1494. It was the best season for navigating the Greater Antilles, when the trades can be depended on by day and there is an offshore breeze at night; the air is still cool, and there is no danger of a hurricane. On the 29th they crossed the Windward Passage to Cape Alpha and Omega, as Columbus had named Cape Maisi on his First Voyage. He landed there, set

457

up a column and a cross, and again took formal possession of Cuba for Spain. On the advice of his officers, the Admiral decided to range the south rather than the north coast, "because should there be anything good it would rather be to the southward than the northward." This was Aristotle's ancient theory, supported by Portuguese experience in Africa, that the further south one sailed, the more gold and precious wares would be encountered.

From Cape Maisi on, the Spaniards made fresh discoveries. They sailed west by south for fifty miles along a cliff-rimmed coast, noting (as we did in our ketch *Mary Otis*) the sweet scent of the land, a combination of sea grape, cactus flowers, and other aromatic plants. As evening fell on the last day of April, they entered a great sickle-shaped harbor which Columbus named *Puerto Grande.* (This was Guantán- amo Bay, seat of an important United States naval base in the twentieth century). A shore party ascertained that the natives had fled in the midst of cooking a gigantic dinner of fish, iguana, and hutía (the small Cuban quadruped), to entertain a visiting cacique. Diego persuaded the cooks to return and share the feast with the Spaniards. They were well paid with hawks' bells and other trifles for their trouble of catching more fish to regale the cacique, and were relieved that their uninvited guests refused to touch iguana meat, roast iguana being the favorite native delicacy.

On May Day morning the fleet departed with the land breeze. As the ships sailed close to the bold shore, multitudes flocked to the water's edge or paddled out in canoes, offering cassava bread and sweet water, and begging the "men from the sky" to call. There had been no unfortunate incidents between Spaniards and natives in Cuba. Race relations there were still "of the Golden Age," and Columbus, to his credit, kept them so.

Forty miles west of Guantánamo the Admiral noted a break in the sierra and sailed through a narrow, cliff-bordered channel into the great bay where twenty years later Diego de Velásquez founded the city of Santiago de Cuba. Again, relations with the natives, who had "the loveliest gardens in the world," were idyllic. Departing at dawn 2 May, the fleet sailed through the waters in which, four centuries later, the Battle of Santiago concluded the long and glorious history of Spanish sea power in the New World.

After sailing all night, Columbus on 3 May, feast of the Discovery

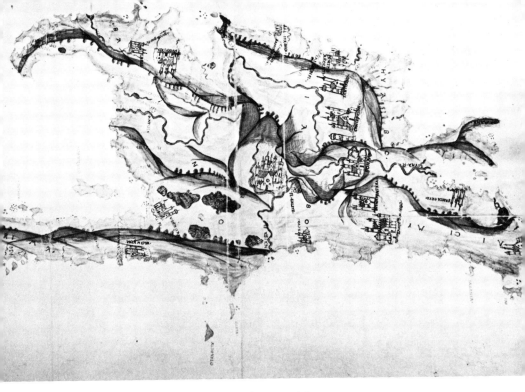

Peter Martyr's map of Hispaniola, 1516.

of the True Cross, landed at a cape that he named Cabo de Cruz, and it is still so called. Instead of turning into the Gulf of Guacanayabó, he decided to take off for Jamaica, of whose existence he had been told by the natives of Santiago. Here he hoped to find gold; for Cuba, so far as he could ascertain, had none.

The trades blew up strong and the fleet had a rough passage of two days, part of the time hove-to. When it moderated enough to make sail, and all hands had been on deck for many hours, the Admiral considerately sent everyone below to rest while he himself set about making sail all alone. I do not imagine he could have done much more than cast off a few gaskets and trim the braces before the sleepers were awakened by the slatting of sails and the change of motion, and came topside to help. But this incident illustrates a pleasant side of Columbus's character and helps to explain the loyalty of common sailors to him.

On 5 May the fleet anchored in St. Ann's Bay, Jamaica, which

Jamaica, Portland Bight. David Crofoot photo.

Columbus named *Santa Gloria*. He declared that this island, half the area of Sicily, was "the fairest that eyes have beheld," mountainous and heavily populated. Sixty or seventy Indian warriors came out in dugout canoes to meet the fleet and showed every sign of giving fight; but a blank cannon shot sent them paddling furiously shoreward. Columbus proceeded to the next port west, Rio Bueno. There the natives made another hostile demonstration, but Columbus attacked with his ships' boats, armed with crossbowmen who "pricked them well and killed a number." Then he set upon them a great dog which "bit them and did them great hurt, for a dog is worth ten men against Indians." These tactics of worrying Indians with big, savage dogs were practised in the New World, as earlier they had been on the Guanches in the Canaries. The natives of Rio Bueno, also Tainos, appeased the Spaniards with provisions but were unable to produce gold. So the Admiral made but one more call in Jamaica, at Montego Bay, then sailed back on the starboard tack to Cape Cruz.

The fleet now resumed its exploration of the south Cuban coast, alert for evidences of Chinese culture. They sailed around the Gulf of Guacanayabó, and at sunrise 15 May 1494 sighted an archipelago of small islands. These were the inshore group of the Laberinto de Doze Leguas. Columbus named this archipelago *El Jardín de la Reina*, the Queen's Garden. According to his description, these cays were then very beautiful; some under cultivation and others adorned with royal palms and calabash trees. The Spaniards admired the flamingoes— "great birds like cranes, but bright red"—and watched the natives hunting turtle with a fish hound. An Indian would catch and train a pilot fish (which has suckers on its head) and let it out on a leash when turtles were about. The fish would then attach itself to a shell, which his Indian master had only to haul in to capture the turtle; the pilot fish was politely thanked and rewarded with bits of meat. This was one of Columbus's tales that Europeans found most difficult to believe, but it was true; and when I sailed through those waters more than thirty years ago, I was told that native Cubans still practised the same method of catching turtle. But we found the "Queen's Garden" a sad disappointment. Mangrove had driven all other plants off the cays, and most of the mangrove had been killed in a hurricane. The channels are so intricate and shallow that we felt Columbus must have been as good a navigator in shoal water as on the ocean.

The three caravels put to sea through the Boca Grande, then shaped a course for the Sierra de Trinidad. As they sailed along this bold coast, natives again flocked to the shore bearing gifts and welcoming the Spaniards as "men from the sky." But not one Chinese junk or sampan or temple or bridge! Could it be that the culture of Cathay had not reached this outlying part of the Grand Khan's dominions? Or was this only one more big island?

Columbus missed the narrow entrance to the bay where Cienfuegos later rose, but investigated the Gulf of Cochinos, which in 1961 acquired notoriety as the "Bay of Pigs," scene of an abortive invasion by exiled Cubans. He observed the subterranean streams that break out from under the sea and enable sailors to fill their water casks without going ashore. "The water was so cold, and of such goodness and so sweet," said Columbus, "that no better could be found in the world." He and a shore party "rested there on the grass by those springs amid the scent of the flowers, which was marvelous, and the sweetness of the singing of little birds, so many and so delightful, and under the shade of those palms, so tall and fair that it was a wonder to see it all." Andrés Bernáldez set all this down from the Admiral's own lips.

We hardly need labor the point that Columbus's appreciation of the beauties of nature was equal to that of eighteenth-century romancers, and unique among pioneers in the age of discovery.

The little fleet now entered the Gulf of Batabanó, where the Admiral saw a phenomenon that has intrigued many later navigators: the sea water turning as white as milk, and then black as ink. The white is caused by fine marl becoming roiled by waves in the shallow waters, and the inky color by black sand similarly stirred up. The shores of this gulf, said the Admiral in vivid language, were of mangrove "so thick a cat couldn't get ashore." By 27 May he reached the tip end of the Zapata Peninsula, which he called *Punta del Serafín* because it was the feast of All Angels; he crossed the Ensenada Broa and anchored near the present town of Batabanó.

And as yet no sign of China!

Sailing westward along the southern shore of the Province of Pinar del Rio, the caravels became involved in the worst shoals yet experienced. They could get through some channels only by the laborious process of kedging—rowing an anchor ahead, dropping it, and hauling the vessel up to it by the windlass while her keel scraped the mud. They even passed the limit of Taino culture and entered the last stronghold of the Siboney. Diego the interpreter could not understand them.

Somewhere along this line, a contemporary manuscript called the Sneyd Codex states that Columbus took off to the southward and discovered South America. Nothing to it! He didn't have time.

Columbus now figured out by mathematics that he was at least half the way around the world; actually he was at longitude 84° West of Greenwich, less than one-quarter around. Assuming the Bahia Cortés, where Cuban land trends south, to be the Gulf of Siam, he believed that he was hot on the trail of the Strait of Malacca. So, why not return to Spain around the world, hooking up with the tracks of Bartholomew Dias and Vasco da Gama?

Fortunately the common sense of a good seaman came to his rescue. The caravels were leaky because of frequent groundings; their rigging had deteriorated to shreds and tatters; provisions were low, and the seamen were growling and grumbling. So the Admiral decided to reverse course. Following the precedent established by Dias in 1488 when forced to turn back from the very gates of India, Columbus took a deposition from almost every man in his little fleet to the effect that Cuba must be part of a continent, that it was useless to sail further to prove it, since no island of that length could exist! Actually, they were then about fifty miles from Cape San Antonio, the western promontory of Cuba. This procedure did not convince even Juan de La Cosa, who represents an insular Cuba on his famous mappemonde dated 1500.

The return to Isabela began on 13 June 1494. For the most part it was a tiresome beat to windward among the same cays as on the outward passage, because the fleet could make no progress in deep water against the trade winds and the westward-flowing current. "If the ships in the Indies only sail with the wind abaft the beam," wrote Columbus, "it is not from bad design or clumsiness; the great currents, which run there in the same direction as the wind, so make it that nobody attempts to struggle close-hauled, for in one day they would lose what they gained in seven; nor do I except caravels, even Portuguese lateeners." His good windward record with *Niña* and *Pinta* in 1493 had been made in deep water with little or no current. Sailing vessels never could cope with the conditions Columbus describes until the advent of the modern racing yachts, and even they usually do so by "turning on the juice." William Hickey, writing at St. Mary's, Jamaica, in the last years of the eighteenth century, tells of watching a ship trying to beat ten miles eastward from Kingston to Port Morant. Every day for eight days she stood out to sea close-hauled on the port tack, and every evening, sailing close-hauled on the starboard tack, she returned to the same position.

Columbus now learned that the only way to make progress to windward in the Caribbean was to stay in smooth water, avoid the current, and work the land breeze at night. It took him 25 days to make good about 200 miles. By the time he reached the Queen's Garden he could stand no more mud navigation, and made for blue water. And then it took him ten days to make 180 miles to windward. Provisions had to be rationed to a pound of weevily biscuit and a pint of sour wine a day, and the sailors worked constantly at the pumps. Finally, on 18 July, they reached Cabo de Cruz and were well entertained by friendly Indians. Rather than endure another long beat to windward along the ironbound coast of Oriente Province, the Admiral decided to ease off his sheets and learn more about Jamaica.

Montego Bay he again entered on 21 July. From that future scene of sport and fashion he passed close aboard the pretty harbor of

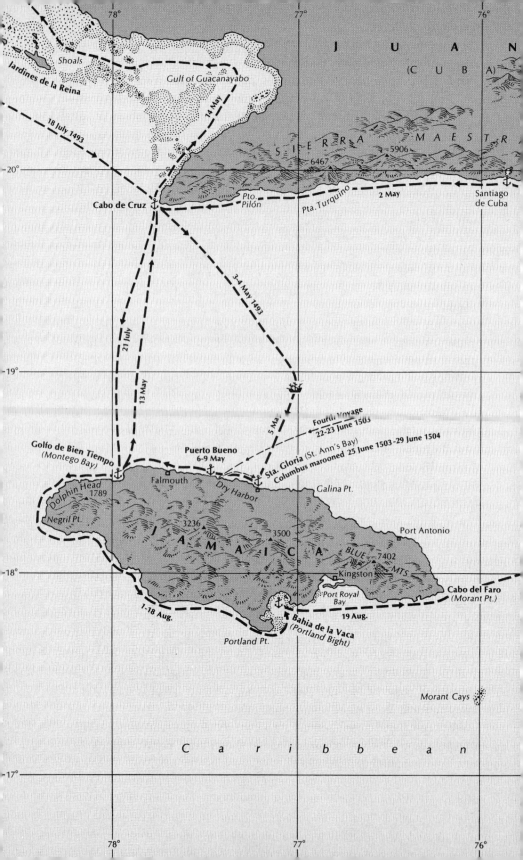

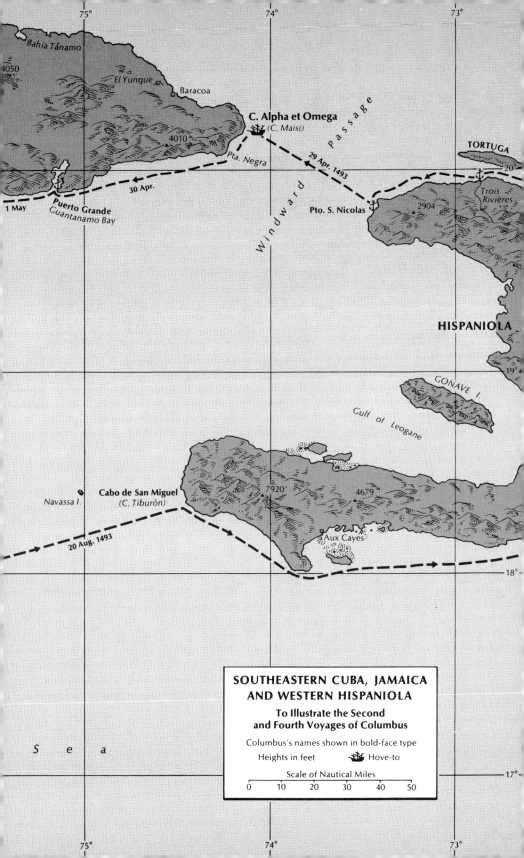

Bahía Tánamo

4050

El Yunque

Baracoa

4010

C. Alpha et Omega
(C. Maisi)

Pta. Negra

29 Apr. 1493

W i n d w a r d   P a s s a g e

TORTUGA

20°

Trois
Rivières

2904

30 Apr.

1 May

Puerto Grande
Guantanamo Bay

Pto. S. Nicolas

HISPANIOLA

19°

GONAVE I.

Gulf   of   Leogane

Navassa I.

Cabo de San Miguel
(C. Tiburón)

7920

4679

20 Aug. 1493

Aux Cayes

18°

S   e   a

17°

**SOUTHEASTERN CUBA, JAMAICA
AND WESTERN HISPANIOLA**

**To Illustrate the Second
and Fourth Voyages of Columbus**

Columbus's names shown in bold-face type

Heights in feet   Hove-to

Scale of Nautical Miles

0   10   20   30   40   50

75°   74°   73°

Jamaica: Lucea Harbor. David Crofoot photo.

Lucea, then hauled around the western end of Jamaica to the south coast and edged along, anchoring every night. The Indians were friendly; one cacique embarrassingly so. He came out to the flagship with a fleet of canoes, his family and suite dressed in magnificent parrot-feather headdresses and little else. The cacique wore a coronet of small polished stones and some large disks of gold and copper alloy that he must have obtained from Central America. In the bow of his canoe stood a herald wearing a cloak of red feathers and carrying a white banner. His wife was similarly adorned with native jewelry, although she wore nothing that could be called clothing except "a little cotton thing no bigger than an orange peel." Their beautiful daughters, aged about 15 and 18, were completely naked. When they drew alongside, the Admiral was in his cabin, so absorbed in reading the office of terce that he did not notice them until they were on board. The cacique then proposed, through Diego Colón, that he and his family sail to Spain with the Admiral to visit the Catholic Sovereigns, "and to see the wonders of Castile." Here was a golden opportunity for Columbus to make a hit at court, but humanity prevailed. He thought of the cold weather on the voyage home, of the indignities that the pretty daughters might suffer from the sailors, and of the effect of a complete change of climate on these innocent souls. So he sent them ashore with gifts, after receiving the cacique's homage and fealty to Ferdinand and Isabella.

On 19 August the fleet cleared Morant Point, the eastern cape of Jamaica, crossed the Windward Passage, and sighted Cape Tiburón, Haiti. By the end of the month they reached Alta Vela, the sail-like rock which marks the southernmost point of Hispaniola.

Saona Island, behind which the three caravels anchored to ride out a hurricane, was so named for Savona, the home town of Michele de Cuneo, the Admiral's merry guest. A total eclipse of the moon took place on 14 September while the fleet lay there, and Columbus, who had an almanac which gave the time of the eclipse at Nuremberg, tried by timing it at Saona to calculate the longitude. It was a simple enough calculation—15 degrees to an hour's time—but something went wrong and the Admiral worked out a longitude too far west by 23 degrees. Building on that gross error, it was easy for Columbus to persuade

Alta Vela: David Crofoot photo.

himself that he had been well on his way around the world when he turned back from Cuba.

The Admiral intended to make a side trip to Puerto Rico, but in the Mona Passage he fell ill. His symptoms suggest a nervous breakdown as the result of lack of sleep, frequent drenching, and inadequate food. Probably he also had the beginning of arthritis, which troubled him gravely during the last ten years of his life. His officers held a council and decided to scud before the wind to Isabela, where the three caravels anchored on 29 September 1494. The Admiral had to be carried ashore in the arms of his seamen.

Although Columbus had not found the empire of the Grand Khan, he had accomplished a great deal on this round voyage of five months from Isabela. He had opened up what proved to be the most valuable of Spain's insular possessions. He had discovered Jamaica. He had demonstrated that he was no less apt at coastal piloting and island hopping than at charting a course across the ocean and conducting a fleet off soundings. Shipmates of that voyage never tired of extolling his feats of navigation, his humanity, and his consideration for them.

Hispaniola and Home

Good news met the Admiral upon landing at Isabela. His brother Bartholomew, whom he had not seen for six years, had arrived. News traveled so slowly from Spain to France that Bartholomew never heard about the success of the First Voyage until too late to embark on the Second. But Ferdinand and Isabella were highly impressed by "Don Bartolomé," as they called him, gave him command of three caravels to take provisions to Hispaniola, and conferred the title of *Adelantado,* advancer. He was not only an expert sailor and cartographer but a far better administrator than his brilliant brother. Intelligent without being an intellectual, he had an innate sense of leadership. Curt in speech and tough with subordinates, he lacked the "sweetness and benignity" that Las Casas saw in Christopher, but he never lost courage or fell ill. Unexpected situations on land or sea he met with promptness and resolution.

It is most regrettable that Bartholomew missed the Second Voyage because he, if anyone, could have averted the appalling situation in Hispaniola which his weak younger brother Diego had allowed to develop. It must be said, however, that the three Columbus brothers had two strikes against them from the start: they were Genoese and the colonists were Spaniards. Spain was the most fiercely nationalistic of European nations, and her sons who went to the New World to seek their fortunes were not only brave and rugged but often greedy and unreasonable. Oviedo, in his *History of the Indies* that came out in 1535, wrote that any early governor of Hispaniola, "to succeed, must be superhuman." And Christopher had already made two bad mistakes—appointing Diego his deputy, and turning Ojeda and Margarit loose in the interior.

During the Admiral's absence, Diego heard about the cruelty and rapacity of Margarit and sent him an order to mend his ways, which so enraged the Spaniard that he roared into Isabela demanding retraction—or else. When he didn't get it, he joined other malcontents in seizing the caravels which Bartholomew had brought out from Spain, and sailed home, where he circulated slanders against the Columbus brothers. A Sevillian goldsmith of the party even declared openly that none of the gold in Hispaniola was genuine.

Before the end of 1494, Antonio de Torres arrived at Isabela in command of four caravels bringing provisions and supplies. He delivered a friendly letter to the Admiral from the King and Queen, who urged him to leave Hispaniola in charge of his "brother or some other person" and come home to help them negotiate with Portugal. Columbus made a great mistake in not accepting this invitation; pride compelled him to try to master the local situation, and to provide a profitable export to Spain. To do that, he adopted the questionable policy of rounding up and enslaving Indians who had resisted Margarit's men. Time and again Columbus had asserted that the Tainos were the most kindly, peaceful, and generous people in the world, and the Sovereigns had particularly enjoined him to treat them as such. But, by the close of February 1495, when Torres was ready to sail to Spain, the Columbus brothers had collected 1500 Indian captives at Isabela. Torres loaded 500 of them, all his four ships could take. The Admiral then allowed every Spaniard at Isabela to help himself to as many of the remainder as he chose, and the rest were told to get out. Cuneo records how these wretched captives, when released, fled as far as they could from the Spaniards; women even abandoned infants in their fear and desperation to escape further cruelty. But at least they were free; the lot of the slaves shipped home was worse. Some two hundred died at sea. The survivors were landed at Seville where Andrés Bernáldez, the clerical chronicler, saw them put up for sale "naked as they were born." He added that they were "not very profitable since almost all died, for the country did not agree with them."

A cacique named Guatiguaná now tried to unite the Indians of Hispaniola, estimated to be at least 250,000 in number, against the Spaniards. He managed to collect a formidable army in the Vega Real to march on Isabela. The Spaniards took the offensive. The Admiral, Bartholomew, and Ojeda marched to the Puerto de los Hidalgos with 20 horse, 20 hounds, and 200 foot, half of them armed with arquebuses. The fire from these primitive muskets alarmed the Tainos more than it harmed them, but when Ojeda charged at the head of the cavalry, dashing into the closely huddled mass of Indians, and at the same time unleashed the savage dogs, their rout became complete. This, the first pitched battle between Europeans and Indians, took place at the end of March 1495. Ojeda followed up his victory by capturing Caonabó, toughest of the caciques, who had been responsible for exterminating the Navidad garrison.

The original Isabela beachhead now expanded to cover the entire island. The Admiral himself made a triumphal march across Hispaniola, which by 1496 was so thoroughly subdued that a Spaniard could safely go wherever he pleased and help himself to the Indians' food, women, and gold.

For almost a year the Columbus brothers were occupied with subjugating and organizing Hispaniola in order to obtain as much gold as possible. Several forts were built in the interior, and armed men were sent to force the natives to deliver a gold tribute. The *repartimientos* system, which later spread to all Spanish America, was begun by Columbus. This meant that grants were made to the individual colonist *with the natives there living*, who were his to have and hold, exploit, punish, or torture, as he chose; subject always (Spanish apologists are fond of pointing out) to the Laws of the Indies which enjoined conversion and kind treatment. But these were seldom enforced. This cruel policy initiated by Columbus and relentlessly pursued by his successors resulted in genocide. Of the estimated native population of 250,000 in 1492, not 500 remained alive in 1538.

Lest we become smug about modern progress and humanity, I wish to remind the reader that exactly the same policy of *repartimientos*, this time to obtain wild rubber and unpaid native labor, was applied to blacks in the Belgian Congo at the turn of this century, and a few years later to Indians in the Portumayo, the upper Amazon, by Peru and a British company. Brian Inglis's noble biography of Roger Casement, who did his best to abolish this atrocious state of things, has evidence that in the Portumayo, at least, virtual slavery of the Indians existed as late as 1970.

The calumnies of Fray Buil, Margarit, and others against Columbus made their mark on the Sovereigns, who sent Juan Aguado, a colonist who had returned to Spain with Torres, to investigate the charges and report to them. He arrived at Isabela in command of four provision ships in October 1495 and at once began throwing his weight around. Columbus now realized he had better return home to mend his political fences. The Spanish population of the island, mostly concentrated at Isabela, had now fallen to 630, partly owing to deaths from disease, partly because many had gone home. A large number of those left behind were sick, and all were discontented. In this rich, fertile land with beautiful climate, they were still dependent on imported provisions. Nobody, unless under compulsion, would trouble to sow grain, said Cuneo, because "nobody wants to live in these countries"; and the most potent oath heard at Isabela was, "As God may take me to Castile, I'm telling you the truth!"

Finally, naming brother Bartholomew governor in his absence, Columbus sailed home in *Niña* on 10 March 1496.

This return from the Second Voyage was a sad contrast to the pomp, pride, and superb equipment of the outward passage in 1493. *Niña*'s sole consort was a 50-tun caravel named *India* which had been built at Isabela from the timbers of two vessels wrecked in a hurricane. The two caravels were dangerously overcrowded with 225 Spaniards and 30 Indian slaves. Columbus was eager to make best speed home, but so few return passages had yet been made that nobody knew the quickest route; and he decided to jump off from the Leeward Islands. That was the shortest rhumb-line to Spain, but it turned out to be the longest in time, because of the necessity to buck headwinds most of the way. The caravels took twelve days to clear Hispaniola, and two weeks more to reach Guadeloupe, where the Admiral wished to lay in a supply of native provisions. Here his first shore party was met by an army of Carib women armed with bows and arrows, from which he concluded that this was the Isle of Amazons. Only by securing as hostages three boys and ten women, one of them a cacique's lady, were the Spaniards able to force the Caribs to provide a supply of cassava roots. These, if properly prepared so as to eliminate the poison, a process that the Indians taught the Spaniards, produced a flour which made a nourishing and palatable bread. The lady cacique and her daughter, so Columbus declared, volunteered to accompany him to Spain, and were accepted. They died en route, or shortly after.

On 20 April 1496, *Niña* and *India* departed Guadeloupe. We have no details of the next month's sailing except that it was very slow, and mostly beating to windward. After a month at sea, all hands were put on a short allowance of six ounces of cassava bread and a cup of water per diem. About that time, providentially, they caught a westerly breeze south of the Azores, but hunger increased daily. Some Spaniards proposed eating the Indians, starting with the Caribs who were man-eaters themselves; it wouldn't be a sin to pay them in their own coin! Others proposed that all natives be thrown overboard so that they would consume no more rations. Columbus, in one of his humanitarian moods, argued that after all Caribs were people and should be treated as such. The debate was still undecided on 8 June when they made landfall on the Portuguese coast almost exactly where the Admiral intended, about 35 miles north of Cape St. Vincent. The several pilots on board thought they were still hundreds of miles from shore and heading for Galicia. Columbus's success at hitting the land "on the nose" after six weeks at sea, much of it sailing a zigzag course, convinced all the seafaring tribe of his high competence at dead-reckoning navigation. The only doubts have been raised by library navigators of recent decades.

On 11 June 1496, Columbus's Second Voyage to America ended in the Bay of Cadiz. Every available banner was broken out and all pendants run up to make as brave an appearance as possible, but it was a sad show at best, what with the miserable Indians and Spanish passengers whom an onlooker described as wasted in their bodies and with "faces the color of saffron."

Two years and nine months had passed since the Admiral's great fleet of seventeen sail departed Cadiz with hearts high and grandiose expectations of founding a valuable colony and locating the emperor of China. From the point of view of the average intelligent Spaniard, all that had been a phantom, and Columbus now seemed an impractical

Autograph Letter of Columbus. To the Bank of St. George, Genoa, 2 April 1502, with his signature. Relating to his *mayorazgo*, or entail, which the Bank is to administer. Courtesy Archives of Genoa.

dreamer. Cuba was no limb of China; anyone who talked with a member of the exploring expedition could see that. His town of Isabela, instead of being a rich trading factory like the Portuguese São Jorge da Mina on the Gold Coast, was a miasmic dump which even the Columbus brothers were abandoning. Instead of the promised gold mine of the Cibao, gold was diffused in small quantities over the island and could only be produced by slave labor. Instead of golden-age simplicity and peacefulness, the natives were beginning to show fight. Nor was there even the consoling thought that before being killed the Indians had been assured of eternal life; none save the few brought home to Spain had yet been baptized. And so loud and angry were the cries of returned Spaniards against the Columbus brothers that the Sovereigns must have been tempted to dismiss them and forget about the Indies. Possibly that is what they would have done had they not heard that the king of Portugal was about to fit out a new expedition to India (Vasco da Gama's), and that Henry VII of England had engaged John Cabot to find a short, high-latitude ocean route to China.

✳ XVIII ✳

Third Voyage, Mainland Discovered

Preparations

Columbus frequently "wrestled with God" to find out why things turned out so badly for him. He performed his religious duties regularly and did his best to convert the Indians to the True Faith; so why did Providence frown on his undertakings? He had served the Sovereigns faithfully, respected their every wish and guarded their interests, and had won for them a new empire overseas; why, then, did they listen to his enemies and send out a low fellow to insult him? He had made all practical preparations, kept his ships staunch, his people healthy, and his powder dry; but now, it would seem, every Spaniard's hand was against him. Why? Why? Why? The Book of Job afforded him consolation, but no clue. Perhaps it was because he had embraced the deadly sin of pride after his First Voyage, had worn excessive apparel (as befitted the rank of admiral), had consorted too much with high company, partaken of rich viands and rare vintages? Pride, to be sure, is a deadly sin. So, upon arrival at Cadiz and ever after, Columbus assumed the coarse brown habit of a Franciscan as evidence of humility, and instead of accepting invitations to castles and palaces, he put up in religious houses with rough quarters and coarse fare. While awaiting

475

a royal command to appear at court, he stayed with a priest named Andrés Bernáldez, chaplain to the archbishop of Seville.

The Admiral might be ostentatiously simple in his habits, but he knew very well the value of publicity. So, when an invitation came from the Sovereigns to visit them, he organized another impressive cavalcade. Two members of the cacique Caonabó's family accompanied him on muleback. Servants rode ahead with cages of brightly colored parrots whose screams heralded the arrival of the hero and his suite. Whenever they entered an important town, Caonabó's brother wore around his neck a massy gold collar, and on his head the cacique's crown, "very big and tall, with wings on its sides like a shield and golden eyes as large as silver cups." Unfortunately, none of these priceless objects has survived, but many others of the kind have since been dug up and preserved in the museums of Europe and America.

Columbus found the King and Queen and his sons Diego and Ferdinand, pages to the Queen, at Valladolid. He was courteously received, especially after presenting the Sovereigns with a clutch of gold nuggets as big as pigeons' eggs. Promptly he put in a plea to be outfitted for a Third Voyage. Five ships he wished to be laden with provisions for Hispaniola and three for himself, to seek out a continent which, as he put it, the king of Portugal believed to be in the ocean south or southeast of the Antilles, and the existence of which had been confirmed by hints received from the Indians. D. João II of Portugal was dead, but the fact that he believed in the existence of this continent stimulated Ferdinand and Isabella to get there first. But Columbus could get nothing but vague promises from the Sovereigns until news from Portugal indicated that João's successor, D. Manuel I, was fitting out a big overseas expedition under Vasco da Gama that was almost ready to depart, destination unknown. Might he not be looking for this same part of the world?

The Sovereigns confirmed Columbus's rights, titles, and privileges and ordered him to recruit three hundred colonists for Hispaniola at the royal expense. Wages started at about fourteen cents a day for a common workman or soldier and rose to forty-two gold dollars a year for farmers and gardeners, plus eight cents a day for keep. Also, they authorized Columbus to recruit for the expedition thirty women who received neither pay nor keep but were expected to work their passage and marry upon arrival. These were the first Christian women to go to the New World since Leif Ericsson's scandalous kindred. All malefactors confined in jail, excepting traitors and heretics, were offered pardon if they would sail with the Admiral to the Indies and stay a year or two. Hispaniola had been so discredited that this was supposed to be the only way to obtain emigrants to the future "Land of Promise." Columbus sent these fellows in the squadron direct to Hispaniola, which he later had reason to regret.

The Admiral found it very difficult to equip his new fleet, because most of it had to be done on credit. He had numerous rows with Bishop Fonseca, who had immediate charge of preparations, and on one occasion became so exasperated with a rascally ship chandler as to knock him down. But, as may be seen by the following task organization, every ship and most of the officers came from Palos. This indicates a lasting confidence in the Admiral by the shipowners and seamen of the town where he obtained his first recruits in 1492.

In January 1498 *Niña* and *India* left for Hispaniola; and three more caravels followed shortly with supplies. These were commanded respectively by Alonso Sánchez de Carvajal, one of Columbus's most faithful captains, and a veteran of his Second Voyage; Pedro de Harana, brother to the Admiral's mistress; and "Gianetto" Colombo, the Admiral's first cousin. We shall encounter this fleet later. The list of those on the Third Voyage of Discovery, and of a second Hispaniola replenishment squadron, follows:—

THIRD VOYAGE TASK ORGANIZATION *
CAPTAIN GENERAL: CHRISTOPHER COLUMBUS

DISCOVERY SQUADRON

Flagship, SANTA MARIA DE GUÍA, *nao* of 101 tuns. Cristóbal Quintero of Palos, master and owner; Bartolomé Ruiz of Palos, assistant master.

Caravel LA CASTILLA (nicknamed VAQUEÑOS), 70 tuns, Pedro de Terreros, captain; Andrés García Galdin, master.

Caravel LA GORDA (nicknamed CORREO), 60 tuns, Hernán Pérez, captain.

The Hispaniola Squadron, which went direct from Ferro to Santo Domingo, consisted of three more caravels under Carvajal.

* Compiled from Capitán de Corbeta Roberto Barreiro-Meiro, "Las Naves del Tercer Viaje de Colón," *Revista General de Marina*, Feb. 1970, which corrects and augments my *Admiral of the Ocean Sea*, I, 228–32.

Third Voyage, to Trinidad

Both squadrons assembled at Seville and departed during the last week of May 1498—the same week that Vasco da Gama arrived at Calicut in India. All six dropped down the Guadalquivir to the roadstead of Sanlúcar da Barrameda, where the Admiral came on board, and on 30 May the Third Voyage to America began.

Columbus decided to sail a more southerly course than heretofore, both in hope of finding D. João's predicted continent, and to seek more gold, holding to the ancient belief that all precious things were to be found in abundance near the Equator. So he planned to sail south to the supposed latitude of Sierra Leone, where the Portuguese had found Guinea gold, and then sail due west. Again, old-fashioned latitude sailing. The Admiral knew very well that he must do something spectacular on this voyage or the whole Enterprise of the Indies might be abandoned. He sometimes compared himself to David, who was commanded to perform incredible tasks and did so, but each time fell into greater disfavor with Saul. He had discovered a western route to the Indies, but that was not enough. He had led a great fleet to Hispaniola, founded a colony there, discovered the Lesser Antilles, Puerto Rico, and Jamaica, explored Cuba, but that was not enough. He must now discover more gold and a continent (which he did)—even that was not enough. Of course he could now have retired with a title, a castle, and a pension, and left brother Bartholomew to rule Hispaniola; but he felt that there was a lot more discovering to be done in the Indies, that he was the one person capable of doing it; and he owed it to the Sovereigns to do just that. Columbus was not the kind of man to sell out. Had he been, we would never have heard of him.

At Funchal in Madeira, where he had formerly resided, he was now received as a hero. Thence he made a three-day run to the familiar roadstead of San Sebastián, Gomera. The romance with Doña Beatriz had evidently died, since all that Columbus or anyone else wrote about this call at her capital was, "We loaded cheeses." It was probably well for the Admiral that this flirtation never ripened into marriage, for Doña Beatriz was cruel as well as beautiful. A gentleman of Gomera who spread rumors of her unchastity after Columbus's previous call was invited to visit her at the castle. This "tea for two" abruptly ended when the lady rang for her retainers and ordered them to hang her guest on a rafter in the castle hall, until he died. To rub it in and discourage gossips, she then had his corpse strung up outside his own residence. Eventually she married D. Alonso de Lugo, captain and conqueror of the Grand Canary, a very suitable husband.

At Gomera, Carvajal's Hispaniola squadron of three caravels, one commanded by the Admiral's cousin "Gianetto" Colombo, parted from the exploring expedition. They made the Dominica landfall as directed, but afterward got into trouble, as we shall see.

From the Canaries, Columbus shaped a course for the Cape Verde Islands, covering 750 miles in six days. He made a brief stop at Boavista to salt down goat mutton, the only meat available; then, on 1 July, called at Santiago in the hope of obtaining cattle to breed in Hispaniola. After staying a week there in heat so intense that many of his people fell ill, he departed with no cattle. On 7 July the trades sprang up, and Columbus shaped a course southwest, seeking the parallel of Sierra Leone. But the wind grew more and more soft, and finally died completely on 13 July when the fleet had reached about latitude 9° 30′ N, longitude 29° W. They were in the doldrums, and for the next eight days drifted with the equatorial current. Their crews, who would have thought it suicidal to strip down and cultivate sun-tans, sweltered in their thick woolen clothes. The Admiral profited (as he thought) from the calm to observe the North Star with his quadrant, but as usual in his efforts at celestial navigation, made so many mistakes that he found the latitude to be 5° N, over 250 miles too far south. He was pleased to believe that he had reached 5° N for a curious reason. Many years before, José Vizinho, a famous Portuguese navigator, had taken the latitude of the Los Islands off the coast of Sierra Leone and found it to be 5° N, as Columbus had been informed. But even Portuguese navigators were not always impeccable; the true latitude of the Los Islands is 9° 30′ N, very close to where Columbus's fleet actually was! The only result of his four-and-a-half-degree error was to throw off all subsequent latitude calculations on this voyage.

On 22 July 1498, a fresh trade wind sprang up from the ESE, slack lines became taut, limp sails bellied out, the ships quickly gathered way, the temperature dropped, and the sailors, who had half expected to rot and die in mid-ocean (for none had before experienced whole days of calm), began talking about the gold they were going to find. The

Cabo de la Galera, Trinidad.

Admiral set the course due west, and for nine days, with a prosperous blast from the trade winds, his fleet made an average speed of six knots or better.

This leg of the voyage must have been almost pure delight to Columbus and his men; we know that, as we followed the same route in our *Capitana* in 1939. Day and night the fleet made exceptional speed. In the trades, vessels always roll a good deal, but the fair and steady wind singing in the rigging, the sapphire white-capped sea, the rush of great waters alongside, and the endless succession of puffy trade-wind clouds lift a seaman's spirits. The old-time Spanish mariners called these broad waters *El Golfo de las Damas*, the Ladies' Sea; so easy is the navigation, so mild and genial the climate. Occasionally a black squall makes up from windward but passes harmlessly with a brief lash of rain. For days the sheets and braces need no attention except to alter the nip on the block so that the lines will not chafe. Flying fish and dorados play about, and the pelagic birds, petrels and the like, pay brief visits.

Sailors can always find something to grumble about and now it was the continual fair wind. How will we ever get back to Spain if we go on this way? said they. But even though the Admiral's latitude was screwy, he was keeping a good dead reckoning and knew almost exactly where he was, relative to the discoveries of the Second Voyage. On 31 July he announced that he was on the meridian of the Lesser Antilles, which was correct, and since the supply of fresh water was dangerously low, he would make a northern detour to water up in Dominica or some other Caribee isle. That very morning he altered the course to N by E.

At noon the Admiral's servant Alonso Pérez, having gone aloft, sang out that he saw land to the westward in the form of three hills. "All glorified the divine bounty and with great joy and merriment they repeated, singing, the *Salve Regina* with other devout canticles and prayers which glorify God and Our Lady, according to the custom of mariners." Columbus, having placed this voyage under the special protection of the Holy Trinity, regarded the three hills of the landfall an answer to prayer, and named the island Trinidad.

Changing course to approach the land, they sighted the southeastern point of the island. Columbus named it *Cabo de la Galera*, Galley Cape, because its peaked cliffs resemble lateen sails, and diagonal marks on the rocks suggest a bank of oars. The fleet arrived off this cape about 9:00 p.m. and, as the moon was nearly full, jogged westward all night.

Next day, the first of August, the Admiral continued along the south coast of Trinidad, searching for a bay that would have a river emptying into it. With his usual good judgment, he chose the best watering place on that coast, now called Erin Bay, where a stream of cool, sweet water crosses the beach. The men went ashore, washed their clothes, wallowed in the fresh water to sluice the caked salt and sweat from their bodies. and had a fine time splashing and yelling, and hallooing into the jungle in the hope that some pretty native girls might respond.

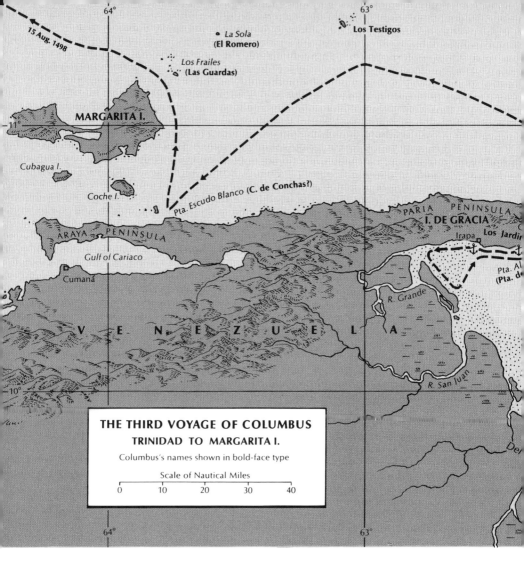

Columbus's names shown in bold-face type

THE THIRD VOYAGE OF COLUMBUS
TRINIDAD TO MARGARITA I.

Scale of Nautical Miles

| 0 | 10 | 20 | 30 | 40 |

First Continental Landing

Columbus weighed anchor at Erin Bay on 2 August and sailed through
the Boca de la Sierpe into the great Gulf of Paria that lies between
Trinidad and the mainland. He must have sailed through the Boca at
turn of tide, for he made no remark about the current that swirls
dangerously around the mid-channel rock, which he named *El Gallo*
(the cock); it is now Soldado. Columbus anchored in the lee of Icacos
Point, Trinidad, and ordered all hands ashore in relays for a few days'

482

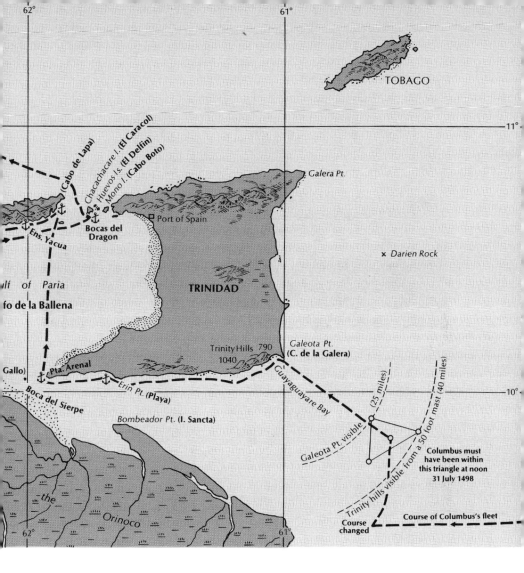

relaxation. They amused themselves fishing and gathering oysters, while the Admiral caused the Boca to be sounded, and marveled at the speed and fury of the current.

His only contact with the natives at this point was mildly comic. He had been hoping to encounter either Chinese mandarins or black potentates like those on the Gold Coast. But when a dugout canoe approached, he observed with disgust that it contained only naked Indians looking very like Caribs. Fortunately, they had better manners. He derived some consolation from the fact that they wore cotton

El Gallo (Soldado Rock).

bandannas like those obtained by the Portuguese in Sierra Leone. With this apparent confirmation of Aristotle's theory of the same latitude producing the same things the world over, he was sure to find Guinea gold around the corner! The Admiral, hoping to start trade, caused some brass chamber pots and other shining objects to be enticingly displayed over the bulwarks, but the Trinidad Indians were not impressed by these common objects of the European home. Next, the Admiral tried putting on a show for their benefit; he ordered a pipe-and-tabor player to sound off, tambourines to be jingled, and the ships' boys to dance. The Indians mistook this to be the strangers' method of warming up for a fight, and let fly a shower of arrows, none of which hit.

On 4 August, as the ships were weighing anchor and about to explore the Gulf, the Spaniards had probably the greatest fright of their lives. An enormous bore or tidal wave, evidently caused by a volcanic disturbance, roared through the Boca, snapped the anchor cable of *Vaqueños*, raised the flagship to what seemed an immense height, and dropped her so low that one could see bottom. The Admiral decided that this was no place to linger, and named that strait *La Boca de la Sierpe*, the Serpent's Mouth.

He now steered due north, attracted by the sight of mountains across the Gulf, on the Paria peninsula. Approaching the tip end of the peninsula, he enjoyed the same gorgeous view that greets a sailor today. Astern lay the placid Gulf, its far shores below the horizon; westward under the setting sun stretched a succession of mountains and rugged headlands; eastward were the high, broken islands that divide the famous Bocas del Dragón, and behind them rose the mountains of Trinidad. Far to the northeast, as it was a very clear evening, Columbus sighted an island which may have been Tobago but more probably was a northern promontory of Trinidad. He anchored for the night at Bahia Celeste near the tip of the Paria peninsula, and next day turned west to explore its southern shore along the Gulf.

Of many harbors, Ensenada Yacua, a little round cove with a sand beach between two rocky headlands, is probably the one that Columbus chose for a landing. He found a large thatched house and a fire burning; but the natives had fled, their places taken by swarms of monkeys who chattered indignantly at the Spaniards. This was the first place where the Admiral or his men set foot on the mainland of America; the first time, indeed, that any European had done so since the Vinland voyages.* As usual, the Admiral did not know what he had discovered; he still believed that Paria peninsula was an island. The date was Sunday, 5 August 1498.

Since it would have been undignified to take formal possession for Spain with only monkeys as audience, Columbus postponed the ceremony until two days later when a horde of friendly natives appeared at the mouth of the Rio Guiria. The Admiral, suffering severely from sore eyes, stayed on board and sent his senior captain, Pedro de Terreros, to take formal possession of this region, which the Indians told him was called Paria. It is still called the Paria peninsula, part of the Republic of Venezuela.

After a preliminary distribution of beads, sugar, and hawks' bells the Indians came out in a fleet of canoes, bringing fruits of the country and a beer called *chicha* fermented from maize. This they still brew in Venezuela. As ornaments they displayed great polished disks made of an alloy of copper and gold that they called *guanin*, and which

---

* John Cabot in 1497 may be credited only with an insular landfall (see pp. 52-56, above) and Vespucci's alleged 1497 landing on the mainland should be dated 1499.

First landing on continent. Ensenada Yacua. David Crofoot photo.

modern archaeologists have named *tumbaga*. By smelting copper with gold, the melting point is greatly reduced, an advantage to these primitive metallurgists; and as they had to import the copper from Central America, it was more valuable to them than gold. So, greatly to the Spaniards' delight, these natives of Paria were willing to swap their gold for articles of the same weight in brass or copper. Columbus had entered a new area of native culture which extends from the Guianas to Honduras.

On 8 August the fleet resumed exploration of the Gulf, rounded the long, tapering Punta Alcatraz (which Columbus called *Aguja*, the Needle), and found a rich lowland with native gardens and groves of big, glossy-leaved mahogany and fustic. So he named it *Los Jardines*. The women of one village came on board wearing necklaces of fine pearls which Columbus ascertained came from the other side of the peninsula. That caused great excitement among the Spaniards. The Indians were willing to sell what pearls they had for the usual trading truck, but unfortunately they had few to spare; so the Admiral begged them by sign language to accumulate a few bushels against his return. At this pleasant place the natives were so friendly that a whole boat's crew accepted an invitation to a feast in a big thatched house, and returned to the ship fat and happy.

Again the Admiral turned west in search of an outlet to the sea. The water, already brackish, shoaled and became fresh and turbid. Caravel *Correo,* sent ahead to reconnoiter because of her light draft, reported four river channels to the westward. These were the mouths of the Rio Grande, and a mouth of the Orinoco emptied a few miles away. Columbus, stubborn as usual in his geographical ideas, would not yet admit that this river flowed from a continent, but he gave up the search for an outlet that was not there and turned east again at the rising of the moon, on 11 August.

All day the land breeze held, and with a favoring current from the river, he reached the Bocas the same night and anchored in a neat little port named *Puerto de Gatos* (Monkey Harbor) on Chacachacare Island. In the small hours of the 13th, the fleet weighed and stood into Boca Grande. There they found the usual turmoil between the fresh water flowing out and the salt tide roaring in, and "thought to perish" when the wind dropped and the caravels drifted toward the rocks; but the fresh water prevailed over the salt, carrying them slowly out, and to safety. Columbus named this strait *Boca del Dragón,* and the name is still used for all four channels that connect the Gulf of Paria with the Caribbean. Dangerous they still are for small craft.

On the way out, Columbus sighted to the northward, over sixty miles distant, the island of Grenada and named it *Asunción* because it was the vigil of the Feast of the Assumption. At dawn 15 August, he sighted an island that he named Margarita, after the charming and witty Infanta Margarita of Austria.

Columbus did not tarry to look for the pearls that were there in abundance, as he was in a great hurry to get to Santo Domingo. That decision, as it turned out, was a mistake. Conditions in Hispaniola would have been no worse had he stayed another month; bringing home a quantity of pearls would have enhanced his prestige, and, worst of all, Ojeda and Bastidas stole his secret of the Pearl Coast and cashed in on it.

Puerto de las Cabañas. Huevos Island, Boca del Dragón. David Crofoot photo.

An "Other World"

On this Feast of the Assumption it suddenly dawned on the Admiral that he had seen the mainland. In his Journal he recorded, "I believe that this is a very great continent, until today unknown. And reason aids me greatly because of that so great river and fresh-water sea, and next, the saying of Esdras . . . that the six parts of the world are of dry land, and one of water. . . . And if this be a continent, it is a marvelous thing, and will be so among all the wise, since so great a river flows that it makes a fresh-water sea of 48 leagues."

This passage, "his very words," Las Casas assures us, is typical of the workings of Columbus's mind. For two weeks he had been sailing along the coast of the continent that he sought, yet refused to believe that it was one because it did not match his idea of a continent. Finally, the evidence of the vast volume of fresh water changed his mind, and at once the old Esdras "six parts out of seven," odd scraps of Scholastic learning, and vague gestures of Caribs, flew together in his mind to prove it.

These lands, he said, are an Other World (*otro mundo*), as indeed they were. It was mere chance that he did not write *nuevo mundo*, New World, which would have entitled him to the credit afterward accorded to Amerigo Vespucci for having recognized it as such. Actually, the two phrases as Columbus and Vespucci used them (and as Peter Martyr had already used *mundus novus*), meant the same thing: a region hitherto unknown to Europeans, not mentioned in Ptolemy's Geography. It distinctly did not mean the "New World" that we use to denote the two Americas. Columbus believed that the mainland he had just coasted along had the same relation to China and the Malay Peninsula as the present Republic of Indonesia actually does.

But Columbus was never satisfied to make two and two equal four; they must make twenty-two. A couple of days later, he confided to his Journal that this continent was the Terrestrial Paradise, the Garden of Eden! Several medieval writers quoted in his favorite bedside book, *Imago Mundi*, on the basis of Genesis ii.8, "And Lord God planted a garden eastward in Eden," located that famous garden at the furthest point of the Far East, where the sun rose on the day of creation. Turning again to the second chapter of Genesis, Columbus read of trees "pleasant to the sight, and good for food," and of the river with "four heads" that watered the garden; and caravel *Correo* had reported four mouths. "And the gold of that land is good;" certainly it was, even though the silly natives liked copper better. He then jumped to the wild conclusion that the globe at this point had a bump on it like a woman's breast, in order to bring Terrestrial Paradise nearer Heaven!

Did not the violent currents in the Bocas prove that water was running down a steep slope?

Although Columbus did suffer from arthritis and inflamed eyes, he was not out of his mind, as these weird theories might suggest; equally strange hypotheses were common among stay-at-home geographers in that era. And he always kept account of his daily positions by dead reckoning. From Margarita on 15 August he set a course NW by N for Saona Island off Hispaniola, as a good point whence to coast down-wind to Santo Domingo, the new island capital. And that *was* the correct airline course! Imagine all the factors Columbus had to feed into his mental computer to get this result—Hispaniola to Cape St. Vincent and Cadiz in 1496; Sanlúcar to Madeira, Gomera, and the Cape de Verdes in 1498; Cape de Verdes to Trinidad, and then through the Gulf of Paria and out by the Bocas to Margarita. And without sighting any land known to Europeans after the Cape de Verdes.

Although he had the direct course to Saona, two factors prevented him from making his desired landfall. One was the westward-running equatorial current which he had no means of gauging; the other, due to his very proper fear of running a reef in the dark of the moon, was cautious navigation. He ordered the caravels to jog or heave-to every night, heaving the lead frequently, and to make sail only by day when dangerous reefs could be detected by changes in the color of the water. This lengthened the passage and so increased his set to leeward. The result was that the fleet made landfall on Alta Vela, 120 miles southwest of Santo Domingo. "It weighed on him to have fallen off so much," wrote Las Casas, but he decided correctly that his miscalculation was caused by a strong current. Could any modern navigator, amateur or professional, provided only with Columbus's knowledge and instruments, have done the like? If not superb dead reckoning, he must have had divine guidance; perhaps a combination of the two!

On 21 August when anchored near Alta Vela in the shelter of Beata Island (which the Admiral named *Madama Beata*, the Blessed Lady), they saw a little caravel approaching from the direction of Santo Domingo. This was the first ship his fleet had sighted since leaving Spain. The stranger fired a gun, luffed up alongside the flagship, and to the Admiral's delight he was hailed by brother Bartholomew. The Adelantado was engaged in pursuing the provision squadron under Carvajal, which he had sighted from shore but which had stupidly continued to sail westward. After this happy reunion, the four caravels beat up to the new capital in eight days, good going against wind and current.

The flagship, *Correo*, and *Vaqueños* anchored in the Ozama River, the inner harbor of Santo Domingo, on the last day of August 1498. Another voyage had been brilliantly carried through. The Admiral had found the gateway to a vast territory for the expansion of the Spanish race, language, and culture, extending from the Rocky Mountains to the Strait of Magellan. What matter if he did think it to be the Garden of Eden? Note his prophetic words in his Journal of this voyage on the day he reached furthest west in the Gulf of Paria:

> And your Highnesses will gain these vast lands, which are an Other World, and where Christianity will have so much enjoyment, and our faith in time so great an increase. I say this with very honest intent and because I desire that your Highnesses may be the greatest lords in the world, lords of it all, I say; and that all may be with much service to and satisfaction of the Holy Trinity.

Superb faith, marvelous prophecy! At a time when Spain's first overseas colony was languishing, and settlers had to be recruited from the jails; when few people of any importance believed in Columbus or thought his discoveries worth the smallest of the Canary Islands, he foretold the vast revenue that Spain would obtain from these conquests, making her the first power in Europe. He predicted that Christianity, whose territory had been shrinking since the rise of Islam, would advance triumphantly into his Other and New World.

Home in Chains

At court, in the meantime, the Admiral's stock was falling. Spaniards who returned from Hispaniola, claiming overtime, were making nuisances of themselves, assaulting King Ferdinand whenever he stirred abroad with cries of, "Pay! Pay!" Columbus's younger son remembered bitterly how he and his brother Diego, pages to Queen Isabella, were mortified by these wretches hooting at them and shouting, "There go the sons of the Admiral of the Mosquitoes, of him who discovered lands of vanity and delusion, the ruin and the grave of Castilian gentlemen!"

Yet we must admit that the three Columbus brothers had failed as administrators. They had been weak when they should have been firm, and ruthless at the wrong time; they had not saved the Indians from exploitation, and had alienated most of the Spaniards. The Sovereigns, before receiving news that the rebel Francisco Roldán had made his peace with the Admiral, appointed Francisco de Bobadilla to go to Hispaniola as royal commissioner, with unlimited powers over persons and property. Bobadilla arrived at Santo Domingo 24 August 1500, when the Admiral was at La Vega, brother Bartholomew at Xaragua, and brother Diego in charge of the city. The first thing that the Spaniard saw upon landing was a gallows from which seven Spanish corpses were hanging, and Diego cheerfully remarked that five more were due to be hanged next day. These men, having rebelled under Adrián de Moxica, had been defeated and captured with Roldán's assistance. Bobadilla, without waiting to hear the Columbus side, took over both fort and government, tossed Don Diego into the brig of his flagship, impounded all the Admiral's effects, won over the populace by proclaiming a general freedom to gather gold anywhere; and, when the Admiral appeared in obedience to his summons, had him fettered and confined in the capital's calaboose. Bartholomew, then in the interior with a loyal army, might have marched on the capital and released his brothers, but the Admiral neither dared nor cared to defy the royal authority Bobadilla represented. On his advice, Bartholomew, too, submitted and was thrown into jail.

The royal commissioner, after compiling a file of anti-Columbus depositions from discontented and mutinous Spaniards, decided to send all three brothers home for trial. In early October of 1500 the Admiral and Diego, both chained, were placed on board caravel *La Gorda*, bound for Spain; Bartholomew sailed in another vessel. The captain of *La Gorda* "would have knocked off the Admiral's irons," says son Ferdinand, but his father "would not permit it, saying that they had been put on him by regal authority and only the Sovereigns could order them struck off."

To a sensitive man like Columbus, these indignities were far more humiliating than they would have been to the average tough *hombre* of that era. On his way home he wrote to a true friend at court, Doña Juana de Torres, a long letter which is at once a cry of distress, a bill of complaints, and a proud vindication of his own conduct. Our Lord, he said, had made him the messenger of the "new heavens and a new earth" envisioned in the Apocalypse and prophesied in Isaiah lxv.17. The Queen, as a reward for understanding this, had been made heiress to this Other World, and in her name he went out and took possession. Yet none of her subjects is so vile that he cannot now insult the Admiral with impunity. He is accused of illegal actions, although he put down two rebellions against the Sovereigns' authority. He safeguarded their Highnesses' interests in the collection of gold. Then Bobadilla arrived, listened to the calumnies of rogues, threw him and his brothers into jail, and removed all restrictions on gold collection so that one rascal made a small fortune in four hours! Columbus ended with a poignant expression of outraged dignity and sense of justice:—"By divine will I have placed under the sovereignty of the King and Queen our lords an Other World, whereby Spain, which was reckoned poor, is become the richest of countries." That was the plain truth.

Fair winds attended the homeward voyage of *La Gorda*, as if the Ocean Sea had wished to shorten the miseries of her Admiral. Before the end of October 1500 he landed at Cadiz, still in chains. Accompanied by his jailer, he lodged at the monastery of Las Cuevas in Seville. The spectacle of Columbus in chains is said to have made a lamentable impression on the populace, but six weeks elapsed before the Sovereigns ordered him released from his fetters, and summoned him to court.*

The three brothers presented themselves to the King and Queen at the Alhambra in Granada shortly before Christmas, 1500. Diego Colón, now in his twenty-first year, was there too, with Ferdinand, a boy of twelve. Imagine their mortification to see their father dressed in Franciscan brown and with marks of iron fetters on his wrists!

The Sovereigns now spoke to Columbus in a kindly and consoling manner, and promised that justice would be done and privileges restored. Weeks stretched into months, but nothing happened. More urgent business than the affairs of distant Hispaniola occupied the atten-

---

* As Ogden Nash summed up the Admiral's career, with a poet's economy:

> So Columbus said, Somebody show me the sunset
>   and somebody did and he set sail for it.
> And he discovered America and they put him in jail for it,
> And the fetters gave him welts,
> And they named America after somebody else.

The Face Is Familiar (Boston, 1940), p. 209, by permission of Mrs. Ogden Nash.

tion of Ferdinand and Isabella. Nothing less than complete restoration of his rights, properties, titles, and offices would satisfy Columbus. He spent time and effort compiling a Book of Privileges, containing all his agreements with and orders and letters from the Sovereigns. But it was futile for him to expect to get everything back. He and his brothers had made too much of a mess of things in Hispaniola, to be entrusted again with the overseas government. And as the coast of South America gradually opened up, it was idle to suppose that the Sovereigns would confirm tithes and similar privileges over a vast continent which originally had been granted in the expectation of his setting up a trading factory or discovering a few islands. Again, Columbus would have been well advised to settle for a castle, a pension, and a new title; but he was not the man to give up anything. Had he been, he would never have discovered the New World.

After waiting eight months from New Year's Day 1501, Columbus learned the worst in September. Instead of being returned in triumph to Hispaniola, he was formally replaced as governor by Don Nicolás de Ovando. Columbus did obtain permission to keep his now empty titles of Viceroy and Admiral, and to send out an agent in Ovando's fleet to make Bobadilla disgorge the moneys which were his. Ovando departed in February 1502 with a magnificent fleet of 30 sail, carrying 2500 sailors, soldiers, and colonists.

Eager to embark once more on his proper element, Columbus now asked for the means to make a Fourth Voyage to the Indies. The Sovereigns so ordered, only a month after Ovando sailed for Hispaniola.

Bibliographic Note

Sources. Las Casas abstracted the now lost Columbus *Diario* or Journal of the Third Voyage. Facsimile and printed text by Carlos Sanz, *Descubrimiento del Continente Americano* (Madrid, 1962), in his serias *Biblioteca Americana Vetutissima.* Translation in my *Journals and Other Documents,* pp. 259–312, together with Columbus's letters, to the Sovereigns of 18 October 1498, to Juana de Torres of October 1500, and the Royal Mandate of 27 September 1501 ordering restitution of the Admiral's property and rights. My *Admiral of the Ocean Sea,* II, 269–74, discusses various controversies about Columbus's route in the Gulf of Paria.

Landfall. We in our *Capitana* in 1939, twenty days out from the Canaries, reached a position within a mile or two of the one where Columbus made that landfall, and had the pleasure of watching, as they rose from the sea, the three hills which seemed to Columbus a happy omen on the last day of July 1498. The name *Cabo de la Galera*, through a misunderstanding, has been transferred to the northeast point of Trinidad; Columbus's landfall is now called Galeota Point.

The Mariner's Day

Time and Watches

Before we take up the rest of Columbus's explorations which were launched immediately after Columbus's Third, suppose we describe a day at sea in his time, which will also go for the entire sixteenth century. Information on this subject, since everyone then took knowledge of it for granted, is very scarce; one can only pick up bits and pieces from sea journals. Fortunately, a humorous Spanish official, Eugenio de Salazar, wrote a very detailed account of what he observed in a voyage from Spain to Santo Domingo in 1573. Without him this chapter would have been mostly blank.

A decent formality has always been observed in ships at sea. The watches are changed and the tiller or wheel is relieved according to formula, solar and stellar observations are made at fixed hours, and any departure from the settled custom is resented by mariners. In Spanish and Portuguese ships these formalities were observed with a quasi-religious ritual, which lent them a certain beauty and served to remind the seamen every half-hour of the day and night that their ship depended for safety not only on her staunchness and their own skill, but on the grace of God.

Until the late sixteenth century, the only ship's clock available was

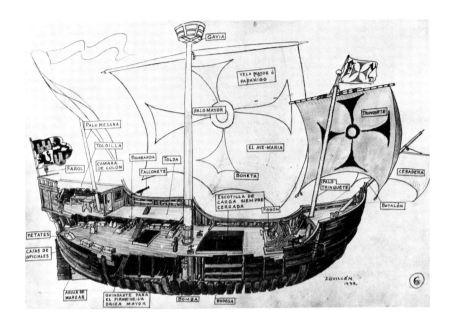

Admiral Guillén's "cut-out" of *Santa Maria*. Courtesy of Naval Museum, Madrid.

the *ampoletta* or *reloj de arena* (sand clock), a half-hour glass containing enough sand to run from the upper to the lower section in exactly thirty minutes. Made in Venice, these glasses were so fragile that many spares were usually carried—Magellan had eighteen on his flagship. It was the duty of a ship's boy in each watch to mind the *ampolleta* and reverse it promptly when the sand ran out. A very rough sea might retard the running of the sand, or the boy might go to sleep; Columbus on one occasion expressed indignation with a lazy lad who lost count. As a ship gains time sailing east and loses it sailing west, even the most modern ship's clock has to be corrected daily by radio. The only way one could mark correct sun time in the era of discovery was to erect a pin or gnomon on the center of the compass card, and watch for the exact moment of noon when the sun's shadow touched the fleur-de-lis that marked north (or, if in the Southern Hemisphere, south) and then turn the glass. Even that could not be counted on to give true noon nearer than 15 or 20 minutes.

The *marineros*, *grumetes*, and *oficiales* of the ship's company (able seamen, apprentice seamen, and petty officers such as caulker and cooper) were divided into two watches (*cuartos* or *guardias*) of four hours each. An officer commanded each watch according to a fixed rule of precedence: captain, pilot, *maestre* (master), *contramaestre* (master's mate or chief boatswain).* From sundry entries in Columbus's Journal, it is clear that his watches were changed at 3, 7, and 11 o'clock. These hours seem odd to a modern seaman, who by immemorial usage expects watches to change at 4, 8, and 12, and I believe they were so changed from 1500 on. Presumably the afternoon watch was "dogged" (i.e., split into two 2-hour watches) as the merchant marine still did in the nineteenth century, in order that the men might change their hours nightly. On a sailing vessel which might be many weeks or even months at sea, it was fairer to dog the watches daily so that each man would have the unpopular "graveyard watch" from midnight to 4:00 a.m. (or from 11 to 3) on alternate nights.

Mariners in those days thought of time less in terms of hours than of *ampolletas* and *guardias*, glasses and watches, eight glasses to a watch. The system of half-hourly ship's bells that we are familiar with began as a means of accenting the turning of the glass. No ship's bell is mentioned in any of the Spanish sea journals of the sixteenth century that I have seen, and García de Palacio's *Instrucción Náutica* (1587), the Mexican seaman's first Bowditch, says nothing of them. Drake's flagship *Golden Hind* carried no bell, but his men "liberated" one from the church at Guatulco, Mexico, in 1579. They hung it in an improvised belfry on board, where a Spanish prisoner reported that it was "used to summon the men to pump." Since pumping ship was the first duty of every watch, it is evident that the bell was used for summons, and that this use of the bell was new to Spaniards, if not to Englishmen.

At night in the Northern Hemisphere whenever the weather was clear and the latitude not too low, your sixteenth-century navigator could tell sun time from the Guards of the North Star. The Little Bear or Little Dipper swings around Polaris once every 24 hours, sidereal time. The two brightest stars of that constellation, *beta* (Kochab) and *gamma*, which mark the edge of the Dipper furthest from the North Star, were called the Guards; and if you knew where Kochab (the principal Guard) should be at midnight, you could tell time as from a clock hand. The early navigators constructed a diagram of a

* In Portuguese ships, curiously, pilot came below master.

little man with Polaris in his belly, his forearms pointing E and W, and his shoulders NE and NW. That gave eight positions for Kochab. As this star moved from one major position to another in three hours, you could tell time at night if you knew its position at midnight on that date. For that purpose a very simple instrument, the nocturnal, sufficed. It had a hole in the center through which you sighted Polaris, and a movable arm representing the Guards, which you moved until it pointed at Kochab; then you read the time off a scale on the outer disk. Nocturnals were in use for centuries. With a little practice, almost anyone on a long voyage can learn to tell time by this method within a quarter-hour.

Ritual and Religion

In the great days of sail, before man's inventions and gadgets had given him a false confidence in his power to conquer the ocean, seamen were the most religious of all workers on land or sea. The mariner's philosophy he took from the Vulgate's 107th Psalm: "They that go down to the sea in ships and occupy their business in great waters; these men see the works of the Lord, and his wonders in the deep. For at his word, the stormy wind ariseth, which lifteth up the waves thereof." It behooved seamen to obey the injunction of the Psalmist, "O that men would therefore praise the Lord for his goodness, and declare the wonders that he doeth for the children of men!" That is exactly what they did, after their fashion. The Protestant Reformation did not change the old customs of shipboard piety, only the ritual; Spanish prisoners on Drake's *Golden Hind* reported a daily service which featured the singing of psalms.

Although the captain or master, if no priest were present, led morning and evening prayers, the little semi-religious observances which marked almost every half-hour of the day were performed by the youngest lads on board, the *pajes de escober* (pages of the broom). This I suppose was on the same principle as having family grace said by the youngest child; God would be better pleased by the voice of innocence.

According to Eugenio de Salazar, the ritual which he describes always prevailed when venturing on unknown seas where the divine protection was imperatively needed. No pious commander would have omitted aught of these traditional observances. I repeat them here just as Salazar reports them, with a translation.

A young boy of the dawn watch saluted daybreak with this ditty:

Bendita sea la luz,	Blessed be the light of day
y la Santa Veracruz	and the Holy Cross, we say;
y el Señor de la Verdad,	and the Lord of Veritie
y la Santa Trinidad;	and the Holy Trinity
bendita sea el alma,	Blessed be th'immortal soul
y el Señor que nos la manda;	and the Lord who keeps it whole,
bendito sea el día	blessed be the light of day
y el Señor que nos lo envía.	and He who sends the night away.

He then recited *Pater Noster* and *Ave Maria*, and added:

> *Dios nos dé buenos días; buen viaje; buen pasaje haga la nao, señor Capitán y maestre y buena compaña, amén; así faza buen viaje, faza: muy buenos días dé Dios a vuestras mercedes, señores de popa y proa.*
>
> God give us good days, good voyage, good passage to the ship, sir captain and master and good company, amen; so let there be, let there be a good voyage; many good days may God grant your graces, gentlemen of the afterguard and gentlemen forward.

Before being relieved the dawn watch was supposed to have the deck well scrubbed down with salt water hauled up in buckets, using stiff besoms made of twigs. At 6:30 or 7:30 the *ampolleta* was turned up for the seventh and last time on that watch, and the boy sang out:

Buena es la que va,	Good is that which passeth,
mejor es la que viene;	better that which cometh,
siete es pasada y en ocho muele,	seven is past and eight floweth,
mas molerá si Dios quisiere,	more shall flow if God willeth,
cuenta y pasa, que buen viaje faza.	count and pass makes voyage fast.

As soon as the sands of the eighth successive glass ran out, the boy in turning up said, instead of his usual ditty:

> *Al cuarto, al cuarto, señores marineros de buena parte, al cuarto, al cuarto en bueno hora de la guardia del señor piloto, que ya es hora; leva, leva, leva.*
>
> On deck, on deck, Mr. Mariners of the right side,* on deck in good time you of Mr. Pilot's watch, for it's already time; shake a leg!

* Meaning the watch, port or starboard, that is due on deck.

The new watch need no time to dress, for nobody has undressed; when they went below in early morn, each man sought out his favorite soft plank, or some corner wherein he could brace himself against the ship's rolling and pitching. The mariners coming on duty are soon awake, rubbing their eyes and grumbling, and each man grabs a ship biscuit, some garlic cloves, a bit of cheese, a pickled sardine, or whatever is on for breakfast, and shuffles aft to the break in the poop. The helmsman gives the course to the captain of his watch, who repeats it to the new helmsman, who repeats it again. Little chance for error! A lookout is posted forward, another aft, the off-going captain of the watch transfers his reckoning from slate to logbook, and the ship's boy wipes the slate clean for the new captain. Chips the carpenter (or *calafate* the caulker if he goes on watch) primes the pump, and if the ship has made water during the night, two or three hands pump her dry. The off-going watch eat breakfast and curl up somewhere out of the sun to sleep.

Now the decks are dry, the sun is yardarm high, and the ship is dancing along before the trades with a bone in her teeth. The captain, whose servant has brought him a bucket of sea water, a cup of fresh water, and a bit of breakfast in his cabin, comes on deck, looks all around the horizon, ejaculates a pious *gracias a Dios* for fair weather, and chats with the master or pilot.

Each watch is responsible for the ship during its hours of duty, except in case of tempest or accident, when all hands are summoned. The usual duties are keeping the decks both clear and clean, making and setting sail as required, trimming sheets and braces; and when there is nothing else to do, scrubbing the rails, making spun yarn and chafing-gear out of old rope, and overhauling other gear. In the morning watch, as soon as the running rigging has dried from the night dews, it has to be swayed up, and every few days the lanyards or tackles that connect the shrouds with the bulwarks must be taken up—but not too taut.

One question to which every old salt wants the answer is about "Crossing the Line." Since the principal southern voyages after 1498 crossed the Equator and entered the Southern Hemisphere, did they do it with ceremony? Did the Portuguese and Spanish navigators relieve the tension of a long voyage with the now time-honored ceremony of Crossing the Line? Did a burlesque Neptune and court come on board over the bows, subjecting the "pollywogs" or neophytes to various humorous indignities to turn them into "shellbacks"? Existing sources indicate that they did not; this ceremony belonged to the northern nations. It was derived from the medieval custom of Norman, Hanseatic, and Dutch sailors holding a quasi-religious service when they passed a well-known landmark such as the Pointe du Raz in Brittany or the Berlingas off Portugal.

The earliest known reference to a ceremony at the Equator is a con-temporary account of the voyage of the Parmentier brothers of Dieppe to Sumatra in 1529. "Tuesday 11 May in the morning, about 50 of our people were made *chevaliers* and received the accolade in passing below the Equator; and the mass *Salve Sancta Parens* was sung from notes to mark the day's solemnity; and we took a great fish called albacore and some bonito, of which a stew was made for supper, solemnizing this feast of chivalry." The next, in order of time, oc-curred on the voyage of a French ship captained by Jean de Léry, to Brazil in 1557. Here is the first reference to the now traditional pranks: "This day the 4th of February, when we passed the World's Center, the sailors went through their accustomed ceremonies . . . namely, to bind [a man] with ropes and plunge him into the sea, or blacken his face well with an old rag rubbed on the bottom of the kettle and then shave it off, so as to give those who had never before passed the Equator something to remember. But one can buy oneself off and be exempt from all that by paying for wine for all hands, as I did."

Parmentier's and Léry's ships were French. When did the Portu-guese and Spanish adopt this genial way to break the monotony of a long voyage? Gossipy Pigafetta, who sailed with Magellan and Elcano around the world in 1519–22, never mentions anything of the sort, which suggests that they had not yet done so.

Sixty years passed, and the account by Jan Huygen van Linschoten of a voyage to Goa in an official Portuguese fleet indicates that sailors of this nation had taken over the custom and developed it in their own fashion. Linschoten's ship sailed in February 1583; on 26 May she passed the Equator off Guinea, and on the 29th the business began. Each ship, following "an ancient custome," elected someone as "Em-peror," who became lord of misrule. On this occasion the pranksters and the drinking went too far, and "by meanes of certain words that passed out of their mouths, there fell a great strife and contention among us at the banquet; at the least a hundred rapiers drawne, without respecting the Captaine or any other, for he lay under foote, and they trod upon him, and had killed each other," had not a distinguished passenger, the new archbishop of Goa, burst forth from his cabin, and commanded every man, under pain of excommunication, to hand over his weapons. This they did, and the strife ended.

No record exists, to my knowledge, of any Spanish ship holding a Crossing the Line ceremony before the eighteenth century. The Portuguese must have adopted it from their many North European friends.

Returning to daily life at sea, on big ships the master's or pilot's orders were transmitted to the men through the *contramaestre* or chief boatswain, who carried a pipe or whistle on a lanyard around his neck and on it played a variety of signals. There is no mention of a pipe on Columbus's ships, probably because they were so small that the captain of the watch gave orders orally. Salazar said he had never seen an order so well and promptly obeyed by soldiers as those of his pilot. Let him but cry, *Ah! de proa!* (Hey, up forward!) and they all come aft on the run "like conjured demons" awaiting his pleasure. Here are some samples of the orders.

dejad las chafaldetas	well the clewlines
alzá aquel briol	heave on that buntline
empalomadle la boneta	lace on the bonnet
tomad aquel puño	lay hold of that clew
entren esas badasas aprisa por esos ollaos	pass them toggles through the latches quick
levá el papahigo	hoist the main course
izá el trinquete	raise the foresail
dad vuelta	put your back into it
enmará un poco la cebadera	give the spritsail a little sheet
desencapillá la mesana	unbend the mizzen
ligá la tricia al guindaste	belay the halyard on the bitts
tirá de los escotines de gabia	haul in on the topsail sheets
suban dos á los penoles	two of you up on the yardarm
untá los vertellos	grease the parrel trucks
amarrá aquellas burdas	belay them backstays
zafá los embornales	clear the scuppers
juegue el guimbalete para que la bomba achique	work that pump brake till she sucks

Nautical Castilian, like nautical English of the last century, had a word for everything in a ship's gear and a verb for every action; strong, expressive words that could not be misunderstood when bawled out in a gale.

For any lengthy operation like winding in the anchor cable or hoisting a yard, the seamen had an appropriate *saloma* or chantey, and of these Salazar gives an example which it is useless to translate. The chanteyman sang or shouted the first half of each line, the men hauled away on the "o" and joined in on the second half, while they got a new hold on the halyard:

> *Bu izá*
> *o dio—ayuta noy*
> *o que somo—servi soy*
> *o voleamo—ben servir*
> *o la fede—mantenir*
> *o la fede—de cristiano*
> *o malmeta—lo pagano*
> *sconfondi—y sarrahin*
> *torchi y mori—gran mastín*
> *o fillioli—dabrahin*
> *o non credono—que ben sia*
> *o non credono—la fe santa*
> *en la santa—fe di Roma*
> *o di Roma—está el perdón*
> *o San Pedro—gran varón*
> *o San Pablo—son compañón*
> *o que ruegue—a Dio por nos*
> *o por nosotros—navegantes*
> *en este mundo—somo tantes*
> *o ponente—digo levante*
> *o levante—se leva el sol*
> *o ponente—resplandor*
> *fantineta—viva lli amor*
> *o joven home—gauditor*

And so on, improvising, until the halyard is "two-blocks," when the captain of the watch commands, *Dejad la driza, amarrá* (Well the halyard, belay!).

When not ordering the men about, the captain of the watch kept station on the high poop, conning the helmsman through a hatch in the deck just forward of the binnacle. On all but the smaller vessels the helmsman had a second compass to steer by, but he could not see ahead, and so had to be an expert at the feel of the ship to keep her on her course. Salazar gives us some specimens of the orders to the helmsman:—

botá a babor	port your helm
no boteis	steady
arriba	up helm
goberná la ueste cuarta al sueste	steer W by S

Besides a nautical language, a nautical slang had developed. Just as modern seamen with mock contempt speak of "this wagon" or "the old crate," a Spaniard called his ship *rocín de madera* (wooden jade) or *pájaro puerco* (flying pig). The nickname for the firebox meant "pot island." People on board got in the habit of using nautical phrases for other things; Salazar, for instance, says, "When I want a pot of jam I say, *saca la cebadera*, break out the spritsail; if I want a table napkin I say, *daca el pañol*, lead me to the sail-locker. If I wish to eat or drink in form I say, *pon la mesana*, set the mizzen. When a mariner upsets a jug he says, *oh! cómo achicais*, Oh how she sucks! When one breaks wind, as often happens, someone is sure to cry, *Ah! de popa*, Hey there, aft!"

Naturally there was a good deal of joking about the seats hung over the rail forward and aft, for the seamen and afterguard to ease themselves. These were called *jardines*, perhaps in memory of the usual location of the family privy. Salazar writes in mock sentiment of the lovely views they afforded of moon and planets, and of the impromptu washings that he there obtained from the waves. A later voyager, Antonio de Guevara, complained of the indecency of thus exposing a Very Reverend Lord Bishop to the full view of the ship's company, and adverts bitterly to the tarred rope-end which performed the function assigned by North American folklore to the corncob.

Food and Drink

Apparently the seamen on Spanish and Portuguese ships enjoyed but one hot meal a day. This must have come around noon, so that the watch below could get theirs before coming on deck, and the watch relieved could eat after them.

Who did the cooking? I wish I knew! There was no rating of cook on any of Columbus's ships or even on Magellan's. The earliest man especially designated as cook that I have found on a ship's roll sailed on Sebastian Cabot's flagship in 1526. García de Palacio's *Instrucción Náutica* of 1587, which gives all ratings and tells everyone's duties, mentions neither cook nor cooker; although the steward, he says, has charge of the fire. My guess is that the hard-worked ship's boys took turns at the firebox, except that the captain's servant would naturally have cooked for him, and pages of gentlemen volunteers served them. On board the big Mexico-bound galleons described by Palacio, a table was set for the men forward, the boatswain presided, and the pages served and cleared away. On small ships it is probable that foremast hands took their share in a wooden bowl and ate it with their fingers wherever they could find a place. How the little *fogón* or open firebox could cook food for over a hundred people on a small caravel, as it must have on *Niña*'s voyage home in 1496, staggers the imagination.

The only drinks mentioned in Spanish or Portuguese inventories are water and wine, both of which were kept in various types of wooden casks. It was the cooper's job to see that these were kept tight and well stowed or lashed down so that they would not roll. South Europeans, unlike the English and French, did not carry beer or cider, which always went sour on a long voyage; coffee and tea did not reach Europe until the following century. The staff of life for Spanish seamen was wine, olive oil, salt meat, salt codfish, and bread in the form of sea biscuit or hardtack baked ashore from wheat flour and stowed in the driest part of the ship. The only sweetening came in the form of honey, sugar being too expensive. Columbus's ideas of the proper provisioning of vessels on an American voyage are given in a letter to the Sovereigns of about 1498–1500:

> Victualling them should be done in this manner: the third part of the breadstuff to be good biscuit, well seasoned and not old, or the major portion will be wasted; a third part of salted flour, salted at the time of milling; and a third part of wheat. Further there will be wanted wine, salt meat, oil, vinegar, cheese, chickpeas, lentils, beans, salt fish and fishing tackle, honey, rice, almonds, and raisins.

Olive oil, carried in huge earthenware jars, was used for cooking fish, meat, and legumes. Salted flour could be made into unleavened bread and cooked in the ashes, as Arab seamen do today. Barreled salt sardines and anchovies are frequently mentioned among ships' stores of the time, and garlic would certainly not have been forgotten. The sixteenth-century mariners fared as well as peasants or workers ashore, except during a storm, or weather so rough that no fire could be kept—or when provisions brought from Europe gave out.

Dinner for the afterguard was announced by a ship's boy in this wise:

> *Tabla, tabla, señor capitán y maestra y buena compaña, tabla puesta; vianda presta; agua usada para el señor capitán y maestre y buena compaña. Viva, Viva el Rey de Castilla por mar y por tierra! Quien le diere guerra que le corten la cabeza; quien no dijere amén, que no le den á beber. Tabla en buena hora, quien no viniere que no coma.*
>
> Table, table, sir captain and master and good company, table ready; meat ready; water as usual for sir captain and master and good company. Long live the King of Castile by land and sea! Who says to him war, off with his head; who won't say amen, gets nothing to drink. Table is set, who don't come won't eat.

Salazar describes how the pages would slam on the officers' table a great wooden dish of stringy, ill-cooked salt meat, when everyone would grab his share and attack it with a sheath knife as if he were a practitioner of anatomy; and how every bone was left "clean as ivory." The table conversation, he says, was mostly sighing for what you couldn't have—"Oh! how I'd fancy a bunch of Guadalajara white grapes!—I could manage a few turnips of Somo Sierra!—If we only had on board a plate of Ilescas strawberries!"

What they longed for, obviously, were anti-scorbutics. Nothing then was known about vitamins, and, for want of fresh vegetables, fruit, or fruit juice, scurvy in its most hideous forms raged among the seamen on almost every long voyage. The officers fared better, as they always carried personal luxuries such as figs, raisins, prunes, and pots of jam which kept the dread disease away. By the end of the next century (as Abbé Labat tells us) the French managed to sail with salad plants set out in flats, so that the afterguard enjoyed green salad almost daily; but they had to set a twenty-four-hour guard over their shipboard garden to keep off rats and sailors.

Although Chaunu's compilation of voyages to the Indies mentions several instances of food giving out on an unduly long return voyage, that was comparatively rare on the West Indies routes. But, as we shall see, no master mariner prior to Drake managed to feed his crew adequately on voyages that went south of the Line, especially those which reached the Pacific. There simply was not room enough, or storage tight enough, to preserve basic foodstuffs such as wine, hard bread, flour, and salt meat for so long a time. Hence the resort to penguin meat, seal, and other loathsome substitutes; and occasionally to the desperate eating of rats and chewing leather chafing-gear. Drake's men made out comparatively well, only because he stripped every prize ship of all desirable food stores, gear, and weapons. There is not one of these southern voyages on which the modern blue-water yachtsman, used to refrigeration and canned goods, would have been happy.

Navigation

On this subject I have little to add to what has already been related earlier in this volume (pages 26–32). During the sixteenth century, "rutters," manuals of navigation, such as Medina's *Arte de Navegar* (1545), proliferated; but sailors, the most conservative of men, were reluctant to try anything new. It was the pilot's business to keep track of the ship's position; but despite the education given pilots before they could be licensed as such, throughout the sixteenth century most pilots depended on dead reckoning.

Captain Teixeira da Mota, after meticulous search into both manuscript and printed rutters of the sixteenth century, has concluded convincingly that the best Portuguese pilots early in that century had plotted the trade winds (which they called *os ventos gerais*), as well as the equatorial current which runs from the bulge of Africa to the Caribbean. They pointed out very early the important fact—known to any square-rig master in the last century—that vessels sailing from the Cape Verde Islands to Brazil must not allow themselves to be carried to the north (leeward) to Cape San Roque, but steer for Cabo Santo Agostinho. Similarly the Spaniards, owing to their increasing trade with Hispaniola, Cuba, and Mexico, found out about the Gulf Stream and so planned their return routes to Spain that this mighty ocean current would help them to whip around Florida and up into the zone of the westerlies.

If one studies the rutters rather than actual voyages, one too easily concludes that Portuguese pilots of the sixteenth century knew everything. But when we read the *Tratado da Sphera* of 1537 by Pedro Nunes (Nonius), the famous Portuguese-Jewish mathematician who discovered the vernier, we wonder how useful these pilots really were. "Why do we put up with these pilots, with their bad language and barbarous manners?" wrote Nunes. "They know neither sun, moon nor stars, nor their courses, movements or declinations; neither latitude nor longitude of the places on the globe, nor astrolabes, quadrants, cross staffs or watches, nor years common or bissextile, equinoxes or solstices." Yet they were supposed to have learned all these things before being licensed by the Casa de Contratación, or by the corresponding board at Lisbon.

Columbus was a dead-reckoning navigator. He made colossal mistakes every time he tried to determine latitude from a star until, marooned at Jamaica, he had plenty of time to make repeated observations. He knew no way (nor did anyone else in the sixteenth century) of determining longitude except by timing an eclipse. Regiomontanus's *Ephemerides* and Zacuto's *Almanach Perpetuum* gave the predicted hours of total eclipses at Nuremberg and Salamanca respectively, and by comparing those with the observed hour of the eclipse by local sun time, multiplying by 15 to convert time into arc, you could find the longitude west of the almanac-maker's meridian. This sounds simple enough, but Columbus with two opportunities (1494 and 1503) muffed both, as did almost everyone else for a century. At Mexico City in 1541 a mighty effort was made by the intelligentsia to determine the longitude of that place by timing two eclipses of the moon. The imposing result was 8h 2m 32s (120° 38′) west of Toledo; but the correct difference of longitude between the two places is 95° 12′. Thus the Mexican savants made an error of some 25½ degrees, putting their city into the Pacific! Even in the late seventeenth century Père Labat, the earliest writer (to my knowledge) to give the position of Hispaniola correctly, adds this caveat: "I only report the longitude to warn the reader that nothing is more uncertain, and that no method used up to the present to find longitude has produced anything fixed and certain."

In the previous chapter we related a telling example of Columbus's excellent dead-reckoning on his Third Voyage. Dead-reckoning is still the foundation of celestial navigation, but the modern navigator

Boxwood Nocturnal "for both Bears," dated 1724. Courtesy Peabody Museum, Salem.

checks his D.R. daily (if weather permits) by latitude or longitude sights or both, which Columbus never learned to do. And, as an error of half a point in your course will mean an error of about 250 miles in landfall on an ocean crossing, it is evident that Columbus's dead-reckoning was extraordinarily careful and accurate. Andrés Bernáldez, who had information directly from the Admiral after his Second Voyage, wrote, "No one considers himself a good pilot and master who, although he has to pass from one land to another very distant without sighting any other land, makes an error of 10 leagues, even in a crossing of 1000 leagues, unless the force of the tempest drives and deprives him of the use of his skill." No such dead-reckoning navigators exist today; no man alive, limited to the instruments and means at

Columbus's disposal, could obtain anything near the accuracy of his results.

By the time Magellan sailed, in 1519, great advances had been made in taking meridian altitudes of the sun with a quadrant or mariner's astrolabe, and working out latitude from a simple formula. Albo, Magellan's pilot whose logbook we have, recorded latitudes of newly discovered places fairly accurately. And there was considerable improvement during the century, as we can ascertain by the positions recorded in Drake's voyage.

The most surprising thing about Columbus's voyages, after his uncanny perception of profitable courses, was the speed that his vessels made; *Niña* and *Pinta*, for instance, making 600 miles in four days of February 1493 and approaching a speed of 11 knots. He and the

Shooting the Sun with an Early Quadrant. Engraving by Ph. Lansbergen, 1628. The caption says, "Here we reckon how far off Heaven is. Psalm 36.5 (Thy mercy, O Lord, is in the heavens.) Courtesy Maritiem Museum "Prins Hendrik," Rotterdam.

Heere uwe goetheyt reyckt foo wijt als den hemel is, Pfalm. 36.verf. 5

Pinzón brothers must have been what men in the clipper ship era called "drivers," not comfortable joggers-along; they refused to shorten sail every night or at the appearance of every black cloud. On his first two voyages Columbus made the Grand Canary in six and seven days from Andalusia; compare that with the average time of that run for Spanish merchantmen in the half-century 1550–1600—just double. His first three ocean crossings of 2500 to 2700 nautical miles—33 days in 1492, 29 days in 1493, 40 days on the Third Voyage in 1498, were good; and that of 21 days on the Fourth Voyage, 1502, was phenomenal. According to Pierre Chaunu, it has seldom been equaled and never surpassed in the colonial era. Even the twelve-ship convoy under Antonio de Torres, by following his master's directions, arrived home in 35 days from Isabela, a record never equaled under sail. For 53 homeward-bound convoys from Havana, 1551–1650, the average time was over 67 days.*

Part of the explanation of these remarkable bursts and sensational stretches of speed lies in the lines and sail plan of the caravel. Would that one of these brave little vessels were dug up, like the Viking ships in Norway, so we could guess at her secret! Naturally a lightly laden caravel, in the early voyages, could sail circles around a heavily laden 200- or 300-tun *nao* on the later trade routes. But the design of those full-rigged and wide-hulled ships also improved through the century. The "round tuck" at the stern of the first *Santa Maria* gave way to a square stern, upon which the high superstructure was built, as an integral part of the vessel. Toward the end of the century, the Dutch began to save manpower by cutting sails smaller and shortening the yards. Perhaps the most important improvement was that of sheathing, to thwart the teredos. Drake's flagship was double-planked, and toward the end of the century Henri IV of France, when outfitting a fleet against Spain, insisted on not only double sheathing but a pad of superior German felt between the planks, and copper-plating below the waterline.

End of a Day at Sea

At 3:00 or 4:00 p.m. the first dog watch is set. The day's work of scrubbing, splicing, seizing, and making repairs is now done; and if the

* See above, Chapter XIV, for the speed of *Niña*.

wind is such that the sails need no handling before nightfall, the men sit about talking and spinning yarns, tending a fishline, washing in buckets of salt water. Peninsular seamen were a cleanly lot. Columbus, at least twice on his First Voyage, mentions their going swimming in a mid-ocean calm, and they never missed a chance to wash themselves and their clothes upon landing near a river. They certainly needed it, since hygiene (in the sixteenth century) required them to wear woolen clothes from neck to feet no matter how hot the climate.

In the second dog watch and before the first night watch is set, all hands are called to evening prayers. The ceremony begins with a ship's boy trimming the binnacle lamp and singing, as he brings it aft along the deck:

> *Amén. Dios nos dé buenas noches, buen viaje, buen pasaje haga la nao, Señor Capitán y Maestre y buena compaña.*
>
> Amen. God give us a good night and good sailing; may the ship make a good passage, Sir Captain and Master and good company.

The boys then lead the ship's company in what was technically called *la doctrina cristiana*. All hands say *Pater Noster, Ave Maria*, and *Credo*, and sing *Salve Regina*. This beautiful hymn, one of the oldest Benedictine chants, fittingly closed the day. The music has come down to us so that we can in some measure re-create that ancient hymn of praise to the Queen of Heaven that floated over uncharted waters every evening as a fleet of discovery slipped along.

We are not to suppose that the seamen kept very close to this music. Columbus once refers to the "*Salve Regina*, which the seamen sing or say after their own fashion," and Salazar wrote his friend: "Presently begins the *Salve*, and we are all singers, for we all have a throat. . . For as mariners are great friends of divisions, and divide the four winds into thirty-two, so the eight tones of music they distribute into thirty-two other and different tones, perverse, resonant, and very dissonant, as if we had today in the singing of the *Salve* and *Litany* a tempest of hurricanes of music, so that if God and His glorious Mother and the Saints to whom we pray should look down upon our tones and voices and not on our hearts and spirits, it would not do to beseech mercy with such a confusion of bawlings!"

The boatswain or boatswain's mate, whichever is on watch, extinguishes the cooking fire before the first night watch is set. As the *ampolleta* is turned up, the boy chorister sings:—

Bendita la hora en que Dios nació,	Blessed be the hour in which God was born
Santa María que le parió	Saint Mary who bore Him
San Juan que le bautizó.	Saint John who baptized Him.
La guarda es tomada,	The watch is called,
La ampolleta muele,	the glass floweth;
buen viaje haremos	We shall make a good voyage
si Dios quisiere.	if God willeth.

On sail the ships through the soft tropic night. Every half hour the boy turns his *ampolleta* and sings his little ditty:

Una va pasada	One glass is gone
y en dos muele;	and now the second floweth;
más molerá	more shall run down
si mi Dios querrá	if my God willeth.
á mi Dios pidamos,	To my God let's pray
que bien viaje hagamos;	to give us a good voyage;
y á la que es Madre de Dios y abogada nuestra,	and through His blessed Mother our advocate on high,
que nos libre de agua de bomba y tormenta.	protect us from the waterspout and send no tempest nigh.

Then he calls to the lookout forward:

Ah! de proa, alerta, buena guardia! Hey you! forward, look alive, keep good watch!

At which the lookout was supposed to make a shout or grunt to prove that he was awake (like our "Lights burning brightly, sir!"). Every hour the helm and the lookout are relieved, but the captain of the watch keeps the quarterdeck for the whole watch, pacing up and down and peering into the binnacle to see if the helmsman is holding his course. If the night is quiet, all members of the watch not on lookout or at the helm lean over the fore bulwarks, watching entranced the phosphorescent sea, dreaming of epic morrows in that marvelous New and Other World.

SALVE REGINA

Sal - ve Re - gi - na   Ma - ter Mi - se - ri - cor - di - ae,

Vi - ta, Dul - ce - do,   et spes no - stra sal - ve.

Ad Te cla - ma - mus   ex - su - les Fi - li - i E - vae.

Ad Te sus - pi - ra - mus Ge - men - tes   et flen - tes

In hac la - cri - ma - rum val - le.   E - ia er - go

Ad - vo - ca - ta no - stra,   il - los   tu - os

Mi - se - ri - cor - des o - cu - los   ad nos con - ver - te.

Et Je - sum Be - ne - di - ctum fru - ctum ven - tris tu - i,

No - bis post hoc ex - si - li - um o - sten - de.   O cle - mens,

O   Pi - a,   O   Dul - cis Vir - goMa - ri - a.

✳ XX ✳

Columbus's Fourth Voyage

1502-1504

The "High Voyage"

We left Columbus in Spain in early 1502, forlornly watching the fleet of Governor Ovando, his successor, depart for Santo Domingo. He felt that the only thing left for him to do, now that he had been deprived of all governmental privileges, was to embark on a new voyage. Hence his Fourth, and last, Voyage to America, a highly interesting one to sailors. The Admiral evidently thought so too, as he always referred to it as *El Alto Viaje*.

Almost fifty-one years old at the start and fifty three when he returned, the Admiral was already an old man by the standards of the day, but on this voyage he showed the highest qualities of seamanship, courage, and fitness to command. Unfortunately, by sailing out into the blue he did not dispense with court influence and administrative problems. The treasurer of Castile, on whom he depended for the seamen's pay, insisted on his taking two Porras brothers, one as captain of a caravel and the other as crown comptroller, since their sister was his mistress. An odd way of pleasing a mistress; but that is what she and the "boys" wanted, and they would have returned as heads of the expedition had the Columbus brothers not been a little too much for them.

516

The celerity with which the Admiral got away this time, and the ample provision made for his fleet, strongly suggest a desire on the part of Ferdinand and Isabella to get rid of him. He asked for the fleet on 26 February 1502; the Sovereigns authorized it on 14 March, and ordered him to make all convenient speed westward, "since the present season is very good for navigation" (which it was not!). He actually organized an expedition of four caravels in a little more than two weeks.

The main object of this voyage was to find a strait between Cuba (still assumed to be a promontory of China) and the continent discovered in 1498. As we have seen, Ojeda, Bastidas, and others had pushed along the Spanish Main as far as the Gulf of Urabá or Darien; but the shores and waters of the Caribbean west of a line drawn from Darien to Bahia Cortés, Cuba, including the entire Gulf of Mexico, were still unexplored by Europeans. Here, Columbus believed, was the key to the great geographical riddle: the relation of his discoveries to Asia. Here he expected to find the strait through which Marco Polo had sailed from China into the Indian Ocean. And the Sovereigns gave him a letter of introduction to Vasco da Gama, outward bound on his second voyage to India around the Cape of Good Hope, in the hope that the two would meet somewhere in the Indian Ocean! Everyone still regarded *the* Ocean Sea as one and indivisible, and the "great sea of India" as a mere bay of it, like the Mediterranean, which would be readily accessible from Europe if only you could find an opening in the western Caribbean.

The Admiral had hoped to have built for him some bergantinas, shoal-draft lateeners with banks of oars, which would make it possible to sail to windward, up rivers, and against a contrary current—but there was no time for that. He had to take what ships he could get, and they were not too bad. Each of his four caravels was square-rigged with small main topsails, and of about the same burthen as *Niña*. Columbus and his son Ferdinand sailed in the largest (70 tuns), the name of which we do not know. He always referred to her as *La Capitana*, the flagship. Diego Tristán, who had been with the Admiral on his Second Voyage, served as her captain. She carried a crew of two officers, 14 able seamen, 20 boys, and 7 petty officers, including trumpeters, presumably to provide a dignified entrance for the Admiral to Oriental ports. The second vessel of this fleet, called *La Gallega* (the Galician), mounted a bonaventure mizzen, a tiny fourth mast stepped on the taffrail like the jigger of a modern yawl. Pedro de Terreros, the only man who is known to have sailed in all four of Columbus's voyages, commanded her; and Juan Quintero, her owner, shipped as master. She carried a boatswain, 9 able seamen, 14 gromets, and one gentleman volunteer. Next in burthen came *Santiago de Palos*, nicknamed *Bermuda* after her owner and master Francisco Bermúdez. Her captain was the lord treasurer's crony Francisco Porras, whose brother Diego sailed with him as comptroller. Since this precious pair had never been to sea, Columbus fortunately insisted on brother Bartholomew's sailing in *Bermuda* as a passenger, with orders to take command in time of stress, when the Porras brothers cowered below. She carried 11 able seamen and a boatswain, 6 gentlemen volunteers, 12 boys, and 4 petty officers. Smallest of the fleet, measuring about 50 tuns, was *Vizcaina* (the Biscayan), commanded by Bartolomeo Fieschi, scion of a leading Genoese family which had befriended the Colombos in times past. She carried a boatswain, 3 gentlemen, 8 able seamen, 10 boys, and the fleet chaplain Fray Alejandro.

All except the Columbus family were on the royal payroll; the captains touched 4000 maravedis (about $27 in gold) a month; able seamen were paid one-quarter of that, and apprentice seamen about $5. Everyone received an unusual advance of six months' pay, and those who survived the voyage had a pot of money coming to them. Collecting it, of course, was another matter.

Comparing the crew list with that of the First Voyage, the only other that we have, one notes the large number of boys between 12 and 18 years old carried in this Fourth Voyage. The Admiral had evidently learned that on a voyage of discovery and high adventure, young fellows make better seamen and obey orders more briskly than old shellbacks who grumble and growl. "What's the idea? Old Captain So-and-So didn't do it that way!" and declare that the new islands are not worth a ducat apiece, and hanker after the fleshpots of Marseilles, Naples, and Lisbon.

The fleet sailed from Seville, 3 April 1502, and on the way down river careened at Casa de Viejo to cleanse the ships' bottoms and pay them with pitch to discourage teredos. On this voyage, unfortunately, the teredos seemed to like pitch; they ate right through it and, within a few months, had riddled the planking. From the river mouth the caravels proceeded to Cadiz, where Columbus and his twelve-year-old son Ferdinand came on board.

At Cadiz the fleet was delayed by foul winds until 11 May, when it sailed with a favoring northerly. After a courtesy call at Arzila on the coast of Morocco, where the Portuguese were reportedly hard-pressed by the Moors, the fleet reached Las Palmas on 20 May and sailed from the Grand Canary on the 25th. "West and by South," the same course as the Second Voyage, was set by the Admiral. We have no details of the ocean passage, completed in only 21 days, a middle-Atlantic record for many years. On 15 June they made landfall on Martinique, next island south of Dominica, tarried there three days for rest and refreshment (apparently undisturbed by Caribs or Amazons), and then ranged the chain of Antilles discovered on the Second Voyage.

On 29 June the Admiral hove-to in the roadstead off the Ozama River mouth, Santo Domingo. He had been forbidden by the Sovereigns to visit his viceroyalty lest he and Ovando run afoul of each other; but the Admiral had several good excuses, if not reasons, to look in at his former capital. He knew that Ovando was about to dispatch a fleet home and that a hurricane was making up, and he wished to take refuge. Columbus had already experienced two hurricanes and recognized the portents only too well. An oily swell rolled in from the southeast, veiled cirrus clouds tore along through the upper air, light gusty winds played over the surface of the water, low-pressure twinges were felt in his arthritic joints, and (a sign unknown to modern hydrographers) various denizens of the deep such as seal and manatee gamboled on the surface in large numbers. So, heaving-to in the outer roadstead, the Admiral sent Captain Terreros ashore with a note to Governor Ovando, predicting a hurricane within two days and requesting permission to take refuge there, and begging the governor to keep all ships in port and double their mooring lines. Ovando had the folly not only to disregard both warning and request but to read the Admiral's note aloud with sarcastic comments to his heelers, who roared with laughter over this "soothsayer" who pretended to be able to predict the winds. And the great fleet proceeded to sea as the governor had planned.

Retribution came swiftly. Ovando's fleet had just rounded into

Mona Passage with the harborless southeastern coast of Hispaniola on the port hand, when the hurricane burst upon it from the northeast. Ships foundered at sea or were driven onto the lee shore and destroyed; and among those that went down with all hands was the flagship commanded by Antonio de Torres, carrying Bobadilla as passenger and a cargo estimated at over half a million dollars in gold. Nineteen ships sank with all hands, six others were lost but left a few survivors, and four scudded safely around Saona into Santo Domingo, arriving in a sinking condition. The only ship that got through to Spain was the smallest, named *Aguja*, bearing Columbus's agent Carvajal with gold belonging to the Admiral which he had forced Bobadilla to disgorge.

Denied shelter at Santo Domingo, the Admiral sought it off the mouth of the Rio Jaina, a short distance to the westward. For he rightly estimated that the hurricane would pass through the Mona Passage and along the north coast of Hispaniola, so that the wind would blow off the southern shore, affording a lee to his ships. As night closed in, the north wind reached the height of its fury, probably a hundred miles per hour. The three smaller caravels parted their cables and drove out to sea, but were well handled (*Bermuda* by Bartholomew Columbus, as Captain Porras took to his bunk) and escaped with only superficial damage. The Admiral had every bit of ironmongery on board frapped to *Capitana*'s cables, and she rode it out. As he remarked in a letter home, "What man ever born, not excepting Job, would not have died of despair when in such weather, seeking safety for son, brother, shipmates and myself, we were forbidden the land and the harbor that I, by God's will and sweating blood, won for Spain!"

By God's will and good seamanship his little fleet came through and made rendezvous in the landlocked harbor of Puerto Viejo de Azua, some fifty miles to the west of Santo Domingo. Columbus and his captains could not have done better if they had received storm warnings by radio. One ship's boat and three anchors were the only serious losses.

After resting a week or ten days at Azua, they put to sea again, steering southwest to the Alta Vela Channel and then west across the Windward Passage, and along the south shore of Jamaica; thence northwest to a cay, probably Cayo Largo off the south coast of Cuba.

Bonacca Island. Señora Obregón photo.

On 27 July the wind turned northeast and the fleet crossed the Caribbean, 360 miles wide at this point, in three days. When the wind moderated, a lookout sighted a group of islands off the coast of Honduras.

At Bonacca or Guanaja, first of the lofty, highly colored, and spectacular Bay Islands, where the Spaniards anchored, they encountered the biggest native canoe any of them had seen: "Long as a galley," beamy, with a cabin amidships for passengers. She carried cotton cloth, copper implements and crucibles for smelting ore, gourds full of beer made from the hubo fruit, and cacao beans which the Jicaque Indians of Honduras used, even recently, as currency. The canoe had come from the mainland, and after trading with the Bay Islands, was bound for Coronel Island off the Yucatan coast, a native emporium for Caribbean traffic. Columbus forcibly detained the skipper, whom he renamed Juan Pérez, as guide and interpreter.

After crossing the thirty-mile strait to Cape Honduras (now called Punta Castilla) on the mainland, the fleet anchored off the site of Trujillo, later founded by Cortés. Here began in earnest the Admiral's search for *the* strait. Should he turn west or east? West would be easier going but hard to get back from against the prevailing wind. So eastward he turned, and that let him in for a long and distressing beat to windward lasting twenty-eight days, from Rio Romano to Cape Gracias a Dios.

> It was one continual rain, thunder and lightning [wrote Columbus]. The ships lay exposed to the weather, with sails torn, and anchors, rigging, cables, boats and many of the stores lost; the people, exhausted and so down in the mouth that they were all the time making vows to be good, to go on pilgrimages and all that; yea; even hearing one another's confessions! Other tempests I have seen, but none that lasted so long or so grim as this. Many old hands whom we looked on as stout fellows lost their courage. What griped me most were the sufferings of my son; to think that so young a lad, only thirteen, should go through so much. But Our Lord lent him such courage that he even heartened the rest, and he worked as though he had been to sea all of a long life. That comforted me. I was sick and many times lay at death's door, but gave orders from a doghouse that the people clapped together for me on the poop deck. My brother was in the worst of the ships, the crank one, and I felt terribly having persuaded him to come against his will.

The wind blew steadily from the east, and the current too ran counter to their course. Every morning the caravels had to weigh anchor, make sail, and claw off shore on the starboard tack, often in heavy rain. At noon the fleet wore to the port tack, stood inshore again, and at sundown anchored off a sodden coast in an open roadstead, the caravels pitching and tossing all night, and the crew fighting mosquitoes from the swamps. Some days they gained a few miles; on others they fetched up opposite the same grove of mangroves off which they had spent the previous night. The average distance made good was only six miles a day. But the Admiral had to be getting on; he dared not tarry for a fair wind, nor to stand out to sea lest he miss the strait. It was the most exhausting sail of his entire career.

At last, on 14 September 1502, the fleet doubled a cape that the Admiral named *Gracias a Dios* (Thanks be to God). Since the land here trended southward, this marked the end of his long dead-beat; now they were able to jog along on the port tack a safe distance from shore.

A Nicaraguan beach, Cape Gracias a Dios in distance. Señora Obregón photo.

They anchored off the Rio Grande de Nicaragua, 120 miles south of Gracias a Dios, to obtain wood and water; Columbus sent a boat over the bar safely, but on the return it was capsized and two sailors were drowned, so the Admiral named this place *Rio de los Desastres.* Off its mouth today there is bar which the chart says is dangerous, and it certainly looks so from the air. They passed at night at Rio San Juan del Norte, missing a chance to sail up to Lake Nicaragua within fifteen miles of the Pacific, and entered a region that the Indians called Cariai, the present Costa Rica.

Ten days were passed at anchor behind Uvita Islet, off the present Puerto Limón. Here they had friendly though somewhat aloof relations with the local Talamanca Indians. The usual roles were reversed, the natives eager to do business and the Spaniards somewhat coy. First, the Indians swam out to the caravels with a line of cotton shirts and ornaments of *guanin*, the gold and copper alloy that Columbus had found in Paria on the Third Voyage. Evidently *guanin* did not sell in Spain, for Columbus would have none of it, but gave the would-be traders some presents to take ashore. Next, to break down "sales resistance," the Indians sent on board two virgins, one about eight and the other about fourteen years old. "They showed great fortitude," recorded Ferdinand (who was then about the same age as the elder), "gave no signs of grief or fear but always looked cheerful and modest. The Admiral . . . had them clothed and fed and had them sent ashore." (Columbus, on the contrary, wrote that they were immodest hussies.) Spanish continence astonished the natives; and when, next day, Bartholomew went ashore to take formal possession, the Indians took his writing materials (ink in a cow's horn, quill pen and paper) to be magical apparatus, and tossed brown powder into the air as "good joss" to counteract these apparently sexless sorcerers from Spain.

To reconnoiter this part of Costa Rica, Columbus sent an armed party upcountry. They reported an abundance of game—deer, puma, and the turkey-like currosow bird. And they brought back as a pet a spider monkey which one of the crossbowmen had wounded. In the meantime, the Indians at Puerto Limón had presented the Admiral with a pair of peccaries, one of which he kept. It was so fierce and aggressive that his Irish wolfhound remained below deck as long as the porker was on board. Piggy met his match, however, in the spider monkey which, wounded though it was, coiled its tail around the peccary's snout, seized him by the nape of the neck, and bit him until he screamed with pain. This "novel and pretty sport," as Columbus called it, he wrote about in full detail to the Sovereigns. Ferdinand, at least, would have enjoyed it.

On 5 October the search for the strait was renewed, and toward evening Columbus believed that he had found it in a channel, the Boca del Dragón, that leads into a great bay now named *Almirante* after him. Once inside, he found Indians wearing on their breasts "mirrors," disks of fine gold. For the standard price of three hawks' bells, value about a penny, the Spaniards were able to buy a gold disk worth ten ducats, about twenty-five dollars.

Having allowed "Juan Pérez" to go home, the Spaniards from now on had no interpreter. So, when Columbus asked in sign language for a strait to a wide ocean, the Indians waved him on to a narrow passage (now Split Hill Channel) that led out of the lagoon. The caravels sailed through this channel, so narrow that their yards brushed

Split Hill Channel in foreground. Columbus sailed through, but not to Indian Ocean. Señora Obregón photo.

the trees, and were rewarded by the sight of a great expanse of water. But, alas, there were mountains on every side; this was not the Indian Ocean but Chiriqui lagoon.

For ten days the fleet idled about the shores of this lagoon, the Guaymi Indians plying a brisk trade in gold disks and bird-shaped amulets which the Spaniards called eagles. Columbus learned from them that he was on an isthmus between two seas, but a high cordillera barred his way. He also picked up from the Indians, or misunderstood them to say, that the Ganges River was only ten days' sail away. Referring to his Bible, the Admiral inferred that this region was the Ophir of 2 Chronicles viii. 18, whence the servants of Hiram brought 450 talents of gold to Solomon. Apparently he also satisfied himself that no strait existed, since from now on he concentrated on gathering gold and establishing a trading post.

On 17 October 1502, a day of westerly wind, the fleet left Chiriqui lagoon by the eastward channel, passed a little shield-shaped island that the Admiral named *El Escudo,* and sailed along Miskito Gulf, working its way east against the trades. From here to Limón Bay (now the Caribbean entrance to the Panama Canal), a distance of over 125 miles, there are no harbors except where a river mouth has built up a bar over which only a canoe can enter, and only when the bar is not breaking. Because of this, and also because the Indians made menacing gestures (howling, spitting, beating drums, blowing conch-shell trumpets, and brandishing spears) at the roadsteads where he anchored, Columbus pressed forward as fast as westerly winds would take him, hoping to find a more hospitable spot for a trading post. On 2 November the four caravels entered a fine harbor which he named *Puerto Bello* and is still so called; during the Spanish colonial regime it became a thriving city at the northern end of the trans-isthmian mule track.

Had Columbus decided to locate there, his garrison would certainly have heard of the Isthmus of Panama and obtained a glimpse of the Pacific Ocean ten years before Balboa did. But the local Indians, though friendly, could not be understood. The Admiral stayed less than a week, obtained provisions and cotton, and continued his voyage on 9 November, when the wind forced them back several miles to a harbor which Columbus named *Puerto de Bastimentos*, Harbor of Provisions. Ten years later, Diego de Nicuesa renamed it *Nombre de Dios* and founded a town which long shared the transit trade with Puerto Bello, and so was sacked by Francis Drake. There the Columbus fleet remained twelve days, making minor repairs while the wind stayed in the east. Again, the Admiral missed a chance to start a settlement at a suitable site.

Their next stop was at a tiny harbor which they called *El Puerto del Retrete*, now called Escribanos. It was so small that the four caravels had to tie up alongside the banks, as to a wharf. This gave the men a chance to sneak off to Indian villages and do private trading with a gun, and that made trouble. Indians gathered on the beach and made threatening gestures, and the Admiral had to mow down a few with gunfire before the rest would disperse.

Tired of waiting for the wind to change, Columbus now decided to sail back to Veragua and take measures to obtain more of the gold which the natives displayed so abundantly in their personal jewelry. On 5 December the fleet returned to Puerto Bello. Next day the wind whipped around into the west again. For a month, the caravels were batted back and forth. The current always changed with the wind;

it was no use trying to buck it. The weather was unusually foul. "I don't say it rained," recorded Columbus, "because it was like another deluge," with thunder and lightning whenever the wind changed. Once the fleet was threatened by a tremendous waterspout, but it passed harmlessly after the Admiral had exorcised it by reading aloud from the Gospel according to St. John the account of that famous tempest on the Sea of Galilee concluding, "It is I: be not afraid." Then, clasping the Bible in his left hand, with drawn sword he traced a cross in the sky and a circle around the fleet. That night *Vizcaina* lost sight of her consorts but found them again after three very dark, tempestuous days. The people were so worn out, said the Admiral, that they longed for death to end their sufferings. Then came two days of calm, during which great schools of shark lashed around the caravels; many were taken and some eaten, as provisions were running low. Ferdinand remembered that the hardtack had become so full of weevils that some men waited for darkness to eat a porridge made of it, but others did not even trouble to wait, "because they might lose their supper had they been so nice."

Two days before Christmas, the fleet put in at the present harbor of Cristóbal, Panama Canal Zone, and there kept Christmas and New Year's Day 1503, very miserably, riding at anchor off the site of the present-day Coco Solo naval base. Here, had he only known it, Columbus was within a few miles of solving the riddle of the strait. He might have gone up the Chagres in borrowed Indian canoes. From the head of navigation he would have been only twelve miles by land from the Pacific Ocean. But he and his men were so beaten down by their long buffeting, so drained of energy and enterprise, and so incapable of communicating with the natives, that they did nothing. Thus Columbus missed by a few miles the most important geographical discovery he could have made on the High Voyage.

Santa Maria de Belén

Sailing back, westward along the inhospitable coast of Veragua, Columbus searched for a likely place to found a trading post which would draw on the abundant gold of that region. On 6 January he anchored off the mouth of a river that he named *Belén* (Bethlehem) because it was Epiphany, the Feast of the Three Kings who brought gifts of gold, frankincense and myrrh, to the infant Jesus. A good omen! Sounding from the boats, he found seven feet of water over the bar and towed his caravels inside, where the river forms a deep basin. They were just in time, as next day another storm worked up a heavy sea which broke on the river bar.

The coastal plain here narrows to a few hundred yards' width, and behind it rises rugged, broken country covered by an impenetrable rain forest; and behind that, mountains whose summits are usually concealed by clouds. The coast consists of long sand beaches separated by rocky bluffs. It is a dangerous place to anchor, and in most places impossible to land from small boats. Rainfall is so excessive that agriculture on any large scale is unprofitable. The few people who live along that shore today have no means of communication with the outside world except by dugout canoes, which can be launched only when the sea is exceptionally calm. We on the Harvard Columbus Expedition found this the most difficult region of all discovered by the Admiral, to examine. Only through the co-operation of the Panama government, providing us with a diesel-powered trading sloop and a good native pilot, did we manage to effect a landing (after sundry tumblings in the surf) at the Río Belén.

A few days after the Feast of the Epiphany, Bartholomew Columbus took the ships' boats westward along the coast and rowed up the next river (the Veragua) toward the seat of a cacique known as the Quibián. Dignified but friendly, the Quibián came downstream with a fleet of canoes to greet the visitors, and next day called on the Admiral in *Capitana*.

Veragua has one of the heaviest rainfalls in the world, and the ground is so thoroughly soaked that every storm starts a freshet. Columbus experienced this on 24 January 1503. Following a rainstorm in the mountains, a torrent roared down on the caravels in the Belén mooring basin. *Capitana* dragged, fouled *Gallega*, and carried away her bonaventure mizzen; and only by smart work with the ground tackle were both vessels kept from broaching on the bar. Two weeks of rain and flood followed; it was not until 6 February that the sea was calm enough for the boats to come out. Bartholomew then made a return visit to the Quibián and marched upcountry along an Indian trail with native guides. In one day, with no other implements but their knives, the Spaniards collected about ten dollars' worth of gold apiece.

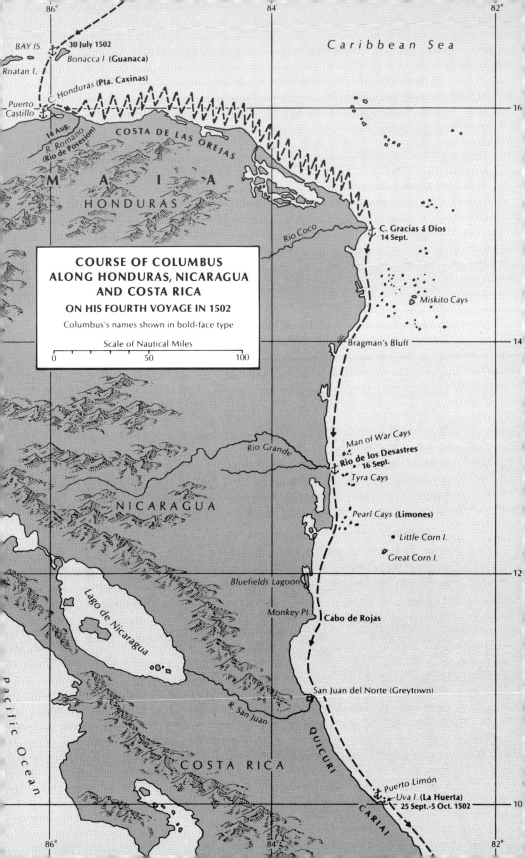

**COURSE OF COLUMBUS
ALONG HONDURAS, NICARAGUA
AND COSTA RICA**

ON HIS FOURTH VOYAGE IN 1502

Columbus's names shown in bold-face type

Scale of Nautical Miles

0   50   100

Caribbean Sea

BAY IS.
30 July 1502
Bonacca I. **(Guanaca)**
Roatan I.
C. Honduras (Pta. Caxinas)
*Puerto
Castillo*
14 Aug.
*R. Romano
(Rio de Posesion)*
COSTA DE LAS OREJAS

M A I A

HONDURAS

Rio Coco

**C. Gracias á Dios
14 Sept.**

Miskito Cays

Bragman's Bluff

Rio Grande

Man of War Cays
**Rio de los Desastres
16 Sept.**
Tyra Cays

NICARAGUA

Pearl Cays **(Limones)**

Little Corn I.

Great Corn I.

Bluefields Lagoon

Lago de Nicaragua

Monkey Pt. **Cabo de Rojas**

San Juan del Norte (Greytown)

R. San Juan

Pacific Ocean

COSTA RICA

QUICURI

Puerto Limón
Uva I. **(La Huerta)**
25 Sept.-5 Oct. 1502

CARIAI

16

14

12

10

86°   84°   82°

Discovery of this auriferous region so pleased the Admiral that he decided to build a fortified trading post at Belén, leave his brother in charge, and return to Spain for reinforcements. A little hill near the mouth of the river was chosen for the site, and the men began to construct the post, which Columbus named *Santa Maria de Belén*. He had chosen about the worst spot on the coast of Central America to establish a beachhead.

In 1940, when we were ranging this coast to check up on Columbus, we encountered an old prospector who explained why Veragua had never been really exploited for gold. Years before, he went up one of the rivers with a partner and an Indian guide. "Where do we find gold?" he asked, after paddling many miles. "Right here!" said the Indian, who pulled out a clasp knife, dug some clay from the river bank and panned out plenty of gold grains! The prospector and his partner began at once to plan how to spend their first million dollars. They returned to the nearest town for supplies and lumber and built sluice boxes, the product of which should have made them rich. But in the next freshet all this gear was washed into the Caribbean. That has happened again and again during the last four and a half centuries. There is still "gold in them thar hills," but only the Indians know how to get it out.

Rio Belén now fell so low that the caravels could not cross the bar. And at this juncture, when they were trapped inside, there came the inevitable change of attitude on the part of the Guaymi Indians. Sailors had been sneaking off by twos and threes to trade with a gun and get women. The Quibián could put up with a good deal of that if he believed that his importunate visitors would shortly depart; but since they now showed every intention of settling down, he decided to give them "the treatment." He sent men in canoes to reconnoiter Belén. They acted so suspiciously that Diego Méndez, one of the Admiral's gentlemen volunteers, offered to row along the coast to learn what was going on. After a few miles he came upon a camp of a thousand howling warriors. Méndez, with that amazing nerve of the Spaniard in face of danger, stepped ashore alone to confront them; then, returning to his boat, kept just out of arrow range all night, observing the Indians' movements. They, realizing that surprise had been lost, retreated to the Quibián's village. Méndez followed them thither, and in the midst of a horrible uproar, coolly pulled out a barber's kit and had his hair cut by his companion, Rodrigo de Escobar. This not only stopped the yelling but so intrigued the Quibián that he ordered his hair to be trimmed. Méndez did so and presented him with the shears, mirror, and comb, after which the Spaniards were allowed to return in peace.

Columbus should now have taken the hint that his trading post would be untenable in the face of the hostility of thousands of Indians who could sneak up under cover of the jungle and overwhelm it. Instead, he made another bad decision—to seize the Quibián and hold him as hostage for his people's good behavior. The cacique and about thirty others were ambushed by an armed party of Spaniards and carried down river. But the Quibián broke his bonds, escaped, and raised his people against the intruders.

In the meantime, seamen were towing three of the four caravels over the bar, intending to leave behind *Gallega* as a floating fortress for the use of Bartholomew and the Belén garrison. On 6 April, while farewells were being said and only twenty men and the Irish wolf-hound were guarding the fort, it was attacked by hundreds of Indians armed with bows and arrows and spears. They were beaten off, largely through the rough work of the hound. But the Indians promptly got their revenge by killing Captain Diego Tristán of *Capitana* who, with a boat party, insisted on carrying out orders issued by the Admiral before the fight started, to fill the flagship's water casks upstream. Only one Spaniard of the boat party escaped, and ten were killed. Ferdinand contrasts this Spaniard's stolid courage with that of Bastiano, an Italian member of the garrison. Méndez caught him running away from the fight and ordered him "About face!" to which Bastiano replied, "Let me go, you devil! I am going to save myself!" and did.

The Admiral, ill with malaria, remained alone on board *Capitana* anchored outside the bar; all his crew had gone ashore to help the garrison. He climbed to the main top and shouted to the men to return, but they could not hear his voice above the hideous screams of the Indians. He became delirious, saw visions, and heard a voice which he believed to be that of God Almighty reminding him that He had done as much for Columbus as for Moses and David, that his tribulations were "written on tablets of marble," and that he was to fear not but trust Him.

Río Belén. Santa Maria de Belén was on the left-hand hill

Here was a tough situation. Three caravels were lying in the open roadstead outside the bar, at the mercy of any storm that might blow up; one (*Gallega*), which the Admiral intended to leave for the garrison's use, lay trapped inside. Indians continued to prowl about the settlement, raising horrid whoops and yells; and there were no hostages for their good behavior, since those imprisoned on board the flagship either escaped or hanged themselves in the hold. Columbus now realized that he had made the Indians implacable enemies and that the trading post must be evacuated or the garrison would meet the fate of Navidad. Having only one small boat left, and that too deep to get over the bar, Columbus had to send orders to his brother by a stout swimmer, Pedro de Ledesma. He returned with Bartholomew's urgent request that the garrison be evacuated promptly, and Columbus consented. Diego Méndez built a raft upon which all the Spaniards ashore, with most of their stores and gear, were lightered across the bar.

Gallega was abandoned, and Santa Maria de Belén reverted to wilderness.

No subsequent attempt to found a European settlement on that coast ever succeeded. The descendants of the Guaymi have retreated to the interior, and except for a few clearings where a handful of half-breeds live in poverty, the coast of Veragua is as wild, wet, and forbiddingly beautiful as when Columbus landed there on the Feast of the Three Kings in 1503.

Marooned in Jamaica

On Easter Sunday, 16 April 1503, *Capitana*, *Bermuda*, and *Vizcaina* departed Belén roads, hoping to make Santo Domingo by Whitsuntide. Columbus, estimating his longitude to be many degrees west of the meridian of Hispaniola, and knowing by experience that it was almost

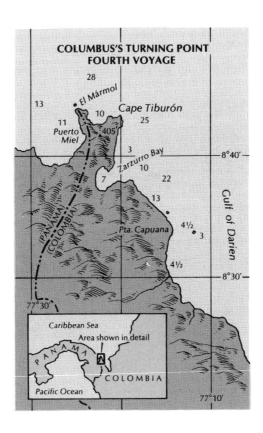

impossible to beat against the easterly trades and the equatorial currents, planned to edge along the coast by working the land breeze and anchoring in bad weather. Then, when he had reached an estimated point due south of Hispaniola, to fetch Santo Domingo on the starboard tack. This sensible decision caused murmurings among the men because the pilots, wrong as usual, estimated that they were already due south of Santo Domingo, or even Puerto Rico. And the three caravels were riddled with teredos. Columbus, being blamed for this, answered thus in his report to the Sovereigns:—

"Let those who are fond of blaming and finding fault, while they sit safely at home, ask, 'Why did you not do thus and so?' I wish they were on this voyage; I well believe that another voyage of a different kind awaits them, or our faith is naught."

In other words, to hell with them!

As the coastwise voyage progressed, all hands were kept busy at the pumps or bailing with buckets and kettles. Nevertheless, *Vizcaina* had to be abandoned in a hopelessly leaky condition at Puerto Bello, where her carcass was found by Nicuesa in 1509. Her crew was divided between *Capitana* and *Bermuda*. These two crawled along into the Gulf of San Blas. All hands were too busy trying to keep afloat to admire the scenery, where a jagged cordillera rises behind gleaming white beaches and a tropical rain forest of mahogany, ebony, and other hard woods. Their foliage makes a glossy-leaved canopy above which an occasional giant of the forest thrusts a top bursting with pink or orange blossoms, as though a torch were being held up from the dark jungle. And the Cuna Cuna or San Blas Indians have retained their integrity and independence to this day.

On 1 May the two caravels reached a headland that Columbus named *El Mármol*, the Marble Cape, because of conspicuous white strata on the cliffs. In that aspect it is unique on this coast, and so has enabled Señor Obregón and myself to identify it positively as Cape Tiburón, on which a small monument marks the boundary between the republics of Colombia and Panama. As the coast here trends southeast into the Gulf of Darien, the pilots and captains, hopefully figuring that they were already east of Guadeloupe, ganged up on Columbus and practically forced him to leave the coast and strike northward. Actually they were on the meridian of Kingston, Jamaica, and about

El Mármol (Cape Tiburón) with its white strata. Señora Obregón photo.

900 miles west of Guadeloupe! The Admiral was so beaten down by arthritis, malaria, and apparent failure that he gave in.

So, on May Day 1503, worm-eaten *Capitana* and riddled *Bermuda* stood northward, sailing as close to the wind as possible, but continually set to leeward by the current. Ten days later they passed the Little Cayman island northwest of Jamaica, and on the 12th made a most unwelcome landfall on the Cuban archipelago which Columbus had formerly named the Queen's Garden. "Full of hunger and trouble," as Ferdinand records, the caravels dropped anchor in a little harbor with poor holding ground at Cayo Breton. The people had "nothing to eat but hardtack and a little oil and vinegar, exhausted by

535

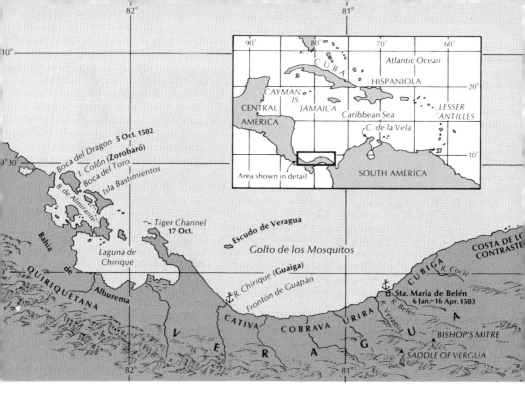

working three pumps day and night because the vessels were ready to sink from the multitude of worms that had bored into them." On top of that, one of the night thunderstorms for which this coast is notorious burst upon them, causing *Bermuda* to part her cable and foul *Capitana*. The flagship passed her a line, and *Capitana*'s one remaining anchor fortunately held them both.

After six days the wind moderated and the caravels, with planking "like a honeycomb" and the sailors "spiritless and desperate," continued to struggle eastward along the Cuban coast. By about 10 June 1503 when they were still west of Santiago, Columbus decided that the only way to save their lives was to stand out to sea on the port tack, hoping for a favorable slant that would take them across Windward Passage to Hispaniola. But when the caravels had reached a point estimated to be about a hundred miles from Cape Tiburón, the water gained on *Bermuda* at so alarming a rate that the Admiral ordered both caravels to square away for Jamaica. Since wooden ships labor less and sail faster with the wind aft, his decision to seek refuge in Jamaica saved their lives.

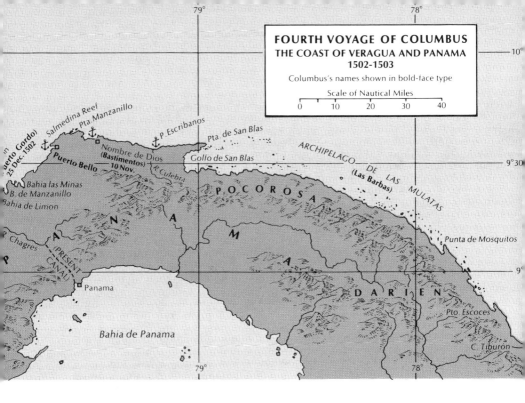

FOURTH VOYAGE OF COLUMBUS
THE COAST OF VERAGUA AND PANAMA
1502-1503

Columbus's names shown in bold-face type

Scale of Nautical Miles

0   10   20   30   40

On 25 June the wretched vessels, their decks almost awash, entered
St. Ann's Bay, Jamaica, which Columbus had named *Santa Gloria* on
the Second Voyage. (Here Spain founded her first Jamaican settlement, in 1509.) He ran them aground side by side on a sand beach,
and shored them up to keep them on an even keel. High tides rose almost to their decks, upon which palm-thatched cabins were built for
the 116 people.

And there they stayed for a year.

These Spaniards marooned on Jamaica were fairly well situated for
defense; the ships' hulks made a dry home and no mean fortress. A
large and friendly Indian village lay nearby. Columbus, who knew by
bitter experience that the natives would not long remain friendly if
his people were allowed to mingle with them, allowed nobody to go
ashore without his permission.

The first thing that needed attention was food. Diego Méndez and
three men set forth on a foraging expedition. They traveled almost to
the east end of the island, purchased a dugout canoe, loaded it with
native provisions, and returned to Santa Gloria in triumph; and, to en-

537

Santa Gloria (St. Ann's Bay), Jamaica, where Columbus spent a year. The clearing at right center indicates the excavation for Nueva Sevilla, the first Spanish settlement, founded in 1509.

sure a continuing supply, Méndez drew up a tariff agreement with the neighboring Indians to sell a cake of cassava bread for two glass beads, two of the big rodents called hutia for a lace point, and a great quantity of anything, such as fish or maize, for a hawk's bell. Why these Spaniards and Genoese could not fish for themselves or plant their own cornfields has never been explained; it is clear that if the Indians had not fed them they would have starved to death.

But how to get home? This final resting place of the two caravels commanded a wide sea view, but the chance of any Spanish or other vessel coming there was infinitesimal, since Columbus had broadcasted "no gold in Jamaica." *Capitana* and *Bermuda* were beyond repair. In later voyages we find Spaniards and Englishmen cheerfully constructing bergantinas and pinnaces on any wooded coast; but these crews appear to have been as incapable of building a small vessel as of feeding themselves. So the only possible way to avoid spending the rest of their lives in Jamaica was to send a messenger to Hispaniola.

As usual, everyone said, "Let Diego Méndez do it!" That faithful and indefatigable Spaniard hauled out the big dugout canoe he had purchased, fixed a false keel and washboards, and fitted a mast and sail. On his first attempt he was captured by Indians somewhere near Northeast Point, escaped, and returned to Santa Gloria. On the next he had plenty of assistance. Bartolomeo Fieschi, the Genoese captain of *Bermuda*, undertook to pilot a second canoe with him to Hispaniola, and the Adelantado organized an armed escort in the shape of a fleet of dugouts to protect them in Jamaican waters. At or near Northeast Point, farewells were exchanged and the two canoes pushed out into Windward Passage.

More to-do was made about this canoe trip than about anything else on the High Voyage. In comparison with numerous lifeboat and raft voyages in World War II, it does not seem a particularly long or difficult passage—only 108 miles from island to island, with a break at Navassa 78 miles out; and the month was July, when the trades die down and hurricanes are few. But neither the Spaniards nor these Indians were used to small-boat journeys, and they certainly took this one hard. Each captain had a crew of six Christians and ten Indian paddlers. The first day out was calm and the following night cool, but the natives drank up all their water rations. By the second sunset, one Indian had died of thirst and others were too weak to paddle.

And a third night fell with no sight of land. But when the moon rose, Diego Méndez observed the outline of Navassa Island against its lower limb. They reached the island in about 72 hours from Jamaica, a little better than a mile an hour. On Navassa everyone drank his fill of fresh water (some of the Indians dying of it), a fire was kindled and shellfish cooked. Now they could see the lofty mountains of Hispaniola, and the following evening they made Cape Tiburón, Haiti. Obtaining fresh Indian paddlers, Méndez and Fieschi continued along the coast to Azua, and thence marched inland to meet Ovando and request succor for the Admiral. It was now August 1503. The governor, by no means grieved at the prospect of Columbus dying in Jamaica, refused to send one of his station ships to rescue him and for seven months continued putting off Méndez. Finally, in March 1504, he was allowed to go to Santo Domingo and there charter a vessel.

Columbus and his men had no means of knowing whether their messengers had arrived or had perished. After six months had elapsed and the winter northers began to make their position on the grounded ships uncomfortable, a mutiny formed around the Porras brothers, the political appointees. They spread the word that Columbus was serving out a term of banishment and had no desire or intention to go to Santo Domingo. So, me lads, if you want to get out of this hell hole and back to Spain, join us; we'll grab a few guns, impress some Indian paddlers, and get ourselves to Hispaniola. Let that cursed Genoese and his infatuated followers stay here and rot!

Forty-eight men, about half the total, began the mutiny on the day after New Year's, 1504. Crying the watchword "To Castile! To Castile!" the mutineers piled into ten dugout canoes and started eastward along the coast, robbing the Indians wherever they called. They had made only about fifteen miles toward Northeast Point when a freshening breeze from the east forced them to put back. All their plunder had to be thrown overboard, and most of the Indian paddlers too. Two more attempts were made to cross, but both failed. So the Porras party abandoned their canoes and trudged back to Santa Gloria, living off the country.

In the meantime those loyal to Columbus were becoming very hungry. The Indians had no surplus stocks of food, and "consumer demand" for beads, lace points, and hawks' bells was exhausted. Moreover, said Ferdinand, every Spaniard consumed enough food for twenty Indians. At this critical juncture, the Admiral pulled his famous eclipse trick. He had an almanac which predicted a total eclipse of the moon on the last night of February 1504. So that day he summoned the nearby caciques and chief men on board stranded *Capitana*, told them that God desired the Indians to supply his people with food, and would presently give them a clear token from Heaven of divine displeasure at their failure to do so. Let them watch the moon that night! The eclipse began at moonrise, and as the blacked-out area increased, the Indians flocked to the ships, howling and lamenting, praying the Admiral to stop it. Columbus retired to his cabin while the eclipse lasted, emerged when he was sure that the total phase was almost over, and announced that he had interceded with the Almighty and promised in their name that they would provide the food the Christians wanted, in return for which God consented to take away the shadow. It worked perfectly, and there was no more food shortage.

At the end of March 1504, more than eight months had elapsed since the canoe messengers had left for Hispaniola, and nothing had been heard of or from them. Suddenly a small caravel sailed in to St. Ann's Bay and anchored near the Spanish camp. It had been sent by Ovando to report on Columbus, especially whether he were still alive. The governor was mean enough to order the captain, Diego de Escobar, not to take anyone to Hispaniola—but she did bring a message from Méndez that he was doing his best to charter a rescue ship. And also a welcome gift—two casks of wine and a side of salt pork.

The morale of the Spaniards hit an all-time low when this caravel disappeared over the horizon. Columbus made advances to the Porras party, knowing that he would be blamed if that pair of brothers did not get home. The Porrases rejected his offers (which included a share of the salt pork), in the hope of suborning the Admiral's men and seizing the stranded boats. They marched on Santa Gloria and the Columbus brothers mustered loyal men to meet them. A pitched battle, fought with knives and swords for want of gunpowder, took place on 29 May, and the loyalists won. The local Indians, who had ringside seats for this fight, doubtless enjoyed seeing the Christians carve each other up. One man had the sole of one foot sliced so neatly that it hung down like a slipper!

Rescue was not much longer in coming. Diego Méndez finally managed to charter a little caravel in Santo Domingo and sent her to

The Morisons and Obregóns home from their flight covering Columbus's Last Voyage.

Jamaica under command of Diego de Salcedo, a loyal servant of the Admiral. He made Santa Gloria in the latter part of June 1504, took everyone on board, and on the 29th departed for Hispaniola. The survivors of the Fourth Voyage, about a hundred strong, had been in Jamaica a year and five days. The little caravel was in poor condition with a sprung mainmast, rotten sails, and a foul bottom; she leaked so badly that they feared she would founder, and it took her six and a half weeks to reach Santo Domingo. There Columbus chartered another vessel and embarked for Spain on 12 September with his brother, his son, and twenty-two others of his company. A majority of the Fourth Voyage survivors elected to remain in Santo Domingo rather than risk another ocean passage. They had had enough work on the pumps to last ten lives.

We know not the route taken by this chartered ship, but the passage of fifty-six days was long and tempestuous, and although the mainmast broke, the Columbus brothers contrived a jury mast out of a spare yard. They finally reached Sanlúcar de Barrameda on 7 November 1504.

The High Voyage was over, after two and a half years at sea, including the year marooned in Jamaica. The most adventurous of the Admiral's four voyages, it was also the most disappointing. He had not discovered the Strait, since none there was; the isthmus that he reported was of no interest to the Sovereigns, and the gold-bearing Veragua that he discovered was unexploitable. But he had done his best. As he wrote to son Diego shortly after his arrival:

"I have served their Highnesses with as great diligence and love as I might have employed to win paradise and more; and if in somewhat I have been wanting, that was impossible, or much beyond my knowledge and strength. Our Lord God in such cases asketh nothing more of men than good will."

Death of the Admiral

After this long and distressing voyage, Columbus expected at least to be summoned to court to tell his story, a favor accorded to almost every captain of an overseas voyage, however insignificant. But the report he had sent home by Diego Méndez did not make a good impression. This *Lettera Rarissima* is rambling and incoherent. It contains some interesting information, together with a superfluity of self-justification and numerous unconvincing "proofs" that he had been sailing along the Malay Peninsula or somewhere in the Far East.

By the time the Admiral reached Seville, 8 or 9 November, the Sovereigns were holding court at Segovia and the Queen was suffering an illness that turned out to be her last. She died on 26 November 1504, greatly to Columbus's grief and loss. Isabella had never sneered at him. She understood what he was trying to do, respected his rights, and protected him from envy and detraction. Ferdinand, too, had supported him, but the Indies were the Queen's overseas kingdom, not his.

The Admiral, now living in a hired house in Seville, was sick in heart and body, but not badly off in this world's goods. He retained a share of the gold acquired on the Fourth Voyage, and Carvajal had brought home a substantial sum for him in *Aguja*, which survived the hurricane of 1502. Two years later, Ovando delivered to him a chest of gold, and he claimed about $180,000 more, still at Hispaniola with his mark on it. But Columbus felt that he had been defrauded and repeatedly besought his son to obtain confirmation of what he called his tithes, eighths, and thirds. The tithe meant 10 per cent of the net exports from all lands that he discovered, as guaranteed by the original contract of 1492. Columbus complained that the government allowed him only a tenth of their fifth of the gold; that is, 2 instead of 10 per cent. The eighth meant the Admiral's guaranteed investment in one-eighth part of the lading of any vessel trading with the Indies. He complained that Bobadilla or Ovando impounded his eighth in sundry cargoes without payment. The third was preposterous. Columbus's grant as Admiral of the Ocean Sea stated that it carried "pre-ëminences and prerogatives . . . in the same manner as . . . the Grand Admiral of Castile." Having ascertained that this Grand Admiral collected 33⅓ per cent tax on trade between Spain and the Canary Islands, Columbus claimed a similar cut on the entire inward and outward trade between Spain and the Indies! Obviously, if the crown had admitted that, little profit would have been left for anyone. As it was, even by collecting a mere 2 per cent of the gold, the Admiral was a rich man according to the standards of his day, and able to leave substantial legacies to his sons.

There is no evidence known to me to indicate that Columbus ever changed his cosmographical ideas, or realized the vast extent of the continent which he had discovered. Peter Martyr very early and Rodrigo Fernández de Santaclla (the editor of the first Spanish edition of Marco Polo) in 1503, among others, questioned whether Columbus's Indies were the real Indies, but the Discoverer ignored them. He died believing that his *Otro Mundo* was but an extension of the Malay Peninsula for several hundred miles.

Even on his deathbed Columbus planned to finance a new crusade, and tried to provide for it in his last will and testament. He spent practically nothing on himself or on keeping up appearances, and he always intended to use the profits of his discoveries to recover the Holy Sepulchre from the infidel. But he also concerned himself over collecting pay for his seamen on the Fourth Voyage who had returned with him. Poor men with no other means of support, they now had two years' wages due. Thrice the Admiral begged the treasurer of Castile to pay them off, without result. They even sent a delegation to court to demand their back pay, with letters from the Admiral to his son and to other persons of influence backing them up; but for years nobody received anything.

Columbus now wisely concluded it was hopeless to expect to be sent back to Hispaniola as viceroy and governor; his poor health and "advanced age" of fifty-three made that impracticable. So he concentrated on having the viceroyalty and admiralty conferred on his son Diego. That boy, a clever courtier, had made himself solid by marrying a lady of royal blood, Doña Maria de Toledo. And, three years after his father's death, Diego was appointed governor of Hispaniola and confirmed in some of his father's hereditary titles.

By the spring of 1505 Columbus felt well enough to travel, provided he could ride a mule; a horse's gait was too rough for him. The crown, under pressure by the horse breeders of Andalusia, had forbidden the use of mules for riding, so the Admiral had to beg for a special permit. That the King granted, and in May 1505 the Admiral started on his long journey to the court at Segovia, north of Madrid.

Ferdinand received him graciously and proposed that an arbitrator be appointed to settle his claims against the crown. Columbus refused because the King insisted that his viceroyalty and admiralty be adjudicated as well the pecuniary claims, and he was too proud to arbitrate anything to which he had a clear legal title. The King then hinted that if he would renounce all titles, offices, and revenues, he would be granted a handsome estate with a fat rent roll. Columbus rejected that absolutely. He considered it dishonorable. He would have all or nothing, and nothing he got.

As the court moved to Salamanca and on to Valladolid, the Admiral painfully followed. A year passed, nothing happened, and in the meantime his arthritis grew worse, and he became bedridden. But he felt so certain of justice being done that he made a will providing legacies out of his expected revenues, such as a sinking fund for the crusade, a house in Genoa to be kept open perpetually for his descendants, a chapel in Hispaniola so endowed that daily Masses might be said for his soul forever. In his simplicity he seemed to feel that these pious bequests would attract the attention of the Almighty, who would compel the King to make them practicable.

Almost at the last moment of his life, Columbus had his hopes raised by the arrival in Spain of the Infanta Doña Juana to claim her mother's throne of Castile. She had been at court when Columbus first returned from the Indies, and looked wide-eyed at his artifacts and his Indians, so he hoped that she might confirm the favors granted by her sainted mother. He was too ill to move, so he sent brother Bartholomew to kiss the young sovereign's hands and bespeak her favor.

During Bartholomew's absence, the Admiral failed rapidly. On 19 May 1506 he ratified his final will, creating son Diego his principal heir and commending to his benevolence all other relatives, including Ferdinand's mother Beatriz de Harana. Next day he suddenly grew worse. Both sons, brother Diego, and a few faithful followers such as Diego Méndez and Bartolomeo Fieschi gathered at his bedside. A priest, quickly summoned, said Mass, and everyone in the devoted circle of relatives, friends, and domestics received the sacrament. After the concluding prayer, the Admiral, remembering the last words of his Lord and Saviour, murmured as his own, *In manus tuas, Domine, commendo spiritum meum*—"Into Thy hands, O Lord, I commend my spirit."

A poor enough funeral followed for the "Admiral of the Ocean Sea, Viceroy and Governor of the Islands and Mainlands in the Indies." The court sent no representative; no bishop, no great dignitary attended, and the official chronicle failed to mention either death or funeral. Columbus had the ill fortune to die at the moment when his discoveries were slightly valued and his personal fortunes and expectations were at their lowest ebb.

Little by little, as his life receded into history and the claims of others to be the "real" discoverers of America faded into the background, his great achievements began to be appreciated. Yet it is one of the ironies of history that the Admiral himself died ignorant of what he had really accomplished, still insisting that he had discovered a large number of islands, a province of China, and an "Other World"; but of the vast extent of that Other World, and of the ocean that lay between it and Asia, he had neither knowledge nor suspicion.

Now, more than five hundred years after his birth, when the day of

Columbus's first landfall in the New World is celebrated throughout the length and breadth of the Americas, his fame and reputation may be considered secure, despite the efforts of armchair navigators and nationalist maniacs to denigrate him. A glance at a map of the Caribbean may remind you of what he accomplished: discovery of the Bahamas, Cuba, and Hispaniola on the First Voyage; discovery of the Lesser Antilles, Puerto Rico, Jamaica, and the south coast of Cuba on his Second, as well as founding a permanent European colony; discovery of Trinidad and the Spanish Main, on his Third; and on the Fourth Voyage, Honduras, Nicaragua, Costa Rica, Panama, and Colombia. No navigator in history, not even Magellan, discovered so much territory hitherto unknown to Europeans. None other so effectively translated his north-south experience under the Portuguese flag to the first east-west voyage, across the Atlantic. None other started so many things from which stem the history of the United States, of Canada, and of a score of American republics.

And do not forget that sailing west to the Orient was his idea, pursued relentlessly for six years before he had the means to try it. As a popular jingle on the occasion of the four hundredth anniversary put it:

> What if wise men as far back as Ptolemy
> Judged that the earth like an orange was round,
> None of them ever said, "Come along, follow me,
> Sail to the West and the East will be found."

Columbus had his faults, but they were largely the defects of qualities that made him great. These were an unbreakable faith in God and his own destiny as the bearer of the Word to lands beyond the seas; an indomitable will and stubborn persistence despite neglect, poverty, and ridicule. But there was no flaw, no dark side to the most outstanding and essential of all his qualities—seamanship. As a master mariner and navigator, no one in the generation prior to Magellan could touch Columbus. Never was a title more justly bestowed than the one which he most jealously guarded—*Almirante del Mar Océano* —Admiral of the Ocean Sea.

Magellan's fleet leaving Seville.
(Painting in Naval Officer's Club, Valparaiso de Chile)

✳ XXI ✳

Ferdinand Magellan

It is an old saying that God gave the Portuguese a very small country to live in, but all the world to die in. A son of Lusitania who nobly exemplified this is the navigator known to a large part of the world as Ferdinand Magellan. About the year 1480 he was born in one of the northernmost provinces of Portugal, either Trás-os-Montes or Entre-Douro-e-Minho. Forty years later he died in the Philippines after conducting the crucial part of the most remarkable voyage in recorded history, the first circumnavigation of the globe.

Trás-os-Montes is in a sense the Portuguese Switzerland. The Serra do Gerez on the Galician (Spanish) border rises to a height of over 5000 feet. Another serra, the Marão, divides it from the province of Entre-Douro-e-Minho on the west. Along its southern border the River Douro flows through deep gorges. Snow lies late on the ground. Hunting deer, wolves, and the wild boar were more important than agriculture in Magellan's day, and in our day they still afford good sport. Guillemard, the English biographer of our hero, found nothing in Trás-os-Montes to interest the tourist "save a certain gloomy grandeur in its scenery," and quotes a Portuguese observation about the climate: *Nove meses de inverno, e três de inferno*—Nine months of winter and three of hell! He declares that our hero inherited the

FERDIN·MAGELLANVS·SVPERATIS
ANTARTIC¹   FRETI·ANGVS
    TIIS·   CLARISS·

Portrait of Magellan. Courtesy Kunsthistorisches Museum, Vienna.

"gloomy and superstitious" character of the people. On my brief in-
cursion into Trás-os-Montes I found the scenery, with steep valleys
and intensively cultivated small farms, strikingly beautiful; and the
people, pleasant and polite to the stranger from overseas—whither a
large proportion has emigrated in search of work. To me, this region
was no more gloomy than Switzerland or Norway. My guess is that

the province contributed to her most famous son a tough but not a gloomy character; rugged strength and the power of prompt decision, qualities which may be learned hunting the wild boar as well as in warfare.

Fernão de Magalhães * was probably born in the Quinta de Souta, parish of Sabrosa, Trás-os-Montes. At least such was his accepted origin until this present century, during which several Portuguese scholars have argued that Terra da Nóbrega, in the adjoining province of the Minho, was the family seat; and still others that he was born and brought up in Oporto, the metropolis for both provinces. The Magalhães were a noble family who had come to Portugal from Normandy with the Count of Boulogne, who became Afonso III in 1248. By more than one marriage they were allied with the great Sousa family who were cousins to the royal house of Aviz. We shall see later how these arms got Ferdinand into trouble in Seville. His first cousin, trying to recover debts to the navigator's heirs in 1563, stated that two brothers, Rui (Ferdinand's father) and Lourenço, had "similar tastes and adventurous inclinations, friends of navigation, and ingenious and extraordinary pilgrims." The mother of the great navigator was Alda de Mesquita, and he had one or two sisters and a brother. His parents having died when he was ten or twelve years old, it was arranged by his Sousa cousins that he be received as a page in the household of Dona Leonor, queen of D. João II, who died in 1495. D. João's successor, D. Manuel I, took the young nobleman into his service; and finding him to be a likely youth, tough and ambitious, allowed him to volunteer under D. Francisco de Almeida, who was about to embark for India as the first Portuguese viceroy.

Few European governors have left India with a better reputation than Almeida, a man of honor, blameless in his actions, devoid of arrogance and greed. His fleet of at least twenty sail departed Lisbon 25 March 1505, and 22 July made Kilwa on the east coast of Africa. After capturing that town and laying the foundations of a fortress, Almeida continued to Mombasa, took this important Arab trading center by storm, left a garrison, and sailed to Anjidiv Island,

---

* As he signed himself, and this has become the usual Portuguese spelling of his name. It became Anglicized and Gallicized shortly after his death as Ferdinand Magellan, the form now followed in almost all Western languages except Spanish, where it is Hernando de Magallanes.

the key to Goa; that place became a Portuguese colony and so re-mained until the end of 1961. Almeida's policy was to establish as many fortified trading posts as possible on the shores of the Indian Ocean and to co-operate with local potentates tired of the Arab monopoly of sea trade. The "Moors" did not take this lying down; there were sea fights and land battles, almost all won by the Christians. Magellan was wounded in one of them and always walked with a slight limp.

We know little else about Magellan's part in the successful campaigns of the Portuguese in the Far East. In 1508, with his bosom friend Francisco Serrão, he sailed in a small fleet of four ships from Cochin on the Malabar coast to Malacca, which commanded the important strait of that name and had become an emporium similar to Singapore. Here Magellan distinguished himself by giving warning of a Malay plot to capture the ships when most of their crews were ashore, and thereby thwarting it.

An episode which early Portuguese historians took pains to relate shows the measure of the man. In January 1510, when he was about thirty years old, two ships of a homeward convoy from Cochin, with Magellan on board, struck on the Padre shoals near the Maldive Islands. Magellan took command, sent the ships' boats with the captains and gentlemen passengers to Cannanore—a journey of eight days—and himself remained in charge of the two wrecks with the greater part of their crews. They, but for confidence in him, would have rushed the boats to get away, or starved. During the several weeks before a rescue vessel arrived, Magellan had the wrecked hulks shored up for safety, kept constant watch against a pirate attack, took care that ra-tions were served out fairly and that there was no pilfering of the valuable cargo. It was considered so remarkable for an officer to do that instead of saving himself, that even the early historians who considered him a traitor to Portugal, praised his courage and his men's loyalty. Magellan was always a sailor's sailor, and *os rudos marinheiros,* as Camoëns called the common "matlow" of that era, always stood by him in his contests with officers.

Governor Afonso de Albuquerque now sent a fleet under António d'Abreu to conquer Malacca in the summer of 1511, and Magellan sailed with him. Malacca fell after a siege of six weeks. Here the Portu-guese received breath-taking accounts of the Spice Islands (the Moluc-cas) that more than substantiated the earlier reports of the Italian traveler Varthema, and Albuquerque decided without delay to reconnoiter this spicy paradise. Three ships were equipped under Abreu, who commanded *Santa Catarina;* Magellan's friend Francisco Serrão commanded the *Sabaia,* and Magellan himself the third, a caravel. This little fleet, destined to open a new era of opulence for Portugal, departed Malacca at the end of 1511, and with a local pilot reached Ambon and Banda. There nutmegs were so plentiful that Abreu loaded up and turned back to Malacca. Serrão's vessel struck a reef and became a total loss. By a ruse he captured the vessel of some pirates who were looking for him, and in her sailed back to Ambon and on to Ternate. Thence he wrote enthusiastic letters to his friend Magellan about the amenities of the Spice Islands and the abundance of clove, cinnamon, and nutmeg.

The fact that Magellan sailed with Abreu as far east as Ambon and Banda justifies us in naming him as the first person of any race to circumnavigate the globe. For Ambon is on longitude 128° E of Greenwich, and Banda is two degrees further east; whilst Mactan in the Philippines, where Magellan met his death, is on longitude 124° E. Thus his furthest west in 1521 overlapped his furthest east in 1511 by four to six degrees of longitude. Later, we shall consider the counterclaim of Magellan's slave Enrique to be first around the world.

Serrão stayed on in Ternate as an unofficial Portuguese resident, and hoped to meet his friend on his way westward around the globe; but both were killed before they could meet.

Magellan returned to Portugal a veteran sailor and soldier, expert at navigation, and with an important plan. He was certain that the Moluccas could be got at more easily by following Columbus's original idea, sailing west, than by the long, difficult voyage around the Cape of Good Hope and through Malacca Strait. From his own, or Serrão's, observations, the Spice Islands were relatively civilized, with local governments under Moslem or pagan sultans who were eager to trade with Europeans. But an essential part of this grand design was to find a strait through Spanish America. Magellan believed he knew where he could find one.

While waiting for a proper opportunity to present this project to D. Manuel, Magellan embarked as a volunteer in a Portuguese army sent to Morocco. There he got in trouble with his commander on the charge of selling surrendered cattle back to the enemy. He therefore

left Africa for Lisbon to clear himself with his sovereign. At the interview he tactlessly asked for an increase of his *moradia* or retaining fee
by the modest sum of about one gold dollar a year.* D. Manuel refused
to listen and sent him back to Morocco to answer the charges. There
they were dropped by his military superiors. They probably had been
involved in the graft, if graft there were; but, after all, what could you
do with a captured herd of cattle but sell it, if you couldn't eat it all?
So Magellan returned to Lisbon, where the king again turned a deaf ear
to his grand design, "The king always loathed him," wrote Barros, a
chronicler of D. Manuel's reign; nobody knows why. The refusal to
increase his *moradia* rankled in Magellan, as he saw hundreds of subordinate officers and mere hangers-on at court receiving more than he
did; Portuguese courtiers were rated socially according to the amount
they received. Far more important, however, than the *moradia* was the
king's rejection of Magellan's enterprise to find the American strait
through which he could sail west to the Spice Islands.

   While living under the shadow of royal displeasure, Magellan made
a personal alliance with a fellow countryman named Rui Faleiro, a
scholar in celestial navigation, of which Magellan by this time was no
mean practitioner himself. Together they worked out the theory that
the famous Line of Demarcation between Spanish and Portuguese
spheres of influence laid down in the Treaty of Tordesillas (1494), if
continued around the globe, would pass west of the Spice Islands, and
thus place them in the Spanish half of the world. A Spanish voyage to
prove it would be their anchor to windward, in case D. Manuel were
so stupid as to sneer at the westward route. The king, however, already
controlled one good route to the Spice Islands and he had sent Gon-
çalo Coelho on two American voyages, looking for another without
success. So he declined. Thus D. Manuel lost his chance to promote
one of the world's two greatest voyages, as his predecessor D. João II
had dismissed the other, that of Columbus.

   What kind of a man was Magellan when, at the age of about thirty-
seven he shook the dust of Lisbon from his feet and entered the
Spanish service? Dark-complexioned, somewhat short in stature but
broad in body, strong and agile in all his members; but above all, tough,
tough, TOUGH. Fortunately for us, Bishop Las Casas, then at Valladolid,

---

* The *moradia* in varying amounts was paid to all courtiers as commutation of
the king's obligation to feed and lodge them. The increase demanded by Magellan
was a beggarly 850 reis per annum.

recorded his impression of Magellan at an interview with the king of Spain:—

> Magellan brought with him a well-painted globe showing the entire world, and thereon traced the course he proposed to take, save that the Strait was purposely left blank so that nobody could anticipate him. . . . I asked him what route he proposed to take, he replied that he intended to take that of Cape Santa Maria (which we call Rio de la Plata) and thence follow the coast up [south] until he found the Strait. I said, "What will you do if you find no strait to pass into the other sea?" He replied that if he found none he would follow the course that the Portuguese took. But, according to what an Italian gentleman named Pigafetta of Vicenza who went on that voyage of discovery with Magellan, wrote in a letter, Magellan was perfectly certain to find the Strait because he had seen on a nautical chart made by one Martín of Bohemia, a great pilot and cosmographer, in the treasury of the King of Portugal the Strait depicted just as he found it. And, because said Strait was on the coast of land and sea, within the boundaries of the sovereigns of Castile, he [Magellan] therefore had to move and offer his services to the king of Castile to discover a new route to the said islands of Molucca and the rest.

Las Casas now gives us the most vivid picture we have of Magellan's appearance and personality:—

> This *Hernando de Magallanes* must have been a brave man, valiant in thought and for undertaking great things, although his person did not carry much authority, since he was of small stature and did not look like much, so that people thought they could put it over him for want of prudence and courage.

They certainly learned better! Three Spanish courtiers and a priest left their bones in Patagonia for having underrated Magellan's valor and toughness.

His finest qualities of courage, decision, and leadership he now offered to Spain. This change of allegiance brought upon him furious attacks by Portuguese writers for more than two centuries after his death. It is difficult to figure out why, since Columbus of Genoa and the Cabots of Venice had offered their enterprises to four different courts, and were thought of none the worse for that. Señor Mauricio Obregón suggests that the reason was this: Magellan, no *roturier* like Columbus or Cabot, belonged to a royal court, which made his desertion of his monarch reprehensible. Yet the law recognized that a vassal could change his allegiance at will. And Magellan's reputation fared no better with his new associates. His short way with mutineers was bitterly resented, and both Esteban Gómez and Juan Sebastián de Elcano brought home a cargo of lies about him to Spain to cover their own misdeeds. His sea journal and other personal records were impounded by the Portuguese when they seized his flagship in the Spice Islands, and are lost. No letter of his written during the voyage has survived. Yet, Magellan's greatness stands out, despite all attempts to disparage him. He not only had the gift of making the right decision at the right time; he was able to outwit enemies who were plotting to kill him, and to keep the loyalty of his men. And, as the Portuguese sailor who wrote the Leiden Narrative recorded, he was "an industrious man, and never rested," the kind of sea captain who slept little and woke at a moment's notice for anything like a change of wind. As a mariner and navigator he was unsurpassed; and although he did not live to complete the greatest voyage of discovery in the world's history, he planned it, and discovered the "Strait that shall forever bear his name," as well as the Marianas and the Philippines where no European had touched before. I cannot do better than quote Edward G. Bourne's masterly summary:

> There was none of the prophetic mysticism of Columbus in the makeup of the great Portuguese. Magellan was distinctly a man of action, instant, resolute, enduring. . . . The first navigation of the Straits of Magellan was a far more difficult problem of seamanship than crossing the Atlantic. . . . Columbus's voyage was over in thirty-five days; but Magellan's had been gone a year and weathered a subarctic winter before the real task began —the voyage over a trackless waste of waters exactly three times as long as the first crossing of the Atlantic. . . . Magellan is to be ranked as the first navigator of ancient or modern times, *and his voyage the greatest single human achievement on the sea.*

Aye, aye, say I!

✳ XXII ✳

Armada de Molucca

1517-1519

Preparations

In the fall of 1517 Magellan broke with Portugal. He had the civility to seek a final audience with D. Manuel and there formally to ask permission "to go and live with someone who would reward his services." The King coldly replied that he could do as he pleased. Magellan requested the honor of kissing the hand of the monarch he had served so long and faithfully, but D. Manuel refused even that slight boon. Magellan promptly went to Seville, arriving 20 October 1517. Shortly after, he signed the formal papers making him a Spanish subject.

In contrast to eastward-oriented Lisbon, Seville was humming with Western Ocean and New World activity, and Magellan found himself in the midst of it. The year before he arrived, Charles I, son of Felipe el Hermoso of Austria and grandson of Ferdinand and Isabella, had become king of Castile, Leon, and Aragon at the age of sixteen; and in June 1518 he was elected king of the Romans, meaning that he would be Emperor as soon as he could get the Pope to crown him in Rome. That did not take place for two years, but the Pope consented that he adopt the style and title of emperor at once. Thus he is known to history as Carlos Quinto, Charles-Quint, or Charles V, Emperor of the Holy Roman Empire.

Let us pause for a few words on that remarkable young man, successor to the Caesars at the age of nineteen. Charles was an intelligent man of great energy, in both respects above contemporary monarchs. He cared a good deal about exploration and discovery, certainly much more than did his contemporaries Henry VIII and François-premier. But, although he adopted as a motto *Plus Ultra* (More Beyond), wrapped around the Pillars of Hercules, the king's primary interest was Spain's position in Europe. He regarded America and the Far East principally as sources of specie and other convertible wealth, to pursue his European objectives. And these objectives were so costly as to be unobtainable:—to recover for his empire the old kingdom of Burgundy with its capital at Dijon and western boundary on the Rhône, to dominate Italy by balance-of-power politics, and to fight that "upstart" power France. It cost Charles almost a million ducats ($2,320,000 in the gold of 1934) to bribe the electors of the Holy Roman Empire to elect him King of the Romans; he had to borrow most of it from the bankers, who never got it all back. The specie flowing in from Mexico and Peru helped, but he never had enough to get out of the red; and many master mariners who devoted their lives to discovery were rewarded either with a pittance or a jail sentence.

Please look at this portrait of the Emperor at the age of about twenty-five by the Dutch painter Jan Cornelisz Vermeyen. This is the Charles V whom Magellan met, before he began dressing his hair in the new Italian fashion and letting his beard grow. Note the pendulous lower lip and the "whopper-jaw," Hapsburg characteristics which he inherited from his father, Philip of Austria, and transmitted to his descendants, even to Alfonso XIII. When he first came to Spain, Charles could hardly speak Spanish; but he soon learned, and did other things to please his new subjects such as showing a good leg on horseback, taking command of infantry in the field, and even jumping into the ring and killing a bull in a *corrida*.

More often than not, Charles V was absent from Spain—visiting his Burgundian inheritance at Brussels, traveling through Italy, on campaigns against France. Like Columbus, his great dream was to head a new crusade to liberate the Holy Land from the infidel; but it was all he could do to prevent the Ottoman Empire's able sultan, Suleiman the Magnificent, from conquering Vienna. On the whole, Charles V paid more attention to problems of discovery, exploration, and overseas conquest than did any contemporary monarch. Although individuals like Magellan generally took the initiative for a voyage of discovery, and merchants like Cristóbal Haro paid most of the bills, Charles V did leave to his son Philip II a greater empire than the modern world had ever known. And that, forty years before England, France, or any other country had established a single colony in the New World.

Everything seemed to be on the move during the first four years of Charles's reign. In the same month that Magellan came to Seville, Martin Luther nailed his famous Ninety-Five Theses against current Catholic practice to the church door at Wittenburg. While Magellan was at sea. Cortés conquered Mexico for Spain. In 1516–17 were written or published some of the greatest books of the High Renaissance:—Machiavelli's *Prince*, Erasmus's *Institution of a Christian Prince*, Thomas More's *Utopia*. Nationalism was rising, and there were other ambitious princes besides those on the Iberian Peninsula, eager to contest a threatened Spanish world hegemony based on the wealth of "the Indies."

Despite the rivalry between Spain and Portugal for this wealth, many Portuguese entered the Spanish service. Among those at Seville who supported Magellan were Diogo Barbosa, alcalde of the arsenal and knight commander of the Order of Santiago. He invited Magellan to stay in his house. His son Duarte (probably the man of that name who had sailed the Eastern seas for Portugal and written a book about them) joined the great voyage. Magellan fitted into the Barbosa family so agreeably as to woo and win Beatriz, Diogo's daughter and Duarte's sister. They were married in 1518, and she brought him a sizable dowry, 600,00 maravedis (about $42,000 in gold). A boy, Rodrigo, was born of this marriage about six months before Magellan sailed; but he died while his father was at sea. Doña Beatriz, wounded by the lies about her husband that successful mutineers brought to Spain, and hearing from Portuguese sources of his death in battle, died of a broken heart in 1521. With her, Ferdinand Magellan's line became extinct. Unlike Columbus, he left no sons to maintain his honor and confound malicious enemies.

Although Magellan had promised his partner Faleiro not to breathe a word of their joint project before Faleiro joined him at Seville, Magellan felt he could not miss an opportunity to lay it before the

The Emperor Charles V. Portrait by Jan Vermeyen; R. Todd-White photo.
Courtesy of owner, Lady Merton of Maidenhead Thicket.

The Empress Isabel. Portrait by Jan Vermeyen; R. Todd-White photo.
Courtesy of owner, Lady Merton of Maidenhead Thicket.

Casa de Contratación. This was the official board at Seville which handled most of Spain's colonial business. The Casa heard and shelved Magellan's scheme; but one member, Juan de Aranda, took the Captain aside, wormed every detail out of him, and promised to promote his cause at court in return for a 20 per cent cut of the expected profits. Faleiro, having arrived in Seville, became so furious over his partner's apparent breach of faith as to quarrel and subsequently break with him; but he did accompany his partner and Aranda to court at Valladolid. Magellan brought along a slave he had bought at Malacca, christened Henrique, who was destined to accompany him on his circumnavigation, and also a pretty girl slave from Sumatra.

At this conference (a description of which by Las Casas we have already quoted), Magellan put up a strong argument for the Spice Islands' being on the Spanish side of the Line of Demarcation if the line were carried around the world. His guess received influential support from Cristóbal Haro, an international figure in merchant banking who had outstanding claims against Portugal which the government of D. Manuel ignored.

It must be emphasized that Magellan had not the remotest idea of the width of the Pacific Ocean, uncrossed as yet by any European. Schoener's globe of 1515, a copy of which Magellan probably showed to Charles V,* places Japan a few hundred miles off Mexico; and the historian López de Gómara asserts that, in his negotiation with Charles V, Magellan declared that the Spice Islands were "no great distance from Panama, and the Gulf of San Miguel which Vasco Núñez de Balboa discovered."

A great personage with whom Magellan had to deal was Juan Fonseca, bishop of Burgos and the most influential member of the Casa de Contratación. He had done his best to hamper and discourage not only Columbus but Balboa and Cortés. Fonseca pretended to like Magellan, and as he was also a member of the royal council immediately under the king, that was important. But it is highly probable, though not proved, that, after placing several relatives and favorites as captains of Magellan's ships, Fonseca encouraged them to take over the command and run away with the expedition. They very nearly did, as we shall see.

The king, a hard-headed young man, snapped at a chance to enlarge

* See below, Chapter XXIV.

his already extensive dominions by annexing the Spice Islands, or at least sharing their trade with Portugal. On 28 March 1518 Charles issued a *capitulación* or agreement pertaining to it. He promised to provide Magellan and Faleiro, joint "captains general of the armada," with an annual salary of 50,000 maravedis each (about $1200), and almost tripled Magellan's before sailing. A fleet of five ships carrying some 250 officers and men would be provided; the partners would receive one-fifth of the profits, and the king promised to send out no rival expedition within ten years. Hypocritically, Charles ordered them not to explore within the territories of his "dear and well-beloved uncle and brother the King of Portugal" *—which was the main object of the expedition. If they discovered any new lands not claimed by any Christian prince, they could become hereditary adelantados thereof, but that chance never occurred. Members of the expedition found it more expedient to trade with the sultans and rajahs of the Far East than to conquer their kingdoms; Magellan lost his life trying to prove the contrary.

The preparations for this important voyage took much longer than expected—as with almost every great voyage under sail for the last four hundred years. In Magellan's case the usual difficulties of equipping ships for sea were multiplied by waterfront rascality and by the inveterate opposition of Portugal. Letters of Portugal's ambassador to Spain prove that he did everything possible to wreck the enterprise before it started, even offering Magellan a bribe to drop the whole thing and return to Portugal. One of D. Manuel's counsellors and confessors, Bishop Vasconcellos, even advocated the assassination of Magellan. Another difficulty was the irascible interference of Rui Faleiro, obviously going mad; he finally had to be left behind. The Casa de Contratación, lukewarm about the enterprise, needed several strong letters from the king to help Magellan get to sea. Portugal's consular agent at Seville noted with pleasure that the five ships procured for Magellan were "very old and patched up"; he "would not care to sail to the Canaries in such old crates; their ribs are soft as butter." Sour grapes, no doubt. Magellan could never have been fobbed off with a rotten ship for a long ocean voyage. The fleet went to sea sound and

---

* Charles V's elder sister Leonor had already married D. Manuel, and his younger sister Catarina married D. Manuel's heir who became D. João III in 1521. In 1525 Charles V married D. Manuel's daughter the Infanta Isabel.

Exterior, Church of Santa Ana, Triana, Seville

staunch, and none of the many casualties on this voyage were due to defects in the vessels but to wear and tear, inadequate provisioning, and human depravity. Bishop Fonseca's hostility did not extend to the fitting out, as he expected his friends to take over the armada at sea; but he winked at cheating by the fleet's furnishers.

Faleiro had been acting so strangely that on 26 July 1519, only a fortnight before the fleet sailed, Charles V ordered him replaced by Juan de Cartagena as captain of *San Antonio* and inspector general of the fleet. "Señor" Cartagena, as he was called in the letter of appointment, had neither rank, title, nor sea experience. A bumptious young courtier, he owed this extraordinary promotion to the fact that he was Bishop Fonseca's "nephew"; i.e., the fruit of some episcopal indiscretion. Antonio de Coca, a bastard of the bishop's brother, was appointed *contador*, fleet accountant. Two other ship's captains, both royal appointees, were Luis de Mendoza, described as a "friend" of the archbishop of Seville, captain of *Victoria* and fleet treasurer with an annual salary of 60,000 maravedis; and Gaspar de Quesada, captain of *Concepción*, also a "servant of the Archbishop" (Fonseca), but beyond that we know naught of his country or family. Thus Fonseca had his men, mostly bastards, spotted in very significant positions in the fleet. But we must credit the episcopal nepotist with one excellent royal appointment, that of Gonzalo Gómez de Espinosa as *alguacil mayor* (chief marshal) of the fleet, commanding all shipboard soldiers. He remained steadfastly loyal to Magellan, and after Magellan's death commanded flagship *Trinidad*. The only captain Magellan could really count on was Juan Serrano of little *Santiago*, like himself a voluntary exile from Portugal. Brother or cousin to Francisco Serrão, Magellan's intimate friend whom he hoped to meet in the Spice Islands, Serrano was an experienced mariner. Portuguese, too, was Esteban Gómez, flag pilot; but he hated Magellan and pulled off the only successful mutiny of the voyage.

Further to emphasize Cartagena's exalted position, Fonseca allowed him to bring along ten servants, all on the payroll, and the Emperor permitted him to draw his court stipends during the expedition in addition to his pay of 60,000 maravedis a year. Was he also joint captain general with Magellan, as Faleiro would have been? The royal cédula of 26 or 28 July 1519, appointing Cartagena captain of *San Antonio* in place of Faleiro, does indeed describe him as *conjunta persona* with Magellan. Cartagena naturally regarded this as giving him joint authority with Magellan; but that is certainly not what Charles V intended. For in his commission and other documents the Emperor always referred to Magellan as *Capitán Mayor* or senior captain, which is usually translated Captain General. And he ordered all officers of the fleet at the before-sailing ceremony in Seville to swear to obey Magellan *en todo*, in all respects.

Everyone who has written about this voyage has had to decide whether Cartagena was legally joint commander with Magellan. In my opinion, the *conjunta persona* phrase in the July cédula was simply a clerical oversight, the scribe assuming that the king wished to grant Cartagena all Faleiro's rights and duties. Had there been any doubt of his position, surely Cartagena would have raised it before the fleet left Sanlúcar, instead of waiting until they had been at sea for over a month and then challenging Magellan in a manner which led to his death.

Charles V made Magellan knight commander of the Order of Santiago before sailing, an honor he did not confer on Cartagena or, after
the voyage, on Elcano.

One would like to know what age these captains were, and what
maritime experience, if any, they had had. I infer from the fact that
José Toribio Medina was unable to find anything about them prior to
1519, that they were all fairly young and completely inexperienced.
By exception, he found that Espinosa was then thirty-two. Magellan
himself had reached his thirty-ninth birthday when he embarked.
Curiously enough, we have data on the ages of many of the common
sailors in 1519. The youngest was a page fourteen years old; the eldest,
an ancient mariner of forty-four.

Besides the usual wrangles and jangles on getting ready for sea,
Magellan, in common with Columbus, had the extra handicap of being
a foreigner. For this reason, probably, the King warned him not to
engage more than five Portuguese for the fleet. An incident on 22
October 1518 indicated that he was on slippery ground at Seville. His
intended flagship, *Trinidad*, was being careened to cleanse her bottom.
On such occasions, naval etiquette required a king's ship to show the
royal ensign at a masthead, and the captain's flag on each capstan head.
Since all her royal ensigns and other Spanish flags had been sent to be
newly painted, Magellan had nothing to show aloft, and he used flags
with his own arms to cover the capstan. On them the Magalhães family
arms were quartered with the Portuguese royal arms, owing to their relationship with the Sousa family. A crowd of idlers gathered on the
Seville graving beach to view this interesting operation. Pretty soon
they began to growl and grumble that the banners and ensigns of their
own king had been replaced by Portuguese arms on the capstans. One
of Magellan's friends, Canon Marienzo of the cathedral, suggested that
he remove his arms from the capstans to appease the mob. That he
did, but to slight effect; for the captain of the port and other officials
appeared, roaring with patriotic zeal, to arrest Magellan for *lèse
majesté*. When the Canon tried to dissuade them by pointing out that
the Captain General was a royal officer, they rushed upon him with
drawn swords, screaming threats of murder. Magellan kept his cool,
and with furious Sevillians thrusting naked swords under his nose,
remarked that the vessel was in a dangerous position with an inrushing
tide, and if they did not leave him and his crew to do what had to be

done, she would be swamped through the open hatches, and they would be responsible for the loss of a king's ship. That sent the officials slinking away, and the shore mob contented itself with more muttering and bawling. Magellan recounted the whole sorry affair in a letter to the King, who ordered all officials who had had a part in the riot to be severely punished. There is no evidence that they ever were.

As this incident shows, the Portuguese were very unpopular in Andalusia. Magellan had to send all over Spain to obtain sailors for his armada; the final lists show, besides a majority of Spaniards, numerous Portuguese, Genoese, Sicilians, French, Germans, Flemings, blacks, and one Englishman. Charles V himself discharged Rui Faleiro and had to order another troublemaker, Luis de Mendoza, flag treasurer and captain of *Victoria*, to render unhesitating obedience to Magellan. This he notoriously failed to do, and it would have been well for him had he been left in Spain instead of providing food for the vultures in Patagonia. The Portuguese historian A. Teixeira da Mota argues that Faleiro must have been responsible for Magellan's general ideas on cosmography, or he would not have taken him to Spain. Pigafetta's *Regole sull' Arte del Navigare* (Rules on the Art of Navigation), it now appears, is merely a free translation of Faleiro's *Regimento da Altura de Leste-Oeste* (Rules for Finding Longitude); but neither tract helped Magellan to determine longitude. Faleiro apparently did not stay long in the *casa de locos* in which he was placed when Magellan sailed. He quarreled with his family, returned to Portugal (where he was put in jail), and after serving the sentence came back to Spain to sue for the salary he would have been paid had he gone to sea. He died in 1544 in poverty.

From Barcelona on 8 May 1519 Charles V issued minute instructions for the voyage—no fewer than 74 paragraphs! Magellan's initial reaction must have been, "Does His Highness suppose I have never been to sea?" Most of the instructions were routine, such as never to overload, always to be kind and just to the natives, to treat the crews "lovingly," and to forbid gambling, brawling, bawdry, and blasphemy. Every member, from captains down to the smallest ship's boy was to have a designated amount of free freight—the system later known as "primage"—for his personal investment in the Far East; captains could bring 8000 pounds' weight; ship's boys 75 pounds each, an unusually generous allowance. Someone close to the king tried to imagine everything that might happen, to include in these instructions; but never anticipated the terrible things that did happen—starvation, mutiny, and the leader's death.

Ships and Crews

From documents in the Spanish archives we know many details of Magellan's fleet and complement. To spare my non-nautical readers, I am here stating the bare outline.

Flagship *Trinidad*, 100 tuns, Magellan captain, succeeded by Duarte Barbosa, João Carvalho, and Gonzalo Gómez de Espinosa.

San Antonio, ship of 120 tuns, Juan de Cartegena captain, succeeded by Antonio de Coca, Álvaro de Mezquita, and Hierónimo Guerra.

Concepción, ship of 90 tuns, Gaspar de Quesada captain; succeeded by Rodríguez Serrano and Luis de Gois.

Victoria, ship of 85 tuns, Luis de Mendoza captain, succeeded by Duarte Barbosa, Cristóbal Rebelo, and Juan Sebastián de Elcano.

Santiago, caravel of 75 tuns, Juan Serrano captain.

Nothing is known about the antecedents of these vessels, except that *Victoria* was built in Guipuzcoa. No contemporary painting or model can be identified as one of them. *Victoria* does indeed appear crossing the Pacific, winged Victory perched on her bowsprit, in Ortelius's atlas of 1589, a picture often copied (even for Drake's flagship!), but she has only two masts and is of a later design than any Magellanic ship. *La Dauphine*, Verrazzano's flagship in his attempt to find a northern strait in 1524, measured 100 tuns; and we have at least a conjectural portrait of her.* The nearest ship pictures, in time, to those of our *Armada de Molucca* (the official name of Magellan's fleet) are those in the Diego Ribero mappemonde of 1529, where two pair of ships, each captioned *voyamaluco* ("I'm going to the Moluccas"), are shown; one pair sailing before the wind off the Chilean coast, the other approaching Surigao Strait. These may (somewhat cautiously) be assumed to be Ribero's idea of *Trinidad* and *Victoria*. The ships in João de Castro's *Roteiro de Goa a Suez* (1541) and those in the Miller Atlas (1525) may also be considered similar to Magellan's. All these are depicted by Portuguese; but so far as I can learn there was then no

* See p. 48, above.

difference between the architecture and rigging of Spanish and Portuguese ships, except that the Portuguese went in heavily for caravels, and only one of Magellan's was of that rig. According to the historian Herrera, Magellan's vessels had exceedingly high sterncastles, to accommodate the unusually large number of officers. The sterncastle had by this time evolved from a square *toldilla* looking like a loose box, to a functional, two- to three-deck superstructure, carrying out the lines of the afterbody and the square stern. That had replaced the neat round "tuck" of Columbus's ships.

This "cage work" (as the English called it) or *obras muertas* "dead wood" (the Spanish phrase) was not so great a detriment to navigation as one might think; the very light woodwork and the high sides helped a ship to sail. Each of Magellan's vessels carried three masts, two square-rigged and the mizzen lateen. The high turn of speed shown by the fleet between Guam and Samar (see Chapter XXV, below) suggests that Magellan's vessels crossed very long main yards and spread big billowing courses, as shown in the Miller I and Ribero maps.

The fleet was amply armed, with 62 culverins, 10 falconets, and 50 arquebuses, in addition to the ordnance that came with the ships. But, as explorers still depended on *l'arme blanche* rather than gunpowder, hundreds of steel pikes, halberds, and swords were carried as well as one hundred complete suits of armor, and the personal suits of mail and plumed helmets owned by the leading officers. Several hundred crossbows, and many long bows, were also taken. The provision of navigation instruments reflects Magellan's interest in the science, as well as that of Andrés de San Martín, the *astrólogo* or top navigator of the fleet. There were 23 charts by Nuño García, an Italian cartographer employed by the Council of the Indies; 6 pair of dividers, 7 astrolabes (one of brass), 21 wooden quandrants such as Columbus used, 35 magnetized needles for the compasses, and 18 half-hour glasses for keeping time. The Portuguese who seized *Trinidad* in the Spice Islands impounded San Martín's books, two planisphere maps by Pedro Reinel, and all other charts and instruments. None have survived.

The fleet carried chests full of trading truck to barter with natives, such as 20,000 hawks' bells in three sizes, 500 pounds of glass beads, brass bracelets, fishhooks, silk, cotton, and woolen cloth of many colors, 400 dozen German knives "of the worst quality," a thousand "little hand mirrors, 100 of them better quality," and a ton of mercury—this, presumably, for medical purposes as its metal-extracting properties had not yet been discovered. When Vasco da Gama presented this sort of truck to the sultans and rajahs of the Indian Ocean, they indignantly rejected it as cheap junk; so Magellan, having had experience with Far Eastern potentates, saw to it that his fleet also carried presents suitable for royalty. Unfortunately we have no list of them, but in the Phillipines and the Moluccas he presented the chieftains with silk robes "made in the Turkish fashion," and sundry bolts of woolen and silk cloth.

As in Columbus's ships, there was no rating of cook. Apparently, apprentice seamen still took turns at the skillet, using a wood fire in an open cook box under the overhang of the forecastle. Important people like Cartagena had personal servants and possibly their own particular cook boxes; in the bigger ships, these were probably below decks. The list of equipment shows utensils of iron and copper, and the provisions included seemingly ample quantities of wine, olive oil, vinegar, beans, lentils, garlic, flour, rice, cheese, honey, sugar, anchovies, sardines, salt cod, salt beef, and salt pork. Each ship carried a few live cattle and swine to slaughter en route. One curious item is 35 boxes of *carne de membrillo*—quince jelly or preserve—for *Trinidad*, whilst other vessels rated but four boxes each. The flagship, too, carried twice as many raisins as her consorts.

Officers and gentlemen volunteers such as Pigafetta had individual cabins or at least bunks in the sterncastle. Some petty officers such as the chief gunner may have lodged there too; but the common sailor slept anywhere on the main deck, in his clothes. Each ship had a *batel*, a longboat, which was usually towed, and several small boats which could be nested in the waist or taken apart and stowed below. The fleet had so many small boats that the simple natives of Rio de Janeiro, seeing them all in the water alongside the ships, assumed them to be the ships' children being suckled like a farrow of pigs! The ships were amply provided with anchors, cables, spare sails, and colors. Charles V and Magellan intended their *Armada de Molucca* to make a brave show.

Information about officers is scarce, especially on the three Spanish captains Cartagena, Mendoza, and Quesada. Magellan himself managed to sign on four relatives—his brother-in-law Duarte Barbosa, his natural son Cristóbal Rebelo, and two cousins, Álvaro de Mezquita and

Martín de Magallanes; the first three rose to command, but Mezquita proved to be a weakling. Barbosa—murdered at Cebu—had had sea experience under the Portuguese almost equal to Magellan's. Born in Lisbon, he spent the years 1501–16 in Portuguese service in the Far East. Happening to be at his father's house in Seville when Magellan married his sister, he signed up with no definite rating but proved a tower of strength to the Captain General, whom he survived for only a week.

Magellan had so much trouble recruiting sailors that he persuaded the king to raise the permitted number of Portuguese from five to more than thirty; even so, we find that a number of Portuguese sailors were put on the beach at the last minute and Spanish substitutes found, because the allotted number had been exceeded. Enemies later accused Magellan of having purposely beefed up his Portuguese contingent to ensure loyal support against mutinous Spaniards—and, God knows, he needed them! But it is not necessary to believe this. Spanish sailors were by now a privileged class, like American-born sailors in the American merchant marine during the last century. There were hardly enough of them to man the well-established and profitable routine voyages to the West Indies, to which they naturally preferred sailing, with prospects of gold, silver, and girls, rather than embarking on a dubious enterprise; and although Magellan attempted to conceal his destination lest recruits be repelled by anything so extraordinary, some rumor of it must have leaked out on the waterfront. Little *Santiago* was more than half manned by foreigners; *Concepción*'s crew, on the other hand, was mostly Andalusian, and *San Antonio* had a large number of Galicians; flagship *Trinidad* and *Victoria*, the one that finally rounded the world, were very mixed in their complements. All the gunners were French, Flemish, German, or English. Charles V must have considered the artillerymen of northern Europe to be better than Spaniards. All five ships had Portuguese pilots. This was natural, as only Portuguese had navigated the coasts of Brazil, East Africa, and Indonesia; everyone bound away wanted a Portuguese pilot, just as all British tramp steamers in the nineteenth century insisted on Scots engineers. All Magellan's pilots were professionals, certified by the board that preceded the Casa de Contratación. They drew 10,000 maravedis annual pay from the crown, and a few thousand extra for piloting Magellan. There were many Genoese, the most prestigious seamen in

Europe, and a scattering of Greeks, Cypriots, and Sicilians. Also one Englishman, "Master Andrew of Bristol," and the inevitable Irishmen from Galway, Guillermo Ires and Juanillo Ires—"Irish Bill" and "Irish Johnny." The five or six blacks on board were slaves to the top officers—"Antón de color negro" followed his master Gonzalo Gómez de Espinosa as a prisoner to India. No such internationally-manned fleet had ever put forth for discovery; at least not since Jason's Argonauts, to whom classically educated writers like Maximilianus were wont to compare Magellan's crew—to the Argonauts' disadvantage.

The sources used by Medina for seamen's pay indicate that a *marinero* (able seaman) drew 1200 maravedis a month, gromets or apprentice seamen 800 maravedis, and the men-at-arms the same. Everyone on board, even Juan de Cartagena's ten personal servants and Magellan's Malay slave Enrique, was on the payroll, and almost everyone received four months' advance pay.

One important foreigner who joined the flagship as a gentleman volunteer and who appears on her crew list as "Antonio Lombardo," was Antonio Pigafetta of Vicenza in Lombardy, where his family house, recently still standing, is marked by a tablet. Despite the fact that he wrote the most famous sea narrative of his century, we have slight knowledge of Pigafetta's life before he came to Spain in the suite of the papal ambassador to Charles V. Since this envoy and Peter Martyr d'Anghiera were opposite numbers—protonotaries—at the papal and Spanish courts, it was natural for them to get together, and for Pigafetta to pick up information about the forthcoming expedition. He tells us himself that, "prompted by a craving for experience and glory," he applied for and received permission from the king and ambassador to sign up with Magellan. In May 1519 he arrived at Seville in time to participate in last preparations, to collect more navigational instruments, and to attend a solemn ceremony in the chapel of Santa Maria de la Victoria in Triana, Seville. There Magellan was presented with a royal standard, all officers swore to obey him in every respect, and every member of the expedition received communion. Several of those who swore obedience to Magellan were already plotting to kill him and take over.

On the face of it. Magellan's fleet, ships, matériel, and people were well suited to the enterprise. The one thing wrong with it came from the apparent political necessity of filling top ranks with bishops' bas-

Nuestra Señora de Victoria, in Church of Santa Ana. Sanchez Obregón photo.

tards, and letting them bring along a pack of pages and other "idlers" "only fit to keep the bread from moulding," as North American sailors used to say. With fewer idle hands and hungry bellies there might have been less starvation and suffering than the crews of *Trinidad*, *Concepción*, and *Victoria* endured in their long, lonely crossing of the Pacific.

Under Way

The Emperor showed himself very eager for Magellan to get going, and that he did on 10 August 1519. Even with expert river pilots it took the fleet several days to drop down the Guadalquivir to Sanlúcar de Barrameda, the outport for Seville. There it anchored in a wide bend of the river, almost under the castle of the Duke of Medina Sidonia. Shipmasters favored this anchorage because, no matter from what direction the wind blew, they could weigh and fill away without making short tacks. And there they stayed for more than a month, until 20 September. A good part of this time was spent in adding to the provisions. Owing to the discovery that "land sharks" had cheated on supplies, furnishing short-weight or putrid meat and old, weevily biscuit, Magellan refused to put to sea until these deficiencies were made good. This meant boat trips to Seville and finding barges to float fresh supplies down to Sanlúcar. Even so, he did not discover half the cheating until the fleet reached Patagonia.

Nuestra Señora de Barrameda, the waterfront church of Sanlúcar where the mariners worshipped, has disappeared. But the Capuchin monastery on the high part of the town still shelters a celebrated image of the Virgin and Child, called Our Lady of the Good Voyage, she holding a silver ship in one hand. In 1519 this image was in a little hermitage on the same spot, and many of Magellan's men must have gone there to pray for a safe voyage. At Sanlúcar the sailors were given daily shore leave on condition that they attend Mass. That duty accomplished, they were free to drink and otherwise disport themselves, for Magellan absolutely refused to allow women on board.

At Seville on 24 August 1519 Magellan signed his last will and testament. Therein he describes himself as Hernando de Magallanes, Comendador (of the Order of Santiago) and His Imperial Majesty's Captain General of the Armada bound for the Moluccas. He declares his firm belief in the Christian faith and in Our Lady as intercessor. He makes several tiny legacies to churches, shrines, and *cofradías* in Seville, and to the sacristy chapel in Seville Cathedral where he usually received holy communion. He hopes to be buried in a grave that he has reserved at Santa Maria de la Victoria in Triana; or, if he dies at sea, to be buried in the nearest church dedicated to Our Lady. The

Sanlúcar de Barrameda: Sketch by Samuel de Champlain, 1598. Courtesy
John Carter Brown Library.

View from the city in 1971. Courtesy D. Alfonso d' Orleáns y de Borbón.

575

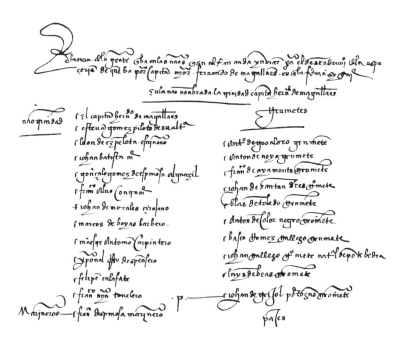

Part of the ship's roll of *Trinidad*. "Roll of the people going in the ships bound to the Indies and the discovery of the Spicery, of which Fernando de Magallanes was Captain General." Courtesy Archivo General de Indias.

600,000 maravedis that he had received as dowry should be repaid to his widow before any other legacies. One-tenth of all he may gain from the voyage to the Moluccas is to be set apart for legacies; one-third to build a new chapel around Santa Maria de la Victoria, where the monks may forever pray for the repose of his soul; two-thirds to be divided three ways—between Santa Maria de Monserrate near Barcelona, San Francisco at Aranda in the Douro valley, and Santo Domingo de las Dueñas in Oporto. His servant (and natural son) Cristóbal Rebelo is to receive 30,000 maravedis; and his slave "Enrique, mulatto, native of Malacca," his freedom and 10,000 maravedis "because he is a Christian, and that he may pray God for my soul." There are elaborate provisions for a *mayorazgo* or trust fund for the benefit of his widow, their children, his sister Isabel, and his Sousa cousins. His executors are his father-in-law Diogo Barbosa and Canon Marienzo of Seville, the one who intervened during the graving of *San Antonio*.

Alas, none of these generous and pious provisions were ever carried out. Doña Beatriz, their son, and the baby not yet born died before *Victoria* returned to Spain. Enrique deserted in Cebu. All attempts of the Barbosa and Magellan families to recover the Captain General's property from the crown, or even to have his long-overdue salary paid, failed. Had he been a convicted murderer, his family could not have been worse treated by the king-emperor whose dominions he had so notably increased, and in whose reign Magellan's voyage stands out as one of the most glorious events.

In September, when ready to sail, Magellan addressed to the king-emperor a memorial stating what he believed to be the longitude of certain islands in relation to the Line of Demarcation. Again he expressed the opinion that the already famous Spice Islands or Moluccas— Ternate, Tidore, and the rest—discovered for Portugal by Serrão in 1512, lay on the Spanish side of that north-south line. This confirms the belief that he expected to enlarge the Spanish empire at the expense of the Portuguese. The positions correspond closely to those on a world map by Maiollo, a copy of which he may have seen or acquired.

On Monday, 19 September 1519, all hands went ashore in relays to confess and receive absolution, and on Tuesday the 20th every ship weighed anchor and shaped her course southwest. Three years would elapse before any of these men except successful mutineers would return.

✳ XXIII ✳

Magellan's Voyage to the Strait

1519-1520

From Sanlúcar to the River Plate

Before finally setting sail from Sanlúcar on 20 September 1519 in the dark of the moon, Magellan issued stringent rules and regulations designed to keep his fleet together and under his control. Flagship *Trinidad* at all times will sail ahead of the others. Each vessel must approach her toward nightfall and ask for orders, and then follow lights kindled in iron cressets on her stern; the *farol*, the principal light, to be made from a torch of pitchy wood or an old hemp rope soaked in oil. The flagship will show two lights if the fleets is to come about or wear, three as a signal to reduce sail, four to strike sail. Any ship from which land is sighted should fire a gun. Three watches were set on each ship nightly: the first at nightfall, the second (called the *modeno*) at midnight, and the third (the *diane*) at daybreak. All men accordingly were divided into three watches, the first under the captain or the *contramaestre*, the second under the pilot or the boatswain's mate, and the third under the master. Instead of "dogging" the watches, as in recent times,* their order was changed nightly to ensure that every three days only did the men have to stand the *modeno*, which American sailors used to call the "graveyard watch."

---

* Splitting 4:00 to 8:00 p.m. watch in two, thus bringing the next day's watch on duty at a different hour.

Once outside the harbor of Sanlúcar, Magellan set the course *sudo-este*—southwest, and with a fair wind his fleet romped south and reached Tenerife in the Canaries on 26 September. There they topped off with water, wood, and fresh meat, bought a load of salt codfish from a caravel, and pitch for caulking seams. Before they cleared from Tenerife, another caravel arrived with an ominous message to Magellan from his father-in-law, Diogo Barbosa. It warned him that his three Spanish captains Cartagena, Mendoza, and Quesada were planning to kill him. Pigafetta confirms this: "Although I don't know why they hated him, except that he was Portuguese and they Spaniards." Magellan sailed handicapped by the bitter hostility of his top Spanish officers; and it is not the least of his glories that he had the wit and fortitude to dispose of them.

Magellan sent a stout reply to Barbosa by the caravel, that what e'er betide he would do his duty as a servant of the king-emperor, if it took his life.

The fleet departed Tenerife at midnight 3 October 1519 with a soft land breeze and a first-quarter moon. At sea it followed a southwest course down to latitude 27° N, and then changed to south by west. Juan de Cartagena, running *San Antonio* under the flagship's stern, demanded of the Captain General why he had changed course? Magellan replied, *Que le siguiessen y no pidiessen mas cuenta*—"Follow me and ask no questions!"

Magellan had good reason to follow a course skirting the African coast. The shipmaster who sold him the salt fish told him that the king of Portugal had sent out a fleet to apprehend him on his Atlantic crossing. D. Manuel had, in fact sent two intercepting fleets, just as D. João II did to catch Columbus. Magellan figured that the way to elude them was to avoid the direct course to Brazil and parallel the African coast to a low latitude, then nip across the Atlantic Narrows. He was right, but the maneuver cost the fleet both time and discomfort.

On 18 October, off Sierra Leone with a last-quarter moon shining balefully through overcast, the fleet underwent a series of storms that sorely tried the seamen. There were furious squalls succeeded by flat calms, in which shoals of sharks cruised around. St. Elmo's fire—Camoëns's "living light, which sailors hold as sacred"—blazed for two hours from the flagship's masthead. Pigafetta, whose natural history observations are somewhat lacking in accuracy, blew up the St. Elmo's fire to a light so powerful that the entire crew went blind for "near a quarter hour" after it went out! He also states that they saw a bird which had no anus, and another bird whose hen, having no feet, laid her eggs on the back of the cock and never touched earth. Here is the ancient myth of the bird-of-paradise, about which the Spaniards heard more in the Moluccas. There was a good deal of Sinbad in Pigafetta; but his tall tales, though sometimes incredible, are always amusing. He repeats the story, already told by Columbus and still current among sailors, of the boatswain bird's eating other birds' excrement. This was based on the big bird's mean practice of watching a booby stuff himself with fish, then swooping at him, screaming, and frightening the poor booby into vomiting; the boatswain bird then caught and swallowed the regurgitated fish.

The fleet now paid for the Captain General's cautious sailing close to the African coast, by running into equatorial calms after shaping a southerly course for Brazil. For many days the five ships were becalmed. The heat became oppressive, as it had been for Columbus in the more northerly doldrums, and inactivity proved a good medium for sedition.

Cartagena probably brooded over the snub he had received from Magellan on changing course; after all, the king had named him *conjunta persona*. In any event, he decided to take issue over a matter of ceremony at sea. The Captain General had ordered each vessel to close the flagship every evening to hail him and receive his oral orders; they could do that even in a flat calm by manning their sweeps. The proper hail, as used on Columbus's voyages, was, *Dios vos salve, señor capitán-general, y maestro y buena compaña*—"God keep you, sir Captain General and master, and good company." One evening, Juan de Cartagena caused the *general* to be omitted and sent a petty officer to sing out—a double insult to Magellan, who answered that in future he expected to be addressed properly, and by the captain himself. Cartagena impudently retorted that he had sent his best man to give the hail, and if Magellan didn't like it he would send a page to do it next time. Magellan has been criticized for treating Juan de Cartagena too roughly. But remember that the Captain General was a Portuguese nobleman of ancient stock who would not suffer insolence from a bishop's bastard, especially one who was plotting to usurp his command and take his life.

Three days later, still in a flat calm and after two repetitions of the insult, Magellan summoned all four captains on board the flagship to participate in a court-martial of *Victoria*'s quartermaster for sodomy with a ship's boy. After the trial (in which both parties were found guilty and condemned to death), Magellan remained in the flag cabin with Captain Cartagena of *San Antonio*, Captain Quesada of *Concepción*, Captain Mendoza of *Victoria*, and Captain Serrano of *Santiago*. The first three were in the plot. Cartagena, hoping to provoke a fight in which the Captain General would be killed, taunted Magellan for having got them into the calm belt through bad navigation. The Captain General kept his cool; Cartagena, mistaking this for timidity, roared out that he for one would no longer obey Magellan's orders. The Captain General expected this. At his signal, the alguacil of *Trinidad*, Gonzalo Gómez de Espinosa, well armed and armored, broke into the cabin, closely followed by Duarte Barbosa and Cristóbal Rebelo with drawn swords. Magellan sprang on Cartagena, grabbed him by the front of his elegant shirt, forced him to stay seated, and cried out, "Rebel, this is mutiny! You are my prisoner, in the king's name!" Cartagena screamed at his confederates Mendoza and Quesada to plunge their daggers into Magellan "according to plan"—thus giving away his prior intention—but they dared not move; Gómez de Espinosa hustled Cartagena down to the main deck and clapped him into a pair of stocks normally occupied by common seamen guilty of petty offenses. Mendoza and Quesada begged the Captain General to afford him more dignified treatment; and as neither of them had committed himself as a mutineer, Magellan consented to release Cartagena and entrust him for safekeeping to Mendoza in *Victoria*. Then, after sounding trumpets to attract everyone's attention in the fleet, the Captain General announced the appointment of Antonio de Coca captain of *San Antonio* in Cartagena's stead.

Ocean currents finally floated the armada out of the doldrums, the blessed trade wind made up, and the ships filled away and gathered speed. Magellan called *Concepción*'s pilot, João Lopes Carvalho, to the *Trinidad* to be flag pilot, because he knew the coast better than

Entering Rio de Janeiro, 1971. Courtesy of the Brazilian Consul at Barcelona.

Gómez did. Magellan also had a copy of the *Livro da Marinharia*, by the chief pilot of Portugal, which gives fairly accurate latitudes of places on the Brazilian coast down to 35° S; and he must have learned from earlier Portuguese experience that if you hit the coast near Cape San Roque at 5° S, the hump of the Brazilian bulge, you are likely to be stuck there for a long, long time. Consequently he aimed for Cabo Santo Agostinho (which marks the harbor of Pernambuco, now Recife) at latitude 8°20′ S, and made it on 29 November 1519.

Since Magellan knew that the Portuguese had already established a *feitoria* at Recife, and wished to avoid being sighted, he did not stop but headed south, keeping the shore in sight. Finally, on Carvalho's assurance that no Portuguese would be encountered at Rio de Janeiro (latitude 22°54′ S), he decided to call there for rest and refreshment. In the small hours of 13 December 1519 the fleet passed Cape Frio, and that afternoon rounded into the spectacular bay. *Trinidad* proudly led the way through the channel, past the now famous *Pão de Açúcar* or Sugar Loaf, and anchored further up the harbor, off the site of the city, in seven fathom. Since this was the feast day of St. Lucy, Magellan named the bay *Santa Luzia* after her. But Coelho and Vespucci had already entered it in the first week of January 1502 and then named it *Rio de Janeiro*, River of January.

The happiest part of the voyage for all hands, and the last fun for most of them, was spent in the two weeks that they tarried at Rio, although the quality of the fun would have shocked St. Lucy, virgin and martyr. Immediately after anchoring, swarms of naked Indians boarded each ship. Carvalho warned the sailors that Guarani husbands were jealous and would resent advances to their wives; but that young girls were free for all, provided their brothers were paid for their services. And the pilot arranged a good deal: every sailor could have his girl for the price of one of those German knives "of worst quality" carried in the slopchests, paid to her brother. Mariners and Indian girls certainly enjoyed each other; nightly revels were held ashore, under a waning moon, and the more attractive lassies earned bonuses, in the shape of Venetian beads, hawks' bells, and red cloth, over the agreed-upon ten-cent knife. One day a beautiful young woman, says Pigafetta, selected her own gift. Coming on board alone when most of the crew were ashore, she peered into the unoccupied master's cabin and spied a long iron nail, more valuable to her than gold. "Picking it up, with great skill and gallantry, she thrust it between the lips of her vagina and, bending low, departed, the Captain General and I having witnessed this."

Carvalho himself collected a bonus: his former Brazilian mistress turned up with their seven-year-old son. The pilot signed up the boy as a *criado* or servant, but he could not persuade Magellan to take the mother along. The Captain General never allowed women on board ship at sea. Before he left any port where there had been goings-on, he caused the alguacil to search every nook and corner of each ship to root out girl stowaways.

The Christians found good trading at Rio, and not only in girls. The Indians loved playing cards and would give eight chickens for one king out of a pack. You could buy a slave with a hatchet; but Magellan forbade slave trade, not only to avoid offending the Portuguese, but because he wanted no extra mouths to feed.

At Rio, mutiny raised its ugly head for a second time. On board *San Antonio* Captain Coca, Bishop Fonseca's nephew, released Juan de

Cartagena and other prisoners. Magellan sent Gómez de Espinosa with men-at-arms to put the mutiny down, but once more entrusted the safe-keeping of Coca and Cartagena to Captain Mendoza of *Victoria*. He then appointed his cousin Álvaro de Mezquita, who had shipped as supernumerary in the flagship, captain of *San Antonio*. That was a mistake; Mezquita, promoted over many others, was not tough enough to deal with such hardbitten *hombres* as he now found under him.

Magellan and his pilots put their heads together and tried to determine the longitude of Rio by timing a conjunction of the moon and Jupiter and comparing it with the time that their almanac gave for it in Cadiz. As usual in such attempts, starting with Columbus's in Jamaica, they messed up the figures so that the result was worthless; later, however, they made a good educated guess at the longitude of Rio Santa Cruz. Magellan's pilots and navigators were the best of their era at celestial navigation. They managed to take an almost correct latitude of Cape Frio, 23° S—only a mile out; even João de Lisboa had made it 25° S.

The fleet kept Christmas off the site of the city of Rio de Janeiro and departed next morning, 26 December 1519. It weighed anchor to the sound of dolorous music, the wailing of abandoned native "brides." Goodby forever to the magnificent bay and harbor, and to the hospitable native Cariocas.

And, as they sailed south, it was goodby to many familiar stars. The Great Bear or Dipper which Homer described as "ever circling . . . with no part in the baths of Ocean," dipped below the northern horizon astern, and already had risen the Southern Cross, almost outshining even brilliant Orion.* The great southern stars only fitfully seen in the north, golden Canopus and Fomalhaut, ruddy Antares and Achenar, dominated the sky.

Now began the serious search for the Strait. Unlike his emulator Verrazzano who sailed so far off shore that he missed all the big bays, Magellan sailed as close to shore as he dared, frequently heaving the lead and investigating every big opening. Once only, between Rio de Janeiro and the River Plate, on 8 January 1520, did the fleet anchor at

* *Odyssey*, v, 274-75. Camoëns in *Lusiads*, V, 15 and VIII, 72, alludes to the "now-bathing Bear." The Southern Cross is apt to disappoint travelers from the north at first sight; but in comparison with other stars of the Southern Hemisphere, one ends in feeling, with Dante, "Heaven in their flames seemed to rejoice."

Punta del Este, Uruguay. Magellan's Cabo de Santa Maria, where he anchored for several days in January 1520. Courtesy of the American Embassy, Montevideo.

night, the moon but four days full. Two or three days later Pilot Carvalho recognized, by three conspicuous hills, Cabo Santa Maria, which he had seen on an earlier voyage. (It is now Punta del Este, Uruguay.) Rounding the Isla de Lobos where now a tall lighthouse marks the eastern entrance to the great Rio de la Plata estuary, Albo's shot of the sun worked out as latitude 35° S. Correct; latitude 35° passes halfway between the Point and the Island. Keeping the coast close aboard, they sighted a conspicuous mountain, doubtless the 1640-foot Cerro Las Ánimas which loomed up as we steamed by Punta del Este in 1972. Magellan cried out, "Monte Video!" and Montevideo is the name of the modern city and capital of Uruguay, sixty miles to the westward.

Magellan, eager to explore the Rio de la Plata (later Englished as the River Plate) then opening up, sailed on. He called it Rio de Solis after the man murdered there by natives in 1516. Hoping that this estuary would turn out to be the Strait (which the Schöner globe of 1515 placed at about latitude 35° S, and both Juan de Solis and João de Lisboa reported it to be there), the Captain General sent *Santiago*, his lightest-draft vessel, up-river to look for an outlet. Captain Serrano found the bay narrowing and shoaling, and reported plenty of evidence that one or more big rivers emptied into it. But, in order to make sure that he had not missed anything, Magellan sent the longboat of each ship to make a detailed search, while the fleet lay at anchor under Punta del Este, off the present beach resort. This boat exploration found the water becoming brackish and then fresh, proving it to be no arm of the sea, but a river.

Convinced that the Strait could not be much further south, the Captain General insisted on going on, hoping to find it before the Antarctic winter closed in.

The Coast of Patagonia

A very difficult part of the voyage now began. The ships departed their anchorage near Montevideo on Candlemas Day, 2 February 1520. This was the right season for a coastal voyage; the official Pilot Chart shows mostly force-four winds from the northwest quadrant and few calms or variables, and Magellan started with a full moon. He crossed the great estuary on course due south, and first anchored off the modern Cabo San Antonio. He usually anchored at night so as not to miss anything—for João de Lisboa's sailing directions ended at Cabo Santa Maria; and sailing within sight of shore was not difficult. Sailors have a rule of thumb for this coast—"as many miles as fathoms"; i.e., on an eight miles' offing you will find a depth of eight fathom. This works very well from Cabo San Antonio to Mar del Plata; the ten-fathom line runs just about ten miles from shore.

At anchor 13 February (off the modern lighthouse of Bahia Blanca), their cables held during a terrific thunderstorm, during which *Victoria* took a number of *culadas* (literally, "arse-hits") on her keel. A particularly beautiful corposant or St. Elmo's fire played about the spars, a "spiritual comfort" to the sailors. Magellan thought Bahia Blanca worth investigating, and they threaded their way among the islands of that now important port and beach resort. Here, or earlier, Magellan adopted a twenty-four-hour schedule, sailing one league from the land by day, and five or six leagues off shore by night.

On 24 February, at latitude 40°40′ S, Magellan opened the mouth of a sixty-mile-wide bay receding more than eighty miles. He brushed this off as a dead-end (which it was) and because his dipsey lead would not

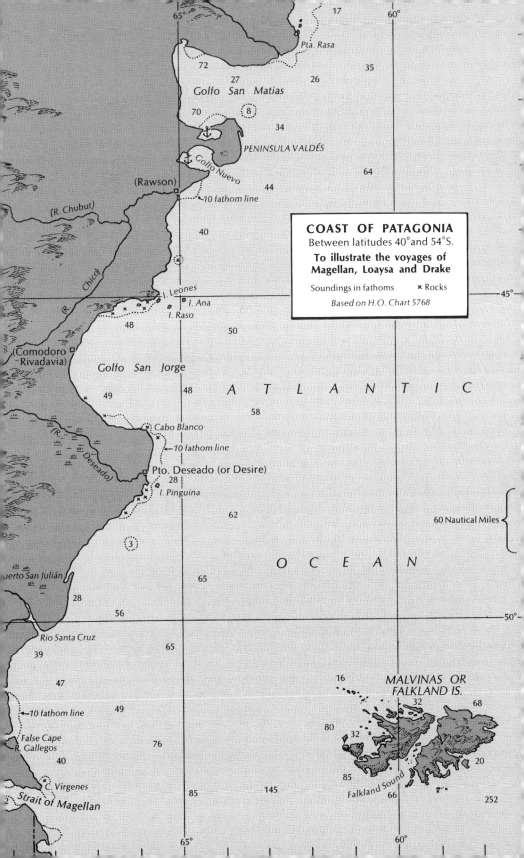

17

60°

Pta. Rasa

72   35

27   26

Golfo San Matias

70   8

34

PENINSULA VALDÉS

Golfo Nuevo

(Rawson)

64

(R. Chubut)

10 fathom line

44

40

COAST OF PATAGONIA
Between latitudes 40° and 54° S.

**To illustrate the voyages of
Magellan, Loaysa and Drake**

Soundings in fathoms   × Rocks

Based on H.O. Chart 5768

45°

(R. Chico)

I. Leones

I. Ana

I. Raso

48   50

(Comodoro
Rivadavia)

Golfo San Jorge

A   T   L   A   N   T   I   C

49   48

58

(R. Deseado)

Cabo Blanco

10 fathom line

Pto. Deseado (or Desire)

28

I. Pinguina

62

60 Nautical Miles

3

O   C   E   A   N

Puerto San Julián

65

28

56

50°

Rio Santa Cruz

39

65

47

16

*MALVINAS OR
FALKLAND IS.*

10 fathom line   49

32   68

False Cape
R. Gallegos

40

76

80

32

85

20

C. Virgenes

85   145

Falkland Sound

66   252

Strait of Magellan

65°   60°

reach bottom—on the Ribero map of 1529 it is called *Bahia sin fondo*, Bottomless Bay. For shelter he chose a snug little harbor just south of Valdés, which he named *Puerto de San Matias* since this was the vigil of St. Matthias. It is now called Golfo Nuevo, a pleasant, well-protected spot to spend a few days. On 27 February they lay off a broad bay that they called *Bahia de los Patos*, owing to the immense number of penguins, for which Europeans as yet had no name except *patos sin alas*—wingless ducks. The boat sent ashore to replenish found plenty of elephant seal and penguin, which the men were still slaughtering when an offshore gale sprang up and blew the fleet out to sea. The wretched shore party had to cover themselves with dead seal and rotting penguin to avoid freezing to death. When the fleet, returning, rescued them, they were smelling horribly. This locality I take to have been the shallow bay at Cabo dos Bahias, and the three islands off it.

The name of these islands, Sanson, evidently refers to the stature of the natives; for Magellan had discovered (and shortly would name) a vast region called Patagonia. It was often described by nineteenth-century travelers, usually in uncomplimentary terms. But the natural grass, nutritious for sheep as it had been for the guanaco, made Patagonia eventually a rival to Australia for sheep raising. The country is not flat but undulating, covered with grass, green in the Antarctic spring, brown the rest of the year. It is well watered, crossed by numerous rivers which rise on the eastern slopes of the Andes, some of which Magellan felt he had to investigate. In his time, these undulating plains were pastures for enormous herds of guanaco, the southern llama, and of puma and rhea, the American ostrich.

Physically, Patagonia corresponds to the North American West between the Great Plains and the Rockies and it, too, inspires both love and hatred. Martinic quotes the farewell of an early explorer: "Patagonia, thou art the land of the strong man and the free soul!"

Storm after storm now pursued the fleet. These were the infamous *pamperos*, line squalls that blow with great ferocity off the land. Six stormy days were ridden out in a small bay that Magellan called *Bahia de los Trabajos*, "Bay of Travail," identified as Port Desire or *Puerto Deseado* at latitude 47°46′ S. Darwin, who kept Christmas 1833 there in *Beagle*, called it "a wretched place," but in 1972 we found the shores neither so rugged nor so picturesque as Darwin's artist Conrad Martens depicted them. The present-day official sailing directions warn one that

Port Desire in 1833. Drawing by Conrad Martens of the *Beagle* expedition.

"heavy gales . . . rising without warning" are prevalent. Magellan's fleet, once outside, suffered more battering, and for three weeks they made only about 120 miles southwesterly, and no sun appeared. Finally they entered *Puerto San Julián*, as Magellan named it, on the last day of March, the eve of Palm Sunday. Summer (January, February, March) was almost over in these high latitudes, and winter so near that the Captain General announced the fleet would stay there until better weather offered some prospect of finding the Strait. And there they stayed for five months, until 24 August.

Puerto San Julián still offers a spacious inner harbor, but a depressing aspect. The entrance between the hundred-foot-high gray cliffs (Cabos Curioso and Desengaño) narrows to a half-mile-wide bottleneck. The tidal range is twenty to twenty-five feet, and the current at the narrow entrance runs up to six knots. So, when things got sticky, Magellan found it wise to moor his flagship in the bottleneck so that any vessel trying to escape would have to cross his cannon range.

Two months elapsed before the Spaniards met one soul ashore. According to Pigafetta, "One day suddenly we saw a naked man of giant stature on the shore of the harbor, dancing, singing, and throwing dust on his head. When the giant was in the Captain General's and our presence, he marveled greatly, and made signs with one finger raised upward, believing that we had come from the sky. He was so tall that we reached only to his waist, and he was well proportioned."

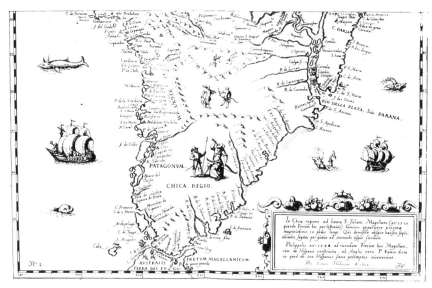

A Patagonian swallowing an arrow. From the Hulsius map of 1602, courtesy British Museum.

He was painted all over and partially dressed in guanaco skins. His feet, shod with guanaco-hide buskins stuffed with straw, looked enormous, which caused Magellan to name him *patagón* (big-foot), and his country, Patagonia. Although Pigafetta greatly exaggerated the Patagonian's stature, many later explorers described these natives as taller than the average European. They led a nomadic and pastoral life, "like Cingani" (gypsies), said Pigafetta, following the wild herds of guanaco which they caught by using captured calves as decoys. They lived largely off that animal, much as the North American Indians of the Great Plains used to do off the buffalo.

This first encounter between Europeans and natives of the region passed off well. The Captain General gave the "man of giant stature" a clutch of rosary beads, some tinkly hawks' bells, a comb in the hope that he might use it on his filthy, tangled locks, and a mirror. This last gift set off a comic scene. The poor savage was so terrified at seeing his hairy mug in the glass that he recoiled, knocking down, as he did so, four little Spaniards. Other natives turned up with their tame guanaco and their beasts of burden—the women. These were short

590

and squat, with breasts hanging down half a fathom, repulsively ugly to Magellan's crews. The men, to amuse the Spaniards, performed a primitive version of the old sword-swallowing trick, shoving arrows down their gullets and drawing them out without hurt.

Some eighteen Patagonians were entertained on board the ships, and later one stayed with them for at least a week, allowed himself to be christened Juan, and learned to say *Jesu, Ave Maria,* and a few other words; he was delighted to eat all the rats and mice that were caught on board, and left clothed and apparently happy. But he never turned up again.

A fortnight later, however, four natives appeared and Magellan kidnapped two by a very mean trick. He heaped their cupped hands with trading truck, and then brought out two pair of leg irons. The giants admired them (as they did everything of iron) but indicated they could hold no more. Carvalho suggested that they could be carried on the legs, and the innocent giants acquiesced "When they saw later that they were tricked," wrote Pigafetta, "they raged like bulls, calling for their god Setebos to aid them." These were the only contacts with the natives that Magellan made in the five dreary months at Puerto San Julián.

Now for the mutiny, which began earlier. Maximilianus Transylvanus, first to interview the few Spaniards who returned home to Spain, recorded shipboard gossip and what he calls a "shameful and foul conspiracy" among the Spanish officers and men. They accused Magellan of planning to cast away the entire fleet, or else of luring Charles V for years with vain hopes of doing the impossible—reaching the Spice Islands via the Antarctic. Anyway, he was a Portuguese, so to hell with him!

Elcano's excuse for participating in the disloyalty, when examined in 1522 was this: Magellan and Cartagena were joint commanders; hence the latter should have been consulted before every decision. In an earlier chapter I concluded emphatically that Cartagena was never joint commander—but he may well have imagined that he was. Magellan alone was the Emperor's Captain General. He alone had the title. In his commission he is given absolute power over all persons sailing with him; or, as Correia put it, *poder de baraco e cutello*— "power of rope and knife." And in the religious ceremony before departure, all officers swore to obey him, and no other commander.

The Narrows, Puerto San Julián. James F. Nields photo.

The very eve of their arrival at San Julián, 31 March, Magellan, after reducing rations, held a colloquy with deputations from all five ships. The men urged him to restore full rations and return to Spain; they doubted whether any strait existed, feared that to continue the voyage southward would lead only to starvation and a frozen death. Magellan replied that he would rather die than give up his quest for the Strait, which the king had ordered; that plenty of food could be found in Puerto San Julián, and they still had enough bread and wine from Spain; and he pointed out that the Strait, which would certainly be found, would lead them to languorous islands and girls even kinder and more beautiful than those of Rio. Finally, he exhorted them not to be wanting in the valor for which Castilians had ever been distinguished. The men, apparently placated, returned to their duty. But the conspiracy continued among the officers.

Next day, Palm Sunday, Magellan summoned all officers to hear Mass ashore, and invited the captains to dine with him afterward in the flag cabin. Only his kinsman Álvaro de Mezquita accepted. That was ominous, and a most unholy Holy Week followed. On Palm Sunday night the mutineers took possession of three ships—*San Antonio* (Captain Mezquita), *Concepción* (Captain Quesada), and *Victoria* (Captain Mendoza). Cartagena, the deposed captain of *San*

Antonio, stabbed but failed to kill Elorriaga, the loyal master of *San Antonio*, and clapped Captain Mezquita in irons; this took care of the biggest ship, while Quesada and Elcano overawed the crew of *Concepción*, and Mendoza got control of *Victoria*.

On Monday of Holy Week Quesada sent a message in *Concepción*'s longboat (manned by stout oarsmen to breast the strong current) to Magellan in flagship *Trinidad*. Coca commanded the boat. The message, signed by the three leading mutineers, took the high ground that the Captain General was disobeying royal instructions by leading them so far south. No longer would they recognize him as Captain General, but would follow his lead as senior captain if he promised to take them back to Spain. Magellan made no reply, but performed a very clever bit of strategy. Detaining this boat and crew, he dressed thirty of his own men in their clothes so that they would not be recognized, manned the boat with them, and let her out on a long hawser so that the tide would carry her near enough to *Victoria* in case she was wanted. (There was a strong ebb current from the flagship to her, and they had plenty of light under the paschal moon, two nights short of full.) Magellan then dispatched alguacil Gómez de Espinosa in his own gig with five or six armed men to *Victoria* with a letter ordering Mendoza to return to his duty and report on board the flagship; if the rebel captain refused to obey, Magellan instructed Espinosa to kill him. Mendoza allowed the alguacil and his men to board *Victoria*, and admitted Espinosa and one man-at-arms to his cabin on the alguacil's assertion that he had a private message for the captain. Mendoza, after reading Magellan's letter, crumpled it as if to throw it away, laughing scornfully. That was his last laugh. Espinosa, stretching forth his left hand as if to take the rejected letter, grasped Mendoza's beard, jerked back his head, and with a dagger thrust in the throat killed him, while his man-at-arms, to make it certain, stabbed the victim's head.

The longboat, full of armed men and commanded by Duarte Barbosa, was standing by a few yards upstream, awaiting a signal. Espinosa waved a cloth, Barbosa ordered his hawser to be cast off, the current quickly took the boat alongside *Victoria*, and the men-at-arms swarmed aboard that ship before her people even knew of their captain's death. Barbosa, promptly appointed by Magellan captain of *Victoria*, ordered anchors aweigh, and with sweeps working, a foresail to catch the evening breeze, and the longboat towing, approached the flagship and anchored alongside. Loyal Serrano followed, anchoring his caravel off *Trinidad*'s other board.

Quesada, captain of *Concepción*, seeing that Magellan now controlled three of the five ships, lost his nerve and tried to sneak out of Puerto San Julián under cover of night in company with *San Antonio*, of which Cartagena had usurped command. This scheme did not work because, before Quesada was ready to sail, a loyal sailor cut *Concepción*'s cable and she drifted with the evening ebb tide within range of Magellan's flagship *Trinidad*. And the almost-full moon helped. When she came near enough, the Captain General gave her a point-blank broadside, and men in the fighting tops raked her decks with crossbow fire and lances. Quesada in full armor on the sterncastle of his ship, with arrows and crossbow bolts bouncing off his steel corselet, vainly tried to rally his crew to fight back. Magellan now had himself rowed to *Concepción*, boarded her, and with drawn sword forced Quesada to surrender his ship.

The Captain General, after clapping both Quesada and Coca in irons on board *Trinidad*, continued the good work. Rowed by Espinosa to *San Antonio*, he hailed her. Cartagena, in armor, abjectly answered the hail in loyal terms. Espinosa boarded the ship and placed him under arrest.

Thus by sheer audacity, wit, and ability to seize opportunities, Magellan who in the morning was master only of his flagship and *Santiago*, by evening ruled the entire fleet. A very serious mutiny had been quenched with injury to but one loyal man, Juan de Elorriaga. As the author of the Leiden Narrative wrote, "After the punishment of these persons all the people were in peace, and there were no more mutinies." Nobody dared again to challenge Magellan's authority—at least not when he was around.

Next day—Tuesday of Holy Week—Magellan had Mendoza's body taken ashore and quartered, and cried him through the fleet as a traitor. He then called a formal court-martial which found Mendoza (represented by his quartered corpse), Cartagena, Coca, Elcano, Quesada, and Quesada's servant Molino, guilty of treason and condemned them to death. There followed a grim celebration of Easter Sunday. Molino won his life as reward for executing his master, which apparently he did with relish; and Quesada's body was hanged on a gibbet next to Mendoza's remains, probably on the Isla Justicia upriver. Magellan commuted all other sentences to hard

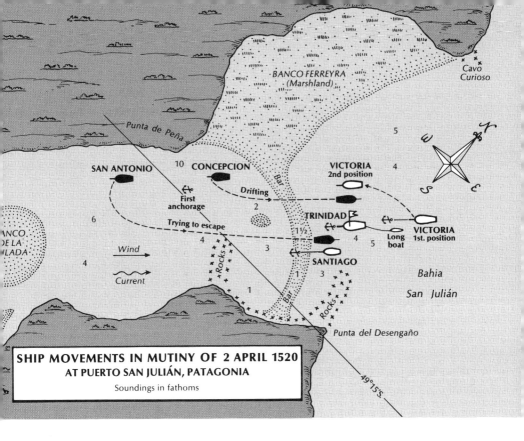

BANCO FERREYRA
(Marshland)

Cavo
Curioso

Punta de Peña

SAN ANTONIO

10 CONCEPCION

5

VICTORIA
2nd position

4

First
anchorage

Drifting

2

Bar

Trying to escape

TRINIDAD

VICTORIA
1st. position

ANCO.
DE LA
LADA.

6

4

Wind

4

3

1½

Long
boat

4

5

Current

1

Rocks

SANTIAGO

1

3

Bahia

San Julián

Rocks

Punta del Desengaño

**SHIP MOVEMENTS IN MUTINY OF 2 APRIL 1520
AT PUERTO SAN JULIÁN, PATAGONIA**
Soundings in fathoms

49°15'S

labor, and all except Cartagena were organized into a sort of chain gang, cutting wood and pumping out ships through the rest of that long winter. Elcano laid this up against Magellan and did his best, after returning to Spain, to destroy his reputation.

Magellan's leniency to Cartagena was misplaced. He was caught using one of the chaplains, Pero Sánchez de Reina, to stir up the men to fresh mutiny. Another court-martial found both, layman and priest, guilty and sentenced them to be marooned.

One force that helped Magellan to quell this serious mutiny was the loyalty of the enlisted men. They had sailed under him long enough to size him up as an experienced mariner, firm yet just; but the three Spanish captains, as they had ample opportunity to observe, were not even sailors.

During the five and a half chilly months at San Julián, Magellan had his men build barracks ashore and (as he well knew sailors must be kept busy) set them a-fishing, hunting game, and curing their catch with salt extracted from natural salt pans at the head of the bay. Sailors also made themselves guanaco and sealskin coats to keep out the bitter cold. More provisions were urgently wanted because, when the ships were unladen in preparation for "rummaging" * them ashore, the scribes and clerks made the appalling discovery of more dirty work by the Sevillian land sharks. Owing to an ingenious method of fraudulent checking, the ships had stores for only six months instead of for a year and a half.

Alan Villiers' curse on rascally ship chandlers, purveyors of rotten spars, substandard cordage, and spoiled or insufficient food, I cheerfully second. Magellan's men, Captain Cook's, and countless others suffered from the diabolical cheating of these human teredos. Their callously selfish peculations have sent countless thousands of poor sailors prematurely to Fiddler's Green. Damn their eyes, one and all!

In search of provisions, and because Captain Serrano was "an industrious man and never rested" (as the author of the Leiden Narrative said), the Captain General sent *Santiago* south under him to try to locate the Strait. Through no fault of her captain, *Santiago* met her fate about three leagues south of the entrance to Rio Santa Cruz, on 3 May 1520. She anchored off a beach, an onshore wind suddenly arose, and before she could make sail her anchor cables parted and she drifted ashore. The men jumped aground dry-shod, all except black Juan, the captain's slave. *Santiago* floated off on the next spring flood, only to ground again a short distance away; this time they could not get her off. Later, much of her cargo was salvaged. After the first grounding, two members of the crew volunteered to walk to San Julián for help. First they had to build a boat from *Santiago*'s timbers to cross the river. From there the distance overland, as the crow flies, is a good sixty miles, and their route must have been at least half again as long. It took them eleven days' stumbling over the partially snow-covered pampas, and with very little o eat as they were unable to shoot guanacos or big birds. Magellan promptly sent a rescuing force by boat to Santa Cruz, and all *Santiago*'s survivors were brought back safely after a month's privation.

Weary of inaction and eager to get on, Magellan now resolved to spend the rest of the Antarctic winter at Rio Santa Cruz. The last sight his men saw as they departed unhappy Puerto San Julián in

---

* Careening, and throwing out the stone ballast to be cleansed by the tide; scraping out accumulated filth in the hold, sprinkling it with vinegar and replacing the ballast. Magellan also had topsides below the waterline smeared with pitch to keep out teredos.

September, was Juan de Cartagena and the priest kneeling at the water's edge and bawling for mercy. Firearms, gunpowder, wine, and hardtack were left with them, but whether they starved to death or were killed by the Indians we know not. Theirs are not the only bones of marooned men left at San Julián. Drake executed Thomas Doughty, convicted of attempted mutiny, at the same spot fifty-one years later. A sinister place indeed.

Magellan has been criticized by sundry armchair admirals for tarrying so long in Patagonian ports. They point out that Drake got through the Strait in seventeen days in August-September 1578, the Antarctic winter. But Drake, on leaving the Strait, ran into a series of northerly and westerly gales which delayed him over a month, and lost two of his three ships; whilst Magellan debouched into a calm, pacific sea. That alone was worth waiting for.

It took the fleet but two days to reach Rio Santa Cruz, so named because they entered on 14 September, feast of the Exaltation of the Holy Cross. The people, however, called it the River of Shad, because they caught so many of that tasty fish. The Genoese pilot estimated this harbor to be on latitude 50° S, and he was correct. There they stayed until 18 October. Santa Cruz, unlike San Julián, lay at the mouth of a navigable river, as Magellan realized after ascertaining the water to be fresh. Captain FitzRoy of H.M.S. *Beagle*, and Charles Darwin, explored 140 miles of Rio Santa Cruz in 1834, and forty-three years later an Argentinian, F. P. Moreno, reached the source in Lago Argentino.

Magellan's officers now thought up a new scheme to avoid worse cold and discomfort; to sail east to the Spice Islands around the Cape of Good Hope. The Captain General rejected this out of hand, but promised to consider it if he found no strait above latitude 75° S.* This did not satisfy the officers, and Esteban Gómez, now pilot of *San Antonio*, proposed another mutiny, but Captain Mezquita decided to follow Magellan. Gómez bided his time.

By 17 October, Magellan judged the Antarctic spring to be sufficiently advanced to proceed. All hands went ashore, confessed to Pedro de Valderrama the flag chaplain, and attended Mass. Next day the four ships, *Trinidad, San Antonio, Concepción*, and *Victoria*, sailed out of Rio Santa Cruz; and this time they were not disappointed in finding *el paso*, the Strait.

* Navarrete, IV, p. lvii. I think this is a misprint for 57° S.

✳ XXIV ✳

"The Strait
That Shall Forever Bear His Name"

October-November 1520

Strait Discovered

On 21 October 1520, the feast of St. Ursula and the Eleven Thousand Virgins, the fleet raised a prominent peninsula which Magellan named after the seagoing Cornish princess and her martyred shipmates. Cabo Vírgenes or Cape Virgins it still is, on latitude 52°20′ S, longitude 68°21′ W. Albo was only twenty miles off in latitude, and made a good guess at the longitude. The Cape is a long flat stretch of grass-topped clay cliffs rising about 135 feet above the water. The landmarks for it (said Uriate on Loaysa's voyage) are a white sand hill four leagues north and "three great mountains of sand which look like islands but are not." On top of this cape the Chile-Argentine boundary turns a right angle and reaches the Atlantic a few yards east of the Chilean lighthouse on Punta Dungeness, the flat and gravelly extension of Cape Virgins. It then drops due south, leaving to Argentina one-third of Tierra del Fuego down to the Beagle Channel, and giving Chile both sides of the Strait.

Although the cape is conspicuous enough, the fact that a strait opens here is by no means obvious, and the tidal currents are so strong and confusing that an uncertain mariner would be tempted to sheer off.

America and Asia on the Schöner globe of 1515, simplified and reduced.
From História da Colonização do Brasil.

Joshua Slocum in 1898 was blown outside Cape Virgins for thirty hours
by a southwest gale; the next "loner," Louis Bernicot in *Anahita,* also
without power, was twice blown out to sea; even steamers have been
forced to scud all the way to the Falklands and there await a change of
wind. Pigafetta writes that but for Magellan they would never have
found the Strait, "for we all thought and said that it was closed on all
sides." (The men evidently imagined a strait as something one could
look through, like that of Gibraltar.) Pigafetta continues: "But the
Captain General found it. He knew where to sail to find a well-hidden
strait, which he saw depicted on a map in the treasury of the king of
Portugal, made by that excellent man Martin de Boemia." That "excellent man" must have been Martin Behaim, to whose globe of 1492–

599

Sketch of Cape Virgins, in Guillemard's *Magellan*.

93 we have already referred; but what was the map? Behaim died in
1507; he never, so far as we know, went on a voyage of discovery, and
no chart by him subsequent to the famous globe is known to exist.

Every biographer of Magellan, and many historians, have discussed
the question, "What chart did Magellan see in Lisbon?" To me, the most
reasonable answer in that he had seen one or more charts which ended
South America with a strait, on the south side of which was the supposed Antarctic continent running around the world. The globe made
in 1515 by the German geographer Johannes Schöner (1477–1547) is a
good example of the chart that Magellan might have seen and thought
to be Behaim's, since both Behaim and Schöner were Nurembergers,
and their style was very similar. As we have seen, Magellan brought a
painted globe to the Spanish court to prove his point; may not this have
been a copy of Schöner's? Pigafetta's word *carta* need not put us off,
since in those days the word could mean a flat map or one spread on a
globe.

A globe like this could have assured Magellan that a strait existed
either at the River Plate or further south. And Schöner makes the
Pacific Ocean encouragingly narrow. *Zipangri* (Japan) is smack up to
Parias (Central America), and the Spice Islands are no farther from
the west coast of South America than the Lesser Antilles are from
Florida. Had they indeed been so near to America, Magellan's idea that
a round-the-world extension of the Line of Demarcation would give
them to Spain would have proved correct. Spain, in fact, would have
got all Asia up to the Ganges.

Two geographical factors unknown to Magellan thwarted him, although, curiously enough, he discovered both. One was the Strait's
extreme southern position, and the other was the enormous breadth

600

of the Pacific Ocean. These, combined, made the western route to the
Far East so long and arduous as to be almost impracticable until ways
were found to cross Mexico. Even so, the Portuguese Cape of Good
Hope route remained the shorter and less difficult of the two. Magellan
shared Columbus's basic idea of sailing from Europe to Asia "in a few
days." America and the unexpected width of the Pacific thwarted both
discoverers. And Magellan's exploits were never properly appreciated
until Schouten and Le Maire capped them with the discovery of Cape
Horn.

From Cape Virgins to Cape Pillar

It was now 21 October 1520; moon two days past first quarter. Having
passed Cabo Vírgenes and avoided the many off-shore rocks and shoals
which there await unwary mariners, the Captain General determined to
investigate this break in the coast, and make sure whether it really
was *the* Strait. He nipped around Punta Dungeness, the flat southern
prolongation of Cabo Vírgenes. Mooring his flagship and *Victoria* in
Bahia Posesión, hoping that this would turn out to be fair holding
ground (which it was not), the Captain General sent ahead *Concepción*, now commanded by his faithful friend Serrano, and *San
Antonio*, commanded by his kinsman Mezquita, to reconnoiter.

One of the sharp northeast gales characteristic of this region blew
up the night of 21–22 October. *Trinidad* and *Victoria* weighed and
jilled around inside the bay; the two others, too deeply embayed to
beat against the gale, sailed west, giving themselves up for lost. Miraculously, as it seemed, the two-mile-wide Primera Angostura (First Narrows) opens up, and they roared through into Bahia Felipe where
they found shelter and holding ground. Further on, they found another and broader narrows (Segunda Angostura) which led to a big
bay, Paso Ancho (Broad Reach). Serrano and Pilot Carvalho put their
heads together and decided that they really were in *the* Strait. After
the gale had blown itself out and the wind turned west, *Concepción*
and *San Antonio* returned to Bahia Posesión and announced themselves
to *Trinidad* and the Captain General by breaking out gay banners,
sounding trumpets, firing gun salutes, shouting, and cheering. Each
pair had feared the loss of the other.

When all four ships were safely anchored, they "thanked God and the Virgin Mary," and Magellan decided to follow whither *San Antonio* and *Concepción* had led. Since it was now 1 November, All Saints' Day, the Captain General named the strait *Todos los Santos*. On early maps that name appears only for sections of the Strait; the whole Strait is almost invariably called *Estrecho de Magallanes*, Magellan's Strait.

The Captain General and his shipmates would have roared with laughter, could they have read the modern official sailing directions for the Strait: "The passage is safe for steamers"; but in thick weather, "both difficult and dangerous, because of incomplete surveys, the lack of aids to navigation, the great distance between anchorages, the strong current, and the narrow limits for the maneuvering of vessels." Magellan might say, "What about us? With no power, other than sail and oar, no survey, no aid to navigation?" The same manual assumes that no ship without power would be so foolhardy as to try the Strait.

Captain James Cook stated in his Journal of the *Endeavour's* voyage (1769), "The doubling of Cape Horn is thought by some to be a mighty thing, and others to this Day prefer the Straits of Magellan." After Cook's fast passage of Cape Horn became known, the big sailing ships in general shunned the Strait and suffered all the buffetings of "Cape Stiff" rather than face the dangers of the shorter route. But the Strait has since come back as a major sea highway. Not only small freighters destined for Chile and Peru, but the mammoth oilers of the 1970's, use the Strait regularly, and an average of about three a year run aground or are lost there. Few realize how long the Strait is—334 nautical miles. This is equivalent to the entire length of the English Channel from Bishop Rock to Dover Strait, or from the Gulf of St. Lawrence to Montreal, or from the Panama Canal entrance to Barranquilla.

Magellan and his captains wisely did not attempt to sail here at night; but as they entered the Strait in the Antarctic spring, darkness lasted but three to five hours.

A boat sent ashore from *Trinidad* in Bahia Felipe between the two Angosturas, reported a dead whale and a native cemetery with a couple of hundred corpses raised on stilts, but nothing alive. No Magellan source mentions his fleet having had any contact with live natives in the Strait. He saw their signal fires almost every night—hence the name that he gave to the country on the south side, *Tierra del Fuego*. The name is particularly applicable today, since this region has struck oil;

the gas from sundry oil wells burns in smoky flares on each side of the Strait's eastern entrance.

In seeing no Fuegians, Magellan's men missed viewing these examples of human fortitude in the face of hostile nature. Probably among the first arrivals from the Asiatic invasion tens of thousands of years earlier, continually pushed south by more powerful and enterprising tribes, these Indians had reached a dead end. Accommodating themselves to available food, though not to dress as the Eskimos did in the far north, they lived on the big, succulent mussels of the Strait and on such fish and birds as they could shoot or snare, burning the wood of the Tepu tree (*Tepularia stipularis*), and stripping bark for canoe hulls from various species of the evergreen Antarctic beech (*Nothofagus antarctica pomilio*, etc.) which clothe the lower slopes of the mountains. Charles Darwin thus described a canoeful of Fuegians whom he en-encountered in the *Beagle:* "These poor wretches were stunted in their growth, their hideous faces bedaubed with white paint, their skins filthy and greasy, their hair entangled, their voices discordant, and their gestures violent." They seemed not to mind sleet falling on their almost naked bodies.

Undeterred by sinister hints of the native graveyard, Magellan's fleet worked through the wider Second Narrows and came to an anchor in Paso Real between Isabel Island and the main. Here, and well into Paso Ancho or Broad Reach, the landscape on each side is pampas: green-to-brown rolling country with no hint of a strait. Even Paso Ancho looks like a dead-end because in clear weather, sixty miles to the southward, the mountains on Dawson Island and on the Cordillera Darwin rise like an impenetrable barrier. On the land side the aspect today is pastoral. In February, hayfields white with daisies roll down to the sea, sheep and cattle pastures are everywhere, and a few neat villas planted with evergreen to shield them from the furious winds, indicate that this region is livable winter or summer. Paso Ancho (15 miles broad), when low-hanging clouds hide the distant snowy mountains, looks very much like any broad bay in Maine, Nova Scotia, or Scotland. The great scenery begins within sight of Cape Froward.

Magellan's fleet, continuing south through Paso Ancho and passing the site of Punta Arenas, again separated. The Captain General sent *San Antonio* and *Concepción* to investigate two openings eastward which turned out to be dead-ends—Bahia Inútil (Useless Bay) and

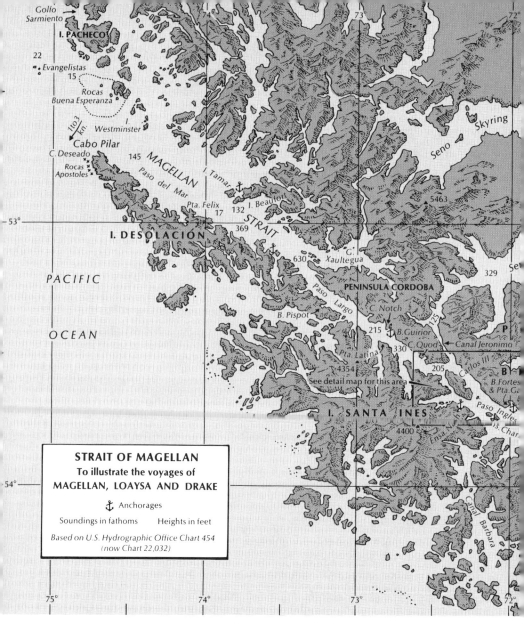

Golfo
Sarmiento
I. PACHECO

22
Evangelistas
15
Rocas
Buena Esperanza
I.
Westminster
1 to 3 km.
Cabo Pilar
C. Deseado   145
Rocas
Apostoles
MAGELLAN
Paso del Mar
I. Tamar
Skyring
Seno

5463

— 53° —

I. DESOLACIÓN
Pta. Felix
17   132   I. Beaufort
369
STRAIT
630   Xaultegua
G.
PENINSULA CORDOBA
329   Se

Paso Largo
C. Notch

PACIFIC

B. Pispot
215   B. Guirior
Pta. Latina   330   C. Quod   Canal Jeronimo   P

OCEAN

4354   See detail map for this area
205   Carlos III   B
B. Fortes
& Pta. Ga
Paso Ingle

I. SANTA INES
4400
Ens.
Is. Char

— 54° —

STRAIT OF MAGELLAN
To illustrate the voyages of
MAGELLAN, LOAYSA AND DRAKE
⚓ Anchorages
Soundings in fathoms   Heights in feet
Based on U.S. Hydrographic Office Chart 454
(now Chart 22,032)

Canal
Barbara

75°   74°   73°   72°

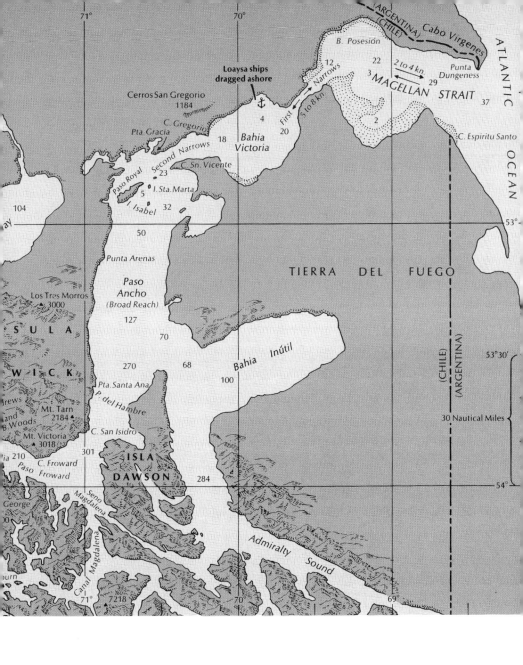

71°　　　　　　　　　　　　70°

(ARGENTINA)　Cabo Vírgenes
(CHILE)

B. Posesión

ATLANTIC

Loaysa ships dragged ashore

12
22
2 to 4 kn.
Punta Dungeness

Cerros San Gregorio
1184

29

3
MAGELLAN STRAIT
37

C. Gregorio
Pta. Gracia

4
First
Narrows
5 to 8 kn.

OCEAN

18
Bahía Victoria
20
2

C. Espíritu Santo

Paso Royal
Second Narrows
23
C. Sn. Vicente

104
5
I. Sta. Marta

I. Isabel
32

53°

50

Punta Arenas

TIERRA DEL FUEGO

Paso Ancho
(Broad Reach)

Los Tres Morros
3000

127

S U L A

70

Bahía Inútil

53°30'

W I C K

270
68

100

rews
Mt. Tarn
2184
and
B. Woods

Pta. Santa Ana
P. del Hambre

53°30'

Mt. Victoria
3018

C. San Isidro

30 Nautical Miles

ia 210
C. Froward
301

ISLA

Paso
Froward

DAWSON
284

54°

George

Seno
Magdalena

Admiralty
Sound

(CHILE)
(ARGENTINA)

urn
71°
7218

70°

69°

Seno del Almirantazgo (Admiralty Bay)—while he in the flagship with *Victoria* sailed along what fortunately turned out to be the real Strait.

Just before this separation, Magellan held a captains' conference to decide whether or not to push on. All were in favor of doing so except Esteban Gómez, now pilot of *San Antonio*. Although a Portuguese, Gómez "hated the Captain General exceedingly" (says Pigafetta), because he had hoped to command the entire fleet, and his simmering hate blew hot when Magellan, after eliminating Cartagena, conferred the captaincy of *San Antonio* on his cousin Mezquita instead of on Gómez. Magellan, *muy compuesto* (with his usual cool), replied that he was resolved to go on, "even if they had to eat the leather chafing-gear on the ships' yards." And that is exactly what they did.

While *San Antonio* was exploring Useless and Admiralty bays, Esteban Gómez pulled off the one successful mutiny of this long voyage. He managed to suborn the stoutest fellows in the crew, clapped weak Captain Mezquita in irons, gave his fellow conspirator Hierónimo Guerra command of the ship, and piloted her back to Spain, arriving at the end of March 1521. He made no attempt to put in at San Julián to pick up marooned Cartagena and the priest. At Seville, both Gómez and his victim Mezquita were flung into jail. Gómez managed to parley his way out and into the royal favor to such good purpose that he got a new ship to go in search of a better strait than Magellan's. But poor Álvaro de Mezquita, the most frustrated officer of the fleet, remained in jail until after *Victoria* arrived home, when he found witnesses to put his conduct in a more favorable light. Charles V eventually ordered Mezquita to be released, and he returned to Portugal on D. Manuel's invitation.

In the meantime Magellan in *Trinidad* with *Victoria* sailed west again down Broad Reach. About thirty miles south of the site of Punta Arenas they passed, behind Punta Santa Ana, the site of Rey Don Felipe, one of two outposts established by Sarmiento de Gamboa in 1583 to guard the Strait. Port Famine, the name given to it by Cavendish in 1587, is still the southernmost settlement on the Strait; not a soul lives to the south and west. Near here, wrote Captain Slocum in 1900, "I had my first experience with the terrific squalls called williwaws, which extended from the point on through the Strait to the Pacific. These were compressed gales of wind that Boreas handed down over the hills in chunks. A full-blown williwaw will throw a ship, even

STRAIT OF MAGELLAN
Paso Ingles, Bahia Fortescue,
Crosstides and Paso Tortuoso
Soundings and heights in meters
Based on Chilean Navy Chart 1114

without sail set, over on her beam ends." Sailing directions warn mariners always to be prepared for a williwaw. They give no notice of their coming, and are apt to hit a vessel with such force as to strip off her sails, or even to capsize her.

Magellan's fleet sailed into spectacular scenery as soon as it passed Mount Tarn, which Darwin was the first to climb. Magellan's people had never seen anything like this combination of ocean strait with snow mountains; nor had Darwin. They rounded Cape Froward, a noble headland rising almost 1200 feet at latitude 53°54′ S, the southernmost point on the American continent. Here the Strait, about five miles wide, turns abruptly northwest, and after another twenty-five to thirty miles becomes a deep, narrow cut through the Andes, as if some giant hand had cleft the mountains millions of years ago.

Entering this part of the Strait, as we did in February 1972, one seems to be entering a completely new and strange world, a veritable Never-Never Land. The Strait never freezes except along the edges, and the evergreen Antarctic beech, with its tiny, matted leaves, grows thickly along the lower mountain slopes. The middle slopes support a coarse

Down the Strait: Cape Froward (above). Antarctic beech groves (below).

grass which turns bronze in the setting sun; and above, the high peaks are snow-covered the year round; when it rains in the Strait, it snows at 6000 feet. One misses, in the Antarctic autumn, the brilliant colors of New England and Canada (since Patagonia and Tierra del Fuego lack birch and other deciduous trees); but by way of compensation, they harbor no mosquitoes, which cannot stand the wind! There is no sign of human life south and west of Port Famine, except for a few small unattended lighthouses at dangerous points. The Indians are extinct, and with no coastal road or path or any means of land transportation, neither Chilean nor foreigner has attempted to settle or even to camp here.* Even the birds are different—the sinister gray *Carnero* which picks out the eyes of shipwrecked sailors, the Steamboat Duck whose whirling wings, resembling the churning paddle wheels of early steamers, enable him to pace an eight-knot vessel on the surface. In spring, when Magellan sailed through, both banks are gay with many-colored flowers, and saturated peat moss makes a sort of tundra in the hollows. Although glaciers are everywhere visible and some descend nearly to the sea, icebergs are missing; the glaciers "calve" only small bits of ice, not bergs. Waterfalls tumble directly into the bays. It is "fascinating sailing," wrote H. W. Tilman, who sailed through in his little sloop *Mischief* in an Antarctic summer not long ago. One rounds miniature capes and peeps into hidden coves: "It had the powerful appeal of an untrodden land." In several places, such as Paso Inglés by Rupert and Carlos Islands, and Crosstides, the channel is less than a mile wide, but in the center the depths run to 800 fathom; and from the narrow ribbon of practicable holding ground near shore, a ship is liable to be wrenched by a sudden williwaw.

The little bight which Magellan named River of Sardines, because its waters were swarming with small edible fish, one can identify as Fortescue Bay, just east of Cabo Gallant at latitude 53°42′ S. The Captain General may even have entered the inner landlocked harbor, Caleta Gallant. Both have excellent holding ground; the Chilean *Derrotero* (Sailing Directions) calls Fortescue the best anchorage in the Strait for all classes of vessels. And it is an exceptionally charming spot. The soft summer night of 24 February 1972, when we lay there in *Orompello* of the Chilean Navy, will be ever memorable for the Milky Way

* An exception: Bahia Cutter, up the Canal San Jerónimo, where there is a small copper mine with about a dozen employees.

rising in a great "whoosh" of sparkling light, and on top of it the Southern Cross flashing brilliantly. Next morning we went ashore on the pebble beach of Bahia Fortescue, wreathed with white flowers resembling gigantic marguerites; a few rods inland we found other flowers, brightly colored, and calafate bushes bearing big red berries. Magellan evidently chose this fair place to celebrate the first Mass in the future Chile. The inner Caleta Gallant, "difficult of access," says the modern *Derrotero*, but not too difficult for Magellan's ships, offers perfect protection and holding ground, with two rivers to replenish water and plenty of beechwood for fuel.

While he waited here, the Captain General fitted out, provisioned, and manned his flag longboat to explore the Strait further in the hope of finding an outlet. "The men returned within three days," says Pigafetta, "and reported that they had seen the cape and the open sea." Roldán de Argote, a Flemish gunner of the fleet, climbed a mountain (later named after him), sighted the ocean, and reported it to the Captain General who "wept for joy," says Pigafetta, "and called that *Cabo Deseado*, for we had long been desiring it." The name is still applied to one of the two prongs of Desolation Island which mark the Pacific entrance to the Strait; Cabo Pilar, the better known later name, is the northern prong.

Solicitous about his other two ships, Magellan turned back to search for them. Having already roughly charted the eastern half of the Strait, he avoided the great masses of kelp that mark rocky ledges, and had leisure to examine the striking scenery. Here, as Herrera tells us, "is the most beautiful country in the world—the Strait a gunshot across, separating high sierras covered with perpetual snow, whose lower slopes were clothed with magnificent trees."

Soon they met *Concepción* sailing alone. Captain Serrano had no news of *San Antonio*, but Magellan refused to write her off, and spent five or six days searching for her, even up Admiralty Sound; *Victoria* sailed all the way to Cape Virgins to look for the errant ship. The Captain General now turned to his chief pilot Andrés de San Martín, who combined astrology with navigation. After plotting the stars and consulting a book, Andrés, reported that she had returned to Spain with Captain Mezquita in chains. He was right, as we have seen.

After *Victoria* rejoined the flagship, Magellan decided to press forward, and information from the boat exploration saved him from wast-

Our landing at Fortescue Bay (Magellan's *Rio de Sardinas*), 24 February 1972. Sanchez Obregón photo.

Going ashore. Flowers at Caleta Gallant, the inner harbor. Sanchez Obregón photo.

ing time on dead ends. He sailed up the main channel, Paso Inglés, the most dangerous reach of the Strait (although not the most narrow), and passed Carlos III Island (where Captain Joshua Slocum in his sloop *Spray* foiled an attack by Fuegians by sprinkling carpet tacks on her deck at night). On this island of many hills Magellan erected a cross.

As one approaches the meeting of waters that some English navigator appropriately named Crosstides, where Canal San Jerónimo empties into the Strait, anyone might wonder which was the Strait and which the Canal. But the longboat crew must have observed as they got nearer, what Ensign Thornton of *Orompello* pointed out to me, that the waters of the Canal are lighter in color than those of the Strait, and that the nearer one approaches, the wider the real Strait appears to be. So Magellan wasted no time, and avoided the dead end. He passed safely through Paso Tortuoso with its 330-fathom deep, and entered Paso Largo with depths up to 810 fathom.

Here again the character of the scenery changes. The mountains of Desolation Island on the port hand are of ribbed granite with stunted vegetation only in the clefts, reminding one of the Labrador; no more trees. Great Pacific surges roll in and break on both sides. You feel that you are coming out into something enormous and unpredictable. Magellan passed Bahia Corkscrew, Cape Providence, and the bold island of Tamar, off which a 2½-fathom rock has wrecked many an incautious ship. Here in mid-Strait, with 800-foot deeps on each side, is the dangerous Bajo Magallanes which breaks when heavy swells roll in from the ocean. At the end of Paso del Mar is the worst of many bad places in the Strait to be caught in a strong westerly.

After thirty miles of this, on 28 November 1520 (moon four days past full) *Trinidad, Concepción,* and *Victoria* passed Cabo Pilar (which Magellan named *Deseado*) on Desolation Island. Only one of these ships, and about 35 out of the 150 members of their crews, ever returned to Spain.

Antonio de Herrera, the late-sixteenth-century Spanish historian who seems to have cared most for Magellan, wrote of his entry into the great Pacific: "On the 27th of November he came out into the South Sea, blessing God, who had been pleas'd to permit him to find what he so much desir'd, being the first that ever went that way, which will perpetuate his Memory for ever. They guessed this Streight to be about one hundred Leagues in Length. . . . The sea was very Black and

Out of the Strait: Desolation Island begins (above). Cabo Pilar, from the west (below).

Boisterous, which denoted a vast Ocean. Magellan order'd publick Thanksgiving, and sail'd away to the Northward, to get out of the Cold."

All in all, Magellan had a "very good chance," as sailors say, especially as he had sailed thrice over at least 250 miles of the 334-mile length of the Strait, looking for *San Antonio*. He did not experience, or at least none of his three literary shipmates noted, any sharp squalls or particular hazards. He managed to moor safely every night by running a hawser from the stern to a tree ashore in one of the many anchorages suitable for small ships. Frequently the sailors landed to gather an excellent anti-scorbutic, the wild celery (*Apium australe*) which grew in abundance near springs or rivers. Later voyagers described the natural bowers that wind-blown beech and pine made in the woods. Their matted branches kept out excessive snow and cold; in this shelter herbs flourished the year round, and in the spring there is a gorgeous show of wild flowers. Magellan's men caught plenty of fish—albacore, bonito, and flying fish. After they had passed safely through, Pigafetta wrote, "I believe that there is not a more beautiful or better strait in the world than that one." Beautiful, yes, but terrible as well; and one must study the history of later voyages through the Strait, and if possible traverse it oneself, to appreciate the grandeur and the magnitude of Magellan's achievement. For say what you will of him, detractors, *he did it.* As Alonso de Ercilla wrote in *La Araucana*,

> Magallanes, Señor, fué el primer hombre
> Que abriendo este camino, le dió nombre.*
> Magellan, Sir, was the first man
> Both to open this route and to give it name.

"Wednesday, November 28, 1520," writes Pigafetta, "we debouched from that Strait, engulfing ourselves in the Pacific Sea." One of the great moments of a great voyage. The Pacific, shimmering under a westering sun, spread for half a circumference before Magellan's eyes. Vasco Núñez de Balboa, to be sure, had seen the ocean from a peak in Darien seven years before, and even earlier Abreu had sailed into its western edge which laved the Moluccas. But Magellan now faced a waste of water thousands of miles wide, and entered it without fear or hesitation. Here too he navigated well, for this forefront of the great ocean is studded with breaking reefs; the entire coast is smoky with

* Canto 1, strophe 8; first published in 1569.

their white spray. If you let a west wind and flood tide throw you off from Cabo Pilar, you are likely to strike the extensive rocky shoals hopefully if unsuitably named by early sailors *Buena Esperanza* and *Las Evangelistas*—Good Hope and The Evangelists.

Albo tells us that from Cabo Deseado they steered northwest, north, and north-northeast for two days and three nights, and on the morning of 1 December sighted land and found their latitude to be 48° S. They were well on their way to penetrate the greatest of oceans, hitherto unknown to Europeans except by rare glimpses of its distant verges.

✳ XXV ✳

Across the Pacific

North from Cabo Pilar

The fleet that Magellan led out of the Strait on 27 or 28 November
1520 comprised flagship *Trinidad*, *Concepcion* now commanded by
Juan Serrano, and *Victoria* commanded by Duarte Barbosa. According to Pilot Albo, they steered northwest, north, and north-northeast
for two days and three nights; proper courses for avoiding the
dangerous southern coast of Chile, especially the Buena Esperanza
and Evangelista rocks which lie in wait for the unwary mariner. This
portion of the Chilean coast resembles that of Norway, deeply indented with fjord-like bays, rocky and lofty shores; the modern sailing directions four and a half centuries after Magellan warn: "not yet
closely examined; strangers should be on their guard!" "On the morning of 1 December," says Albo, "we saw bits of land like hillocks"
sticking over the horizon. These ran together to make a mountainous
promontory, a "bold and remarkable headland" rising to 1300 feet.
This sounds like Cabo Tres Montes in latitude 47° S. Albo says 48°,
the latitude of Campana Island; but Campana is not nearly so conspicuous as Tres Montes, so we must allow the pilot an occasional
error. He usually calculated his latitude too far south.

From this place Magellan really shoved off into the Pacific Ocean, as he then named it, the winds being steady and the weather fair in comparison with what he had experienced in the Atlantic. "Well was it named Pacific," wrote Pigafetta, "for during this period"—three months and twenty days—"we met with no storm."

Here let us pause a moment and contemplate what lay ahead of Magellan. The Pacific Ocean was a watery wilderness as completely unknown to Europeans as Australia or Amazonia. Balboa had sighted it and the Portuguese had touched its western verge; but in the absence of any method to find longitude, nobody knew how wide this ocean could be; and all estimates in Magellan's hands, whether literary or cartographical, were at least 80 per cent short of the truth. Although Polynesians for centuries had been circulating through the thousands of Pacific islands and atolls in their outrigger canoes, Europeans knew nothing of them whatsoever. Magellan's lengthy voyage from the mouth of the Strait to Guam traced almost as many new routes for commerce as Columbus; and, in fact, realized (after the deaths of both men) Columbus's dream of tapping the wealth of the Indies by sailing west. Actually, mapmakers for a century after Magellan underestimated the width of the Pacific by as much as 40 per cent.

Pigafetta at this point gives us one of the earliest descriptions of the constellations in the Southern Hemisphere. "The Antarctic Pole is not so steady as the Arctic. Many small stars clustered together are seen, which have the appearance of two clouds of mist." These are *nubecula major* and *minor*, now the Magellanic Clouds. "In the midst of them," continues Pigafetta, "are two large and not very bright stars, which move but slightly. Those two stars are the Antarctic Pole." He probably meant two stars of the constellation Hydra which moves around the southern celestial pole, just as Ursa Minor circles its northern counterpart. "When we were in the midst of that Gulf," continues Pigafetta, "we saw a cross with five extremely bright stars straight toward the west, and they are equally spaced one with the other." Richard Eden's early translation of Pigafetta adds, "This crosse is so fayre and bewtiful, that none other hevenly body may be compared to it." Since the Southern Cross would have been low in the southeastern sky, Pigafetta must have made a mistake in identification. It could not have been Orion's Belt, which would have been due west at that time, since Orion was familiar; it might have been a cross-like constellation, *Grus* the Crane, which shone low in the southwest, about to set.

At Cabo Pilar, Pilot Albo picks up his narrative, which enables us roughly to plot the fleet's course across the Pacific. Here is a sample of it; the dates begin at noon of the day mentioned:

2–3 Dec. 1520, course NW, taking the fleet to latitude 46°30' S.

12–13 Dec. 1520, course NE by N, taking them to latitude 40° S.

1–2 Jan. 1521, course WNW, taking them to latitude 24° S.

19–20 Jan. 1521, course NW by W, taking them to latitude 15° S.

All fair winds and good sailing so far. Albo records southwest courses for two days, 21–22 January 1521, indicating head winds for the only time on this fourteen-week voyage to Guam. Correia the Portuguese historian declared that they sailed for five months (really three, Cabo Pilar to Guam) without shortening sail; and evidently very little shifting of the lines except to freshen a halyard's nip in the block.

It is a disappointment to the historian that none of Magellan's chroniclers, not even Pigafetta, has a word to say about the beauty of the Pacific or the day-by-day ritual. Nevertheless, anyone who has "spooned" before Pacific trade winds can imagine the scene. *Trinidad, Concepción,* and *Victoria* roll along with wind astern or on the quarter, all square sails set and mizzen furled to help the steering. Bluest of blue seas, white fleecy clouds flying to leeward, frequent bursts of flying fish pursued by dorados, and (until February or March) plenty to eat; ships' boys singing their little ditties every half-hour when the glass is turned, and longer ones at change of watch; at dusk, *Concepción* and *Victoria* closing *Trinidad* so that Captains Serrano and Barbosa can make the proper hail: *Dios vos salve, capitán general y señor maestro y buona compaña!* At noon Pilot Albo shoots the sun and figures out the latitude. Velvet nights with the old familiar stars returning—the Bear (no longer indulging in his daily bath), Orion, and friendly Polaris, the navigator's best friend, appear. The incredible beauty of dawn at sea, heralded by the zodiacal light in the east. Does not the memory of it wring the heart of every old salt?

Magellan had no ship's bells to mark the passing time, only half-hour glasses; but he and his captains held morning and evening prayers regularly, just as all the great navigators did.

On the respective sailing qualities of his three ships I can find no data in any source. *Trinidad*, 110 tuns' burthen, was presumably faster than *Concepción* of 80 tuns, or *Victoria* of 85 tuns; but by this time they had learned to adjust their speed by lacing on or removing bonnets from their sails, to keep the fleet speed uniform. And from Guam to Samar, even if Albo slipped a couple of days in his log, they made the amazingly fast speed of eight knots, considering that they had not been careened and their bottoms cleansed since Patagonia.

Alan Villiers's poignant words on Captain Cook's fleet apply equally to Magellan's: "On sailed the little vessels, feeble, man-made, windblown chips upon a hostile immensity, held to their course only by the ability and iron will of the great seaman commanding them." * In Magellan's case, the Pacific was unusually kind to the man who first named her and crossed her. Fair winds wafted him on, and by following where they took him, he avoided possible shipwreck in the dark of the moon on any one of a thousand islets and atolls. He could have done no better had he enjoyed full information about the great ocean's winds and currents. Drake later in the same century, Bougainville and Wallis in the eighteenth, learned to their cost that no sailing vessel could safely stretch out to the westward right after clearing the Strait; she must sail north, preferably to latitude 25° S between November and March, before benefiting from the southeast trade winds.

Why, when all this was unknown, did Magellan sail north before turning west? The obvious, common-sense seaman's answer is, "to stay with fair winds." His "Genoese pilot" gives us an additional reason: "As he had information that there were no provisions at Maluco [the Spice Islands], he said that he would go in a northerly direction as far as 10° or 12° North. And they reached to as far as 13° N, and in this latitude they navigated to the W, and W by S."

It is true that not much food except rice and fresh fish could be had in the Spice Islands, as we shall see from *Victoria*'s later experience; Magellan's friend Serrão had probably so informed him. Several modern historians argue that Magellan was heading for Okinawa and the Ryukyus. Duarte Barbosa called the Ryukyus *los Lequíos* in his book, which Magellan may have read, and identified them with biblical Tarshish and Ophir. Señor Obregón and I, however, believe

* Villiers, *Captain James Cook*, p. 245.

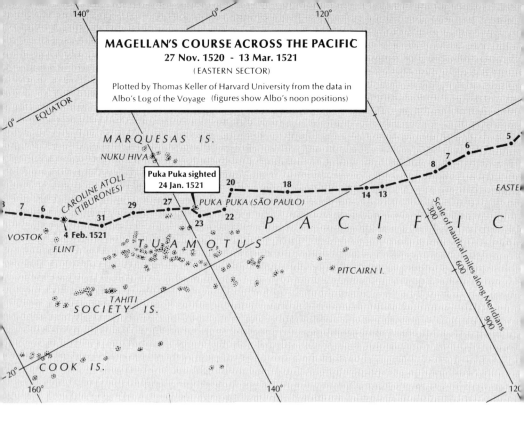

MAGELLAN'S COURSE ACROSS THE PACIFIC
27 Nov. 1520 - 13 Mar. 1521
(EASTERN SECTOR)

Plotted by Thomas Keller of Harvard University from the data in
Albo's Log of the Voyage (figures show Albo's noon positions)

that, apart from the provision problem, Magellan had learned about prevailing winds in the Moluccas during his early Portuguese voyage, and wanted to be in a good position to coast down to the Spice Islands when the northeast trades struck in. Be that as it may, we need no better motive than simple acquisitiveness to lead Magellan so far north. He must have heard of the Philippine Islands in Malacca, where there was a colony of some five hundred Filipinos, and he probably hoped to secure them for Spain before proceeding to his main objective, the Spice Islands.

Referring to our chart where Albo's courses are plotted, the fleet could not have sailed a more lonely course across the Pacific if Magellan had been the captain of a modern solo, non-stop cruise looking for publicity and prizes. First, he missed the two Juan Fernandez Islands well off Valpariso. Then, crossing a wide space where there are no islands, he left to port the Tuamotou and Manihiki archipelagos except (as we state below) for two uninhabited atolls. Had Magellan

620

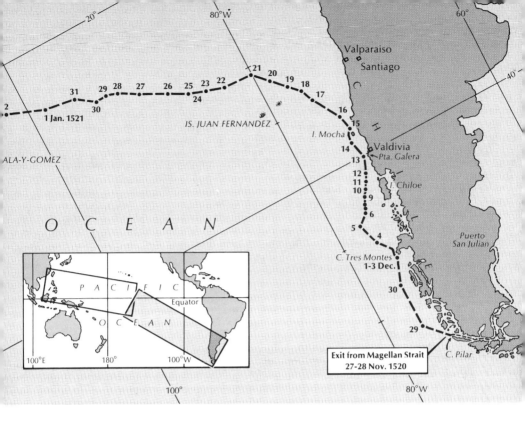

steered only three degrees further north, he would have seen the lofty Marquesas, which would have led to Nuka Hiva and the rest of that superb archipelago. Had he steered the same distance south, he might have made glamorous Tahiti. His fleet must have passed within a hundred miles or so of the northernmost Marshall Islands—Bikar, Bikini, and Eniwetok.

In considering this course, I agree with Alan Villiers that a kind providence was looking after Magellan. Further south he would have run into hundreds of islands and atolls, each a coral-baited trap for European ships. Semi-starvation and scurvy were bad, but better than running aground and being stripped bare by nimble Polynesians. He could hardly have shaped a better course if he had had modern sailing directions, not only avoiding dangerous, island-studded waters but making best use of prevailing winds and currents. Cast your eye over the United States government Pilot Chart of the South Pacific for January and February, and you will see that Magellan followed

621

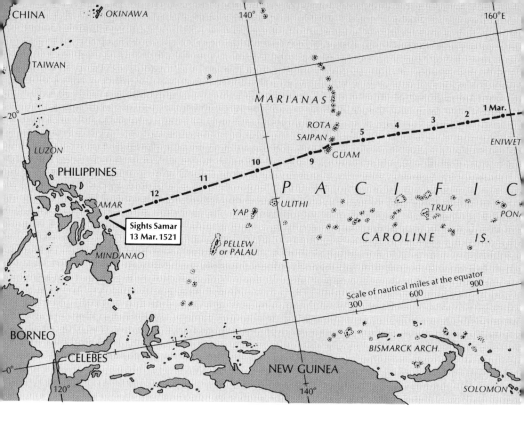

the recommended sailing route from Cape Horn to Honolulu until he got into the zone of the southeast tradewinds, and then steered before them, northwesterly, into the great open spaces.

Magellan's logistics have also been criticized. Why should his men have starved and been forced to eat chafing-gear and rats? First, because (at the government's behest) he had too many pages and other idlers on board. Second, because of cheating by the ship chandlers of Seville. Third, because of the unprecedented and unexpected length of the voyage. Have you never heard of hunger and scurvy on a long sailing voyage? Even three centuries after Magellan, with courses laid down on accurate charts, sailors expected to suffer both and often did. Instead of criticizing Magellan for his losses and sufferings, one should praise him for getting as far as Cebu. Note also that the Loaysa Expedition of 1525, although piloted by the experienced Elcano, fared even worse than Magellan's fleet; and so did most of the other trans-Pacific voyages.

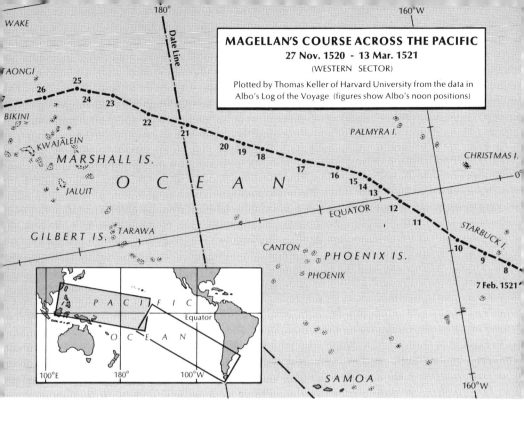

MAGELLAN'S COURSE ACROSS THE PACIFIC
27 Nov. 1520 - 13 Mar. 1521
(WESTERN SECTOR)

Plotted by Thomas Keller of Harvard University from the data in
Albo's Log of the Voyage (figures show Albo's noon positions)

In plotting the fleet's course we have to consider whether or not to apply the compass variation, which in that part of the Pacific is now 15° to 20° East, and we can only assume that it was probably about the same in 1520. The "Genoese pilot" (as quoted by Skelton) says, "We northeasted the compass box two points," which indicates that Albo's courses were taken from a compass adjusted for 22.5° E. variation. This can be proved by checking Albo between two known points, Guam and the entrance to Leyte Gulf. There we find his west by south course to be exact to the "true" bearing within a quarter-point, or 2.8°. This seems to indicate that Albo's compass bearings were accurate but that his day ran too short; that the fleet was making better speed than he allowed. The northward Humboldt Current along the west coast of South America is not strong enough to explain the discrepancy.

A remark on navigation by Pigafetta has aroused no end of controversy. "Daily," he says of the earlier part of the Pacific voyage, "we made runs of 50, 60, or 70 leagues *a la catena ho apopa*" (at the *catena*, which was at the stern). What does *catena* mean? Some have identified it as the chip log—but that was not yet invented. Others, including my respected Dutch acquaintance Mr. Crone, believe it to have been a trailed line for measuring the angle between a vessel's keel and her wake, in order to determine leeway. But no sixteenth-century log or book on navigation mentions anything like that, and every old salt to whom I have put the question answers that no accurate estimate of leeway could possibly be made by trailing a rope and measuring its angle to the wake. Furthermore, Pigafetta's mention of the word is in the context of speed, not angle of drift. My explanation is simple: *catena* in those days meant not only a chain but two important cross-beams in a vessel's hull, the first under the forecastle and the second well aft. Mariners stationed on the deck above each beam could time the seconds required for a piece of flotsam to pass between them as the ship sailed; when it passed the fellow at the stern, he sang out and the bow man stopped counting. Knowing the linear distance between these two beams, and the elapsed time, anyone who knew a little mathematics could figure out the ship's speed in knots—nautical miles per hour. This well known method of estimating a ship's speed was called by the English, "the Dutchman's Log." But, you may object, how could they count time without a watch? Why, just as navigators do today in counting seconds between a celestial observation with the sextant and consulting the chronometer, thus:

> *One* chimpanzee, *two* chimpanzees, *three* chimpanzees, etc.; or,
> *One* two three four, *two* two three four, *three* two three four, etc.

Las Islas Infortunatas

On 24 January 1521, after the fleet had dropped slightly south owing to a two-day head wind, and two days after full moon, they "found an islet wooded but uninhabited. We sounded and found no bottom, and so continued on our course, and this islet we named *San Pablo*, because it was the day of his conversion." So says Pilot Albo.

What was this deserted and unpromising island? Puka Puka, northernmost atoll but one of the Tuamotu archipelago. Albo says that they found it "in the neighborhood" of latitude 16°20′ S;

Las Islas Infortunatas: Puka Puka—Magellan's *San Pablo*. From the southeast, two miles distant. Courtesy of Captain Vallaux, French Navy (above). Caroline atoll—Magellan's *Isla de Tiburones*.

Pigafetta says flatly that it lay on 15° S. The center of Puka Puka, according to the latest French surveys, is on latitude 14°50′ S, only ten miles north of Pigafetta's estimate. Albo is definitely faulted on this point, for if Magellan really had sighted an island at 16°20′ S, he would have run into a flock of big atolls of the Palliser group.

There are other reasons, too, for a firm identification of Magellan's San Pablo as the modern Puka Puka. It rides out so far ahead of the Tuamotu archipelago as to catch the eye of anyone crossing the Pacific at around 15° S. To this day there is "no practicable anchorage," according to the French authorities. It was the first island after Juan Fernandez, seen in 1616 by Le Maire and Schouten, and it was the first island seen by Thor Heyerdahl in his voyage across the Pacific on the raft *Kon Tiki*.

After inspecting this island and deciding not to land, Magellan sailed NW, WNW, and W by N until on the eleventh day, 4 February 1521, he found (according to Albo) another "uninhabited island, where we caught many sharks, and so gave it the name *Isla de los Tiburones*." This, he says, lay on latitude 10°40′ S.

This shark-infested atoll must have been one of the three little islands which form an isosceles triangle with legs about 125 miles long: Flint (latitude 11°28′ S), Vostok (10°06′ S), and Caroline (10° 00′ S). It must have been Caroline, the biggest, and the only one with a lagoon; for it is common knowledge in the Pacific that lagoons attract sharks. And why did not Magellan at least call at one of these islands? Lack of holding ground, no doubt. The soundings nearest to them on the latest French chart are 2010 meters (Puka Puka), and 1370 meters (Caroline). We in 1971 could see plenty of coconut palms and pandanus on Caroline, but no sign of human life. Overcast prevented us from seeing Flint or Vostok Island, but both are rocky pinnacles rising from a great depth, and Flint has been such a favorite breeding and roosting place for sea birds that it became the scene of guano diggings in the last century.

Starvation at Sea, Relief at Guam

According to the "Genoese pilot," having reached latitude 13° N, "They navigated to the West by South, a matter of a hundred leagues, where on 6 March 1521 they fetched two islands inhabited by many people."

Albo, more convincingly, describes the course as northwest from 5 to 15 February, when the fleet reached latitude 01°45′ N, having crossed the Line on the 13th. They steered west-northwest from 15 to 25 February, and due west along latitude 13° N between 1 and 6 March.

Pigafetta is no help to us in tracking this last leg across the Pacific, but his description of the crews' sufferings is vivid and moving. The most trying part of the crossing took place after passing the two atolls, when they had already been two and a half months from the last place where they could have taken on food and water. "We were three months and twenty days without refreshment from any kind of fresh food. We ate biscuit which was no longer biscuit but its powder, swarming with worms, the rats having eaten all the good. It stank strongly of their urine. We drank yellow water already many days putrid. We also ate certain ox hides that had covered the top of the yards to prevent the yards from chafing the shrouds, and which had become exceedingly hard because of the sun, rain and wind. We soaked them in the sea for four or five days, then placed them for a short time over the hot embers and ate them thus, and often we ate sawdust. Rats were sold for half a ducat [$1.16 in gold] apiece, and even so we could not always get them."

Alan Villiers and I guess that the leather chafing-gear may not have been too bad as a hunger-stopper. Squareriggers needed an enormous amount of chafing-gear to prevent sails' slatting themselves threadbare against spars and rigging. Magellan, with his sea experience, would certainly have loaded plenty of guanaco hide in Patagonia for spares, and a relatively fresh guanaco hide would have made a more nutritious meal for a starving man than sawdust or old boots. Provided, of course, that the diner's teeth were sound and not rotted by scurvy!

The worst affliction, even above hunger and thirst, was scurvy. In Pigafetta's words, "The gums of both the lower and upper teeth of some of our men swelled, so that they could not eat under any circumstances." Thirty men got it in the arms, legs, and elsewhere, and, according to our chronicler, nineteen men died in the three ships. He, "by the grace of God, suffered no sickness," and neither did the Captain General. Magellan's supply of quince preserve doubtless came in useful as an anti-scorbutic for the afterguard; and let us hope that he issued some of it to the common sailors. "Had not God and His blessed mother given us such good weather," concluded Pigafetta, "we would

S. E. Morison, M. Obregón, and Pan Am crew. Sanchez Obregón photo.

Umatac harbor and village from site of old fort. Sanchez Obregón photo.

all have died of hunger in that exceeding vast ocean. I verily believe no such voyage will ever again be made."

Alas, Antonio, there have been very many such voyages, in which sailors have died of thirst, scurvy, and starvation after eating leather boots, scrapings from the inside of casks, and even, on occasion, each other. The nineteen deaths which he reports on Magellan's three ships were nothing extraordinary, and the official score is eleven. But why did not Magellan call at one of those *Islas Infortunatas* to fish, gather coconuts, and perhaps dig a well for fresh water? Probably because he felt that in another day or two he would raise some big island and find plenty of food.

On the next leg of their trans-Pacific run to Guam, which took exactly one month (5 February to 6 March 1521), they steered, according to Albo, northwest and west-northwest in February and west in March. Pigafetta here makes a curious statement: "We passed . . . a short distance from two exceedingly rich islands," one in latitude 20° N "by name Cipangu . . . and the other in 15° [N] by name *Sumbdit Pradit*." Cipangu means Japan, whose southernmost point of Kyushu lies on latitude 31° N and bears northwest from Guam many hundreds of miles. But a reference to Schöner's globe will show why Magellan thought he had passed it. What he meant by *Sumbdit Pradit* is still anybody's guess.

At last, on 6 March 1521, 98 or 99 days out from the Strait, the weary voyagers found their first relief, combined with plenty of excitement. They sighted two lofty islands, first lucky break of the Pacific voyage; for these were Guam and Rota. The fleet sailed between them, turned south, and followed the coast of Guam looking for a harbor. Soft green hills rose to jagged peaks, coconut palms lined the shore, and everything looked green and lush; but the hungry sailors could find no break in the reef until they were almost at the southern end of the island, when providentially a harbor now called Umatak, with no reef barrier, opened up. A group of thatched huts could be seen at the head of it, and a fleet of native sail engaged in fishing. These were *praos*, lateen-rigged dugout canoes, each with an outrigger. Marvelously fast and maneuverable, they sailed circles around the three ships. Magellan therefore called Guam and Rota *Las Islas de Velas Latinas*, Isles of Lateen Sails, but he soon found reason to change the name to the opprobrious *Islas de Ladrones*, Isles of Thieves.

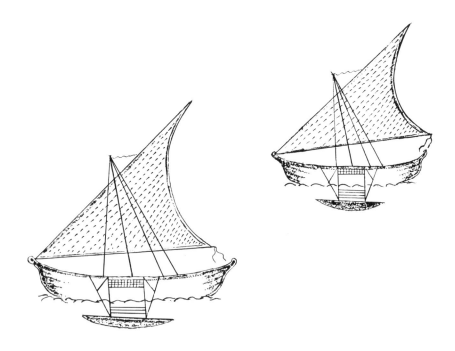

Chamorro praos, sketched at Palau in late sixteenth century. Courtesy Archivo General de Indias, Seville.

The natives promptly swarmed on board the flagship, which alone had entered the harbor, and proceeded to pick up everything on deck or below not nailed down; every bit of iron, crockery, belaying pin, or length of line cut off the rigging. Doubtless they would have "stolen the paint off the deck" (the traditional mariners' description of harbor thieves), if paint there had been. The debilitated flagship crew could neither dissuade them from stealing nor persuade them to go away; so Magellan finally gave orders to his men-at-arms to shoot a few with crossbows. That temporarily got rid of the boarders; one native pulled a crossbow bolt right out of his side and looked with amazement at the spurting blood. After this brawl terminated, the sailors observed that the longboat had been stolen from right under *Trinidad*'s stern!

These people were Chamorros, an agile, handsome, brown-skinned Polynesian race who had raided Guam several centuries earlier, conquered the native Macronesians, and become an arrogant ruling caste. Probably they had already dealt with errant Chinese junks; certainly they were neither awed by the ships nor afraid of Spaniards. In the next century, after having been converted by Spanish priests and their island group renamed *Las Marianas,* the Chamorros became friendly, peaceful, and charming. During their forty-two years under American rule (1899–1941), they conformed to Western ways, and under a harsh Japanese domination remained steadfastly loyal to the United States.

But that was in our time. Magellan's immediate problems were to procure fresh food and get back his boat. He acted with his usual coolness and decision. When night fell he ordered his fleet to jill about in the offing. At daybreak he approached the shore and attacked the village, having manned the other two ships' longboats with forty armed men. The landing force burned forty to fifty huts and many praos, recovered the stolen boat, and obtained a supply of rice, fruit, and fresh water which gave the fleet a comparatively balanced diet en route to the Philippines. Pigafetta notes that some of the sick on board begged the landing party to bring them a few buckets' full of the enemy's guts as a sure cure for scurvy—presumably a medical superstition of the time, or perhaps a means of satisfying their craving for fresh meat. Although seven Chamorros were killed in this brawl, hundreds of them cheerfully sailed out to the ships next day.

It was now 9 March 1521, the day after new moon, and Magellan immediately got under way. One wishes there had been an artist on board to depict his departure from Umatac. About a hundred praos made sail and romped around the slow-moving ships, their crews laughing and shouting; one fellow even had the impudence to sail right across the painter of a towed longboat. Others approached the ships holding up fish and offering by signs to toss them on board; if the Spaniards "bit" and bade them come nearer, they would drop the fish and throw a shower of stones at the sailors on deck, then sail away laughing their heads off. "Light-hearted masters of the waves," indeed.

From Samar to Cebu

The Captain General set course west by south. Whether he knew this would take him to Leyte Gulf, the best entrance to the Philippines, or simply made a good guess, we do not know. For five days they made unusual speed—an average of seven to eight knots. It was a happy run, with plenty of fresh food to cure the sick; all except Chief Gunner Andrew of Bristol, the only Englishman on board. Too far gone, he died the first day out from Guam.

On 15 March 1521 they saw the mountains of Samar rising from the sea. Magellan changed course to close; but, after observing the coast to be cliffy, with no harbor, altered his course again to due south, making the tiny but conspicuous island of Suluan on latitude 10°45′ N. There he anchored for the night. It was the fifth Sunday of Lent in the church calendar, dedicated to Lazarus; so Magellan named this archipelago after him. Only after the visit by Villalobos in 1542 was it renamed *Las Islas Filipinas*, after the Infante of Spain who became Philip II.

From Suluan they sailed to the much bigger island of Homonhon. *Trinidad, Concepción,* and *Victoria* were now in waters ever memorable for the greatest naval battle in recorded history, that of Leyte Gulf, 24–26 October 1944. Forty to forty-five miles across Leyte Gulf from Homonhon lies the coast of Leyte, where the American amphibious forces landed. Magellan, either by chance or acting upon information gained in his former Portuguese voyages to Malacca, had hit upon one of the two principal entrances to the Philippine archipelago, Surigao Strait.

The Captain General, solicitous for the health of scurvy victims, caused two tents to be pitched on Homonhon Island for their shelter, and a live sow (picked up at Guam) to be slaughtered to give them fresh meat. There, on Monday, 18 March, Europeans made their first contact with Filipinos, and sized them up as a far more civilized and sophisticated race than the Chamorros. A boat from Suluan approached with nine men on board. Magellan enjoined silence on his men while they landed and walked up to the tents. Their leader made "signs of joy" to Magellan, and left with him five of the best dressed members of his suite, says Pigafetta. Magellan, seeing that these were "men of reason," gave them something to eat and presented them with red caps, mirrors, combs, hawks' bells, ivory, fine linen cloth, and other articles. Impressed by the Captain General's courtesy, they presented him with fresh fish, a jar of palm wine "which they called *uraca*" (arrack), figs "more than a palm long" (bananas), and two *cochi* (coconuts).

Homonhon Island. Sanchez Obregón photo.

Limasawa Island. Sanchez Obregón photo.

That was all they had on hand. But the people made signs that they would return in four days' time bringing *umay* (rice), coconuts, and many other victuals, and they kept their word. Pigafetta describes in detail the native process of making palm wine and other products; he had never before seen a coconut or a banana. Two coconut palms, he said, can provide food and drink for ten people; and, he might have added, clothing, housing, and other things as well. "These people became very familiar with us," he says. "We took great pleasure with them, for they were very pleasant and talkative"—by the sign language, presumably. They are *caphri* (heathen) *, all except the chiefs go naked; they are "dark, fat and painted"—i.e., tattooed. Magellan showed them over *Trinidad*, exhibiting samples of spices and gold which he hoped to find in great quantities.

The ships stayed at Homonhon for a week, Magellan daily visiting the sick ashore, himself serving them drinks of refreshing coconut milk. On 25 March, as they were about to weigh anchor, Pigafetta fell overboard and just saved himself by seizing a main clewline trailing in the water, and hallooing for help. Apparently he had never learned to swim. He ascribed his rescue to "the mercy of that font of charity," the Virgin Mary, since it was the feast of her Annunciation.

Having made sail, the fleet shaped a west-southwest course into Surigao Strait, passing Hibuson, Dinagat, and other islands. (Here, 423 years and seven months later, occurred the last great naval action between battleships and their attendant destroyers. That night in 1944, Surigao Strait was brilliantly lighted by shell bursts and burning Japanese warships, and roaring with explosions.) But all was quiet on Thursday, 28 March 1521, when there occurred a dramatic and significant event.

The fleet had anchored off the little island of Limasawa at the southern entrance to Surigao Strait. A small boat put out and approached flagship *Trinidad;* eight men were on board. At the Captain General's order, his slave Enrique de Malacca hailed them. "They immediately understood him and came alongside." West had met East at last by circling the globe. Enrique may have been the first man to do it.

---

* From the Arabic *kafir*, non-believer; generally used in the Far East by Moors for people who did not worship God. Hence the Cafres or Kaffirs of South Africa.

Two hours later, two *balanghai* (native barges) full of men approached and on the quarterdeck of the larger sat a high personality under an awning of mats. He, the ruler Rajah Colambu, refused to come on board but allowed his people to do so, and Magellan showered them with gifts. His highness in return offered the Captain General a bar of gold and a basket of ginger, which were refused. Magellan's policy, which he impressed on all his men, was to pretend to undervalue gold, since he had observed that wherever European sailors showed greed for it, the price soared; he even refused to swap six strings of glass beads for a pointed coronet of massy gold. Both at Limasawa and Cebu he was rewarded for this continence by the natives' giving gold for iron almost pound for pound—"changey-changey," as sailors used to say.

Next day, Good Friday of 1521, Magellan sent Enrique ashore to assure the Rajah of his friendship and to buy food; Colambu himself came out with baskets of fresh provisions, embraced the Captain General and presented him with three dorados and three porcelain jars filled with rice. Magellan countered with a red cap and a red-and-yellow robe made "Turkish fashion," with which the Rajah was delighted. He was shown over the flagship and given a collation, after which Magellan demonstrated the value of European steel plate. A soldier put on a suit of armor, three others struck him repeatedly with swords and daggers, to no effect. The Rajah *resto casi fora dise* (was struck speechless) and then remarked that one such man in armor was worth a hundred local troops. Magellan capped that admission by boasting that he had two hundred such men on board each of his three ships—a gross exaggeration.

Next item in this West-meets-East business was a royal luncheon party attended by Pigafetta and two other officers. They took seats on a grounded *balanghai*, ate pork, and at every mouthful drank a toast in palm wine. The natives drank from a cup held in the right hand; at the same time they extended the left fist as if to strike their favored guest, but the Christians soon learned that this gesture was friendly. All became somewhat fuddled by the number of toasts. By suppertime Pigafetta had so far sobered up as to write down the names of things, phonetically of course, in the local language; and before leaving he had compiled a long vocabulary. Supper was served in the Rajah's palace, which reminded Pigafetta of a hay barn raised on stilts; and there they were joined by a brother rajah from Mindanao named Siaui. Dinner consisted of roast fish, fresh-gathered ginger, and more palm wine. The Italian and the guest rajah, who became intoxicated, spent the night there on a bamboo mat. When a boat came for Pigafetta and his two companions next morning, Rajah Colambu kissed their hands, and they reciprocated.

Now came the vigil of Easter Sunday, the first Easter that the fleet had passed at sea since leaving the Strait. Early next morning, Magellan caused High Mass to be celebrated on Limasawa by the flag chaplain. Fifty men landed "in theyr best apparel withowte weapons or harnesse" (i.e., armor), according to Eden's translation of Pigafetta, and marched with the two rajahs to the place where an altar had been set up. Both rajahs kissed the cross after Magellan, but were not allowed to partake of the sacred elements. At the elevation of the host, Magellan's body-guard fired a salvo from their arquebuses, and the ships discharged a blank broadside. Magellan next laid on a fencing contest between his men-at-arms, which greatly pleased the rajahs, and Colambu gave him permission to set up a cross on the nearest mountain. That they did on Easter afternoon. Each Christian present venerated the cross, repeating *Pater Noster* and *Ave Maria*, and the rajahs followed suit. Somewhere in the course of these entertainments, Colambu and Magellan performed the rite of *casi-casi* or blood brotherhood. This consisted, mainly, of each tasting a drop of the other's blood.

Although a good time was had by all who went ashore at Limasawa, not many provisions were available; and Colambu, upon being asked where more could be obtained, not only suggested Cebu but offered himself to pilot them there as soon as his own crop of rice was gathered. Magellan, to expedite this, sent details of mariners to help get in the harvest; they became so drunk on palm wine the first day ashore that they were not much good to anyone.

The gentle Limasawans, says Pigafetta, went about nearly naked, but the men were tattooed all over and the women wore tapa-cloth skirts. Both sexes wore heavy earrings of gold and ivory, and constantly chewed betel nut. Here, and at Cebu, he describes a sexual practice known as *palang*. "The males, large and small, have their penis pierced from one side to the other near the head, with a gold or tin bolt as large as a goose quill. In each end of the bolt some have what resembles a star, with points; others are like the head of a cart nail. . . . In the middle of the bolt is a hole, through which they urinate." Their excuse for this "lewd way of intercourse," as it was called by a Spanish official in Manila many years later, was that their women liked it that way, spur rowels and all; from the age of six he adds, young girls had their vaginas artificially stretched so as to admit this load of phallic hardware. Pigafetta, however, asserts that "the women loved us very much more than their own men."

After a stay of one week, the fleet left Mazaua (as Pigafetta calls Limasawa) and, piloted by the rajah in his private dugout canoe, sailed through Canigao Channel with Leyte on the starboard hand, into the Camotes Sea. They anchored one night at an island which Pigafetta calls Gatighan (which Robertson identifies as one of the Cuatro Islas off Leyte—but I rather think it was one of the Camotes). Here the men killed and ate a big fruit-eating bat and said it tasted like chicken. They then coasted into the principal harbor on the east coast of Cebu, behind the small but fatal island of Mactan.

It was now Low Sunday, 7 April 1521. On approaching the town of Cebu, on the same site as the present city, Magellan ordered his ships to be dressed with all their colors, struck all sails, and fired salutes as they dropped anchor. This created consternation ashore, but when the Captain General sent "a foster-son of his"—probably his bastard Rebelo—as ambassador to the sultan, accompanied by Enrique, the natives were reassured. Enrique told them that the Christians came in peace, their master the Captain General, subject to the greatest prince in the world, was "going to discover Malucho" (the Spice Islands). He now called on the sultan of Cebu at the suggestion of his blood-brother Colambu, to exchange merchandise for provisions. The sultan (named Humabon) consented, provided the Europeans paid tribute, which a Moorish junk from Siam had done only four days before. Enrique officiously replied that his master was subject of too great a king to pay tribute to anyone, and if Humabon "wanted peace, peace he would have; if war, war." At that the Moslem master of the junk (who was standing by) interposed, saying, "Watch out, sir; these are the same lot who have conquered Calicut, Malacca and Greater India. If well treated they will respond in kind, but if treated ill they will raise hell." Humabon replied that he would think it over. Next day, Colambu landed and backed up the Moro; and after the flag notary had explained through Enrique that the Captain General demanded no tribute

from him, Humabon not only consented to trade but performed the
casi-casi ceremony. A plentiful supply of food was purchased with
hawks' bells and glass beads.

All this inaugurated a precarious peace. The Sultan, his heir apparent, the Moro junk captain, eight chief men, and Rajah Colambu came
on board *Trinidad*. Magellan received them seated in a red velvet chair,
leather chairs were set out for the Spanish officers, and rugs or mats for
the visitors, as it embarrassed them to sit on chairs. The Captain General
made a long speech describing the elements of the Christian religion
and inviting them to be converted. Sultan Humabon appeared willing
to have all his people baptized. Magellan promised to present him with
a suit of armor that he admired; and added that if the girls too were
baptized, his men "could have intercourse with their women without
committing a very great sin"—a strange if amusing argument for Christian conversion! The Sultan and the Rajah promised to do everything
he wanted. Magellan embraced them, weeping with joy; and, clasping
hands with Sultan Humabon and the crown prince, promised that "by
his faith in God and in the Emperor his lord, and by the habit of Santiago which he wore," * he would give them perpetual peace with the
king of Spain.

Following an exchange of gifts, Pigafetta, Enrique, and a few others
walked up to the town and were received by the Sultan. "He was
short and fat and tattooed in various designs," noted Pigafetta, clad
only in a G-string, an embroidered head scarf, and jewelry. He was
regaling himself with a beaker of palm wine drunk through no fewer
than four straws, and occasionally reached out to pluck a turtle egg
from a porcelain bowl. The Italian, after investing his highness with an
Oriental-style robe, red cap, and string of Venetian beads, proceeded
with Enrique to the young prince's house, where they were entertained
by a four-piece orchestra of "very beautiful, almost white" girls playing on gongs and drums; after the music they threw off their already
scanty clothes and danced with the delighted Christians. The two visitors returned on board that night.

A crew member having died, Magellan obtained permission to bury
him in the public plaza after consecrating the spot, and set up a cross
over the grave. He also obtained the Sultan's consent to hold a sort of

---

* This habit featured the Santiago cross, whose arms and head are tipped with
fleurs-de-lys.

bazaar in a bamboo shed ashore. The Christians there displayed a variety of trade goods, which they swapped for gold, livestock, and rice. For fourteen pounds of iron the natives gave ten pieces of gold weighing a ducat and a half each.

The Sultan, having shown a wish to be baptized, now caused a platform to be set up in the plaza. On Sunday, 14 April, the ceremony was performed by the flagship's chaplain with all the pomp and circumstance the Christians could lay on, Magellan appropriately wearing a white robe. Humabon was renamed Don Carlos after the Emperor; Rajah Colambu became Don Juan after the Infante, and the Moslem junk captain, who also desired to be converted, became Don Cristóbal. Threatened with death if they did not conform, most of the chiefs did. Following their baptisms, at least 500 male subjects were christened. Mass was said ashore and the ships discharged their artillery as a salute to this new batch of converts. Next, the Sultana and forty women were baptized, and Magellan gave the lady a small image of a smiling Christ Child. This *Santo Niño* is the only object still preserved that once belonged to Magellan.

These picturesque and moving ceremonies, especially the conversion of the Moslem junk captain, mark another historic meeting of East and West. Islam had moved around the world from Arabia eastward; Christianity had moved westward from Jerusalem and Rome. Here they met. Which way would they go now? For the moment, the cross prevailed over the crescent, but not for long, and the conflict has never entirely ceased. When we were flying over these waters at Christmastide 1971, Christians and Moros were fighting in Mindanao.

The next four days were spotted with ceremony. Magellan came ashore daily to hear Mass celebrated by the flag chaplain, Father Valderrama. The Sultana (now christened Lisabeta), "young and beautiful and entirely covered with a white and black cloth," wearing a palm-leaf hat crowned with a sort of tiara, attended Mass and brought her ladies-in-waiting and many of her subjects. "Altogether we baptized 800 souls," recorded Pigafetta; and "before that octave had elapsed, all the persons of that island and some from the other islands were baptized." The Spaniards followed their now standard procedure of cross in one hand, sword in t'other. "We burned one hamlet in a neighboring island because it refused to obey the king or us," recorded Pigafetta. That was on Mactan, and Mactan did not forget.

Views on Cebu and Mactan: prao anchored off a village, and the Magellan
monument, Mactan.

Religious ecstasy reached its height when Magellan accepted a challenge to cure a sick brother to the crown prince, if he would burn a set of heathen idols to which he was making daily sacrifices. Magellan and Father Valderrama put on "a procession from the plaza to the house of the sick man with as much pomp as possible." They found him speechless and unable to move. The priest baptized him, together with both his wives and ten girls. Magellan asked him how he felt; he spoke at once and declared that he already "felt very well." Magellan administered a draught of specially prepared *mandolata* (milk of almonds), set up a complete bed to replace his crummy mat, and plied him daily with various soothing concoctions. On the fifth day the man began to walk, and people ran about the island shouting, "Castilla! Castilla!" and destroying every idol they could lay hands on.

Up to a point, the stay at Cebu was the most delightful of the entire voyage, even better than Rio de Janeiro. The men had plenty to eat and drink; the women were kind both before and after conversion. Magellan felt very proud over being the means of saving a thousand souls and acquiring a new province for Spain. Alas, if he could only have let well enough alone!

Battle of Mactan and Death of Magellan

Magellan was obsessed by the urge to attack Sultan Humabon's enemies. At Limasawa he had asked Rajah Colambu whether he would not like to take him on a raid to chastise his nearest enemy, but the cagey rajah declined on the ground that it was not the right season. Now Magellan intervened between Cebu and Mactan, although the newly baptized sultan showed no enthusiasm for battle. Tiny Mactan had two rajahs: Zula, friendly to Cebu, and hostile Lapu Lapu; but Humabon could live with that situation. Nevertheless, he accepted Magellan's offer to attack the recalcitrant Lapu Lapu, and contributed a thousand men to the expeditionary force.

There was nothing new in Magellan's strategy. Almost every group of European intruders into Africa and America felt that to cement an alliance with the nearest tribe of natives they must deploy fire power against next-door enemies. The Portuguese had done it repeatedly in Africa and India. Cortés marched on Mexico City against Montezuma with more native rebels than Spanish soldiers; Champlain pleased his

Canadian allies by fighting the Iroquois, inaugurating a century of warfare between them and the French. Even the English, who in general
managed to stay out of native rivalries, pitted one tribe against another
in the Carolinas. But for Magellan to do it here, when he had the local
situation well in hand, was utter folly. And what made it worse is the
fact that Humabon did not even demand this military action against
Lapu Lapu. Zula, who did ask for it, requested but one boatload of
men-at-arms, but the Captain General decided to send three, in the
ships' longboats. "We begged him repeatedly not to go," said Pigafetta,
"but he, like a good shepherd, refused to abandon his flock." He insisted on attacking on Saturday, 27 April, believing it to be his lucky
day.

In this fatal operation, Magellan broke every rule of amphibious
warfare, as we learned them in World War II; and the comparison is
not irrelevant because amphibious assault is the oldest form of naval
warfare, and many of its principles have never changed. Briefly, he
did not attempt surprise, he made no provision for gunfire support,
he chose an unsuitable beach full of natural obstacles which prevented
the boats from getting within shooting distance of the shore, he timed
the assault at low water when the rocks were most prominent, and he
failed to co-ördinate his attack with native allies, who remained idle
spectators of the ensuing slaughter.

Here is what happened; the sources are in surprising agreement. At
midnight 26–27 April 1521, the Christian assault force of sixty men
embarked in the three ships' longboats, and Sultan Humabon, some of
his chief men, and numerous warriors embarked in twenty to thirty
big native canoes and mostly played a spectator role. The moon was
five days past full. All boats were rowed or paddled through the narrow channel between Cebu city and Mactan, rounded Bantolinas Point
and paused before the big cove (now called Magellan Bay) on the
northeast side of Mactan. *Trinidad, Victoria,* and *Concepción* anchored within cannon shot of the shore, but, coming late, took no
significant part in the fight. Magellan's and Humabon's landing craft
reached their objective three hours before the break of day. Here was
an excellent chance for surprise, which Magellan lost by sending a
message via the Siamese trader to Lapu Lapu, "that if his subjects
would obey the king of Spain and recognize him as their lord, and pay
tribute, he would be their friend; if they wished otherwise, they would

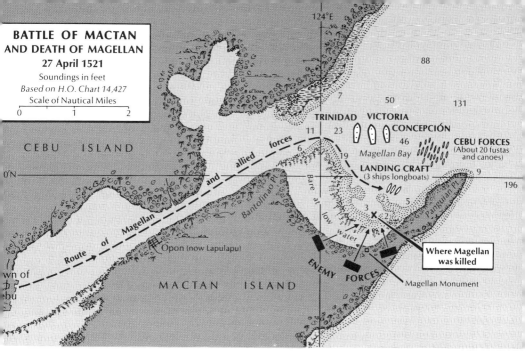

**BATTLE OF MACTAN
AND DEATH OF MAGELLAN**
27 April 1521
Soundings in feet
Based on H.O. Chart 14,427
Scale of Nautical Miles
0   1   2

124°E

88

7

50   131

TRINIDAD   VICTORIA

11   23   CONCEPCIÓN

46   **CEBU FORCES**
(About 20 fustas
and canoes)

Magellan Bay

LANDING CRAFT
(3 ships longboats)

9

196

CEBU   ISLAND

6

19

0°N

3   2

2   5

**Where Magellan
was killed**

Opon (now Lapulapu)

ENEMY   FORCES

MACTAN   ISLAND

Magellan Monument

Route *of* *Magellan*

and *allied* *forces*

Bantolinao Pt.

Bare at low water

Panguan Pt.

wn of
フ?
:bu

feel the iron of our lances." Lapu Lapu replied that he feared not the Christians' steel, having plenty of "fire-hardened spears and stakes of bamboo," and Magellan could attack when he chose.

At first light, the landing craft having approached as near the beach as they could at low water, Magellan and forty-eight of his men leaped into water knee to thigh deep, and slowly waded toward shore. The other eleven Spaniards guarded the boats, which stood by, distant from the beach "two crossbow flights"—a little over a mile. By the time the Christians landed, Lapu Lapu had organized his forces, "more than 1500 men," in three divisions—one at the head of the wide bay in front of their village, and one on each flank. "When they saw us, they charged down upon us with exceeding loud cries," wrote Pigafetta. The assault force swivel guns were out of range and the ships had not yet come up, so Magellan received no gunfire support. He formed his pitifully small landing force into two groups and fought back, both to the right and to the left, with arquebuses and crossbows. It was no use; the shots, at too great a range, were deflected by the enemy's wooden shields. Magellan ordered *no tirar*, "cease firing," but his men paid no attention and shot off all their ammunition. Now the enemy yelled even louder and "leaped about, covered by their shields" and "shooting so many arrows and hurling so many bamboo spears (some tipped with iron) that we were put on the defensive." At this point, Magellan should have retreated, but he counter-attacked, landed, and set fire to native huts ashore, "to terrify them." That aroused the enemy to greater fury. The Captain General, shot through the right leg with a poisoned arrow, ordered his landing party to retire to the boats, and most of them did so precipitately; but Magellan with six or eight faithful men, including Pigafetta, covered their retreat. The enemy pursued them into the water, hurled spears abundantly, and knocked Magellan's helmet off twice; "but he always stood firmly like a good knight." Finally he made a fatal tactical error, taking a stand with his devoted band beyond the range of ships or armed boats.

"Thus did we fight for more than one hour," wrote Pigafetta, up to their knees or more in water, and with no help from anyone—a valiant little group about their Captain General. He could have saved himself by retreating helter-skelter with the rest, but like a *preux chevalier* of old, he felt obliged to cover the retirement of his men. With more and more native warriors swarming about, the end was inevitable. A man of Mactan hurled a spear at Magellan's face, missed, and was immediately killed by the Captain General's lance. Since the lance stuck fast in the native's body, Magellan tried to draw his sword but could not because his sword arm had been wounded; and when the Mactanese observed this weakness, all hurled themselves upon him. One wounded him in the leg with a scimitar, he fell face down in the water, the enemy rushed upon him with spear and sword and slashed the life out of him.

"Thus," wrote Pigafetta, "they killed our mirror, our light, our comfort and our true guide. When they wounded him, he turned back many times to see whether we were all in the boats. Then, seeing him dead, we wounded made the best of our way to the boats, which were already pulling away. But for him, not one of us in the boats would have been saved, for while he was fighting the rest retired." At the last moment, too late, the three ships started to cannonade the crowded ranks of the enemy.

Pigafetta's eulogy of his captain is a classic: "Among the other virtues which he possessed, he was always the most constant in greatest adversity. He endured hunger better than all the rest, and, more ac-

Magellan Bay, Mactan. Site of Magellan's death.

curately than any man in the world, he understood dead reckoning and celestial navigation. And that this was the truth appeared evident, since no other had so much talent, nor the ardor to learn how to go around the world, as he almost did." "I hope," said Pigafetta to the man to whom he dedicated his narrative, "that through the efforts of your illustrious self the fame of so noble a captain will never die."

☆ XXVI ☆

Philippines and Spice Islands

Massacre at Cebu

Sultan Humabon wept when he heard of Magellan's death. He demanded the Captain General's body, asking the victorious rajah to name his own price; but Lapu Lapu refused to give it up "for all the riches in the world," and nobody knows what happened to Magellan's remains. A skull dug up on Mactan in 1971, with the remains of a Spanish sword, may possibly be his, but there is nothing to identify it.

The casualties in this fight, few but important, were eight Christians, including Magellan and Cristóbal Rebelo who had been promoted to captain of *Victoria*, together with four recently baptized natives of Cebu, and an estimated fifteen of the enemy. That afternoon the surviving officers chose Duarte Barbosa, Magellan's brother-in-law, to be captain of *Trinidad* and Captain General, dignities he enjoyed for barely three days.

Enrique de Malacca, the slave who had fought beside Magellan at Mactan, now turned lazy and surly when he could have been most useful, for he knew Spanish as well as Malay, and handled all communications with the rulers and people of Cebu. Enrique now declared that his master's death released him from servitude, which was correct; Magellan's last will and testament not only freed him but left him a legacy of 10,000 maravedis. So the former slave took to his bunk, nursing a slight wound he had received in the fight. This exasperated Captain General Barbosa, who spoke to Enrique somewhat in this wise: "Rise and shine, you lazy son-of-a-bitch, or I'll have you triced up and well flogged!" At any rate, he called him a dog and threatened to have him whipped, thus arousing all the man's native pride and vindictiveness, and costing Barbosa and some twenty-five shipmates their lives.

Enrique's revenge, doubtless sweet to him, widely outmeasured the offense. He convinced Sultan Humabon that the Christians planned to kidnap him, and then plotted to forestall treachery by treachery. This the Sultan did by means of a state banquet on 1 May, in the dark of the moon. Christians of every rank and rating were invited, and about thirty accepted, including Serrano and Barbosa. Of these, only Gómez de Espinosa and Carvalho survived because, smelling treachery, they sneaked out in time to save their lives and returned to their ships. Carvalho, now in temporary command, heard the tumult and saw natives throwing down the cross set up by Magellan and kicking it about. It took no great wit to guess what was up; Carvalho ordered each vessel to weigh and make sail, first approaching near enough to throw a few broadsides into the town. When *Trinidad* came within hailing distance, Captain Serrano was led to the shore, bound and bleeding, begging his countrymen to ransom him.

Carvalho is accused by Pigafetta and others of cold-bloodedly sailing away, leaving shipmate Serrano to his fate; but the Portuguese author of the Leiden Narrative tells a different story. Serrano called out that the ransom demanded for his life was two lombards, ships' cannon. Carvalho agreed, and sent a pair of these guns ashore in his skiff. The natives then declared these were not enough, and bargained for more. The boat party said they would give anything to recover Serrano, but he must be put in a safe place where they could pick him up. That they refused to do, and Serrano nobly urged his shipmates to break off the parley and get out, as he believed the natives were stalling until reinforcements arrived, to try to capture the ships, and they had better escape quickly "since it were better for him to die than that all should perish." Even as they were shifting sail to stand off shore, the Spanish sailors saw the men guarding Serrano turn on him, and heard shrieks which told only too well that another murder was being committed. The other victims of Enrique's revenge and the Sultan's treason in-

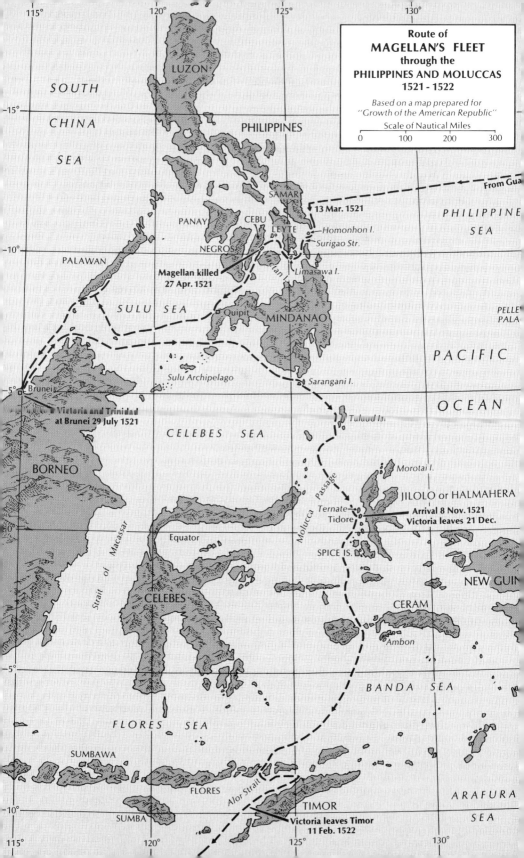

cluded three captains (Barbosa, Serrano, and Luis Alfonso de Gois), Andrés de San Martín, Father Valderrama, two secretaries, several petty officers and servants, and a dozen mariners and apprentice seamen. All were killed in the brawl or shortly after, sold as slaves to China. What became of Enrique we do not know; presumably he enjoyed an ill-earned eminence at the Sultan's court.

Cebu immediately relapsed into paganism, and every evidence of its brief experiment with Christianity was destroyed except El Santo Niño, the statue of the Christ Child.

Through the Philippines to the Spiceries

The three Spanish ships sailed to a beach somewhere on Bohol Island, and there reorganized. A conclave of officers elected Carvalho captain general, a responsibility he did not deserve and proved incompetent to perform. The alguacil, Gonzalo Gómez de Espinosa, then replaced him as captain of *Trinidad*. Since the fleet's complement had been reduced by starvation, fighting, and massacre to about 110 men, only enough properly to man two ships, it was decided to scrap *Concepión*, already riddled with ship worms. They saved anything that might be of value on the long voyage home, dividing her gear and stores between the two other ships, and burned her hull to the water's edge so that the natives could not pick her bones. Elcano, her master, soon emerged as captain of *Victoria*.

Sailing south-southwest, *Trinidad* and *Victoria* passed close to the tiny island of Panglao off southern Bohol, and were surprised to find it inhabited by "black men like those living in Ethiopia," says Pigafetta. These were the Negritos, as primitive a people as the Australian aborigines. Thence they made a leisurely tour of the southern Philippines and parts of the future Indonesia, apparently in no hurry to reach the Spice Islands. Probably they felt that, having come so far, they might as well discover all they could for Spain and pick up valuables for themselves. They were not, to be sure, discovering "new" countries like those of America, or even Guam. For the rest of the voyage they were visiting civilized communities with organized governments which had well established trading relations with China, Thailand, and India, as well as islands already familiar to the Portuguese. Nonetheless, to the crews of *Trinidad* and *Victoria* all these places were new and exciting, and I beg the reader to indulge me in carrying the story of this wonderful voyage to its conclusion.

Debouching into the Sulu Sea, the two ships called at a place called Quipit (now Kipit) on the Zamboanga peninsula of Mindanao. Here is a lofty, beautiful green-clad coast where rivers with ochre-colored water empty into the Sulu Sea, creating a golden pool amid the ocean sapphire; and the tiniest of white beaches nestle between rocky headlands. Calanao the local rajah performed the *casi-casi* ceremony with Carvalho, but had no food to spare. Pigafetta and other officers were rowed for two hours up river by the completely naked Rajah and his chiefs, introduced to the Ranee, and served a supper of rice and excessively salt fish, washed down by palm wine. There they passed the night, returning on board ship next day.

Sailing almost due west across the Sulu Sea, the ships called at the little island of Cagayan Sulu, whose inhabitants were Moros banished from Borneo. They shot game with poisoned arrows from blow-pipes. Again, no food; but the next island, about 120 miles to the northwestward, was lengthy, fabulous Palawan, where provisions of all kinds were abundant. "We called that land the Land of Promise," says Pigafetta, "because we suffered great hunger before we found it." At one of the numerous bays on the south coast of this opulent island, not improbably the future Puerto Principesa, they traded with friendly people, some pagan and some Moslem. Here the Christians saw their first cock fight, a form of sport that apparently had not reached Spain, and enjoyed the local arrack (rice wine) which had more kick than the palm wine of Cebu.

At beautiful Palawan, still an island paradise, they lingered a full month. There is a dreamy quality about summer sailing in the Philippines. The winds are mild, the sun warm, the sea teeming with fish. The land is so fertile that for more than half the year, after the main crops are gathered, the people have nothing to do but enjoy themselves. There was nothing very dreamy, however, in the way these Spaniards treated the natives. Wanting a pilot from Palawan to Borneo, they captured a ship about to enter the harbor and impressed her three Moro pilots to conduct them. The two ships departed enchanted Palawan on 21 June 1521, day of the full moon, and arrived at Brunei in northeastern Borneo on 9 July.

No "wild men of Borneo" greeted them here, but a most sophisticated society; the Spaniards might have thought they had found the land of a Thousand and One Nights. The Shahbender (title of the ruler of Brunei) sent out to meet *Trinidad* and *Victoria* a beautiful prao with gilt work on bow and stern. She flew a blue-and-white banner surmounted by peacock feathers; a band on board played on native instruments, and eight elderly chiefs closed the Spanish ships and came on board bearing gifts. Next, the Shahbender sent three music-making praos which encircled the ships "with great pomp," presented the Spaniards with various foodstuffs made of rice, and granted them permission to land.

This man was the most prestigious prince the Spanish had yet encountered; and his independent sultanate has lasted to our own day. Three hundred men-at-arms holding naked scimitars at the ready, guarded him in a vast, richly adorned palace. He remained in his private apartments adjoining the harem, refusing to communicate except by speaking tube, and that with a palace official. Pigafetta and the six men who went ashore to make a formal call and present gifts were transported from the harbor to an official's house on elephants bearing silk trappings and castles on their backs. A dozen porters followed to carry the gifts. Cotton mattresses were provided by their host. Next morning the elephants carried them to the palace to present their credentials and receive permission to trade. They observed the protocol of raising hands over head, stepping up each knee, and bowing deeply toward the Shahbender. At him they were graciously permitted to peek as he lolled on a sofa in his private apartments, chewing betel nut and playing with one of his many young sons. After a thirty-two-course dinner at the official's, and a second night in real beds, the deputation enjoyed another elephant ride to the port.

This visit to Brunei did not end on the same gay note. On the morning of 29 July 1521 the Spanish sailors saw a fleet of over a hundred praos approaching their anchorage from one side, and a fleet of junks advancing from the other. Anticipating treachery, as at Cebu, they hastily made sail and attacked the junks, capturing four and killing a number of men. On board one junk was the son of the Rajah of Luzon who, as the Shahbender's captain general, had sacked and destroyed the town of a disobedient chief and carried off three beautiful girls. Carvalho released him (secretly receiving a fat ransom in gold) and kept the three girl captives to start a harem of his own. Having completed this steal, Carvalho found it expedient to leave Brunei, abandoning his own eight-year-old Brazilian son who had been invited ashore to play with a son of the Shahbender. This boy never saw his father again. What became of the three girls we are not told; probably they were released at Ternate after Carvalho's death. Magellan would never have allowed them to sail in his fleet, but discipline had become lax since his death and the Spaniards behaved as if they had all the time in the world.

Retracing their course toward Palawan, on 7 September 1521 *Victoria* and *Trinidad* called at an island they called Combonbon, which was probably Banguey on the south side of Balabac Strait. Here they stayed forty-two days, during which "we labored hard," said Pigafetta, to grave, caulk and repair the ships and lay in a supply of firewood, going "barefoot in the forest" to cut it. The service of graving and pitching to deter the teredo, essential to keep a wooden ship afloat in tropical seas, must have been properly attended to, as *Victoria* made the long voyage home despite leaks. At Banguey they found many kinds of fish and shellfish including *Tridacena gigas*, the giant clam which can kill a man by clamping down on his arm or leg.

Proceeding eastward again, they spoke an important junk in which were embarked Tuan Mahmud, the Shahbender's governor of Palawan, and his son and brother. As she refused to strike sail, they captured and sacked her. The Tuan was so liberal with gifts over and above what had been stolen from him, that the Spaniards gave him expensive presents such as a yellow damask robe, a green cloth robe, and a blue cloth cloak. At the September full moon the fleet officers, feeling that Carvalho was becoming much too big for his boots as well as a menace to their future safety by acts of piracy, degraded him to his former rank of flag pilot, elected Gómez de Espinosa captain general as well as captain of *Trinidad*, and appointed Juan Sebastián de Elcano captain of *Victoria*, fleet treasurer and accountant.

The two ships, directed by one of the impressed pilots, crossed the Sulu Sea, passed through Basilan Strait into Moro Gulf, and passed the site of the modern city of Zamboanga. En route they encountered the ancestors of the latter-day Sámal Laut or sea-gypsies, who live on board their boats and follow the monsoon. Although Carvalho had been deposed, the crews of *Victoria* and *Trinidad* continued to practise piracy. For no apparent need or reason, they captured a big prao

Tidore (really Ternate). A Dutch fleet attacking the Portuguese in early seventeenth century. After De Bry. From his *Peregrinates in Indiam Orientalem*, 1607.

with a crew of eighteen, all chiefs of Mindanao, killed seven and saved one to act as co-pilot, since he claimed to know the course to the Spice Islands. He did; this man knew his business.

On 26 October 1521 in the Celebes Sea and the dark of the moon, the two ships encountered their first storm since leaving the Strait of Magellan, and they had to strip down to bare poles. Three corposants—St. Elmo's on the maintop, St. Nicholas's on the mizzentop, and Santa Clara's on the foretop—appeared and "dissipated the darkness." The mariners promised, if saved, to donate a slave to each saint, but Pigafetta does not explain the proposed method of delivery.

At a harbor between the two islands of Bahut and Sarangani—latitude 6°07′ N, says Pigafetta, which is close—the Spaniards shanghaied two more native pilots who guided them southeasterly through the uninhabited Karakelong group and past the Sangi Islands, where all but

Ternate and Tidore, 1972. The two islands and the tiny one between.
Sanchez Obregón photo.

one of the impressed pilots managed to escape by swimming ashore.
Finally, on 6 November 1521, they raised four conspicuous islands,
and "The pilot who still remained with us told us that those four
islands were *Maluco*"—the long-sought Spiceries. "So we thanked
God, and for joy discharged all our artillery. And no wonder we were
so joyful, for we had spent twenty-seven months less two days in our
search for Molucca," counting from the day they left Spain.

They really had arrived. Here was what Columbus had been looking
for, what Magellan had been sent to find. As Camoëns put it,

> Olha cá pelos mares do Oriente
> As infinitas ilhas espalhadas.
> Ve Tidore e Ternate co fervente
> Cume que lança as flamas ondeadas.
> As árvores verás do cravo ardente,
> Co sangue Português inda compradas.

Through all these Oriental waters / sprinkled with islands innumerable,/ behold Tidore and Ternate from whose burning / summit plumes

of fire flare; / trees of ardent cloves you may see, / which Lusitanian blood has purchased.

These were names to conjure with; John Milton tells of a fleet

> by equinoctial winds
> Close sailing from Bengala, or the isles
> Of Ternate and Tidore, whence merchants bring
> Their spicy drugs . . .

Henry Thoreau, wintering in his cabin on Walden Pond, mused that the ice there harvested "with favoring winds" would go "floating by Ternate and Tidore" to be "landed in ports of which Alexander only heard the names." *

On the afternoon of 8 November 1521, *Trinidad* and *Victoria*, firing another salute, entered the harbor of Tidore, most important of the five principal Moluccas. The others are Ternate, Motir, Makyan, and Batchian. They stretch in a north-south line, from latitude 4° N to the Equator, parallel to the big island of Halmahera (Jilolo), also counted as a Spice Island. All six islands are lofty and verdure-covered. Ternate and Tidore are so tiny—the first, almost round and only six and a half miles in diameter, and Tidore barely ten miles long—that it is difficult to believe that in the sixteenth century they inspired momentous voyages, supported independent rulers in high state, and caused thousands of deaths among Europeans fighting to control their fragrant riches.

And why were spices—especially clove, cinnamon, nutmeg, mace, and pepper—so avidly sought after in this era? They were part of life in both the European and Asiatic worlds. They flavored all kinds of cooked food. They were used in perfumes and (like myrrh) for embalming. Spices were among the most important ingredients of *materia medica*. Before tea, coffee, and chocolate had been introduced to Europe, spices pepped up beer and wine, and in lieu of refrigeration they masked the unpleasant savor of decomposing food. Even today, how would you like to live without pepper, nutmeg, or cinnamon?

Urdaneta reported to the king of Spain in 1537, after living several years in Molucca, that from all six Spice Islands the annual export varied from 5000 to 11,600 quintal (hundredweight) of cloves; that when he arrived there, the value of a *bahar* (over four quintal) of cloves was two ducats, and in five years it went up to ten. Maxi-

---

* Lusiads, x.132, *Paradise Lost*, ii.638, *Walden*, end of chap. xvi.

Morisons and Obregóns under clove tree, Ternate. Sanchez Obregón photo.

Informal reception committee, Ternate. Sanchez Obregón photo.

milianus Transylvanus, who obtained from *Victoria*'s survivors a fairly accurate account of how spices were grown, wrote, "The natives share groves of this tree among themselves, just as we do vineyards." Since about 1515 the Portuguese had been distributing the clove harvest from Lisbon throughout Europe, and also (by virtue of their superior navigation and business sense) throughout the Far East. No wonder that they, the first Europeans to reach the Moluccas, were determined to hold them in strict monopoly.

Returning to our voyage, on 9 November 1521, after the two Spanish ships had anchored in the harbor of Tidore, Sultan Abuleis, a Moslem about forty-five years old, came out to greet them in a prao. He was seated under a silk awning, accompanied by one of his sons bearing a scepter, two hand-washers with water in gold jars, and two men bearing gold caskets filled with betel-nut. The Sultan bade the Christians welcome; he had even dreamed of their coming. Boarding the flagship, he condescended to sit on a velvet-covered chair whence he "received us as children," says Pigafetta, and declared that he and all his people wanted nothing better than to be vassals of imperial Charles.

657

The Portuguese, who had been called in by his predecessor ten years earlier to break the Arab monopoly, had evidently outstayed their welcome.

Abuleis informed the Christians that Magellan's old friend Francisco Serrão had died on Ternate some eight months earlier, but tactfully concealed the circumstances. The rulers of Tidore and Ternate were enemies; Serrão supported Ternate, where he had been living since 1512, and so effectively that Abuleis put poison into his drink when, after concluding peace, he visited Tidore to buy cloves. Next, a few days after he had greeted the Spaniards, Abuleis himself was poisoned by his daughter, wife of the sultan of Batchian, "under pretext of trying to bring about peace between the kings of these two islands; but he recovered." Princely politics in the Moluccas are somewhat difficult to follow.

Pigafetta gives us some interesting figures on the sexual habits of these Moro princes. The sultan of Tidore had one principal wife and some two hundred girls in his harem; every family in the island had to furnish him with one or two daughters to keep it full. In the neighboring island of Halmahera (Jilolo) were two sultans who respectively fathered 526 and 666 children, surpassing Augustus the Strong of Saxony, who boasted only 364 bastards. Jessu, the elder with the top score, visited Ternate while the Christians were there and exchanged gifts, but not wives.

The weeks spent here were pure joy to Pigafetta. He describes how clove trees were grown and the harvest gathered, and the preparation of sago, the bread of these islands. The sultan of Ternate himself came to the Spanish ships and traded quantities of cloves. The sultan of Tidore swore "by Allah and the Koran" that he would always be a friend to the king of Spain. The sultan of Batchian made a state visit in a gaily beflagged prao, a veritable trireme with three banks of oars on each side and 120 rowers moving to the cadence of banging gongs. The Spaniards attended a banquet given in their honor by the local sultan; every man sat between two young girls "clad in silk garments from the waist to the knees."

New sails were now bent on the ships and painted with the cross of Santiago. The Christians left some of their arquebuses and culverins as a parting present with the sultan of Tidore, who gave them in return one slave, ten *bahar* of cloves, and two stuffed birds of paradise. These birds were supposed to live wholly in the air, never reaching earth until they died; and as the specimens which Elcano brought home had no feet, this was assumed to be true.

To have a double chance of getting home with these valuable cargoes, the officers of the fleet decided that, now the easterly monsoon had started, *Victoria* should return via the Cape of Good Hope, and *Trinidad* await the westerly monsoon and head for Nueva España. There her cargo would be carried across the Isthmus of Panama and shipped to Spain. Departure was delayed because *Trinidad* sprang a leak at anchor and the men had to careen and unload her to get at it. Leaving her in the harbor of Tidore, *Victoria* under Captain Elcano set sail 21 December 1521 with 47 of her original crew and 13 natives on board; Gómez de Espinosa stayed behind with 53 men to sail *Trinidad*. The last moon of the year had entered last quarter, a bad time to start. *Victoria* endured a nine months' voyage and many vicissitudes before Captain Elcano got her back to Spain with eighteen Christian and three native survivors.

✳ XXVII ✳

Homeward Bound

1522

Trinidad's Fatal Attempt

Trinidad and *Victoria* have now sailed far beyond the limits set by this book. When they dropped Mindanao below the northern horizon, they had passed the last land which, by any stretch of imagination, could be called America, or new discoveries. Most of the native inhabitants, whether Moslem or heathen, were organized, sophisticated, and prosperous, and the Portuguese had been coming to Indonesia for fifteen years or more. Judging, however, that my readers would like to see this greatest of all voyages through, we shall finish the story of Magellan's two surviving ships.

First, let us relate the unsuccessful attempt of *Trinidad* to return home eastward. Owing to necessary repairs, she did not depart Tidore until more than three months after *Victoria*. Gonzalo Gómez de Espinosa commanded her, and Carvalho would have been her pilot had he not died at Tidore in February 1522. Juan Bautista de Punzorol, probably the one known to fame as the "Genoese pilot," replaced him.

Leaving one officer and four men ashore as nucleus of a trading factory to pursue the spice trade, *Trinidad*, carrying a cargo of almost 1000 quintal—nearly fifty ton—of cloves, set sail for Tidore 6 April 1522, in the full of the paschal moon. She passed Jilolo (Halmahera) and Morotai, into the Philippine Sea, revictualed at Komo, and for a time steered east by north; but head winds forced her to fall off to the northward. She called at one of the Marianas, where three men deserted; and, continually baffled by easterly winds, stormy weather, and what seemed to the crew to be intense cold, struggled as far north as latitude 43° N, that of Hakodate in Japan. Then Gómez de Espinosa decided to return to Tidore. It took him six weeks to reach an island that he calls Bonaconora, probably Morotai or another small island north of Jilolo. By that time, thirty of the crew of fifty-three had died, and so many more were disabled by scurvy that they had become incapable of handling the ship.

During her absence a fleet of seven Portuguese naval vessels under Captain António de Brito, who had been scouring the eastern seas looking for Magellan, put in at Tidore, mopped up the little Spanish garrison, and reduced the sultan to a tearful renunciation of his new friends and abject obedience to Portugal. Espinosa, at Bonaconora, received news of these doings, and in his helpless condition sent Brito a letter by boat, begging for succor. The pitiless Portuguese replied by sending a caravel to take possession of *Trinidad* and sail her to Ternate, where he impounded her papers and log-books, discharged her valuable cargo for his benefit, and stripped her of sails, lines, and all valuable gear. In that condition a squall struck her at anchor and she dragged ashore, broke up, and became a total loss.

Sad indeed was the once proud flagship's fate, and tragic that of most of her remaining crew. Brito beheaded a beachcomber whom Espinosa had picked up, on the ground that he was a Portuguese subject who had deserted. He seriously considered having the "Genoese pilot" and a few others slaughtered forthwith, but (he cynically explains in his letter to the king), "I detained them in Maluco because it is an unhealthy country, with the intention of having them die there," which most of them did. The boatswain and the carpenter were set to work for Brito himself, and the rest were sent to Governor Albuquerque of India, to dispose of as he chose. Their fate is unknown, except that Espinosa's slave, Antón "de color Negro," was presented by Albuquerque to his sister.

Of the four members of *Trinidad*'s crew who eventually returned to the Iberian Peninsula, Juan Rodriguez, at forty-four the oldest man in Magellan's fleet, escaped in a Portuguese ship. Espinosa and Ginés de Mafra were taken to the Banda Islands—Java, Malacca, and Cochin —where they endured hard labor for two years and were then shipped with Hans Vargue the German gunner to Lisbon. All three were there thrown into prison. Faithful Hans died in jail, pathetically bequeathing all his property—back pay and a packet of cloves and nutmegs— to his commanding officer. The Portuguese passed on Espinosa and Ginés de Mafra to Seville, where the Spanish authorities clapped them into jail. After seven months' incarceration, both were released and given their day in court in 1527—almost eight years after leaving home. Ginés found that his wife, believing him dead, had married again and spent all his property. After a legal hassle over that, he returned to the Indies. Pedro de Alvaredo employed him as chief pilot on a coastal voyage in the Pacific in 1536, and six years later he became pilot to Ruy López de Villalobos on his voyage to the Philippines. Espinosa, whose courageous support of Magellan in the San Julián mutiny saved the voyage, spent four and a half years in captivity in the East before returning to Spain.

Diogo Barbosa, Magellan's father-in-law, in a memorial to the king-emperor, remarked bluntly that mutineers in *San Antonio* "were very well received and treated at the expence of Your Highness, while the captain and others who were desirous of serving Your Highness were imprisoned and deprived of all justice. From this," he added, "so many bad examples arise—heartbreaking to those who try to do their duty." True enough. Magellan, too, had he returned to Spain, would certainly have been jailed on some excuse.

Charles V later made it up to Espinosa, so far as lay in his power. He granted him noble status and a coat of arms with a motto on a global crest differing slightly from Elcano's: "Thou wert one of the first to go around me." His back pay, even though the officials of the Casa de Contratación would allow him no salary for years spent in prison, amounted to a large sum of money. The king gave him 15,000 maravedis as heir of Hans Vargue, a pension of 30,000 maravedis, and a job paying 43,000 maravedis per annum as inspector of ships bound to the Indies. He still held that position in 1543, when we finally lose sight of this valiant captain and loyal supporter of Magellan. We do not know where or when he died. Peace to his soul!

Victoria's Voyage Home

Juan Sebastián de Elcano received full honors for sailing *Victoria* home, which caused his part in the San Julián mutiny to be over-looked and forgiven. A younger man than Magellan (born 1486 or 1487 at Guetaria in the northern province of Guipúzcoa, third of eight children to a middle-class family), he had commanded a ship bigger than any of Magellan's before the great voyage. Nobody ever denied the high quality of his seamanship. But what of his personality? Neither Pigafetta nor the Portuguese author of the Leiden Narrative, both of whom sailed with Elcano from Tidore to Seville, ever mentions him. Possibly they had not forgotten the mutiny at San Julián; more probably they had suffered personal slights. Since Magellan forgave Elcano for his part in the mutiny, so should we; but it is hard to overlook his lying at Magellan's expense about the mutiny at San Julián in 1527. Anyway, as captain of *Victoria* he never wavered on the difficult voyage home.

Her crew took leave of their fellow countrymen and new friends at Tidore on 21 December 1521 and sailed with a complement of sixty, thirteen of them natives. Steering almost due south along the line of Spice Islands, she called at the islet off Tidore to pick up a load of firewood that had been cut for her, left the other Spice Islands astern, saw the last new moon of 1521 arise, and passed to starboard the Xulla (Suela) Islands which tail off from the Celebes. In Manipa Strait between Ceram (Sarang) and Buru (Boeroe) she anchored in Jakiol Bay on 27 December and there obtained fresh provisions. Now turning southeast (having evidently shipped a native pilot who knew his business), *Victoria* passed through the great Indonesian island barrier by Alor Strait.* In the Savu Sea a severe storm arose, and all hands made vows to perform a pilgrimage to a shrine of the Virgin if she would deign to save them; but they had no opportunity to do that before Seville. *Victoria* scudded east before the storm along the ironbound south shores of Pantar and Alor Islands, reaching an island then called Malua, where she found a harbor and stayed a fortnight caulking and

---

* Most authorities say by the narrow Flores Strait, further west; but Albo makes it clear that they chose the wider Alor Strait, as any prudent pilot would do.

Beach on Timor

making other repairs. On 25 January 1522 she crossed the fifteen-mile channel to the great and lofty (9580 feet) island of Timor. The eastern half of this island remains Portuguese, last remnant except Macao of her Far-Eastern empire; but in 1522 no conquering Lusitanians had yet arrived.

Timor, described by Camoëns as that "isle which yields sandalwood salubrious and sweet to smell," received a good name from Pigafetta. "White sandalwood is found in that island and nowhere else. Also, ginger, water buffaloes, swine, goats, fowls, rice, figs [bananas], sugar-cane, oranges, lemons, wax, almonds, kidney beans, and other things. . . . We found a junk from Luzon there, which had come to buy sandalwood," and Elcano brought a packet of the fragrant wood home to Spain. The people were all heathen and (after some initial misunderstanding) willing to trade; but as they were riddled with the "disease of St. Job" (syphilis), the crew avoided the girls. For three weeks *Victoria* coasted the superb scenery of northwestern Timor, from Balibo (west of Dilli) to Kuping, buying provisions wherever they could be found.

Pigafetta, who seems to have understood the Moros with whom he conversed, picked up at Timor a series of yarns about China and the Far East. The tallest of them, which later European travelers have confirmed, is about a variation of the *palang* in the courtship habits of young gentlemen of Java. In his own words, "When the young men of Java are in love with any gentlewoman, they sew certain little bells between their member and the foreskin, stand under the window of their innamorata and, making a show of urinating and shaking their member, they make the little bells tinkle and so continue until the listening lady hears the sound. She then comes out and they take their pleasure; always with those little bells in place, for the women like hearing them ring inside."

On the night of the full moon, 10–11 February 1522, *Victoria* sailed from Timor with the land breeze into "the great open sea called Laut Chidol"—the Indian Ocean. Elcano dared not call at Bali, Java,

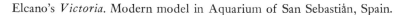

Elcano's *Victoria*. Modern model in Aquarium of San Sebastián, Spain.

or Sumatra for fear of being attacked by the Portuguese, and the fate of *Trinidad* proved the wisdom of his decision. But he paid for it with suffering. To double the Cape he steered straight across the Indian Ocean. Two more moons waxed and waned and a third became almost full, before he sighted Africa. This leg of the voyage reduced his crew to a state of misery equal to that which they had endured in the Pacific. Magellan's ships never could carry enough sea stores for a prolonged voyage. In this case, owing to the scarcity of salt in the Spice Islands and Timor, the barreled meat and fish, insufficiently pickled, turned putrid in the hold. And in early March the monsoon petered out and westerlies set in, head winds which raised enormous seas against which *Victoria* found it difficult to contend. Twice or thrice she had to lay-to, tossing and rolling, while the captain kept his men busy repairing leaks and splicing the now ragged rigging so that it would help get them home. Fortunately he had had a new suit of sails made in Tidore.

On 18 March 1522, just as Pilot Albo was shooting the sun, they sighted a "very high island." Twice they tried to fetch it but, thwarted by head winds, gave it up. This must have been the one that the Dutch later named Amsterdam, in latitude 37° 50′ S. Some of the sailors were so cold, hungry, and sick as to beg Elcano to put in at Portuguese Mozambique, which they wrongly estimated to be close at hand; but the majority, "more desirous of honor than of their own life, determined to go to Spain living or dead." Brave boys, hurrah for them!

For several more weeks *Victoria* shaped courses between west by south and west by north, twice venturing below latitude 40° S and being forced to lay-to for a couple of days. Elcano finally decided that sailing in the "roaring forties" did not pay, closed South Africa, sighted it on 8 May, and landed at a port, probably Mossel Bay or Port Elizabeth. No natives were encountered or food obtained here; and —O bitter disappointment!—they ascertained from the lay of the land, and the high mountains, that they had not yet doubled the Cape. So on *Victoria* struggled, bucking the Agulhas Current and contrary winds, carrying away her foretopmast and springing her main yard. Finally, on a fair May day she doubled Cape Agulhas, Africa's furthest south (latitude 34° 50′ S) and the nearby Cape of Good Hope, sighting both in the misty distance.

"Then we sailed north for two months continually without taking on any refreshment," wrote Pigafetta. On 8 June 1522, with a full moon, *Victoria* crossed the Equator for the fourth time since leaving Spain. Between Timor and the Cape de Verdes, she lost fifteen of her own men and ten Indonesians, more than had died on board Magellan's three ships in crossing the Pacific. Pigafetta thought it significant that when the corpses were committed to the sea, the Christians floated on their backs, facing heaven, and the pagans floated face down, toward hell!

On 9 July *Victoria* anchored in the port of Ribeira Grande on the Cape de Verdes island of Santiago. There the officers were disturbed to find that their count of the calendar was wrong; they thought it was Wednesday, but the people ashore assured them it was Thursday. This was a serious matter, since it meant that they had eaten meat (when they had it) on Friday, and kept Easter on Monday. A grievous if not mortal sin! Not until they reached Seville could anyone find the explanation that they had lost a day by sailing westward with the sun. In the meantime, all hands swore to do penance for this mistake, if they ever got home.

In order to deceive the Cape Verde Portuguese as to where they had been, Elcano instructed his shore party to declare that they had lost their way returning from the Caribbean. This worked at first, and the shore party brought out a boatload of rice. After resting at anchor four or five days with constant pumping, Elcano sent his biggest boat ashore manned by thirteen sailors, to get more food and buy slaves to spell out his exhausted men at the pumps. Having no cash, he sent several parcels of cloves for the purchase, and that put the Portuguese authorities wise to the fact that *Victoria* had been poaching on "their" Spice Islands. They detained the crew and sent out one of their own boats, ordering Elcano to surrender his ship. The Captain, unlike Columbus whose *Niña* had been similarly treated in the Azores in 1493, did not feel strong enough to shoot it out with the Portuguese; and, seeing several armed vessels in the harbor making sail apparently to overhaul him, he hastily departed on 15 July. This time, by the corrected calendar.

It was another long haul against the northerly "Portuguese trades" to get home, and in some respects this leg of the voyage was the toughest. For not only did the eighteen men have to do the work

normally done by fifty; they had to work the pumps day and night
to prevent *Victoria* from foundering. She sighted Tenerife 28 July.
As usual with African traders returning home against the north wind,
she had to make a wide sweep to the northwest on the starboard tack
to the Azores. Tall Pico thrust its volcanic cone above the horizon on
7 August. With light variables, she jilled around the Azores for over
a week, gravely in need of provisions but not daring to land in Portuguese territory. On 21 August she got a good slant for Cape St. Vincent and picked up that prominent landmark on 4 September, the
eve of *Victoria*'s last full moon at sea.

The winds now favored the weary mariners. On Saturday, 6 September, *Victoria* entered the harbor of Sanlúcar de Barrameda. After
one night (and, we hope, fresh food), Elcano procured a long boat
with a crew of stout oarsmen, who helped pull her up the Guadalquivir on two flood tides. On the 8th she anchored off a quay at
Seville hard by the Church of Santa Maria de la Victoria; and by a
happy coincidence found that it was the feast day of this particular
virgin, the friend of mariners. It was three years and one month from
the time *Victoria* had sailed thence.

Only eighteen Christians were left to perform penitential vows. On
Tuesday the 9th, barefoot and clad only in their shirts, each man
carrying a long lighted candle, they marched into the Minorite convent at the Triana waterfront to pray before Santa Maria de la Victoria, then crossed the old pontoon bridge to Seville proper, and after
a walk of well over a mile, entered the great Cathedral and worshipped
at the venerated shrine of Santa Maria de l'Antigua.

Juan Sebastián de Elcano was not committed to jail, the fate of so
many master mariners returning from a great discovery. He lost no
time making a report, in which he shows commendable concern for
his fellow survivors. Charles V had returned to Spain after more than
two years' absence, well pleased with himself; a rebellion in Castile had
been suppressed, and although France had declared war, Henry VIII
(whose daughter Mary the Emperor intended to marry) declared war
on France. Elcano was summoned to his presence at Valladolid, together with picked members of *Victoria*'s crew, who first were issued

Arms of Elcano

new clothes and an installment of their wages. The Emperor received
his captain graciously and granted him an annual pension of 500 ducats
($1160 in gold). The herald's office provided him with a very ap-
propriate coat of arms. Here is the blazon: Chief, a castle *or* on field
gules, and on the other half a field *or*, with two crossed cinnamon
sticks, three nutmegs and twelve cloves. Crest: a globe bearing the
motto *Primus circumdedisti me* (Thou first circumnavigated me).
Supporters: two Malay kings, crowned, each holding a branch of a
spice tree, proper.

Charles V demanded of his brother-in-law D. João III (now king of
Portugal) the return of the thirteen sailors marooned in the Cape
Verdes, and this was done fairly promptly. They with the rest of the
eighteen Christians who finished this voyage were received at court;
what happened to the three Indonesian survivors is unrecorded.
Adding the five men from *Trinidad* who eventually reached the
Peninsula, we have 35 survivors from the four ships which originally
left Spain and the Canaries in 1519; *San Antonio*, which defected,

669

CIRCIVS·VEL·RESIAS·

CAVRVS·CORVS·VEL·LAPIXSI·VIGESTES·

CIRCVLVS·ARTICVS·

CATAIO·PROVI

FAVONIV
VE·ZEPHIR

TROPICVS·CANCRI·

INSVLE·MALVCHE·

AEQVINOCTIALIS·   p·à·los·pulucunos
                  p·de·s·paulo

TROPICVS·CAPRICORNI·

CIRCVLVS·ANTARTICVS·

AFRICVS·VE·LIBVS·

LIBONOTVS·EVRO·AVSTE

msu

Pinguela

R·IO·D
PLAT

al·stretto·dri

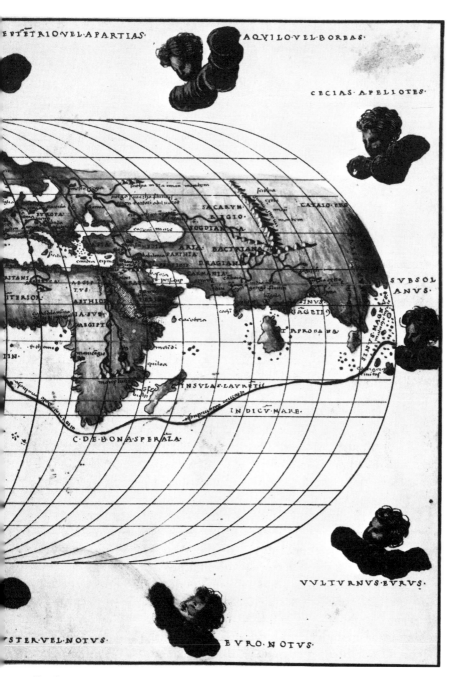

Battista Agnese map of 1568, showing course of Magellan and Elcano, and Panama route to west coast. Courtesy, Library of Congress.

would account for 50 to 55 more. Many had trouble collecting back pay. Miguel de Rodas, assistant master of *Victoria*, when presented to the Emperor, was given arms similar to Elcano's, and granted an annual pension of 50,000 maravedis; but three years later he testified that he had received none of it. Nevertheless, he liked seafaring so much that he shipped in the Sebastian Cabot expedition, to his subsequent sorrow. Juan de Acurio, one of the lucky eighteen, complained two years later that he had gained naught from *Victoria*'s voyage but "glory, experience, and a bale of cloves" weighing 75 pounds!

It is probable—although not provable—that the successful outcome of this great voyage convinced Charles V that God intended him to enlarge his empire to embrace the world. From his Hapsburg-Austrian forebears he had inherited not only a prominent jaw and a firm character, but the motto A.E.I.O.U., initials for *Austriae Est Imperare Orbi Universo* (Austria Is Destined To Rule the Entire Globe). Hitherto this prophecy had been supposed to apply only to the European world known to the ancients; but here was Elcano bringing home treaties with Oriental potentates. Perhaps Columbus's idea of Spain's drawing the Grand Khan into her diplomatic orbit was not extravagant. But, how could Charles V rule the Far East while he had the Grand Turk and France on his back? First things first; implementation of Magellan's voyage must wait.

The scientific value of this voyage is beyond doubt. There must have been old fogies who said, "What's the use? Everyone knew you could sail around the world, but who would want to?" Any European interested in geography knew that this was a great feat of navigation. Magellan and Elcano had contributed more to geographical knowledge than any navigator since Columbus.

Victoria, which should have been preserved as a monument, met her death in the merchant service. After extensive repairs to make her tight, she made one round voyage to the West Indies; but upon attempting a second, she disappeared with all hands.

Pigafetta traveled from court to court, presenting kings and queens with extracts from his narrative. From the Seignory of Venice he obtained permission to publish it there, but he never did; the first edition of his narrative, in French, came out in Paris in 1525. Through this, and several Italian editions prior to 1540, and the English translation by Richard Eden in 1555, knowledge of Magellan's voyage became well disseminated. Pigafetta, now created a knight of Malta, "dined out" on the Magellan voyage for several years but died fairly young in his home town Vicenza.

Cristóbal de Haro and others who financed the voyage struck it rich despite all losses. *Victoria* brought home 520 quintal (25 to 26 long tons) of cloves, which sold for 7,888,634 maravedis (about $22,680 in gold), and the packs of cinnamon, mace, and nutmeg brought about $1800 more. This exceeded by at least a thousand dollars the original cost of the entire expedition.

Almost everyone who knows the sea and has considered this subject, feels that Magellan's was the greatest and most wonderful voyage in recorded history. But for two centuries that "noble captain," the leader, organizer, and (until his death) Captain General, received little or no credit other than Pigafetta's encomium. The Portuguese denounced him as a traitor, the Spanish execrated him, owing to stories of his harshness and mistakes in navigation brought home by Esteban Gómez and Elcano. In Spain the Basque master mariner received all the credit; his home town and San Sebastián are full of monuments and memorials, and a heroic statue to him is about to be erected in Seville.

Doña Beatriz Magellan and her two little children died before *Victoria* reached Seville, and Magellan's legal heirs were unable to collect his salary from the government of Charles V. From the expedition to which he gave his life, Magellan reaped only fame. Killed when performing the last of many gallant acts, his remains lie in an unmarked grave, or were scattered to the winds near where he fell.

Of the three greatest navigators in the age of discovery—Columbus, Magellan, and Vasco da Gama—Magellan stands supreme. Gama first reached India, pushing the voyage of Dias to its logical conclusion. Columbus, with the boldest concept, broke the Atlantic barrier once and for all, and crossed the Western Ocean and back four times, but in its kindest zone. Magellan, however, conquered the tempestuous southern waters and overcame mutiny, starvation and treachery to cross the Pacific Ocean, which he named. Elcano, to be sure, finished the circumnavigation, but he was only carrying out Magellan's plan.

Magellan's real monument is the Strait that he opened to the world:

> Forever sacred to the hero's fame,
> Those foaming straits shall bear his deathless name.

✸ XXVIII ✸

Drake's Voyage of Circumnavigation

1577-1579

From Plymouth to Puerto San Julián

The World Encompassed by Sir Francis Drake is the title of a proud narrative of this first English circumnavigation, by the Rev. Francis Fletcher. It began mainly as a privateering voyage, a campaign in the yet undeclared war between England and Spain; but Drake also made two new discoveries—islands south of Tierra del Fuego, and part of the west coast of North America. Although he definitely did not discover Cape Horn—Le Maire and Schouten did that in 1616—Drake made a new furthest south: Henderson Island at latitude 53°35′ S, which lies only about sixty miles northwesterly from the true Cape Horn. And the first New England was Drake's Nova Albion on the coast of California.

Francis Drake, born in Devonshire about 1541, was the son of an ardently Protestant chaplain to the royal dockyard of Chatham. His first sea experience came with John Lovell's and John Hawkins's slave-trading voyages to the West Indies. He commanded the fifty-tun *Judith* of Hawkins's "third and troublesome voyage" of 1568, and in her escaped from the treacherous attack of the Spaniards at San Juan de Ulua. This seems to have given him an inextinguishable lust for revenge. Many times, in his great voyage, he told Spanish prisoners that he was merely getting back a "bit of his own" from that defeat. He first expended his rage against Spain in 1571, by a raid on the Isthmus of Panama in the twenty-five-tun pinnace *Swan*. Next year he commanded both her and the 70-tun *Pasco* belonging to John Hawkins. At isolated Port Pheasant (now Puerto Escocés) near the Gulf of Darien, he assembled three knocked-down pinnaces and captured Nombre de Dios on the Isthmus in a brilliant amphibious operation. But he failed to carry off the stacked-up bars of silver, owing to the combination of a bad wound and a torrential downpour. Learning that no more treasure would move across the Isthmus for many months, Drake raided Cartagena and Santa Marta and captured several coastal ships. Near the end of January 1573, informed by Cimaroons (runaway slaves who looked on the English as liberators), Drake with his lieutenant John Oxenham, eighteen Englishmen and twenty blacks, marched across the Isthmus and captured a mule train. It yielded only victuals; but the two leaders, climbing a tall tree near Old Panama, sighted both the town and the Pacific Ocean, and made a vow that some day they would sail those waters. Again, in alliance with Guillaume le Testu, Drake waylaid a treasure train. He captured rich booty but his French ally was killed.

John Oxenham, with a hundred-tun ship, two knocked-down pinnaces, and fifty men, tried to capture the Isthmus of Panama in 1576. After the local Spaniards under Gabriel de Loarte captured most of his shipping, Oxenham with amazing energy built a forty-five-foot pinnace at the head of navigation of the Rio Chucunaque, which flows into the Pacific, and rowed her to the Pearl Islands in the Gulf of Panama. There he spent a month, capturing a number of Spanish ships; but the unexpected energy and good tactics of Loarte captured his party and most of them were hanged.

Long before Oxenham's fate was known in England, Drake had embarked on the enterprise that led him around the world. It was a southern counterpart to the Northwest Passage idea which Michael Lok, Martin Frobisher, and the Company of Cathay had been promoting. England should enter the Pacific by the Strait of Magellan, sail to latitude 40° or 50° N, seek out the Northwest Passage at its western terminus, and find a good location for an English colony somewhere on the west coast of America. That is what the careful historian James A. Williamson infers to have been the main object of Drake's famous

Sir Francis Drake. Portrait by unknown artist, 1581. Courtesy National Portrait Gallery, London.

voyage. Others deem it to have been nothing more than an exalted privateering expedition against Spain, using the west coast as a new and untouched source of plunder. In my opinion, Drake was an opportunist. His first object was to reach the Pacific; but what he would do when he got there would depend on wind, weather, luck, and circumstances.

A syndicate comprising the Earl of Leicester, Sir Francis Walsingham, Sir Christopher Hatton, the Earl of Lincoln (then Lord High Admiral), Sir William Winter and his brother George, both high officials in the Royal Navy, and John Hawkins the navy treasurer, was formed to finance this voyage. Drake himself put in £1000, presumably prize money, for he had no inherited wealth. All this must have been done with Queen Elizabeth's knowledge and her tacit or ambiguous consent; one can well imagine her saying, with a toothy grin, "Go forward, and God bless ye; but fail not lest I disavow the lot o' ye!" In the summer of 1577 this syndicate issued instructions to Drake to pass through the Strait of Magellan and explore the continental coast beyond, from latitude 42° S to 30° S, "as not being under the obedience of any Christian prince." He should prospect for mineral wealth, spy out places fit for vending English goods, and return by the way he came. The 50°–30° bracket obviously meant Chile and possibly Peru, since the English did not know how far south the Spanish had settled. But everyone agrees that there was a secret, unavowed motive for the expedition, to spoil the Spaniard in a region full of treasure, where he felt completely safe from enemies. The leader himself revealed that the Queen had said to him, "Drake! So it is that I would gladly be revenged on the King of Spain for divers injuries that I have received!" And he had on board some sort of royal commission which made him a privateer, not a pirate.

The task organization, vessels which assembled at Plymouth during the summer of 1577, was as follows:

CAPTAIN GENERAL: FRANCIS DRAKE
Captain of men-at-arms, Thomas Doughty

Ship PELICAN (later renamed GOLDEN HIND), the "Admirall" (flagship); 100–120 tuns, 16 to 18 guns on two decks; Drake captain

Ship ELIZABETH, "vice-admirall," 80 tuns, 16 guns, John Winter captain

Bark MARYGOLD, 30 tuns, 16 guns, John Thomas captain

Flyboat SWAN, acting as storeship, 50 tuns, 5 guns, John Chester captain

Pinnace BENEDICT, 12 tuns, 1 gun

Pinnace CHRISTOPHER, 15 tuns, Thomas Moore captain

Elizabeth and *Benedict* belonged to John Winter, *Christopher* to Drake himself. *Pelican* (*Golden Hind*) has been more intensely studied than any other historic ship between Columbus's *Santa Maria*

and the Pilgrim Fathers' *Mayflower*. A fairly new vessel, built in France, she was owned by the Hawkinses, who had probably bought her from a Huguenot sea-rover. She was a fine, stout vessel, double-sheathed with a layer of tarred horsehair between the two skins to foil teredos. Her gun ports could be closed and caulked tight and the guns stowed below. She usually towed her longboat. Even so, with up to eighty men on board, her main deck must have been uncomfortably crowded. Drake, anticipating a long voyage, had a forge and black-smith's shop fitted up somewhere—probably under the forecastle—and by helping himself from Spanish prizes and shore raids, he kept well supplied with dry provisions, wine, cordage, sails, and all manner of sea stores. After his great voyage the Queen ordered *Golden Hind* to be preserved ashore at Deptford, but the house planned to cover her was never built and she rotted away. From the plans of this projected house, Gregory Robinson infers that she was 90 feet long, 19 feet beam, with a depth of hold of 9 feet 6 inches. The Spanish captives on board *Golden Hind* were greatly impressed by her and invariably over-estimated her burthen by 100 to 500 tuns.

Among the important gentlemen volunteers were John Doughty (half brother to Thomas), two Hawkinses, Drake's youngest brother Thomas, and his cousin John. The total complement, including sailors, soldiers, and volunteers, amounted to something between 150 and 164, of which fourteen were boys. Almost all were English or Irish, except that Drake had a "black moore" named Diego, who was mortally wounded in the raid on Valparaiso.

After the usual delays in provisioning and getting to sea, this fleet made a fair start from Plymouth on 13 December 1577. An earlier at-tempt ran into a gale in which *Pelican* was forced to cut away her mainmast and *Marygold* drove ashore but successfully floated. On Christmas Day 1577, Drake put in at the island of Mogador on the outer Barbary Coast south of Safi. There he set up one of the prefabri-cated pinnaces carried in a ship's hold, and for the first time disclosed to his company their true objectives. Alexandria had earlier been the "official" destination. On the way to Cape Blanco they took several Spanish or Portuguese prizes, and at the Cape the fleet was "washed and trimmed." A forty-tun Spanish fisherman of a type called a *canter* or *caunter* was exchanged with her owner for *Benedict* and given that pinnace's name. And here they first sighted the Southern Cross. The

The *Golden Hind*. From Gregory Robinson, *The Elizabethan Ship* (1956), illustration by P. A. Jobson. Courtesy Longman Group Ltd.

native inhabitants of Mogador gave them no trouble, but Master Fletcher regarded the "Arabs" as the most filthy and degraded people he ever encountered; they performed all bodily functions, copulation included, in full view of a crowd containing English sailors.

Before the end of January 1578, the fleet called at Maio and Santiago in the Cape de Verdes, where Fletcher gratified his Protestant prejudices by throwing down a cross erected by the Portuguese, and regaled himself on delicious coconut and grapes. At Santiago they easily captured a Portuguese ship from Oporto, named *Maria*, "laden with singuler wines, sacks & Canaryes with woolens and Linen Clothes, silkes and velveets & many other good commodityes which stood us in that stead that shee was the life of our voyage, the neck of which otherwise had been broken for the shortnes of our provisions." Drake exchanged her for the second newly assembled pinnace and sent the Portuguese crew home in pinnace *Christopher* with "a Butte of wine, and some victuals and their wearing clothes." *Maria* he placed under the command of Thomas Doughty, and that was a mistake. Doughty misbehaved; and when Drake, to keep an eye on his old friend, made him master of flagship *Pelican*, he threw his weight around to such ill purpose that Drake "disgraded" him and sent him on board flyboat *Swan*.

At volcanic Fogo, Drake dismissed all Portuguese taken prisoner except pilot Nuno da Silva (called Silvester by the English), who volunteered to pilot the fleet in Brazil, which he did well and became very intimate with his commander.

The fleet, now reduced to six sail, dropped Fogo in the dark of the moon on 2 February, crossed the Line on the 17th, and approached the Brazilian coast at the latitude of Porto Alegre (30° S) on 5 April; but before they could work up the lagoon into the harbor a severe gale blew them out to sea. They finally anchored off Punta del Este, Uruguay. Francis Fletcher the chaplain and chronicler observed that they lost sight of Polaris at one degree north of the Equator and picked up the Guards of the South Celestial Pole one degree south of that. He made the same observation about shipboard lice as had Columbus: from England to the Tropic of Capricorn the vessel grew lousier and lousier; then of a sudden the lice "all dyed and consumed away of themselves."

Proceeding from Punta del Este to El Rincon roadstead, in the lee of a rocky island, they remained until 20 April, briefly explored the lower River Plate, and put out to sea on the 25th, with a full moon. Drake, having the latest Spanish maps of South America, sailed south, aiming at Cabo Tres Puntas which they sighted 12 May. Here the Captain General almost lost his life exploring in a ship's boat. For two weeks they lay at anchor in Port Desire, and on 20 June reached Puerto San Julián.

The parallel between Drake's voyage and Magellan's, more than half a century earlier, cannot have escaped the reader. The only landmark

Beagle Channel.

What Drake saw.

False Cape Horn.

that Drake could see upon entering San Julián was a gibbet, which they assumed to be the one on which Quesada and Mendoza had been hanged; but could that sinister tree have survived fifty-eight winters?

At the previous port of call, Drake's men made their first acquaintance with naked, painted Patagonians, who did some friendly trading for "toyes and trifles," and revealed the name of their god "Settaboth" —Pigafetta's Setebos. Here, however, they had a serious brawl. Drake went ashore with six men including master gunner Oliver. This fellow, shooting with bow and arrow to amuse or impress the natives, broke his bowstring; the Indians "tooke present advantage, and charging his bowe clapt an arrow into the body of him and through his Lunges." The Captain General acted promptly. Picking up Oliver's arquebus, heavily charging it "with a bullet and haile shot," he dispatched the beginner of the quarrel, tearing out his guts. "His cry was so hideous and horrible a roare, as if ten bulls had joyned together in roaring." That panicked the Patagonians who (says *The World Encompassed*) were "nothing so monstrous or giant as they were reported" by Pigafetta, and no taller than a tall Englishman, but most repulsive to the view.

"This bloody Tragedie being ended, another more grevious ensueth," observes the reverend chronicler. He meant the trial and execution of Master Doughty for mutiny. Doughty had been Drake's companion in arms in Ireland and a true friend, or so he thought. Fletcher could not explain why so Christian a gentleman, "a sweet Orator, a pregnant Philosopher, a good gift for the Greeke tongue and a Reasonable tast of Hebrew, . . . and in Ireland an aproved Soldier and not behind many in the Study of the Law," should have acted as he did. The court-martial brought out the fact—or hearsay—that he conducted among the mariners in every ship that he commanded a sort of whispering campaign against Drake. Certain modern writers believe in a deep, dark plot of Doughty as stooge for Lord Treasurer Burghley, to usurp command of the fleet and take it home, in order to avoid offending Spain. In my opinion clashing personalities were the main cause. On these long Southern voyages the "top brass" got on each other's nerves, so that vague suspicion and idle gossip became magnified into mutiny and treason, and Drake by fair means or foul acquired such an antipathy to Doughty that he had to go. One remembers Magellan's executions at this very spot, and others by Mendoza and Sebastian Cabot further north.

The court, over forty in number, comprising all officers and gentlemen volunteers of the fleet, met on an island inside Puerto San Julián. So many proofs, both oral and written, were produced of Doughty's disloyalty that he broke down and confessed "that he conspired, not onely the overthrow of the action, but of the principall actor also . . . a deare and true friend," and admitted that he deserved to· die. The court rendered the verdict "that it would be unsafe to let him live." Drake, apparently devastated by these revelations, sentenced Doughty to death, giving him the choice of three methods: execution then and there, marooning, or being sent to England "to answer his deed before the Lords of her Majesties Cowncell." Doughty chose immediate execution, desiring only the favor that he and Drake might receive communion together, "and that he might not die other than a gentleman's death."

There followed one of those pious and pathetic scenes that the Elizabethans loved—mutual forgiveness, dinner with the Captain General, last communion, Doughty "preparing at once his necke for the axe, and his spirit for heaven," head severed from body by an executioner of his choice. They buried him on the "Bloody Island" under the old gibbet, the grave marked by "a great grinding stone," carved with his name "in Latin, that it might the better be understood by all that should come after us." Next day all hands heard Master Fletcher preach a hortatory sermon, followed by holy communion and psalm singing. And—indicating that even in those days men liked grim souvenirs—the flag cooper made tankards of the gibbet for any sailor who wanted one.

Doughty's execution did not end grumblings and mutterings among the men, for Puerto San Julián, as Magellan had found, is no snug winter harbor. So Drake decided to risk a winter passage of the Strait rather than wait six months for summer. Before leaving, he preached a sermon ashore. This was the famous discourse in which he laid down the rules of discipline which should govern any hazardous undertaking: equal sharing of hardship and labor, no privilege of rank save that of an officer in the expedition, entire subordination to the commander. He chided the mariners for unruliness, but more weightily reproved the gentlemen for "stomaching daintiness in face of toil. . . . I must have

Psalms sung on board *Golden Hind*. From *The Whole Booke of Psalmes Collected into English by Thomas Sternhold and John Hopkins* (London: John Daye, 1578), p. 73. Courtesy Harvard College Library.

the gentleman to haul and draw with the mariner and the mariner with the gentleman. What! let us show ourselves all to be of a company, and let us not give occasion to the enemy to rejoice at our decay and overthrow. I would know him that would refuse to set his hand to a rope, but know there is not any such here." He then dismissed each and every officer from his post; and after another ringing appeal for all to rise to the occasion, reinstated them "as servants of the Queen under her General Francis Drake, to sail against the Spaniard at his sole command."

Sunday, 17 August 1578, the fleet, now reduced to three ships (*Pelican, Elizabeth,* and *Marygold*) and two pinnaces (*Swan* having been abandoned as unseaworthy), departed San Julián with a fair north wind and moon two days short of full. On the 20th they sighted Cabo Vírgenes, which the pilot recognized as the entrance to the Strait. It reminded Fletcher of Cape St. Vincent. Drake, always observing great occasions with ceremony, ordered a time-honored naval salute, striking topsails "upon the bunt" as "homage to our soveraigne lady the Queenes majesty"; and each ship held a service of thanksgiving to God for having brought them so far in safety. As a special accent, Drake proclaimed with sound of trumpet that flagship *Pelican* would henceforth be called *Golden Hind*. He chose this name because a golden hind *trippant* was the crest of his principal supporter at court, Sir Christopher Hatton. Ordinarily, renaming a ship in the course of a voyage would have been considered unlucky and caused grumbling among the sailors. So, why did Drake do it? Possibly Doughty had been part-owner of the ship; probably Drake regarded "the pelican, whose bill can hold more than his belly can," as a bird unworthy to be the eponym of an important ship.

"These things thus accomplished, wee joyfully entered the Streight with hope of Good Success." It was 21 August 1578.

Through the Strait to Furthest South

And good success they had. Magellan the pioneer took thirty-seven days to get through; Cavendish took forty-nine, and Richard Hawkins in 1593, forty-six days. Drake's ships did the 363 miles in only sixteen days, including calls to take on water and kill penguins. Pilot Silva records that the wind blew steadily from between northeast and east-northeast, which accounted for their speed, but the *Famous Voyage* account in Hakluyt declares: "we had the wind often against us, so that some of the fleet recouering a Cape or point of land, others should be forced to turne backe agayne, and to come to an anker where they could." It was still Antarctic winter, the mountains were snow-covered, and the beech forests "seeme to stoope with the burden of the weather." Hakluyt's narrator describes the "monstrous and wonderfull" mountains, rising tier after tier, "reaching themselves above their fellowes so high, that between them did appeare three regions of cloudes." We marveled at the same effect in 1972.

On 24 August 1578, having passed through the two Narrows, "We fell [in] with three Ilands, bearing triangle-wise one from another; one of them was very faire and large and of a fruitfull soile, upon which, being next unto us and the weather very calme, our Generall with his gentlemen and certaine of his mariners, then landed, taking possession thereof in her Majesties name, and to her use, and called the same *Elizabeth* Iland."

Drake certainly had nerve to claim this land for the Queen, seeing that Magellan's and several other Spanish fleets had passed it long before he did; but, surprisingly, the name he gave to the largest of the three islands has survived in Spanish translation: Isla Isabel. The other two, mere rocks (now named Santa Marta and Santa Magdalena) were "exceeding useful," as covered by helpless birds "which the Welch men named Pengwin." "In the space of one day we killed no less than 3000," wrote Fletcher. "They are a very good and wholesome victuall." Maybe so for a time, when properly pickled; but penguin meat quickly cloys and goes putrid. Nuno da Silva the Portuguese pilot agreed that their flavor was good, not fishy, and that the lightest of them weighed ten pounds.

From Elizabeth Island the fleet sailed south, rounded Cape Froward and then steered northwest, following Magellan's course and often beating to windward. Fletcher left a very vivid picture of a williwaw: "Two or three of these winds would com togeather & meet . . . in one body whose forces . . . did so violently fall into the sea whirleing, or as the Spanyard sayth with a Tornado, that they would peirse into the verry bowells of the sea & make it swell upwards on every syde. . . . Besides this the sea is so deep in all this passage that, upon life and death, there is no coming to Anker." Nuno da Silva, on the contrary, recorded, on the south side, "many small bays or coves in which one could . . . safely anchor." This they obviously did. Master Fletcher tells us that the Antarctic beech branches made natural arbors where flourished herbs and "simples" such as wild celery, thyme, marjoram, scurvy grass, and "other strange plants." At this juncture, "nearly all" the flagship's crew were down with scurvy, but Drake had the juice squeezed from some of the herbs, and, administering it in wine, cured all but two men, who died. Drake had a big beech tree cut down and a section of the trunk placed in the *Golden Hind*'s hold; good evidence, observed pilot Silva, that he never intended to return that way.

Having worked through Paso Inglés, Paso Tortuoso, and Paso

Largo, "We had such a shutting up to the Northwards, and such large and open fretes toward the South, that it was doubtfull which way wee should passe." The same thing had happened to Magellan. Drake brought his fleet to anchor under an island (probably Providence or Beaufort), and had himself rowed to check the entrance to the Pacific. At that time the fleet received a visit from friendly Fuegians in a beech-bark canoe with a high bow and stern, so well framed and proportioned that the English thought it must have been built "for the pleasure of some great and noble personage, yea, of some Prince"—but the poor Fuegians had no prince. They were "of a meane stature" compared with the Patagonians, "gentile & familiar to strangers, heavily painted and almost naked." Nomads, they lived in skin wigwams and slept on the hard ground. "The women," wrote Fletcher, "weare chaines of white shells upon their armes & som about their Necks whereof they seem to be verry proud. They are well spedd [equipped] for Bellyes, Brests & Buttocks, but nothing in Comparison with the Giant women" of Patagonia.

On 6 September, under a new moon, the fleet passed Cabo Pilar and "entered into the South Sea or *Mare del Zur*." There Drake's luck changed. The Pacific (Fletcher said it should better have been named the Furious) Ocean was in one of her ugly moods. Drake intended now to sail north toward the Line, to get away from "the nipping cold, under so cruell and frowning a winter," but the ships could make no headway against the north wind and heavy seas. For an entire month, to 7 October, the three vessels * were batted about and driven south, even down to latitude 57° S says Fletcher; Nuno da Silva's log agrees that they made land at latitude 57° and anchored for an hour in forty fathom. It is anyone's guess where that was. One night, during the second watch, *Marygold*, with Captain Thomas, Master Bright, and twenty-eight men, disappeared; last seen "spooming" away from the flagship toward the iron-bound Chilean coast. She probably sought to raise Cabo Pilar and take refuge within the Strait. Fletcher guessed that they "were swallowed up with horrible & unmercifull waves or rather Mountains of the sea"; for he and another man on watch in the *Golden Hind* "did heare their feareful cryes"; but Drake long hoped that the *Marygold* had survived and would rejoin him.

Prayers coming from the *Hind* finally were heeded. At the end of

* The two pinnaces appear to have been abandoned.

this terrible month, sun, moon, and stars came out, the wind moderated, the tempestuous seas were stilled, and she began crawling north again. In the last week of October she sighted land, and anchored off what Drake believed to be "the uttmost Iland of *terra incognita*, to the Southward of America." He gave it no name, but called the group to which it belonged, "the Elizabeth Isles."

This island, identified by Wagner (and by myself in 1972) as Henderson Island at longitude 69°05′ W, latitudes 55°32′ to 55°37.5′ S, had never yet been seen by a European. Drake was certain that he had attained "the uttermost Cape or hedland . . . without which there is no maine nor Iland to be seene to the Southwards, but that the Atlanticke Ocean and the South Sea, meete in a most large and free scope." No Antarctic continent, my masters. "The West Occidental [the Western Ocean] and the South Sea are but one!" But it took

Drake's furthest south, Henderson Island, 55°35′ S. Saunderson Island in foreground. Courtesy of the photographer Bill Ray.

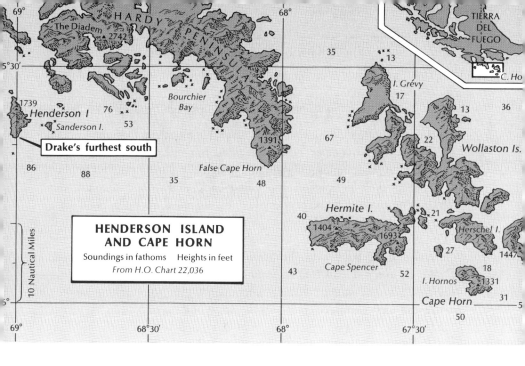

cartographers about a century to get over depicting a great land mass extrapolated from Tierra del Fuego and circling the earth. Australia represents all that remains of this geographical myth.

Cape Horn, the southernmost land of any consequence until you hit the Palmer Peninsula of the real Antarctic, lies some sixty miles southeast of Henderson Island, on latitude 55°59′ S. The International Oceanographic Conference of London in 1919 fixed the meridian of Cape Horn as the boundary between Atlantic and Pacific. But Drake had proved the two great oceans to be one, and opened the way for Schouten and Le Maire's discovery of Cape Horn in 1616.

Golden Hind anchored off Henderson Island on 24 October 1578 and tarried until a new moon rose on 1 November. Master Fletcher went ashore with the Captain General, walked down the grassy slopes, found them thick with delicious wild currants, and on its southernmost point set up a stone and carved thereupon the date and the Queen's name. Drake later told Hawkins that he "grovelled"—threw himself on his belly—at the uttermost tip of this cape and stretched out his arms as far as he could toward the South Pole, so he could boast that no man had been so near it as himself. So typical of Drake— always something of the big boy in him.

689

The Buccaneering Phase

Of the gallant fleet of six that sailed from Plymouth in December 1577 there now (1 November 1578) remained but one, the *Golden Hind*. *Elizabeth*, the second largest ship, had parted company in early October without Drake's permission and sailed back to England through the Strait. For over three centuries this was assumed to be a plain case of desertion by Captain Winter, like that of Gómez from Magellan; but Winter's tale excuses if not justifies his action. During the foul weather he had ducked back into the Strait as a refuge and there anchored. Drake, he averred, had told him, when they last exchanged words during a lull in the storm, that he intended to give up bucking violent north and west winds, to re-thread the Strait and make for the Moluccas via the Cape of Good Hope. So Winter tarried for a month, lighting signal fires at night; then, assuming that Drake had been cast away, he put his Cape of Good Hope plan to *Elizabeth*'s crew. To a man they protested that they had had enough, and rejected it. Captain Winter gave in and sailed for England, arriving in June 1579 after calling at Belle Isle on the French coast, where he did his best to blacken Drake's name.

Weather exerted an overriding influence on the boldest mariners in days of sail. Drake, having made furthest south, and the winds having turned fair, decided to sail *Golden Hind* north along the coasts of Chile and Peru and see what he could pick up.

And plenty did he pick up! In the previous thirty years Spain, as we have seen, had extended her empire along the west coast as far as Valdivia, Chile, on latitude 40° S. Most of the settlements were very small, with fewer men-at-arms than Drake had on board *Golden Hind*, thus easily captured and sacked. Spain employed a considerable fleet of coast-built merchantmen to carry silver and other treasures from the ports of Bolivia, and from Callao, port of Lima, to Old Panama. *Golden Hind* played wolf among sheep to this merchant fleet, for none were armed with cannon, never expecting to encounter anything bigger than an Indian balsa raft in the Pacific. The Englishmen embarked on this adventure in the spirit of schoolboy pranksters; even Master Fletcher the preacher enjoyed the fun. Finding a Spaniard ashore asleep beside thirteen barrels of silver, a flock of sheep, and "much *charqui*," * they "freed him of his charge" but left him screaming with rage and resentment. At another point, encountering a hidalgo driving a train of llamas loaded with silver, "we could not indure to see a gentleman Spaniard turned carrier . . . therefore we offered our own service and became drivers." Capturing a vessel laden with linen, "we thought [it] might stand us in some stead and therefore tooke it with us."

At Mocha Island near Valdivia they encountered tough resistance from the local Indians, who with arrows "thick as gnatts in the sonn" attacked the party when watering. Not one Englishman escaped having two or more arrows stuck into him; two men were killed outright; and two more, cut off from the boat, were killed and eaten most horribly—the barbarians cutting "gubblets" of their flesh, tossing them in the air, catching them while dancing, and devouring them "like doggs." The rest of the crew wanted to take revenge by cannonfire, but Drake refused, saying that the cruel Spaniards made the Indians act that way, and there were too many on hand (an estimated 2000) for one ship to punish.

Drake's tactics were to surprise, capture, and sack a Spanish settlement with all shipping in the harbor, and when he had looted everything valuable, turn ships and sailors loose, but with no sails to enable them to pursue him. Whilst Drake always remained a hero to his countrymen, he was usually denounced by Spanish and other Catholic writers as a cruel, ruthless, and unprincipled pirate. But since the publication of documents from Spanish archives by the Hakluyt Society in 1914, this view has become untenable; for his Spanish prisoners uniformly praised *El Draque* for humanity and generosity; nor did he ever kill anyone in cold blood. His men, rushing ashore, desecrated churches, stole sacred vessels, and destroyed statues, paintings, and crucifixes; but they did not rape or kill. Incidentally, Drake spoke Spanish well enough to converse with his prisoners.

Entering the great harbor of Valparaiso, the Englishmen were invited on board a small Spanish vessel whose crew, assuming that they too were Spaniards, beat a drum in welcome, invited them on board, and broke out "a Buttizo of wine of Chile." The guests' nationality was given away by their tough red-haired boatswain Tom Moone, who had been with Drake on his West Indies voyages and hated the dons. He

* Jerked beef, which the English learned to eat in Spanish America.

not only struck a Spaniard but aggravated the offense by crying to him, *abaxo perro*, "Down dog!" The English boarding party then clapped the Spanish sailors under hatches and joined their friends in "rifling" the town. Since Valparaiso then contained barely nine houses, they confined their ravages to the church, "the spoyle whereof our Generall gave to M. Fletcher his minister," and a warehouse which yielded several pipes of wine. The English sailors so relished the "buttizo" that they became patrons of Chilean wine and carried away so much of it from various ships and ports that it never gave out until mid-Pacific, if then.

At Quillóta and Coquimbo it was much the same story. At Valdivia they captured the ship that had been Mendaña's *Capitana* on his voyage of discovery to the Solomon Islands, with 24,000 *pesos d'oro*,* and took her along with a genial cargo of 1700 jars of wine captured ashore. Nuno da Silva tells us they had to heave overboard six pipes of tar to make room for the wine. Who wouldn't? Drake landed at Bahia Saleda (latitude 27°55′ S) on 20 December and tarried a whole month to assemble the last of his knocked-down pinnaces; it speaks ill for Chilean communications that this delay did not alert the entire west coast. Arica, on the present border between Chile and Peru, port for Potosí and other silver mines, he reached on 7 February 1579, moon at first quarter. Loot from two vessels riding there yielded "about forty bars" of silver, a chest of pieces of eight, and "some wine." Passing Punta Chala ("Chawley" to Fletcher), Drake captured a ship from which he learned that a rich haul was awaiting him in Callao, seaport of Lima, the "City of Kings" and capital of the Peruvian viceroyalty.

Golden Hind sailed by the south channel, unheralded and unseen, into Callao harbor. There the men plundered a dozen or more ships "aboard whom we made somewhat bold to bid ourselves welcome," says Fletcher, and looted 1500 "barres of plate," a chestful of silver reals, and a quantity of linen and silk. This alerted the authorities at Lima, and the Viceroy himself, mounted and in armor, led two hundred men to the waterfront to repel invaders. Too late! It was 14 February, and *Golden Hind* had already slipped out to sea, towed by her longboat in the early morning calm, to pursue *Nuestra Señora de la Concepción*, a

---

* Sarmiento *dixit* (Nuttall, *New Light on Drake*, p. 60), but the Spanish official report from Callao (*ibid.*, p. 92) says 1,400,000 pesos! This ship Drake later destroyed (p. 169).

treasure-laden ship headed for Panama. Drake offered a gold chain to whoever first sighted her, and his fifteen-year-old cousin John Drake won it. The attempt of the viceroy of Peru, D. Francisco de Toledo, to pursue, in two hastily armed vessels, was a complete flop. His ships were so clumsily handled as to get becalmed near shore while Drake went zooming along in a fresh breeze. But (wrote Sarmiento de Gamboa), "the most imperative reason for returning seemed to be that many of the gentlemen were very seasick and in no condition to stand, much less to fight." These weak-stomached defenders of Peru were all severely punished on their return. This was typical of the many bumbling attempts of the Spanish authorities, owing largely to confused orders and bad seamanship, to catch Drake. He showed them all a clean pair of heels; but in truth, as one Spanish witness wrote to the king, "in this South Sea there is no vessel or vessels that can harm him, for they are small in size and their crews are inexperienced."

Drake's target on this occasion was the famous vessel generally known by her Spanish nickname *Cacafuego*, which nice North American and English writers have translated "Spitfire"; it really means "Shitfire." The name is not only indecent but inappropriate, as she mounted no heavy ordnance. Her master, San Juan de Antón, suspecting no harm, allowed *Golden Hind* to sail alongside and grapple. Antón turned out to be a Basque who had lived in Southampton and spoke English well. According to his report, Drake's men shouted, "We're English, strike sail! . . . If not, look out for you will be sent to the bottom!" He answered, "What England is this? Come on board and strike the sails yourselves!" A bosun's whistle shrilled, a trumpet sounded, and a volley crashed out from Drake's arquebuses. This was followed by crossbow bolts and chain shot which severed the Spaniard's mizzen mast. Drake's new pinnace laid aboard her on the larboard side, and "about 40" archers scrambled up the channels and took possession of the ship. Antón was hustled on board *Golden Hind* and into the flag cabin where Drake, in the act of removing his armor, greeted him thus: "Have patience, such is the usage of war." Next day, 2 March 1579, Drake breakfasted on board *Cacafuego* and left orders with his own steward to prepare meals for the Spanish captain as if for himself.

It took three days for the English pinnace to transfer to *Golden Hind* all the plunder, which amounted (says San Juan de Antón) to 447,000 pesos in specie, equivalent to about half a million dollars in gold; and two other Spaniards present deposed that it was "more than 360,000 pesos." At the end of this process an impudent Spanish pilot's boy remarked that his ship should no longer be called *Cacafuego* but *Cacaplata*—the English thought this to be a wonderful witticism. Before releasing the Spanish captain and his ship, Drake gave to every member of her crew, clothing, knives, weapons, and a fistful of pesos; a merchant passenger received fans and mirrors "for his lady," and to Captain Antón a German-made musket, six hundred pounds of iron, a barrel of powder, a gilt corselet, a silver-gilt bowl inscribed "Francisqus Draques," a safe-conduct in case he met the two missing English ships, and a plea to the viceroy of Peru to spare the lives of John Oxenham and the Englishmen captured with him. One touch of gallantry that particularly appealed to the Spaniards was Drake's allowing one of his prizes to keep her royal ensign flying, saying, "Leave the arms of King Philip where they are, for he is the best king in the world."

No wonder Antón and his crew parted from Drake in good humor, regarding him a very proper *caballero*. But the viceroy of Peru paid no attention to his plea for mercy to Oxenham and his men. All were executed in 1580. Drake himself always showed mercy to captives. A black slave seized at Arica, unhappy at sea, begged to be allowed to return to his master; Drake said, "Go, with God's blessing," and let Antón take him ashore.

On his way to catch *Cacafuego*, Drake captured a vessel "laden with ropes and tackles for ships," and a golden crucifix "with goodly great Emerauds set in it." These were probably the same emeralds that he later set in a new crown for his Queen.

Drake now turned north, to evade certain pursuit, and anchored behind Caño Island off the coast of Costa Rica. Sighting a vessel sailing in the offing, Drake sent out his pinnace to capture it, which was easily done. This fifteen-tun *fragata*, belonging to one Rodrigo Tello, carried a cargo of silver and sarsaparilla, but more important were two professional pilots who were about to take the annual Acapulco galleon to the Philippines. Drake impounded all their Pacific charts and tried to bribe or threaten one of them, Alonso Sánchez Colchero by name, to pilot him across the Pacific. For refusing, he was threatened with the noose but let off with no hurt, and a gift of fifty pesos for his wife. Drake, however, kept the charts.

After graving *Golden Hind* rather ineffectively on a beach near Caño Island, and with Tello's *fragata* as prize, Drake continued northward. On 2 April 1579 his calculated latitude was 13°20′ N. Next day he surprised and captured a small vessel upon which a Spanish nobleman, Dr. Francisco de Zárate, a cousin to the Duke of Medina Sidonia, had embarked as passenger. Zárate has left us an impressive picture of Drake's style and courtesy. He dined with the Captain General in the flag cabin, and tells in his narrative that Drake gave him food from his own plate and told him "not to grieve, that my life and property were safe." Next day being Sunday, *Golden Hind* dressed ship. Drake "decked himself very finely," went on board the prize and took four chests of Chinese porcelain and several packs of linen and fine silks, and a gold falcon with an emerald in its breast which belonged to Don Francisco, giving him in return a silver brazier. Zárate describes Drake as a man about thirty-five years old, short in stature, and bearded, "one of the greatest mariners that exist, both as a celestial navigator and in knowledge of command. . . . He treats his men with affection, and they treat him with respect." One prisoner reported that "all his men trembled before him" and bowed low, hats in hand, whenever they passed him on deck; but several whom Don Francisco questioned, declared that they "adored" him. Nine or ten young gentlemen volunteers, and pilot Nuno da Silva, dined in the Captain General's mess, where they were served "on silver dishes with gold borders and gilded garlands within which are his arms"; and the fiddlers played both at dinner and supper. Most important, from a legal point of view, Drake displayed his *provisiones*, his commission from the Queen, and other legal documents.

Drake now calculated that the entire west coast of South America would be alerted, and armed ships buzzing like angry hornets whose nest has been disturbed. So there was no question of returning home the way he came. His last call in settled Spanish America was at Guatalco, Mexico, mainly to obtain water and provisions for a long voyage, but also to top off with more silver. His men captured an entire court of justice from judge to black prisoners, haled them on board ship, and forced the judge to write a letter to the town fathers permitting the English to water there. After so doing, they "ransaked the town," completely cleaning out from the church the communion plate, vestments, holy images, even the bell. Tom Moone, Drake's red-haired and pock-marked boatswain, acquired "a chaine of gold and some other jewells, which we intreated a gentleman Spaniard to leave behinde him, as he was flying out of the towne." The gentleman probably did not think it so funny. When Drake regaled two leading citizens with wine in his flag cabin, one complained that the town had nothing to eat, all Indians having fled to the woods; so Drake sent ashore, to help keep the population alive, two bags of flour, two jars of wine, one of oil, and two sugar-loaves. He kept the black prisoners but later released them, together with a wench belonging to Zárate, on a Pacific island.

At Guatulco, Drake released Don Francisco and Nuno da Silva, who had served him well as pilot but knew nothing of the waters to come. Once ashore, Nuno wrote interesting reports of his experience with Drake, together with a lively description of him: "Francis Drake is a man aged 38. He may be two years more or less. He is short in stature, thickset and very robust. He has a fine countenance, ruddy of complexion, and a fair beard. He has the mark of an arrow wound in his right cheek which is not apparent if one looks not with special care. In one leg he has a ball of an arquebus which was shot at him in the Indies. . . . He had seated at his table the captain, pilot and doctor. He also read the psalms and preached. . . . He carries a book in which he enters his log, and paints birds, trees and sea-lions. He is an adept in painting and carries along a boy [John Drake] a relative of his, who is a great painter. When they both shut themselves up in his cabin they were always painting." (All these sketches and paintings, alas, have perished.) Nuno also had a high opinion of Drake as a mariner.

This straightforward account of Nuno's got him into trouble with the Mexican branch of the Spanish Inquisition, which accused him of having complacently attended Drake's shipboard Protestant services where psalms were sung. The singing of translated psalms, the only hymns used in the Anglican church for centuries, appears to have been particularly irritating at that time to Catholics. Nuno defended himself by saying that he "attended" no regular service but could not help hearing the English heretics bellowing their unauthorized psalms. The Inquisition sentenced him to perpetual exile from the Indies. But he did escape the torch if not the rack, and is even said to have visited England before he died. In any case, the Admiralty restored to him the value of the merchandise on board his ship, when Drake captured it in the Cape de Verdes.

Sailing from Guatulco under the paschal moon on Maundy Thursday, 16 April 1579, *Golden Hind* struck out into the Pacific "to get a winde," finally caught the northwest trades, and, sailing close-hauled, on 5 June made land somewhere in the present state of Oregon.

Before leaving Mexico for the north, Drake destroyed the three biggest prizes he had taken, keeping only Tello's fragata for a tender. One of those he relinquished with regret because of her speed on the wind; when sailing in company with *Golden Hind*, Drake had to order her to tow anchors wrapped in old sails, so she would not thrust ahead of him. Colchero and the other pilot whom Drake set free reported to the viceroy that he would undoubtedly make the coast of Alta California, "because the season for navigation to China is now past . . . and the winds are contrary." *Golden Hind*, already leaking from the strain of her heavy cargo, badly needed a good careening, graving, and caulking.

Bibliographic Note

The earliest account of Drake's voyage to be printed is "The Famous Voyage" in Hakluyt's *Voyages*, 1589 edition. Hakluyt threw in a signature on the subject when the book was already in press; it follows II, 643. The Hakluyt Society's reproduction of this edition is the one I refer to as *The Famous Voyage*.

Henry R. Wagner, *Sir Francis Drake's Voyage Around the World, Its Aims and Achievements* (San Francisco, 1926), is still the best book on this voyage. Wagner (1862–1957), a California businessman and collector, studied all known sources and investigated many localities; and his corpus of documents is comprehensive. Unfortunately, his reproductions of maps, whether ancient or modern, are mostly illegible. Written before the "Plate of Brass" (see below) was discovered, Wagner's book is supplemented by an 18-page pamphlet printed in 1970 for the Zamorano Club of Los Angeles: *Drake on the Pacific Coast. Henry R. Wagner. With an Introduction and Notes by Ruth Frey Axe*, his research assistant. This gives Wagner's emphatic opinion against the Plate and the San Francisco Bay hypothesis. The same Club printed his autobiography, *Bullion to Books*, but therein he says nothing about the Plate and little about Drake.

A number of California gentlemen interested in Drake in 1954 incorporated themselves as The Drake Navigators' Guild, with Fleet Admiral Chester W. Nimitz USN as honorary chairman. Over the years they have done meticulous research on Drake in California and issued a number of valuable publications, of which the most comprehensive is Raymond Aker, *Report of Findings Relating to Identification of Sir Francis Drake's Encampment at Point Reyes National Seashore* (461 pp. mimeographed and illustrated, Point Reyes [1970]). It is to be hoped that this will be printed, together with the riposte by the Bodega Bay proponents, Robert F. Heizer, John H. Kemble, and Andrew Rolls, *Analysis of Raymond Aker's Report* (mimeographed, Point Reyes, 1970).

Two more important monographs, Robert W. Allen and Robert W. Parkinson, *Identification of the Nova Albion Conie,* and *Examination of the Botanical References . . . at Nova Albion,* both illustrated, were published by the Guild in 1971.

✳ XXIX ✳

Drake in California

1579

Nova Albion

Everyone, including Drake, with whom the Spanish prisoners talked on board *Golden Hind*, reported that he intended to sail home around the world. Nuno da Silva, however, felt confident that he was going north first. Did Drake change his mind, or had he always intended to seek the fabled Strait of Anian, the Northwest Passage which attracted so much misguided effort by his English contemporaries? We simply do not know. It has been surmised that he picked up from the Spanish pilot, his unwilling captive, the timetable of the Manila galleons, which always cleared Acapulco by 27 March, and that he considered mid-April too late for fair winds on a Pacific crossing. Hardly credible; weather reports of the Manila ships were not so accurate as to deter a navigator like Drake who had successfully threaded the Strait of Magellan in winter. Or he may have felt that the fifty days' supply of water that he took on board at Guatulco was not enough for a trans-Pacific voyage. Or he may have decided he must find a safe place to repair *Golden Hind*, whose heavy cargo of silver had started a number of leaks. Actually this leg of the voyage, to somewhere in Alta California on 5 June 1579, took almost exactly fifty days; a very neat calculation, or merely Drake's usual good luck.

Golden Hind and the Tello pinnace made a wide sweep into the Pacific and then headed for the west coast, close-hauled on the port tack. The mariners at sea were "grievously pinched" with "extreme and nipping cold," says *The Famous Voyage*, "complained of the extremitie thereof, and the further we went, the more colde increased upon us." Hence Drake started his sheets "to seeke the land." The wind veered northward on 5 June 1579, when Drake's ships "were forced by contrary windes to runne in with the Shoare, which we then first descried, and to cast anchor in a bad bay, the best roads we could for the present meete with." This bay spoken of so disparagingly was probably the little cove just south of Cape Arago on the coast of Oregon at latitude 43°20′ N. There the two vessels were subjected to "extreme gusts and flawes" and these were succeeded by "most vile, thicke, and stinking fogges." "In this place was no abiding for us," wrote Fletcher; the only direction in which anyone wanted to go was south. And that is what Drake did. He abandoned his search for the Strait of Anian—if that had ever been his intention.

In June they coasted south for a good five degrees, always with moonlight, saw snow-covered mountains of the Coast Range in the distance, and suffered from more "nipping cold." Master Fletcher, anticipating criticism from "chamber champions," men "who lye on their feather beds till they go to sea," and whose teeth chatter when drinking "a cup of cold Sack and sugar by the fire," became indignant over slug-abed criticism of this southerly turn, as are we. California weather is not all golden sunshine and gentle rain; there were ten days of frost and snow at Oakland in the winter of 1972–73, and why should Fletcher have reported foul weather had it been fair? The cold cannot possibly have been anything like what northern discoverers such as Frobisher and Davis had endured, but the temperature did drop to the point where the lines froze; and by comparison with the equatorial heat they had been through, and lacking winter clothing, the men doubtless were very uncomfortable. So were the crew of the famous Captain Cook on this same coast almost two centuries later.

More astonishing to us (and repugnant to west coast tourist bureaus) is Master Fletcher's statement that the face of the earth all along the west coast appeared "unhandsome and deformed . . . shewing trees without leaves, and the ground without greenes in those moneths of June and July." But that may be explained by drought, or normal

Cape Arago and South Cove. Robert W. Allen photo.

midsummer parching. We in May 1973 found the coast beautifully green.

Since Drake's shipmates seldom if ever recorded their impressions of scenery, we cannot scold them for not alluding to the beauty of the California coast that they followed so assiduously. Rolling hills come right down to the shore and, as often as not, break off as cliffs. Trees are scarce except in sheltered valleys, as the prevalent west and northwest winds will not let them grow tall. Surf continually roars upon the shore, and even today sea birds are plentiful; we plowed through vast sheets of tiny paddling phalaropes dipping for plankton, and there was hardly a moment when gulls, terns, cormorants, and many others were not crossing our bows in flight. The water is chilled summer and winter by a southward flowing current, into which the cold Japan current feeds. Partly because this makes bad sea bathing, but mostly because Californians have foresightedly made this shore into state parks or reservations, the coast that Drake examined has escaped "development." One can gaze on a Drake's Bay almost as untouched by humans as when the "Generall" passed that way.

From the 43° landfall (state two out of the three original narratives) *Golden Hind* coasted south in search of a comfortable harbor and found it at 38° N. (The third narrative says 38°15′.) Here they put in on 17 June 1579 and tarried until 23 July; and 38° N is the exact latitude of Point Reyes, some thirty-six miles north of the Golden Gate.

Before examining the question of where Drake spent those five weeks in June and July 1579, let us relate what happened there. The most important thing, after graving the *Golden Hind*, was the friendly attitude of the natives, Indians known as the Coast Miwok tribe who lived from about Cape Mendocino to San Francisco Bay. When Drake careened his flagship on a beach so that her leak could be got at, he built a fortified camp ashore. This drew a multitude of Indians armed with bows and arrows; for like other natives of America, they instinctively resented foreigners who gave the impression of having come to stay. Drake was expert enough at the universal sign language to allay their suspicions, especially after he had distributed liberal gifts of cloth, shirts, and "other things. "

These Miwok were great talkers, delivering lengthy orations in a language that no Englishman could make head or tail of, and relentless singers and dancers after their fashion. The men went completely naked; and the women, who wore miniskirts of bulrushes, had a curious habit which has puzzled later ethnologists, of lacerating cheeks and torsos with their fingernails until the blood flowed in torrents, and, as further self-punishment, casting themselves on rough ground or briars. The English sources say nothing of sexual relations between the two races, but it is difficult to believe that they did not occur, considering the long time that Drake's men had been at sea.* These natives amiably augmented the Englishmen's rations during their five weeks' stay, mostly with broiled fish and a root that they called *petáh*. This was the bulb of a wild lily that they ground into meal and ate, and they also made bread of acorns; but they had no corn or manioc to offer, and it puzzles one how Drake managed to provision his ship for the long

---

* It may be significant that in the numerous Spanish reports of Drake's incursions on the west coast, his men were never accused of raping, or even molesting the Indian girls.

voyage ahead. Presumably his men shot and cured the small rodents that they called "conies." This has been identified recently as *Thomomys bottae bottae*, the Bötta Pocket Gopher, although some authorities still assert that it was the common ground squirrel. Maybe they cured fish on shore, as in Newfoundland. But where could they have obtained salt?

One of the earlier yelling and lacerating orgies by native visitors was broken up by Drake's calling on Preacher Fletcher to conduct divine service, complete with psalm-singing. The Indians then stopped their clamor to listen, stare, and occasionally shout. "Yea, they tooke such pleasure in our singing of Psalmes, that whensoever they resorted to us, their first request was commonly this, *Gnaáh*, by which they intreated that we would sing." The historian J. Franklin Jameson once sagely observed that *gnaáh* proved that all Englishmen, and not only the Puritans, sang psalms through their noses!

On one occasion, at least, the native visitors brought their chief, distinguished by several necklaces of local shells, a mantle of gopher skins, a wood "septer or royall mace," and a knitted cap in which feathers were stuck, as a crown. He greeted Drake with the title of *Hyó*, "set a rustic crown on his head, inriched his necke with all their chains," and laid on a special song and dance. What the natives meant by all this is anyone's guess, but Drake chose to regard it as a feudal ceremony in which these humble creatures placed themselves under the protection of Queen Elizabeth. Consequently, shortly before his July departure, Drake named the country *Nova Albion*, "for two causes; the one in respect of the white bancks and cliffes, which lie toward the sea; the other, that it might have some affinity, even in name also, with our own country, which was sometime so called." (Albion was the Greek name for England.) He then "set up a monument of our being there . . . a plate of brasse, fast nailed to a great and firme post; whereon is engraven" the Queen's name, the date, and the fact of the king and people freely acknowledging her sovereignty, the Queen being represented by a silver sixpence with her effigy, and "our Generall" by his name. So says Fletcher; more about this Plate anon. But the white cliffs are right there on Drake's Bay, outside the Estero, and they bear a striking resemblance to those on the English Channel.

After *Golden Hind* had been graved, repaired, and floated, Drake "with his gentleman and many of his company, made a journey up

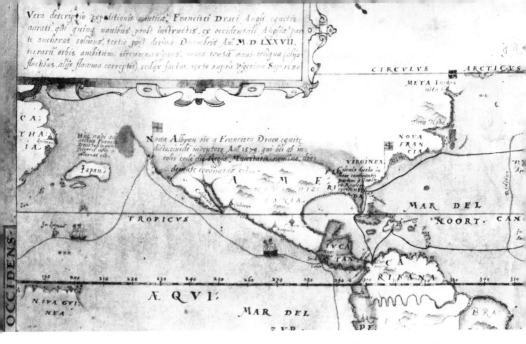

The Mellon-Drake map, 1517. In Mr. and Mrs. Paul Mellon's Collection, Upperville, Va. Photo Courtesy Robert H. Power.

into the land." The inland parts they found "farre different from the shoare, a goodly country, and fruitfull soyle, stored with many blessings fit for the use of man" such as great herds of deer. It is indeed a beautiful rolling country, reminding one of the downs along the English Channel. Those who do not know this region may wonder why this inland excursion did not reveal San Francisco Bay to Drake and his merry men. The answer is simple: a day's walk along the valley as far as Olema at the head of Tomales Bay is screened from San Francisco Bay by high ridges and Mount Tamalpais of 2600 feet altitude.

Drake's men never wore out their welcome. As the Indians observed preparations for departure, "so did the sorrowes and miseries of this people" seem to increase; more lacerations by the women, more "wofull complaints and moanes, . . . refusing all comfort." Which certainly indicates that those Englishmen had behaved with singular kindness and patience, and suggests that if only the Northwest Passage had opened up, Nova Albion might have become an earlier New England with a more salubrious climate and better race relations.

Tello's pinnace was abandoned, probably because Drake no longer had enough men to work her as well as *Golden Hind*. The flagship left California with between fifty and sixty men on board.

"The 23 of July," says Fletcher, the Indians "tooke a sorrowfull farewell of us, but being loath to leave us, they presently ranne to the top of the hills to keepe us in their sight as long as they could, making fires before and behind, and on each side of them." Drake never returned, nor did any other Englishman for centuries.

Now, in which bay did *Golden Hind* spend those five golden weeks?

The Good Bay of Nova Albion

Numerous scholars and amateurs from California and elsewhere have attempted to answer this question. Each selects his bay and despises any other solution. And, after my short coastal reconnaissance, I have become as positive as any!

If we accept the contemporary statements that the bay lay on or around latitude 38° N, the choice boils down to Bodega Bay at 38°20′ N, Drake's Bay at 38°00′ N, and San Francisco Bay, entering by the Golden Gate at 37°49′ N.

Data available in the three contemporary accounts are as follows:

1. Drake hit the coast at or around latitude 43° N (Cape Arago) on 5 June, sailed southward looking for a suitable harbor to careen and repair *Golden Hind*, and found it between 38° and 38°30′ N on 17 June. These latitudes we must accept, for Drake and his pilots knew perfectly well how to take accurate sights ashore, and they had five weeks in which to find fair days and clear nights to shoot the sun and Polaris.

2. Fogs were common, and lasted for days on end; but the grass was still brown and the weather chilly.

3. "White bancks and cliffes which lie toward the sea" were seen, reminding Drake of the familiar south-coast cliffs in old England, and suggesting the name *Nova Albion*.

4. Fish, clams, mussels, and pocket gophers were abundant, and the natives ground meal out of a lily root.

5. Jodocus Hondius's map of about 1589-90 has an inset of *Portus Novae Albionis*. Everybody thinks this fits "his" bay neatly; and ingenious attempts have been made to identify it as Bodega Harbor, the Estero of Drake's Bay, and the part of San Francisco Bay where the

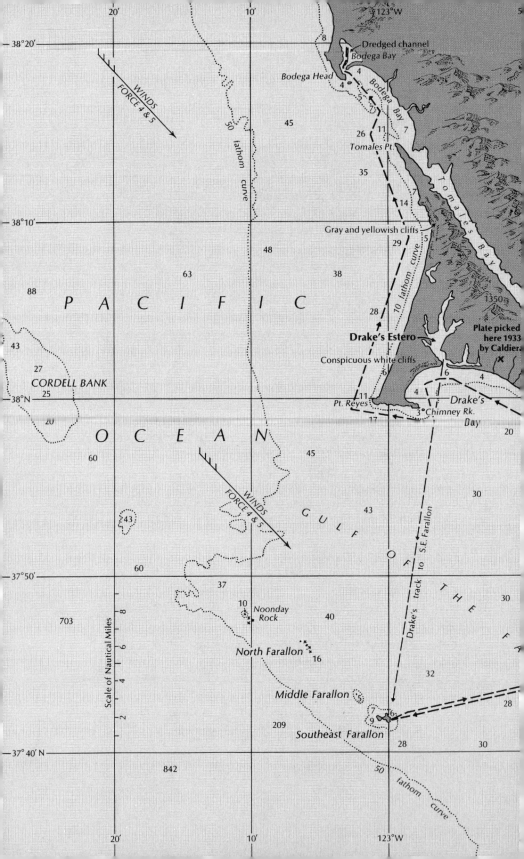

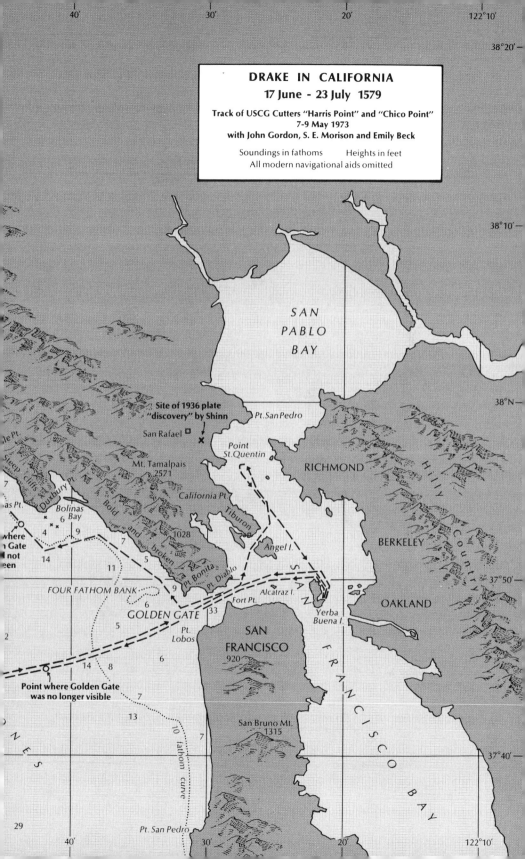

Brass Plate was last picked up. I cannot see any resemblance to any of them. It looks a bit like Trinidad Bay up north, but that was no place to careen a ship safely, and the three contemporary authorities state that the bay was at 38°30′ or 38° N.

Rounding Cape Mendocino at latitude 40°26.5′, the next good harbor you reach is Bodega Bay, latitude 38°20′ N, one of the favorites. Bodega Head is a fist-like, conspicuous headland, altitude 228 feet. Passing it, sailing south, you find a narrow inlet with (nowadays) a dredged depth of seven feet at the entrance, leading into Bodega Harbor, home port for several hundred salmon-fishing boats. The neighboring country resembles the downs along the English Channel, but no more so than the country around Drake's Bay.

The absence of white cliffs is the principal reason for rejecting Bodega Bay as Drake's. The outer shores of the Tamales Peninsula are indeed bold, and the cliffs are of a pale gray color flecked with yellow, which might by a stretch of the imagination be called white; but they certainly do not resemble those of the south coast of old England. As for the long but shoal Tamales Bay running thirteen miles southeasterly from Bodega Bay, no careful seaman would have let his ship be trapped in that pocket.

Eighteen to twenty miles to the southward of Bodega Head, and right on latitude 38° N, is Point Reyes, protecting what is now officially called Drake's Bay. When we visited it in May 1973, we found the shores to be almost as wild and devoid of human touch as four centuries ago. The first thing that strikes one here are conspicuous white cliffs, highest on the coast, and closely resembling the group called the Seven Sisters of Beachy Head on the English Channel. In the northern bight of Drake's Bay there opens a shallow estuary now officially named Drake's Estero. Its mouth is now closed by a bar of sand and silt, but in the U. S. Coast Guard chart of 1860 it could be entered by a channel with least depth of eight feet, and there are records of coastal schooners using it as a refuge early in the twentieth century. The anchorage in the outer Bay is hard and bad,* but the Estero, with a good mud and sand bottom, is ample in extent and would have offered Drake a perfect shelter to careen and repair the

---

* In March 1973 the German training ship *Deutschland*, 4400 tons, anchored here hoping to clean up in preparation for an official visit to San Francisco, but found it too rough to launch a boat, and dragged her anchors.

Ketch *Little Revenge* rounding Point Reyes. Courtesy Drake Navigators Guild.

leaks in *Golden Hind*. George Davidson, professor of geodesy and astronomy at Berkeley, made a special study of Drake's California in the 1880's, and decided that he landed there, which led to both state and nation officially naming it Drake's Bay and Drake's Estero. I see no reason to disagree.

The subsequent history of Drake's Bay is interesting. Sixteen years after Drake's voyage, Sebastián Rodríguez Cermeño, in command of the Spanish ship *San Agustín*, examined this coast on his way from Manila to Mexico. *San Agustín* was cast away in November 1595 in this same bay, which her captain named San Francisco. In his narrative Cermeño reports three fathom of water on the bar to the Estero. He heard nothing about Drake from the Indians, who were still friendly, and saw nothing to suggest that anyone had been there before. He explored the Estero, which he valued largely for its supply of fresh

Ketch *Little Revenge* and the "white cliffs of Albion" in Drake's Bay. Courtesy Drake Navigators Guild.

water. Before he got around to bringing *San Agustín* inside, an onshore wind drove her on the beach and he never got her off. Some old ship timbers which are still in Drake's Bay may be hers. Cermeño then caused a pinnace (which he called a *luncha*) to be assembled on the spot, and in her sailed to Mexico, arriving 31 January 1596 at Acapulco with some eighty people on board. His name San Francisco has led to much confusion, but everyone now agrees that Cermeño's bay was the one now named Drake's.

The next important Spanish voyage thither was that of Sebastian Vizcaíno in January, 1603, Although first to chart the Farallons, Vizcaíno never sighted the Golden Gate, which was so named by John C. Frémont in 1849. The annual Manila galleons returning to Acapulco passed along this coast, within sight of the shore, for two hundred years, without ever seeing the Golden Gate. San Francisco Bay was finally discovered in 1769 by an overland expedition led by Gaspar de Portolá, the first Spanish governor of Alta California; and the first ship known to have entered it is Juan Manuel de Ayala's *San Carlos* in 1755.

No mariner who knows the California coast will find this surprising. The lay of the land is such that one can sail almost up to the Golden Gate without realizing that there is an opening; headlands and the Berkeley-Oakland hills look like a continuous land mass. On a clear May day in 1973 we could not see the Golden Gate when eight miles away, at the outer buoy to the dredged ship channel. Approaching it from the north, as Drake might have done had he clung to the coast

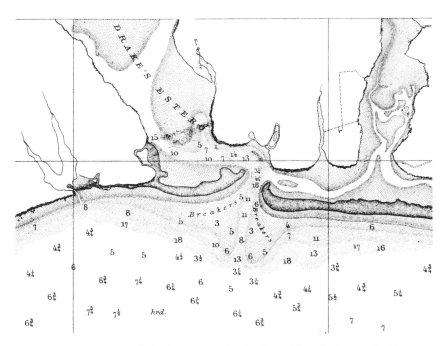

Drake's Estero, Drake's Bay. From U. S. Coast Guard Chart of 1860.

Nineteenth-century square-rigger entering Golden Gate. Courtesy Gabriel Moulin Studios.

before sighting the Farallons, one cannot see the Golden Gate three miles away. And that Drake could have entered this gorgeous bay, one of the world's finest, without describing it, is incredible. In the great gold rush of the 1850's it was not infrequent for sailing ships coming from Cape Horn to miss the Golden Gate and pile up on a rocky shore nearby. Innumerable cases of the sort could be cited; almost any seaman with experience of this coast will think it preposterous that Drake could have seen this entrance.

Nevertheless, there are many advocates for San Francisco Bay having been Drake's bay. Edward Everett Hale in Justin Winsor's *Narrative and Critical History*, predicted that "it will not be long, probably, before the question is decided," and "does not hesitate" to give the palm to San Francisco Bay. Too bad Dr. Hale could not have lived another fifty years, when he would have found the dispute blown sky-high and the site thrown into San Francisco's lap by the discovery of the now famous "Drake Plate of Brass."

My conclusion, and that of my shipmates on our brief examination of the Marin County coast, is that Drake's Bay is correctly so named; that here he spent five weeks, repaired *Golden Hind*, sang psalms for the Indians, and marched up country. The white cliffs like those of Albion "on the side of the sea" (from the Estero) were for us the determining factor. If Drake or any of his men had climbed Mount Tamalpais, they would have seen the magnificent panorama of San Francisco Bay and probably sailed in to investigate it; but Englishmen in those days did not climb a mountain for fun.

The Plate of Brass—or Was It Lead?

The World Encompassed states that Drake caused a plate of brass to be engraved with a record of his taking possession, and nailed it to a post, together with an English sixpence bearing Queen Elizabeth's effigy. *The Famous Voyage* in Hakluyt says substantially the same thing, without stating the metal of the plate. The *Anonymous Narrative*, however, says that in this "harborow where he grounded his ship to trim her, while they were graving of their ship . . . in this place Drake set up a greate post and nayled there on a sixpence which the contraye people woorshipped as if it had bin god [space] also he nayled upon this post a plate of lead and scratched therein the Queenes name."

So, brass or lead? Lead is the more probable, because every seagoing ship in that era carried sheet lead for covering leaks, keckling (wrapping) cables to prevent their chafing in a hawse-hole, and a variety of uses. Brass, on the other hand, was then little used on ships, and it would have been unusual to find a sheet of this size among the *Golden Hind*'s sea stores or in her shipboard forge.

For many years, Professor Herbert E. Bolton of the University of California at Berkeley, lecturing to his classes on early west coast history, quoted *The World Encompassed* story about the brass plate, and begged his students to keep their eyes open; and if it were found, bring it to him. Anyone with a knowledge of undergraduate humor would regard that as an invitation to a student "rag" or "gag."

In the summer of 1936 a man named Beryle Shinn picked up a tarnished brass plate "on a pile of rocks on the brow of a hill on the north shore of Corte Madera Inlet, in Marin County, overlooking the waters of San Francisco Bay," near San Quentin. He tossed it into the trunk of his car, thinking it might do for repairs; but in February 1937, a neighbor who had been a pupil of Professor Bolton, and who helped Shinn to cleanse it, noticed the name "Francis Drake." He then took it to Bolton, who promptly pronounced it genuine, as did Mr. Allen L. Chickering, president of the California Historical Society. Shinn played coy about selling the plate, but finally accepted $3500 as an "award," and the plate is now prominently displayed near the entrance to the Bancroft Library, Berkeley. Here is the inscription:

> BEE IT KNOWNE VNTO ALL MEN BY THESE PRESENTS
> IVNE 17 1579
> BY THE GRACE OF GOD AND IN THE NAME OF HERR
> MAIESTY QVEEN ELIZABETH OF ENGLAND AND HERR
> SVCCESSORS FOREVER I TAKE POSSESSION OF THIS
> KINGDOME WHOSE KING AND PEOPLE FREELY RESIGNE
> THEIR RIGHT AND TITLE IN THE WHOLE LAND VNTO HERR
> MAIESTIES KEEPEING NOW NAMED BY ME AN TO BEE
> KNOWNE VNTO ALL MEN AS NOVA ALBION.
> FRANCIS DRAKE

At the lower right corner is a jagged hole through which, presumably, the bemused Indians could see the effigy of their new queen on a silver sixpence.*

The place where Shinn found the plate has ever since been a leading argument of the proponents of San Francisco as having been Drake's

---

* Here, for comparison, is exactly what Fletcher wrote in *The World Encompassed* (Penzer ed., p. 62; facsimile ed., p. 80): "Before we went from thence, our Generall caused to be set vp a monument of our being there, as also of her maiesties and successors right and title to that kingdome; namely, a plate of brasse, fast nailed to a great and firme post; whereon is engrauen her graces name, and the day and yeare of our arriuall there, and of the free giuing vp of the prouince and kingdome, both by the king and people, into her maiesties hands: together with her highnesse picture and armes, in a piece of sixpence currant English monie, shewing itselfe by a hole made of purpose through the plate; vnderneath was likewise engrauen the name of our Generall, etc."

bay. But it is difficult to see what the Plate contributes to this argument. For, during the early publicity about this "discovery," a chauffeur named William Caldeira alleged that he had picked up the Plate in 1933 on a roadside about two and a half miles from the shore of Drake's Bay, washed it enough to see the word "Drake" but (since his employer was not interested) discarded it as useless about half a mile from the place where Shinn found it. Nobody seems to have reflected that a heavy object like a brass plate, after the post to which it was attached had rotted, would in the course of over 350 years have buried itself in the ground and been completely overgrown by turf; so if Caldeira found it on the surface, someone must have dug it up, or forged it, and placed it there. Shinn does indeed describe the position of his find as "embedded in the ground with a rock partly overlaying it"; but it could not have been deeply embedded since he saw a corner of it sticking out, and the rock was small enough for him to pick up and roll down the hill. Thus the claim of sundry writers that the Plate had been right there waiting, for 350 years, to be discovered, cannot be sustained:

Experts disagree as to whether or not the brass is contemporary with Drake. Analysis by Colin J. Fink of Columbia University and George R. Harrison of Massachusetts Institute of Technology, declared it to be hundreds of years old. But Henry R. Wagner, a practising metallurgist before he shifted to the less exact field of history, declared that, judging from its zinc content, this particular piece of brass could not have been more than sixty or seventy years old. And Professor Calley of Princeton, who also analyzed it, states that the zinc content was much too great for it to have been Elizabethan. A faker could have picked it up in an old junk shop.

Apart from provenance, the contents condemn the Plate as a fraud. No such odd lettering, especially the capital B which resembles a four-paned window, can be found in the British Isles. Mr. Reginald Haselden, curator of manuscripts at the Huntington Library at the time of the discovery, declared it to be a forgery. Experts in the British Museum pronounced it an undoubted fake; no such letter forms for the M and N exist in Elizabethan graffiti or manuscripts. The language, too, is wrong for the era. "By the Grace of God" should have come after "Elizabeth" and before "of England," as anyone with

Drake's or Fletcher's education would have known.* Among other spellings, *herr*, used twice, is also suspect. The *New English Dictionary*, V, 228, gives over twenty different spellings to this possessive of the pronoun *she*, but not one of them is *herr*. I am reminded of the remark of an eminent philologist at Copenhagen with whom I discussed alleged runic inscriptions in America: "If you dig up an alleged Greek vase sitting on a telephone directory, there is no need to argue further." Since the letters and language of the Drake Plate are not of the period, there is no sense quibbling about the age of the brass or who picked it up and where.

In my opinion, the Plate is a hoax perpetrated by some collegiate joker who knew little about Drake except what he had heard from Dr. Bolton and read in one of the modern editions of *The World Encompassed*. He naturally chose that text to be blown up for the inscription, tried to give it a "quaint" look by odd lettering and spelling, then dropped it at a place where it was likely to be picked up. "Drake's Plate of Brass" is as successful a hoax as the Piltdown Man or the Kensington Rune Stone.

Voyage Home

On 24 July 1579, the day after *Golden Hind* left her anchorage, she sighted the Farallon Islands and "called them the Islands of St. James," as it was the vigil of that saint's feast. They landed on the Southeast Farallon, the biggest, whose 350-foot hill, from a distance, looks like a miniature Rock of Gibraltar. Here Drake topped off his provisions with sea-lion meat and the eggs and flesh of numerous wild fowl which nest there. This seems an odd thing to do at the beginning of a long voyage; but maybe the native provisions obtained at Drake's bay were deemed insufficient.

Golden Hind made a westerly passage of sixty-five or sixty-six days without sighting land. Her first call was on 30 September at a group of islands where the natives were great thieves and pestered the English sailors by hurling stones at them from outrigger dugouts. One remembers Magellan's experience at Guam in the Ladrones; but Fletcher gives the latitude as "about" 8° N, which won't do for Guam, latitude

---

* For instance, the grant to Adrian Gilbert in 1583 begins, "Elizabeth, by the Grace of God, of England, France and Ireland Queene."

My Drake Reconnaissance. The Morison Team: Emily Beck; Lt. Roger Piquet, USN; Lt. Commander John Gordon, USNR.

The Southeast Farallon.

13° N. It was probably an island of the Pelew or Palau group. From this Isle of Thieves, *Golden Hind* sailed along the south coast of Mindanao and then took off for the fabulous Ternate, where the ships of Magellan and Loaysa had tarried after the death of their captain general. Drake found Ternate to be much the same as Elcano had reported it sixty years earlier. The rajah, Babù by name, sent out to check the strange ship and, having ascertained that she was neither Spanish nor Portuguese, invited her into port, sending four big canoes to tow her in during a calm. Babù was enchanted to open trade with a rival to the monopolizing Portuguese. He flew into a rage when Drake declined to pay heavy export duty on six tons of cloves that he bought, but the Captain appeased him with valuable gifts and discussed the possibility of setting up an English factory at Ternate.

Drake spent but four or five days at Ternate, departing 6 November 1579. *Golden Hind* again needed a complete bottom-cleansing and rummaging, so Drake sought out an uninhabited island to do it.* He found one, which the men called Crab Island because it was full of big king crabs, "One whereof was sufficient for hungrie stomachs at a dinner." Drake stayed there twenty-six days, "a wonderful refreshing to our wearied bodies." Upon departing, he left behind two blacks he had picked up somewhere in the eastern seas, "and likewise the negro wench Maria, being gotten with childe in the ship." Maria had been a slave to Francisco Zárate and as she had been on board about eight months, Fletcher's statement is probably correct. Drake's purpose in leaving these three on the isle of the king crabs, says the *Anonymous Narrative*, was to start a settlement. What became of the marooned blacks we know not.

Departing Crab Island 12 December, *Golden Hind* followed the east coast of Celebes, blown by the northeast monsoon. On the night of 8 or 9 January 1580, Drake almost lost his ship and his voyage. *Golden Hind* ran on a shelving reef off shore. To get her off, he jettisoned several big bronze cannon, half his precious cargo of Ternate cloves, and even some sacks of flour and beans; but nothing could move her. Then Preacher Fletcher tried prayer and administered holy communion to

---

* Heaving down and graving left a ship and her company as defenseless as a lobster changing its shell; that is why captains from Columbus down, if unable to do it in a friendly civilized port, had to seek out a lonely spot. Drake's place is identified by Wagner as one of the small islands in the Banggai archipelago.

every member of the crew, which now numbered but fifty-eight. That seems to have done the trick. The wind changed, and by setting all sail, the ship slid off into deep water and resumed her voyage, undamaged. The poor parson, instead of being thanked for invoking divine aid, was disgraced for remarking, when things looked very bad, that this accident was divine punishment for the execution of Doughty. Drake, incensed, played God himself, excommunicated the minister from the Church of England, and condemned him to wear about his arm a paper declaring, "FRANCIS FLETCHER YE FALSEST KNAVE THAT LIVETH." But Drake seldom stayed angry long, and within a few days Fletcher was again leading shipboard prayers and preaching sermons.

Golden Hind, following much the same course as Elcano's Victoria sixty years earlier, called frequently and with no trouble at Moslem-held islands for provisions, Drake even signing treaties with the local rajahs. At Tjilatjap, Java, "as many as nine kings came and entered the vessel," and were much pleased with the music and the banquets that the Englishmen gave them. From there, she crossed the Indian Ocean, rounded the Cape of Good Hope about 18 June 1580, and, avoiding the islands under Spanish or Portuguese sovereignty, called at a river mouth in Sierra Leone to replenish water (which was down to half a pint a day for three men), and provisions. It is obvious that Drake had learned from Pigafetta's narrative, a copy of which he had on board, the urgent necessity of keeping his crew well fed. Sailing from Sierra Leone 24 July, Golden Hind avoided the usual route of Portuguese East Indiamen returning home, and sailed into Plymouth on 26 September 1580, the day of full moon. It was three years less eleven weeks since the day she left England.

The first question Drake is said to have asked ashore was about the health of his Queen. For he sensed that had she died, he might be repudiated as an unauthorized pirate. His second request was to straighten out his calendar; for, like Elcano, he had lost a day sailing west and could not make out why.

By any standards, this was a great and memorable voyage, even though it came sixty years later than Magellan's and brought meager results in actual discovery. Drake had shown consummate seamanship throughout. He had kept most of his men alive, well fed, and healthy. Despite one non-stop run of sixty-three days in the Atlantic, two of fifty and sixty-eight days in the Pacific, and a third of at least seven weeks' duration in the Indian Ocean and South Atlantic, they suffered very little from illness. Only seventeen men, including those killed in brawls with Indians or Spaniards, lost their lives during the voyage. That is a remarkably good record for the sixteenth century, or indeed for the next two centuries. Moreover, he took good care of his ship, heaving her down often enough to keep her bottom clean and tight. For his countrymen he opened a new seaway to wealth and glory in the East Indies. The proposed English "factory" at Ternate was never set up; but after a few years, both English and Dutch were plucking the feathers of Portugal in the Far East.

Golden Hind brought home more valuable plunder than any ship of any nation, prior to Cavendish's prize *Santa Ana*. Exactly how much, historians have been unable to figure out because there was a great deal of smuggling bars of silver ashore at night. She sailed to London in November 1580 and unloaded considerable bar silver at the Tower. Drake had already delivered some of it to a royal treasury official, who stowed it in Saltash Castle at Plymouth, and he sent a few horse-loads of silver and gold to Sion House, Richmond, where the Queen was staying, as a harbinger of plenty to come.

Bernardo de Mendoza, the Spanish ambassador to England, made every effort to persuade Elizabeth to repudiate Drake and return his booty to Spain. Characteristically, she stalled him along for months, not being ready for a complete breach with Spain, and in the meantime secretly ordered £10,000 of the spoil, lying in the Tower, to be delivered to Drake personally. Wagner estimated the total value of his booty in gold, silver, and precious stones at 950,000 *pesos d'oro*, equivalent to £332,000 in the currency of the day; contemporary rumor, which Treasurer Tremayne vainly tried to verify by interrogating leading members of the crew, put it at £1,500,000. A good part went to the government; but the "undertakers" who paid for fitting out the fleet at an estimated cost of £4000, were said to have received 1000 per cent on their investment.

Drake enjoyed the Queen's personal favor to a high degree, and he presented her with a diamond cross and a new crown made of Peruvian silver and emeralds. At her orders he was knighted on 4 April 1581 on the deck of his flagship at Deptford. That marked her defiance to Spain, and the beginning of Philip II's organization of the "invincible armada" to conquer England and depose Elizabeth. Drake bought Buck-land Abbey in his ancestral county of Devon, where he set himself up as a country gentleman. His first wife (Mary Newman) having died in 1583, he married, two years later, Elizabeth Sydenham. They left no children; but Drake's heir, his brother Thomas, is ancestor to the present Drake family.

Sir Francis never ceased to work for further humiliation of Spain, and of his activities after 1581 we have written briefly in *Northern Voyages*. He took a leading part in the defeat of the Spanish Armada, and sailed to the West Indies on his last cruise against the dons in 1595. The following year he died of yellow fever on board his flagship off Nombre de Dios, Panama, and was buried at sea.

During his lifetime and ever since, Drake became a folk hero to the English, in a class with King Alfred and Lord Nelson; and rightly so. He loved God, loved England and hated her enemies, loved the sea, loved fighting, loved fame and fortune. The late Alfred Noyes wrote an epic on Drake in twelve books, and tells in his poem "The Admiral's Ghost" of the Devonshire tradition that Nelson was one of them. Another legend of the gallant captain is told in "Drake's Drum," Sir Henry Newbolt's poem:—

> Drake he's in his hammock an' a thousand mile away,
>   (Capten, art tha sleepin' there below?),
> Slung atween the round shot in Nombre Dios Bay,
>   An' dreamin' arl the time o' Plymouth Hoe.
> Yarnder lumes the Island, yarnder lie the ships,
>   Wi' sailor lads a-dancin' heel-an'-toe,
> An' the shore-lights flashin', an' the night-tide dashin',
>   He sees et arl so plainly as he saw et long ago.
> Drake he was a Devon man, an' ruled the Devon seas,
>   (Capten, art tha sleepin' there below?),
> Rovin' tho' his death fell, he went wi' heart at ease,
>   An' dreamin' arl the time o' Plymouth Hoe.
> "Take my drum to England, hang et by the shore,
>   Strike et when your powder's runnin' low;
> IF THE DONS SIGHT DEVON, I'LL QUIT THE PORT O' HEAVEN,
>   AN' DRUM THEM UP THE CHANNEL AS WE DRUMMED THEM LONG AGO."

List of Illustrations

(All maps drawn by Vaughn Gray)

Index

Guadeloupe I., 439, 442, 443, 471-2
Guam, 629-31, 716, 718
Guanaco, 588, 590
Guanahini, *see* San Salvador
Guantánamo Bay, 458
Guarani Indians, 583
Guatiguaná, 470
Guaymi Indians, 525, 530, 533
Guerra, Hierónimo, 568, 606
Guevara, Antonio, 505
Guillemard, F. H. H., 549-50
Guillén y Tato, Adm. Julio, 384
Guise, Jean, Cardinal, 151
Gutiérrez, Pedro, 388, 451
Guyon, Jean, seigneur de Thaumetz, 235*n*

Hakluyt, Richard, 37, 127, 197, 208, 250, 259, 263, 320, 327, 331; on Drake, 685-6, 697, 700, 713; on Hore's cruise to Newfoundland, 103-5; Verrazzano's letter translated, 142, 144
Hale, Edward Everett, 712-13
Half-hour glass, 12, 282, 393-4, 497, 498
Hall, Charles F., 302, 304
Hall, Christopher: with Frobisher, 281, 287, 293, 307, 308, 312; log of Frobisher's *Gabriel*, 285, 286, 287
Hall, James, Stockholm Chart, 94
Hall's I., 287, 288, 293, 295, 296, 298-9, 318, 319, 339
Hamilton Inlet, 340, 348
Hanseatic League, 47, 383
Harana, Beatriz Enriquez de, 375, 430, 546
Harana, Diego de, 385, 388-9, 417, 451
Harana, Pedro de, 477
Hare I., 227, 228, 245
Harfleur, 110, 113, 124
Haró, Cristóbal, 559, 562, 673
Harrington Is., 218, 264, 265
Harrison, George R., 715
Harry Grace à Dieu, 124
Harvey, Edward, 308
Haselden, Reginald, 715
Hastings Manuscript, 4, 9, illus. 10-11, 15, 29, 31, 36, 49
Hatteras, Cape, 144
Hatton, Sir Christopher, 676, 685
Havana, 254
Hawkins, John, 674, 675, 676
Hawkins, Richard, 685
Hawkins family, 678
Head Harbor, 189

Heere, Lucas de, drawing of Eskimo, 305-6
Henderson I., 674, 688, 689
Henri II, 115, 171, 273
Henri IV, 127, 512
Henrique, *see* Enrique de Malacca
Henry VII, 379; and Anglo-Azorean Syndicate, 79, 84, 85, 86; and John Cabot, 41-2, 56, 66, 68-70, 72, 131, 474; portrait, 42; and Sebastian Cabot, 86
Henry VIII, 87, 99, 105, 166, 254, 260, 668; François I compared with, 131; and Rut's voyage, 100, 103; Thorne's letter to, 99-100
Henry, Cape, 147
Henry the Navigator, Prince (Infante Dom Henrique), 352, 353, 354
Heptaméron, 154, 265-6, 272
Hermine, L', 124; see also *Grande Hermine*
Hermine (weasel), significance of, 213
Herrera, Antonio de, 569, 610, 612, 614
Herring, 108, 124, 127, 199
Heyerdahl, Thor, 626
Hickey, William, 463
Hispaniola: colonies, 415-17, 451-6, 468-74, 487; Columbus brothers fail as administrators, 491-2; Columbus in, on first voyage, 411-18; Columbus in, on second voyage, 435, 450-56, map 465, 468-74; Columbus in, on third voyage, 490-91; Columbus replaced as governor, 494; Columbus's report to Ferdinand and Isabella on, 429-30; Peter Martyr's map, 459
Hochelaga (St. Lawrence River), 219, 223
Hochelaga (site of Montreal), 230-31, 234-9, 258; plan, 236-7
Holometer, 282
Homem, Diogo, Map, 97-8
Homonhon I., 632, 633
Hondius, Jodocus, Map, 705
Honduras, 521, map 529
Honfleur, 108, 110
Honguedo, 204*n*, 219
Hopewell, 30, 307
Hore, Richard, 99; tourist cruise to Newfoundland, 103-5
Horn, Cape, 601, 602, 674, 689; False Cape Horn, 681
Howard, Lord Charles, of Effingham, Lord High Admiral, 323; portrait, 324